International Relations

TENTH EDITION 2012–2013 UPDATE

Joshua S. Goldstein

American University, Washington, D.C.
University of Massachusetts, Amherst

Jon C. Pevehouse

University of Wisconsin, Madison

PEARSON

Boston   Columbus   Indianapolis   New York   San Francisco   Upper Saddle River
Amsterdam   Cape Town   Dubai   London   Madrid   Milan   Munich   Paris   Montréal   Toronto
Delhi   Mexico City   São Paulo   Sydney   Hong Kong   Seoul   Singapore   Taipei   Tokyo

IN MEMORY OF PROF. DEBORAH J. "MISTY" GERNER

Senior Acquisitions Editor: Vikram Mukhija
Editorial Assistants: Beverly Fong, Isabel Schwab
Executive Marketing Manager: Wendy Gordon
Senior Media Editor: Paul DeLuca
Production Manager: Eric Jorgensen
Project Coordination, Text Design, and Electronic
  Page Makeup: Integra Software Services, Inc.
Cover Designer/Manager: Wendy Ann Fredericks
Cover Photos: *Clockwise from top left*: Child soldier in
  Libya, 2011, © Reuters/Yannis Behrakis.
  Demonstration at European Central Bank,
Frankfurt, Germany, 2011, © Arne
Dedert/dpa/Corbis. Israeli and Palestinian leaders
with U.S. Secretary of State, 2010, © Alex
Wong/Getty Images. Refugees from Kyrgyzsran
receive help from UNICEF, 2010, © Shamil
Zhumatov/Reuters/Landov.
Photo Researcher: Brandi M. Ford
Senior Manufacturing Buyer: Roy L. Pickering, Jr.
Printer and Binder: Quad/Graphics-Taunton
Cover Printer: Lehigh-Phoenix Color/Hagerstown

For permission to use copyrighted material, grateful acknowledgment is made to the
copyright holders on p. 517, which are hereby made part of this copyright page.

Library of Congress Cataloging-in-Publication Data

Goldstein, Joshua S., 1952–
    International relations/Joshua S. Goldstein, Jon C. Pevehouse—10th ed. update.
      p. cm.
    Includes bibliographical references and index.
      ISBN 978-0-205-87526-9
    1. International relations—Textbooks.   I. Pevehouse, Jon C.   II. Title.
    JZ1242.G652 2013
    327—dc23
                                                          2011052955

1 2 3 4 5 6 7 8 9 10—QGT—15 14 13 12

www.pearsonhighered.com

ISBN-13: 978-0-205-87526-9
ISBN-10:   0-205-87526-2

Brief Contents

Detailed Contents

Note: Each chapter ends with a summary, key terms, and critical thinking questions.

Preface

We all live in an increasingly interconnected world. These connections bring significant benefits to our everyday lives: the ability to communicate instantaneously around the world sharing one's culture and beliefs, the possibility of directly helping a person affected by an earthquake through a global network of charities, the ability to purchase a product made from parts manufactured in a dozen different countries each using its specialized knowledge to create a better product—these are some of the potential benefits of the interconnected world. Yet, these connections may also worsen existing problems: terrorist networks use the technology of these connections to carry out attacks; some types of global commerce can put undue strain on our natural environment; and millions of people still live with few global connections that are enjoyed by citizens of wealthier countries.

Despite these increasing connections and their implications for everyday life, many students begin college misinformed about basic facts of international relations (IR) such as the extent of poverty and levels of foreign assistance given to the developing world and the trend toward fewer wars over the past two decades. An introductory textbook plays a key role in students' education about international affairs, and we have worked hard to make this one timely, accurate, visually appealing, and intellectually engaging. We hope this textbook can help a generation develop knowledge and critical thinking in order to find its voice and place in the changing world order.

IR is not only an important topic but also a fascinating one. The rich complexity of international relationships—political, economic, and cultural—provides a puzzle to try to understand. The puzzle is not only an intellectual challenge but also emotionally powerful. It contains human-scale stories in which the subject's grand themes—war and peace, intergroup conflict and community, integration and division, humans and their environment, poverty and development—play out.

New to the Tenth Edition 2012–2013 Update

The tenth edition 2012–2013 update includes important revisions throughout to keep the book current in a year of historic changes in the international system. New developments such as the Arab Spring revolutions and the European financial crisis are featured in text and photos throughout the book.

In international security affairs, this edition gives particular attention to the Arab Spring uprisings that overthrew governments in Tunisia, Egypt, and Libya and continue (at this writing) in Syria and Yemen. These movements represent the latest of a series of waves of democratization in recent decades that are reshaping the nature of the international community. The UN-authorized NATO intervention in Libya's revolution, generally considered a successful humanitarian intervention, is a related development covered in this edition. The U.S. killing of Osama bin Laden in Pakistan, new uses of armed drones, the withdrawal of U.S. forces from Iraq, and the start of their withdrawal in Afghanistan are also important security developments of the past year. Palestine's bid for UN membership, South Sudan's independence, and Ivory Coast's installation of a legitimate president after a violently disputed election are also important security topics covered in this edition.

In international political economy, the financial turmoil that has rocked the world economy since 2008 has changed international relationships and institutions, especially in the European Union, where a struggle for the future of the euro zone has been unfolding amid street clashes in Greece, bailout negotiations in Brussels, and funding appeals directed to China and Brazil. Meanwhile, Russia's 17-year quest to join the World Trade Organization has succeeded, bringing the largest of the remaining nonmembers into the fold and corresponding with Vladimir Putin's return to Russia's presidency. The United States, for its part, advanced trade by finalizing new agreements with South Korea, Colombia, and Panama since the last edition of this book.

New developments in technology also receive coverage here. Internet, cell phone, and social media capabilities played critical roles in the organizing of protests against repressive governments in the Arab Spring countries and, indeed, throughout the world. Meanwhile, the Stuxnet computer worm, evidently a product of U.S.-Israeli collaboration, successfully infected Iran's nuclear program and destroyed centrifuges used to enrich uranium, setting Iran's drive for nuclear weapons back by several years without firing a shot. And as world population passed 7 billion, conflicts over natural resources heightened, such as when China cut off exports of rare earth minerals, over which it holds a near monopoly. This update edition discusses all these major development of the past eventful year.

This edition retains the overall flow of the theory chapters in the tenth edition: Chapter 2 discusses realist theories, while Chapter 3 now discusses alternatives to realism, including liberal and social theories. Chapter 4 returns to a discussion of foreign policy, including how domestic politics (traditionally the purview of American and comparative politics scholars) influences international relations in both positive and negative ways.

We have updated the tables and figures with the most recent available data. This includes new data on GDP, reflecting the recovery from the global recession; on migration and refugees; on the debt burden in the developing world; on the HIV/AIDS epidemic; and on UN peacekeeping operations, to name a few.

This update edition contains significant revisions to the photo program. Dozens of new photos, many of them from 2011, draw visual attention to current events while reinforcing key concepts in the text.

Finally, this update includes the new boxed feature introduced in the tenth edition, "Seeking the Collective Good." The purpose of this new section is to emphasize our core theme of the book: the collective goods problem. Each chapter contains an example of a collective good that states are attempting to achieve. Each box then explores how the three core principles laid out in Chapter 1—dominance, reciprocity, or identity—have been used by states in an attempt to supply the collective good. We hope these new examples can provide a meaningful anchor for students to consider the concept of collective goods problems and the three potential approaches to solving them.

Structure of the Book

This book's aim is to present the current state of knowledge in IR in a comprehensive and accessible way—to provide a map of the subject covering its various research communities in a logical order. This map is organized around the subfields of international security and international political economy. These subfields, although separated physically in this book, are integrated conceptually and overlap in many ways. Common core principles—dominance, reciprocity, and identity—unify the book by showing how theoretical models apply across the range of topics in international security and political economy.

The overall structure of this book follows substantive topics, first in international security and then in international political economy. Chapter 1 introduces the study of IR; explains the collective goods problem and the core principles of dominance, reciprocity, and identity; and provides some geographical and historical context for the subject. The historical perspective places recent trends, especially globalization, in the context of the evolution of the international system over the 20th century, while the global orientation reflects the diversity of IR experiences for different actors, especially those in the global South. Chapters 2 and 3 lay out the various theoretical approaches to IR: realism, liberal theories, social theories (constructivist, postmodern, and Marxist), peace studies, and gender theories.

Chapter 4 discusses the formulation and implementation of foreign policy including a discussion of the key institutions involved in that process. Chapter 5 introduces the main sources of international conflict, including ethnic, religious, territorial, and economic conflicts. The conditions and manner in which such conflicts lead to the use of violence are discussed in Chapter 6, on military force and terrorism. Chapter 7 shows how international organizations and law, especially the United Nations, have evolved to become major influences in security relations, and how human rights have become increasingly important. The study of international organizations also bridges international security topics with those in international political economy.

The remaining chapters move through the various topics that make up the study of international political economy, beginning with microeconomic principles and national economies through trade and finance, international integration, the environment, and North-South relations, focusing heavily on development. Chapter 8 introduces theoretical concepts in political economy (showing how theories of international security translate into IPE issue areas) and discusses the most important topic in international political economy, namely, trade relations. Chapter 9 describes the politics of global finance and multinational business operations in an era of globalization. Chapter 10 explores the processes of international integration, telecommunications, and cultural exchange on both a regional scale—the European Union—and a global one. Chapter 11 shows how environmental politics and population growth expand international bargaining and interdependence both regionally and globally. Chapter 12 addresses global North-South relations, with particular attention given to poverty in the global South. Chapter 13 then considers alternatives for economic development in the context of international business, debt, and foreign aid. Chapter 14—a brief postscript—reflects on the book's central themes and encourages critical thinking about the future.

Pedagogical Elements

In a subject such as IR, in which knowledge is tentative and empirical developments can overtake theories, critical thinking is a key skill for college students to develop. At various points in the text, conclusions are left open-ended to let students reason their way through an issue, and in addition to the critical thinking questions at the end of each chapter, the boxed features support deeper and more focused critical thinking.

As noted earlier, the "Seeking the Collective Good" boxes focus on the core organizing concept of the textbook: the collective goods problem. Each box discuss a collective good and the problems encountered by states in attempting to achieve cooperation to provide the good. In each example, we highlight how one or more of the core principles (dominance, reciprocity, and identity) has been used successfully (or unsuccessfully) in the provision of the good.

The one-page "Policy Perspectives" feature in each chapter places students in the decision making perspective of a national leader. This feature bridges international relations theory to policy problems while demonstrating the trade-offs often present in political decision-making and highlighting the interconnectedness of foreign and domestic politics.

The "Let's Debate the Issue" boxes help students develop opinions on controversial topics. The topics in each chapter are chosen to pick up on important concepts discussed in that chapter. Thus, this feature deepens the treatment of particular topics, while reinforcing the general themes in each chapter.

Last, the "Careers in International Relations" feature at the end of Chapter 1 helps students think about job possibilities in the field. These pages, devoted to careers in nongovernmental organizations, government and diplomacy, international business, and teaching and research, respond to the question "How will this class help me find a job?" and include books and Web sites to further pursue the issue.

Many people find information—especially abstract concepts—easier to grasp when linked with pictures. Thus, the book uses color photographs extensively to illustrate important points. Photo captions reinforce main themes from each section of the text and link them with the scenes pictured, including in this edition many 2011 photos.

Students use different learning styles. Students who are visual learners should find not only the photos but also the many color graphics especially useful. The use of quantitative data also encourages critical thinking. Basic data, presented simply and appropriately at a global level, allow students to form their own judgments and to reason through the implications of different policies and theories. The text uses global-level data (showing the whole picture), rounds off numbers to highlight what is important, and conveys information graphically where appropriate.

IR is a large subject that offers many directions for further exploration. The footnotes in this book, updated for the tenth edition, suggest further reading on various topics. Unless otherwise noted, they are not traditional source notes. (Also, to save space in the notes, publisher locations are omitted and major university or state names refer to their university presses, although this is not a correct research paper style.)

JOSHUA S. GOLDSTEIN
JON C. PEVEHOUSE

MyPoliSciLab for *International Relations*

The moment you know.

Educators know it. Students know it. It's that inspired moment when something that was difficult to understand suddenly makes perfect sense. Our MyLab products have been designed and refined with a single purpose in mind—to help educators create that moment of understanding with their students.

MyPoliSciLab delivers *proven results* in helping individual students succeed. It provides *engaging experiences* that personalize, stimulate, and measure learning for each student. And it comes from a *trusted partner* with educational expertise and a deep commitment to helping students, instructors, and departments achieve their goals.

MyPoliSciLab can be used by itself or linked to any learning management system. To learn more about how MyPoliSciLab combines proven learning applications with powerful assessment, visit **www.mypoliscilab.com**.

MyPoliSciLab delivers *proven results* in helping individual students succeed.

- Pearson MyLabs are currently in use by millions of students each year across a variety of disciplines.
- MyPoliSciLab works, but don't take our word for it. Visit **www.pearsonhighered.com/elearning** to read white papers, case studies, and testimonials from instructors and students that consistently demonstrate the success of our MyLabs.

MyPoliSciLab provides *engaging experiences* that personalize, stimulate, and measure learning for each student.

- *Assessment.* Track progress and get instant feedback on every chapter, video, and multimedia activity. With results feeding into a powerful gradebook, the assessment program identifies learning challenges early and suggests the best resources to help.
- *Personalized Study Plan.* Follow a flexible learning path created by the assessment program and tailored to each student's unique needs. Organized by learning objectives, the study plan offers follow-up reading, video, and multimedia activities for further learning and practice.
- *Pearson eText.* Just like the printed text, highlight and add notes to the eText online or download it to a tablet.
- *Flashcards.* Learn key terms by word or definition.
- *Video.* Analyze current events by watching streaming video from major news providers.
- *Mapping Exercises.* Explore interactive maps that test basic geography, examine key events in world history, and analyze the state of the world.
- *Simulations.* Engage world politics by experiencing how political actors make decisions.
- *PoliSci News Review.* Join the political conversation by following headlines in *Financial Times* newsfeeds, reading analysis in the blog, taking weekly current events quizzes and polls, and more.
- *ClassPrep.* Engage students with class presentation resources collected in one convenient online destination.

MyPoliSciLab comes from a *trusted partner* with educational expertise and an eye on the future.

- Pearson support instructors with workshops, training, and assistance from Pearson Faculty Advisors so you get the help you need to make MyPoliSciLab work for your course.
- Pearson gathers feedback from instructors and students during the development of content and the feature enhancement of each release to ensure that our products meet your needs.

To order MyPoliSciLab with the print text, use ISBN 0-205-84402-2.

Supplements

Pearson is pleased to offer several resources to qualified adopters of *International Relations* and their students that will make teaching and learning from this book even more effective and enjoyable. Several of the supplements for this book are available at the Instructor Resource Center (IRC), an online hub that allows instructors to quickly download book-specific supplements. Please visit the IRC welcome page at **www.pearsonhighered.com/irc** to register for access.

Instructor's Manual/Test Bank   This resource includes chapter summaries, learning objectives, lecture outlines, multiple-choice questions, true/false questions, and essay questions for each chapter. Available exclusively on the IRC.

Pearson MyTest   This powerful assessment generation program includes all of the items in the instructor's manual/test bank. Questions and tests can be easily created, customized, saved online, and then printed, allowing flexibility to manage assessments anytime and anywhere. To learn more, please visit **www.mypearsontest.com** or contact your Pearson representative.

PowerPoint Presentation Organized around a lecture outline, these multimedia presentations also include photos, figures, and tables from each chapter. Available exclusively on the IRC.

Sample Syllabus This resource provides suggestions for assigning content from this book and MyPoliSciLab. Available exclusively on the IRC.

Longman Atlas of World Issues (0-205-78020-2) From population and political systems to energy use and women's rights, the *Longman Atlas of World Issues* features full-color thematic maps that examine the forces shaping the world. Featuring maps from the latest edition of *The Penguin State of the World Atlas*, this excerpt includes critical thinking exercises to promote a deeper understanding of how geography affects many global issues. Available at no additional charge when packaged with this book.

Goode's World Atlas (0-321-65200-2) First published by Rand McNally in 1923, *Goode's World Atlas* has set the standard for college reference atlases. It features hundreds of physical, political, and thematic maps as well as graphs, tables, and a pronouncing index. Available at a discount when packaged with this book.

The Penguin Dictionary of International Relations (0-140-51397-3) This indispensable reference by Graham Evans and Jeffrey Newnham includes hundreds of cross-referenced entries on the enduring and emerging theories, concepts, and events that are shaping the academic discipline of international relations and today's world politics. Available at a discount when packaged with this book.

Research and Writing in International Relations (0-205-06065-X) With current and detailed coverage on how to start research in the discipline's major subfields, this brief and affordable guide offers the step-by-step guidance and the essential resources needed to compose political science papers that go beyond description and into systematic and sophisticated inquiry. This text focuses on areas where students often need help—finding a topic, developing a question, reviewing the literature, designing research, and last, writing the paper. Available at a discount when packaged with this book.

Acknowledgments

Many scholars, colleagues, and friends have contributed ideas that ultimately influenced the ten editions of this book. The book owes a special debt to the late Robert C. North, who suggested many years ago that the concepts of bargaining and leverage could be used to integrate IR theory across four levels of analysis. For help with military data issues, we thank the late Randall Forsberg. For suggestions, we thank our colleagues, and the students in our world politics classes. For help with the footnotes and glossary, thanks to Louis Cooper and Peter Howard. For developing earlier versions of the "Let's Debate the Issue" boxes, we thank Mir Zohair Husain. For help with data research and bibliographic work, we thank Tana Johnson, Felicity Vabulas, Stephanie Dufek, Ben Zimmerman, and Roberta Braga. Thanks to Mark Lilleleht for assistance on the Careers feature. Finally, we appreciate the years of support we received from our colleague, teacher, and friend Deborah "Misty" Gerner, who passed away in 2006 and to whom this edition is dedicated.

The following reviewers made many useful suggestions: Catherine Adams, King's College London; Karen Adams, University of Montana; Philip Baumann, Minnesota State University Moorhead; Robert G. Blanton, University of Memphis; Robert E. Breckinridge, Mount Aloysius College; Jeff Cavanaugh, Mississippi State University; Brian Champion, Brigham Young University; Gregory A. Cline, Michigan State University; Myles Clowers, San Diego City College; Cynthia Combs, University of North Carolina at Charlotte; Michael Corgan, Boston University; Paul D'Anieri, University of Florida; Patricia Davis, University of Notre Dame; Elizabeth DeSombre, Colby College; June Teufel Dreyer, University of Miami; Larry Elowitz, George College and State University; George Emerson, Miami Dade Community College; Mark Everingham, University of Wisconsin–Green Bay; Jonathan Galloway, Lake Forest College; Marc Genest, University of Rhode Island; the late Deborah J. Gerner, University of Kansas; Emily O. Goldman, University of California, Davis; Vicki Golich, California State University, San Marcos; Robert Gregg, School of International Service, American University; Wolfgang Hirczy, University of Houston; Piper Hodson, Saint Joseph's College; Steven W. Hook, University of Missouri; Ted Hopf, Ohio State University; Mir Zohair Husain, University of South Alabama; Akira Ichikawa, University of Lethbridge; W. Martin James, Henderson State University; Matthias Kaelberer, Iowa State University; Aaron Karp, Old Dominion University; Joyce Kaufman, University of Maryland at College Park; John Keeler, University of Washington; Michael Kelley, University of Central Arkansas; Jane K. Kramer, University of Oregon; Mark Lagon, Georgetown University; William Lamkin, Glendale Community College; Wei-Chin Lee, Wake Forest University; Christopher Leskin, University of the Cumberlands; Renée Marlin-Bennett, Johns Hopkins University; James Meernick, University of North Texas; Karen Mingst, University of Kentucky; Richard Moore, Lewis-Clark State College; Layna Mosley, University of North Carolina; Mark Mullenbach, University of Central Arkansas; Todd Myers, Grossmont College; John W. Outland, University of Richmond; Salvatore Prisco, Stevens Institute of Technology; David Rapkin, University of Nebraska at Lincoln; Edward Rhodes, Rutgers University; Leonard Riley, Pikes Peak Community College; Trevor Rubenzer, University of South Carolina-Upstate; Richard Rupp, Purdue University–Calumet; Houman Sadri, University of Central Florida; Henry Schockley, Boston University; Keith St. Clair, Grand Rapids Community College; Paul Vasquez, Wabash College; Paul Vicary, Florida International University; Thomas J. Volgy, University of Arizona; and David Wilsford, Institute for American Universities, France. The errors, of course, remain our own responsibility.

To the Student

The topics studied by scholars are like a landscape with many varied locations and terrains. This textbook is a map that can orient you to the main topics, debates, and issue areas in international relations. Scholars use specialized language to talk about their subjects. This text is a phrase book that can translate such lingo and explain the terms and concepts that scholars use to talk about international relations. However, IR is filled with many voices speaking many tongues. The text translates some of those voices—of presidents and professors, free traders and feminists—to help you sort out the contours of the subject and the state of knowledge about its various topics. In this tenth edition, we have especially tried to streamline and clarify this complex subject to help you not just understand but deeply understand international relations. But ultimately, the synthesis presented in this book is that of the authors. Both you and your professor may disagree with many points. Thus, this book is only a starting point for conversations and debates.

With map and phrase book in hand, you are ready to explore a fascinating world. The great changes taking place in world politics have made the writing of this textbook an exciting project. May you enjoy your own explorations of this realm.

J. S. G.
J. C. P.

A Note on Nomenclature

In international relations, names are politically sensitive; different actors may call a territory or an event by different names. This book cannot resolve such conflicts; it has adopted the following naming conventions for the sake of consistency. The United Kingdom of Great Britain (England, Scotland, Wales) and Northern Ireland is called Britain. Burma, renamed Myanmar by its military government, is referred to as Burma. The 1991 U.S.-led multinational military campaign that retook Kuwait after Iraq's 1990 invasion is called the Gulf War. The war between Iran and Iraq in the 1980s is called the Iran-Iraq War. The country of Bosnia and Herzegovina is generally shortened to Bosnia (with apologies to Herzegovinians). The former Yugoslav Republic of Macedonia is called Macedonia. The People's Republic of China is referred to as China. The Democratic Republic of the Congo (formerly called the Belgian Congo and then Zaire) is here called Democratic Congo. Elsewhere, country names follow common usage, dropping formal designations such as "Republic of."

International Relations

CHAPTER 1

The Globalization of International Relations

New York Philharmonic Orchestra and North Korean audience, 2008.

Globalization, International Relations, and Daily Life

International relations is a fascinating topic because it concerns peoples and cultures throughout the world. The scope and complexity of the interactions among these groups make international relations a challenging subject to master. There is always more to learn. This book is only the beginning of the story.

Narrowly defined, the field of **international relations (IR)** concerns the relationships among the world's governments. But these relationships cannot be understood in isolation. They are closely connected with other actors (such as international organizations, multinational corporations, and individuals); with other social structures and processes (including economics, culture, and domestic politics); and with geographical and historical influences. These elements together power the central trend in IR today—globalization.

Indeed, two key events of recent years reflect globalization. The terrorists who plotted and carried out the September 11, 2001, attacks used the Internet to assist in planning, coordination, and fundraising for the attacks. And the global economic recession of 2008–2009, which began with a collapse of the U.S. home mortgage market, spread quickly to other nations. Highly integrated global financial markets created a ripple effect across the globe that is still being felt today. Thus, two hallmarks of globalization—expanding communications technology and integrated markets—facilitated events that directly impacted our daily lives.

Not only large-scale events influence our daily lives. The prospects for getting jobs after graduation depend on the global economy and international economic competition. Those jobs also are more likely than ever to entail international travel, sales, or communication. And the rules of the world trading system affect the goods that students consume every day, such as electronics, clothes, and gasoline.

Globalization has distinct positive impacts on our daily lives as well. As technology advances, the world is shrinking year by year. Better communication and transportation capabilities constantly expand the ordinary person's contact with people, products, and ideas from other countries. Globalization is internationalizing us.

In addition to feeling the influence of globalization and international relations on our daily lives, individual citizens can influence the world as well. Often, international relations is portrayed as a distant and abstract ritual conducted by a small group of people such as presidents, generals, and diplomats. Although leaders do play a major role in international affairs, many other people participate. College students and other citizens participate in international relations every time they vote in an election or work on a political campaign, buy a product or service traded on world markets, and watch the news. The choices we make in our daily lives ultimately affect the world we live in. Through those choices, every person makes a unique contribution, however small, to the world of international relations.

The purpose of this book is to introduce the field of IR, to organize what is known and theorized about IR, and to convey the key concepts used by political scientists to discuss relations among nations. This first chapter defines IR as a field of study, introduces the actors of interest, and reviews the geographical and historical aspects of globalization within which IR occurs.

Read and Listen to **Chapter 1** at **mypoliscilab.com**

Study and **Review** the **Pre-Test & Flashcards** at **mypoliscilab.com**

3

TOUCHED BY WAR

IR affects our lives in many ways. This woman's boyfriend died in Iraq in 2006.

Explore the Simulation "Why Study International Relations" on mypoliscilab.com

Core Principles

The field of IR reflects the world's complexity, and IR scholars use many theories, concepts, and buzzwords in trying to describe and explain it. Underneath this complexity, however, lie a few basic principles that shape the field. We will lay out the range of theories and approaches in Chapters 2 through 4, but here we will present the most central ideas as free from jargon as possible.

IR revolves around one key problem: How can a group—such as two or more countries—serve its *collective* interests when doing so requires its members to forgo their *individual* interests? For example, every country has an interest in stopping global warming, a goal that can be achieved only by many countries acting together. Yet each country also has an individual interest in burning fossil fuels to keep its economy going. Similarly, all members of a military alliance benefit from the strength of the alliance, but each member separately has an interest in minimizing its own contributions in troops and money. Individual nations can advance their own short-term interests by seizing territory militarily, cheating on trade agreements, and refusing to contribute to international efforts such as peacekeeping or vaccination campaigns. But if all nations acted this way, they would find themselves worse off, in a chaotic and vicious environment where mutual gains from cooperating on issues of security and trade would disappear.

This problem of shared interests versus conflicting interests among members of a group goes by various names in various contexts—the problem of "collective action," "free riding," "burden sharing," the "tragedy of the commons," or the "prisoner's dilemma." We will refer to the general case as the **collective goods problem,** that is, the problem of how to provide something that benefits all members of a group regardless of what each member contributes to it.[1]

In general, collective goods are easier to provide in small groups than in large ones. In a small group, the cheating (or free riding) of one member is harder to conceal, has a greater impact on the overall collective good, and is easier to punish. The advantage of small groups helps explain the importance of the great power system in international security affairs and of the G20 (Group of Twenty) industrialized countries in economic matters.[2]

[1] Olson, Mancur. *The Logic of Collective Action.* Harvard, 1971 [1965].
[2] At the G20 meeting in 2009, leaders of the major industrial countries announced that the G20 would replace the G8 as the key group coordinating global financial matters.

The collective goods problem occurs in all groups and societies, but is particularly acute in international affairs because each nation is sovereign, with no central authority such as a world government to enforce on individual nations the necessary measures to provide for the common good. By contrast, in domestic politics *within* countries, a government can force individuals to contribute in ways that do not serve their individual self-interest, such as by paying taxes or paying to install antipollution equipment on vehicles and factories. If individuals do not comply, the government can punish them. Although this solution is far from perfect—cheaters and criminals sometimes are not caught, and governments sometimes abuse their power—it mostly works well enough to keep societies going.

Three basic principles—which we call dominance, reciprocity, and identity—offer possible solutions to the core problem of getting individuals to cooperate for the common good without a central authority to make them do so (see Table 1.1 on p. 8). These three principles are fundamental across the social sciences and recur in such disciplines as the study of animal societies, child development, social psychology, anthropology, and economics, as well as political science. To explain each principle, we will apply the three principles to a small-scale human example and an IR example.

Dominance   The principle of **dominance** solves the collective goods problem by establishing a power hierarchy in which those at the top control those below—a bit like a government but without an actual government. Instead of fighting constantly over who gets scarce resources, the members of a group can just fight occasionally over position in the "status hierarchy." Then social conflicts such as who gets resources are resolved automatically in favor of the higher-ranking actor. Fights over the dominance position have scripted rules that minimize, to some extent, the harm inflicted on the group members. Symbolic acts of submission and dominance reinforce an ever-present status hierarchy. Staying on top of a status hierarchy does not depend on strength alone, though it helps. Rather, the top actor may be the one most adept at forming and maintaining alliances among the group's more capable members. Dominance is complex, and not just a matter of brute force.

In international relations, the principle of dominance underlies the great power system, in which a handful of countries dictate the rules for all the others. Sometimes a 4so-called *hegemon* or superpower stands atop the great powers as the dominant nation. The UN Security Council, in which the world's five strongest military powers hold a veto, reflects the dominance principle.

The advantage of the dominance solution to the collective goods problem is that, like a government, it forces members of a group to contribute to the common good. It also minimizes open conflict within the group. However, the disadvantage is that this stability comes at a cost of constant oppression of, and resentment by, the lower-ranking members in the status hierarchy. Also, conflicts over position in the hierarchy can occasionally harm the group's stability and well-being, such as when challenges to the top position lead to serious fights. In the case of international relations, the great power system and the hegemony of a superpower can provide relative peace and stability for decades on end but then can break down into costly wars among the great powers.

Reciprocity   The principle of **reciprocity** solves the collective goods problem by rewarding behavior that contributes to the group and punishing behavior that pursues self-interest at the expense of the group. Reciprocity is very easy to understand and can be "enforced" without any central authority, making it a robust way to get individuals to cooperate for the common good.

But reciprocity operates in both the positive realm ("You scratch my back and I'll scratch yours") and the negative ("An eye for an eye, a tooth for a tooth"). A disadvantage

TRAVEL COMPANIONS

Collective goods are provided to all members of a group regardless of their individual contributions, just as these migrant workers crossing the Sahara desert in Niger in 2006 all depend on the truck's progress even while perhaps jostling for position among themselves. In many issue areas, such as global warming, the international community of nations is similarly interdependent. However, the provision of collective goods presents difficult dilemmas as players seek to maximize their own share of benefits.

of reciprocity as a solution to the collective goods problem is that it can lead to a downward spiral as each side punishes what it believes to be negative acts by the other. Psychologically, most people overestimate their own good intentions and underestimate the value of the actions of their opponents or rivals. To avoid tit-for-tat escalations of conflict, one or both parties must act generously to get the relationship moving in a good direction.

In international relations, reciprocity forms the basis of most of the norms (habits; expectations) and institutions in the international system. Many central arrangements in IR, such as World Trade Organization agreements, explicitly recognize reciprocity as the linchpin of cooperation. For instance, if one country opens its markets to another's goods, the other opens its markets in return. On the negative side, reciprocity fuels arms races as each side responds to the other's buildup of weapons. But it also allows arms control agreements and other step-by-step conflict-resolution measures, as two sides match each other's actions in backing away from the brink of war.

Identity   A third potential solution to the collective goods problem lies in the identities of participants as members of a community. Although the dominance and reciprocity principles act on the idea of achieving individual self-interest (by taking what you can, or by mutually beneficial arrangements), the **identity** principle does not rely on self-interest. On the contrary, members of an identity community care about the interests of others in that community enough to sacrifice their own interests to benefit others. The roots of this principle lie in the family, the extended family, and the kinship group. But this potential is not limited to the close family; it can be generalized to any identity community that one feels a part of. As members of a family care about each other, so do members of an ethnic group, a gender group, a nation, or the world's scientists. In each case, individual members will accept solutions to collective goods problems that do not give them the best deal as individuals, because the benefits are "all in the family," so to speak. A biologist retiring at a rich American university may give away lab equipment to a biologist in a poor country because they share an identity as scientists. A European Jew may give money to Israel because of a shared Jewish identity, or a computer scientist from India may return home to work for lower pay after receiving training in Canada, in order to help the community he or she cares about. Millions of people contribute to international disaster relief funds after tsunamis, earthquakes, or hurricanes because of a shared identity as members of the community of human beings.

In IR, identity communities play important roles in overcoming difficult collective goods problems, including the issue of who contributes to development assistance, world health, and UN peacekeeping missions. The relatively large foreign aid contributions of Scandinavian countries, or the high Canadian participation in peacekeeping, cannot be explained well by self-interest, but arise from these countries' self-defined identities as members of the international community. Even in military forces and diplomacy (where dominance and reciprocity, respectively, rule the day), the shared identities of military professionals and of diplomats—each with shared traditions and expectations—can take the edge off conflicts. And military alliances also mix identity politics with raw self-interest, as shown by the unusual strength of the U.S.-British alliance, which shared interests alone cannot explain as well as shared identity does.

Nonstate actors, such as nongovernmental organizations or terrorist networks, also rely on identity politics to a great extent. The increasing roles of these actors—feminist organizations, churches, jihadists, and multinational corporations, for example—have brought the identity principle to greater prominence in IR theory in recent years.

An Everyday Example   To sum up the three core principles, imagine that you have two good friends, a man and a woman, who are in a romantic relationship. They love each other and enjoy the other's company, but they come to you for help with a problem: When they go out together, the man likes to go to the opera, whereas the woman enjoys going to boxing matches.[3] Because of your training in international relations, you quickly recognize this as a collective goods problem, in which the shared interest is spending time together and the conflicting individual interests are watching opera and watching boxing. (Of course, you know that the behavior of states is more complicated than that of individuals, but put that aside for a moment.) You might approach this problem in any of three ways.

First, you could say, "Traditionally, relationships work best when the man wears the pants. For thousands of years the man has made the decision and the woman has followed it. I suggest you do the same, and buy season tickets to the opera." This would be a dominance solution. It could be a very stable solution, if the woman cares more about spending time with her true love than she cares about opera or boxing. It would be a simple solution that would settle all future conflicts. It would give one party everything he wants, and the other party some of what she wants (love, company, a stable relationship). This might be better for both of them than spending all their evenings arguing about where to go out. On the other hand, this solution might leave the woman permanently resentful at the unequal nature of the outcome. She might feel her love for her partner diminish, over time, by a longing for respect and a nostalgia for boxing. She might even meet another man who likes her *and* likes boxing.

Second, you could say, "Look, instead of fighting all the time, why don't you establish a pattern and trade off going to boxing one time and opera the next." This would be a reciprocity solution. You could help the couple set up agreements, accounting systems, and shared expectations to govern the implementation of this seemingly simple solution. For example, they could go to boxing on Friday nights and opera on Saturday nights. But what if opera season is shorter than boxing season? Then perhaps they would go to opera more often during its season and boxing more often when opera is out of season. What if one of them is out of town on a Friday night? Does that night count anyway or does it earn a credit for later? Or does the one who is in town go out alone? What if the man *hates* boxing but the woman only mildly dislikes opera? Do you set up a schedule of two operas for each boxing match to keep each side equally happy or unhappy? Clearly, reciprocity

---

[3] This scenario is adopted from the game theory example "Battle of the Sexes."

solutions can become very complicated (just look at the world trade rules in Chapter 8, for example), and they require constant monitoring to see if obligations are being met and cheating avoided. Your friends might find it an irritant in their relationship to keep close track of who owes whom a night at the opera or at a boxing match.

Third, you could say, "Who cares about opera or boxing? The point is that you love each other and want to be together. Get past the superficial issues and strengthen the core feelings that brought you together. Then it won't matter where you go or what you're watching." This would be an identity solution. This approach could powerfully resolve your friends' conflict and leave them both much happier. Over time, one partner might actually begin to prefer the other's favorite activity after more exposure—leading to a change in identity. On the other hand, after a while self-interest could creep back in, because that loving feeling might seem even happier with a boxing match (or opera) to watch. Indeed, one partner can subtly exploit the other's commitment to get past the superficial conflicts. "What's it matter as long as we're together," she says, "and oh, look, there's a good boxing match tonight!" Sometimes the identity principle operates more powerfully in the short term than the long term: the soldier who volunteers to defend the homeland might begin to feel taken advantage of after months or years on the front line, and the American college student who gives money once to tsunami victims may not want to keep giving year after year to malaria victims.

TABLE 1.1   Core Principles for Solving Collective Goods Problems

Principle	Advantages	Drawbacks
Dominance	Order, Stability, Predictability	Oppression, Resentment
Reciprocity	Incentives for Mutual Cooperation	Downward Spirals; Complex Accounting
Identity	Sacrifice for Group, Redefine Interests	Demonizing an Out-Group

SEEKING THE COLLECTIVE GOOD

Introduction

In explaining how countries behave in IR, a central concept is the "collective goods problem" (p. 4). This recurring problem results when two or more members of a group share an interest in some outcome of value to them all, but have conflicting individual interests when it comes to achieving that valued outcome. For example, the world's countries share a desire to avoid global warming, but each one benefits from burning fossil fuels to run its economy. If a few members of a group fail to contribute to a collective good, the others will still provide it and the few can "free ride." But if too many do so, then the collective good will not be provided for anyone. For instance, if too many countries burn too much fossil fuel, then the whole world will suffer the effects of global warming.

Within domestic societies, governments solve collective goods problems by forcing the members of society to contribute to common goals, such as by paying taxes. In international affairs, no such world government exists. Three core principles—dominance, reciprocity, and identity—offer different solutions to the collective goods problem. These principles underlie the actions and outcomes that make up IR.

To help tie together a central topic in a chapter with the core principles used throughout the book, each

DOMINANCE

RECIPROCITY

IDENTITY

An IR Example   Now consider the problem of nuclear proliferation. All countries share an interest in the collective good of peace and stability, which is hard to achieve in a world where more and more countries make more and more nuclear weapons. Within a society, if individuals acquire dangerous weapons, the government can take them away to keep everyone safe. But in the society of nations, no such central authority exists. In 2006, North Korea tested its first nuclear bomb and Iran continues uranium enrichment that could lead to a nuclear bomb—defying UN resolutions in both cases.

One approach to nuclear proliferation legitimizes these weapons' ownership by just the few most powerful countries. The "big five" with the largest nuclear arsenals hold veto power on the UN Security Council. Through agreements like the Non-Proliferation Treaty (NPT) and the Proliferation Security Initiative, the existing nuclear powers actively try to keep their exclusive hold on these weapons and prevent smaller nations from getting them. This is a dominance approach. In 2003, when the United States thought Iraq's Saddam Hussein might have an active nuclear weapons program, as he had a decade earlier, it invaded Iraq and overthrew its government. Similarly, in 1982, when Iraq had begun working toward a nuclear bomb, Israel sent jets to bomb Iraq's nuclear facility, setting back the program by years. One drawback to these dominance solutions is the resentment they create among the smaller countries. Those countries point to an unenforced provision of the NPT stating that existing nuclear powers should get rid of their own bombs as other countries refrain from making new ones. And they ask what gives Israel the right to bomb another country, or the United States the right to invade one. They speak of a "double standard" for the powerful and the weak.

Reciprocity offers a different avenue for preventing proliferation. It is the basis of the provision in the NPT about the existing nuclear powers' obligation to disarm in exchange for smaller countries' agreement to stay nonnuclear. Reciprocity also underlies arms control agreements, used extensively in the Cold War to manage the buildup of nuclear bombs by the superpowers, and used currently to manage the mutual reduction of their arsenals. Deterrence also relies on reciprocity. The United States warned North Korea in 2006 against selling its bombs (an action that would be in North Korea's short-term self-interest),

chapter contains a Seeking the Collective Good box. Each box will discuss how the world's states deal with an important issue in IR using one (or more) of the core principles. Examples include stopping genocide (Chapter 7), enhancing world trade (Chapter 8), and slowing global warming (Chapter 11).

Canadian smokestack, 2009. Global climate stability is a collective good.

threatening to retaliate against North Korea if any other actor used such a bomb against the United States. And when Libya gave up its nuclear weapons program in 2003, the international community gave it various rewards, including the ending of economic sanctions, in exchange.

The identity principle has proven equally effective against nuclear proliferation, if less newsworthy. Many nations that have the technical ability to make nuclear weapons have *chosen* not to do so. They have constructed their national identities in ways that shape their self-interests so as to make nuclear bombs undesirable. Some, like Sweden, do not intend to fight wars. Others, like Germany, belong to alliances in which they come under another nation's nuclear "umbrella" and do not need their own bomb. South Africa actually developed nuclear weapons in secret but then dismantled the program before apartheid ended, keeping the bomb out of the hands of the new majority-rule government. Nobody forced South Africa to do this (as in dominance), nor did it respond to rewards and punishments (reciprocity). Rather, South Africa's identity shifted. Similarly, Japan's experience of the catastrophic results of militarism, culminating in the destruction of two of its cities by nuclear bombs in 1945, continues generations later to shape Japan's identity as a country that does not want nuclear weapons, even though it has the know-how and even the stockpile of plutonium to make them.

Collective goods problems fascinate social scientists, and especially scholars of IR, precisely because they have no easy solutions. In later chapters, we will see how these three core principles shape the responses of the international community to various collective goods problems across the whole range of IR issues.

IR as a Field of Study

IR is a rather practical discipline. There is a close connection between scholars in colleges, universities, and think tanks and the policy-making community working in the government—especially in the United States. Some professors serve in the government (for instance, Professor Condoleezza Rice became national security advisor in 2001 and secretary of state in 2005 under President George W. Bush), and sometimes professors publicize their ideas about foreign policy through newspaper columns or TV interviews. Influencing their government's foreign policy gives these scholars a laboratory in which to test their ideas in practice. Diplomats, bureaucrats, and politicians can benefit from the knowledge produced by IR scholars.[4]

Theoretical debates in the field of IR are fundamental, but unresolved.[5] It will be up to the next generation of IR scholars—today's college students—to achieve a better understanding of how world politics works. The goal of this book is to lay out the current state of knowledge without exaggerating the successes of the discipline.

As a part of political science, IR is about *international politics*—the decisions of governments about foreign actors, especially other governments.[6] To some extent, however, the

---

[4] Walt, Stephen M. The Relationship between Theory and Policy in International Relations. *Annual Review of Political Science* 8, 2005: 23–48.

[5] Art, Robert J., and Robert Jervis, eds. *International Politics: Enduring Concepts and Contemporary Issues.* 8th ed. Longman, 2006. Dougherty, James E., Jr., and Robert L. Pfaltzgraff. *Contending Theories of International Relations: A Comprehensive Survey.* 5th ed. Longman, 2001. Doyle, Michael W. *Ways of War and Peace: Realism, Liberalism, and Socialism.* Norton, 1997.

[6] Carlsnaes, Walter, Thomas Risse, and Beth Simmons, eds. *Handbook of International Relations.* Sage, 2002. Waever, Ole. The Sociology of a Not So International Discipline: American and European Developments in International Relations. *International Organization* 52 (4), 1998: 687–727.

POLICY PERSPECTIVES

Overview

International policy makers confront a variety of problems every day. Solving these problems requires difficult decisions and choices. "Policy Perspectives" is a box feature in each chapter that places you in a particular decision-making perspective (for example, the prime minister of Great Britain) and asks you to make choices concerning an important international relations issue.

Each box contains four sections. The first, "Background," provides information about a political problem faced by the leader. This background information is factual and reflects real situations faced by these decision makers.

The second section, "Domestic Considerations," reflects on the implications of the situation for domestic politics within the leader's government and society. How will the lives of ordinary citizens be affected?

The third section, "Scenario," suggests a new problem or crisis confronting the leader. Although these crises are hypothetical, all are within the realm of possibility and would require difficult decisions by the leaders and their countries.

The fourth section, "Choose Your Policy," asks you to make a choice responding to the Scenario. With each decision, think about the trade-offs between your options. What are the risks and rewards in choosing one policy over another? Do alternative options exist that could effectively address the problem within the given constraints? Does one option pose bigger costs in the short term, but fewer in the long term? Can you defend your decision to colleagues, the public, and other world leaders? How will your choice affect your citizens' lives and your own political survival?

As you consider each problem faced by the decision maker, try to reflect on the process and logic by which you have reached the decision. Which factors seem more important and why? Are domestic or international factors more important in shaping your decision? Are the constraints you face based on limited capability (for example, money or military power), or do international law or norms influence your decision as well? How do factors such as lack of time influence your decision?

You will quickly discover that there are often no "right" answers. At times, it is difficult to choose between two good options; at other times, one has to decide which is the least bad option.

---

field is interdisciplinary, relating international politics to economics, history, sociology, and other disciplines. Some universities offer separate degrees or departments for IR. Most, however, teach IR in political science classes, in which the focus is on the *politics* of economic relationships, or the *politics* of environmental management to take two examples. (The domestic politics of foreign countries, although overlapping with IR, generally make up the separate field of *comparative politics*.)

Political relations among nations cover a range of activities—diplomacy, war, trade relations, alliances, cultural exchanges, participation in international organizations, and so forth. Particular activities within one of these spheres make up distinct **issue areas** on which scholars and foreign policy makers focus attention. Examples of issue areas include global trade, the environment, and specific conflicts such as the Arab-Israeli conflict. Within each issue area, and across the range of issues of concern in any international relationship, policy makers of one nation can behave in a cooperative manner or a conflictual manner—extending either friendly or hostile behavior toward the other nation. IR scholars often look at international relations in terms of the mix of **conflict and cooperation** in relationships among nations.

The scope of the field of IR may also be defined by the *subfields* it encompasses. Some scholars treat topics such as this book's chapters (for example, international law or international development) as subfields, but here we will reserve the term for two macro level topics. Traditionally, the study of IR has focused on questions of war and peace—the subfield of **international security** studies. The movements of armies and of diplomats, the crafting of treaties and alliances, the development and deployment of military capabilities—these are the subjects that dominated the study of IR in the past, especially in the 1950s and 1960s, and they continue to hold a central position in the field. Since the Cold War, regional conflicts and ethnic violence have received more attention, while interdisciplinary peace studies programs and feminist scholarship have sought to broaden concepts of "security" further.[7]

The subfield of **international political economy (IPE),** a second main subfield of IR, concerns trade and financial relations among nations and focuses on how nations have cooperated politically to create and maintain institutions that regulate the flow of international economic and financial transactions. Although these topics previously centered on relations among the world's richer nations, the widening of globalization and multilateral economic institutions such as the World Trade Organization has pushed IPE scholars to focus on developing states as well. In addition, they pay growing attention to relations between developed and developing nations (often labeled North-South relations), including such topics as economic dependency, debt, foreign aid, and technology transfer. Also newly important are problems of international environmental management and of global telecommunications. The subfield of IPE is expanding accordingly.[8]

The same principles and theories that help us understand international security (discussed in the first half of this book) also help us understand IPE (discussed in the second half). Economics is important in security affairs, and vice versa.

Theoretical knowledge accumulates by a repeated cycle of generalizing and then testing. For a given puzzle, various theories can explain the result (though none perfectly) as a case of a more general principle. Each theory also logically predicts other outcomes, and these can be tested empirically. A laboratory science, controlling all but one variable, can test theoretical predictions efficiently. IR does not have this luxury, because many variables operate simultaneously. Thus, it is especially important to think critically about IR events and consider several different theoretical explanations before deciding which (if any) provides the best explanation.

Actors and Influences

▶ Watch
the **Video**
**"Conflict Diamonds
and the Kimberley
Process"**
on **mypoliscilab.com**

The principal actors in IR are the world's governments. Scholars of IR traditionally study the decisions and acts of those governments in relation to other governments. The international stage is crowded with actors large and small that are intimately interwoven with the decisions of governments. These actors are individual leaders and citizens. They are bureaucratic agencies in foreign ministries. They are multinational corporations and terrorist groups. But the most important actors in IR are states.

---

[7] Neack, Laura. *Elusive Security: States First, People Last.* Rowman & Littlefield, 2007. Booth, Ken, ed. *Critical Security Studies and World Politics.* Rienner, 2005. Buzan, Barry, Ole Waever, and Jaap de Wilde. *Security: A New Framework for Analysis.* Rienner, 1997.

[8] Cohen, Benjamin J. *International Political Economy: An Intellectual History.* Princeton, 2008. Gilpin, Robert. *Global Political Economy: Understanding the International Economic Order.* Princeton, 2001. Keohane, Robert O., and Joseph S. Nye, Jr. *Power and Interdependence.* 3rd ed. Longman, 2001.

State Actors

A **state** is a territorial entity controlled by a government and inhabited by a population. The locations of the world's states and territories are shown in the reference map at the back of this book, after the Jobs section. Regional maps with greater detail appear there as well.

A state government answers to no higher authority; it exercises *sovereignty* over its territory—to make and enforce laws, to collect taxes, and so forth. This sovereignty is recognized (acknowledged) by other states through diplomatic relations and usually by membership in the United Nations (UN). (The concepts of state sovereignty and territoriality are elaborated in Chapter 2.) The population inhabiting a state forms a *civil society* to the extent that it has developed institutions to participate in political or social life. All or part of the population that shares a group identity may consider itself a *nation* (see "Nationalism" on pp. 160–161). The state's government is a *democracy* to the extent that the government is controlled by the members of the population rather than imposed on them. (Note that the word *state* in IR does not mean a state in the United States.) In political life, and to some extent in IR scholarship, the terms *state*, *nation*, and *country* are used imprecisely, usually to refer to state governments.

With few exceptions, each state has a capital city—the seat of government from which it administers its territory—

POWERS THAT BE

States are the most important actors in IR. A handful of states are considered great powers and one a "superpower." The BRICS countries—Brazil, Russia, India, China, and South Africa—are large, growing countries outside Europe and North America. Here, their leaders meet in 2011.

and often a single individual who acts in the name of the state. We will refer to this person simply as the "state leader." Often he or she is the *head of government* (such as a prime minister) or the *head of state* (such as a president, or a king or queen). In some countries, such as the United States, the same person is head of state and government. In other countries, the positions of the president or royalty, or even the prime minister, are symbolic. In any case, the most powerful political figure is the one we mean by "state leader," and these figures are the key individual actors in IR, regardless of whether these leaders are democratically elected or dictators. The state actor includes the individual leader as well as bureaucratic organizations (such as foreign ministries) that act in the name of the state.

The **international system** is the set of relationships among the world's states, structured according to certain rules and patterns of interaction. Some such rules are explicit, some implicit. They include who is considered a member of the system, what rights and responsibilities the members have, and what kinds of actions and responses normally occur between states.

The modern international system has existed for less than 500 years. Before then, people were organized into more mixed and overlapping political units such as city-states, empires, and feudal fiefs. In the past 200 years the idea has spread that *nations*—groups of people who share a sense of national identity, usually including a language and culture—should have their own states. Most large states today are such **nation-states**. But since World War II, the decolonization process in much of Asia and Africa has added many new states, some not at all nation-states. A major source of conflict and war at present is the frequent mismatch between perceived nations and actual state borders. When people identify with a nationality that their state government does not represent, they may fight to form their own state and thus to gain sovereignty over their territory and affairs. This substate nationalism is only one of several growing trends that undermine the present system of states. Other such trends include the globalization of economic processes, the power of telecommunications, and the proliferation of ballistic missiles.

The independence of former colonies and, more recently, the breakup into smaller states of large multinational states (the Soviet Union, Yugoslavia, and Czechoslovakia) have increased the number of states in the world. The exact total depends on the status of a number of quasi-state political entities, and it keeps changing as political units split apart or merge. The UN had 193 members in 2012.

The population of the world's states varies dramatically, from China and India with more than 1 billion people each, to microstates such as San Marino with fewer than 40,000. With the creation of many small states in recent decades, the majority of states now have fewer than 10 million people each, and more than half of the rest have 10 to 50 million each. But the 15 states with populations of more than 70 million people together contain about two-thirds of the world's population.

States also differ tremendously in the size of their total annual economic activity—**Gross Domestic Product (GDP)**[9]—from the $14 trillion U.S. economy to the economies of tiny states such as the Pacific island of Tuvalu ($30 million). The world economy is dominated by a few states, just as world population is. Figure 1.1 lists the largest countries by population and economy. Each is an important actor in world affairs.

A few of these large states possess especially great military and economic strength and influence, and are called *great powers*. They are defined and discussed in Chapter 2. The most powerful of great powers, those with truly global influence, have been called *superpowers*. This term generally meant the United States and the Soviet Union during the Cold War, and now refers to the United States alone.

Some other political entities are often referred to as states or countries although they are not formally recognized as states. Taiwan is the most important of these. It operates independently in practice but is claimed by China (a claim recognized formally by outside powers) and is not a UN member. Formal colonies and possessions still exist; their status may change in the future. They include Puerto Rico (U.S.), Bermuda (British), Martinique (French), French Guiana, the Netherlands Antilles (Dutch), the Falkland Islands (British), and Guam (U.S.). Hong Kong reverted from British to Chinese rule in 1997 and retains a somewhat separate economic identity under China's "one country, two systems" formula. The status of the Vatican (Holy See) in Rome is ambiguous, as is Palestine. Including various such territorial entities with states brings the world total to about 200 state or quasi-state actors. Other would-be states such as Kurdistan (Iraq), Abkhazia (Georgia), and Somaliland (Somalia) may fully control the territory they claim but are not internationally recognized.

---

[9] GDP is the total of goods and services produced by a nation; it is very similar to the Gross National Product (GNP). Such data are difficult to compare across nations with different currencies, economic systems, and levels of development. In particular, comparisons of GDP in capitalist and socialist economies, or in rich and poor countries, should be treated cautiously. GDP data used in this book are mostly from the World Bank. GDP data are adjusted through time and across countries for "purchasing-power parity" (how much a given amount of money can buy). See Summers, Robert, and Alan Heston. The Penn World Table (Mark 5): An Expanded Set of International Comparisons, 1950–1988. *Quarterly Journal of Economics* 106 (2), 1991: 327–68. GDP and population data are for 2008 unless otherwise noted.

FIGURE 1.1 Largest Countries, 2010

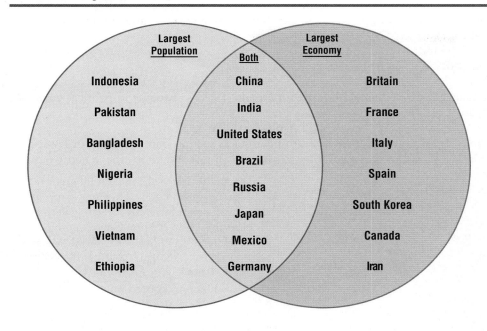

Note: Left and center columns listed in population order, right column in GDP order. GDP calculated by purchasing parity.

Source: CIA. *World Factbook.*

Nonstate Actors

National governments may be the most important actors in IR, but they are strongly influenced by a variety of **nonstate actors** (see Table 1.2). These actors are also called *transnational actors* when they operate across international borders.

First, states often take actions through, within, or in the context of **intergovernmental organizations (IGOs)**—organizations whose members are national governments. IGOs fulfill a variety of functions and vary in size from just a few states to virtually the whole UN membership. The Organization of Petroleum Exporting Countries (OPEC), the World Trade Organization (WTO), military alliances such as NATO, and political groupings such as the African Union (AU) are all IGOs.

Another type of transnational actor, **nongovernmental organizations (NGOs)**, are private organizations, some of considerable size and resources. Increasingly NGOs are being recognized, in the UN and other forums, as legitimate actors along with states, though not equal to them. Some of these groups have a political purpose, some a humanitarian one, some an economic or technical one. Sometimes NGOs combine efforts through transnational advocacy networks.[10] There is no single

---

[10] Keck, Margaret E., and Kathryn Sikkink. *Activists Beyond Borders: Advocacy Networks in International Politics.* Cornell, 1998. Batliwala, Srilatha, and L. David Brown. *Transnational Civil Society: An Introduction.* Kumarian, 2006.

IN THE ACTION

Nonstate actors participate in IR alongside states, although generally in less central roles. Nongovernmental organizations (NGOs) are becoming increasingly active in IR. Here the group Human Rights Watch calls for Yemen to investigate possible war crimes in recent fighting, 2010.

pattern to NGOs. Together, IGOs and NGOs are referred to as international organizations (IOs).[11] By one count there are more than 25,000 NGOs and 5,000 IGOs. IOs are discussed in detail in Chapters 7 and 10.

Multinational corporations (MNCs) are companies that span multiple countries. The interests of a large company doing business globally do not correspond with any one state's interests. MNCs often control greater resources, and operate internationally with greater efficiency, than many small states. They may prop up (or even create) friendly foreign governments, as the United Fruit Company did in the "banana republics" of Central America a century ago. But MNCs also provide poor states with much-needed foreign investment and tax revenues. MNCs in turn depend on states to provide protection, well-regulated markets, and a stable political environment. MNCs as international actors receive special attention in Chapters 9 and 13.

Various other nonstate actors interact with states, IOs, and MNCs. For example, the terrorist attacks since September 11, 2001, have demonstrated the increasing power that technology gives terrorists as nonstate actors. Just as Greenpeace can travel to a remote location and then beam video of its environmental actions there to the world, so too can al Qaeda place suicide bombers in world cities, coordinate their operations and finances through the Internet and the

TABLE 1.2 Types of Nonstate Actors

Type		Who Are They?	Examples
IGOs[a]	Intergovernmental Organizations	Members are national governments	United Nations, NATO, Arab League
NGOs[a]	Nongovernmental Organizations	Members are individuals and groups	Amnesty International, Lions Clubs, Red Cross
MNCs	Multinational Corporations	Companies that span borders	ExxonMobil, Toyota, Wal-Mart
Others		Individuals, Cities, Constituencies, etc.	Bono, Iraqi Kurdistan, al Qaeda

[a]Note: IGOs and NGOs together make up International Organizations (IOs).

---

[11] Armstrong, David, Lorna Lloyd, and John Redmond. *International Organization in World Politics*. Palgrave, 2003.

global banking system, and reach a global audience with videotaped appeals. "Global reach," once an exclusive capability of great powers, now is available to many others, for better or worse.

Some nonstate actors are *substate actors*: they exist within one country but either influence that country's foreign policy or operate internationally, or both. For instance, the state of Ohio is entirely a U.S. entity but operates an International Trade Division to promote exports and foreign investment, with offices in Belgium, Japan, China, Canada, Israel, India, Australia, and Mexico. The actions of substate economic actors—companies, consumers, workers, investors—help create the context of economic activity against which international political events play out, and within which governments must operate.

In this world of globalization, of substate actors and transnational actors, states are still important. But to some extent they are being gradually pushed aside as companies, groups, and individuals deal ever more directly with each other across borders, and as the world economy becomes globally integrated. Now more than ever, IR extends beyond the interactions of national governments.

Both state and nonstate actors are strongly affected by the revolution in information technologies now under way. The new information-intensive world promises to reshape international relations profoundly. Technological change dramatically affects actors' relative capabilities and even preferences. Telecommunications and computerization allow economics, politics, and culture alike to operate on a global scale as never before. The ramifications of information technology for various facets of IR will be developed in each chapter of this book.

Levels of Analysis

The many actors involved in IR contribute to the complexity of competing explanations and theories. One way scholars of IR have sorted out this multiplicity of influences, actors, and processes is to categorize them into different *levels of analysis* (see Table 1.3). A level of analysis is a perspective on IR based on a set of similar actors or processes that suggests possible explanations to "why" questions. IR scholars have proposed various level-of-analysis schemes, most often with three main levels (and sometimes a few sublevels between).[12]

The *individual* level of analysis concerns the perceptions, choices, and actions of individual human beings. Great leaders influence the course of history, as do individual citizens, thinkers, soldiers, and voters. Without Lenin, it is said, there might well have been no Soviet Union. If a few more college students had voted for Nixon rather than Kennedy in the razor-close 1960 election, the Cuban Missile Crisis might have ended differently. The study of foreign policy decision making, discussed in Chapter 3, pays special attention to individual-level explanations of IR outcomes because of the importance of psychological factors in the decision-making process.

The *domestic* (or *state* or *societal*) level of analysis concerns the aggregations of individuals within states that influence state actions in the international arena. Such aggregations include interest groups, political organizations, and government agencies. These groups operate differently (with different international effects) in different kinds of societies and states. For instance, democracies and dictatorships may act differently from one another,

[12] Singer, J. David. The Level-of-Analysis Problem in International Relations. *World Politics* 14 (1), 1961: 77–92. Waltz, Kenneth. *Man, the State, and War: A Theoretical Analysis*. Rev. ed. Columbia, 2001.

TABLE 1.3 Levels of Analysis

Many influences affect the course of international relations. Levels of analysis provide a framework for categorizing these influences and thus for suggesting various explanations of international events. Examples include:

Global Level

North-South gap	Religious fundamentalism	Information revolution
World regions	Terrorism	Global telecommunications
European imperialism	World environment	Worldwide scientific and
Norms	Technological change	business communities

Interstate Level

Power	Wars	Diplomacy
Balance of power	Treaties	Summit meetings
Alliance formation	Trade agreements	Bargaining
and dissolution	IGOs	Reciprocity

Domestic Level

Nationalism	Dictatorship	Gender
Ethnic conflict	Domestic coalitions	Economic sectors and industries
Type of government	Political parties and elections	Military-industrial complex
Democracy	Public opinion	Foreign policy bureaucracies

Individual Level

Great leaders	Psychology of perception and decision	Citizens' participation (voting,
Crazy leaders	Learning	rebelling, going to war, etc.)
Decision making in crises	Assassinations, accidents of history	

and democracies may act differently in an election year from the way they act at other times. The politics of ethnic conflict and nationalism, bubbling up from within states, plays an increasingly important role in the relations among states. Within governments, foreign policy agencies often fight bureaucratic battles over policy decisions.

The *interstate* (or *international* or *systemic*) level of analysis concerns the influence of the international system upon outcomes. This level of analysis therefore focuses on the interactions of states themselves, without regard to their internal makeup or the particular individuals who lead them. This level pays attention to states' relative power positions in the international system and the interactions (trade, for example) among them. It has been traditionally the most important of the levels of analysis.

To these three levels can be added a fourth, the *global* level of analysis, which seeks to explain international outcomes in terms of global trends and forces that transcend the interactions of states themselves.[13] The evolution of human technology, of certain worldwide beliefs, and of humans' relationship to the natural environment are all processes at the global level that reach down to influence international relations. The global level is

---

[13] North, Robert C. *War, Peace, Survival: Global Politics and Conceptual Synthesis.* Westview, 1990. Dower, Nigel. *An Introduction to Global Citizenship.* Edinburgh, 2003.

also increasingly the focus of IR scholars studying transnational integration through worldwide scientific, technical, and business communities (see Chapter 10). Another pervasive global influence is the lingering effect of historical European imperialism—Europe's conquest of Latin America, Asia, and Africa (see "History of Imperialism, 1500–2000" in Chapter 12).

Levels of analysis offer different sorts of explanations for international events. For example, many possible explanations exist for the 2003 U.S.-led war against Iraq. At the individual level, the war could be attributed to Saddam Hussein's gamble that he could defeat the forces arrayed against him, or to President Bush's desire to remove a leader he personally deemed threatening. At the domestic level, the war could be attributed to the rise of the powerful neoconservative faction that convinced the Bush administration and Americans that Saddam was a threat to U.S. security in a post–September 11 world. At the interstate level, the war might be attributed to the predominance of U.S. power. With no state willing to back Iraq militarily, the United States (as the largest global military power) was free to attack Iraq without fear of a large-scale military response. Finally, at the global level, the war might be attributable to a global fear of terrorism, or even a clash between Islam and the West.

Although IR scholars often focus their study mainly on one level of analysis, other levels bear on a problem simultaneously. There is no single correct level for a given "why" question. Rather, levels of analysis help suggest multiple explanations and approaches to consider in explaining an event. They remind scholars and students to look beyond the immediate and superficial aspects of an event to explore the possible influences of more distant causes. Note that the processes at higher levels tend to operate more slowly than those on the lower levels. Individuals go in and out of office often; the structure of the international system changes rarely.

Globalization

Globalization encompasses many trends, including expanded international trade, telecommunications, monetary coordination, multinational corporations, technical and scientific cooperation, cultural exchanges of new types and scales, migration and refugee flows, and relations between the world's rich and poor countries. Although globalization clearly is very important, it is also rather vaguely defined and not well explained by any one theory. One popular conception of globalization is as "the widening, deepening and speeding up of worldwide interconnectedness in all aspects of contemporary social life. . . . "[14] But at least three conceptions of this process compete.[15]

One view sees globalization as the fruition of liberal economic principles. A global marketplace has brought growth and prosperity (not to all countries but to those most integrated with the global market). This economic process has made traditional states obsolete as economic units. States are thus losing authority to supranational institutions

---

[14] Held, David, Anthony McGrew, David Goldblatt, and Jonathan Perraton. *Global Transformations: Politics, Economics and Culture.* Stanford, 1999: 2. Held, David, and Anthony McGrew. *Globalization/Anti-Globalization: Beyond the Great Divide.* Polity, 2007.

[15] Friedman, Thomas L. *The World Is Flat.* Farrar, Straus, and Giroux, 2007. Stiglitz, Joseph E. *Globalization and Its Discontents.* Norton, 2002. Drezner, Daniel W. *All Politics Is Global.* Princeton, 2008. Rudra, Nita. *Globalization and the Race to the Bottom in Developing Countries: Who Really Gets Hurt?* Cambridge, 2008. Kapstein, Ethan B. *Economic Justice in an Unfair World: Toward a Normal Playing Field.* Princeton, 2007. Cusimano, Maryann K. *Beyond Sovereignty: Issues for a Global Agenda.* Palgrave, 1999.

THINK GLOBALLY

As the world economy becomes more integrated, markets and production are becoming global in scope. This Hong Kong container port ships goods to and from all over the world, 2008.

such as the International Monetary Fund (IMF) and the European Union (EU), and to transnational actors such as MNCs and NGOs. The values of technocrats and elite, educated citizens in liberal democracies are becoming global values, reflecting an emerging global civilization. The old North-South division is seen as less important, because the global South is moving in divergent directions depending on countries' and regions' integration with world markets.

A second perspective is skeptical of these claims about globalization. These skeptics note that the world's major economies are no more integrated today than before World War I (when British hegemony provided a common set of expectations and institutions). The skeptics also doubt that regional and geographic distinctions such as the North-South divide are disappearing in favor of a single global market. Rather, they see the North-South gap as increasing with globalization. Also, the economic integration of states may be leading not to a single world free trade zone, but to distinct and rival regional blocs in America, Europe, and Asia. The supposed emerging world civilization is disproved by the fragmenting of larger units (such as the Soviet Union) into smaller ones along lines of language, religion, and other such cultural factors.

A third school of thought sees globalization as more profound than the skeptics believe, yet more uncertain than the view of supporters of liberal economics.[16] These "transformationalists" see state sovereignty as being eroded by the EU, the WTO, and other new institutions, so that sovereignty is no longer an absolute but just one of a spectrum of bargaining leverages held by states. The bargaining itself increasingly involves nonstate actors. Thus globalization diffuses authority. State power is not so much strengthened or weakened by globalization, but transformed to operate in new contexts with new tools.

While scholars debate these conceptions of globalization, popular debates focus on the growing power of large corporations operating globally, the disruptive costs associated with joining world markets (for example, job loss and environmental impacts), the perception of growing disparities between the rich and the poor, and the collusion of national governments in these wrongs through their participation in IOs such as the

---

[16] Rosenau, James N. *Distant Proximities: Dynamics beyond Globalization.* Princeton, 2003.

WTO and the IMF.[17] Policies to expand free trade are a central focus of antiglobalization protesters (see pp. 313–314). Street protests have turned host cities into besieged fortresses in Seattle (1999); Washington, D.C. (2000 IMF and World Bank meetings); Quebec (2001 summit working toward a Free Trade Area of the Americas); and Genoa, Italy (2001 G8 summit), where protesters engaged police in battles that killed one person. The key 2001 WTO meeting to launch a new trade round was held in Qatar, where protesters had little access. At the 2003 WTO meeting in Cancun, Mexico, thousands of protesters marched against the talks and the economic elites conducting them, but were kept away from the WTO conference center. At the 2005 Hong Kong WTO meeting, protesters blocked nearby roads and some even tried to swim across Hong Kong harbor to disrupt the meeting.

Just as scholars disagree on conceptions of globalization, so do protesters disagree on their goals and tactics. Union members from the global North want to stop globalization from shipping their jobs south. But workers in impoverished countries in the global South may desperately want those jobs as a first step toward decent wages and working conditions (relative to other options in their countries). Window-smashing anarchists meanwhile steal media attention from environmentalists seeking to amend the trade agenda. Thus, neither globalization nor the backlash to it is simple.

Globalization is changing both international security and IPE, as we will see in the coming chapters, but it is changing IPE more quickly and profoundly than security. The coming chapters address a broad range of topics, each affected by globalization. Chapter 4 shows how nonstate actors influence foreign policies of states. Chapter 7 discusses global institutions, international law, and human rights, all of growing importance as globalization continues. Chapters 8 and 9 look at economic globalization in trade, finance, and business, where globalization's influences are most apparent. Chapter 10 considers the information technology side of globalization, as the world becomes wired in new ways. Chapter 11 discusses the global environment and examines how increasing interaction through globalization influences our physical environment. Chapters 12 and 13 cover the global North-South divide, which is central to the concept of globalization.

The rest of *this* chapter takes up two contextual aspects of globalization that shape the issue areas discussed in subsequent chapters—(1) the relations among the world's major regions, especially the rich North and poor South; and (2) the evolution of the international system over the past century.

Global Geography

To highlight the insights afforded by a global level of analysis, this book divides the world into nine regions. These *world regions* differ from each other in the number of states they contain and in each region's particular mix of cultures, geographical realities, and languages. But each represents a geographical corner of the world, and together they reflect the overall larger divisions of the world.

The global **North-South gap** between the relatively rich industrialized countries of the North and the relatively poor countries of the South is the most important

Watch the **Video** "Global Food Prices and Changing Diets" on **mypoliscilab.com**

[17] Broad, Robin. *Citizen Backlash to Economic Globalization.* Rowman & Littlefield, 2002. Milani, Brian. *Designing the Green Economy: The Post-Industrial Alternative to Corporate Globalization.* Rowman & Littlefield, 2000.

FIGURE 1.2 Nine Regions of the World

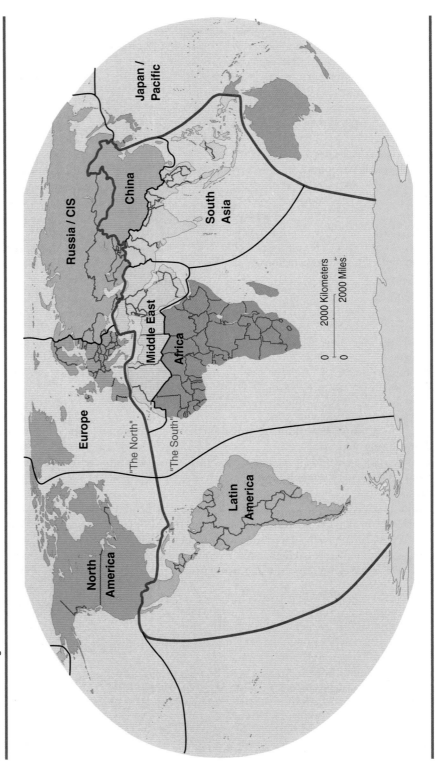

geographical element at the global level of analysis. The regions used in this book have been drawn so as to separate (with a few exceptions) the rich countries from the poor ones. The North includes both the West (the rich countries of North America, Europe, and Japan) and the old East, including the former Soviet Union (now Russia) and the *Commonwealth of Independent States (CIS)*, a loose confederation of former Soviet republics excluding the Baltic states.[18] The South includes Latin America, Africa, the Middle East, and much of Asia. The South is often called the *third world* (third after the West and East)—a term that is still widely used despite the second world's collapse. Countries in the South are also referred to as "developing" countries or "less-developed" countries (LDCs), in contrast to the "developed" countries of the North. The world regions are shown in Figure 1.2.

Several criteria beyond income levels help distinguish major geographically contiguous regions. Countries with similar economic levels, cultures, and languages have been kept together where possible. States with a history of interaction, including historical empires or trading zones, are also placed together in a region. Finally, countries that might possibly unify in the future—notably South Korea with North Korea, and China with Taiwan—are kept in the same region. Of course, no scheme works perfectly, and some states, such as Turkey, are pulled toward two regions.

Most of these regions correspond with commonly used geographical names, but a few notes may help. *East Asia* refers to China, Japan, and Korea. *Southeast Asia* refers to countries from Burma through Indonesia and the Philippines. Russia is considered a European state although a large section (Siberia) is in Asia. The *Pacific Rim* usually means East and Southeast Asia, Siberia, and the Pacific coast of North America and Latin America.[19] *South Asia* only sometimes includes parts of Southeast Asia. Narrow definitions of the *Middle East* exclude both North Africa and Turkey. The *Balkans* are the states of southeastern Europe, bounded by Slovenia, Romania, and Greece.

Table 1.4 shows GDP for each of the world's countries, organized by region. Table 1.5 shows the approximate population and economic size (GDP) of each region in relation to the world as a whole. As the table indicates, income levels per capita are, overall, more than five times as high in the North as in the South. *The North contains only 20 percent of the world's people but 60 percent of its goods and services.* The other 80 percent of the world's people, in the South, have only 40 percent of the goods and services.

Within the global North, Russia and the CIS states lag behind in income levels, having suffered declines in the 1990s. In the global South, the Middle East, Latin America, and (more recently) China have achieved somewhat higher income levels than have Africa and South Asia, which remain extremely poor. Even in the somewhat higher-income regions, income is distributed quite unevenly and many people remain very poor. Note that more than half of the world's population lives in the densely populated (and poor) regions of South Asia and China. IR scholars have no single explanation of the huge North-South income gap (see Chapter 12).

---

[18] Note that geographical designations such as the "West" and the "Middle East" are European-centered. From Korea, for example, China and Russia are to the west, and Japan and the United States are to the east. On world-level geography, see Kidron, Michael, Ronald Segal, and Angela Wilson. *The State of the World Atlas.* 5th ed. Penguin, 1995. Boyd, Andrew, and Joshua Comenetz. *An Atlas of World Affairs.* McGraw-Hill, 2007.

[19] Ikenberry, G. John, and Michael Mastanduno. *International Relations Theory and the Asia-Pacific.* Columbia, 2003. Pempel, T. J. *Remapping East Asia.* Cornell, 2005.

TABLE 1.4 States and Territories with Estimated Total GDP, 2010
(In Billions of 2011 U.S. Dollars)

North America

United States	14,000	Canada	1,400	Bahamas	10

Europe

Germany[a]	3,000	Norway	300	Latvia	30
Britain[a]	2,200	Portugal[a]	200	Bosnia and Herzegovina	30
France[a]	2,200	Denmark[a]	200	Albania	30
Italy[a]	1,900	Finland[a]	200	Estonia[a]	20
Spain[a]	1,400	Hungary[a]	200	Cyprus[a]	20
Netherlands[a]	700	Ireland[a]	200	Macedonia	20
Poland[a]	700	Slovakia[a]	100	Iceland	10
Belgium[a]	400	Bulgaria[a]	100	Malta[a]	10
Austria[a]	300	Serbia	80	Montenegro	7
Greece[a]	300	Croatia	80	Liechtenstein	4
Sweden[a]	300	Lithuania[a]	60	Andorra	4
Switzerland	300	Slovenia[a]	60	Monaco	1
Romania[a]	300	Luxembourg	40	San Marino	1
Czech Republic[a]	300				

Japan/Pacific

Japan	4,400	Fiji	4	Nauru	0
South Korea	1,500	Guam/Marianas[b]	3	Marshall Islands	0
Australia	800	Solomon Islands	1	Palau	0
New Zealand	100	Samoa	1	Kiribati	0
North Korea	40	Vanuatu	1	Tuvalu	0
Papua New Guinea	20	Tonga	0	Micronesia	0

Russia/CIS

Russia	2,300	Azerbaijan	100	Kyrgyzstan	10
Ukraine	300	Turkmenistan	40	Tajikistan	10
Kazakhstan	200	Armenia	20	Moldova	10
Belarus	100	Georgia	20	Mongolia	10
Uzbekistan	80				

China

China	9,500	Hong Kong[b]	300	Macau[b]	20
Taiwan[b]	700				

Middle East

Turkey	900	Morocco/W. Sahara	200	Oman	70
Iran	800	Kuwait	100	Yemen	60
Saudi Arabia	600	Iraq	100	Lebanon	60
Egypt	500	Libya	100	Jordan	40
Algeria	300	Syria	100	Bahrain	30
United Arab Emirates	300	Qatar	100		
Israel/Palestine	200	Tunisia	90		

Latin America

Brazil	2,300	Bolivia	50	Suriname	4
Mexico	1,500	Panama	50	Guyana	3
Argentina	600	El Salvador	40	Netherlands Antilles[b]	3
Colombia	400	Uruguay	40	Belize	3
Venezuela	400	Paraguay	30	Virgin Islands[b]	2
Chile	300	Honduras	30	French Guiana[b]	2
Peru	300	Trinidad & Tobago	30	St. Lucia	2
Cuba	100	Jamaica	20	Antigua & Barbuda	2
Ecuador	100	Nicaragua	20	Grenada	1
Dominican Republic	90	Haiti	10	St. Vincent & Grenadines	1
Puerto Rico[b]	70	Martinique[b]	7	St. Kitts & Nevis	1
Guatemala	70	Barbados	6	Dominica	1
Costa Rica	50	Bermuda[b]	5		

South Asia

India	4,100	Bangladesh	200	Brunei	20
Indonesia	1,100	Singapore	200	Laos	20
Thailand	500	Sri Lanka	100	Bhutan	4
Pakistan	500	Burma (Myanmar)	60	Maldives	2
Malaysia	400	Nepal	30	East Timor	1
Philippines	300	Cambodia	30		
Vietnam	300	Afghanistan	20		

Africa

South Africa	500	Mauritius	20	Somalia	6
Nigeria	400	Gabon	20	Sierra Leone	5
Angola	100	Burkina Faso	20	Zimbabwe	4
Sudan	90	Zambia	20	Central African Republic	4
Ethiopia	80	Chad	20	Eritea	3
Kenya	60	Mali	20	Lesotho	3
Tanzania	50	Congo Republic	20	Burundi	4
Cameroon	50	Niger	10	Reunion[b]	3
Uganda	40	Rwanda	10	Gambia	3
Ghana	40	Namibia	10	Cape Verde	2
Côte d'Ivoire (Ivory Coast)	40	Benin	10	Djibouti	2
Botswana	30	Guinea	10	Seychelles	2
Democratic Congo	20	Malawi	10	Liberia	2
Mozambique	20	South Sudan	10	Guinea-Bissau	2
Equatorial Guinea	20	Mauritania	7	Comoros Islands	1
Senegal	20	Swaziland	6	São Tomé & Principe	0
Madagascar	20	Togo	6		

[a]European Union.

[b]Nonmember of UN.

Note: GDP data are inexact by nature. Estimates for Russia, CIS, China, and other nonmarket or transitional economies are particularly suspect and should be used cautiously. Numbers below 0.5 are listed as 0.
Sources: Data are authors' estimates based on World Bank. Data are at purchasing-power parity. See footnote 9 on p. 14.

TABLE 1.5 Comparison of World Regions, 2010

Region	Population (Millions)	GDP (Trillion $)	GDP per Capita (Dollars)
The North			
North America	340	$15	$44,000
Europe	530	16	30,000
Japan/Pacific	240	7	29,000
Russia/CIS	280	3	10,700
The South			
China	1,330	10	6,800
Middle East	450	4	9,200
Latin America	590	6	10,500
South Asia	2,190	8	3,000
Africa	850	2	2,300
Total North	**1,390 (20%)**	**41 (58%)**	**29,500**
Total South	**5,410 (80%)**	**30 (42%)**	**5,300**
World Total	**6,800**	**$71**	**$10,400**

Note: Data adjusted for purchasing-power parity. 2010 GDP estimates (in 2011 dollars) are from Table 1.5; those for Russia, CIS, and China, should be treated especially cautiously.

The Evolving International System

Watch the **Video** "**August 1991: The Collapse of the Soviet Union**" on **mypoliscilab.com**

The basic structures and principles of international relations are deeply rooted in historical developments. Throughout this book we will review the history that bears on topics such as the great power system (Chapter 2), imperialism (Chapter 12), and nationalism (Chapter 5). Here we will review briefly the key events of the 20th century and focus in particular on the post–Cold War era since 1990.

The Two World Wars, 1900–1950

World War I (1914–1918) and World War II (1939–1945) occupied only ten years of the 20th century (see Figure 1.3). But they shaped the character of the century.[20] Nothing like those wars has happened since, and they remain a key reference point for the world in which we live today. With perhaps just two other cases in history—the Thirty Years' War and the Napoleonic Wars—the two world wars were global or hegemonic wars in which almost all major states participated in an all-out struggle over the future of the international system.[21]

For many people, World War I symbolizes the tragic irrationality of war. It fascinates scholars of IR because it was a catastrophic war that seems unnecessary and perhaps even

---

[20] Ferguson, Niall. *The War of the World: Twentieth-Century Conflict and the Descent of the West*. Penguin, 2006.
[21] Dockrill, Michael. *Atlas of Twentieth Century World History*. HarperCollins, 1991. Ferguson, Niall. *The Pity of War: Explaining World War I*. Basic Books, 1999. Keegan, John, ed. *The Times Atlas of the Second World War*. HarperCollins, 1989. Weinberg, Gerhard L. *A World at Arms: A Global History of World War II*. Cambridge, 1994.

accidental. After a century of relative peace, the great powers marched off to battle for no good reason. There was even a popular feeling that Europe would be uplifted and reinvigorated by a war—that young men could once again prove their manhood on the battlefield in a glorious adventure. Such ideas were soon crushed by the immense pain and evident pointlessness of the war.

The previous major war had been the Franco-Prussian War of 1870–1871, when Germany executed a swift offensive using railroads to rush forces to the front. That war had ended quickly, decisively, and with a clear winner (Germany). People expected that a new war would follow the same pattern. All the great powers made plans for a quick railroad-borne offensive and rapid victory—what has been called the *cult of the offensive*. They believed that the one to strike first would win. Under these doctrines, one country's mobilization for war virtually forced its enemies to mobilize as well. Thus, when a Serbian nationalist assassinated Archduke Ferdinand of Austria in 1914 in Sarajevo, a minor crisis escalated and the mobilization plans pushed Europe to all-out war.[22]

Contrary to expectations, the war was neither short nor decisive, and certainly not glorious. It bogged down in *trench warfare* along a fixed front. For example, in 1917 at the Battle of Passchendaele (Belgium), the British in three months fired five tons of artillery shells per yard of front line, over an 11-mile-wide front, and then lost 400,000 men in a failed ground attack. The horrific conditions were worsened by chemical weapons and by the attempts of Britain and Germany to starve each other's population into surrender.

Russia was the first state to crumble. Revolution at home removed Russia from the war in 1917 (and led to the founding of the Soviet Union). But the entry of the United States into the war on the anti-German side that year quickly turned the tide. In the *Treaty of Versailles* of 1919, Germany was forced to give up territory, pay reparations, limit its future armaments, and admit guilt for the war. German resentment against the harsh terms of Versailles would contribute to Adolf Hitler's rise to power in the 1930s. After World War I, U.S. president Woodrow Wilson led the effort to create the **League of Nations**, a forerunner of today's United Nations. But the U.S. Senate would not approve U.S. participation, and the League did not prove effective. U.S. isolationism between the world wars, along with declining British power and a Russia crippled by its own revolution, left a power vacuum in world politics.

In the 1930s, Germany and Japan stepped into that vacuum, embarking on aggressive expansionism that ultimately led to World War II. Japan had already occupied Taiwan and Korea after defeating China in 1895 and Russia in 1905. In World War I, Japan gained some German colonies in Asia. In 1931, Japan occupied Manchuria (northeast China) and set up a puppet regime there. In 1937, Japan invaded the rest of China and began a brutal occupation that continues to haunt Chinese-Japanese relations.

Meanwhile, in Europe in the 1930s, Nazi Germany under Hitler had re-armed, intervened to help fascists win the Spanish Civil War, and grabbed territory from its neighbors under the rationale of reuniting ethnic Germans in those territories with their homeland. Hitler was emboldened by the weak response of the international community and the League of Nations to aggression by fascist regimes in Italy and Spain. In an effort to appease German ambitions, Britain and France agreed in the **Munich Agreement** of 1938 to let Germany occupy part of Czechoslovakia (known as the Sudetenland). Appeasement has since had a negative connotation in IR, because the Munich Agreement seemed only to encourage Hitler's further conquests.

In 1939, Germany invaded Poland, leading Britain and France to join the war against Germany. Hitler signed a nonaggression pact with his archenemy, Joseph Stalin of the

---

[22] Van Evera, Stephen. The Cult of the Offensive and the Origins of the First World War. *International Security* 9 (1), 1984: 58–107. Snyder, Jack L. *The Ideology of the Offensive: Military Decision Making and the Disasters of 1914*. Cornell, 1984.

FIGURE 1.3 The Two World Wars, 1900–1950

Category	1900	1910	1920	1930	1940	1950
Europe	mobilization plans developed	Balkan crises · Sarajevo · U.S. enters war		Italy invades Ethiopia · Munich Agreement	U.S. enters war · D-Day	
Germany	naval arms race with Britain →	Defeat · Weimar Republic	hyperinflation	Hitler wins power · rearmament · occupation of Austria, Czech. · invasion of Poland	The Holocaust · strategic bombing · occupation of Europe · Defeat	occupied by Allied forces
Russia		Russian Revolution · (civil war) · USSR formed		(industrialization) · pact with Hitler	German invasion · Victory	
Asia	U.S. in Philippines · Russo-Japanese War	Japan neutral in WW I		Japan occupies Manchuria (China) · Japan invades China · Japan quits League of Nations	Pearl Harbor · Japan occupies S.E. Asia · island battles · Hiroshima	Occupied by U.S.
International Norms & Law	Hague Peace Conferences	Versailles treaty · League of Nations → · Washington Naval Treaty		U.S. isolationism	Nuremberg Tribunal	United Nations →
Technology	destroyers	submarines · trench warfare · chemical weapons · tanks		mechanized armor	air war · radar · nuclear weapons	

World War I · World War II

Soviet Union, and threw his full army against France, occupying most of it quickly. Hitler then double-crossed Stalin and invaded the Soviet Union in 1941. This offensive ultimately bogged down and was turned back after several years. But the Soviet Union took the brunt of the German attack and suffered by far the greatest share of the 60 million deaths caused by World War II. This trauma continues to be a powerful memory that shapes views of IR in Russia and Eastern Europe.

The United States joined World War II against Germany in 1942. The U.S. economy produced critically important weapons and supplies for allied armies. The United States played an important role with Britain in the strategic bombing of German cities—including the firebombing of Dresden in February 1945, which caused 100,000 civilian deaths. In 1944, after crossing the English Channel on June 6 (*D-Day*), British-American forces pushed into Germany from the west while the Soviets pushed from the east. A ruined Germany surrendered and was occupied by the allied powers. At its peak, Nazi Germany and its allies had occupied virtually all of Europe, except Britain and part of Russia.

While the war in Europe was raging, Japan fought a war over control of Southeast Asia with the United States and its allies. Japan's expansionism in the 1930s had only underscored the dependence on foreign resources that the expansionism was intended to solve: the United States punished Japan by cutting off U.S. oil exports. Japan then destroyed much of the U.S. Navy in a surprise attack at *Pearl Harbor* (Hawaii) in 1941 and seized desired territories (including Indonesia, whose oil replaced that of the United States). The United States, however, built vast new military forces and retook a series of Pacific islands in subsequent years. The strategic bombing of Japanese cities by the United States culminated in the only historical use of nuclear weapons in war—the destruction of the cities of *Hiroshima* and *Nagasaki* in August 1945—which triggered Japan's quick surrender.

The lessons of the two world wars seem contradictory. From the failure of the Munich Agreement in 1938 to appease Hitler, many people have concluded that only a hard-line foreign policy with preparedness for war will deter aggression and prevent war. Yet in 1914 it was just such hard-line policies that apparently led Europe into a disastrous war, which might have been avoided by more conciliatory policies. Evidently the best policy would be sometimes harsh and at other times conciliatory, but IR scholars have not discovered a simple formula for choosing (see "Causes of War" in Chapter 5).

The Cold War, 1945–1990

The United States and the Soviet Union became the two superpowers of the post–World War II era (see Figure 1.4).[23] Each had its ideological mission (capitalist democracy versus communism), its networks of alliances and clients, and its deadly arsenal of nuclear weapons. Europe was divided, with massive military forces of the United States and its *North Atlantic Treaty Organization (NATO)* allies on one side and massive military forces of the Soviet Union and its *Warsaw Pact* allies on the other. Germany itself was split, with three-quarters of the country—and three-quarters of the capital city of Berlin—occupied by the United States, Britain, and France. The remainder, surrounding West Berlin, was occupied by the Soviet Union. Crises in Berlin in 1947–1948 and 1961 led to armed confrontations but not war. In 1961, East Germany built the Berlin Wall separating East from West Berlin. It symbolized the division of Europe by what Winston Churchill had called the "iron curtain."

---

[23] Gaddis, John Lewis. *We Now Know: Rethinking Cold War History.* Oxford, 1997. Zubok, Vladislav, and Constantine Pleshakov. *Inside the Kremlin's Cold War: From Stalin to Khrushchev.* Harvard, 1996. Garthoff, Raymond. *Détente and Confrontation: American-Soviet Relations from Nixon to Reagan.* Brookings, 1985. Larson, Deborah Welch. *Anatomy of Mistrust: U.S.-Soviet Relations During the Cold War.* Cornell, 1997. Trachtenberg, Marc. *A Constructed Peace: The Making of the European Settlement, 1945–1963.* Princeton, 1999.

FIGURE 1.4 The Cold War, 1945–1990

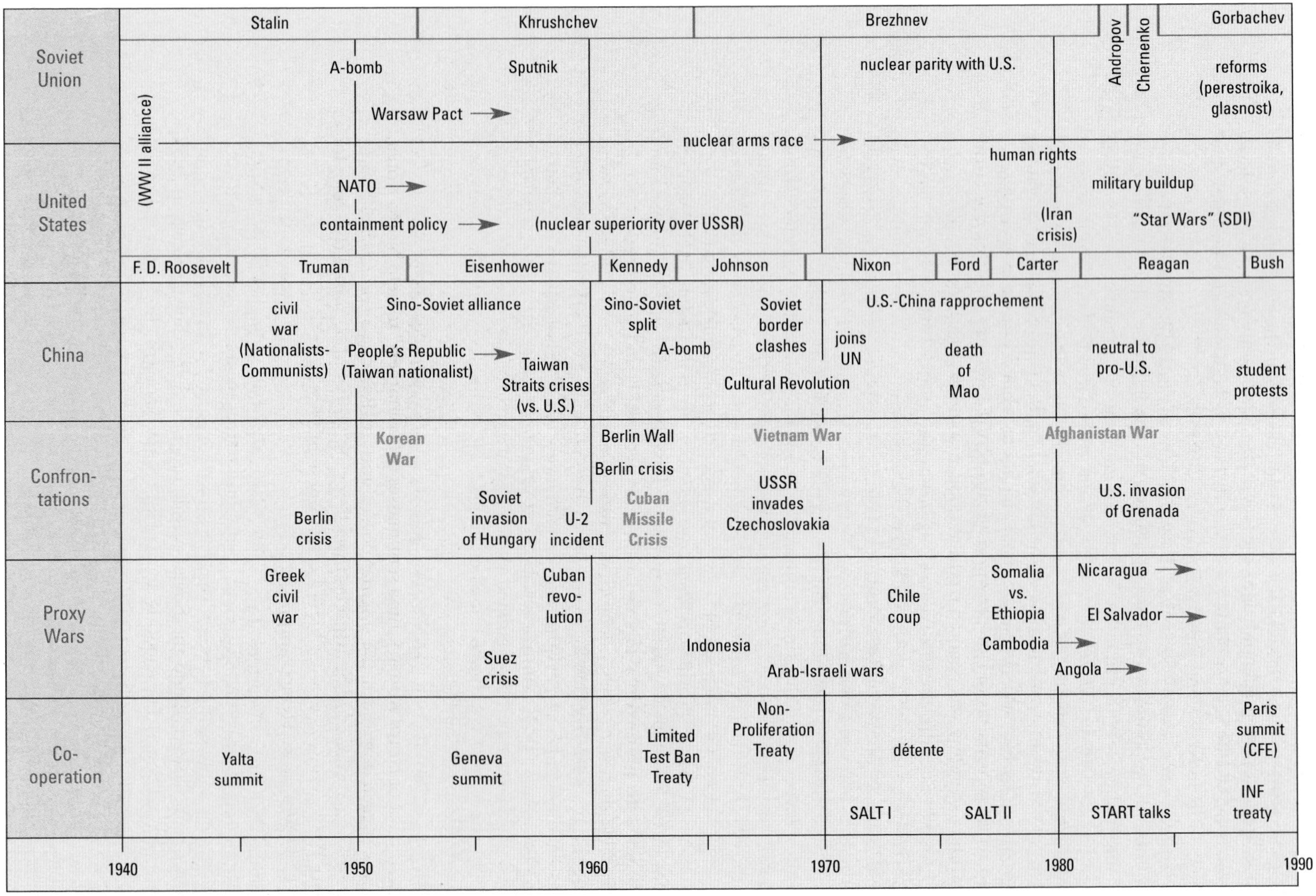

Timeline: 1940 — 1950 — 1960 — 1970 — 1980 — 1990

Soviet Union (leaders: Stalin, Khrushchev, Brezhnev, Andropov, Chernenko, Gorbachev)
- A-bomb
- Warsaw Pact →
- Sputnik
- nuclear parity with U.S.
- reforms (perestroika, glasnost)

United States (leaders: F. D. Roosevelt, Truman, Eisenhower, Kennedy, Johnson, Nixon, Ford, Carter, Reagan, Bush)
- (WW II alliance)
- NATO →
- containment policy →
- (nuclear superiority over USSR)
- nuclear arms race →
- human rights
- (Iran crisis)
- military buildup
- "Star Wars" (SDI)

China
- civil war (Nationalists-Communists)
- People's Republic (Taiwan nationalist)
- Sino-Soviet alliance
- Taiwan Straits crises (vs. U.S.) →
- Sino-Soviet split
- A-bomb
- Soviet border clashes
- Cultural Revolution
- joins UN
- U.S.-China rapprochement
- death of Mao
- neutral to pro-U.S.
- student protests

Confrontations
- Berlin crisis
- Korean War
- Soviet invasion of Hungary
- U-2 incident
- Berlin Wall
- Berlin crisis
- Cuban Missile Crisis
- Vietnam War
- USSR invades Czechoslovakia
- Afghanistan War
- U.S. invasion of Grenada

Proxy Wars
- Greek civil war
- Suez crisis
- Cuban revolution
- Indonesia
- Arab-Israeli wars
- Chile coup
- Somalia vs. Ethiopia
- Cambodia
- Angola →
- Nicaragua →
- El Salvador →

Co-operation
- Yalta summit
- Geneva summit
- Limited Test Ban Treaty
- Non-Proliferation Treaty
- détente
- SALT I
- SALT II
- START talks
- Paris summit (CFE)
- INF treaty

Despite the hostility of East-West relations during the **Cold War,** a relatively stable framework of relations emerged, and conflicts never escalated to all-out war between the largest states. At a U.S.-Soviet-British meeting at *Yalta* in 1945, when the defeat of Germany was imminent, the Western powers acknowledged the fact of the Soviet army's presence in Eastern Europe, allowing that area to remain under Soviet influence. Although the Soviet bloc did not join Western economic institutions such as the IMF, all the world's major states joined the UN. The United Nations (unlike the ill-fated League of Nations) managed to maintain almost universal membership and adherence to basic structures and rules throughout the Cold War era.

The central concern of the West during the Cold War was that the Soviet Union might gain control of Western Europe—either through outright invasion or through communists' taking power in war-weary and impoverished countries of Western Europe. This could have put the entire industrial base of the Eurasian landmass (from Europe to Siberia) under one state. The *Marshall Plan*—U.S. financial aid to rebuild European economies—responded to these fears, as did the creation of the NATO alliance. Half of the entire world's military spending was devoted to the European standoff. Much spending was also devoted to a superpower nuclear arms race, in which each superpower produced tens of thousands of nuclear weapons (see pp. 221–222).

Through the policy of **containment**, adopted in the late 1940s, the United States sought to halt the expansion of Soviet influence globally on several levels at once—military, political, ideological, economic. The United States maintained an extensive network of military bases and alliances worldwide. Virtually all of U.S. foreign policy in subsequent decades, from foreign aid and technology transfer to military intervention and diplomacy, came to serve the goal of containment.

The *Chinese communist revolution* in 1949 led to a Sino-Soviet alliance (*Sino* means "Chinese"). But China became fiercely independent in the 1960s following the **Sino-Soviet split**, when China opposed Soviet moves toward *peaceful coexistence* with the United States.[24] In the late 1960s, young radicals, opposed to both superpowers, ran China during the chaotic and destructive *Cultural Revolution*. But feeling threatened by Soviet power, China's leaders developed a growing affiliation with the United States during the 1970s, starting with a dramatic visit to China by U.S. president Richard Nixon in 1972. This visit led to U.S.-Chinese diplomatic relations in 1979. During the Cold War, China generally tried to play a balancer role against whichever superpower seemed most threatening at the time.

In 1950, the *Korean War* broke out when communist North Korea attacked and overran most of U.S.-allied South Korea. The United States and its allies (under UN authority obtained after the Soviets walked out of the Security Council in protest) counterattacked and overran most of North Korea. China sent masses of "volunteers" to help North Korea, and the war bogged down near the original border until a 1953 truce ended the fighting. The Korean War hardened U.S. attitudes toward communism and set a negative tone for future East-West relations, especially for U.S.-Chinese relations in the 1950s.

The Cold War thawed temporarily after Stalin died in 1953. The first **summit meeting** between superpower leaders took place in Geneva in 1955. This thaw in relations led both sides to agree to reconstitute Austria, which had been split into four pieces like Germany. But the Soviet Union sent tanks to crush a popular uprising in Hungary in 1956 (an action it repeated in 1968 in Czechoslovakia), and the Soviet missile program that orbited *Sputnik* in 1957 alarmed the United States. The shooting down of a U.S. spy plane (the *U-2*) over the Soviet Union in 1960 scuttled a summit meeting between superpower leaders Nikita Khrushchev and Dwight D. Eisenhower. Meanwhile in Cuba, after Fidel Castro's communist revolution in

---

[24] Zhang, Shu. *Economic Cold War: America's Embargo Against China and the Sino-Soviet Alliance, 1949–1963.* Stanford, 2002.

IRON CURTAIN

During the Cold War, the U.S. and Soviet sides sought spheres of influence. Europe was divided, and Germany itself was split, with its capital, Berlin, also divided. In 1961 the communist side built the Berlin Wall, seen here in 1962, to keep its population from leaving. It was dismantled as the Cold War ended in 1989.

1959, the United States attempted a counterrevolution in the botched 1961 *Bay of Pigs* invasion.

These hostilities culminated in the **Cuban Missile Crisis** of 1962, when the Soviet Union installed medium-range nuclear missiles in Cuba. The Soviet aims were to reduce the Soviet Union's strategic nuclear inferiority, to counter the deployment of U.S. missiles on Soviet borders in Turkey, and to deter another U.S. invasion of Cuba. U.S. leaders, however, considered the missiles threatening and provocative. As historical documents revealed years later, nuclear war was quite possible. Some U.S. policy makers favored military strikes before the missiles became operational, when in fact some nuclear weapons in Cuba were already operational and commanders were authorized to use them in the event of a U.S. attack.[25] Instead, President John F. Kennedy imposed a naval blockade to force their removal. The Soviet Union backed down on the missiles, and the United States promised not to invade Cuba in the future. Leaders on both sides were shaken, however, by the possibility of nuclear war. They signed the *Limited Test Ban Treaty* in 1963, prohibiting atmospheric nuclear tests, and began to cooperate in cultural exchanges, space exploration, aviation, and other areas.

The two superpowers often jockeyed for position in the global South, supporting **proxy wars** in which they typically supplied and advised opposing factions in civil wars. The alignments were often arbitrary. For instance, the United States backed the Ethiopian government and the Soviets backed next-door rival Somalia in the 1970s; however, when an Ethiopian revolution caused the new government to seek Soviet help, the United States switched its support to Somalia instead.

One flaw of U.S. policy in the Cold War period was to see all regional conflicts through East-West lenses. Its preoccupation with communism led the United States to support unpopular pro-Western governments in a number of poor countries, nowhere more disastrously than during the *Vietnam War* in the 1960s. The war in Vietnam divided U.S. citizens and ultimately failed to prevent a communist takeover. The fall of South Vietnam in 1975 appeared to signal U.S. weakness, especially combined with U.S. setbacks in the Middle East—the 1973 Arab oil embargo against the United States and the 1979 overthrow of the U.S.-backed shah of Iran by Islamic fundamentalists.

In this period of apparent U.S. weakness, the Soviet Union invaded Afghanistan in 1979. But, like the United States in Vietnam, the Soviet Union could not suppress rebel armies supplied by the opposing superpower. The Soviets ultimately withdrew after almost

---

[25] May, Ernest, and Philip Zelikow, eds. *The Kennedy Tapes: Inside the White House during the Cuban Missile Crisis.* Harvard, 1997. Munton, Don, and David A. Welch. *The Cuban Missile Crisis: A Concise History.* Oxford, 2006.

a decade of war that considerably weakened the Soviet Union. Meanwhile, President Ronald Reagan built up U.S. military forces to record levels and supported rebel armies in the Soviet-allied states of Nicaragua and Angola (and one faction in Cambodia) as well as Afghanistan. Superpower relations slowly improved after Mikhail Gorbachev, a reformer, took power in the Soviet Union in 1985. But some of the battlegrounds of the global South (notably Afghanistan and Angola) continued to suffer from brutal civil wars (fought with leftover Cold War arms) into the new century.

In retrospect, it seems that both superpowers exaggerated Soviet strength. In the early years of the nuclear arms race, U.S. military superiority was absolute, especially in nuclear weapons. The Soviets managed to match the United States over time, from A-bombs to H-bombs to multiple-warhead missiles. By the 1970s the Soviets had achieved strategic parity, meaning that neither side could prevent its own destruction in a nuclear war. But behind this military parity lay a Soviet Union lagging far behind the West in everything else—wealth, technology, infrastructure, and citizen/worker motivation.

In June 1989, massive pro-democracy demonstrations in China's capital of Beijing (Tiananmen Square) were put down violently by the communist government. Hundreds were shot dead in the streets. Later that year, as the Soviet Union stood by, one Eastern European country after another replaced its communist government under pressure of mass demonstrations. The toppling of the Berlin Wall in late 1989 symbolized the end of the Cold War division of Europe. Germany formally reunified in 1990. The Soviet leader, Gorbachev, allowed these losses of external power (and more) in hopes of concentrating on Soviet domestic restructuring under his policies of *perestroika* (economic reform) and *glasnost* (openness in political discussion). China remained a communist, authoritarian government but liberalized its economy and avoided military conflicts. In contrast to the Cold War era, China developed close ties with both the United States and Russia and joined the world's liberal trading regime.

Scholars do not agree on the important question of why the Cold War ended.[26] One view is that U.S. military strength under President Reagan forced the Soviet Union into bankruptcy as it tried to keep up in the arms race. A different position is that the Soviet Union suffered from internal stagnation over decades and ultimately imploded because of weaknesses that had little to do with external pressure. Indeed, some scholars think the Soviet Union might have fallen apart earlier without the United States as a foreign enemy to bolster the Soviet government's legitimacy with its own people.

The Post–Cold War Era, 1990–2010

The post–Cold War era began with a bang while the Soviet Union was still disintegrating. In 1990, perhaps believing that the end of the Cold War had left a power vacuum in its region, Iraq occupied its neighbor Kuwait in an aggressive grab for control of Middle East oil. Western powers were alarmed—both about the example that unpunished aggression could set in a new era and about the direct threat to energy supplies for the world economy. The United States mobilized a coalition of the world's major countries (with almost no opposition) to counter Iraq. Working through the UN, the U.S.-led coalition applied escalating sanctions against Iraq.

When Iraq did not withdraw from Kuwait by the UN's deadline, the United States and its allies easily smashed Iraq's military and evicted its army from Kuwait in the *Gulf War*. But the coalition did not occupy Iraq or overthrow its government. The costs of the Gulf War were shared among the participants in the coalition, with Britain and France making military

---

[26] Herrmann, Richard K., and R. Ned Lebow. *Ending the Cold War: Interpretations, Causation, and the Study of International Relations.* Palgrave, 2004. Brooks, Stephen G., and William C. Wohlforth. Clarifying the End of the Cold War Debate. *Cold War History* 7 (3), 2007: 447–54.

commitments while Japan and Germany made substantial financial contributions. The pass-the-hat financing for this war was an innovation, one that worked fairly well.[27]

The final collapse of the Soviet Union followed only months after the Gulf War.[28] The 15 republics of the Soviet Union—of which Russia was just one—had begun taking power from a weakened central government, declaring themselves sovereign states. This process raised complex problems ranging from issues of national self-determination to the reallocation of property. Russia and the other former republics struggled throughout the 1990s against economic and financial collapse, inflation, corruption, war, and military weakness, although they remained political democracies. A failed Russian military coup attempt in 1991—and the prominent role of Russian president Boris Yeltsin in opposing it—accelerated the collapse of the Soviet Union.[29] Soon both capitalism and democracy were adopted as the basis of the economies and political systems of the former Soviet states. The republics became independent states and formed the CIS. Of the former Soviet republics, only the three small Baltic states and Georgia are nonmembers.

Western relations with Russia and the other republics have been mixed since the 1990s. Because of their own economic problems, and because of a sense that Russia needed internal reform more than external aid, Western countries provided only limited aid for the region's harsh economic transition, which had drastically reduced living standards. Russia's brutal suppression of its secessionist province of Chechnya in 1995 and 1999 provoked Western fears of an expansionist, aggressive Russian nationalism. Russian leaders feared NATO expansion into Eastern Europe that placed threatening Western military forces on Russia's borders. Meanwhile, Japan and Russia could not resolve a lingering, mostly symbolic, territorial dispute.[30]

Despite these problems, the world's great powers overall increased their cooperation after the Cold War. Russia was accepted as the successor state to the Soviet Union and took its seat on the Security Council. Russia and the United States agreed to major reductions in their nuclear weapons, and carried them out in the 1990s.

Just after the Gulf War in 1991, the former Yugoslavia broke apart, with several of its republics declaring independence. Ethnic Serbs, who were minorities in Croatia and Bosnia, seized territory to form a "Greater Serbia." With help from Serbia, which controlled the Yugoslav army, they killed hundreds of thousands of non-Serb Bosnians and Croatians and expelled millions more, to create an ethnically pure state.

The international community recognized the independence of Croatia and Bosnia, admitting them to the UN and passing dozens of Security Council resolutions to protect their territorial integrity and their civilian populations. But in contrast to the Gulf War, the great powers showed no willingness to bear major costs to protect Bosnia. Instead they tried to contain the conflict by assuming a neutral role as peacekeeper and intermediary.[31] In 1995, Serbian forces overran two UN-designated "safe areas" in eastern Bosnia, expelling the women and slaughtering thousands of the men. Finally, two weeks of NATO airstrikes (the alliance's first-ever military engagement), along with losses to Croatia on the ground, induced Serbian forces to come to terms. The treaty to end the war (authored by U.S. negotiators) formally held Bosnia together but granted Serbian forces autonomy on half of their territory, while placing about 60,000 heavily armed (mostly NATO) troops on the ground to maintain a cease-fire. Meanwhile, Serbian strongman Slobodan Milosevic was

---

[27] Freedman, Lawrence, and Efraim Karsh. *The Gulf Conflict: 1990–1991*. Princeton, 1993.

[28] Fukuyama, Francis. *The End of History and the Last Man*. Free Press, 1992.

[29] McFaul, Michael. *Russia's Unfinished Revolution: Political Change from Gorbachev to Putin*. Cornell, 2001.

[30] Ikenberry, G. John. *After Victory*. Princeton, 2000.

[31] Gow, James. *Triumph of the Lack of Will: International Diplomacy and the Yugoslav War*. Columbia, 1997. Rieff, David. *Slaughterhouse: Bosnia and the Failure of the West*. Simon & Schuster, 1995. Malcolm, Noel. *Bosnia: A Short History*. New York University, 1994.

indicted for war crimes by the UN tribunal for the former Yugoslavia, was delivered to the tribunal in 2001, and died in 2006 near the end of a lengthy trial.

In contrast to their indecision early in the Bosnia crisis, the Western powers acted decisively in 1999 when Serbian forces carried out "ethnic cleansing" in the Serbian province of Kosovo, predominantly populated by ethnic Albanians. NATO launched an air war that escalated over ten weeks. NATO came under criticism from Russia and China for acting without explicit UN authorization and for interfering in Serbia's internal affairs. (The international community and the UN considered Kosovo, unlike Bosnia, to be a part of Serbia.) In the end, Serbian forces withdrew from Kosovo and NATO has controlled the province ever since.[32] In 2008, with the UN Security Council still deadlocked over its status, Kosovo declared independence, bringing protests from Serbia and its allies. In 2010, the World Court declared Kosovo's *declaration* of independence legal, although its substantive status remains in dispute.

Other Western military intervention decisions since 1990 were less effective. In Somalia, a U.S.-led coalition sent tens of thousands of troops to suppress factional fighting and deliver relief supplies to a large population that was starving. However, when those forces were drawn into the fighting and sustained casualties, the United States abruptly pulled out.[33] In Rwanda in 1994, the genocide of more than half a million civilians in a matter of weeks was virtually ignored by the international community. The great powers, burned by failures in Somalia and Bosnia, decided that their vital interests were not at stake. In 1997, the Rwanda conflict spilled into neighboring Zaire (now Democratic Congo), where rebels overthrew a corrupt dictator. Neighboring countries were drawn into the fighting, but the international community steered clear even as conditions worsened and millions of civilians died. The U.S. military intervened in Haiti to restore the elected president, but today Haiti remains mired in poverty and political instability.

New rifts opened in 2001 between the United States and both China and Europe—possibly signaling a realignment against U.S. predominance in world affairs. The United States stood nearly alone against the rest of the international community on a range of issues—missile defenses, the Kyoto treaty on global warming, a treaty to enforce the prohibition on biological weapons, a proposal to curb international small-arms sales, the proposed International Criminal Court, and a proposal to curb tobacco marketing in poor countries. Russia and China signed a treaty of friendship in 2001, and European countries helped vote the United States off two important UN commissions.

These divisive issues receded when the United States was attacked by terrorists on September 11, 2001. The attack destroyed the World Trade Center in New York and a wing of the Pentagon in Washington, D.C., killing thousands of Americans and citizens of about 60 other countries. The attacks mobilized support for the United States by a very broad coalition of states, out of a realization that terrorism threatens the interstate system itself. President Bush declared a "war on terrorism" that was expected to last years and span continents, employing both conventional and unconventional means. In late 2001, U.S. and British forces and their Afghan allies ousted the Taliban regime in Afghanistan, which had harbored and supported the al Qaeda network (led by Osama bin Laden) responsible for attacks on the United States.

The great power divisions reappeared, however, as the United States and Britain tried to assemble a coalition to oust Iraq's Saddam Hussein by force in early 2003. France and Germany (along with Russia and China) bitterly opposed the war, as did millions of protesters around the

---

[32] Bacevich, Andrew J., and Eliot A. Cohen. *War over Kosovo*. Columbia, 2002. Mertus, Julie A. *Kosovo: How Myths and Truths Started a War*. California, 1999. Vickers, Miranda. *Between Serb and Albanian: A History of Kosovo*. Columbia, 1998.

[33] Clarke, Walter S., and Jeffrey I. Herbst, eds. *Learning from Somalia: The Lessons of Armed Humanitarian Intervention*. Westview, 1997. Rutherford, Kenneth R. *Humanitarianism Under Fire: The U.S. and UN Intervention in Somalia*. Kumarian, 2008.

WAVE OF CHANGE

Peaceful trends mark the post–Cold War era, though war and terrorism continue. The Arab Spring popular uprisings in 2011 brought the world's latest wave of democracy to the Middle East. They overthrew governments in Tunisia, Egypt, and Libya; weakened those in Syria and Yemen; and reshaped the international dynamics of the region. Here, protesters in Tahrir Square—in the capital of Egypt, at the heart of the Arab world—demand that the military government continue with reforms after the ouster of Egypt's president 2011.

world. The dispute brought the Atlantic alliance to a low point and wrecked France's dream of leading a unified European foreign policy. The war on Iraq also weakened the UN's post–Cold War security role, because the U.S.-led coalition went forward despite its failure to win Security Council authorization for war.

The invasion itself was brief and decisive. A U.S. military force of 250,000 troops with advanced technology overpowered the Iraqi army in three weeks. Many Iraqis welcomed the end of a dictatorial regime, as had most Afghans in late 2001, but the war inflamed anti-American sentiment, especially in Muslim countries. Insurgent forces in Iraq gained strength as the U.S. occupation stretched on for years, and by 2006 U.S. public opinion had turned against the war as violence escalated. After a U.S. troop surge in 2007, and the arming of Sunni communities fed up with foreign Islamist radicals, violence in Iraq fell.[34] U.S. forces withdrew from Iraq in 2009–2011, but violence continued. Estimates of Iraqi deaths caused by the war range from tens of thousands to more than 600,000. Elections in 2010 were relatively peaceful, but left the country divided among several political parties who could not form a government for months afterward.

In Afghanistan, fighting worsened beginning in 2007 as the Taliban began an insurgency campaign from bases in Pakistan. Disputed elections in the summer of 2009 only exacerbated violence and increased political uncertainty. President Obama then pledged 30,000 more U.S. troops to help stabilize Afghanistan, yet also announced a date to start withdrawing troops from that country in the summer of 2011.

At the same time, the United States faced new crises involving nuclear weapons programs. North Korea restarted its program, producing possibly a half-dozen nuclear bombs and testing two in 2006 and 2007. Starting in 2004, Iran made and broke several agreements with Europe to suspend the enrichment of uranium that could be used to build nuclear weapons. In response, the UN Security Council passed a series of sanctions against Iran, demanding that it stop its enrichment program. In 2010, with Iran seemingly a few years away from successfully building a weapon, centrifuges key to its enrichment program began mysteriously destroying themselves, and investigation turned up a highly sophisticated computer "worm" called Stuxnet that had infected Iran's control computers. The worm, evidently a creation of Israeli and American defense scientists, set back Iran's program by several years and deferred a discussion of whether to bomb Iran's nuclear facilities.

---

[34] Woodward, Bob. *State of Denial: Bush at War, Part III.* Simon & Schuster, 2006. Gordon, Michael R., and Gen. Bernard E. Trainor. *Cobra II: The Inside Story of the Invasion and Occupation of Iraq.* Pantheon, 2006. Ricks, Thomas E. *The Gamble: General David Patraeus and the American Military Adventure in Iraq, 2006–2008.* Penguin, 2009.

The post–Cold War era may seem a conflict-prone period in which savage wars flare up with unexpected intensity around the world, in places such as Bosnia and Rwanda—even New York City. Yet, *the post–Cold War era has been more peaceful than the Cold War* (see p. 85). World military spending decreased by about one-third from its peak in the 1980s, although it has risen partway back since 2001. Old wars have ended faster than new ones have begun.[35] Latin America and Russia/CIS have nearly extinguished wars in their regions, joining a zone of peace already encompassing North America, Europe, Japan/Pacific, and China.

Warfare is diminishing even in the arc of conflict from Africa through the Middle East to South Asia. Since 1990, long, bloody wars have ended in South Africa, Mozambique, Angola, southern Sudan, and Ethiopia-Eritrea, as did the Cold War conflicts in Central America and most recently Sri Lanka. More recent wars in Ivory Coast, Rwanda, and Indonesia have also largely wound down. After the Cold War, world order did not spiral out of control with rampant aggression and war.

However, the Israeli-Palestinian conflict, which saw rising expectations of peace in the 1990s, worsened in 2000 after a proposed deal fell through. With the 2006 Palestinian election victory of the militant Islamist party Hamas, responsible for many terrorist bombings in Israel, hopes for a durable peace faded. In 2006 Israel fought a brief but intense war with Hezbollah guerrillas in southern Lebanon, and in 2008–2009 Israel and Hamas traded major airstrikes and rocket attacks, culminating in the Israeli invasion of Gaza.[36]

In international economic relations, the post–Cold War era is one of globalization. New hubs of economic growth are emerging, notably in parts of Asia with remarkable economic growth. At the same time, disparities between the rich and poor are growing, both globally and within individual countries. Globalization has created backlashes among people who are adversely affected or who believe their identities are threatened by foreign influences. The resurgence of nationalism and ethnic-religious conflict— occasionally in brutal form—results partly from that backlash. So does the significant protest movement against capitalist-led globalization.

With increasing globalization, transnational concerns such as environmental degradation and disease have become more prominent as well. Global warming looms as an ever more present danger, underscored in 2005 by the toll of Hurricane Katrina on New Orleans and the accelerating melting of arctic ice. In 2008–2009, a virulent swine flu (known as H1N1) spread worldwide, triggering efforts to control the virus through quarantines and a new vaccine. Major oil spills in the Gulf of Mexico and China in 2010 refocused international attention on the issue of pollution and the environment, especially in the context of the global race for natural resources.

China is becoming more central to world politics as the 21st century begins. Its size and rapid growth make China a rising power—a situation that some scholars liken to Germany's rise a century earlier. Historically, such shifts in power relations have caused instability in the international system. China is the only great power that is not a democracy. Its poor record on human rights makes it a frequent target of Western criticism from both governments and NGOs.

China holds (but seldom uses) veto power in the UN Security Council, and it has a credible nuclear arsenal. China adjoins several regional conflict areas and affects the global proliferation of missiles and nuclear weapons. It claims disputed territory in the resource-rich South China Sea, but has not fought a military battle in 25 years. With the transfer of Hong Kong from Britain in 1997, China acquired a valuable asset and turned to hopes of someday reintegrating Taiwan as well, under the Hong Kong formula of "one country, two systems." China is the only great power from the global South. Its population size and

---

[35] Human Security Centre. *Human Security Report 2005: War and Peace in the 21st Century.* Oxford, 2006.
[36] Booth, Ken, and Tim Dunne, eds. *Worlds in Collision: Terror and the Future of Global Order.* Palgrave, 2002.

rapid industrialization from a low starting point make China a big factor in the future of global environmental trends such as global warming. All these elements make China an important actor in the coming decades.

It remains to be seen whether, in the coming years, the international system can provide China with appropriate status and respect to reflect its rising power and historical importance, and whether China in turn can come to conform with international rules and norms. The 2008 Olympic games in Beijing, a successful coming-of-age party for China on the world stage, focused attention on these processes. So will the Chinese leadership's decisions about whether to encourage or discourage the rising tide of nationalism among China's young people as communist ideology loses its hold.

The transition into the post–Cold War era has been a turbulent time, full of changes and new possibilities both good and bad. It is likely, however, that the basic rules and principles of IR—those that scholars have long struggled to understand—will continue to apply, though their contexts and outcomes may change. Most central to those rules and principles is the concept of power, to which we now turn.

✓—⸢ **Study**
and **Review**
the **Post-Test &**
Chapter Exam
at **mypoliscilab.com**

CHAPTER REVIEW

SUMMARY

- IR affects daily life profoundly; we all participate in IR.

- IR is a field of political science concerned mainly with explaining political outcomes in international security affairs and international political economy.

- Theories complement descriptive narratives in explaining international events and outcomes, and although scholars do not agree on a single set of theories or methods, three core principles shape various solutions to collective goods problems in IR.

- States are the most important actors in IR; the international system is based on the sovereignty of about 200 independent territorial states of varying size.

- Nonstate actors such as intergovernmental organizations (IGOs), nongovernmental organizations (NGOs), and multinational corporations (MNCs) exert a growing influence on international relations.

- Four levels of analysis—individual, domestic, interstate, and global—suggest multiple explanations (operating simultaneously) for outcomes in IR.

- Globalization is conceived differently by various scholars, but generally refers to the growing scope, speed, and intensity of connectedness worldwide. The process may be weakening, strengthening, or transforming the power of states. Antiglobalization activists oppose growing corporate power but disagree on goals and tactics.

- World Wars I and II dominated the 20th century, yet they seem to offer contradictory lessons about the utility of hard-line or conciliatory foreign policies.

- For nearly 50 years after World War II, world politics revolved around the East-West rivalry of the Cold War. This bipolar standoff created stability and avoided great power wars, including nuclear war, but turned states in the global South into proxy battlegrounds.

- The post–Cold War era holds hope of general great power cooperation despite the appearance of new ethnic and regional conflicts.

- A "war on terrorism" of uncertain scope and duration began in 2001 after terrorist attacks on the United States.

- The U.S. military campaign in Iraq overthrew a dictator, but divided the great powers, heightened anti-Americanism worldwide, and led to years of insurgency and sectarian violence.

KEY TERMS

international relations
  (IR)   3
collective goods
  problem   4
dominance   5
reciprocity   5
identity   6
issue areas   11
conflict and
  cooperation   11
international
  security   12
international political
  economy (IPE)   12

state   13
international
  system   13
nation-states   13
Gross Domestic
  Product (GDP)   14
nonstate actors   15
intergovernmental
  organization
  (IGO)   15
nongovernmental
  organization
  (NGO)   15
globalization   19

North-South
  gap   21
League of
  Nations   27
Munich Agreement   27
Cold War   31
containment   31
Sino-Soviet
  split   31
summit meeting   31
Cuban Missile
  Crisis   32
proxy wars   32

CRITICAL THINKING QUESTIONS

1. Pick a current area in which interesting international events are taking place. Can you think of possible explanations for those events from each of the four levels of analysis? (See Table 1.3, p. 18.) Do explanations from different levels provide insights into different aspects of the events?

2. The Cold War is long over, but its influences linger. Can you think of three examples in which the Cold War experience continues to shape the foreign policies of today's states?

3. In what ways does international economics affect our daily lives? Is this true for all people in all places? Or do economic processes such as globalization affect some regions more than others?

4. Given the contradictory lessons of World Wars I and II, can you think of situations in today's world in which appeasement (a conciliatory policy) would be the best course? Situations in which hard-line containment policies would be best? Why?

5. What do you expect will be the character of the 21st century? Peaceful? War-prone? Orderly? Chaotic? Why do you have the expectations you do, and what clues from the unfolding of events in the world might tell you whether your guesses are correct?

Globalization: Vanishing State Power?

Overview

For over 300 years, the nation-state has been the main organizing principle in the world. State governments fight wars, protect their citizens, collect taxes, and provide services for everyday life (from running transit systems to collecting garbage). The idea of the state as a key organizing principle dates back hundreds of years. Political philosophers such as Thomas Hobbes saw governments as providing individuals protection from the state of nature (where life without the state was "nasty, brutish, and short") and from other groups of individuals.

The idea of a nation-state was European in origin. Prior to colonization, large portions of Africa, Asia, and Latin America were organized in different ways: either by families, clans, or other group units. Yet, as Europeans spread throughout the world in efforts to colonize and settle new lands, they brought the idea of a nation-state with them. In a relatively short period of time, the world was organized as a set of states interacting on the world stage. States became the central actors providing services to individuals, while coming into conflict or cooperating with one another.

Yet in the era of globalization, the power of the state is being challenged. With globalization has come the rise of technology, nonstate actors, fluid state borders, and intergovernmental organizations, all of which are eroding the state's ability to control what goes on within and across its borders. Could we be seeing the beginning of the end of the nation-state as an organizing principle in international relations?

State Power Is on the Decline

Nonstate actors are now as important as the state. Whether they are nongovernmental organizations (NGOs) or multinational corporations (MNCs), nonstate actors play an increasingly important part in world politics. NGOs pressure governments to change human rights practices, MNCs compel states to adapt laws to suit their businesses, and terrorist groups undermine state security. These challenges to state power have grown in the past decade and will continue to grow as globalization allows citizens more access to one another.

States are no longer the key economic actors. Except for the economically largest states such as the United States and Japan, MNCs and private investors control more resources and capital than many nation-states. Add to this list the powerful IGOs such as the World Bank, the World Trade Organization, and the International Monetary Fund, and states are but one category of player in the global economic game.

Many substitutes for nationalism have emerged. While nationalism was a powerful force supporting the state in the past, other ideas have emerged to challenge it. Religion has replaced allegiance to the state for some, and strong ethnic ties also challenge loyalty to the state. If more individuals' primary loyalty is to something besides their nation-state, state power will continue to decline.

States Are Down but Not Out

States have always been challenged, but they have always persevered. States have been under threat for centuries. Whether the threat was from nonstate actors (pirates), from NGOs (the antislavery movement), or from MNCs (the British East India Tea Company), the state has emerged as the central power in international relations. No successful replacement for the state has yet arisen.

States still perform functions that cannot be handed off to other actors. Despite the rise of nonstate actors, certain functions will always fall to states, such as collecting taxes, making laws, and protecting citizens from external threats. States will always need help to perform these duties, but no other entity can perform them outright.

Nationalism will remain a powerful ideological force for the foreseeable future. While alternatives to nationalism exist, none are as widely accepted. Individuals still have strong allegiances to their countries. Witness the number of separatist groups that still try to achieve their independence as a state. If the state did not still have distinct advantages, why would people go to such lengths to achieve statehood?

Questions

- How has globalization played a role in challenging the power of the state? In other words, which of the challenges are attributable to globalization and which are attributable to forces that may run counter to globalization, such as religion?

- Is there an alternative to the nation-state? Are there more natural ways to organize politics? Think about alternatives that are smaller (ethnic groups, tribes, regions) and larger (multistate coalitions like the European Union or world government).

- One way to think about the European Union is as a natural progression into larger political units. Centuries ago, Europe was a series of city-states, then slightly larger kingdoms, then larger principalities, then nation-states, and now a larger union. Can you foresee a similar evolution in any other geographic region, such as Latin America or Africa?

For Further Reading

Zakaria, Fareed. *The Post American World.* Norton, 2008.

Cameron, David. *Globalization and Self-Determination: Is the Nation-State Under Siege?* Routledge, 2006.

Bhagwati, Jagdish. *In Defense of Globalization.* Oxford, 2007.

Stiglitz, Joseph E. *Globalization and Its Discontents.* Norton, 2003.

Jobs in Government and Diplomacy

SUMMARY

Jobs in government and diplomacy offer team players the chance to affect policy, but require patience with large bureaucracies.

BENEFITS AND COSTS Both governments and intergovernmental organizations (IGOs) play key roles in international relations and employ millions of people with interests and training in IR.

Despite differences between careers in IGOs and governments, there are numerous similarities. Both are hierarchical organizations, with competitive and highly regulated working environments. Whether in the U.S. State Department or the UN, entrance into and promotion in these organizations is regulated by exams, performance evaluations, and tenure with the organization.

Another similarity lies in the challenges of being pulled in many directions concerning policies. Governments face competing pressures of public opinion, constituencies, and interests groups—each with distinct policy opinions. IGOs also deal with interest groups (such as NGOs), but an IGO's constituents are states, which in many cases disagree among themselves.

Many employees of IGOs or governments thrive on making decisions that influence policies. Both work environments also attract coworkers with deep interests in international affairs, and the resulting networks of contracts can bring professional and intellectual rewards. Finally, jobs in governments or IGOs may involve travel or living abroad, which many enjoy.

However, promotion can be slow and frustrating. Usually, only individuals with advanced degrees or technical specializations achieve non–entry level positions. It can take years to climb within the organization and the process may involve working in departments far from your original interests. In addition, both IGOs and governments are bureaucracies with formal rules and procedures, requiring great patience. Employees often express frustration that initiative and "thinking outside the box" are not rewarded.

SKILLS TO HONE The key to working in IGOs or government is to get your foot in the door. Be flexible and willing to take entry positions that are not exactly in your area of interest. For example, the State Department is only one of many parts of the U.S. government that deal with IR. Do not assume that to work in foreign affairs, one must be a diplomat.

Foreign language training is also important, especially for work in large IGOs with many field offices. The ability to work well in groups and to network within and across organizations is an important asset. People who can strengthen lines of communication can gain support from many places in an organization.

Finally, strong analytical and writing abilities are extremely important. Both IGOs and governments deal with massive amounts of information daily. The ability to analyze information (even including mathematical or computational analysis) and to write clear, concise interpretations will make one invaluable.

RESOURCES

Shawn Dorman. *Inside a U.S. Embassy: How the Foreign Service Works for America.* 2nd ed. Washington, D.C.: American Foreign Service Assoc., 2003.

Linda Fasulo. *An Insider's Guide to the UN.* New Haven: Yale University Press, 2005.

http://jobs.un.org
http://careers.state.gov
http://jobsearch.usajobs.opm.gov/a9st00.aspx

Jobs in International Business

SUMMARY

Jobs in international business offer high pay, interesting work, and demanding hours for those with language and cultural skills.

BENEFITS AND COSTS As the pace and scope of globalization have accelerated, opportunities to work in international business have blossomed. For many large companies, the domestic/global distinction has ceased to exist. This new context provides opportunities and challenges for potential employees.

Careers in international business offer many advantages. Business jobs can pay substantially more than those in governments or NGOs and can open opportunities to travel extensively and network globally. Foreign-based jobs mean relocation to another country to work and immerse oneself in another culture.

However, such a career choice also has potential costs. Many jobs require extensive hours, grueling travel, and frequent relocation. As with any job, promotion and advancement may fall victim to external circumstances such as global business cycles. And these jobs can be especially hard on families.

International opportunities arise in many business sectors. Banking, marketing (public relations), sales, and computing/telecommunications have seen tremendous growth in recent years. These jobs fall into three broad categories: (1) those located domestically, yet involving significant interactions with firms abroad; (2) domestic jobs working for foreign-based companies; and (3) those based abroad, for foreign or domestic firms.

SKILLS TO HONE One key to landing in the international business world is to develop two families of skills: those related to international relations and those related to business operations. Traditional MBA (Masters in Business Administration) and business school programs will be helpful for all three types of jobs, yet for jobs based abroad, employers often also look for a broader set of skills taught in economics, political science, and communications. Thus, not only traditional business skills, but language and cultural skills, are essential. Employers look for those who have knowledge of a country's human and economic geography as well as culture. Experience with study abroad, especially including working abroad, can help show an ability to adapt and function well in other cultures. Strong analytical and especially writing abilities also matter greatly to employers.

Research also helps in landing a job. Employers often look for knowledge of a particular industry or company, in order to make best use of an employee's language and cultural skills. Of course, while experience in non-international business never hurts, be mindful that the practices, customs, and models of business in one country may not apply well abroad. Cross-cultural skills combined with substantive business knowledge in order to translate the operational needs of companies from the business world to the global realm are highly valued.

RESOURCES

Edward J. Halloran. *Careers in International Business.* 2nd ed. NY: McGraw-Hill, 2003.

Deborah Penrith, ed. *The Directory of Jobs and Careers Abroad.* 12th ed. Oxford, UK: Vacation Work Publications, 2005.

http://www.rileyguide.com/internat.html
http://www.jobsabroad.com/search.cfm
http://www.transitionsabroad.com/listings/work/careers/index.shtml

Jobs in Nongovernmental Organizations

SUMMARY

Jobs in NGOs provide personally rewarding experiences for those willing to work hard for a cause, but pay poorly and are hard to obtain.

BENEFITS AND COSTS Nearly 30,000 NGOs exist, and that number grows daily. Thousands of individuals are interested in working in these organizations. Although all NGOs are different, many perform multiple functions: working in developing countries regarding a variety of issues; public outreach at home and abroad; lobbying governments to change their policies; designing projects to solve problems and attempting to find funding for their implementation.

Working for an NGO has many benefits. Workers often find themselves surrounded by others concerned about the same issues: improving the environment, protecting human rights, advancing economic development, or promoting better health care. The spirit of camaraderie can be exhilarating and rewarding.

While working for an NGO can be extremely rewarding personally, it is rarely rewarding financially. Most NGOs are nonprofit operations that pay workers meagerly for long hours. Moreover, many smaller NGOs engage in a constant fight for funding from governments, think tanks, private foundations, or individuals. The process of fundraising can be quite time consuming.

Despite the large number of NGOs, relatively low pay, and long hours, finding a job with an NGO can be difficult. One key is to be specific. Try to narrow down your interests in terms of substantive areas (e.g., human rights, environment) and/or geographic region. Also think about whether you want to work in your own country or abroad. Positions abroad may be more rewarding but are in lower supply and higher demand.

SKILLS TO HONE NGOs are looking for self-starters. Most have little time and few resources for training. Basic office skills (e.g., computer expertise) are essential, but employees also need to cover a range of duties every day. Anything and everything is in your job description. Writing and communication skills are key, especially when fundraising is part of the job. Foreign language skills also matter since many NGOs maintain or work with field offices abroad.

Often, NGOs ask potential employees to volunteer for a period while they train, before being hired. Increasingly, some companies place workers in an NGO or volunteer opportunity for a price. By paying to work, you can gain a probationary period to develop your skills and familiarize yourself with the operation so as to become efficient before going on the payroll.

Finally, in cities where NGOs cluster (e.g., Washington, D.C.), personal networks play an important role in finding good opportunities. Workers often move from one organization to another. For this reason, many volunteer or accept jobs with NGOs not in their immediate area of interest to gain experience and contacts, which can help future career advancement.

RESOURCES

Sherry Mueller. Careers in Nonprofit and Educational Organizations. In *Careers in International Affairs*. 7th ed. Washington, D.C.: Georgetown School of Foreign Service, 2003.

Richard M. King. *From Making a Profit to Making a Difference: How to Launch Your New Career in Nonprofits*. River Forest, IL: Planning/Communications, 2000.

http://www.ngo.org/links/index.htm
http://www.idealist.org
http://www.wango.org/resources.aspx?section=ngodir

Jobs in Education and Research

SUMMARY

Jobs in teaching and research offer freedom to pursue ideas and work with colleagues, but require years of schooling.

BENEFITS AND COSTS People follow various paths to an interest in teaching and researching in the field of international relations. Your own professor or instructor is likely to have a unique story about how he or she became interested in international affairs.

One advantage of an academic and research career, whether at a teaching-oriented institution or a large research university, is intellectual freedom. One can spend a career approaching a variety of topics that are interesting and constantly evolving, that may involve travel abroad for fieldwork, and that may let you network with hundreds of colleagues interested in similar topics.

Most research positions (e.g., in think tanks) are different in two respects. First, these jobs often give more direction to an individual in terms of the research to be performed. Second, there is little or no teaching involved. Still, for those interested in IR research, such jobs can result in a wider dissemination of one's work to a broader audience that often includes policy makers.

To teach IR at an advanced level or to perform research for think tanks and government agencies usually requires an advanced degree—nearly always a masters degree, often a doctorate (Ph.D.). Masters degree programs often take between one and two years, while a Ph.D. in international relations usually takes a minimum of five years. Often, students take time off between their undergraduate and graduate educations to travel internationally or get work experience to hone their interests. Of course, many students never return to extend their education if they find a job that allows them to achieve their personal and career goals.

Finally, in completing most advanced degrees, a large amount of self-direction is necessary. Coursework is only one part of masters or Ph.D. programs: a thesis is also required. Writing a thesis requires you to work on your own time schedule, balancing other duties (such as work as a teaching or research assistant) that can easily crowd out your own work. Many who complete the coursework for an advanced degree do not finish their thesis or take many years to do so.

SKILLS TO HONE Whether one wants to pursue an advanced degree for the purposes of teaching in an academic setting or engaging in applied research, there are important skill sets to develop. First and foremost is critical thinking. Scholars and researchers must consider many alternatives as answers to questions, while being able to evaluate the validity or importance of those alternatives. Second is writing. Before, during, and after producing a thesis, writing is a key skill for academics and researchers. Finally, think about developing a set of applied skills to use as a toolbox while analyzing questions. The contents of this toolbox might include other languages to facilitate fieldwork abroad. It could include statistics and data skills to facilitate quantitative analysis. Or it could include mathematics to use game theoretic models. No matter which tools you emphasize, specialized skills will help you answer research questions, whether as part of the academy or in a private or governmental research organization.

RESOURCES *The Chronicle of Higher Education* (weekly). Online at chronicle.com/

American Political Science Assoc. *Earning a PhD in Political Science*. 4th ed. Washington, D.C., 2004.

Ernest J. Wilson. Is There Really a Scholar-Practitioner Gap? An Institutional Analysis. *PS: Political Science and Politics,* January 2007.

http://www.apsanet.org
http://www.apsia.org
http://www.isanet.org

CHAPTER 2

Realist Theories

Libyan rebels fire rockets, 2011.

Realism

No single theory reliably explains the wide range of international interactions, but one theoretical framework has historically held a central position in the study of IR. This approach, called realism, is favored by some IR scholars and vigorously contested by others, but almost all take it into account.

Realism (or *political realism*) is a school of thought that explains international relations in terms of power. The exercise of power by states toward each other is sometimes called *realpolitik*, or just *power politics*.

Modern realist theory developed in reaction to a liberal tradition that realists called **idealism** (of course, idealists themselves do not consider their approach unrealistic). Idealism emphasizes international law, morality, and international organizations, rather than power alone, as key influences on international events.[1] Idealists think that human nature is basically good. They see the international system as one based on a community of states that have the potential to work together to overcome mutual problems (see Chapter 3). For idealists, the principles of IR must flow from morality. Idealists were particularly active between World War I and World War II, following the painful experience of World War I. U.S. president Woodrow Wilson and other idealists placed their hopes for peace in the League of Nations as a formal structure for the community of nations.

Those hopes were dashed when that structure proved helpless to stop German, Italian, and Japanese aggression in the 1930s. Since World War II, realists have blamed idealists for looking too much at how the world *ought* to be instead of how it *really* is. Sobered by the experiences of World War II, realists set out to understand the principles of power politics without succumbing to wishful thinking. Realism provided a theoretical foundation for the Cold War policy of containment and the determination of U.S. policy makers not to appease the Soviet Union and China as the West had appeased Hitler at Munich in 1938.

Realists ground themselves in a long tradition. The Chinese strategist *Sun Tzu*, who lived 2,000 years ago, advised the rulers of states how to survive in an era when war had become a systematic instrument of power for the first time (the "warring states" period). Sun Tzu argued that moral reasoning was not very useful to the state rulers of the day, faced with armed and dangerous neighbors. He showed rulers how to use power to advance their interests and protect their survival.[2]

At roughly the same time, in Greece, *Thucydides* wrote an account of the Peloponnesian War (431–404 B.C.) focusing on relative power among the Greek city-states. He stated that "the strong do what they have the power to do and the weak accept what they have to accept."[3] Much later, in Renaissance Italy (around 1500), *Niccolò Machiavelli* urged princes to concentrate on expedient actions to stay in power, including the manipulation of the public and military alliances. Today the adjective *Machiavellian* refers to excessively manipulative power maneuvers.[4]

The English philosopher *Thomas Hobbes* in the 17th century discussed the free-for-all that exists when government is absent and people seek their own self-interests. He called

Read and **Listen** to **Chapter 2** at **mypoliscilab.com**

Study and **Review** the **Pre-Test & Flashcards** at **mypoliscilab.com**

---

[1] Nardin, Terry, and David R. Mapel, eds. *Traditions of International Ethics*. Cambridge, 1992. Long, David, and Peter Wilson, eds. *Thinkers of the Twenty Years' Crisis: Inter-War Idealism Reassessed*. Oxford, 1995.
[2] Sun Tzu. *The Art of War*. Translated by Samuel B. Griffith. Oxford, 1963.
[3] Thucydides. *History of the Peloponnesian War*. Translated by R. Warner. Penguin, 1972, p. 402.
[4] Machiavelli, Niccolò. *The Prince, and the Discourses*. Translated by Luigi Ricci. Revised by E. R. P. Vincent. NY: Modern Library, 1950. Meinecke, Friedrich. *Machiavellism: The Doctrine of Raison d'État and Its Place in Modern History*. Translated by D. Scott. Yale, 1957.

◉─⌐ **Watch**
the **Video**
**"Churchill's Iron
Curtain Speech"**
on **mypoliscilab.com**

it the "state of nature" or "state of war"—what we would now call the "law of the jungle" in contrast to the rule of law. Hobbes favored a strong monarchy (which he labeled a *Leviathan*) to tame this condition—essentially advocating a dominance approach to solve the collective goods problem in domestic societies. Realists see in these historical figures evidence that the importance of power politics is timeless and cross-cultural.

After World War II, scholar *Hans Morgenthau* argued that international politics is governed by objective, universal laws based on national interests defined in terms of power (not psychological motives of decision makers). He reasoned that no nation had "God on its side" (a universal morality) and that all nations had to base their actions on prudence and practicality. He opposed the Vietnam War, arguing in 1965 that a communist Vietnam would not harm U.S. national interests.

Similarly, in 2002, before the U.S. invasion of Iraq, leading realists figured prominently among the 33 IR scholars signing a *New York Times* advertisement warning that "war with Iraq is *not* in America's national interest."[5] Thus realists do not always favor using military power, although they recognize the necessity of doing so at times. The target of the IR scholars' ad was the group of foreign policy makers in the Bush administration known as *neoconservatives*, who advocated more energetic use of American power, especially military force, to accomplish ambitious and moralistic goals such as democratizing the Middle East.

Thus, realism's foundation is the principle of dominance; alternatives based on reciprocity and identity will be reviewed in Chapter 3. Figure 2.1 lays out the various theoretical approaches to the study of IR we discuss in Chapters 2 and 3.

Realists tend to treat political power as separate from, and predominant over, morality, ideology, and other social and economic aspects of life. For realists, ideologies do not matter much, nor do religions or other cultural factors with which states may justify their actions.

FIGURE 2.1 Theories of IR

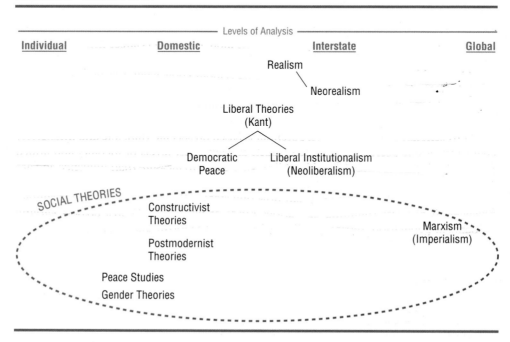

5 Morgenthau, Hans. We Are Deluding Ourselves in Vietnam. *New York Times Magazine*, April 18, 1965. Advertisement, *New York Times*, September 26, 2002.

TABLE 2.1 Assumptions of Realism and Idealism

Issue	Realism	Idealism
Human Nature	Selfish	Altruistic
Most Important Actors	States	States and others including individuals
Causes of State Behavior	Rational pursuit of self-interest	Psychological motives of decision makers
Nature of International System	Anarchy	Community

Realists see states with very different religions, ideologies, or economic systems as quite similar in their actions with regard to national power.[6] Thus, realists assume that IR can be best (though not exclusively) explained by the choices of states operating as autonomous actors rationally pursuing their own interests in an international system of sovereign states without a central authority.[7]

Table 2.1 summarizes some major differences between the assumptions of realism and idealism.

Power

Power is a central concept in international relations—the central one for realists—but it is surprisingly difficult to define or measure.[8]

Defining Power

Power is often defined as the ability to get another actor to do what it would not otherwise have done (or not to do what it would have done). A variation on this idea is that actors are powerful to the extent that they affect others more than others affect them. These definitions treat power as influence. If actors get their way a lot, they must be powerful.

One problem with this definition is that we seldom know what a second actor would have done in the absence of the first actor's power. There is a danger of circular logic: power explains influence, and influence measures power.

Power is not influence itself, however, but the ability or potential to influence others. Many IR scholars believe that such potential is based on specific (tangible and intangible) characteristics or possessions of states—such as their sizes, levels of income, and armed forces. This is power as *capability*. Capabilities are easier to measure than influence and are less circular in logic.

Measuring capabilities to explain how one state influences another is not simple, however. It requires summing up various kinds of potentials. States possess varying amounts of population, territory, military forces, and so forth. *The best single indicator of*

---

[6] Morgenthau, Hans J., and Kenneth W. Thompson. *Politics among Nations: The Struggle for Power and Peace.* 6th ed. Knopf, 1985. Carr, Edward Hallett. *The Twenty Years' Crisis, 1919–1939: An Introduction to the Study of International Relations.* Macmillan, 1974 [1939]. Aron, Raymond. *Peace and War: A Theory of International Relations.* Translated by R. Howard and A. B. Fox. Doubleday, 1966.

[7] Waltz, Kenneth. *Theory of International Politics.* Addison-Wesley, 1979.

[8] Barnett, Michael, and Raymond Duvall. Power in International Politics. *International Organization* 59 (1), 2005: 1–37. Baldwin, David. Power in International Relations. In Carlsnaes, Walter, Thomas Risse, and Beth Simmons, eds. *Handbook of International Relations.* Sage, 2002, pp. 177–91.

POWER AS INFLUENCE

Power is the ability to influence the behavior of others. Military force and economic sanctions are among the various means that states and nonstate actors use to try to influence each other. Russia's position as a major energy supplier to Europe has increased its power in recent years even though its military threat to Europe has decreased. In 2009 Russia shut off natural gas supplies during a price dispute with Ukraine, a dispute shadowed by Russian anger at Ukraine's efforts to join NATO. The shutoff, visible here in a pressure gauge reading zero, left customers across Europe without heat. In 2010 Ukrainians elected a new president more friendly toward Russia.

a state's power may be its total GDP, which combines overall size, technological level, and wealth. But even GDP is at best a rough indicator, and economists do not even agree how to measure it. The method followed in this book adjusts for price differences among countries, but an alternative method gives GDP estimates that are, on average, about 50 percent higher for countries in the global North and about 50 percent lower for the global South including China (see footnote 9 on p. 14). So GDP is a useful estimator of material capabilities but not a precise one.

Power also depends on nonmaterial elements. Capabilities give a state the potential to influence others only to the extent that political leaders can mobilize and deploy these capabilities effectively and strategically. This depends on national will, diplomatic skill, popular support for the government (its legitimacy), and so forth. Some scholars emphasize the *power of ideas*—the ability to maximize the influence of capabilities through a psychological process. This process includes the domestic mobilization of capabilities—often through religion, ideology, or (especially) nationalism. International influence is also gained by forming the rules of behavior to change how others see their own national interests. If a state's own values become widely shared among other states, it will easily influence others. This has been called *soft power*.[9] For example, the United States has influenced many other states to accept the value of free markets and free trade.

As the concept of soft power illustrates, dominance is not the only way to exert power (influence others). The core principles of reciprocity and (in the case of soft power) identity can also work. For example, a father who wants his toddler to stop screaming in a supermarket might threaten or actually administer a spanking (dominance); he might promise a candy bar at the checkout as a reward for good behavior (reciprocity); or he could invoke such themes as "Be a big boy/girl" or "You want to help Daddy, don't you?" (identity). Although realists emphasize dominance approaches, they acknowledge that states often achieve their interests in other ways. Furthermore, even realists recognize

---

[9] Nye, Joseph S., Jr. *Bound to Lead: The Changing Nature of American Power*. Basic Books, 1990.

that power provides only a general understanding of outcomes. Real-world outcomes depend on many other elements, including accidents or luck.

Because power is a relational concept, a state can have power only relative to other states' power. *Relative power* is the ratio of the power that two states can bring to bear against each other. It matters little to realists whether a state's capabilities are rising or declining in absolute terms, only whether they are falling behind or overtaking the capabilities of rival states.

Estimating Power

The logic of power suggests that in wars, the more powerful state will generally prevail. Thus, estimates of the relative power of the two antagonists should help explain the outcome of each war. These estimates could take into account the nations' relative military capabilities and the popular support for each one's government, among other factors. But most important is the total size of each nation's economy—the total GDP—which reflects both population size and the level of income per person (per capita). With a healthy enough economy, a state can buy a large army, popular support (by providing consumer goods), and even allies.

For example, the United States that invaded Iraq in 2003 was the most powerful state in world history, and Iraq had been weakened by two costly wars and a decade of sanctions. The power disparity was striking. In GDP, the United States held an advantage of more than a hundred to one; in population, more than ten to one. U.S. forces were larger and much more capable technologically. In 2003, the United States lacked some of the power elements it had possessed during the 1991 Gulf War—the moral legitimacy conferred by the UN Security Council, a broad coalition of allies (including the most powerful states regionally and globally), and partners willing to pay for most of the costs of the war. Despite these shortfalls, U.S. military power was able to carry out the objective of regime change in Iraq, within a month and with low U.S. casualties.

And yet, years later, the U.S. forces' position in Iraq as well as the stability of the new Iraqi government remained uncertain. An anti-American insurgency proved far stronger than expected, and religious violence among Iraqis took a dramatic toll. Ironically, along with an increase in the number of troops stationed in Iraq (often referred to as "the surge"), U.S. forces began to move toward a reciprocity-based strategy: funding groups that had formerly opposed the American military, in order to gain their support. The difficulties encountered by the world's superpower in trying to establish stable political control in Iraq demonstrate that power—getting others to do what you want—includes many elements beyond just military might. GDP does not always predict who will win a war.

Elements of Power

State power is a mix of many ingredients. Elements that an actor can draw on over the *long term* include total GDP, population, territory, geography, and natural resources. These attributes change only slowly. Less tangible long-term power resources include political culture, patriotism, education of the population, and strength of the scientific and technological base. The credibility of its commitments (reputation for keeping its word) is also a long-term power base for a state. So is the ability of one state's culture and values to consistently shape the thinking of other states (the power of ideas).

THE ECONOMICS OF POWER

Military power such as tanks rests on economic strength, roughly measured by GDP. The large U.S. economy supports U.S. military predominance. In the 2003 U.S. invasion of Iraq, the United States could afford to send a large and technologically advanced military force to the Middle East. Here, U.S. forces enter Iraq, March 2003.

The importance of long-term power resources was illustrated after the Japanese surprise attack on the U.S. fleet at Pearl Harbor in 1941, which decimated U.S. naval capabilities in the Pacific. In the short term, Japan had superior military power and was able to occupy territories in Southeast Asia while driving U.S. forces from the region. In the longer term, the United States had greater power resources due to its underlying economic potential. It built up military capabilities over the next few years that gradually matched and then overwhelmed those of Japan.

Other capabilities allow actors to exercise influence in the *short term*. Military forces are such a capability—perhaps the most important kind. The size, composition, and preparedness of two states' military forces matter more in a short-term military confrontation than their respective economies or natural resources. Another capability is the military-industrial capacity to quickly produce weapons. The quality of a state's bureaucracy is another type of capability, allowing the state to gather information, regulate international trade, or participate in international conferences. Less tangibly, the *support* and *legitimacy* that an actor commands in the short term from constituents and allies are capabilities that the actor can use to gain influence. So is the *loyalty* of a nation's army and politicians to their leader.

Given the limited resources that any actor commands, trade-offs among possible capabilities always exist. Building up military forces diverts resources that might be put into foreign aid, for instance. Or buying a population's loyalty with consumer goods reduces resources available for building up military capabilities. To the extent that one element of power can be converted into another, it is *fungible*. Generally, money is the most fungible capability because it can buy other capabilities.

Realists tend to see *military force* as the most important element of national power in the short term, and other elements such as economic strength, diplomatic skill, or moral legitimacy as being important to the extent that they are fungible into military power. Yet, depending on the nature of the conflict in question, military power may be only one of many elements of power. Robert Gates, as U.S. secretary of defense, called for a "dramatic increase" in spending on diplomacy and economic aid, noting that despite very high military spending, these "other elements of national power" have lagged behind in an era of asymmetric warfare (for example, counterterrorism) in which conflicts are "fundamentally political in nature" and not simply military. Secretary Gates went on to point out that the United States has more members of military marching bands than foreign service officers. In 2009, the top U.S. military officer added that although U.S. leaders had "reached for the military hammer in the toolbox of foreign policy fairly often" in recent years, "armed forces may not always be the best choice" to achieve foreign policy goals.[10] Consistent with this thinking, U.S. spending on foreign aid has increased dramatically (along with military spending) since the attacks of 9/11 (see pp. 35–36).

Morality can contribute to power by increasing the will to use power and by attracting allies. States have long clothed their actions, however aggressive, in rhetoric about their peaceful and defensive intentions. For instance, the 1989 U.S. invasion of Panama was named "Operation Just Cause." Of course, if a state uses moralistic rhetoric to cloak self-interest too often, it loses credibility even with its own population.

The use of geography as an element of power is called **geopolitics**. It is often tied to the logistical requirements of military forces. In geopolitics, as in real estate, the three most important considerations are location, location, location. States increase their power to the extent they can use geography to enhance their military capabilities, such as by securing allies and bases close to a rival power or along strategic trade routes, or by controlling key natural resources. Today, control of oil pipeline routes, especially in Central Asia, is a major geopolitical issue. Military strategists have also pointed out that the melting of the continental ice shelf (see Chapter 11) has opened new shipping routes for military purposes, creating new a geopolitical issue for Russia and the United States.

The International System

States interact within a set of long-established "rules of the game" governing what is considered a state and how states treat each other. Together these rules shape the international system.[11]

Watch the **Video** "Chamberlain's Appeasement Speech" on **mypoliscilab.com**

Anarchy and Sovereignty

Realists believe that the international system exists in a state of **anarchy**—a term that implies not complete chaos or absence of structure and rules, but rather the lack of a central government that can enforce rules.[12] In domestic society within states, governments can enforce contracts, deter citizens from breaking rules, and use their monopoly on legally sanctioned violence to enforce a system of law. Both democracies and dictatorships provide central government enforcement of a system of rules. Realists contend that no such central authority exists to enforce rules and ensure compliance with norms of conduct. This makes collective goods problems especially acute in IR. The power of one state is countered only by the power of other states. States must therefore rely on

[10] Sanger, David. A Handpicked Team for a Sweeping Shift in Foreign Policy. *New York Times*, December 1, 2008. Shanker, Thom. Top Officer Urges Limit on Mission of Military. *New York Times*, January 13, 2009: A9.

[11] Dehio, Ludwig. *The Precarious Balance: Four Centuries of the European Power Struggle*. Translated by Charles Fullman. Vintage Books, 1962 [from the German version of 1948]. Luard, Evan. *Conflict and Peace in the Modern International System: A Study of the Principles of International Order*. Macmillan, 1988. Wight, Martin. *Systems of States*. Leicester, 1977.

[12] Bull, Hedley. *The Anarchical Society: A Study of Order in World Politics*. Columbia, 2002 [1977]. Taylor, Michael. *Anarchy and Cooperation*. Wiley, 1976. Starr, Harvey. *Anarchy, Order, and Integration: How to Manage Interdependence?* Michigan, 1997.

self-help, which they supplement with allies and the (sometimes) constraining power of international norms.

Some people think that only a world government can solve this problem. Others think that adequate order, short of world government, can be provided by international organizations and agreements (see Chapter 7). But most realists think that IR cannot escape from a state of anarchy and will continue to be dangerous as a result.[13] In this anarchic world, realists emphasize prudence as a great virtue in foreign policy. Thus states should pay attention not to the *intentions* of other states but rather to their *capabilities*.

Despite its anarchy, the international system is far from chaotic. The great majority of state interactions closely adhere to **norms** of behavior—shared expectations about what behavior is considered proper.[14] Norms change over time, slowly, but the most basic norms of the international system have changed little in recent centuries.

Sovereignty—traditionally the most important norm—means that a government has the right, in principle, to do whatever it wants in its own territory. States are separate and autonomous and answer to no higher authority. In principle, all states are equal in status, if not in power. Sovereignty also means that states are not supposed to interfere in the internal affairs of other states. Although states do try to influence each other (exert power) on matters of trade, alliances, war, and so on, they are not supposed to meddle in the internal politics and decision processes of other states. More controversially, some states claim that sovereignty gives them the right to treat their own people in any fashion, including behavior that other states call genocide.

The lack of a "world police" to punish states if they break an agreement makes enforcement of international agreements difficult. For example, in the 1990s, North Korea announced it would no longer allow inspections of its nuclear facilities by other states, which put it in violation of the Non-Proliferation Treaty (NPT). The international community used a mix of positive incentives and threats to persuade North Korea to stop producing nuclear material. But in 2002 North Korea withdrew from the NPT and built perhaps a half-dozen nuclear bombs, one of which it exploded in 2006 (the world's first nuclear test in a decade). After reaching an agreement with the United States to stop producing nuclear weapons in 2008, North Korea refused to allow physical inspection of some of its nuclear facilities, noting that "it is an act of infringing upon sovereignty."[15] These examples show the difficulty of enforcing international norms in the sovereignty-based international system.

In practice, most states have a harder and harder time warding off interference in their affairs. Such "internal" matters as human rights or self-determination are, increasingly, concerns for the international community. For example, election monitors increasingly watch internal elections for fraud, while international organizations monitor ethnic conflicts for genocide.[16] Also, the integration of global economic markets and telecommunications (such as the Internet) makes it easier than ever for ideas to penetrate state borders.[17]

States are based on territory. Respect for the territorial integrity of all states, within recognized borders, is an important principle of IR. Many of today's borders are the result

[13] Mearsheimer, John J. *The Tragedy of Great Power Politics.* Norton, 2001.

[14] Franck, Thomas M. *The Power of Legitimacy among Nations.* Oxford, 1990.

[15] *BBC News Online.* North Korea Rejects Nuclear Sampling. November 2, 2008.

[16] Alvarez, R. Michael, Thad E. Hall, and Susan D. Hyde. *Election Fraud: Detecting and Deterring Electoral Manipulation.* Brookings, 2008.

[17] Krasner, Stephen D. *Sovereignty: Organized Hypocrisy.* Princeton, 1999.

of past wars (in which winners took territory from losers) or were imposed arbitrarily by colonizers.

The territorial nature of the interstate system developed long ago when agrarian societies relied on agriculture to generate wealth. In today's world, in which trade and technology rather than land create wealth, the territorial state may be less important. Information-based economies are linked across borders instantly, and the idea that the state has a hard shell seems archaic. The accelerating revolution in information technologies may dramatically affect the territorial state system in the coming years.

States have developed norms of diplomacy to facilitate their interactions. An embassy is treated as though it were the territory of the home state, not the country where it is located (see pp. 261–263). For instance, when the U.S. embassy in China harbored a wanted Chinese dissident for two years after the 1989 Tiananmen Square crackdown, Chinese troops did not simply come in and take him away. To do so

TERRITORIAL LACK OF INTEGRITY

Sovereignty and territorial integrity are central norms governing the behavior of states. Terrorism and secessionist movements present two challenges to these norms. In 2008, Russia and Georgia fought a brief war over pro-Russian breakaway regions of Georgia, which ended up firmly in Russian control. Here, during the war, a tank from the region passes a billboard declaring Russia's Vladimir Putin "our president."

would have violated U.S. territorial integrity. Yet in 1979, Iranian students took over the U.S. embassy in Tehran, holding many of its diplomats hostage for 444 days—an episode that has soured American-Iranian relations ever since.

Diplomatic norms recognize that states try to spy on each other. Each state is responsible for keeping other states from spying on it. In 2002, China discovered that its new presidential aircraft—a Boeing 767 refurbished in Texas—was riddled with sophisticated listening devices. But China did not make an issue of it (the plane had not gone into service), and a U.S.-China summit the next month went forward. In the post–Cold War era, spying continues, even between friendly states.

Realists acknowledge that the rules of IR often create a **security dilemma**—a situation in which states' actions taken to ensure their own security (such as deploying more military forces) threaten the security of other states.[18] The responses of those other states, such as deploying more of their own military forces, in turn threaten the first state. The dilemma is a prime cause of arms races in which states spend large sums of money on mutually threatening weapons that do not ultimately provide security.

The security dilemma is a negative consequence of anarchy in the international system. If a world government could reliably detect and punish aggressors who arm

---

[18] Herz, John. Idealist Internationalism and the Security Dilemma. *World Politics* 2 (2), 1950: 157–80. Jervis, Robert. Cooperation under the Security Dilemma. *World Politics* 30 (2), 1978: 167–214.

themselves, states would not need to guard against this possibility. Yet the self-help system requires that states prepare for the worst. Realists tend to see the dilemma as unsolvable, whereas liberals think it can be solved through the development of institutions (see Chapters 3 and 7).

As we shall see in later chapters, changes in technology and in norms are undermining the traditional principles of territorial integrity and state autonomy in IR. Some IR scholars find states practically obsolete as the main actors in world politics, as some integrate into larger entities and others fragment into smaller units.[19] Other scholars find the international system quite enduring in its structure and state units.[20] One of its most enduring features is the balance of power.

Balance of Power

In the anarchy of the international system, the most reliable brake on the power of one state is the power of other states. The term **balance of power** refers to the general concept of one or more states' power being used to balance that of another state or group of states. Balance of power can refer to any ratio of power capabilities between states or alliances, or it can mean only a relatively equal ratio. Alternatively, balance of power can refer to the *process* by which counterbalancing coalitions have repeatedly formed in history to prevent one state from conquering an entire region.[21]

The theory of balance of power argues that such counterbalancing occurs regularly and maintains the stability of the international system. The system is stable in that its rules and principles stay the same: state sovereignty does not collapse into a universal empire. This stability does not, however, imply peace; it is rather a stability maintained by means of recurring wars that adjust power relations.

Alliances (to be discussed shortly) play a key role in the balance of power. Building up one's own capabilities against a rival is a form of power balancing, but forming an alliance against a threatening state is often quicker, cheaper, and more effective. In the Cold War, the United States encircled the Soviet Union with military and political alliances to prevent Soviet territorial expansion. Sometimes a particular state deliberately becomes a balancer (in its region or the world), shifting its support to oppose whatever state or alliance is strongest at the moment. Britain played this role on the European continent for centuries, and China played it in the Cold War.

But states do not always balance against the strongest actor. Sometimes smaller states "jump on the bandwagon" of the most powerful state; this has been called bandwagoning as opposed to balancing. For instance, after World War II, a broad coalition did not form to contain U.S. power; rather, most major states joined the U.S. bloc. States may seek to balance threats rather than raw power; U.S. power was greater than Soviet power but was less threatening to Europe and Japan (and later to China as well).[22] Furthermore, small states create variations on power-balancing themes when they play off rival great powers against each other. For instance, Cuba during the Cold War received massive Soviet

[19] Aydinli, Ersel, and James N. Rosenau, eds. *Globalization, Security, and the Nation State: Paradigms in Transition.* SUNY, 2005. Rosenau, James N. *Distant Proximities: Dynamics beyond Globalization.* Princeton, 2003.
[20] Weiss, Linda. *The Myth of the Powerless State.* Cornell, 1998.
[21] Gulick, Edward V. *Europe's Classical Balance of Power.* Cornell, 1955. Niou, Emerson M. S., Peter C. Ordeshook, and Gregory F. Rose. *The Balance of Power: Stability and Instability in International Systems.* Cambridge, 1989. Vasquez, John, and Colin Elman, eds. *Realism and the Balance of Power: A New Debate.* Prentice Hall, 2002.
[22] Walt, Stephen M. *The Origins of Alliances.* Cornell, 1987.

subsidies by putting itself in the middle of the U.S.-Soviet rivalry. Other small states may, for domestic reasons, fail to mobilize to balance against threats.[23]

In the post–Cold War era of U.S. dominance, balance-of-power theory would predict closer relations among Russia, China, and even Europe to balance U.S. power. These predictions appear to be on the mark. Russian-Chinese relations have improved dramatically in such areas as arms trade and demilitarization of the border. French leaders have criticized U.S. "hyperpower." Europe and Japan opposed U.S. positions on a range of proposed treaties in 2001 on such subjects as missile defense, biological weapons, small-arms trade, and global warming. The appearance of a common enemy—international terrorists—brought the great powers together temporarily after September 2001. But the 2003 Iraq War brought back a power-balancing coalition of great powers (except Britain)—along with most other countries and world public opinion—against U.S. predominance.

In 2003, world public opinion revealed widespread anti-American sentiment. In Indonesia, Pakistan, Turkey, and Nigeria—containing half of the world's Muslims—more than 70 percent worried that the United States could become a threat to their own countries, a worry shared by 71 percent of Russians. A survey of 38,000 people in 44 nations showed a dramatic drop in support for the United States from 2002 to 2003. As Figure 2.2

FIGURE 2.2 Views of the United States in Nine Countries, 2000–2011 (Percent favorable view in public opinion polls)

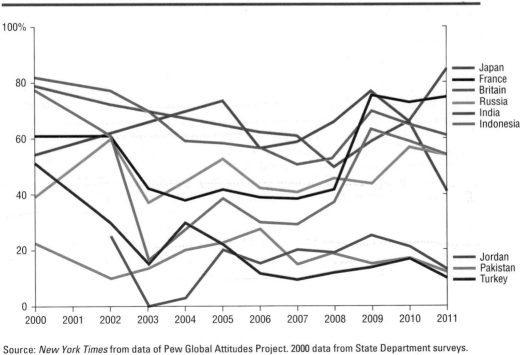

Source: *New York Times* from data of Pew Global Attitudes Project. 2000 data from State Department surveys.

[23] Schweller, Randall L. *Unanswered Threats: Political Constraints on the Balance of Power.* Princeton, 2006.

illustrates, this decline in favorable views of the United States worldwide continued through 2007. Yet, 2008 brought an upturn in opinions of the United States. A survey of 24,000 people in 24 countries found a more positive view of America in ten of those countries, mostly due to optimism about the Obama administration. Still, in recent years, the predominance of U.S. power may have led to counterbalancing, as predicted by balance-of-power theory.[24]

Great Powers and Middle Powers

The most powerful states in the world exert most of the influence on international events and therefore get the most attention from IR scholars. By almost any measure of power, a handful of states possess the majority of the world's power resources. At most a few dozen states have any real influence beyond their immediate locality. These are called the great powers and middle powers in the international system.

Although there is no firm dividing line, **great powers** are generally considered the half-dozen or so most powerful states. Until the past century, the great power club was exclusively European. Sometimes great powers' status is formally recognized in an international structure such as the 19th-century Concert of Europe or today's UN Security Council. In general, great powers are often defined as states that can be defeated militarily only by another great power. Great powers also tend to share a global outlook based on national interests far from their home territories.

The great powers generally have the world's strongest military forces—and the strongest economies to pay for them—and other power capabilities. These large economies in turn rest on some combination of large populations, plentiful natural resources, advanced technology, and educated labor forces. Because power is based on these underlying resources, membership in the great power system changes slowly. Only rarely does a great power—even one defeated in a massive war—lose its status as a great power, because its size and long-term economic potential change slowly. Thus Germany and Japan, decimated in World War II, are powerful today, and Russia, after gaining and then losing the rest of the Soviet Union, is still considered a great power.[25]

What states are great powers today? Although definitions vary, seven states appear to meet the criteria: the United States, China, Russia, Japan, Germany, France, and Britain. Together they account for more than half of the world's total GDP and two-thirds of its military spending (see Figure 2.3). They include the five permanent members of the UN Security Council, which are also the members of the "club" openly possessing large nuclear weapons arsenals.

Notable on this list are the United States and China. The United States is considered the world's only superpower because of its historical role of world leadership (especially in and after World War II) and its predominant military might. China has the world's largest population, rapid economic growth (8–10 percent annually over 15 years), and a large though not very modern military, including a credible nuclear arsenal. Indeed, in 2008, the U.S. National Intelligence Council's long-range planning report noted that China is poised to have a profound effect on the world over the next

[24] Walt, Stephen M. *Taming American Power: The Global Response to U.S. Primacy.* Norton, 2005. Sweig, Julia E. *Friendly Fire: Losing Friends and Making Enemies in the Anti-American Century.* Public Affairs, 2006. Katzenstein, Peter J., and Robert O. Keohane, eds. *Anti-Americanisms in World Politics.* Cornell, 2008.
[25] Levy, Jack S. *War in the Modern Great Power System, 1495–1975.* Kentucky, 1983.

FIGURE 2.3 Great Power Shares of World GDP and Military Expenditures, 2009

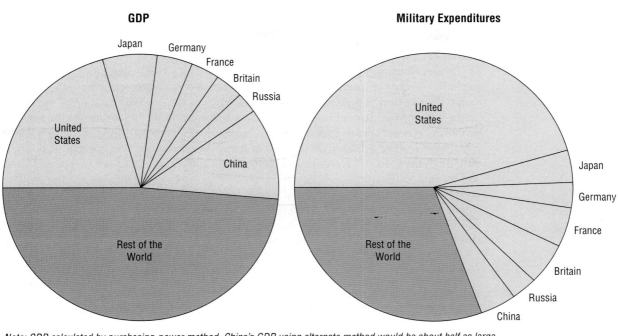

GDP   Military Expenditures

Note: GDP calculated by purchasing-power method. China's GDP using alternate method would be about half as large.
Data sources: World Bank, World Development Indicators 2009; SIPRI, SIPRI Yearbook 2009

20 years—perhaps more than any other state.[26] Japan and Germany are economically great powers, but both countries have played constrained roles in international security affairs since World War II. Nonetheless, both have large and capable military forces, which they have begun to deploy abroad, especially in peacekeeping operations. Russia, France, and Britain were winners in World War II and have been active military powers since then. Although much reduced in stature from their colonial heydays, they still qualify as great powers.

Middle powers rank somewhat below the great powers in terms of their influence on world affairs. Some are large but not highly industrialized; others have specialized capabilities but are small. Some aspire to regional dominance, and many have considerable influence in their regions.

A list of middle powers (not everyone would agree on it) might include midsized countries of the global North such as Canada, Italy, Spain, the Netherlands, Poland, Ukraine, South Korea, and Australia. It could also include large or influential countries in the global South such as India, Indonesia, Brazil, Argentina, Mexico, Nigeria, South Africa, Israel, Turkey, Iran, and Pakistan. Middle powers have not received as much attention in IR as have great powers.[27]

[26] Shane, Scott. Global Forecast by American Intelligence Expects al Qaeda's Appeal to Falter. *New York Times,* November 21, 2008: A1. Rosecrance, Richard. Power and International Relations: The Rise of China and Its Effects. *International Studies Perspectives* 7 (1), 2006: 31–35.

[27] Cohen, Stephen P. *India: Emerging Power.* Brookings, 2001.

Power Distribution

With each state's power balanced by other states, the most important characteristic of the international system in the view of some realists is the *distribution* of power among states. Power distribution as a concept can apply to all the states in the world or just the states in one region, but most often it refers to the great power system.

Neorealism, sometimes called *structural realism*, is a 1990s adaptation of realism. It explains patterns of international events in terms of the system structure—the international distribution of power—rather than in terms of the internal makeup of individual states.[28] Compared to traditional realism, neorealism is more "scientific" in the sense of proposing general laws to explain events, but neorealism has lost some of the richness of traditional realism, which took account of many complex elements (geography, political will, diplomacy, etc.).[29] Recently, *neoclassical realists* have sought to restore some of these lost aspects.[30]

The *polarity* of an international power distribution (world or regional) refers to the number of independent power centers in the system. This concept encompasses both the underlying power of various participants and their alliance groupings. Figure 2.4 illustrates several potential configurations of great powers.

FIGURE 2.4 Power Distribution in the International System

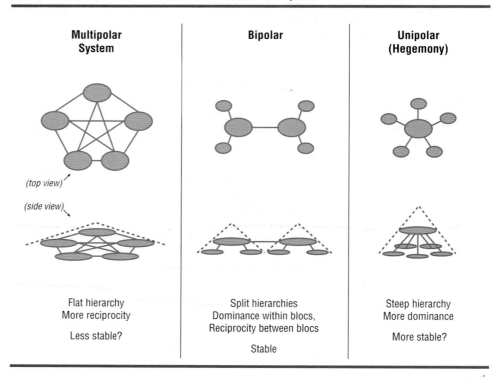

Multipolar System	Bipolar	Unipolar (Hegemony)
(top view)		
(side view)		
Flat hierarchy More reciprocity Less stable?	Split hierarchies Dominance within blocs, Reciprocity between blocs Stable	Steep hierarchy More dominance More stable?

---

[28] Waltz, *Theory of International Politics* (see footnote 7 in this chapter).

[29] Keohane, Robert O., ed. *Neorealism and Its Critics*. Columbia, 1986. Buzan, Barry, Charles Jones, and Richard Little. *The Logic of Anarchy: Neorealism to Structural Realism*. Columbia, 1993.

[30] Vasquez, John A. *The Power of Power Politics: From Classical Realism to Neotraditionalism*. Cambridge, 1999.

A **multipolar system** typically has five or six centers of power, which are not grouped into alliances. Each state participates independently and on relatively equal terms with the others. In the classical multipolar balance of power, the great power system itself was stable but wars occurred frequently to adjust power relations.

Tripolar systems, with three great centers of power, are fairly rare, owing to the tendency for a two-against-one alliance to form. Aspects of tripolarity colored the "strategic triangle" of the United States, the Soviet Union, and China during the 1960s and 1970s. Some scholars imagine a future tripolar world with rival power centers in North America, Europe, and East Asia. A *bipolar* system has two predominant states or two great rival alliance blocs. IR scholars do not agree about whether bipolar systems are relatively peaceful or warlike. The U.S.-Soviet standoff seemed to provide stability and peace to great power relations, but rival blocs in Europe before World War I did not. At the far extreme, a *unipolar* system has a single center of power around which all others revolve. This is called hegemony, and will be discussed shortly.

Some might argue that peace is best preserved by a relatively equal power distribution (multipolarity) because then no country has an opportunity to win easily. The empirical evidence for this theory, however, is not strong. In fact, the opposite proposition has more support: peace is best preserved by hegemony (unipolarity), and next best by bipolarity.

Power transition theory holds that the largest wars result from challenges to the top position in the status hierarchy, when a rising power is surpassing (or threatening to surpass) the most powerful state.[31] At such times, power is relatively equally distributed, and these are the most dangerous times for major wars. Status quo powers that are doing well under the old rules will try to maintain them, whereas challengers that feel locked out by the old rules may try to change them. If a challenger does not start a war to displace the top power, the latter may provoke a "preventive" war to stop the rise of the challenger before it becomes too great a threat.[32]

When a rising power's status (formal position in the hierarchy) diverges from its actual power, the rising power may suffer from relative deprivation: its people may feel they are not doing as well as others or as they deserve, even though their position may be improving in absolute terms. Germany's rise in the 19th century gave it great power capabilities even though it was left out of colonial territories and other signs of status; this tension may have contributed to the two world wars.

It is possible China and the United States may face a similar dynamic in the future. China may increasingly bristle at international rules and norms that it feels serves the interests of the United States. For its part, the United States may fear that growing Chinese economic and military power will be used to challenge U.S. power. In 2010, the U.S. military's strategic review questioned China's "long-term intentions," raising new questions about future power transitions (see "Let's Debate the Issue" at the end of this chapter).

According to power transition theory, then, peace among great powers results when one state is firmly in the top position and the positions of the others in the hierarchy are clearly defined and correspond with their actual underlying power.

Hegemony

Hegemony is one state's holding a preponderance of power in the international system, allowing it to single-handedly dominate the rules and arrangements by which international

---

[31] Organski, A. F. K. *World Politics*. Knopf, 1958. Kugler, Jacek, and Douglas Lemke, eds. *Parity and War: Evaluations and Extensions of the War Ledger*. Michigan, 1996.
[32] Levy, Jack S. Declining Power and the Preventive Motivation for War. *World Politics* 40 (1), 1987: 82–107.

CHINA RISING

Realists emphasize relative power as an explanation of war and peace. The modernization of China's military—in conjunction with China's rapidly growing economy—will increase China's power over the coming decades. Some observers fear instability in Asia if the overall balance of power among states in the region shifts rapidly. Here, a nuclear-powered submarine sails near China's coast, 2009.

political and economic relations are conducted.[33] Such a state is called a *hegemon.* (Usually hegemony means domination of the world, but sometimes it refers to regional domination.) The Italian Marxist theorist Antonio Gramsci used the term hegemony to refer to the complex of *ideas* that rulers use to gain consent for their legitimacy and keep subjects in line, reducing the need to use force to accomplish the same goal.[34] By extension, such a meaning in IR refers to the hegemony of ideas such as democracy and capitalism, and to the global predominance of U.S. culture (see pp. 379–380).

Most studies of hegemony point to two examples: Britain in the 19th century and the United States after World War II. Britain's predominance followed the defeat of its archrival France in the Napoleonic Wars. Both world trade and naval capabilities were firmly in British hands, as "Britannia ruled the waves." U.S. predominance followed the defeat of Germany and Japan (and the exhaustion of the Soviet Union, France, Britain, and China in the effort). In the late 1940s, the U.S. GDP was more than half the world's total; U.S. vessels carried the majority of the world's shipping; the U.S. military could single-handedly defeat any other state or combination of states; and only the United States had nuclear weapons. U.S. industry led the world in technology and productivity, and U.S. citizens enjoyed the world's highest standard of living.

As the extreme power disparities resulting from major wars slowly diminish (states rebuild over years and decades), hegemonic decline may occur, particularly when hegemons have overextended themselves with costly military commitments. IR scholars do not agree about how far or fast U.S. hegemonic decline has proceeded, if at all, and whether international instability will result from such a decline.[35]

[33] Kapstein, Ethan B., and Michael Mastanduno. *Unipolar Politics.* Columbia, 1999. Rupert, Mark. *Producing Hegemony: The Politics of Mass Production and American Global Power.* Cambridge, 1995. Nye, Joseph S. *Paradox of American Power: Why the World's Only Superpower Can't Go It Alone.* Oxford, 2002.

[34] Gramsci, Antonio. *The Modern Prince and Other Writings.* International Publishers, 1959. Gill, Stephen, ed. *Gramsci, Historical Materialism and International Relations.* Cambridge, 1993. Cox, Robert W. *Production, Power, and World Order: Social Forces in the Making of History.* Columbia, 1987.

[35] Kennedy, Paul. *The Rise and Fall of the Great Powers: Economic Change and Military Conflict from 1500–2000.* Random House, 1987. Posen, Barry R. Command of the Commons: The Military Foundations of U.S. Hegemony. *International Security* 28 (1), 2003: 5–46. Ikenberry, G. John, ed. *America Unrivaled: The Future of the Balance of Power.* Cornell, 2002.

Hegemonic stability theory holds that hegemony provides some order similar to a central government in the international system: reducing anarchy, deterring aggression, promoting free trade, and providing a hard currency that can be used as a world standard. Hegemons can help resolve or at least keep in check conflicts among middle powers or small states.[36] When one state's power dominates the world, that state can enforce rules and norms unilaterally, avoiding the collective goods problem. In particular, hegemons can maintain global free trade and promote world economic growth, in this view.

This theory attributes the peace and prosperity of the decades after World War II to U.S. hegemony, which created and maintained a global framework of economic relations supporting relatively stable and free international trade, as well as a security framework that prevented great power wars. By contrast, the Great Depression of the 1930s and the outbreak of World War II have been attributed to the power vacuum in the international system at that time—Britain was no longer able to act as hegemon, and the United States was unwilling to begin doing so.[37]

Why should a hegemon care about enforcing rules for the international economy that are in the common good? According to hegemonic stability theory, hegemons as the largest international traders have an inherent interest in the promotion of integrated world markets (where the hegemons will tend to dominate). As the most advanced state in productivity and technology, a hegemon does not fear competition from industries in other states; it fears only that its own superior goods will be excluded from competing in other states. Thus hegemons use their power to achieve free trade and the political stability that supports free trade. Hegemony, then, provides both the ability and the motivation to provide a stable political framework for free international trade, according to hegemonic stability theory. This theory is not, however, accepted by all IR scholars.[38]

From the perspective of less powerful states, of course, hegemony may seem an infringement of state sovereignty, and the order it creates may seem unjust or illegitimate. For instance, China chafed under U.S.-imposed economic sanctions for 20 years after 1949, at the height of U.S. power, when China was encircled by U.S. military bases and hostile alliances led by the United States. To this day, Chinese leaders use the term *hegemony* as an insult, and the theory of hegemonic stability does not impress them.

Even in the United States there is considerable ambivalence about U.S. hegemony. U.S. foreign policy has historically alternated between *internationalist* and *isolationist* moods.[39] It was founded as a breakaway from the European-based international system, and its growth in the 19th century was based on industrialization and expansion within North America. The United States acquired overseas colonies in the Philippines and Puerto Rico but did not relish a role as an imperial power. In World War I, the country waited three years to weigh in and refused to join the League of Nations afterward. U.S. isolationism peaked in the late 1930s when polls showed 95 percent of the public opposed to participation in a future European war, and about 70 percent against joining the League of Nations or joining with other nations to stop aggression.[40]

---

[36] Keohane, Robert O. The Theory of Hegemonic Stability and Change in International Economic Regimes, 1967–1977. In Holsti, Ole R., R. M. Siverson, and A. L. George, eds. *Change in the International System.* Westview, 1980.

[37] Kindleberger, Charles P. *The World in Depression, 1929–1939.* California, 1973. Lake, David A. *Power, Protection, and Free Trade: International Sources of U.S. Commercial Strategy, 1887–1939.* Cornell, 1988.

[38] Snidal, Duncan. The Limits of Hegemonic Stability Theory. *International Organization* 39 (4), 1985: 579–614. Gruber, Lloyd. *Ruling the World: Power Politics and the Rise of Supranational Institutions.* Princeton, 2000.

[39] Zakaria, Fareed. *From Wealth to Power: The Unusual Origins of America's World Role.* Princeton, 1998.

[40] Free, Lloyd A., and Hadley Cantril. *The Political Beliefs of Americans.* Rutgers, 1967.

PRICE OF HEGEMONY

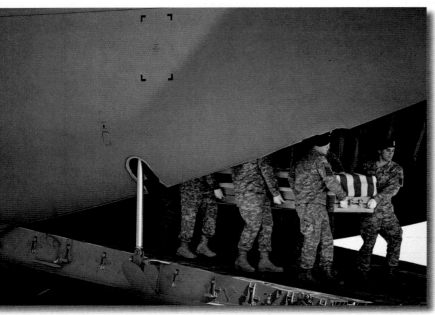

The United States is the world's most powerful single actor. Its ability and willingness to resume a role as hegemon—as after World War II—are important factors that will shape world order, but the U.S. role is still uncertain. America's willingness to absorb casualties will affect its role. Here, soldiers return from Afghanistan, 2009.

Internationalists, such as Presidents Theodore Roosevelt and Woodrow Wilson, favored U.S. leadership and activism in world affairs. These views seemed vindicated by the failure of isolationism to prevent or avoid World War II. U.S. leaders after that war feared Soviet (and then Chinese) communism and pushed U.S. public opinion toward a strong internationalism during the Cold War. The United States became an activist, global superpower. In the post–Cold War era, U.S. internationalism was tempered by a new cost consciousness, and by the emergence of a new isolationist camp born in reaction to the displacements caused by globalization and free trade.[41] However, the terrorist attacks of September 2001 renewed public support for U.S. interventionism in distant conflicts that no longer seemed so distant. Recently, though, opposition to the Iraq War, a protracted conflict in Afghanistan, and difficult economic times at home have spurred a new isolationist trend in the United States.

A second area of U.S. ambivalence is *unilateralism versus multilateralism* when the United States does engage internationally. Multilateral approaches—working through international institutions—augment U.S. power and reduce costs, but they limit U.S. freedom of action. For example, the United States cannot always get the UN to do what it wants. Polls show that a majority of U.S. citizens support working through the UN and other multilateral institutions.[42] However, members of the U.S. Congress since the 1990s, and the George W. Bush administration during its tenure, expressed skepticism of the UN and of international agencies, generally favoring a more unilateralist approach.[43]

In the 1990s, Congress slipped more than $1 billion behind in paying U.S. dues to the UN. In 2001, the new Bush administration declined to participate in such international efforts as a treaty on global warming (see pp. 390–394), a conference on racism, and an International Criminal Court (see p. 275). The international community's united front against terrorism pushed these disputes to the back burner, but they soon reemerged. The 2003 U.S.-led war in Iraq, with few allies and no UN stamp of approval, marked the peak of U.S. unilateralism. The Obama administration, however, has taken a more multilateral approach in these issue areas, and repaid all back dues in 2009.

[41] Haass, Richard N. *The Reluctant Sheriff: The United States after the Cold War.* Brookings, 1997. Lieber, Robert J. *Eagle Rules? Foreign Policy and American Primacy in the 21st Century.* Prentice Hall, 2002.
[42] Kull, Steven, and I. M. Destler. *Misreading the Public: The Myth of a New Isolationism.* Brookings, 1999.
[43] Ferguson, Niall. *Colossus: The Price of America's Empire.* Penguin, 2004. Daalder, Ivo H., and James M. Lindsay. *America Unbound: The Bush Revolution in Foreign Policy.* Wiley, 2005.

The Great Power System, 1500–2000

To illustrate how these concepts such as the balance of power, power transition, and hegemony have operated historically, we briefly review the origins of the modern international system. Noted by the presence of great powers, sovereignty, balance of power, and periods of hegemony, the modern great power system is often dated from the *Treaty of Westphalia* in 1648, which established the principles of independent, sovereign states that continue to shape the international system today (see Figure 2.5). These rules of state relations did not, however, originate at Westphalia; they took form in Europe in the 16th century. Key to this system was the ability of one state, or a coalition, to balance the power of another state so that it could not gobble up smaller units and create a universal empire.

This power-balancing system placed special importance on the handful of great powers with strong military capabilities, global interests and outlooks, and intense interactions with each other. (Great powers are defined and discussed on pp. 54–55.) A system of great power relations has existed since around A.D. 1500, and the structure and rules of that system have remained fairly stable through time, although the particular members change. The structure is a balance of power among the six or so most powerful states, which form and break alliances, fight wars, and make peace, letting no single state conquer the others.

The most powerful states in 16th-century Europe were Britain (England), France, Austria-Hungary, and Spain. The Ottoman Empire (Turkey) recurrently fought with the European powers, especially with Austria-Hungary. Today, that historic conflict between the (Islamic) Ottoman Empire and (Christian) Austria-Hungary is a source of ethnic conflict in the former Yugoslavia (the edge of the old Ottoman Empire).

Within Europe, Austria-Hungary and Spain were allied under the control of the Hapsburg family, which also owned the territory of the Netherlands. The Hapsburg countries (which were Catholic) were defeated by mostly Protestant countries in northern Europe—France, Britain, Sweden, and the newly independent Netherlands—in the *Thirty Years' War* of 1618–1648.[44] The 1648 Treaty of Westphalia established the basic rules that have defined the international system ever since—the sovereignty and territorial integrity of states as equal and independent members of an international system. Since then, states defeated in war might have been stripped of some territories but were generally allowed to continue as independent states rather than being subsumed into the victorious state.

In the 18th century, the power of Britain increased as it industrialized, and Britain's great rival was France. Sweden, the Netherlands, and the Ottoman Empire all declined in power, but Russia and later Prussia (the forerunner of modern Germany) emerged as major players. In the *Napoleonic Wars* (1803–1815), which followed the French Revolution, France was defeated by a coalition of Britain, the Netherlands, Austria-Hungary, Spain, Russia, and Prussia. The *Congress of Vienna* (1815) ending that war reasserted the principles of state sovereignty in reaction to the challenges of the French Revolution and Napoleon's empire.[45] In the *Concert of Europe* that dominated the following decades, the five most powerful states tried, with some success, to cooperate on major issues to prevent war—a possible precedent for today's UN Security Council. In this period, Britain became a balancer, joining alliances against whatever state emerged as the most powerful in Europe.

By the outset of the 20th century, three new rising powers had appeared on the scene: the United States (which had become the world's largest economy), Japan, and Italy. The great power system became globalized instead of European. Powerful states were industrializing, extending the scope of their world activities and the might of their militaries. After Prussia defeated Austria and France in wars, a larger Germany emerged to challenge

---

[44] Rabb, Theodore K., ed. *The Thirty Years' War*. University Press of America, 1981.
[45] Kissinger, Henry A. *A World Restored*. Houghton Mifflin, 1973 [1957].

FIGURE 2.5 The Great Power System, 1500–2000

	1500	1600	1700	1800	1900	2000
Wars		Spain conquers Portugal · Spanish Armada · 30 Years' War	War of the Spanish Succession	7 Years' War · Napoleonic Wars	Franco-Prussian War · World War I	World War II · Cold War
Major Alliances	Turkey (Muslim) vs. Europe (Christian)	Hapsburgs (Austria-Spain) vs. France, Britain, Netherlands, Sweden	France vs. Britain, Spain	France vs. Britain, Netherlands	Germany (& Japan) vs. Britain, France, Russia, United States, China	Russia vs. U.S., W. Eur., Japan
Rules & Norms	Nation-states (France, Austria)	Dutch independence · Grotius on int'l law · Treaty of Westphalia 1648	Treaty of Utrecht 1713	Kant on peace · Congress of Vienna 1815 · Concert of Europe	League of Nations · Geneva conventions · Communism	UN Security Council 1945- · Human rights
Rising Powers	Britain, France	Netherlands · Russia	Netherlands · Netherlands hegemony	Prussia → United States, Germany, Japan, Italy · British hegemony	United States, Germany, Japan, Italy	China · U.S. hegemony
Declining Powers	Venice	Spain	Netherlands · Sweden · Ottoman Empire		Britain, France, Austria, Italy	Russia

62

Britain's position.[46] In *World War I* (1914–1918), Germany, Austria-Hungary, and the Ottoman Empire were defeated by a coalition that included Britain, France, Russia, Italy, and the United States. After a 20-year lull, Germany, Italy, and Japan were defeated in *World War II* (1939–1945) by a coalition of the United States, Britain, France, Russia (the Soviet Union), and China. Those five winners of World War II make up the permanent membership of today's UN Security Council.

After World War II, the United States and the Soviet Union, which had been allies in the war against Germany, became adversaries for 40 years in the Cold War. Europe was split into rival blocs—East and West—with Germany split into two states. The rest of the world became contested terrain where each bloc tried to gain allies or influence, often by sponsoring opposing sides in regional and civil wars. The end of the Cold War around 1990, when the Soviet Union collapsed, returned the international system to a more cooperative arrangement of the great powers somewhat similar to the Concert of Europe in the 19th century.

Alliances

An *alliance* is a coalition of states that coordinate their actions to accomplish some end. Most alliances are formalized in written treaties, concern a common threat and related issues of international security, and endure across a range of issues and a period of time. Shorter-term arrangements, such as the U.S.-led forces in Iraq, may be called a *coalition*. But these terms are somewhat ambiguous. Two countries may have a formal alliance and yet be bitter enemies, such as the Soviet Union and China in the 1960s or NATO members Greece and Turkey today. Or, two countries may create the practical equivalent of an alliance without a formal treaty.

● Watch
the **Video**
**"Normalizing
Sino-Japanese
Relations"**
on **mypoliscilab.com**

Purposes of Alliances

Alliances generally have the purpose of augmenting their members' power by pooling capabilities. For smaller states, alliances can be their most important power element, and for great powers the structure of alliances shapes the configuration of power in the system. Of all the elements of power, none can change as quickly and decisively as alliances. Most alliances form in response to a perceived threat. When a state's power grows and threatens that of its rivals, the latter often form an alliance to limit that power. This happened to Iraq when it invaded Kuwait in 1990, as it had to Hitler's Germany in the 1940s and to Napoleon's France in the 1800s.

Realists emphasize the fluidity of alliances. They are not marriages of love, but marriages of convenience. Alliances are based on national interests, and can shift as national interests change. This fluidity helps the balance-of-power process operate effectively. Still, it is not simple or costless to break an alliance: one's reputation may suffer and future alliances may be harder to establish. So states often adhere to alliance terms even when it is not in their short-term interest to do so. Nonetheless, because of the nature of international anarchy, the possibility of turning against a friend is always present. Realists would agree with the British statesman Lord Palmerston, who told Parliament in 1848, "We have no eternal allies and we have no perpetual enemies. Our interests are perpetual and eternal and those interests it is our duty to follow."[47]

[46] Langer, William L. *European Alliances and Alignments, 1871–1890*. Knopf, 1931.
[47] Remarks in the House of Commons, March 1, 1848.

MARRIAGE OF CONVENIENCE

Alliances generally result from a convergence of practical interests, not sentimental or ideological reasons. Here, a U.S. general gets rival Afghan warlords to patch up relations, 2002.

Examples of fluid alliances are many. Anticommunist Richard Nixon could cooperate with communist Mao Zedong in 1972. Joseph Stalin could sign a nonaggression pact with a fascist, Adolf Hitler, and then cooperate with the capitalist West against Hitler. The United States could back Islamic militants in Afghanistan against the Soviet Union in the 1980s, then attack them in 2001. Every time history brings another such reversal in international alignments, many people are surprised. Realists are not so surprised.

The fluidity of alliances deepens the security dilemma (see p. 51). If there were only two states, each could match capabilities to have adequate defense but an inability to attack successfully. But if a third state is free to ally with either side, then each state has to build adequate defenses against the potential alliance of its enemy with the third state. The threat is greater and the security dilemma is harder to escape.

Alliance cohesion is the ease with which the members hold together an alliance. Cohesion tends to be high when national interests converge and when cooperation within the alliance becomes institutionalized and habitual. When states with divergent interests form an alliance against a common enemy, the alliance may come apart if the threat subsides (as with the U.S.-Soviet alliance in World War II, for instance). Even when alliance cohesion is high, as in NATO during the Cold War, conflicts may arise over who bears the costs of the alliance (**burden sharing**).[48]

Great powers often form alliances (or less formal commitments) with smaller states, sometimes called client states. *Extended deterrence* refers to a strong state's use of threats to deter attacks on weaker clients—such as the U.S. threat to attack the Soviet Union if it invaded Western Europe. Great powers face a real danger of being dragged into wars with each other over relatively unimportant regional issues if their respective clients go to war. If the great powers do not come to their clients' protection, they may lose credibility with other clients, but if they do, they may end up fighting a costly war.[49] The Soviet Union worried that its commitments to China in the 1950s, to Cuba in the

[48] Martin, Pierre, and Mark R. Brawley, eds. *Alliance Politics, Kosovo, and NATO's War: Allied Force or Forced Allies?* Palgrave, 2000.

[49] Snyder, Glenn H. *Alliance Politics.* Cornell, 1997. Leeds, Brett Ashley. Do Alliances Deter Aggression? The Influence of Military Alliances on the Initiation of Militarized Interstate Disputes. *American Journal of Political Science* 47 (3), 2003: 427–40. Menon, Rajan. *The End of Alliances.* Oxford, 2008.

1960s, and to Syria and Egypt in the 1970s (among others) could result in a disastrous war with the United States.

NATO

At present, two important formal alliances dominate the international security scene. By far the more powerful is the **North Atlantic Treaty Organization (NATO)**, which encompasses Western Europe and North America. (The second is the U.S.-Japanese alliance.) Using GDP as a measure of power, the 28 NATO members possess nearly half the world total. Members are the United States, Canada, Britain, France, Germany, Italy, Belgium, the Netherlands, Luxembourg, Denmark, Norway, Iceland, Spain, Portugal, Greece, Turkey, Poland, the Czech Republic, Hungary, Lithuania, Estonia, Latvia, Slovenia, Slovakia, Bulgaria, Romania, Albania, and Croatia. At NATO headquarters in Brussels, Belgium, military staffs from the member countries coordinate plans and periodically direct exercises in the field. The NATO "allied supreme commander" has always been a U.S. general. In NATO, each state contributes its own military units—with its own national culture, language, and equipment specifications.

NATO was founded in 1949 to oppose and deter Soviet power in Europe. Its counterpart in Eastern Europe during the Cold War, the Soviet-led **Warsaw Pact**, was founded in 1955 and disbanded in 1991. During the Cold War, the United States maintained more than 300,000 troops in Europe, with advanced planes, tanks, and other equipment. After the Cold War ended, these forces were cut to about 100,000. But NATO stayed together because its members believed that NATO provided useful stability even though its mission was unclear.[50] Article V, considered the heart of NATO, asks members to come to the defense of a fellow member under attack. It was envisioned as a U.S. commitment to help defend Western Europe against the Soviet Union, but instead was invoked for the first time when Europe came to the defense of the United States after the terrorist attacks in 2001.

The first actual use of force by NATO was in Bosnia in 1994, in support of the UN mission there. A "dual key" arrangement gave the UN control of NATO's actions in Bosnia, and the UN feared retaliation against its lightly armed peacekeepers if NATO attacked the Serbian forces to protect Bosnian civilians. As a result, NATO made threats, underlined by symbolic airstrikes, but then backed down after UN qualms; this waffling undermined NATO's credibility. Later NATO actions in the Balkans (the air war for Kosovo in 1999 and peacekeeping in Macedonia in 2001) went more smoothly in terms of alliance cohesion.

NATO's intervention in Libya in 2011 also proved effective, as air power turned the tide of the rebel war that overthrew Libya's dictator. With UN Security Council and Arab League backing for a no-fly zone, and European countries providing most of the combat planes, NATO rated the operation a great success.

Currently, NATO troops from a number of member countries are fighting Taliban forces in Afghanistan. Since 2006, these forces, known as the International Security Assistance Forces (ISAF), have been under NATO leadership. Over 100,000 troops serve in the ISAF, with NATO states providing the bulk of the forces. Non-NATO states, such as Australia, New Zealand, and Jordan, have also contributed troops to ISAF. International combat forces are scheduled to withdraw by 2014.

The European Union has formed its own rapid deployment force, outside NATO. The decision grew in part from European military weaknesses demonstrated in the 1999 Kosovo war, in which the United States contributed the most power by far. Although this

---

[50] Goldgeier, James M. *Not Whether But When: The Decision to Enlarge NATO.* Brookings, 1999.

Eurocorps generally works *with* NATO, it also gives Europe more independence from the United States. In 2003, the European Union sent military forces as peacekeepers to Democratic Congo—the first multinational European military operation to occur outside NATO. In 2004, NATO and U.S. forces withdrew from Bosnia after nine years, turning over peacekeeping there to the European Union (as they had in Macedonia). But NATO forces including U.S. soldiers remain next door in Kosovo.

The biggest issue for NATO is its recent eastward expansion, beyond the East-West Cold War dividing line (see Figure 2.6). In 1999, former Soviet-bloc countries Poland,

FIGURE 2.6 NATO Expansion

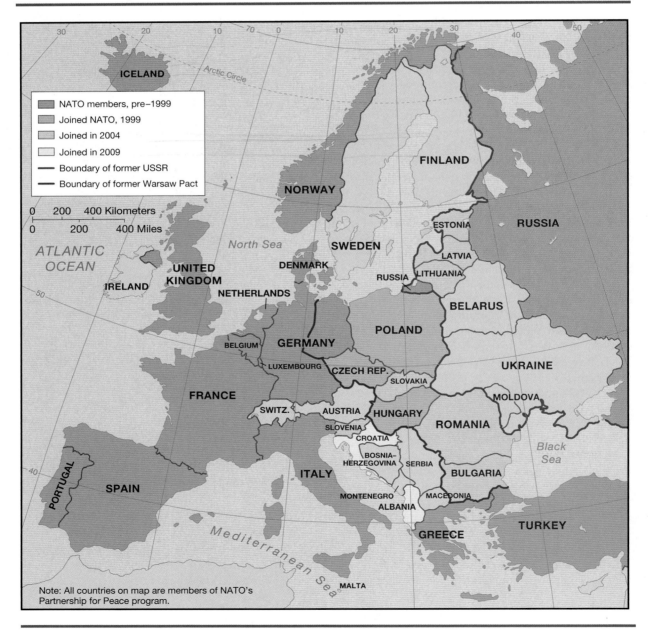

Note: All countries on map are members of NATO's Partnership for Peace program.

the Czech Republic, and Hungary joined the alliance. Joining in 2004 were Estonia, Latvia, Lithuania, Slovakia, Slovenia, Romania, and Bulgaria. In 2009, Albania and Croatia accepted membership in NATO, bringing the total number of members to 28. Making the new members' militaries compatible with NATO was a major undertaking, requiring increased military spending by existing and new NATO members. NATO expansion was justified as both a way to solidify new democracies and as protection against possible future Russian aggression. Yet, the 2003 Iraq War bypassed and divided NATO members. Longtime members France and Germany strongly opposed the war, and Turkey refused to let U.S. ground forces cross into Iraq. At the same time, U.S. leaders began shifting some operations (and money) to

ALLIANCE OF THE STRONG

The NATO alliance has been the world's strongest military force since 1949; its mission in the post–Cold War era is somewhat uncertain. Here, President Kennedy reviews U.S. forces in Germany, 1963.

new members in Eastern Europe such as Romania—with lower prices and a location closer to the Middle East—while drawing down forces based in Germany.

Russian leaders oppose NATO's expansion into Eastern Europe as aggressive and anti-Russian. They view NATO expansion as reasserting dividing lines on the map of Europe, but pushed closer to Russia's borders. These fears strengthen nationalist and anti-Western political forces in Russia. To mitigate the problems, NATO created a category of symbolic membership—the Partnership for Peace—which almost all Eastern European and former Soviet states including Russia joined. However, the 1999 NATO bombing of Serbia heightened Russian fears regarding NATO's eastward expansion, as has NATO cooperation with Ukraine and Georgia, the latter of which fought a short war against Russia in 2008.[51] In response to NATO expansion, Russia has attempted to expand its own military cooperation with states such as Venezuela, a government critical of U.S. foreign policy, and China, with whom it has conducted dozens of joint military exercises recently.

Other Alliances

The second most important alliance is the **U.S.-Japanese Security Treaty**, a bilateral alliance. Under this alliance the United States maintains nearly 35,000 troops in Japan (with weapons, equipment, and logistical support). Japan pays the United States several

[51] Moens, Alexander, Lenard J. Cohen, and Allen G. Sens, eds. *NATO and European Security: Alliance Politics from the End of the Cold War to the Age of Terrorism.* Praeger, 2003.

billion dollars annually to offset about half the cost of maintaining these troops. The alliance was created in 1951 (during the Korean War) against the potential Soviet threat to Japan.

Because of its roots in the U.S. military occupation of Japan after World War II, the alliance is very asymmetrical. The United States is committed to defend Japan if it is attacked, but Japan is not similarly obligated to defend the United States. The United States maintains troops in Japan, but not vice versa. The United States belongs to several other alliances, but Japan's only major alliance is with the United States. The U.S. share of the total military power in this alliance is also far greater than its share in NATO.

Japan's constitution (written by U.S. General Douglas MacArthur after World War II) renounces the right to make war and maintain military forces, although interpretation has loosened this prohibition over time. Japan maintains military forces, called the Self-Defense Forces, strong enough for territorial defense but not for aggression. It is a powerful army by world standards but much smaller than Japan's economic strength could support. Japanese public opinion restrains militarism in general and precludes the development of nuclear weapons in particular after Japanese cities were destroyed by nuclear weapons in World War II. Nonetheless, some Japanese leaders believe that Japan's formal security role should expand commensurate with its economic power. Japanese troops participated in Afghanistan in 2001 and Iraq in 2004 (though not in combat roles), and Japan seeks a permanent seat on the UN Security Council. The UN in turn is pressing Japan to participate fully in peace keeping missions.

SEEKING THE COLLECTIVE GOOD

NATO in Afghanistan
COLLECTIVE GOOD: Defeating the Taliban in Afghanistan

BACKGROUND: After the terrorist attacks in 2001, NATO member states pledged their assistance in fighting the forces of al Qaeda and its Taliban protectors in Afghanistan. Countries formed the multinational International Security Assistance Forces (ISAF), made up of mostly NATO troops deployed in Afghanistan. The forces are trying to provide security for the fledgling Afghan government, train a new military, and build political institutions to prevent the Taliban from retaking power.

Getting an adequate force to prevail in Afghanistan is a collective good. Providing troops and equipment for ISAF is voluntary on the part of NATO members. Regardless of how many troops the different countries send, they share equally the benefit of defeating al Qaeda. But if too many countries are too stingy in

contributing, the overall force will be too small and the goal will not be achieved.

CHALLENGE: After nearly ten years, the war in Afghanistan is as active as ever. The war has become a controversial political issue in nearly every country contributing troops to ISAF. Pro-Taliban forces continue to carry out widespread attacks and threaten to undermine the progress made to date.

NATO members have been stingy in committing troops. Both the Bush and Obama administrations pressured allies to send more troops and money, but with limited results. In the 2010 "surge," America added 30,000 troops and other NATO members only 10,000. The allies face limits

DOMINANCE

For its part, the United States has used the alliance with Japan as a base to project U.S. power in Asia, especially during the wars in Korea (1950–1953) and Vietnam (1965–1975), when Japan was a key staging area. The continued U.S. military presence in Japan (as in Europe) symbolizes the U.S. commitment to remain engaged in Asian security affairs.

However, these U.S. forces have been drawn down somewhat in the past decade in response to high costs, reduced threats, and more American focus on the Middle East. In 2010, the alliance became a major political issue in Japan as its prime minister, Yukio Hatoyama, resigned after reneging on his promise to force the United States to renegotiate certain aspects of the treaty.

Parallel with the U.S.-Japan treaty, the United States maintains military alliances with several other states, including Australia and South Korea, where 25,000 troops are stationed under a bilateral alliance dating to the Korean War. Close U.S. collaboration with militaries in other states such as Israel make them de facto U.S. allies.

The 11 members of the *Commonwealth of Independent States (CIS)* comprise the former Soviet republics except the Baltic states (Estonia, Latvia, and Lithuania). Russia, the official successor state to the Soviet Union, is the leading member and Ukraine the second largest. Although some military coordination takes place through the CIS, initial plans for a joint military force did not succeed. Among the largest CIS members, Kazakhstan and Belarus are the most closely aligned with Russia, while Ukraine is the most independent (and in fact never officially ratified the CIS agreement). In 2009, Georgia withdrew from the CIS, due to its 2008 military conflict with Russia.

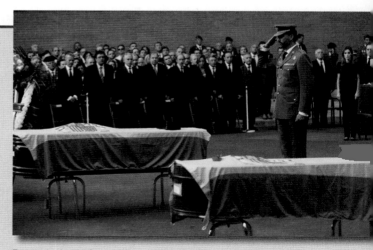

Funeral of two Spanish soldiers killed in Afghanistan, 2010.

because of the war's growing unpopularity, budget pressures due to the global recession, and uncertain prospects for victory. In 2010, the Dutch government lost power when it tried to keep Dutch troops in Afghanistan.

SOLUTION: In theory, NATO operates on reciprocity—its members are equals with all contributing to the common good. The members also share an identity as Western democracies fighting violent religious terrorists. But in the hard currency of boots on the ground and flag-draped coffins coming home, not enough NATO members found these reasons compelling.

The solution to the collective goods problem in this case was for the dominant power to provide the good. NATO is not really a club of equals, but a hierarchy with one member having more military might than the others combined. Being on top of a dominance hierarchy does not just mean ordering around underlings. Often the actors best able to stay on top of a hierarchy are those who form alliances well and use power and wealth to keep other members loyal.

Regional Alignments

Beyond the alliances just discussed and the regional IGOs mentioned earlier, most international alignments and coalitions are not formalized in alliances. Among the great powers, a close working relationship has developed, with China the most independent.

In the global South, many states joined a nonaligned movement during the Cold War, standing apart from the U.S.-Soviet rivalry. This movement, led by India and Yugoslavia, was undermined by the membership of states such as Cuba that were clearly clients of one of the superpowers. In 1992, the nonaligned movement agreed to stay in business, although most of its member states now prefer to cooperate on security matters through more regionally based institutions.

At the turn of the century, the 53-member Organization of African Unity, an IGO with few powers, re-formed as the African Union (AU), a stronger organization with a continent-wide parliament, central bank, and court. The African Union's first real test came with allegations of genocide in the Darfur region of Sudan in 2004. In response, the AU deployed 3,000 troops, joined by a much larger force of UN peacekeepers. The AU has also deployed forces, mostly Ugandan, in Somalia in recent years.

In Asia, China has long been loosely aligned with Pakistan in opposition to India (which was aligned with the Soviet Union). The United States tended to favor the Pakistani side as well, but both U.S.-Indian and U.S.-Chinese relations have improved since the Cold War ended.[52] China also has a loose alliance with North Korea, whom it values as a counterweight to South Korea. Yet, China maintains concerns about the North's political and economic stability, which has implications for China's border regions.

Other long-standing U.S. friends in Asia include the Philippines (where joint antiterrorist operations began in 2002), the Chinese Nationalists on Taiwan (only informally since the 1970s), Singapore, and Thailand.

In the Middle East, the Arab-Israeli conflict created a general anti-Israel alignment of the Arab countries for decades, but that alignment broke down as Egypt in 1978 and then Jordan in 1994 made peace with Israel. As the Israeli-Palestinian peace process moves forward and backward year by year, Arab countries continue to express varying degrees of solidarity with each other and opposition to Israel. Troughs in Israeli-Arab relations came in 2006 when Israel fought a month-long war with Hezbollah guerrillas in southern Lebanon and in 2008 when it invaded the Gaza Strip to fight Hamas militants. Meanwhile, Israel and Turkey formed a close military relationship that amplified Israeli power, but relations deteriorated after Israel killed Turkish protesters on a ship trying to break the blockade of Gaza in 2009. Also, despite its small size, Israel has been the largest recipient of U.S. foreign aid since the 1980s (about $3 billion per year).[53]

The United States has close relations with Egypt (since 1978) and cooperates closely with Turkey (a NATO member), Kuwait, Saudi Arabia, and Morocco. U.S.-Iranian relations remain chilled 30 years after the 1979 revolution. But, oddly, Iran, with its Shi'ite population, has close ties with Iraq's new U.S.-backed government, which is dominated by Shi'ite religious parties. The United States had very hostile relations with Iraq before the

[52] Hemmer, Christopher, and Peter Katzenstein. Why Is There No NATO in Asia? Collective Identity, Regionalism, and the Origins of Multilateralism. *International Organization* 56 (3), 2002: 575–607.

[53] Fawcett, Louise, ed. *International Relations of the Middle East*. Oxford, 2004. Telhami, Shibley. *The Stakes: America and the Middle East*. Westview, 2002.

FIGURE 2.7 Current Alignment of Great and Middle Powers

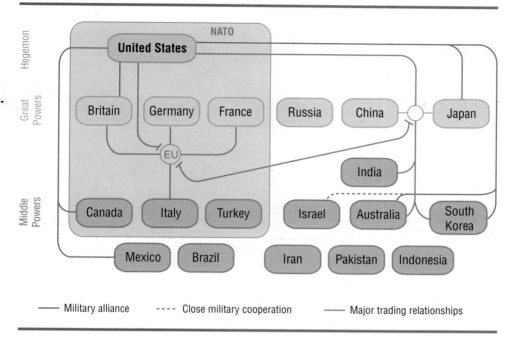

2003 war, and has faced stronger antipathy in the region thereafter. U.S. relations with Libya were also hostile for decades until a 2003 agreement, and became very friendly after Libya's U.S.-backed revolution in 2011.

It is unclear what new international alignments may emerge in the years to come. The fluidity of alliances makes them a wild card for scholars to understand and for policy makers to anticipate. For the present, international alignments—both military alliances and trade relationships—center on the United States (see Figure 2.7). Although several independent-minded states such as China, Russia, and France keep U.S. hegemony in check, little evidence exists of a coherent or formal rival power alignment emerging to challenge the United States.

Strategy

Actors use *strategy* to pursue good outcomes in bargaining with one or more other actors. States deploy power capabilities as leverage to influence each other's actions.[54] Bargaining is interactive, and requires an actor to take account of other actors' interests even while pursuing its own.[55]

Explore the Simulation "The Prisoner's Dilemma: You Are a Presidential Advisor" on mypoliscilab.com

---

[54] North, Robert C. *War, Peace, Survival: Global Politics and Conceptual Synthesis.* Westview, 1990.

[55] Snyder, Glenn H., and Paul Diesing. *Conflict among Nations: Bargaining, Decision Making, and System Structure in International Crises.* Princeton, 1977. Starkey, Brigid, Mark A. Boyer, and Jonathan Wilkenfeld. *Negotiating a Complex World: An Introduction to International Negotiation.* 2nd ed. Rowman & Littlefield, 2005. Telhami, Shibley. *Power and Leadership in International Bargaining: The Path to the Camp David Accords.* Columbia, 1990.

POLICY PERSPECTIVES

Prime Minister of India, Manmohan Singh

PROBLEM *How do you confront a fluid security environment by managing current and formal rivals?*

BACKGROUND As the world's largest democracy, your country faces many challenges both at home and abroad. In particular, in the past 50 years, you have fought wars against your two largest neighbors, China and Pakistan. Both states possess nuclear weapons, as do you. China and Pakistan have cooperated with each other in the past, including on sales of high technology military goods such as missiles.

Your generally hostile relationship with Pakistan grows from a territorial dispute over half of the region of Kashmir, which both of you claim, but India maintains control over. The territory is coveted not only by your respective governments but by the publics in each country as well. While there has been some cooperation between each country, tensions still run high over Kashmir. In the aftermath of the November 2008 terrorist attacks in Mombai, many in your country blamed Pakistan since it is home to Islamic militant groups.

Your hostilities with China have cooled over the years, but China remains a major rival in the region and you still maintain competing claims over territory. Like your own country, China is large economically as well as militarily, and it attempts to exert strong leadership in your region. In the past two years, however, you have increased ties with China and you personally visited China at the beginning of 2008 to open discussions on future trade and military cooperation. In December 2007, your armies (the two largest in the world) held joint training exercises.

DOMESTIC CONSIDERATIONS Within your country, neither Pakistan nor China is a popular choice for allies. Your population is still angered by the Chinese victory in the 1962 Sino-Indian war and the disputed border territory that gave rise to the conflict. Yet your largely Hindu population is also angry at repeated attempts by Muslim Pakistan to gain control of Kashmir. Your advisors also remind you that China still has a healthy relationship with Pakistan, selling large numbers of weapons and giving military assistance to Pakistan. Indeed the main political opposition parties argue that you have been too "soft" on both Pakistan and China in your time as Prime Minister. Any public backlash against your foreign policy on these issues could be widespread and bring calls for new elections that could unseat your government.

SCENARIO Imagine the government of Pakistan begins to suffer from large-scale instability. Islamist militants are close to overthrowing the government there, giving them control of Pakistan's nuclear weapons. They are also calling for Muslims in Kashmir to rise up against Indian control, promising to openly assist a rebellion in that province by providing weapons and intelligence. Your own intelligence service considers the collapse of the current Pakistani government "likely."

CHOOSE YOUR POLICY Do you push for closer relations with China as a result of instability in Pakistan? Can you trust China to support you in a dispute with Pakistan, given those countries' close relationship? Do you ask China to help mediate between your government and Pakistan in the event of hostilities? Or do you continue your course as independently as possible, not trusting Chinese intentions toward your country?

Statecraft

Classical realists emphasize *statecraft*—the art of managing state affairs and effectively maneuvering in a world of power politics among sovereign states. Power strategies are plans actors use to develop and deploy power capabilities to achieve their goals.

A key aspect of strategy is choosing the kinds of capabilities to develop, given limited resources, in order to maximize international influence. This requires foresight because the capabilities required to manage a situation may need to be developed years before that situation presents itself. Yet the capabilities chosen often will not be fungible in the short term. Central to this dilemma is what kind of standing military forces to maintain in peacetime—enough to prevent a quick defeat if war breaks out, but not so much as to overburden one's economy (see pp. 223–224).

Strategies also shape policies for when a state is willing to use its power capabilities. The *will* of a nation or leader is hard to estimate. Even if leaders make explicit their intention to fight over an issue, they might be bluffing.

The strategic actions of China in recent years exemplify the concept of strategy as rational deployment of power capabilities. China's central foreign policy goal is to prevent the independence of Taiwan, which China considers an integral part of its territory (as does the United Nations and, at least in theory, the United States). Taiwan's government was set up to represent all of China in 1949, when the nationalists took refuge there after losing to the communists in China's civil war. Since the international community's recognition of the Beijing government as "China," however, Taiwan has attempted to operate more and more independently, with many Taiwanese favoring independence. China may not have the military power to invade Taiwan successfully, but it has declared repeatedly that it will go to war if Taiwan declares independence. So far, even though such a war might be irrational on China's part, the threat has deterred Taiwan from formally declaring independence. China might lose such a war, but would certainly inflict immense damage on Taiwan. In 1996, China held war games near Taiwan, firing missiles over the sea. The United States sent two aircraft carriers to signal to China that its exercises must not go too far.

Not risking war by declaring independence, Taiwan instead has engaged in diplomacy to gain influence in the world. It lobbies the U.S. Congress, asks for admission to the UN and other world organizations, and grants foreign aid to countries that recognize Taiwan's government (23 mostly small, poor countries worldwide as of 2011).

China has used its own diplomacy to counter these moves. It breaks diplomatic relations with countries that recognize Taiwan, and it punishes any moves in the direction of Taiwanese independence. Half the countries that recognize Taiwan are in the Caribbean and Central America, leading to a competition for influence in the region. China has tried to counter Taiwanese ties with those countries by manipulating various positive and negative leverages. For example, in Panama, where China is a major user of the Panama Canal (which reverted to Panama from U.S. ownership in 1999), Taiwan has cultivated close relations, invested in a container port, and suggested hiring guest workers from Panama in Taiwan. But China has implicitly threatened to restrict Panama's access to Hong Kong, or to reregister China's many Panamanian-registered ships in the Bahamas instead. (The Bahamas broke with Taiwan in 1997 after a Hong Kong conglomerate, now part of China, promised to invest in a Bahamian container port.) Similarly, when the Pacific microstate of Kiribati recognized Taiwan in late 2003 to gain Taiwanese aid, China broke off relations and removed a Chinese satellite-tracking station from Kiribati. Because the tracking station played a vital role in China's military reconnaissance and growing space program—which had recently launched its first astronaut—its dismantling underscored China's determination to give Taiwan priority even at a cost to other key national goals.

Two of the seven vetoes China has used in the UN Security Council were to block peacekeeping forces in countries that extended recognition to Taiwan. These vetoes

AMPLIFYING POWER

Coherent strategy can help a state make the most of its power. China's foreign policy is generally directed toward its most important regional interests, above all preventing Taiwan's formal independence. Despite conflicts with a number of its neighbors, China has had no military engagements for 25 years. Here, China uses its veto in the UN Security Council for only the fifth time ever, to end a peacekeeping mission in Macedonia, which had just established ties with Taiwan, 1999.

demonstrate that if China believes its Taiwan interests are threatened, it can play a spoiler role on the Security Council. When the former Yugoslav republic of Macedonia recognized Taiwan in 1999 (in exchange for $1 billion in aid), China vetoed a UN peacekeeping mission there at a time of great instability in next-door Kosovo (by 2001, Macedonia had switched its diplomatic recognition to China). By contrast, when its Taiwan interests are secure, China cooperates on issues of world order. For example, although China opposed the 1991 Gulf War, it did not veto the UN resolution authorizing it.

These Chinese strategies mobilize various capabilities, including missiles, diplomats, and industrial conglomerates, in a coherent effort to influence the outcome of China's most important international issue. Strategy thus amplifies China's power.[56]

The strategy of **deterrence** uses a threat to punish another actor if it takes a certain negative action (especially attacking one's own state or one's allies). If deterrence works, its effects are almost invisible; its success is measured in attacks that did not occur.[57]

Generally, advocates of deterrence believe that conflicts are more likely to escalate into war when one party to the conflict is weak. In this view, building up military capabilities usually convinces the stronger party that a resort to military leverage would not succeed, so conflicts are less likely to escalate into violence. A strategy of **compellence**, sometimes used after deterrence fails, refers to the threat of force to make another actor take some action (rather than refrain from taking an action).[58] Generally it is harder to get another state to change course (the purpose of compellence) than it is to get it to refrain from changing course (the purpose of deterrence).

[56] Rohter, Larry. Taiwan and Beijing Duel for Recognition in Central America. *New York Times*, August 5, 1997: A7. Zhao, Quansheng. *Interpreting Chinese Foreign Policy: The Micro-Macro Linkage Approach.* Oxford, 1996. Swaine, Michael, and Ashley Tellis. *Interpreting China's Grand Strategy: Past, Present, and Future.* Rand, 2000.

[57] Zagare, Frank C. *Perfect Deterrence.* Cambridge, 2000. Goldstein, Avery. *Deterrence and Security in the 21st Century.* Stanford, 2000. Morgan, Patrick. *Deterrence Now.* Cambridge, 2003. Huth, Paul K. *Extended Deterrence and the Prevention of War.* Yale, 1988. Jervis, Robert, Richard Ned Lebow, and Janice Gross Stein. *Psychology and Deterrence.* Johns Hopkins, 1985. George, Alexander L., and Richard Smoke. *Deterrence in American Foreign Policy: Theory and Practice.* Columbia, 1974.

[58] Schelling, Thomas C. *The Strategy of Conflict.* Harvard, 1960. Art, Robert J., and Patrick M. Cronin, eds. *The United States and Coercive Diplomacy.* U.S. Institute of Peace, 2003.

One strategy used to try to compel compliance by another state is *escalation*—a series of negative sanctions of increasing severity applied in order to induce another actor to take some action. In theory, the less severe actions establish credibility—showing the first actor's willingness to exert its power on the issue—and the pattern of escalation establishes the high costs of future sanctions if the second actor does not cooperate. These actions should induce the second actor to comply, assuming that it finds the potential costs of the escalating punishments greater than the costs of compliance. But escalation can be quite dangerous. During the Cold War, many IR scholars worried that a conventional war could lead to nuclear war if the superpowers tried to apply escalation strategies.

An **arms race** is a reciprocal process in which two (or more) states build up military capabilities in response to each other. Because each wants to act prudently against a threat, the attempt to reciprocate leads to a runaway production of weapons by both sides. The mutual escalation of threats erodes confidence, reduces cooperation, and makes it more likely that a crisis (or accident) could cause one side to strike first and start a war rather than wait for the other side to strike. The arms race process was illustrated vividly in the U.S.-Soviet nuclear arms race, which created arsenals of tens of thousands of nuclear weapons on each side.[59]

INTERNAL DIVISIONS

The unitary actor assumption holds that states make important decisions as though they were single individuals able to act in the national interest. In truth, factions and organizations with differing interests put conflicting pressures on state leaders. In extreme cases, weak states do not control the armed factions within them. These Somali pirates being captured by Turkish commandos in 2009 are just one of the internal groups, ranging from autonomous territories to Islamist militants, that operate with impunity within Somalia.

Rationality in International Relations

Most realists (and many nonrealists) assume that those who wield power while engaging in statecraft behave as **rational actors** in their efforts to influence others.[60] This view has two implications for IR.

[59] Isard, Walter, and Charles H. Anderton. Arms Race Models: A Survey and Synthesis. *Conflict Management and Peace Science* 8, 1985: 27–98. Glaser, Charles. When Are Arms Races Dangerous? Rational versus Suboptimal Arming. *International Security* 28 (4), 2004: 44–84.

[60] Brown, Michael E., Owen R. Cote, Sean M. Lynn-Jones, and Steven E. Miller, eds. *Rational Choice and Security Studies*. MIT, 2000. Lake, David A., and Robert Powell, eds. *Strategic Choice and International Relations*. Princeton, 1999. Fearon, James. Rationalist Explanations for War. *International Organization* 49 (3), 1995: 379–414. Friedman, Jeffrey, ed. *The Rational Choice Controversy: Economic Models of Politics Reconsidered*. Yale, 1996.

First, the assumption of rationality implies that states and other international actors can identify their interests and put priorities on various interests. A state's actions seek to advance its interests. Many realists assume that the actor (usually a state) exercising power is a single entity that can "think" about its actions coherently and make choices. This is called the *unitary actor* assumption, or sometimes the *strong leader* assumption. The assumption is a simplification, because the interests of particular politicians, parties, economic sectors, or regions of a country often conflict. Yet realists assume that the exercise of power attempts to advance the **national interest**—the interests of the state itself.

But what are the interests of a state? Are they the interests of a particular agency within the government? Are they the interests of domestic groups? The need to prevail in conflicts with other states (see Chapter 5)? The ability to cooperate with the international community for mutual benefit (see Chapter 7)? There is no simple answer. Some realists simply define the national interest as maximizing material power—a debatable assumption.[61] Others compare power in IR with money in economics—a universal measure. In this view, just as firms compete for money in economic markets, states compete for power in the international system.[62]

Second, rationality implies that actors are able to perform a **cost-benefit analysis**—calculating the costs incurred by a possible action and the benefits it is likely to bring. Applying power incurs costs and should produce commensurate gains. As in the problem of estimating power, one has to add up different dimensions in such a calculation. For instance, states presumably do not initiate wars that they expect to lose, except when they stand to gain political benefits, domestic or international, that outweigh the costs of losing the war. But it is not easy to tally intangible political benefits against the tangible costs of a war. Even victory in a war may not be worth the costs paid. Rational actors can miscalculate costs and benefits, especially when using faulty information (although this does not mean they are irrational). Finally, human behavior and luck can be unpredictable.

These assumptions about rationality and the actors in IR are simplifications that not all IR scholars accept. But realists consider these simplifications useful because they allow scholars to explain in a general way the actions of diverse actors.

The Prisoner's Dilemma

Game theory is a branch of mathematics concerned with predicting bargaining outcomes. A game is a setting in which two or more players choose among alternative moves, either once or repeatedly. Each combination of moves (by all players) results in a set of payoffs (utility) to each player. The payoffs can be tangible items such as money or any intangible items of value. Game theory aims to deduce likely outcomes (what moves players will make), given the players' preferences and the possible moves open to them. Games are sometimes called formal models.

Game theory was first used extensively in IR in the 1950s and 1960s by scholars trying to understand U.S.-Soviet nuclear war contingencies. Moves were decisions to use nuclear weapons in certain ways, and payoffs were outcomes of the war. The use of game theory to study international interactions has become more extensive among IR scholars in recent

---

[61] Waltz, *Theory of International Politics* (see footnote 7 in this chapter).

[62] Morgenthau and Thompson, *Politics among Nations* (see footnote 6 in this chapter). Mearsheimer, *The Tragedy of Great Power Politics* (see footnote 13 in this chapter).

years, especially among realists, who accept the assumptions about rationality. To analyze a game mathematically, one assumes that each player chooses a move rationally, to maximize its payoff.

Different kinds of situations are represented by different classes of games, as defined by the number of players and the structure of the payoffs. One basic distinction is between **zero-sum games**, in which one player's gain is by definition equal to the other's loss, and *non-zero-sum games*, in which it is possible for both players to gain (or lose). In a zero-sum game there is no point in communication or cooperation between the players because their interests are diametrically opposed. But in a non-zero-sum game, coordination of moves can maximize the total payoff to the players, although each may still maneuver to gain a greater share of that total payoff.[63]

The game called **Prisoner's Dilemma (PD)** captures the kind of collective goods problem common to IR. In this situation, rational players choose moves that produce an outcome in which all players are worse off than under a different set of moves. They all could do better, but as individual rational actors they are unable to achieve this outcome. How can this be?

The original story tells of two prisoners questioned separately by a prosecutor. The prosecutor knows they committed a bank robbery but has only enough evidence to convict them of illegal possession of a gun unless one of them confesses. The prosecutor tells each prisoner that if he confesses and his partner doesn't confess, he will go free. If his partner confesses and he doesn't, he will get a long prison term for bank robbery (while the partner goes free). If both confess, they will get a somewhat reduced term. If neither confesses, they will be convicted on the gun charge and serve a short sentence. The story assumes that neither prisoner will have a chance to retaliate later, that only the immediate outcomes matter, and that each prisoner cares only about himself.

This game has a single solution: both prisoners will confess. Each will reason as follows: "If my partner is going to confess, then I should confess too, because I will get a slightly shorter sentence that way. If my partner is not going to confess, then I should still confess because I will go free that way instead of serving a short sentence." The other prisoner follows the same reasoning. The dilemma is that by following their individually rational choices, both prisoners end up serving a fairly long sentence—when they could have both served a short one by cooperating (keeping their mouths shut).

PD-type situations occur frequently in IR. One good example is an arms race. Consider the decisions of India and Pakistan about whether to build sizable nuclear weapons arsenals. Both have the ability to do so. Neither side can know whether the other is secretly building up an arsenal unless they reach an arms control agreement with strict verification provisions. To analyze the game, we assign values to each possible outcome—often called a *preference ordering*—for each player. This is not simple: if we misjudge the value a player puts on a particular outcome, we may draw wrong conclusions from the game.

The following preferences regarding possible outcomes are plausible: the best outcome would be that oneself but not the other player had a nuclear arsenal (the expense of

[63] O'Neill, Barry. A Survey of Game Theory Models on Peace and War. In Aumann, R., and S. Hart, eds. *Handbook of Game Theory*. Vol. 2. North-Holland, 1994. Powell, Robert. *In the Shadow of Power: States and Strategies in International Politics*. Princeton, 1999. Morrow, James D. *Game Theory for Political Scientists*. Princeton, 1995.

FIGURE 2.8 Payoff Matrix in India-Pakistan PD Game

		Pakistan	
		Cooperate	Defect
India	Cooperate	(3,3)	(1,4)
	Defect	(4,1)	(2,2)

Note: First number in each group is India's payoff, second is Pakistan's. The number 4 is highest payoff, 1 lowest.

building nuclear weapons would be worth it because one could then use them as leverage); second best would be for neither to go nuclear (no leverage, but no expense); third best would be for both to develop nuclear arsenals (a major expense without gaining leverage); worst would be to forgo nuclear weapons oneself while the other player developed them (and thus be subject to blackmail).

The game can be summarized in a *payoff matrix* (see Figure 2.8). The first number in each cell is India's payoff, and the second number is Pakistan's. To keep things simple, 4 indicates the highest payoff, and 1 the lowest. As is conventional, a decision to refrain from building nuclear weapons is called "cooperation," and a decision to proceed with nuclear weapons is called "defection." The dilemma here parallels that of the prisoners—each state's leader reasons: "If they go nuclear, we must; if they don't, we'd be crazy not to." The model seems to predict an inevitable Indian-Pakistani nuclear arms race, although both states would do better to avoid one.

In 1998, India detonated underground nuclear explosions to test weapons designs, and Pakistan promptly followed suit. In 2002, the two states nearly went to war, with projected war deaths of up to 12 million. A costly and dangerous arms race continues, and each side now has dozens of nuclear missiles, and counting. Avoiding an arms race would benefit both sides as a collective good, but the IR system, without strong central authority, does not allow them to realize this potential benefit. This example illustrates why realists tend to be pessimistic about cooperative solutions to collective goods problems such as the one that the PD game embodies.

IR scholars have analyzed many other games beyond PD. For example, *Chicken* represents two male teenagers speeding toward a head-on collision. The first to swerve is "chicken." Each reasons: "If he doesn't swerve, I must; but if he swerves, I won't." The player who first commits irrevocably not to swerve (for example, by throwing away the steering wheel or putting on a blindfold while behind the wheel) will win. Similarly, in the 1962 Cuban Missile Crisis, some scholars argued that President John F. Kennedy "won" by seeming ready to risk nuclear war if Soviet Premier Nikita Khrushchev did not back down and remove Soviet missiles from Cuba. (There are, however, alternative explanations of the outcome of the crisis.)

Chicken sheds light on the concept of deterrence (see p. 74). Deterrence involves convincing another actor not to undertake an action it otherwise would. Just as in the game of Chicken, when one driver commits to not swerving, state leaders attempt to convince others that they will respond harshly if they (or an ally) are attacked. But because not swerving risks disaster for both sides, it is difficult for one side to convince the other that he or she will risk crashing (fighting a war) if the other side decides not to swerve.[64]

---

[64] Goldstein, Joshua S. Dilemmas: Crossing the Road to Cooperation. In Zartman, I. William, and Saadia Touval, eds. *International Cooperation: The Extents and Limits of Multilateralism*. Cambridge, 2010.

Game theory often studies *interdependent decisions*—the outcome for each player depends on the actions of the other.

This chapter has focused on the concerns of realists—the interests of states, distribution of power among states, bargaining between states, and alliances of states. The chapter has treated states as unitary actors, much as one would analyze the interactions of individual people. The actions of state leaders have been treated as concerned with maximizing power through pursuing definable interests through coherent bargaining strategies. But realism is not the only way to frame the major issues of international relations. Chapter 3 re-examines these themes critically, relying less on the core principle of dominance and more on reciprocity and identity.

✓•⌐**Study**
and **Review**
the **Post-Test &**
Chapter Exam
at **mypoliscilab.com**

CHAPTER REVIEW

SUMMARY

- Realism explains international relations in terms of power.
- Realists and idealists differ in their assumptions about human nature, international order, and the potential for peace.
- Power can be conceptualized as influence or as capabilities that can create influence.
- The most important single indicator of a state's power is its GDP.
- Short-term power capabilities depend on long-term resources, both tangible and intangible.
- Realists consider military force the most important power capability.
- International anarchy—the absence of world government—means that each state is a sovereign and autonomous actor pursuing its own national interests.
- The international system traditionally places great emphasis on the sovereignty of states, their right to control affairs in their own territory, and their responsibility to respect internationally recognized borders.
- Seven great powers account for half of the world's GDP as well as the great majority of military forces and other power capabilities.
- Power transition theory says that wars often result from shifts in relative power distribution in the international system.
- Hegemony—the predominance of one state in the international system—can help provide stability and peace in international relations, but with some drawbacks.
- The great power system is made up of about half a dozen states (with membership changing over time as state power rises and falls).
- States form alliances to increase their effective power relative to that of another state or alliance.
- Alliances can shift rapidly, with major effects on power relations.

- The world's main alliances, including NATO and the U.S.-Japanese alliance, face uncertain roles in a changing world order.

- International affairs can be seen as a series of bargaining interactions in which states use their power capabilities as leverage to influence the outcomes. But bargaining outcomes also depend on strategies and luck.

- Rational-actor approaches treat states as though they were individuals acting to maximize their own interests. These simplifications are debatable but allow realists to develop concise and general models and explanations.

- Game theory draws insights from simplified models of bargaining situations. The Prisoner's Dilemma game embodies a difficult collective goods problem.

KEY TERMS

realism 43	power transition theory 57	nonaligned movement 70
idealism 43	hegemony 57	deterrence 74
power 45	hegemonic stability theory 59	compellence 74
geopolitics 49	alliance cohesion 64	arms race 75
anarchy 49	burden sharing 64	rational actors 75
norms 50	North Atlantic Treaty Organization (NATO) 65	national interest 76
sovereignty 50	Warsaw Pact 65	cost-benefit analysis 76
security dilemma 51	U.S.-Japanese Security Treaty 67	game theory 76
balance of power 52		zero-sum games 77
great powers 54		Prisoner's Dilemma (PD) 77
middle powers 55		
neorealism 56		
multipolar system 57		

CRITICAL THINKING QUESTIONS

1. Using Table 1.4 on pp. 24–25 (with GDP as a measure of power) and the maps at the back of the book, pick a state and speculate about what coalition of nearby states might form with sufficient power to oppose the state if it became aggressive.

2. Choose a recent international event and list the power capabilities that participants used as leverage in the episode. Which capabilities were effective, and which were not? Why?

3. The modern international system came into being at a time when agrarian societies relied primarily on farmland to create wealth. Now that most wealth is no longer created through farming, is the territorial nature of states obsolete? How might the diminishing economic value of territory change the ways in which states interact?

4. If you were the leader of a small state in Africa, bargaining with a great power about an issue where your interests diverged, what leverage and strategies could you bring into play to improve the outcome for your state?

5. Given the distinction between zero-sum and non-zero-sum games, can you think of a current international situation that is a zero-sum conflict? One that is non-zero-sum?

Can the United States and China Peacefully Coexist?

ARGUMENT 1

Overview

In this chapter, we noted that realists emphasize the idea of the balance of power—states may ally with one another to prevent another state from becoming too dominant. Yet, in the current system, the United States is clearly unparalleled in military and economic power. Some scholars argue that China will be the state that challenges the leadership position of the United States in the future.

Historically, the relationship between China and the United States has been rocky. During the Cold War, after the United States opened the relationship with China, the two great powers cooperated against a common enemy, the Soviet Union. After the Cold War, that cooperation has varied significantly as China has expanded economically and militarily, filling the global power vacuum left by the collapse of the Soviet Union.

Although China is still smaller economically and less powerful militarily than the United States, if current growth continues, it will eventually surpass the United States in economic might. Armed with such a large economy, it will not take long for China to then catch the United States militarily. These changes are referred to as power transitions (see p. 57). While sometimes these transitions between powerful states are peaceful (the United States replacing Great Britain, for example), oftentimes they are not (Germany's attempts to overtake Great Britain in World Wars I and II). Should China grow to challenge the United States, what does the future hold for these two great powers? Will their relationship be one of peace or hostility?

The United States and China Will Find It Difficult to Peacefully Coexist

U.S. and Chinese allies create conflicts between them. China's ties to North Korea, Iran, and Sudan have strengthened in the past five years. The United States considers each of these states to be hostile, while China has courted each for economic or strategic reasons. On the U.S. side, although there is no formal alliance, American friendliness to Taiwan, which China regards as a renegade province, also creates tensions.

China already promotes its interests in conflict with the United States. China currently pegs its currency to keep its goods cheap in the United States. Despite many protests against this policy, China persists in pegging its currency, which harms domestic manufacturers in the United States.

China is already attempting to compete with the United States as a global superpower. China has expanded foreign aid to Africa (even to states sanctioned by the United States). China has increased weapons sales around the world. China is also courting states with hostile relationships to the United States such as Venezuela and Iran. All signs point to China attempting to compete with the United States for global supremacy.

The United States and China Can Peacefully Coexist

The United States and China agree on many important issues. On issues such as terrorism and nuclear proliferation, China sees eye-to-eye with the United States. As with the United States and the Soviet Union during the Cold War, there is room for agreement on issues of strategic importance that will allow for cooperation between the two great powers. In addition, China's "peaceful rise" strategy has avoided direct conflict with the United States for 30 years.

Nuclear deterrence will keep relations stable. Both states have large, credible nuclear forces that can deter the opponent from attacking. While this may not rule out proxy wars (as in the Cold War), it does suggest that relations will remain civil and stable between the United States and China.

Economic interdependence will keep relations peaceful. The United States and China depend on one another economically. America depends on Chinese goods flowing in at reasonable prices, while China depends on the U.S. market for its export-led growth strategy. This situation of mutual dependence will keep relations warm, since hostility would threaten to undermine these trade relationships.

Questions

- Is conflict inevitable between the United States and China? If China were to become a democracy, would conflict be more or less likely?

- If conflicts occur in the future, are there ways to discourage them? Or are these conflicts just part of global politics between great powers? Can international organizations (such as the United Nations) help to ameliorate the potential for great power conflict?

- Taiwan is an important source of friction between the United States and China. Although the United States does not formally recognize Taiwan, American has signed a friendship treaty with the island. Should the United States risk its relationship with China over honoring its commitments to Taiwan? If China forces the United States to choose between Taiwan and lower tensions, which should the United States choose?

For Further Reading

Kynge, James. *China Shakes the World: A Titan's Rise and Troubled Future—and the Challenge for America.* Houghton Mifflin, 2007.

Mearsheimer, John J. *The Tragedy of Great Power Politics.* Norton, 2003.

Shirk, Susan L. *China: Fragile Superpower.* Oxford, 2008.

Bergsten, C. Fred, Charles Freeman, Nicholas R. Lardy, and Derek J. Mitchell. *China's Rise: Challenges and Opportunities.* Peterson Institute, 2008.

CHAPTER **3** | Liberal and Social Theories

Pakistani women wait for relief assistance, 2010.

The Waning of War

In recent years, a strong trend toward fewer and smaller wars has become evident.[1] To many Americans, the world seems more war-prone and violent than ever, because the country is at war on a scale not seen since Vietnam. Yet for the world as a whole, the current period is one of the least warlike ever.

First consider the long-term trend. In the first half of the 20th century, world wars killed tens of millions and left whole continents in ruin. In the second half of that century, during the Cold War, proxy wars killed millions, and the world feared a nuclear war that could have wiped out our species. Now, in the early 21st century, wars like those in Iraq and Sudan kill hundreds of thousands. We fear terrorist attacks that could destroy a city, but not life on the planet. Generation by generation, the world has moved forward, unevenly but inexorably, from tens of millions killed, to millions, to hundreds of thousands. This is still a large number and the impacts of war are still catastrophic. Perhaps most important, if we could understand and sustain this trend, major wars might fade away altogether, though minor wars and terrorist attacks may continue to kill thousands of people.

Events in the post–Cold War era continue this long-term trend toward smaller wars. The late 1990s and early 21st century saw the termination of lingering Cold War–era conflicts such as in Angola, Northern Ireland, Guatemala, and southern Sudan (following South Africa and Mozambique earlier in the 1990s). Most of the wars that flared up after the Cold War ended, such as in Bosnia, Kosovo, Algeria, Rwanda, Burundi, and Uganda, have also come to an end. This waning of war continues in recent years. Liberia and Ivory Coast established power-sharing governments and brought in international peacekeepers—following in the path of Sierra Leone (which in 2003 held democratic elections). In 2005, the Irish Republican Army finished permanently dismantling its weaponry. India and Pakistan began their first cease-fire in a decade, as did Burma's government and its largest rebel militia.

Today's most serious conflicts consist mainly of skirmishing rather than all-out battles. The last battles between heavily armed forces on both sides (with, for example, artillery, tanks, and airplanes) were the 2003 invasion of Iraq and the 2008 Russian-Georgian war, both short and one-sided affairs. The last sustained interstate war, between Ethiopia and Eritrea, ended in 2000. The last great power war (with great powers fighting each other) ended more than 50 years ago.

In 2010, war continued to abate in Iraq and worsen in Afghanistan. Fighting continued in Sudan and flared in Yemen and Nigeria. In Democratic Congo, small-scale but brutal fighting among various factions has flared since the devastating war there ended in 2003. (UN peacekeepers arrived in 1999.)

Ten years ago, this textbook's list of wars in progress (which appears on p. 154) showed 20 wars and 8 more just ending in transitional cease-fires. Today the list is down to 13. Similarly, deaths caused by all types of war, including actions such as shelling, car bombs, and airstrikes (but not including indirect deaths from disease), have fallen quite dramatically over the past 60 years. Figure 3.1 charts the decline in war-related fatalities since the end of World War II. While some years are higher or lower than others, there is a consistent trend downward in this graph over recent decades, suggesting an overall movement toward less war in the international system.

Read and Listen to **Chapter 3** at **mypoliscilab.com**

Study and **Review** the **Pre-Test & Flashcards** at **mypoliscilab.com**

Watch the **Video** **"The Crisis in Darfur"** on **mypoliscilab.com**

---

[1] Human Security Centre. *Human Security Report 2009: Shrinking Costs of War*. Human Security Centre, 2009.

FIGURE 3.1 Battle-Related Deaths in War, 1946–2008

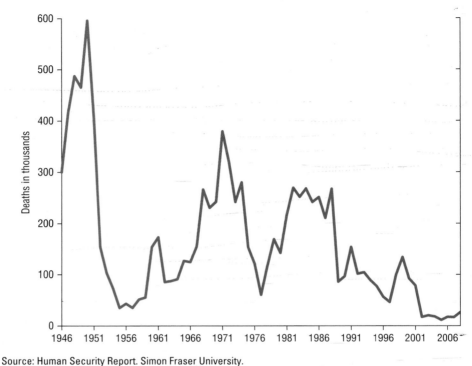

Source: Human Security Report. Simon Fraser University.

Liberal Theories

**Watch
the Video
"Toppling Hussein"
on mypoliscilab.com**

If realism offers mostly dominance solutions to the collective goods problems of IR, several alternative theoretical approaches discussed in this chapter draw mostly on the reciprocity and identity principles (recall Figure 2.1 in Chapter 2). Among other common elements, these approaches generally are more optimistic than realism about the prospects for peace.

Although realists see the laws of power politics as relatively timeless and unchanging, liberal theorists generally see the rules of IR as slowly, incrementally evolving through time and becoming more and more peaceful. This evolution results primarily from the gradual buildup of international organizations and mutual cooperation (reciprocity) and secondarily from changes in norms and public opinion (identity). The main theories discussed in this and the following chapter all hold that we are not doomed to a world of recurring war but can achieve a more peaceful world. In addition, this chapter reviews liberal theories of domestic politics and foreign policy making that, unlike realism, place importance on the domestic and individual levels of analysis in explaining state behavior.

Kant and Peace

Liberal theories of IR try to explain how peace and cooperation are possible. The German philosopher Immanuel Kant 200 years ago gave three answers.[2] The first, based on the

[2] Kant, Immanuel. *Perpetual Peace*. Edited by Lewis White Beck. Bobbs-Merrill, 1957 [1795]. Russett, Bruce, and John Oneal. *Triangulating Peace: Democracy, Interdependence, and International Organizations*. Norton, 2000.

reciprocity principle, was that states could develop the organizations and rules to facilitate cooperation, specifically by forming a world federation resembling today's United Nations. This answer forms the foundation of present-day liberal institutionalism, discussed shortly.

Kant's second answer, operating at a lower level of analysis, was that peace depends on the internal character of governments. He reasoned that republics, with a legislative branch that can hold the monarch in check, will be more peaceful than autocracies. This answer, along with Kant's related point that citizens of any country deserve hospitality in any other country, is consistent with the reciprocity principle, but also relies on the identity principle. Like the social theories discussed later in this chapter, it explains states' preferences based on the social interactions within the state. A variation on Kant's answer, namely that *democracies* do not fight *each other,* is the basis of present democratic peace theory, also discussed later in this chapter. (Kant himself distrusted democracies as subjecting policy to mob rule rather than rationality, a view influenced by witnessing the French Revolution.)

Kant's third answer, that trade promotes peace, relies on the presumption that trade increases wealth, cooperation, and global well-being—all while making conflict less likely in the long term because governments will not want to disrupt any process that adds to the wealth of their state.[3] Moreover, as trade between states increases, they will find that they become mutually dependent on one other for goods. This mutual dependence between states is referred to as economic **interdependence**. Scholars often differentiate situations of *sensitivity,* where one state relies on another to provide an important good but can find alternate suppliers, with *vulnerability,* where there are few or no alternative suppliers.[4]

Realists are skeptical of the peace-promotes-trade argument, however, arguing that one state's reliance on another creates *more* tensions in the short term because states are nervous that another actor has an important source of leverage over them.[5] In particular, states worry about their reliance on other states for strategic minerals needed for military purposes, such as special minerals or alloys for aircraft production and uranium for atomic weapons. Leaders worry about vulnerability giving other countries leverage over them in instances of conflict. Realists point to the fact that arguments about interdependence and peace were common prior to World War I, yet war occurred anyway.

Liberal Institutionalism

Now let us return to Kant's first answer to the question of how peace can evolve, namely the ability of states to develop and follow mutually advantageous rules, with international institutions to monitor and enforce them. Liberal theories treat rational actors as capable of forging short-term individual interests in order to further the long-term well-being of a community to which they belong—and hence indirectly their own well-being. The core principle of reciprocity lies at the heart of this approach, because international institutions operate by reciprocal contributions and concessions among formally equal members (peers). Indeed, in several important institutions, such as the World Trade Organization and the European Union, decisions require *consensus* among all members, making them all equal in governance.

---

[3] Angell, Norman. *The Foundations of International Polity.* Heinemann, 1914. Ward, Michael D., Randolph M. Siverson, and Xun Cao. Disputes, Democracies, and Dependencies: A Reexamination of the Kantian Peace. *American Journal of Political Science* 51 (3), 2007: 583–601.

[4] Keohane, Robert O., and Joseph S. Nye. *Power and Interdependence.* 3rd ed. Longman, 2001.

[5] Mansfield, Edward D., and Brian M. Pollins. *Economic Interdependence and International Conflict: New Perspectives on an Enduring Debate.* Michigan, 2003. McDonald, Patrick. *The Invisible Hand of Peace.* Cambridge, 2009.

HAPPY FAMILY

Liberal theories emphasize the potential for rivalries to evolve into cooperative relationships as states recognize that achieving mutual benefits is most cost effective in the long run. For example, the U.S. and Soviet/Russian space programs began cooperating in the 1960s and continue today, with other countries. Here, astronauts from the United States, Russia, Germany, and Sweden share the International Space Station, 2006.

Kant argued that states, although autonomous, could join a worldwide federation like today's UN and respect its principles even at the cost of forgoing certain short-term individual gains. To Kant, international cooperation was a more rational option for states than resorting to war. Thus, in realist conceptions of rationality, war and violence appear rational (because they often advance short-term state interests), but in liberal theories, war and violence appear as irrational deviations that result from defective reasoning and that harm the (collective, long-term) interests of warring states.

The **neoliberal** approach differs from earlier liberal approaches in that it concedes to realism several important assumptions—among them, that states are unitary actors rationally pursuing their self-interests in a system of anarchy. Neoliberals say to realists, "Even if we grant your assumptions about the nature of states and their motives, your pessimistic conclusions do not follow." States achieve cooperation fairly often because it is in their interest to do so, and they can learn to use institutions to ease the pursuit of mutual gains and the reduction of possibilities for cheating or taking advantage of another state.[6]

Despite the many sources of conflict in IR, states cooperate most of the time. Neoliberal scholars try to show that even in a world of unitary rational states, the neorealists' pessimism about international cooperation is not valid. States can create mutual rules, expectations, and institutions to promote behavior that enhances cooperation.

In particular, reciprocity in IR helps international cooperation emerge despite the absence of central authority. Through reciprocity, not a world government, norms and rules are enforced. In international security, reciprocity underlies the gradual improvement of relations sought by arms control agreements and peacekeeping missions. In international political economy (IPE), in which cooperation can create great benefits through trade, the threat to restrict trade in retaliation for unfair practices is a strong incentive to comply with rules and norms. The World Trade Organization (WTO) and its predecessor, the General Agreement on Tariffs and Trade (GATT), function on this principle—states that defect on their obligations by increasing tariffs must suffer punishment by allowing other states to place tariffs on their goods.

Neoliberals argue that reciprocity can be an effective strategy for achieving cooperation in a situation of conflicting interests.[7] If one side expresses willingness to cooperate

[6] Baldwin, David A., ed. *Neorealism and Neoliberalism: The Contemporary Debate*. Columbia, 1993. Nye, Joseph S., Jr., Neorealism and Neoliberalism. *World Politics* 40 (2), 1988: 235–51. Milner, Helen. International Theories of Cooperation among Nations: Strengths and Weaknesses [review article]. *World Politics* 44 (3), 1992: 466–94. Oye, Kenneth A., ed. *Cooperation under Anarchy*. Princeton, 1986. Keohane, Robert O., and Lisa Martin. The Promise of Institutionalist Theory. *International Security* 20 (1), 1995: 39–51.

[7] Keohane, Robert O. Reciprocity in International Relations. *International Organization* 40 (1), 1986: 1–27. Downs, George W., and David M. Rocke. *Optimal Imperfection? Domestic Uncertainty and Institutions in International Relations*. Princeton, 1995.

and promises to reciprocate the other's cooperative and conflictual actions, the other side has an incentive to work out a cooperative bargain. Because reciprocity is relatively easy to interpret, the vow of future reciprocity often need not be stated explicitly. For example, in 1969 China's relations with the United States had been on ice for 20 years. A U.S. economic embargo against China was holding back the latter's economic development. China's support of North Vietnam was costing American lives. The two states were not on speaking terms. President Nixon (and his advisor Henry Kissinger) decided to slightly relax the U.S. trade embargo against China. Three days later, China released three U.S. citizens whose boat had earlier drifted into Chinese waters.[8] China reciprocated other U.S. initiatives, and in 1972 Nixon visited China in a spirit of rapprochement.

Similarly, in 2009, the Obama administration announced it would stop building a missile defense system in Europe that Russia considered provocative. Some saw this as a move to gain Russian support for sanctions against Iran for its nuclear program. And indeed, in the spring of 2010, the UN Security Council approved tighter sanctions on Iran, with the Russians voting in favor.

Neoliberals use the *Prisoner's Dilemma (PD)* game (see pp. 76–78) to illustrate their argument that cooperation is possible. Each actor can gain by individually defecting, but both lose when both defect. Similarly, in IR, states often have a mix of conflicting and mutual interests. The dilemma can be resolved if the game is played over and over again—an accurate model of IR, in which states deal with each other in repeated interactions. In that case, a strategy of strict reciprocity after an initial cooperative move (nicknamed *tit-for-tat*) can bring about mutual cooperation in a repeated PD game, because the other player must conclude that any defection will merely provoke a like defection in response.[9]

But side by side with the potential for eliciting cooperation, reciprocity contains a danger of runaway hostility. When two sides both reciprocate but never manage to put relations on a cooperative footing, the result can be a drawn-out, nasty, tit-for-tat exchange of punishments. This characterizes Israeli relations with Palestinian militants over the years, for instance. Figure 3.2 charts data tracking the interactions between Israeli and Palestinian actors over a 17-year period. Note that as one actor exhibits conflictual behavior (negative values on the graph), the other matches with negative responses. Likewise, cooperative behavior (positive values on the graph) brings reciprocated cooperation in the immediate time period. Yet, over time, this reciprocity has done little to keep cooperation high—periods of agreement, even those reciprocated by each side, eventually give way to reciprocated conflict.[10]

Building on the reciprocity principle, many norms mediate states' interactions. For example, diplomatic practices and participation in international organizations (IOs) are both strongly governed by shared expectations about the rules of correct behavior. As collective goods problems crop up in IR, states rely on a context of rules, norms, habits, and institutions that make it rational for all sides to avoid the self-defeating outcomes that would result from pursuing narrow, short-term self-interest. Neoliberals study historical and contemporary cases in IR to see how institutions and norms affect the possibilities for

[8] Kissinger, Henry. *White House Years*. Little, Brown, 1979: 179–80.

[9] Axelrod, Robert. *The Evolution of Cooperation*. Basic, 1984. Goldstein, Joshua S., and Jon C. Pevehouse. Reciprocity, Bullying, and International Cooperation: Time-Series Analysis of the Bosnia Conflict. *American Political Science Review* 91 (3), 1997: 515–29.

[10] Goldstein, Joshua S., Jon C. Pevehouse, Deborah J. Gerner, and Shibley Telhami. Reciprocity, Triangularity, and Cooperation in the Middle East, 1979–1997. *Journal of Conflict Resolution* 45 (5), 2001: 594–620.

FIGURE 3.2 Reciprocity in Israeli-Palestinian Conflict and Cooperation, 1979–1997

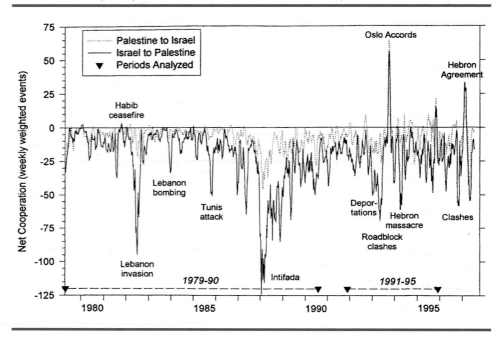

overcoming dilemmas and achieving international cooperation. (As we will soon see, some constructivists emphasize that these norms eventually function without states thinking about self-interest at all.) Thus, for neoliberals the emergence of international institutions is key to understanding how states achieve a superior rational outcome that includes long-term self-interest and not just immediate self-interest.

International Regimes

Achieving good outcomes is not simple, though. Because of the contradictory interpretations that parties to a conflict usually have, it is difficult to resolve conflicts without a third party to arbitrate or an overall framework to set common expectations for all parties. These considerations underlie the creation of IOs.

An **international regime** is a set of rules, norms, and procedures around which the expectations of actors converge in a certain issue area (whether arms control, international trade, or Antarctic exploration).[11] The convergence of expectations means that participants in the international system have similar ideas about what rules will govern their mutual participation: each expects to play by the same rules. (This meaning of regime is not the same as that referring to the domestic governments of states, especially governments considered illegitimate, as in *regime change*.)

---

[11] Krasner, Stephen D., ed. *International Regimes*. Cornell, 1983. Hasenclever, Andreas, Peter Mayer, and Volker Rittberger. *Theories of International Regimes*. Cambridge, 1997.

Regimes can help solve collective goods problems by increasing transparency—because everyone knows what everyone else is doing, cheating is riskier. The current revolution in information technologies is strengthening regimes particularly in this aspect. Also, with better international communication, states can identify conflicts and negotiate solutions through regimes more effectively.

The most common conception of regimes combines elements of realism and liberalism. States are seen as autonomous units maximizing their own interests in an anarchic context. Regimes do not play a role in issues in which states can realize their interests directly through unilateral applications of leverage. Rather, regimes come into existence to overcome collective goods dilemmas by coordinating the behaviors of individual states. Although states continue to seek their own interests, they create frameworks to coordinate their actions with those of other states if and when such coordination is necessary to realize self-interest (that is, in collective goods dilemmas).

Regimes do not substitute for the basic calculations of costs and benefits by states; they just open up new possibilities with more favorable benefit-cost ratios. Regimes do not constrain states, except in a very narrow and short-term sense. Rather, they facilitate and empower national governments faced with issues in which collective goods or coordination problems would otherwise prevent these governments from achieving their ends. Regimes can be seen as *intervening variables* between the basic causal forces at work in IR—for realists, the relative power of state actors—and the outcomes such as international cooperation (or lack thereof). For realists in particular, regimes do not negate the effects of power; more often they codify and normalize existing power relations in accordance with the dominance principle. For example, the nuclear nonproliferation regime protects the status quo in which only a few states have nuclear weapons.

Because regimes depend on state power for their enforcement, some IR scholars argue that regimes are most effective when power in the international system is most concentrated—when there is a hegemon to keep order (see "Hegemony" on pp. 57–60). Yet, regimes do not always decline with the power of hegemons that created them. Rather, they may take on a life of their own. Although hegemony may be crucial in *establishing* regimes, it is not necessary for *maintaining* them.[12] Once actors' expectations converge around the rules embodied in a regime, the actors realize that the regime serves their own interests. Working through the regime becomes a habit, and national leaders may not seriously consider breaking out of the established rules. This persistence of regimes was demonstrated in the 1970s, when U.S. power declined following the

HEALTHY REGIME

International regimes are sets of rules, norms, and procedures, not always codified into institutions, that govern the behavior of actors in IR. The world health regime includes states, IGOs such as the World Health Organization (WHO), nonprofit organizations such as the Gates Foundation, and others, all working with common expectations about activities to improve health and stem epidemics. Here, Cuban doctors give WHO vaccines to children in Haiti, 2010.

---

[12] Keohane, Robert O. *After Hegemony: Cooperation and Discord in the World Political Economy.* Princeton, 1984.

decades of U.S. hegemony since 1945. The international economic regimes adjusted somewhat and survived.

In part, the survival of regimes rests on their embedding in permanent *institutions* such as the UN, NATO, and the International Monetary Fund. These institutions become the tangible manifestation of shared expectations as well as the machinery for coordinating international actions based on those expectations. In international security affairs, the UN and other IOs provide a stable framework for resolving disputes (Chapter 7). IPE is even more institutionalized, again because of the heavier volume of activity and the wealth that can be realized from cooperation.[13]

Institutions gain greater stability and weight than do noninstitutionalized regimes. With a staff and headquarters, an international institution can actively promote adherence to the rules in its area of political or economic life. These bureaucracies, however, can also promote policies not intended by the states that created the institutions (a problem noted by constructivist scholars; see p. 102).

Important institutions in international security and IPE are discussed in Chapters 7 and 8, respectively. Liberal institutionalism also places high value on international law, which receives its own discussion in Chapter 7. The culmination of liberal institutionalism to date is the European Union (EU), which receives in-depth discussion in Chapter 10. After centuries of devastating wars, European states now enjoy a stable peace among themselves with strong international institutions to bind them.

Collective Security

The concept of **collective security**, which grows out of liberal institutionalism, refers to the formation of a broad alliance of most major actors in an international system for

---

[13] Taylor, Paul, and A. J. R. Groom, eds. *International Institutions at Work.* St. Martin's, 1988.

SEEKING THE COLLECTIVE GOOD

Great Nations Pay Their Bills
COLLECTIVE GOOD: The UN Budget

BACKGROUND: Since its founding at the end of World War II, the United Nations has performed many valuable services for its members, the countries of the world. Countries use the UN for diplomacy, peacekeeping, and humanitarian assistance, among other things. These services are a collective good for the world's countries because each country enjoys them regardless of whether it pays more or less of the UN budget. The organization sets dues for its members, and each is supposed to pay on time, but not infrequently, they pay late, or later and later.

CHALLENGE: In the 1980s, the United States got into a series of conflicts with the UN about how much the U.S. dues should be. By the mid-1990s, the UN members owed billions of dollars in back dues, with the United States alone owing more than a billion dollars and Russia about half a billion. Diplomats met in chilled rooms, as the UN could not afford to heat its headquarters building in New York during the winter. U.S. domestic politics contributed to the problem, as the Republican Congress did not approve of President Clinton's budget requests for the UN, which they saw as toothless and ineffective at best, corrupt and anti-American at worst.

SOLUTION: Reciprocity governs UN dues in principle, since all countries contribute according to a formula based on each individual economy's size, but in practice,

IDENTITY

the purpose of jointly opposing aggression by any actor. Kant laid out the rationale for this approach. Because past treaties ending great power wars had never lasted permanently, Kant proposed a federation (league) of the world's states. Through such a federation, Kant proposed, the majority of states could unite to punish any one state that committed aggression, safeguarding the collective interests of all the nations while protecting the self-determination of small nations that all too easily became pawns in great power games.[14]

After the horrors of World War I, the *League of Nations* was formed to promote collective security. But it was flawed in two ways. Its membership did not include all the great powers (including the most powerful one, the United States), and its members proved unwilling to bear the costs of collective action to oppose aggression when it did occur in the 1930s, starting with Japan and Italy. After World War II, the United Nations was created as the League's successor to promote collective security (see Chapter 7). Several regional IGOs also currently perform collective security functions (deterring aggression) as well as economic and cultural ones—the *Organization of American States (OAS)*, the *Arab League*, and the *African Union*.

The success of collective security depends on two points. First, the members must keep their alliance commitments to the group (that is, members must not free ride on the efforts of other members). When a powerful state commits aggression against a weaker one, it often is not in the immediate interest of other powerful states to go to war over the issue. Suppressing a determined aggressor can be very costly.

A second requisite for collective security is that enough members must agree on what constitutes aggression. The UN Security Council is structured so that aggression is defined by what all five permanent members, in addition to at least four of the other ten members, can agree on (see "The Security Council" on pp. 242–245). This collective security system

---

[14] Kant, *Perpetual Peace* (see footnote 2 in this chapter).

countries defected from that formula to promote their own short-term interests. The dominance principle is of little use since the UN cannot use military force to make a country pay its dues.

The UN Foundation, founded in 1998 with a large contribution by media mogul Ted Turner, started a campaign to use the identity principle to solve the problem of U.S. nonpayment of dues. The campaign had the slogan, "Great nations pay their bills." The slogan subtly portrayed the delinquent United States as a deadbeat Dad who has failed to make his child support payments! This appeal to Americans' concept of their nation as great changed the tone of debate about the UN dues. The United States began to catch up on arrears, and in 2009, it paid up the last of its back obligations. Wanting to be, and seen as, a great nation, America paid its bills.

The UN headquarters in New York, 2007.

does not work against aggression by a great power. When the Soviet Union invaded Afghanistan, or the United States mined the harbors of Nicaragua, or France blew up the Greenpeace ship *Rainbow Warrior,* the UN could do nothing—because those states can veto Security Council resolutions.[15]

Collective security worked in 1990–1991 to reverse Iraq's conquest of Kuwait because the aggression brought all the great powers together and because they were willing to bear the costs of confronting Iraq. It was the first time since the founding of the UN that one member state had invaded, occupied, and annexed another—attempting to erase it as a sovereign state. The invasion was so blatant a violation of Kuwaiti sovereignty and territorial integrity that the Security Council had little trouble labeling it aggression and authorizing the use of force by a multinational coalition. The threat Iraq posed to the world's oil supplies provided additional incentive for coalition members to contribute money or troops to solve the problem.

In 2002–2003, by contrast, the Security Council repeatedly debated Iraq's failure to keep the agreements it had made at the end of the Gulf War, in particular the promise to disclose and destroy all its weapons of mass destruction. But the great powers split, and a proposed U.S.-British resolution authorizing military force was withdrawn after France promised to veto it; Germany, Russia, and China had all strongly opposed it and the war. Public opinion around the world, especially in predominantly Muslim countries, also opposed the war. When the UN did not act, the United States, Britain, and Australia sent military forces and overthrew Saddam Hussein by force, comparing the UN to the toothless League of Nations. However, the U.S. forces found no weapons of mass destruction in Iraq, and then found itself in a prolonged counterinsurgency war. In retrospect, although the world's collective security system is creaky and not always effective, bypassing it to take military action also holds dangers.

The concept of collective security has broadened in recent years. For example, *failed states* have very weak control of their territory, making them potential havens for drug trafficking, money laundering, and terrorist bases. Essentially, domestic politics looks rather like international anarchy. Currently, Somalia is such a case. It has an extremely weak government that cannot control large parts of territory, and has become a home to terrorist organizations (see Chapter 5) and pirates (see Chapter 6). In these cases, the international community has a duty to intervene, according to some approaches, to restore law and order.[16]

The Democratic Peace

Kant argued that lasting peace would depend on states' becoming republics, with legislatures to check the power of monarchs (or presidents) to make war. He thought that checks and balances in government would act as a brake on the use of military force—as compared to autocratic governments in which a single individual (or small ruling group) could make war without regard for the effect on the population.

Somewhat similarly, IR scholars have linked democracy with a kind of foreign policy fundamentally different from that of authoritarianism.[17] One theory they considered was that

---

[15] Lepgold, Joseph, and Thomas G. Weiss, eds. *Collective Conflict Management and Changing World Politics.* SUNY, 1998.

[16] Rotbert, Robert. Failed States in a World of Terror. *Foreign Affairs* 81 (4), 2002: 127–41.

[17] Huth, Paul, and Todd Allee. *The Democratic Peace and the Territorial Conflict in the Twentieth Century.* Cambridge, 2003. Bueno de Mesquita, Bruce, et al. *The Logic of Political Survival.* MIT, 2003. Reiter, Dan, and Allan C. Stam. *Democracies at War.* Princeton, 2002. Schultz, Kenneth A. *Democracy and Coercive Diplomacy.* Cambridge, 2001.. Rummel, R. J. *Power Kills: Democracy as a Method of Nonviolence.* Transaction, 1997. Doyle, Michael W. Liberalism and World Politics. *American Political Science Review* 80 (4), 1986: 1151–70.

democracies are generally more *peaceful* than authoritarian governments (fighting fewer, or smaller, wars). This turned out not to be true. Democracies fight as many wars as do authoritarian states. Indeed, the three most war-prone states of the past two centuries (according to political scientists who count wars) were France, Russia, and Britain. Britain was a democracy throughout, France for part of the period, and Russia not at all.

What *is* true about democracies is that although they fight wars against authoritarian states, *democracies almost never fight each other*. No major historical cases contradict this generalization, which is known as the **democratic peace**. Why this is so is not entirely clear. As there have not been many democracies for very long, the generalization could be just a coincidence, though this seems unlikely. It may be that democracies do not tend to have severe conflicts with each other, as they tend to be capitalist states whose trade relations create strong interdependence (war would be costly because it would disrupt trade). Or, citizens of democratic societies (whose support is necessary for wars to be waged) may simply not see the citizens of other democracies as enemies. By contrast, authoritarian governments of other states *can* be seen as enemies. Note that the peace among democracies gives empirical support to a long-standing liberal claim that, because it is rooted in the domestic level of analysis, contradicts realism's claim that the most important explanations are at the interstate level.

Over the past two centuries, democracy has become more widespread as a form of government, and this trend is changing the nature of the foreign policy process worldwide.[18] Many states do not yet have democratic governments (the most important of these is China). And existing democracies are imperfect in various ways—from political apathy in the United States and corruption in Japan to autocratic traditions in Russia.[19] Nonetheless, the trend is toward democratization in most of the world's regions.

DEMOCRATIC TIDE

Upsurges of democratic movements throughout the world in recent years testify to the power of the idea of democracy. Because democracies rarely fight each other, worldwide democratization might lead to lasting peace. Here, Tunisia holds its first free election after leading the Arab Spring and reversing decades of authoritarian rule, 2011.

---

[18] Pevehouse, Jon C. *Democracy from Above? Regional Organizations and Democratization.* Cambridge, 2005.

[19] Zakaria, Fareed. *The Future of Freedom: Illiberal Democracy at Home and Abroad.* Norton, 2003. Collier, David, and Steven Levitsky. Democracy with Adjectives: Conceptual Innovation in Comparative Research. *World Politics* 49 (3), 1997: 430–51.

In the past two decades the trend has accelerated in several ways. New democracies emerged in several (though not all) states of the old Soviet bloc. Military governments were replaced with democratically elected civilian ones throughout most of Latin America as well as in several African and Asian countries. South Africa, the last white-ruled African country, adopted majority rule in 1994. In the late 1990s, long-standing dictatorships and military governments gave up power peacefully to democratic governments in Indonesia and Nigeria, both regional giants. In late 2004 and early 2005, pro-democracy forces won a string of victories in Ukraine, Palestine, Afghanistan, Iraq, and Kyrgyzstan. In 2008, Pakistan's military-run government stepped down to make way for a democratically elected government. And in 2011, the Arab Spring revolutions catalyzed democratic transitions in Tunisia, Egypt, and Libya. However, movement in the other direction still occurs. Military coups took place in Madagascar and Honduras in 2009 and Niger in 2010. Governments in Afghanistan and Iran were also accused of rigging elections in 2009 to ensure their continuation in power. Iran responded to election protests with a brutal crackdown against supporters of the opposition candidate.

We do not know where these trends will lead, but it is now conceivable that someday nearly all of the world's states will be democratically governed. As Kant envisaged, an international community based on peaceful relations may emerge.

However, although mature democracies almost never fight each other, a period of *transition* to democracy may be more prone to war than either a stable democracy or a stable authoritarian government.[20] Therefore the process of democratization does not necessarily bode well for peace in the short term. This theory gained support in early 2006 when Iraqi elections were followed by a rise in sectarian violence, and then Palestinian elections brought to power the militant faction Hamas, which rejects Israel's right to exist.

Finally, it is important to note that while democracy is often associated with peace and cooperation, democratic institutions make cooperation more difficult. For example, pressures for raising trade tariffs often arise from democratically elected legislatures. Some democratic countries may fail to join international organizations because of domestic opposition, as was the case with the United States and the League of Nations after World War I (see Chapter 1). Public opposition can also make attempts to expand existing cooperation difficult, as European Union leaders discovered after their proposal for a new EU constitution was defeated in democratic elections (see Chapter 10). Thus, while liberal scholars often extol the virtues of democracy, these same domestic institutions can make the process of international cooperation more complex.

Liberal theories thus provide a host of alternatives to power-based realist theories. Nearly all liberal theories focus on solving the collective action problem using the reciprocity principle. Whether because of international or domestic institutions, states come to expect reciprocal behavior regarding cooperation from other states. In this way, their calculations of interests move from short-term concerns to long-term considerations. Next, we review another set of alternatives to realism that focus on the identity principle.

Social Theories

Several distinct approaches in IR theory may be grouped together as *social theories*, meaning that they rely on social interaction to explain individuals' and states' preferences. These theories contrast with the assumption of fixed, timeless preferences in

---

[20] Mansfield, Edward D., and Jack Snyder. *Electing to Fight: Why Emerging Democracies Go to War*. MIT, 2005. Snyder, Jack. *From Voting to Violence: Democratization and Nationalist Conflict*. Norton, 2000.

most theories based on realism (states want more power) and liberalism (states, interest groups, and individuals want peace and prosperity).

Constructivism, a fast-growing approach in IR, asks how state's construct their interest through their interactions with one another. It is best described as an approach rather than a theory since, when stripped to its core, it says nothing about IR per se. However, its lessons about the nature of norms, identity, and social interactions can provide powerful insights into the world of IR. In fact, most constructivist explanations draw heavily on the identity principle to explain international behavior.

Identities and Ideas Matter

Constructivism is interested in how actors define their national interests, threats to those national interests, and their interests' relationships to one another. Realists (and neoliberals) tend to simply take state interests as given. Thus, constructivism puts IR in the context of broader social relations.[21] States decide what they want based not only on material needs, but also on "social" interaction. Just as a shopper may decide to buy a particular mp3 player because it will be perceived as cool (that is, more socially acceptable), so states may choose policies based on what they perceive will be "popular" with other states. Yet, just as shoppers may have limits placed on which music player they can afford to buy (limited resources), constructivists also recognize that power is not absent from international relations.[22]

Constructivist research has many strands. One prominent line examines how states' interests and identities are intertwined, as well as how those identities are shaped by interactions with other states.[23] For example, why is the United States concerned when North Korea builds nuclear weapons, but not when Great Britain does? Realists would quickly answer that North Korea poses a bigger threat, but from a pure military power perspective, Great Britain is a *far* superior military force to North Korea. Yet no one would argue that Great Britain is a threat to the United States no matter how many nuclear weapons it builds and no matter how deep disagreements about foreign policy become. Constructivist scholars would point out the shared history, shared alliances, and shared norms that tell Americans and the British they are not a threat to one another although they are very powerful militarily.

The identity of the potential adversary matters, not just its military capabilities and interests. This is a rejection of the realist assumption that states always want more rather than less power and wealth as well as the assumption that state interests exist independently of a context of interactions among states.[24] Constructivists hold that these state identities are complex and changing, and arise from interactions with other states—often through a process of *socialization*. Some constructivist scholars contend that over time, states can conceptualize one another in such a way that there is no danger of a security dilemma, arms races, or the other effects of anarchy. They point to

Explore
the **Simulation**
"Using Theory:
You Are the
New Prime Minister"
on mypoliscilab.com

[21] Legro, Jeffrey W. *Rethinking the World: Great Power Strategies and International Order*. Cornell, 2005. Hopf, Ted. *Social Construction of International Politics: Identities and Foreign Policies, Moscow, 1955 and 1999*. Cornell, 2002. Crawford, Neta C. *Argument and Change in World Politics: Ethics, Decolonization, and Humanitarian Intervention*. Cambridge, 2002. Katzenstein, Peter, ed. *The Culture of National Security*. Columbia, 1996.
[22] Barnett, Michael, and Raymond Duvall. *Power in Global Governance*. Cambridge, 2005.
[23] Hall, Rodney Bruce. *National Collective Identity: Social Constructs and International Systems*. Columbia, 1999. Reus-Smit, Christian. *The Moral Purpose of the State: Culture, Social Identity, and Institutional Rationality in International Relations*. Princeton, 1999. Barnett, Michael. *Dialogues in Arab Politics*. Columbia, 1998.
[24] Wendt, Alexander. *Social Theory of International Politics*. Cambridge, 1999. Guzzini, Stefano, and Anna Leander, eds. *Constructivism and International Relations: Alex Wendt and His Critics*. Routledge, 2006.

CONSTRUCTING IDENTITIES

Constructivist theories, based on the core principle of identity, see actors' preferences as constructed by the actors rather than given "objectively." These theories may do better than realist or liberal approaches in explaining major changes in a state's foreign policy goals and image in the world that arise from internal changes and new self-concepts rather than external constraints or opportunities. Examples might include the breakup of the Soviet Union and the election of Barack Obama as U.S. president. Iran's identity as an Islamic revolutionary state affects its foreign policies. Here, the morals police close a barber shop in Iran for giving Western-style haircuts, 2008.

Europe as an example—a continent that was the center of two military conflicts in the first half of the 20th century that killed millions. By the end of that century, war had become unthinkable. European identities are now intertwined with the European Union, not with the violent nationalism that led to two world wars. For constructivists, power politics, anarchy, and military force cannot explain this change. Institutions, regimes, norms, and changes in identity are better explanations.[25]

Societies as a whole also change over time in what they consider to be threatening. Two hundred years ago, pirates were the scourge of the high seas. These non-state actors invaded ports, pillaged goods, committed murder, and flaunted all international authority. It would not be hard to consider such behavior terrorism even though the pirates had no political goals in their violence. Even if not terrorism, no one would doubt the costs associated with piracy. Many states, including the United States, used their navies in attempts to eradicate pirates. Yet, despite the danger and harm historically caused by these actors, today we celebrate pirates by making them sports mascots, naming amusement rides after them, and glorifying them in movies.

Of course, one could argue that pirates are no longer a threat—even though numerous acts of piracy still occur on the high seas. Even apart from the high-profile pirate hijackings near Somalia in 2008–2009, the threat from piracy has remained high for many years. Yet, we find it acceptable to play down the piracy threat by incorporating them into popular culture. No doubt someone from two centuries ago would find such acceptance odd.

How odd? Imagine in 200 years your great-great-grandchildren riding a terrorist-themed ride at Disneyland or watching the latest *Terrorists of the Persian Gulf* movie. Constructivists are quick to point out that what societies or states consider dangerous is not universal or timeless. Social norms and conventions change, and these changes can have tremendous implications for foreign policy.

States may also come to value and covet something like status or reputation, which are social, not material, concepts. Switzerland, for example, values its role as a neutral,

---

[25] Checkel, Jeffrey. Social Learning and European Identity Change. *International Organization* 55 (3), 2000: 553–88.

nonaligned state (it belongs to neither the European Union nor NATO, and joined the UN only in 2002). This status as a neutral state gives Switzerland prestige and power—not a material power like money or guns—but a normative power to intervene diplomatically in important international affairs. Similarly, Canada's foreign policy contains its own identity-driven imperatives usually revolving around peacekeeping and humanitarian operations.

These identity-based explanations can help to explain the behavior of great powers as well. In 1993, the UN Security Council established a war crimes tribunal for the former Yugoslavia. Its effectiveness was limited in its first years by inadequacy of funding necessary to hire investigators and translators, rent offices and phone lines, and so forth. The contributions of the great powers to support the tribunal varied, with the United States providing the most support (though still not adequate to the need) and Great Britain providing very little.

Liberal theorists would quickly recognize a collective goods problem in paying for the tribunal. The world community benefits from the work of the tribunal (inasmuch as it deters future aggression and genocide), but each individual state gains this benefit—however beneficial it ends up being—regardless of its own contribution. By this logic, Britain was being rational to free-ride because the United States and others were willing to pick up enough of the tab to make the tribunal at least minimally effective.

Realists might well question this explanation. They might see Britain's lack of support as more straightforward. British leaders may not have wanted the tribunal to succeed because Britain tacitly sided with Serbia (a traditional ally), and Serbia was not cooperating with a tribunal that had indicted the Bosnian Serb leaders as war criminals. The same geopolitical factors that led Britain in the past to side with Serbia (and Russia and France) against Croatia (and Germany, Austria, and Turkey) were still operating. War crimes come and go, by this reasoning, but great power interests remain fairly constant.

Both theories seem to have merit, but sometimes history provides "experiments" that, even though we do not control them, help sort out competing explanations. In this case, in 1997 a liberal government headed by Prime Minister Tony Blair replaced the conservative government of John Major. This change did not affect the explanatory "variables" of either theory—the nature of the collective goods problem inherent in the tribunal, and the nature of Britain's strategic and historical interests and alliances in the Balkans. But in fact Blair's government shifted its Bosnia policy dramatically, leading a raid to arrest two war crimes suspects and contributing substantial funds for the tribunal to construct a second courtroom. The fact that a change in political leadership changed British behavior suggests that identity-based explanations do play some role: Blair's idea of Britain's place in the international community drove the outcome of the case.

Another field of constructivist research also relies heavily on international norms and their power to constrain state action. Although realists (and neoliberals) contend that states make decisions based on a *logic of consequences* ("What will happen to me if I behave a certain way?"), constructivist scholars note that there is a powerful *logic of appropriateness* ("How should I behave in this situation?").[26] For example, some cases of humanitarian intervention—military intervention by a state or states to protect citizens or subjects of another state—seem difficult to explain in realist or liberal terms. Why, for example, did the United States in 1992 send troops to Somalia—a country of minimal strategic and economic importance to the United States—as Somalia descended into political chaos and

---

[26] March, James G., and Johan Olsen. The Institutional Dynamics of International Political Orders. *International Organization* 52 (4), 1998: 943–69.

POLICY PERSPECTIVES

President of Ukraine, Victor Yanukovych

PROBLEM *How do you maintain cooperation with international institutions in the face of pressure from a powerful neighbor?*

BACKGROUND After your election in 2010, you halted the process of trying to join NATO. In 2008, your predecessor had applied for NATO membership, an application that was rejected. Although NATO left the door open for future membership, the Ukrainian public was angry over the NATO rejection. Yet, you have continued your cooperation with NATO in several political issue areas.

Your predecessor's desire for stronger NATO ties originated from a more rationalist logic of consequences: tensions between your country and Russia have run high. Russia supplies much of your natural gas and several times has cut off supplies during political disputes, most recently in the winter of 2008–2009. Your country has responded to these cutoffs by closing Russian oil pipelines that pass through your country en route to Western Europe. Entering NATO could provide political support and military protection against any aggressive Russian diplomacy.

You have been much less supportive of NATO membership than your predecessor. You have reassured Russia that, in the short term, Ukraine will not reapply for membership. You have told leaders of several Western European states that you wish your country to remain neutral in international affairs. Finally, you authored a bill passed by the legislature that removed the phrase "NATO membership" from the list of official national security goals.

DOMESTIC CONSIDERATIONS Historically, a major source of opposition to Ukraine's entry into NATO comes from your own population. Opinion polls show that your public opposes Ukraine's membership in NATO by a margin of nearly two to one. Your own party's electoral base is located near the Russian border and favors better relations with Russia.

The public, while opposing NATO membership, does strongly support Ukraine's application to the EU. The public also supported Ukraine's successful application to the World Trade Organization. Public opposition to NATO is not anti-Western per se, but is rooted in the NATO airstrikes against Serbia in 1999 in the war over Kosovo. There is a general desire to reorient Ukraine's foreign policy toward the West, but so far, this desire has excluded NATO membership.

SCENARIO Imagine that Russia again cuts off supplies of natural gas and other resources to your country. The dispute is over your continued cooperation with NATO in political affairs. Russia is demanding that you lessen your cooperation with the NATO alliance or face increasing political pressure and economic pressure. Although NATO membership is not a prerequisite for EU membership, EU members would not look favorably on you abandoning an international regime to which you had committed.

CHOOSE YOUR POLICY Do you lessen ties with NATO, even though coordination with NATO has benefited your country greatly? Do you give in to Russia and abandon this cooperation? Do you change your own position on NATO in response to Russia's bullying and apply for full NATO membership? Can you abandon cooperation with NATO while simultaneously pursuing EU membership?

faced the possibility of mass starvation (see p. 35)? A constructivist explanation might point to changing norms about which kinds of people are worthy of protection. In the 19th century, European powers occasionally intervened to protect Christian subjects of the Ottoman Empire from massacres, but generally ignored non-Christian victims. However, as decolonization enshrined the principle of self-determination and as human rights became widely valued, the scope of humanitarian intervention expanded. Although the international community does not always respond effectively to humanitarian crises, it is no longer acceptable to view only Christians as deserving protection.[27] The United States in this example tried to act in an appropriate fashion rather than according to the dictates of cost-benefit calculations.

Examples of this identity approach can be found in the developing world as well. Some constructivists have argued that countries in Latin America, Africa, and the Middle East have adopted or changed policies in response to international norms—not because it provided large benefits, but rather because it was perceived as the appropriate course of action. For example, many developing states have raced to create science bureaucracies and/or begin technological modernization of their militaries. Constructivists point out that the reason developing states choose to spend their limited resources on such projects is their desire to be perceived as "modern" by the international system. "Modern" states have science bureaucracies and advanced militaries. Ironically, many states that build science bureaucracies have few scientists while many states that build advanced militaries have few enemies.[28] Thus, constructivists emphasize that identities and norms must be used to explain this seemingly puzzling behavior.

How are these international norms spread around the world? In an age of global communication and relative ease of transportation, many possibilities exist. Constructivists emphasize different sets of actors who spread norms. Some contend that individuals, labeled *norm entrepreneurs*, through travel, writing, and meeting with elites change ideas and encourage certain types of norms. Some point to broad-based social movements and nongovernmental organizations, such as the anti-apartheid movement encouraging the development of a global norm of racial equality. Others show how international organizations (such as the UN and NATO) can diffuse norms of what is appropriate and inappropriate behavior. In each case, however, new ideas and norms, rather than power and self-interest, drive state behavior.[29]

Research in the constructivist tradition has expanded rapidly in recent years.[30] Scholars have examined the role of the European Union in socializing elites in new member states[31] as well as the role of the United Nations in conferring legitimacy on

[27] Finnemore, Martha. *The Purpose of Intervention: Changing Beliefs about the Use of Force*. Cornell, 2004.

[28] Finnemore, Martha. International Organizations as Teachers of Norms: The United Nations Education, Scientific, and Cultural Organizations and Science Policy. *International Organization* 47 (4), 1993: 565–97. Eyre, Dana, and Mark Suchman. Status, Norms, and the Proliferation of Conventional Weapons: An Institutional Theory Approach. In Katzenstein, Peter, ed. *The Culture of National Security*. Columbia, 1996.

[29] Keck, Margaret, and Kathryn Sikkink. *Activists Beyond Borders: Advocacy Networks in International Politics*. Cornell, 1998. Klotz, Audie. *Norms in International Relations: The Struggle against Apartheid*. Cornell, 1995. Finnemore, Martha. *National Interests in International Society*. Cornell, 1996. Johnston, Alastair Iain. Treating Institutions as Social Environments. *International Studies Quarterly* 45 (3), 2001: 487–516. Schimmelfennig, Frank. The Community Trap: Liberal Norms, Rhetorical Action, and the Eastern Enlargement of the European Union. *International Organization* 55 (1), 2001: 47–80.

[30] Klotz, Audie, and Cecelia Lynch. *Strategies for Research in Constructivist International Relations*. M. E. Sharpe, 2007.

[31] Checkel, Jeffrey. International Institutions and Socialization in Europe: Introduction and Framework. *International Organization* 59 (4), 2005: 801–26.

the use of force as a source of its power.[32] Others have investigated how international organizations gain authority through their expertise (for example, the IMF on international financial issues) to make decisions that run counter to what their member states desire.[33] Finally, constructivist scholars have begun to investigate how notions of identity and symbolism are important for understanding terrorist movements and counterterrorism policy.[34]

Of course, like any approach or theory of IR, constructivism has its share of critics. Realists suggest that norms are simply covers for state (or personal) interests. Liberals argue that some constructivist scholars pay too little attention to the formal institutions and the politics within them. Moreover, both realists and liberals criticize that it is difficult to tell when a person's identity is genuine or is adopted strategic reasons to bring material benefits (such as more aid, trade, or membership into an exclusive organization).[35] Despite these criticisms, constructivist thinking and its emphasis on the identity principle will continue to be at the core of IR research for years to come.

Postmodernism

Postmodernism is a broad approach to scholarship that has left its mark on various academic disciplines, especially the study of literature. Because of their literary roots, postmodernists pay special attention to *texts* and to *discourses*—how people talk and write about their subject (IR).[36] Postmodern critiques of realism thus center on analyzing realists' words and arguments.[37] A central idea of postmodernism is that there is no single, objective reality but a multiplicity of experiences and perspectives that defy easy categorization. For this reason, postmodernism itself is difficult to present in a simple or categorical way. Postmodern scholarship in IR preceded, set the stage for, and has largely been supplanted by constructivism.

From a postmodern perspective, realism cannot justify its claim that states are the central actors in IR and that states operate as unitary actors with coherent sets of objective interests (which they pursue through international power politics). Postmodern critics of realism see nothing objective about state interests, and certainly nothing universal (in that one set of values or interests applies to all states).

More fundamentally, postmodernism calls into question the whole notion of states as actors. States have no tangible reality; they are "fictions" that we (as scholars and citizens) construct to make sense of the actions of large numbers of individuals. For postmodernists, the stories told about the actions and policies of states are just that—stories. From this

---

[32] Hurd, Ian. *After Anarchy: Legitimacy and Power in the United Nations Security Council*. Princeton, 2008.

[33] Barnett, Michael, and Martha Finnemore. *Rules for the World*. Cornell, 2004.

[34] Leheny, David. Symbols, Strategies, and Choices for International Relations Scholarship after September 11. *Dialogue IO* 1 (1), 2003: 57–70.

[35] Hyde-Price, Adrian. "Normative" Power Europe: A Realist Critique. *Journal of European Public Policy* 13 (2), 2006: 217–34. Zehfuss, Maja. *Constructivism in International Relations: The Politics of Reality*. Cambridge, 2002. Mercer, Jonathan. Anarchy and Identity. *International Organization* 49 (2), 1995: 229–52.

[36] Burke, Anthony. Postmodernism. In Reus-Smit, Christian, and Duncan Snidal, eds. *The Oxford Handbook of International Relations*. Oxford, 2008, pp. 359–77. Jarvis, Darryl S. L. *International Relations and the "Third Debate": Postmodernism and Its Critics*. Praeger, 2002.

[37] Ashley, Richard K., and R. B. J. Walker. Speaking the Language of Exile: Dissident Thought in International Studies [Introduction to special issue]. *International Studies Quarterly* 34 (3), 1990: 259–68. Lapid, Yosef. The Third Debate: On the Prospects of International Theory in a Post-Positivist Era. *International Studies Quarterly* 33 (3), 1989: 235–54. Molloy, Sean. *The Hidden History of Realism: A Genealogy of Power Politics*. Palgrave, 2006.

perspective, an arbitrary distinction leads bookstores to put spy novels on the fiction shelf whereas biographies and histories go on the nonfiction shelf. None of these is an objective reality, and all are filtered through an interpretive process that distorts the actual experiences of those involved.[38] Contrary to realism's claim that states are unitary actors, postmodernists see multiple realities and experiences lurking below the surface of the fictional entities that realists construct (states). The Soviet Union, for example, was treated by realists as a single actor with a single set of objective interests. Indeed, it was considered the second most important actor in the world. Realists were amazed when the Soviet Union split into 15 pieces, each containing its own fractious groups and elements. It became clear that the "unitary state" called the Soviet Union had masked (and let realists ignore) the divergent experiences of constituent republics, ethnic groups, and individuals.

Postmodernists seek to "deconstruct" such constructions as states, the international system, and the associated stories and arguments (texts and discourses) with which realists portray the nature of international relations. To *deconstruct* a text—a term borrowed from literary criticism—means to tease apart the words in order to reveal hidden meanings, looking for what might be omitted or included only implicitly. The hidden meanings not explicitly addressed in the text are often called the **subtext**.[39]

Omissions are an aspect of subtext, as when realist theories of IR omit women and gender, for example. In its emphasis on states, realism omits the roles of individuals, domestic politics, economic classes, MNCs, and other nonstate actors. In its focus on the great powers, realism omits the experiences of poor countries. In its attention to military forms of leverage, it omits the roles of various nonmilitary forms of leverage.

Realism focuses so narrowly because its aim is to reduce IR to a simple, coherent model. The model is claimed to be objective, universal, and accurate. To postmodernists, the realist model is none of these things; it is a biased model that creates a narrow and one-sided story for the purpose of promoting the interests of powerful actors. Postmodernists seek to destroy this model along with any other model (including neoliberalism) that tries to represent IR in simple objective categories. Postmodernists instead want to celebrate the diversity of experiences that make up IR without needing to make sense of them by simplifying and categorizing.[40]

Marxism

Historically most important among social theories, Marxist approaches to IR hold that both IR and domestic politics arise from unequal relationships between **economic classes**. This emphasis on classes—implying that the domestic and economic attributes of societies shape external relations with other states—contrasts with the realist approach to IR with

Watch the **Video** "Castro's Cuba" on mypoliscilab.com

---

[38] Shapiro, Michael J. Textualizing Global Politics. In Der Derian, James, and Michael J. Shapiro, eds. *International/Intertextual Relations: Postmodern Readings of World Politics.* Lexington, 1989, pp. 11–22. Shapiro, Michael J., and Hayward R. Alker, eds. *Challenging Boundaries: Global Flows, Territorial Identities.* Minnesota, 1996.

[39] Campbell, David. *Politics without Principle: Sovereignty, Ethics, and the Narratives of the Gulf War.* Rienner, 1993. Stephanson, Anders. *Kennan and the Art of Foreign Policy.* Harvard, 1989. Chaloupka, William. *Knowing Nukes: The Politics and Culture of the Atom.* Minnesota, 1992.

[40] Walker, R. B. J., and Saul H. Mendlovitz, eds. *Contending Sovereignties: Redefining Political Community.* Rienner, 1990. Walker, R. B. J. *Inside/Outside: International Relations as Political Theory.* Cambridge, 1993. Weber, Cynthia. *Simulating Sovereignty: Intervention, the State and Symbolic Exchange.* Cambridge, 1995. Sjolander, Claire Turenne, and Wayne S. Cox, eds. *Beyond Positivism: Critical Reflections on International Relations.* Rienner, 1994. George, Jim. *Discourses of Global Politics: A Critical (Re)Introduction to International Relations.* Rienner, 1994.

RICH AND POOR

Disparity of wealth is a central aspect of global North-South relations. Marxists see international relations and domestic politics alike as being shaped by a class struggle between the rich and the poor. In São Paulo, Brazil, rich and poor neighborhoods sit side by side.

its separation of domestic and international politics. We will discuss Marxist theories of IR in Chapter 12, as they primarily concern the global divisions of North and South arising from the history of imperialism. Here we will show, briefly, how Marxist theories as social theories contrast with the realist paradigm.

Marxism is a branch of socialism, a theory that holds that the more powerful classes oppress and exploit the less powerful by denying them their fair share of the surplus they create. The oppressed classes try to gain power in order to seize more of the wealth for themselves. This process, called *class struggle*, is one way of looking at the political relationships between richer and poorer people, and ultimately between richer and poorer world regions.

Marxism includes both communism and other approaches. In the mid-19th century, *Karl Marx* emphasized labor as the source of economic surplus. At that time, the Industrial Revolution was accompanied by particular hardship among industrial workers (including children) in Europe. Marxists still believe that the surplus created by labor should be recaptured by workers through political struggle. Today, Marxism is most influential in countries of the global South, where capital is scarce and labor conditions are wretched.

One important class in revolutions during the past century (contrary to Marx's expectations) has been *peasants*.[41] Marxists traditionally consider peasants backward, ignorant, individualistic, and politically passive as compared to the better-educated and class-conscious proletariat. But in practice, the successful third world revolutions have been peasant rebellions (often led by Marxists talking about the proletariat). The largest was the Chinese revolution in the 1930s and 1940s.

Marx's theories of class struggle were oriented toward *domestic* society in the industrializing countries of his time, not toward poor countries or international relations. Traditional Marxists looked to the advanced industrialized countries for revolution and socialism, which would grow out of capitalism. In their view, the third world would have to develop through its own stages of accumulation from feudalism to capitalism before taking the revolutionary step to socialism. What actually happened was the opposite. Proletarian workers in industrialized countries enjoyed rising standards of living and did not make

---

[41] Moore, Barrington. *Social Origins of Dictatorship and Democracy: Lord and Peasant in the Making of the Modern World.* Beacon, 1993 [1966]. Scott, James C. *Weapons of the Weak: Everyday Forms of Peasant Resistance.* Yale, 1986.

revolutions. Meanwhile, in the backward third world countries, oppressed workers and peasants staged a series of revolutions, successful and failed.

Why did revolutions occur in backward rather than advanced countries? The answer largely shapes how one sees North-South relations today.[42] Marxists have mostly (but not exclusively) followed a line of argument developed by *V. I. Lenin*, founder of the Soviet Union, before the Russian Revolution of 1917.[43] Russia was then a relatively backward state, as the global South is today, and most Marxists considered a revolution there unlikely (looking instead to Germany).

Lenin's theory of imperialism argued that European capitalists were investing in colonies where they could earn big profits and then using part of these to *buy off* the working class at home. But Lenin saw that after the scramble for colonies in the 1890s, few areas of the world remained to be colonized. Imperialist expansion could occur only at the expense of other imperialist states, leading to interimperialist competition and wars such as World War I. Seizing on Russia's weakness during that war, Lenin led the first successful communist revolution there in 1917.

Lenin's general idea still shapes a major approach to North-South relations—the idea that industrialized states exploit poor countries (through both formal and informal colonization) and buy off their own working classes with the profits. Through this *globalization of class relations*, world accumulation concentrates surplus toward the rich parts of the world and away from the poor ones. Revolutions, then, would be expected in poor regions.

Many third world revolutionaries sought to break loose from exploitation by the European colonizers. After European colonization ended, the United States as the world's richest country (with large investments in the global South and a global military presence) became the target of revolutionaries agitating against exploitation in poor countries. In a number of countries, imperialists were thrown out (often violently, sometimes not) and revolutionary nationalists took power.

One of the most important such revolutions was in China, where Mao Zedong's communists took power in 1949 on a Leninist platform adapted to the largely peasant-based movement they led. Mao declared that "China has stood up"—on its own feet, throwing off foreign domination and foreign exploitation. In India at the same time, the movement led by Gandhi used a different means (nonviolence) to achieve similar ends—national independence from colonialism. Indonesia threw out the Dutch. Lebanon threw out the French. Cuba threw out the Americans. This pattern was repeated, with variations, in dozens of countries.

According to the revolutionaries in these countries, exploitation of third world countries by rich countries takes away the economic surplus of the global South and concentrates the accumulation of wealth toward the rich parts of the world. By breaking free of such exploitation, third world states can then retain their own surplus and begin to accumulate their own wealth. Eventually they can generate their own self-sustaining cycles of accumulation and lift themselves out of poverty.[44] However, such an approach has not worked well. A policy of self-reliance does not foster growth (see p. 291). And within a single poor country, trade-offs arise between concentrating or distributing wealth. For former colonies, the realities of economic development after independence have been complex. These realities are discussed in Chapter 12.

[42] Brewer, Anthony. *Marxist Theories of Imperialism: A Critical Survey.* 2nd ed. Routledge, 1990. Kubálková, Vendulka, and Albert Cruickshank. *Marxism and International Relations.* Clarendon, 1985.
[43] Lenin, V. I. *Imperialism, the Highest Stage of Capitalism.* 1916.
[44] Tickner, J. Ann. *Self-Reliance versus Power Politics.* Columbia, 1987. Amin, Samir. Self-Reliance and the New International Economic Order. *Monthly Review* 29 (3), 1977: 1–21.

Not all Marxist approaches favor a policy of self-reliance after revolution. *Leon Trotsky*, a Russian revolutionary, believed that after the 1917 revolution, Russia would never be able to build socialism alone and should make its top priority the spreading of revolution to other countries to build a worldwide alliance. Trotsky's archrival Stalin wanted to build "socialism in one country," and he prevailed (and had Trotsky killed).[45] Most third world revolutions since then, including China's, have had a strongly nationalist flavor.

Marxist theories in IR entered a low-visibility phase after the collapse of the Soviet Union and China's turn toward capitalism—events that seemed to discredit Marxist theories. However, in the past few years, Marxists and former Marxists have taken power in a number of Latin American countries. Venezuela and Bolivia, as a result, have become active allies of Cuba, forming an anti-American coalition. In Nicaragua, the former communist leader whom U.S.-organized rebels fought in the 1980s won election as president in 2006. These events, along with China's continuing formal adherence to Marxism, suggest that Marxist theories of IR have ongoing importance in the post–Cold War era.

Peace Studies

Peace studies challenges fundamental concepts behind both realism and neoliberalism.[46] In particular, peace studies seeks to shift the focus of IR away from the interstate level of analysis and toward a broad conception of social relations at the individual, domestic, and global levels of analysis. Peace studies connects war and peace with individual responsibility, economic inequality, gender relations, cross-cultural understanding, and other aspects of social relationships. Peace studies also seeks peace not in the transactions of state leaders but in the transformation of entire societies (through social revolution) and in transnational communities (bypassing states and ignoring borders to connect people and groups globally).[47] Another way in which peace studies seeks to broaden the focus of inquiry is to reject the supposed objectivity of traditional (realist and liberal) approaches. Most scholars of peace studies think that a good way to gain knowledge is to participate in action—not just to observe objectively. This lack of objectivity has been criticized as *normative bias* because scholars impose their personal norms and values on the subject. Scholars in peace studies respond, however, that realism itself has normative biases and makes policy prescriptions.

The development and implementation of peaceful strategies for settling conflicts—using alternatives to violent forms of leverage—are known by the general term **conflict resolution**. These methods are at work, competing with violent methods, in virtually all international conflicts. Recently, the use of conflict resolution has been increasing, becoming more sophisticated, and succeeding more often.[48] Most conflict resolution uses a third party whose role is **mediation** between two conflicting parties.[49] Most of today's international conflicts have one

---

[45] Mandel, Ernest. *From Stalinism to Eurocommunism: The Bitter Fruits of "Socialism in One Country."* Translated by Jon Rothschild. N. L. B., 1978. Howe, Irving. *Leon Trotsky.* NY: Viking, 1978.

[46] Barash, David P., and Charles P. Webel. *Peace and Conflict Studies.* Sage, 2002. Samaddar, Ranabir. *Peace Studies: An Introduction to the Concept, Scope, and Themes.* Sage, 2004.

[47] Cancian, Francesca M., and James William Gibson. *Making War/Making Peace: The Social Foundations of Violent Conflict.* Wadsworth, 1990. Rapoport, Anatol. *Peace: An Idea Whose Time Has Come.* Michigan, 1992. Galtung, Johan. *Peace by Peaceful Means: Peace and Conflict, Development and Civilization.* Sage, 1996.

[48] Wallensteen, Peter. *Understanding Conflict Resolution: War, Peace, and the Global System.* Sage, 2007. Zartman, I. William, and Guy O. Faure, eds. *Escalation and Negotiation in International Conflicts.* Cambridge, 2006. Walter, Barbara. *Committing to Peace: The Successful Settlement of Civil Wars.* Princeton, 2002. Jeong, Ho-Won. *Conflict Resolution: Dynamics, Process, and Structure.* Ashgate, 2000.

[49] Bercovitch, Jacob, ed. *Resolving International Conflicts: The Theory and Practice of Mediation.* Rienner, 1996. Princen, Thomas. *Intermediaries in International Conflict.* Princeton, 1992.

or more mediating parties working regularly to resolve the conflict short of violence. No hard-and-fast rule states what kinds of third parties mediate what kinds of conflicts. The UN is the most important mediator on the world scene. Some regional conflicts are mediated through regional organizations, single states, or even private individuals.[50]

The involvement of the mediator can vary. Some mediation is strictly *technical*—a mediator may take an active but strictly neutral role in channeling communication between two states that lack other channels of communication.[51] For example, Pakistan secretly passed messages between China and the United States before the breakthrough in U.S.-Chinese relations in 1971. Such a role is sometimes referred to as offering the mediator's *good offices* to a negotiating process. In facilitating communication, a mediator listens to each side's ideas and presents them in a way the other side can hear. The mediator works to change each side's view of difficult issues. In these roles, the mediator is like the translator between the two sides, or a therapist helping them work out psychological problems in their relationship.[52] Travel and discussion by private individuals and groups can serve as *citizen diplomacy*, to ease tensions as well.[53]

If both sides agree in advance to abide by a solution devised by a mediator, the process is called *arbitration*. In that case, both sides present their arguments to the arbitrator, who decides on a "fair" solution. For example, when Serbian and Bosnian negotiators could not agree on who should get the city of Brcko, they turned the issue over to arbitration rather than hold up the entire 1995 Dayton Agreement. Arbitration often uses a panel of three people, one chosen by each side unilaterally and a third on whom both sides agree.

Conflicting parties (and mediators) can also use *confidence-building* measures to gradually increase trust. By contrast, *linkage* lumps together diverse issues so that compromises on one can be traded off against another in a grand deal. This was the case, for instance, in the Yalta negotiations of 1945 among the United States, Britain, and the Soviet Union. On the table simultaneously were such matters as the terms of occupation of Germany, the Soviet presence in Eastern Europe, the strategy for defeating Japan, and the creation of the United Nations.

Peace studies scholars argue that war is not just a natural expression of power, but one closely tied to militarism in (some) cultures.[54] **Militarism** is the glorification of war, military force, and violence through TV, films, books, political speeches, toys, games, sports, and other such avenues. Militarism also refers to the structuring of society around war—for example, the dominant role of a military-industrial complex in a national economy, or the dominance of national security issues in domestic politics. Militarism may underlie the propensity of political leaders to use military force. Historically, militarism has had a profound influence on the evolution of societies. War has often been glorified as a "manly" enterprise that ennobles the human spirit (especially before World War I, which changed that perspective). Not only evil acts but also exemplary acts of humanity are brought forth by war—sacrifice, honor, courage, altruism on behalf of loved ones, and bonding with a community larger than oneself.

Examples of less militarized cultures show that realism's emphasis on military force is not universal or necessary. Costa Rica has had no army for 50 years (just lightly armed

[50] Child, Jack. *The Central American Peace Process, 1983–1991: Sheathing Swords, Building Confidence*. Rienner, 1992.

[51] Stein, Janice Gross, ed. *Getting to the Table: The Processes of International Prenegotiation*. Johns Hopkins, 1989.

[52] Crocker, Chester A., Fen Osler Hampson, and Pamela Aall. *Taming Intractable Conflicts: Mediation in the Hardest Cases*. U.S. Institute of Peace, 2004. Kremenyuk, V. A., ed. *International Negotiation: Analysis, Approaches, Issues*. 2nd ed. Jossey-Bass, 2002.

[53] Agha, Hussein, Shai Feldman, Ahmad Khalidi, and Ze'ev Schiff. *Track II Diplomacy: Lessons from the Middle East*. MIT, 2003.

[54] Bacevich, Andrew J. *The New American Militarism: How Americans Are Seduced by War*. Oxford, 2005. Grossman, Dave. *On Killing: The Psychological Cost of Learning to Kill in War and Society*. Little, Brown, 1995.

SHADOW OF WAR

Militarism in a culture, or the lack thereof, can influence foreign policy. In societies at war, children's psychological trauma contributes to intergroup conflicts decades later. Generations of Palestinians have grown up in a society affected by violent conflict. This Palestinian girl, walking between Israeli troops and Palestinian stone-throwers in the West Bank in 2010, has lived around violent conflict her whole life, as have her parents and grandparents.

forces), even during the 1980s when wars occurred in neighboring Nicaragua and Panama. Japanese culture since World War II has developed strong norms against war and violence.

Anthropologists have tried to connect the domestic characteristics of hunter-gatherer societies with their external propensity to engage in warfare. Some evidence shows that war occurs more frequently in societies with internal (especially gender) inequalities, with harsh child-rearing practices, and with fathers who are absent from child rearing. By contrast, relatively peaceful societies are more likely to have open decision-making processes, relative gender equality, and permissive and affectionate child rearing.[55] But all these societal attributes could as well be *effects* of war as causes. And because all kinds of societies seem to have the potential for warfare under some conditions (see Chapter 5), distinctions such as "warlike" are only relative.

Just as war is seen in peace studies as a pervasive aspect of society as a whole, so can peace be reconceptualized in a broader way.[56] Because realism assumes the normalcy of military conflicts, it recognizes only a negative kind of peace—the temporary absence of war. By contrast, **positive peace** refers to a peace that resolves the underlying reasons for war—peace that is not just a cease-fire but a transformation of relationships. Under positive peace, not only do state armies stop fighting each other, they stop arming, stop forming death squads against internal protest, and reverse the economic exploitation and political oppression that scholars in peace studies believe are responsible for social conflicts that lead to war.

Proponents of this approach see broad social and economic issues—assumed by realists to be relatively unimportant—as inextricably linked with positive peace. Some scholars define poverty, hunger, and oppression as forms of violence—which they call *structural violence* because it is caused by the structure of social relations rather than by direct actions such as shooting people. Structural violence in this definition kills and harms many more

[55] Ross, Marc Howard. A Cross-Cultural Theory of Political Conflict and Violence. *Political Psychology* 7, 1986: 427–69. Caprioli, Mary. Primed for Violence: The Role of Gender Inequality in Predicting International Conflict. *International Studies Quarterly* 49 (2), 2005: 161–78.

[56] Lipschutz, Ronnie D., and Mary Ann Tétreault. *Global Politics as If People Mattered.* 2nd ed. Rowman & Littlefield, 2009. Elias, Robert, and Jennifer Turpin, eds. *Rethinking Peace.* Rienner, 1994.

people each year than do war and other forms of direct political violence. Positive peace is usually defined to include the elimination of structural violence.

Advocates of positive peace also criticize militaristic culture. The "social construction of war"—a complex system of rules and relations that ultimately supports the existence of war—touches our lives in many ways: from children's war toys to patriotic rituals in schools; from teenagers' gender roles to military training for young men; from the taxes we pay to the sports we play. The positive peace approach seeks to change the whole system, not just one piece of it.

Positive peace encompasses a variety of approaches to social change. These include alternative mechanisms for conflict resolution to take the place of war; popular pressure on governments through peace movements and political activism; the strengthening of norms against the use of violence (including the philosophy of nonviolence); the development of international or global identity transcending national, ethnic, and religious divisions; and egalitarian relations within societies in the economic, social, and political realms (including changes in gender roles).

The creation of a **world government** has long been debated by scholars and pursued by activists.[57] Some scholars believe progress is being made (through the UN) toward the eventual emergence of a world government. Others think the idea is impractical or even undesirable (merely adding another layer of centralized control, when peace demands decentralization and freedom).

Scholars in peace studies also study how to achieve the conditions for positive peace. Most peace studies scholars share a skepticism that state leaders left to themselves would ever achieve positive peace. Rather, they believe the practice of IR will change only as a result of pressures from individuals and groups. The most commonly studied method of exerting such pressure is through **peace movements**—people taking to the streets in protest against war and militarism.[58] As U.S. president Dwight Eisenhower once said,

FOR PEACE

Peace demonstrators play a role in many international conflicts. Here, marchers in Spain protest the U.S. war in Iraq, 2007.

[57] Pojman, Louis P. *Terrorism, Human Rights, and the Case for World Government.* Rowman & Littlefield, 2006. Mandelbaum, Michael. *The Case for Goliath: How America Acts as the World's Government in the 21st Century.* Public Affairs, 2006.

[58] Breyman, Steve. *Why Movements Matter: The West German Peace Movement and U.S. Arms Control Policy.* SUNY, 2001. Lynch, Cecelia. *Beyond Appeasement: Interpreting Interwar Peace Movements in World Politics.* Cornell, 1999. Carter, April. *Peace Movements: International Protest and World Politics Since 1945.* Longman, 1992.

"People want peace so much that one of these days governments had better get out of their way and let them have it."[59]

The philosophy of *nonviolence* is based on a unilateral commitment to refrain from using any violent forms of leverage in bargaining. No state today follows such a strategy, but substate actors do.[60] *Mahatma Gandhi,* who led India's struggle for independence from the British Empire before 1948, emphasized that nonviolence must be *active* in seeking to prevent violence, to resolve conflicts without violence, and especially to stand up against injustice enforced violently. Gandhi organized Indians to resist the British colonial occupation without resorting to violence, even when British troops shot down unarmed Indian protesters.

Proponents of nonviolence emphasize the practical side of nonviolence in addition to its morality. As a tool of the powerless standing up against injustices by the powerful, nonviolence is often the most cost-effective approach—because the costs of violent resistance would be prohibitive.[61] In the United States, the philosophy of nonviolence spread widely in the 1960s in the civil rights movement, especially through the work of Martin Luther King, Jr. Protesters in the Arab Spring movements in 2011 followed Dr. King's example as well as specific strategies recommended by an American, Gene Sharp, whose ideas were taught to young Arab activists at earlier workshops in Europe. These nonviolent approaches worked spectacularly in Tunisia and Egypt, were quickly swept aside by a violent rebellion in Libya, and led to a protracted standoff in Syria, where government repression killed about 5,000 unarmed demonstrators during 2011.

The dilemma of nonviolence is how to respond to violence.[62] Gandhi believed that there is always a third alternative to passivity or response in kind. Nonviolence does not always succeed when faced with violence, but then neither does violent response. However, political leaders may believe they have done their duty if they respond violently without success, but not if they respond nonviolently without success.

Gender Theories

Scholarship on gender has cut a broad swath across academic disciplines, from literature to psychology to history. In recent years, it has made inroads in international relations, once considered one of the fields most resistant to gendered arguments.[63]

Why Gender Matters

Gender scholarship encompasses a variety of strands of work, but all have in common the insight that gender matters in understanding how IR works—especially in issues relating to war and international security. *Feminist scholarship* in various disciplines seeks to uncover hidden assumptions about gender in how we study a subject. What scholars traditionally claim to be universal often turns out to be true only of males. Some feminist IR scholars argue that the core assumptions of realism—especially of anarchy and sovereignty—reflect the ways in which *males* tend to interact and to see the world. In this view, the realist

[59] Eisenhower, Dwight D. *Ike's Letters to a Friend, 1941–1958.* Edited by Robert Griffith. Kansas, 1984.

[60] Miller, Richard B. *Interpretations of Conflict: Ethics, Pacifism, and the Just-War Tradition.* Chicago, 1991.

[61] Ackerman, Peter, and Jack DuVall. *A Force More Powerful: A Century of Nonviolent Conflict.* St. Martin's, 2001. Wehr, Paul, Heidi Burgess, and Guy Burgess, eds. *Justice without Violence.* Rienner, 1994.

[62] Sharp, Gene. *Civilian-Based Defense: A Post-Military Weapons System.* Princeton, 1990.

[63] Peterson, V. Spike, and Anne Sisson Runyan. *Global Gender Issues.* 2nd ed. Westview, 1999. Tickner, J. Ann. *Gendering World Politics: Issues and Approaches in the Post–Cold War Era.* Columbia, 2001. Meyer, Mary K., and Elisabeth Prügl, eds. *Gender Politics in Global Governance.* Rowman & Littlefield, 1999. Steans, Jill. *Gender and International Relations: An Introduction.* Rutgers, 1998. Whitworth, Sandra. *Feminism and International Relations.* St. Martin's, 1994. Tickner, J. Ann. *Gender in International Relations: Feminist Perspectives on Achieving Global Security.* Columbia, 1992.

approach simply assumes male participants when discussing foreign policy decision making, state sovereignty, or the use of military force.

This critique is somewhat complex. Because the vast majority of heads of state, diplomats, and soldiers *are* male, it may be realistic to study them as males. What the feminist critics then ask is that scholars explicitly recognize the gendered nature of their subject (rather than implicitly assuming all actors are male). In this view, our understanding of male actors in IR can be increased by considering how their gender identity affects their views and decision processes. And females also influence IR (more often through nonstate channels than males do)—influences often ignored by realism. Some feel that women scholars tend to be more interested in these roles and effects than are their male colleagues, who largely ignore gender topics. One list of "fifty key thinkers" in IR includes 4 women, 3 of whom it lists as gender scholars, while none of the 46 males are listed as gender scholars.[64] And when a survey in 2005 listed the 25 most influential IR scholars, all 25 were male.[65]

A GUY THING

Feminists from various theoretical traditions agree that the gender makeup of international summits is important. Here, Germany's chancellor looks outnumbered among leaders of the G8 and African states, 2011.

Beyond revealing the hidden assumptions about gender in a field of scholarship, feminist scholars often *challenge traditional concepts of gender* as well. In IR, these traditional concepts revolve around the assumptions that males fight wars and run states, whereas females are basically irrelevant to IR. Such gender roles are based in the broader construction of masculinity as suitable to *public* and political spaces, whereas femininity is associated with the sphere of the *private* and domestic.

Like realists (see p. 43), gender theorists follow a long line of tradition.[66] Not long before Thucydides, the ancient Greek woman poet Sappho wrote love poems to women on the island of Lesbos. Just before Machiavelli, the Italian-born writer Christine de Pisan praised women's abilities to make peace. A century after Hobbes, Mary Wollstonecraft in Britain argued for equal rights for women. And a century before Morgenthau founded American realism, the American Susan B. Anthony worked tirelessly for pacifism, abolitionism, and suffragism.

Beyond a basic agreement that gender is important, there is no such thing as "the feminist approach" to IR but several such approaches—*strands* of scholarship and theory. Although they are interwoven (all paying attention to gender and to the status of women), they often run in different directions. On some core issues, the different strands of feminism have conflicting views, creating interesting debates *within* feminism.

---

[64] Griffiths, Martin. *Fifty Key Thinkers in International Relations*. Routledge, 1999.
[65] Peterson, Susan, Michael J. Tierney, and Daniel Maliniak. Inside the Ivory Tower. *Foreign Policy* 151, Nov./Dec. 2005: 58–64.
[66] Thanks to Francine D'Amico for these comparisons.

One strand, **difference feminism**, focuses on valorizing the feminine—that is, valuing the unique contributions of women *as* women. Difference feminists do not think women do all things as well as men or vice versa. Because of their greater experience with nurturing and human relations, women are seen as potentially more effective than men (on average) in conflict resolution as well as in group decision making. Difference feminists believe there are real differences between the genders that are not just social constructions and cultural indoctrination (although these contribute to gender roles, too). Some difference feminists believe there is a core biological essence to being male or female (sometimes called *essentialism*), but most think women's difference is more culturally than biologically determined. In either case, feminine perspectives create a *standpoint* from which to observe, analyze, and criticize the traditional perspectives on IR.[67] Another strand, **liberal feminism**, rejects these claims as being based on stereotyped gender roles. Liberal feminists see the "essential" differences in men's and women's abilities or perspectives as trivial or nonexistent—men and women are equal. They deplore the exclusion of women from positions of power in IR but do not believe that including women would change the nature of the international system. Liberal feminists seek to include women more often as subjects of study—such as women state leaders, women soldiers, and other women operating outside the traditional gender roles in IR.

A third approach combines feminism with postmodernism, discussed later in this chapter. **Postmodern feminism** tends to reject the assumptions about gender made by both difference and liberal feminists. Where difference feminists consider gender differences important and fixed, and liberal feminists consider those differences trivial, postmodern feminists find them important but arbitrary and flexible.

The Masculinity of Realism

Difference feminism provides a perspective from which to reexamine the core assumptions of realism—especially the assumption of autonomy, from which flow the key realist concepts of sovereignty and anarchy. To realists, the international system consists of autonomous actors (states) that control their own territory and have no right to infringe on another's territory. Some difference feminists have argued that realism emphasizes autonomy and separation because men find separation easier to deal with than interconnection.

This view rests on a psychological theory that boys and girls grow up from a young age with different views of separateness and connection.[68] In this theory, because a child's primary caretaker is almost always female in the early years, girls form their gender identity around the perception of *similarity* with their caretaker (and by extension the environment in which they live), but boys perceive their *difference* from the caretaker. From this experience, boys develop social relations based on individual *autonomy*, but girls' relations are based on *connection*. As a result, women are held to be more likely than men to fear abandonment, whereas men are more likely to fear intimacy.

In *moral* reasoning, according to this theory, boys tend to apply abstract rules and stress individual rights, but girls pay more attention to the concrete contexts of different situations and to the responsibility of group members for each other. In playing *games*, boys

---

[67] Keohane, Robert O. International Relations Theory: Contributions of a Feminist Standpoint. *Millennium* 18 (2), 1989: 245–53.

[68] Gilligan, Carol. *In a Different Voice: Psychological Theory and Women's Development*. Harvard, 1982. Chodorow, Nancy. *The Reproduction of Mothering*. California, 1978.

resolve disputes through arguments about the rules and then keep playing, but girls are more likely to abandon a game rather than argue over the rules and risk the social cohesion of their group. In *social relations*, boys form and dissolve friendships more readily than girls, who are more likely to stick loyally with friends. (The empirical evidence in psychological research for these theorized gender differences is mixed at best.)

Realism, of course, rests on the concept of states as separate, autonomous actors that make and break alliances freely while pursuing their own interests (but not interfering in each other's internal affairs). Such a conception of autonomy parallels the masculine psyche just described. Thus, some feminist scholars find in realism a hidden assumption of masculinity. Furthermore, the sharp distinction that realists draw between international politics (anarchic) and domestic politics (ordered) parallels the distinction in gender roles

ROLE REVERSAL

Feminist scholars emphasize the importance of gender roles in IR, especially the traditional distinction between males in the political-military roles and females in the domestic-family roles. Changing this division could change IR, they think. Here, top U.S. officials attend the UN General Assembly, 2010.

between the public (masculine) and private (feminine) spheres. Thus, realism constructs IR as a man's world.

By contrast, an international system based on *feminine* principles might give greater importance to the interdependence of states than to their autonomy, stressing the responsibility of people to care for each other with less regard for states and borders. In the struggle between the principles of human rights and of sovereignty (noninterference in internal affairs), human rights would receive priority. In the choice of forms of leverage when conflicts arise between states, violence might be less prevalent.

The realist preoccupation with the interstate level of analysis presumes that the logic of war itself is autonomous and can be separated from other social relationships such as economics, domestic politics, sexism, and racism. Difference feminism, however, reveals the *connections* of these phenomena with war. It suggests new avenues for understanding war at the domestic and individual levels of analysis—underlying causes that realists largely ignore.

From this difference-feminist perspective, neoliberalism has gone backward from traditional liberalism, by accepting the realist assumption of separate unitary states as the important actors and downplaying substate and transnational actors including women.[69] Neoliberalism's conception of cooperation as rule-based interactions among autonomous actors also reflects masculinist assumptions.

---

[69] Moghadam, Valentine M. *Globalizing Women: Transnational Feminist Networks*. Johns Hopkins, 2005.

Gender in War and Peace

In addition to its emphasis on autonomy and anarchy, realism stresses military force as the key form of leverage in IR. Here, too, many difference feminists see in realism a hidden assumption of masculinity. They see war as not only a male occupation, but also the quintessentially male occupation. In this view, men are inherently the more warlike gender, and women the more peaceful.[70] Thus, although realism may accurately portray the importance of war and military force in IR as we now know it, this merely reflects the male domination of the international sphere to date—not a necessary, eternal, or inescapable logic of relations among states.[71]

Difference feminists find much evidence to support the idea of war as a masculine pursuit. Anthropologists have found that in all known cultures, males are the primary (and usually the only) combatants in warfare, despite the enormous diversity of those cultures in so many other ways. (Of course, voting and political leadership were also male domains for most of history, yet feminist scholars would hardly call those activities essentially masculine.)

One supposed link between war and masculinity is the male sex hormone testosterone (along with related hormones), which some biologists have connected with aggressive behavior in animals. However, testosterone does not *cause* aggression. Rather, social interactions "feed back" to affect testosterone levels (winners' testosterone levels rise while losers' levels fall). Thus testosterone is a link in a complex system of relationships between the organism and the social environment. Complex behaviors such as aggression and war cannot be said to be biologically *driven* or predetermined, because humanity's most striking biological capability is flexibility. Even some feminist scholars who see gender differences as strictly cultural, and not biological at all, view war as a masculine construction.[72]

Both biologically and anthropologically, no firm evidence connects women's caregiving functions (pregnancy and nursing) with any particular kinds of behavior such as reconciliation or nonviolence—although females have been studied less than males. The role of women varies considerably from one society to another. Although they rarely take part in combat, women sometimes provide logistical support to male warriors and sometimes help drive the men into a war frenzy by dancing, shaming nonparticipating males, and other activities supportive of war. Yet in other cultures, women restrain the men from war or play special roles as mediators in bringing wars to an end.

The idea of women as peacemakers has a long history. In ancient Athens, the (male) playwright Aristophanes speculated about how women might end the unpopular Peloponnesian War with Sparta, then in progress. (His play *Lysistrata* was read in 1,000 locations in 56 countries on March 3, 2003, to protest the coming Iraq War.) In the play, a young woman named Lysistrata organizes the Athenian and Spartan women to withhold sex from the men until the latter stop the war (the women also make off with the war treasury). In short order, the men come to their senses and make peace.[73] Women have formed their own organizations to work for peace on many occasions. In 1852, *Sisterly Voices* was published as a newsletter for women's peace societies. Bertha von Suttner in 1892 persuaded Alfred

---

[70] Woolf, Virginia. *Three Guineas*. Hogarth, 1977 [1938]. Pierson, Ruth Roach. *Women and Peace: Theoretical, Historical and Practical Perspectives*. Croom Helm, 1987. Burguieres, M. K. Feminist Approaches to Peace: Another Step for Peace Studies. *Millennium* 19 (1), 1990: 1–18. Brock-Utne, Birgit. *Educating for Peace: A Feminist Perspective*. Pergamon, 1985. Reardon, Betty. *Sexism and the War System*. Teachers College, 1985.

[71] Goldstein, Joshua S. *War and Gender: How Gender Shapes the War System and Vice Versa*. Cambridge, 2001. Lorentzen, Lois Ann, and Jennifer Turpin, eds. *The Women and War Reader*. New York University, 1998. Elshtain, Jean Bethke, and Sheila Tobias, eds. *Women, Militarism, and War: Essays in History, Politics, and Social Theory*. University Press of America, 1989.

[72] Hartsock, Nancy C. M. Masculinity, Heroism, and the Making of War. In Harris, Adrienne, and Ynestra King, eds. *Rocking the Ship of State: Toward a Feminist Peace Politics*. Westview, 1989, pp. 133–52.

[73] Aristophanes. *Lysistrata*. Edited by Jeffrey Henderson. Oxford, 1987.

Nobel to create the Nobel Peace Prize (which Suttner won in 1905). During World War I, in 1915, Jane Addams and other feminists convened an international women's peace conference at The Hague. They founded the Women's Peace Party (now called the Women's International League for Peace and Freedom).[74] After World War I, the *suffrage* movement won the right for women to vote. Difference feminists thought that women would vote for peace and against war, changing the nature of foreign policy, but women generally voted as their husbands did. Similarly, decades later when women participated in liberation struggles against colonialism in the global South, some feminists thought such participation would change foreign policies in the newly independent countries, but in general such changes did not materialize (partly because women were often pushed aside from political power after the revolution).

Nonetheless, U.S. public opinion on foreign policy issues since the 1930s partially vindicates difference feminists. A **gender gap** in polls shows that women are about ten percentage points lower than men on average in their support for military actions. This gender gap shrinks, however, when broad consensus on a military action exists, as when U.S. forces attacked terrorist supporters in Afghanistan in late 2001.

Meanwhile, feminists in recent decades have continued to organize women's peace organizations.[75] In the 1980s, Women's Action for Nuclear Disarmament (WAND) opposed the nuclear arms buildup, and women encamped for years at Britain's Greenham Common air base. In 1995, the UN-sponsored Beijing conference on women brought together women activists from around the world, and helped deepen feminists' engagement with global issues such as North-South inequality.

WOMAN POWER

Difference feminists see women as inherently less warlike than men and more adept at making peace because of their potential and actual experiences as mothers. In this view, women play distinct roles in wartime and also have distinct needs. During the long civil war in Liberia in the 1990s, women organized mass protests for peace and insisted the male faction leaders end the war. Their leader, Leymah Gbowee, shared the Nobel Peace Prize in 2011.

In 2000, the UN Security Council passed Resolution 1325, mandating greater inclusion of women and attention to gender in UN peacekeeping and reconstruction. But in several locations, UN peacekeepers participated in local prostitution, rape, and even sex trafficking. In 2004, Secretary-General Annan called "shameful" the reported behavior of UN troops from several countries serving in Democratic Congo. Investigators there found hundreds of cases of sexual crimes by UN personnel.

As a result of Resolution 1325, "gender advisors" have begun to accompany international peacekeeping and relief operations to provide practical advice on more effective operations in the context of local cultures' gender relations. For example, the head of a group of Swedish men sent to build a bridge in Sri Lanka initially said, "Our task is to build a bridge, we don't

[74] Degen, Marie Louise. *The History of the Woman's Peace Party*. Burt Franklin Reprints, 1974 [1939].
[75] Swerdlow, Amy. Pure Milk, Not Poison: Women Strike for Peace and the Test Ban Treaty of 1963. In Harris and King, eds. *Rocking the Ship of State* (see footnote 72 in this chapter), pp. 225–37. Stephenson, Carolyn M. Feminism, Pacifism, Nationalism, and the United Nations Decade for Women. In Stiehm, Judith, ed. *Women and Men's Wars*. Oxford: Pergamon, 1983, pp. 341–48. Kirk, Gwyn. Our Greenham Common: Feminism and Nonviolence. In Harris and King, eds. *Rocking the Ship of State* (see footnote 72 in this chapter), pp. 115–30.

need to worry about gender issues." When asked how it would be used, he replied, "By car mostly," but when asked, "The women too?" he said, "No, they'll probably walk." As a result of this gender perspective, the bridge was redesigned to include a pedestrian walkway.[76]

Through these various actions, difference feminists began developing a feminist practice of international relations that could provide an alternative to the masculine practice of realism. The motto of the UN Educational, Scientific, and Cultural Organization (UNESCO) is, "Since war begins in the minds of men, it is in the minds of men that the foundations for peace should be sought." For difference feminists, war does indeed begin in the minds of men, but the foundations for peace would better be sought in the minds of women.

Women in IR

Liberal feminists are skeptical of difference-feminist critiques of realism. They believe that when women are allowed to participate in IR, they play the game basically the same way men do, with similar results. They think that women can practice realism—based on autonomy, sovereignty, anarchy, territory, military force, and all the rest—just as well as men can. Liberal feminists therefore tend to reject the critique of realism as masculine. (In practice, many feminist scholars draw on both difference feminists' and liberal feminists' views in various proportions.)[77]

Liberal feminism focuses on the integration of women into the overwhelmingly male preserves of foreign policy making and the military. In most states, these occupations are typically at least 90 percent male. For instance, in 1995 the world's diplomatic delegations to the UN General Assembly were 80 percent male overall, and the heads of those delegations were 97 percent male. The U.S. military, with one of the highest proportions of women anywhere in the world or in history, is still 85 percent male.[78] For liberal feminists, the main effect of this gender imbalance on the nature of IR—that is, apart from effects on the status of women—is to waste talent. Liberal feminists think that women have the same capabilities as men, so the inclusion of women in traditionally male occupations (from state leader to foot soldier) would bring additional capable individuals into those areas. Gender equality would thus increase national capabilities by giving the state a better overall pool of diplomats, generals, soldiers, and politicians.

In support of their argument that, on average, women handle power just as men do, liberal feminists point to the many examples of women who have served in such positions. No distinctly feminine feature of their behavior in office distinguishes these leaders from their male counterparts. Rather, they have been diverse in character and policy. Of course, women in traditionally male roles may have been selected (or self-selected) on the basis of their suitability to such roles: they may not act the way "average" women would act. Still, they do show that individuals cannot be judged accurately using group characteristics alone.

Female state leaders do not appear to be any more peaceful, or any less committed to state sovereignty and territorial integrity, than are male leaders (see Table 3.1). Some have even suggested that women in power tend to be more warlike to compensate for being females in traditionally male roles. Overall, women state leaders, like men, seem capable of leading in war or in peace as circumstances demand.[79]

In the U.S. Congress, it is hard to compare men's and women's voting records on foreign policy issues because there have been so few women. The U.S. Senate, which

[76] Genderforce: Sweden. *From Words to Action*. Booklet, circa 2006.

[77] Kelly, Rita Mae, et al., eds. *Gender, Globalization, and Democratization*. Rowman & Littlefield, 2001.

[78] Seager, Joni. *The Penguin Atlas of Women in the World*. Penguin, 2003.

[79] D'Amico, Francine, and Peter R. Beckman, eds. *Women in World Politics: An Introduction*. Bergin & Garvey, 1995. Nelson, Barbara J., and Najma Chowdhury, eds. *Women and Politics Worldwide*. Yale, 1994. Genovese, Michael A., ed. *Women as National Leaders: The Political Performance of Women as Heads of Government*. Sage, 1993. McGlen, Nancy E., and Meredith Reid Sarkees. *Women in Foreign Policy: The Insiders*. Routledge, 1993.

TABLE 3.1 Notable Women State Leaders of Recent Decades

Leader	Country	Record in Office	Time Frame
Rosa Otunbayeva	Kyrgyz Republic	First woman president of former Communist Central Asian state. Calmed ethnic tensions.	2010
Sheikh Hasina Wajed	Bangladesh	Attempting to consolidate democratic transition	2008–
Angela Merkel	Germany	Only current woman leader of a great power; put limits on German troops with NATO forces in Afghanistan	2005–
Ellen Johnson-Sirleaf	Liberia	Struggling to keep country calm after civil war	2006–
Margaret Thatcher	Britain	First woman to lead a great power in a century; went to war to recover Falkland Islands from Argentina	1982
Indira Gandhi	India	Led war against Pakistan	1971
Golda Meir	Israel	Led war against Egypt and Syria	1973
Benazir Bhutto	Pakistan	Struggled to control own military	late 1980s
Corazon Aquino	Philippines	Struggled to control own military	late 1980s
Tansu Çiller	Turkey	Led a harsh war to suppress Kurdish rebels	mid-1990s
Violetta Chamorro	Nicaragua	Kept the peace between factions after civil war	1980s
Chandrika Kumaratunga	Sri Lanka	Tried to make peace with separatists, but returned to war	1990s and since
Megawati Sukarnoputri	Indonesia	Struggled to keep country calm; lost re-election bid	2000s

Note: Other states, such as Finland, Norway, New Zealand, Denmark, Thailand, and Iceland, have had women leaders when war and peace were not major political issues in those countries.

approves treaties and foreign policy appointments, was 98–99 percent male until 1992 (but dropped to 84 percent male in 2007). Women never chaired the key foreign policy committees (Armed Services and Foreign Relations/International Relations) in the Senate or House until 2011—although Rep. Nancy Pelosi became the first woman Speaker of the House, third in line to the presidency, in 2007.

Globally, the number of women serving in legislatures is increasing. A 2008 UN report found that women comprised over 18 percent of members of parliaments across the world, up from 7 percent in 1995. Some nations set aside a certain number of seats for females in parliament.[80] Yet, female candidates often capture more seats than are set aside. In Rwanda, for example, women make up over 50 percent of the lower house of parliament, even though the law requires only 30 percent female representation. Although more women find themselves in politics, the UN report pointed to global shortcomings as well. For example, even though women are increasingly represented in legislatures, they do not hold correspondingly equal numbers in political party leadership positions.

Liberal feminists also believe that women soldiers, like women politicians, have a range of skills and abilities comparable to men's. Again, the main effect of including more women would be to improve the overall quality of military forces.[81] About 200,000 women soldiers serve in the U.S. military (15 percent of the total) and more than 1 million women are veterans. Women perform well in a variety of military roles, including logistical and

[80] Caul, Miki. Political Parties and the Adoption of Candidate Gender Quotas: A Cross-National Analysis. *Journal of Politics* 63 (4), 2003: 1214–29. Tripp, Aili M., and Alice Kang. The Global Impact of Quotas. *Comparative Political Studies* 41 (3), 2008: 338–61.

[81] De Pauw, Linda Grant. *Battle Cries and Lullabies: Women in War from Prehistory to the Present*. Oklahoma, 1998. Francke, Linda Bird. *Ground Zero: The Gender Wars in the Military*. Simon & Schuster, 1997. Stiehm, Judith Hicks, ed. *It's Our Military, Too!* Temple, 1996. Fraser, Antonia. *The Warrior Queens*. Knopf, 1989. Addis, Elisabetta, Valerie E. Russo, and Lorenza Ebesta, eds. *Women Soldiers: Images and Realities*. St. Martin's, 1994. Isaksson, Eva, ed. *Women and the Military System*. St. Martin's, 1988.

medical support, training, and command. Women have also had success in other countries that have allowed them into the military (or, in a few cases, drafted them).

Although women have served with distinction in military forces, they have been excluded from combat roles in most of those forces. In some countries, military women are limited to traditional female roles such as nurses and typists. Even when women may hold nontraditional positions such as mechanics and pilots (as in the United States), most women remain in the traditional roles. And certain jobs still remain off-limits; for instance, women cannot serve in U.S. combat infantry units. (U.S. women have, however, played vital roles in combat support in Iraq and Afghanistan.) Thus relatively few cases exist to judge women's abilities in combat.

Those cases include historical examples of individual women who served in combat (sometimes disguised as men, sometimes not). In the 15th century, Joan of Arc rallied French soldiers to defeat England, turning the tide of the Hundred Years' War. (The English burned her at the stake as a witch after capturing her.) Women have often participated in combat in rebel forces fighting guerrilla wars in Vietnam, Nicaragua, and elsewhere, as well as in terrorist or paramilitary units in countries such as Peru, Germany, Italy, and Palestine. Women in Eritrea's guerrilla forces became part of that country's regular army after independence and then served in frontline combat units during Eritrea and Ethiopia's trench warfare in the late 1990s.

In recent years, U.S. women soldiers have found themselves in combat (today's mobile tactics and fluid front lines make it hard to separate combat from support roles). During the 1991 Gulf War, tens of thousands of U.S. women served, 13 were killed, and 2 were captured as prisoners of war. In the late 1990s, women began serving on some U.S. combat ships and airplanes, but not in ground combat units. In the 2003 Iraq War, women flew all types of airplanes and helicopters, and one woman was in the first group of U.S. POWs captured early in the war. During the subsequent years of war in Iraq, U.S.

COMBAT HERO

Women soldiers have performed as well as men in military tasks, as predicted by liberal feminists. But in state armies, women are barred from virtually all infantry combat units worldwide. Guerrilla forces more often include women, and female U.S. military police in Iraq often participate in fighting. Here, in 2005, a sergeant from the Kentucky National Guard receives the silver star for heroism in combat after fighting off an ambush in Iraq.

---

[82] Katzenstein, Mary Fainsod, and Judith Reppy, eds. *Beyond Zero Tolerance: Discrimination in Military Culture*. Rowman & Littlefield, 1999.

[83] Giles, Wenona, and Jennifer Hyndman, eds. *Sites of Violence: Gender and Conflict Zones*. California, 2004. Carpenter, R. Charli. *Innocent Women and Children: Gender, Norms, and the Protection of Civilians*. Ashgate, 2006. Enloe, Cynthia. *Maneuvers: The International Politics of Militarizing Women's Lives*. California, 2000.

women military police have acquitted themselves well in numerous firefights. All these cases suggest that (at least some) women are able to hold their own in combat.

The main reason that military forces exclude women from combat seems to be fear about what effect their presence might have on the male soldiers, whose discipline and loyalty have traditionally been thought to depend on male bonding and single-minded focus. Liberal feminists reject such arguments and contend that group bonding in military units does not depend on gender segregation. (After all, similar rationales were once given for racial segregation in U.S. military forces.)[82] The effect of war on noncombatant women has also received growing attention.[83] Attacks on women in Algeria, Rwanda, Bosnia, Afghanistan, Democratic Congo, and Sudan pointed to a possible new trend toward women as military targets. Systematic rape was used as a terror tactic in Bosnia and Rwanda, and the Japanese army in World War II operated an international network of sex slaves known as "comfort women." Rape has long been treated as a normal if regrettable by-product of war, but recently certain instances of rape were declared war crimes (see p. 275).

In sum, liberal feminists reject the argument that women bring uniquely feminine assets or liabilities to foreign and military affairs. They do not critique realism as essentially masculine in nature but do criticize state practices that exclude women from participation in international politics and war.

Difference Feminism versus Liberal Feminism?

The arguments of difference feminists and liberal feminists may seem totally at odds. Difference feminists argue that realism reflects a masculine perception of social relations, whereas liberal feminists think that women can be just as realist as men. Liberal feminists believe that female participation in foreign policy and the military will enhance state capabilities, but difference feminists think women's unique abilities can be put to better use in transforming (feminizing) the entire system of international relations rather than in trying to play men's games.

The evidence in favor of both positions can be reconciled to some extent by bearing in mind that the character and ability of an individual are not the same as that of his or her group. Rather, the qualities of individuals follow a bell curve distribution, with many people clustered in the middle and fewer people very high or low on a given capability.

Gender differences posited by difference feminists mean that one bell curve is shifted from the other, even though the two may still overlap quite a bit (see Figure 3.3). To take a simple example, a few women are physically larger than almost all men, and a few men are smaller than almost all women. But on average, men are somewhat larger than women. On various dimensions of capability, the women's curve is above or below the men's on average, but there is still much overlap.

Liberal feminist arguments emphasize the overlap of the two bell curves. They say that individual women—*most* women on most relevant dimensions—are well within the male curve and thus can perform equally with the men. Indeed, women in nontraditional gender roles may well perform better than their male counterparts, because presumably women who self-select into such roles (such as joining the military) are near the high end of the female bell curve, whereas the men are closer to the middle of the male curve (because more of them join). Similarly, women who become state leaders are presumably more adept at foreign policy making than most women (or men), because political processes tend to select women at the high end of the curve in terms of their affinity for realism.

Difference feminists are more interested in the shift in the two bell curves, not their overlap. On average, in this perspective, women tend to see international relations in a somewhat different way than men do. So although *individuals* selected to participate in foreign policy and the military may not differ from their male counterparts, women as a group differ. Women voters display different concerns regarding IR than men (as shown by the gender gap in opinion polls and voting patterns).

FIGURE 3.3 Overlapping Bell Curves

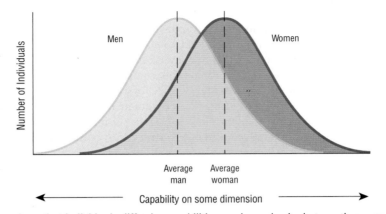

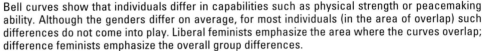

Bell curves show that individuals differ in capabilities such as physical strength or peacemaking ability. Although the genders differ on average, for most individuals (in the area of overlap) such differences do not come into play. Liberal feminists emphasize the area where the curves overlap; difference feminists emphasize the overall group differences.

By this logic, then, profound differences in IR—and a shift away from the utility of realism in explaining state behavior—would occur only if many women participated in key foreign policy positions. That is, a *few* women politicians or women soldiers do not change the masculine foundations of IR. Women foreign policy makers today are surrounded by males (advisors, military officers, political leaders, and foreign state leaders). But a world in which *most* politicians or soldiers were female might be a different story. Then, instead of the selection of women for their ability to fit into men's games, the rules of the game might themselves change to reflect the fact that "average" women would be the main actors in the traditionally important IR roles. Of course, these theories of difference feminists have never been tested, because women have never attained predominance in foreign policy making in any country—much less in the international system as a whole.

In addition to the liberal and difference strands of feminism, the third strand, postmodern feminism, is connected with the rise of postmodernism in the social sciences.

Postmodern Feminism

One line of criticism directed at realism combines feminism and postmodernism.[84] *Postmodern feminism* seeks to deconstruct realism with the specific aim of uncovering the pervasive hidden influences of gender in IR while showing how arbitrary the construction of gender roles is. Feminist postmodernists agree with difference feminists that realism carries hidden meanings about gender roles but deny that there is any fixed inherent meaning in either male or female genders. Rather, feminist postmodernists look at the interplay of gender and power in a more open-ended way. Postmodern feminists criticize liberal feminists for trying merely to integrate women into traditional structures of war and foreign policy. They criticize difference feminists as well, for glorifying traditional feminine virtues.

In studying war, postmodern feminists have challenged the archetypes of the (male) "just warrior" and the (female) "beautiful soul." They argue that women are not just passive

---

[84] Peterson, V. Spike, ed. *Gendered States: Feminist (Re)Visions of International Relations Theory.* Rienner, 1992. Sylvester, Christine. *Feminist Theory and International Relations in a Postmodern Era.* Cambridge, 1994.

bystanders or victims in war, but active participants in a system of warfare tied to both genders. Women act not only as nurses and journalists at the "front" but as mothers, wives, and girlfriends on the "home front."[85] These scholars believe that stories of military forces should not omit the roles of prostitutes at military bases, nor should stories of diplomacy omit the roles of diplomats' wives.[86]

Postmodern feminists reject not only realism but also some of the alternative approaches that emphasize the protection of women and other noncombatants. Just-war doctrine (see pp. 263–264) is considered too abstract—a set of concepts and rules that does not do justice to the richness of each historical context and the varied roles of individual men and women within it.[87]

Postmodern feminists have tried to deconstruct the language of realism, especially when it reflects influences of gender and sex. For instance, the first atomic bombs had male gender (they were named "Fat Man" and "Little Boy"); the coded telegram informing Washington, D.C., that the first hydrogen bomb had worked said simply, "It's a boy" (presumably being born a girl would have indicated a failure). The plane that dropped the atomic bomb on Hiroshima (the *Enola Gay*) had female gender; it was named after the pilot's mother. Likewise the French atom-bomb test sites in the South Pacific were all given women's names.[88] Similarly, pilots have pasted pinup photos of nude women onto conventional bombs before dropping them. In all these cases, postmodern feminists would note that the feminine gender of vehicles, targets, or decorations amplifies the masculinity of the weapon itself.

These efforts find sex and gender throughout the subtext of realism. For example, the terms *power* and *potency* refer to both state capability and male virility. Military force depends on phallic objects—weapons designed to shoot projectiles, penetrate targets, and explode. In basic training, men chant: "This is my rifle [holding up rifle], this is my gun [pointing to crotch]; one's for killing, the other's for fun."[89] Nuclear weapons are also repeatedly spoken of in sexual terms, perhaps due to their great "potency." Female models are hired to market tanks, helicopter missiles, and other "potent" weapons to male procurement officers at international military trade shows.[90] The phallic character of weapons has seemingly persisted even as technology has evolved from spears to guns to missiles.[91]

All three strands of feminist theories provide explanations that often differ from both realist and liberal theories. In the case of response to aggression, feminists might call attention to the importance of gender roles such as the need for state leaders to prove their manhood by standing up to the bad guys. This is connected with the male role as protector of the orderly domestic sphere (home, family, country) against the dangerous and anarchic outside world. Since 2001, gender roles have become increasingly visible on both sides of the "war on terror," with both women's positions in society and men's concepts of masculinity becoming contested territory between the West and armed Islamic groups. Traditional theories of IR that ignore these issues may lack explanatory power as a result.

---

[85] Elshtain, Jean Bethke. *Women and War.* 2nd ed. Chicago, 1995. Braybon, Gail, and Penny Summerfield. *Out of the Cage: Women's Experiences in Two World Wars.* Pandora, 1987.

[86] Enloe, Cynthia. *Bananas, Beaches, and Bases: Making Feminist Sense of International Politics.* California, 1989. Pettman, Jan Jindy. *Worlding Women: A Feminist International Politics.* Routledge, 1996. Moon, Katherine H. S. *Sex among Allies: Military Prostitution in U.S.-Korea Relations.* Columbia, 1997.

[87] Elshtain, *Women and War* (see footnote 85 in this chapter). Ruddick, Sara. *Maternal Thinking: Towards a Politics of Peace.* Women's Press, 1989.

[88] Cohn, Carol. Sex and Death in the Rational World of Defense Intellectuals. *Signs* 12 (4), 1987: 687–718.

[89] Dyer, Gwynne. *War.* Crown, 1985.

[90] Center for Defense Information [Washington, DC]. Weapons Bazaar [slide show]. 1985.

[91] Trexler, Richard C. *Sex and Conquest: Gendered Violence, Political Order, and the European Conquest of the Americas.* Cornell, 1995.

✓•–⌈ **Study**
and **Review**
the **Post-Test &**
Chapter Exam
at **mypoliscilab.com**

Whether states' interests reflect fixed assumptions about power and well-being, or are constructed by states and substate actors based on ideas and social interactions, those interests do sometimes conflict with those of other states. Such conflicts are the subject of the next chapter.

CHAPTER REVIEW

SUMMARY

- The central claims of realism—regarding anarchy, state actors, rationality, and the utility of military force—have been challenged on a variety of grounds.

- Liberals dispute the realist notion that narrow self-interest is more rational than mutually beneficial cooperation.

- Reciprocity can be an effective strategy for reaching cooperation in ongoing relationships but carries a danger of turning into runaway hostility or arms races.

- Neoliberalism argues that even in an anarchic system of autonomous rational states, cooperation can emerge through the building of norms, regimes, and institutions.

- Collective goods are benefits received by all members of a group regardless of their individual contribution. Shared norms and rules are important in getting members to pay for collective goods.

- International regimes—convergent expectations of state leaders about the rules for issue areas in IR—help provide stability in the absence of a world government.

- Hegemonic stability theory suggests that the holding of predominant power by one state lends stability to international relations and helps create regimes.

- In a collective security arrangement, a group of states agrees to respond together to aggression by any participating state; the UN and other IGOs perform this function.

- Democracies have historically fought as many wars as authoritarian states, but democracies have almost never fought wars against other democracies. This is called the democratic peace.

- Constructivists reject realist assumptions about state interests, tracing those interests in part to social interactions and norms.

- Postmodern critics reject the entire framework and language of realism, with its unitary state actors. Postmodernists argue that no simple categories can capture the multiple realities experienced by participants in IR.

- Marxists view international relations, including global North-South relations, in terms of a struggle between economic classes (especially workers and owners) that have different roles in society and different access to power.

- Peace studies programs are interdisciplinary and seek to broaden the study of international security to include social and economic factors ignored by realism.

- For scholars in peace studies, militarism in many cultures contributes to states' propensity to resort to force in international bargaining.

- Feminist scholars of IR agree that gender is important in understanding IR but diverge into several strands regarding their conception of the role of gender.

- Difference feminists argue that men are more warlike on average than women. They believe that although individual women participants (such as state leaders) may not reflect this difference, the participation of large numbers of women would make the international system more peaceful.

- Liberal feminists disagree that women have substantially different capabilities or tendencies as participants in IR. They argue that women are equivalent to men in virtually all IR roles. As evidence, liberal feminists point to historical and present-day women leaders and women soldiers.

- Postmodern feminists seek to uncover gender-related subtexts implicit in realist discourse, including sexual themes connected with the concept of power.

KEY TERMS

interdependence   87
neoliberal   88
international regime   90
collective security   92
democratic peace   95
constructivism   97
postmodernism   102
subtext   103

economic classes   103
Marxism   104
conflict resolution   106
mediation   106
militarism   107
positive peace   108
world government   109
peace movements   109

difference feminism   112
liberal feminism   112
postmodern feminism   112
gender gap   115

CRITICAL THINKING QUESTIONS

1. U.S.-Canadian relations seem better explained by liberal institutionalism than by realism. What other (one or more) interstate relationships have this quality? Show how the contrasting tenets of realism and liberal institutionalism each applies to the relationship(s).

2. Inasmuch as democracies almost never fight wars against each other, do existing democracies have a national security interest in seeing democratization spread to China and other authoritarian states? If so, how can that interest be reconciled with the long-standing norm of noninterference in the internal affairs of other sovereign states?

3. Can you think of a case in which a state's actions clearly followed a constructed identity rather than objective national interests? Where did the key ideas in that identity originate and how did they come to influence the state's actions?

4. Would IR operate differently if most leaders of states were women? What would the differences be? What evidence (beyond gender stereotypes) supports your answer?

5. In what ways do the explanations of IR events change if women are considered primary players rather than peripheral ones? Which women, in which roles, would you consider important?

Legislative Quotas for Women: An Effective Tool for Equality?

Overview

Many countries now use gender quotas when electing legislatures. This is especially true of new democracies in the developing world. As of 2008, 59 countries legally require women to hold some number of seats in at least one house of the national legislature, and 33 countries require women's representation at the regional governmental level. The requirements range from a low of 2 percent of seats in Bangladesh (which also elected a woman to be prime minister in 2009), to nearly 50 percent of seats of the lower house in Rwanda.

These quotas vary not only by the number of seats reserved for women, but also by their implementation. Some countries have amended their constitutions to require more equal representation. Other countries pass laws (which are easier to change at a later time than a constitution) to carve out a minimum number of legislative seats for women, while still other countries place the burden on political parties. In these latter cases, parties must nominate a certain percentage of women to run in elections. This method does not guarantee seats to women (since they could lose the election), but does guarantee an opportunity to hold a seat.

This growing phenomenon of gender quotas has often been encouraged by Western states (especially Europe) and human rights organizations. Should these quotas be encouraged (or even required) by Western states that assist with democratization? Do these quotas help or hurt the goal of female equality in the developing world?

Legislative Quotas Are Important for Equality and Development

Equal representation is important for democratic government. Women make up half the population of most countries. They should thus have an equal say in the political process. A healthy democracy demands that all citizens feel invested in the political process.

Women will face discrimination and slower political acceptance without quotas. In the United States and Europe, despite having the vote, it took years for women to be represented in significant numbers in legislatures. There is no reason to expect the developing world to be different. Quotas will speed the acceptance of women in the political world, giving them more of a say on matters of public policy.

Women's political empowerment will help economic development. Studies have shown that the empowerment of women can accelerate economic growth in the developing world (see Chapter 12). Quotas can accelerate the pace of that empowerment. Moreover, the costs of economic reform often fall disproportionately on women. Giving women more of a say in how that reform takes places is important.

Legislative Quotas Will Not Help Equality and Are Undemocratic

Quotas could create animosity toward women. Reserving seats for women in legislatures risks a backlash against women's rights. Other groups (ethnic, religious, etc.) may push for quotas as well, creating a hostile political environment. The result could be political instability as various groups press their case for legally protected seats in the legislature.

Quotas are undemocratic. The ideal of democracy is to allow anyone to serve as a representative regardless of race, gender, ethnicity, or any other personal quality. By their very nature, gender-based quotas violate this idea, reserving certain seats for one group based on a personal quality irrespective of that person's qualifications.

Quotas achieve a gender equality that is Western-oriented in nature. The idea of individual rights is a Western-oriented concept of human rights. Rather than encouraging gender quotas, other policies should be promoted that are more compatible with local political culture.

Questions

- Should developing countries be encouraged to use gender quotas to bring more women into the political process? Does this practice violate the idea of democratic representation? Would a legislature made up of predominantly men also violate the idea of democratic representation?

- Do you expect similar or different policies coming from a legislature with significant female representation? Recall the views of liberal and difference feminism. What would proponents of those theories predict?

- What might be other ways to encourage female participation in the political process aside from legislative quotas? Are such steps necessary only in countries with no history of democracy or in older, established democracies as well?

For Further Reading

Irving, Helen. *Gender and the Constitution: Equity and Agency in Comparative Constitutional Design.* Cambridge, 2008.

Hartmann, Heidi. *Gendering Politics and Policy: Recent Developments in Europe, Latin America, and the United States.* Routledge, 2006.

Tremblay, Manon. *Women and Legislative Representation: Electoral Systems, Political Parties, and Sex Quotas.* Palgrave, 2008.

Goetz, Anne Marie. *Governing Women: Women's Political Effectiveness in Contexts of Democratization and Governance Reform.* Routledge, 2008.

CHAPTER 4

Foreign Policy

U.S. officials watch Osama bin Laden raid, 2011.

Making Foreign Policy

Models of Decision Making

The foreign policy process is a process of *decision making*. States take actions because people in governments—*decision makers*—choose those actions.[1] Decision making is a *steering* process in which adjustments are made as a result of feedback from the outside world. Decisions are carried out by actions taken to change the world, and then information from the world is monitored to evaluate the effects of these actions. These evaluations—along with information about other, independent changes in the environment—go into the next round of decisions (see Figure 4.1).

A common starting point for studying the decision-making process is the **rational model**.[2] In this model, decision makers set goals, evaluate their relative importance, calculate the costs and benefits of each possible course of action, then choose the one with the highest benefits and lowest costs (see Figure 4.2).

The choice may be complicated by *uncertainty* about the costs and benefits of various actions. In such cases, decision makers must attach probabilities to each possible outcome of an action. For example, will pressuring a rival state to give ground in peace talks work or backfire? Some decision makers are relatively *accepting of risk*, whereas others are *averse to risk*. These factors affect the importance that decision makers place on various alternative outcomes that could result from an action.

Of course, one may believe decision makers are rational, but not accept the realist assumption that states may be treated as unitary actors. Governments are made up of individuals, who may rationally pursue their goals. Yet, the goals of different individuals involved in making a decision may diverge, as may the goals of different state agencies. For example, the U.S. secretary of state may have a different goal than the secretary of

Read and **Listen** to **Chapter 4** at **mypoliscilab.com**

Study and **Review** the **Pre-Test & Flashcards** at **mypoliscilab.com**

FIGURE 4.1 Decision Making as Steering

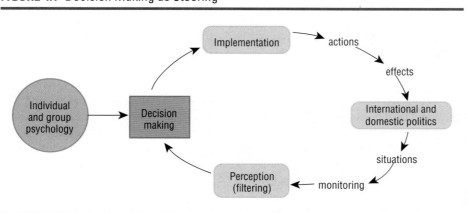

[1] Stein, Janice Gross. Psychological Explanations of International Conflict. In Carlsnaes, Walter, Thomas Risse, and Beth A. Simmons, eds. *Handbook of International Relations*. Sage, 2002, pp. 292–308. Snyder, Richard C., H. W. Bruck, and Burton Sapin. *Foreign Policy Decision Making (Revisited)*. Palgrave, 2002.

[2] The rational model, along with the organizational process and bureaucratic politics models discussed later, derives from Graham Allison; see Allison, Graham T., and Philip Zelikow. *Essence of Decision: Explaining the Cuban Missile Crisis*. 2nd ed. Longman, 1999. Bernstein, Barton J. Understanding Decisionmaking, U.S. Foreign Policy and the Cuban Missile Crisis. *International Security* 25 (1), 2000: 134–64.

FIGURE 4.2 Rational Model of Decision Making

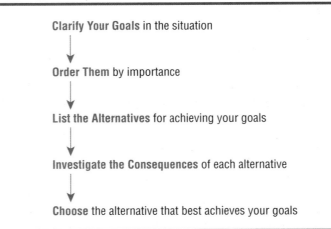

Clarify Your Goals in the situation

↓

Order Them by importance

↓

List the Alternatives for achieving your goals

↓

Investigate the Consequences of each alternative

↓

Choose the alternative that best achieves your goals

Watch
the **Video**
**"The New
European Union"**
on **mypoliscilab.com**

Explore
the **Simulation**
**"Foreign Policy:
You Are the President"**
on **mypoliscilab.com**

defense, just as the Central Intelligence Agency may view a situation differently than the National Security Council does. The rational model of decision making is somewhat complicated by uncertainty and the multiple goals of decision makers. Thus, the rational model may imply that decision making is simpler than is actually the case.

An alternative to the rational model of decision making is the **organizational process model**. In this model, foreign policy decision makers generally skip the labor-intensive process of identifying goals and alternative actions, relying instead for most decisions on standardized responses or *standard operating procedures*. For example, the U.S. State Department every day receives more than a thousand reports or inquiries from its embassies around the world and sends out more than a thousand instructions or responses to those embassies. Most of those cables are never seen by the top decision makers (the secretary of state or the president); instead, they are handled by low-level decision makers who apply general principles—or who simply try to make the least controversial, most standardized decision. These low-level decisions may not even reflect the high-level policies adopted by top leaders, but rather have a life of their own. The organizational process model implies that much of foreign policy results from "management by muddling through."[3]

Another alternative to the rational model is the **government bargaining** (or *bureaucratic politics*) **model**, in which foreign policy decisions result from the bargaining process among various government agencies with somewhat divergent interests in the outcome.[4] In 1992, the Japanese government had to decide whether to allow sushi from California to be imported—a weakening of Japan's traditional ban on importing rice (to maintain self-sufficiency in its staple food). The Japanese Agriculture Ministry, with an interest in the well-being of Japanese farmers, opposed the imports. The Foreign Ministry, with an interest in smooth relations with the United States, wanted to allow the imports. The final decision to allow imported sushi resulted from the tug-of-war between the

---

[3] Avant, Deborah D. *Political Institutions and Military Change: Lessons from Peripheral Wars*. Cornell, 1995.
[4] Welch, David A. The Organizational Process and Bureaucratic Politics Paradigms: Retrospect and Prospect. *International Security* 17 (2), 1992: 112–46. Christiansen, Eben J., and Steven B. Redd. Bureaucrats Versus the Ballot Box in Foreign Policy Decision Making: An Experimental Analysis of the Bureaucratic Politics Model and Poliheuristic Theory. *Journal of Conflict Resolution* 48 (1), 2004: 69–90.

ministries. Thus, according to the government bargaining model, foreign policy decisions reflect (a mix of) the interests of state agencies.

Individual Decision Makers

Every international event is the result, intended or unintended, of decisions made by individuals. IR does not just happen. President Harry Truman, who decided to drop U.S. nuclear bombs on two Japanese cities in 1945, had a sign on his desk: "The buck stops here." As leader of the world's greatest power, he had nobody to pass the buck to. If he chose to use the bomb (as he did), more than 100,000 civilians would die. If he chose not to, the war might drag on for months with tens of thousands of U.S. casualties. Truman had to choose. Some people applaud his decision; others condemn it. But for better or worse, Truman as an individual had to decide, and to take responsibility for the consequences. Similarly, the decisions of individual citizens, although they may not seem important when taken one by one, create the great forces of world history.

The study of individual decision making revolves around the question of rationality. To what extent are national leaders (or citizens) able to make rational decisions in the national interest—if indeed such an interest can be defined—and thus to conform to a realist view of IR? Individual rationality is not equivalent to state rationality: states might filter individuals' irrational decisions so as to arrive at rational choices, or states might distort individually rational decisions and end up with irrational state choices. But realists tend to assume that both states and individuals are rational and that the goals or interests of states correlate with those of leaders.

The most simplified rational-actor models assume that interests are the same from one actor to another. If this were so, individuals could be substituted for each other in various roles without changing history very much. And states would all behave similarly to each other (or rather, the differences between them would reflect different resources and geography, not differences in the nature of national interests). This assumption is at best a great oversimplification;[5] individual decisions reflect the *values* and *beliefs* of the decision maker.

Individual decision makers not only have differing values and beliefs, but also have unique personalities—their personal experiences, intellectual capabilities, and personal styles of making decisions. Some IR scholars study individual psychology to understand how personality affects decision making. Psychoanalytic approaches hold that personalities reflect the subconscious influences of childhood experiences. For instance, Bill Clinton drew much criticism in his early years as president for a foreign policy that seemed to zigzag. A notable Clinton personality trait was his readiness to compromise. Clinton himself has noted that his experience of growing up with a violent, alcoholic stepfather shaped him into a "peacemaker, always trying to minimize the disruption."[6]

Beyond individual *idiosyncrasies* in goals or decision-making processes, individual decision making diverges from the rational model in at least three *systematic* ways. First, decision makers suffer from **misperceptions** and **selective perceptions** (taking in only some kinds of information) when they compile information on the likely consequences of their choices.[7] Decision-making processes must reduce and filter the incoming information on which a decision is based; the problem is that such filtration often is biased. **Information screens** are subconscious filters through which people put the information coming in about the world around them. Often they simply ignore any information that does not fit

---

[5] Farnham, Barbara. *Roosevelt and the Munich Crisis: A Study of Political Decision-Making.* Princeton, 1997.

[6] Collins, Nancy. A Legacy of Strength and Love [interview with President Clinton]. *Good Housekeeping* 221 (5), 1995: 113–15.

[7] Jervis, Robert. *Perception and Misperception in International Politics.* Princeton, 1976.

MADMAN?

Foreign policies often deviate from rationality as a result of the misperceptions and biases of decision makers and populations. Here, South Korea's president meets the reclusive and eccentric late dictator of North Korea, Kim Jong Il, in 2007 as international negotiations seek to curtail Kim's nuclear weapons. These weapons will pose a much greater threat if Kim's son, who took over in 2011, is an irrational madman than if he turns out to be a shrewdly rational actor.

their expectations. Information is also screened out as it passes from one person to another in the decision-making process. For example, prior to the September 2001 terrorist attacks, U.S. intelligence agencies failed to adequately interpret available evidence because too few analysts were fluent in Arabic. Similarly, Soviet leaders in 1941 and Israeli leaders in 1973 ignored evidence of pending invasions of their countries.

Misperceptions can affect the implementation of policy by low-level officials as well as its formulation by high-level officials. For example, in 1988, officers on a U.S. warship in the Persian Gulf shot down a civilian Iranian jet that they believed to be a military jet attacking them. The officers were trying to carry out policies established by national leaders, but because of misperceptions their actions instead damaged their state's interests.

Second, the rationality of individual cost-benefit calculations is undermined by emotions that decision makers feel while thinking about the consequences of their actions—an effect referred to as *affective bias*. (*Positive* and *negative affect* refer to feelings of liking or disliking someone.) As hard as a decision maker tries to be rational in making a decision, the decision-making process is bound to be influenced by strong feelings held about the person or state toward which a decision is directed. (Affective biases also contribute to information screening, as positive information about disliked people or negative information about liked people is screened out.)

Third, *cognitive biases* are systematic distortions of rational calculations based not on emotional feelings but simply on the limitations of the human brain in making choices. The most important of these distortions seems to be the attempt to produce *cognitive balance*—or to reduce *cognitive dissonance*. These terms refer to the tendency people have to try to maintain mental models of the world that are logically consistent (this seldom succeeds entirely).[8]

One implication of cognitive balance is that decision makers place greater value on goals that they have put much effort into achieving—the *justification of effort*. This is especially true in a democracy, in which politicians must face their citizens' judgment at the

---

[8] Vertzberger, Yaacov Y. I. *The World in Their Minds: Information Processing, Cognition, and Perception in Foreign Policy Decisionmaking.* Stanford, 1990. Sylvan, Donald A., and James F. Voss. *Problem Representation in Foreign Policy Decision Making.* Cambridge, 1998.

polls and so do not want to admit failures. The Vietnam War trapped U.S. decision makers in this way in the 1960s. After sending half a million troops halfway around the world, U.S. leaders found it difficult to admit to themselves that the costs of the war were greater than the benefits.

Decision makers also achieve cognitive balance through *wishful thinking*—an overestimate of the probability of a desired outcome. A variation of wishful thinking is to assume that an event with a *low probability* of occurring will *not* occur. This could be a dangerous way to think about catastrophic events such as accidental nuclear war or a terrorist attack.

Cognitive balance often leads decision makers to maintain a hardened image of an *enemy* and to interpret all of the enemy's actions in a negative light (because the idea of bad people doing good things would create cognitive dissonance).[9] A *mirror image* refers to two sides in a conflict maintaining very similar enemy images of each other ("we are defensive, they are aggressive," etc.). A decision maker may also experience psychological *projection* of his or her own feelings onto another actor. For instance, if (hypothetically) Indian leaders wanted to gain nuclear superiority over Pakistan but found that goal inconsistent with their image of themselves as peaceful and defensive, the resulting cognitive dissonance might be resolved by believing that Pakistan was trying to gain nuclear superiority (the example works as well with the states reversed).

Another form of cognitive bias, related to cognitive balance, is the use of *historical analogies* to structure one's thinking about a decision. This can be quite useful or quite misleading, depending on whether the analogy is appropriate.[10] Because each historical situation is unique in some way, when a decision maker latches onto an analogy and uses it as a shortcut to a decision, the rational calculation of costs and benefits may be cut short as well. In particular, decision makers often assume that a solution that worked in the past will work again—without fully examining how similar the situations really are. For example, U.S. leaders used the analogy of Munich in 1938 to convince themselves that appeasement in the Vietnam War would lead to increased communist aggression in Asia. In retrospect, the differences between North Vietnam and Nazi Germany made this a poor analogy (largely because of the civil war nature of the Vietnam conflict). Vietnam itself then became a potent analogy that helped persuade U.S. leaders to avoid involvement in certain overseas conflicts, such as Bosnia; this was called the "Vietnam syndrome" in U.S. foreign policy.

All of these psychological processes—misperception, affective biases, and cognitive biases—interfere with the rational assessment of costs and benefits in making a decision.[11] Two specific modifications to the rational model of decision making have been proposed to accommodate psychological realities.

First, the model of *bounded rationality* takes into account the costs of seeking and processing information. Nobody thinks about every single possible course of action when making a decision. Instead of **optimizing**, or picking the very best option, people usually work on the problem until they come up with a "good enough" option that meets some minimal criteria; this is called **satisficing**, or finding a satisfactory solution.[12] The time constraints

---

[9] Herrmann, Richard K., and Michael P. Fischerkeller. Beyond the Enemy Image and the Spiral Model: Cognitive-Strategic Research after the Cold War. *International Organization* 49 (3), 1995: 415–50. Mercer, Jonathan L. *Reputation and International Politics.* Cornell, 1996. O'Reilly, K. P. Perceiving Rogue States: The Use of the "Rogue State" Concept by U.S. Foreign Policy Elites. *Foreign Policy Analysis* 3 (4), 2007: 295–315.

[10] Khong, Yuen Foong. *Analogies at War: Korea, Munich, Dien Bien Phu, and the Vietnam Decisions of 1965.* Princeton, 1992. Neustadt, Richard E., and Ernest R. May. *Thinking In Time: The Uses of History for Decision Makers.* Free Press, 1986.

[11] Tuchman, Barbara W. *The March of Folly: From Troy to Vietnam.* Knopf/Random House, 1984. Parker, Richard B. *The Politics of Miscalculation in the Middle East.* Indiana, 1993. Bennett, Andrew. *Condemned to Repetition? The Rise, Fall, and Reprise of Soviet-Russian Military Interventionism, 1973–1996.* MIT, 1999.

[12] Simon, Herbert A. *Models of Bounded Rationality.* MIT, 1982.

faced by top decision makers in IR—who are constantly besieged with crises requiring their attention—generally preclude their finding the very best response to a situation. These time constraints were described by U.S. Defense Secretary William Cohen in 1997: "The unrelenting flow of information, the need to digest it on a minute-by-minute basis, is quite different from anything I've experienced before. . . . There's little time for contemplation; most of it is action."[13]

Second, **prospect theory** provides an alternative explanation (rather than simple rational optimization) of decisions made under risk or uncertainty.[14] According to this theory, decision makers go through two phases. In the *editing phase*, they frame the options available and the probabilities of various outcomes associated with each option. Then, in the *evaluation phase*, they assess the options and choose one. Prospect theory holds that evaluations take place by comparison with a *reference point*, which is often the status quo but might be some past or expected situation. The decision maker asks whether he or she can do better than that reference point, but the value placed on outcomes depends on how far from the reference point they are.

Individual decision making thus follows an imperfect and partial kind of rationality at best. Not only do the goals of different individuals vary, but decision makers face a series of obstacles in receiving accurate information, constructing accurate models of the world, and reaching decisions that further their own goals. The rational model is only a simplification at best and must be supplemented by an understanding of individual psychological processes that affect decision making.

Group Psychology

What are the implications of group psychology for foreign policy decision making? In one respect, groups promote rationality by balancing out the blind spots and biases of any individual. Advisors or legislative committees may force a state leader to reconsider a rash decision. And the interactions of different individuals in a group may result in the formulation of goals that more closely reflect state interests rather than individual idiosyncrasies. However, group dynamics also introduce new sources of irrationality into the decision-making process.

Groupthink refers to the tendency for groups to reach decisions without accurately assessing their consequences, because individual members tend to go along with ideas they think the others support.[15] The basic phenomenon is illustrated by a simple psychology experiment. A group of six people is asked to compare the lengths of two lines projected onto a screen. When five of the people are secretly instructed to say that line A is longer—even though anyone can see that line B is actually longer—the sixth person is likely to agree with the group rather than believe his or her own eyes.

Unlike individuals, groups tend to be overly optimistic about the chances of success and are thus more willing to take risks. Participants suppress their doubts about dubious undertakings because everyone else seems to think an idea will work. Also, because the group diffuses responsibility from individuals, nobody feels accountable for actions.

---

[13] *Washington Post*, March 5, 1997: A22.

[14] Davis, James W. *Threats and Promises: The Pursuit of International Influence.* Johns Hopkins, 2000. McDermott, Rose. *Risk-Taking in International Politics: Prospect Theory in American Foreign Policy.* Michigan, 1998. Levy, Jack. Prospect Theory, Rational Choice, and International Relations. *International Studies Quarterly* 41 (1), 1997: 87–112.

[15] Janis, Irving L. *Victims of Groupthink: A Psychological Study of Foreign-Policy Decisions and Fiascoes.* Houghton Mifflin, 1972. Hart, Paul, Eric K. Stern, and Bengt Sundelius, eds. *Beyond Groupthink: Political Group Dynamics and Foreign Policy-Making.* Michigan, 1997.

In a spectacular case of group-think, President Ronald Reagan's close friend and director of the U.S. Central Intelligence Agency (CIA) bypassed his own agency and ran covert operations spanning three continents using the National Security Council (NSC) staff in the White House basement. The NSC sold weapons to Iran in exchange for the freedom of U.S. hostages held in Lebanon, and then used the Iranian payments to illegally fund Nicaraguan Contra rebels. The *Iran-Contra scandal* resulted when these operations, managed by an obscure NSC aide named Oliver North, became public.

The U.S. war in Iraq may also provide cautionary examples to future generations about the risks of misinformation, misperception, wishful thinking, and groupthink in managing a major foreign policy initiative.[16] Some of the problems of individual and group psychology in the policy process—be they in Vietnam, Bosnia, or Iraq—are illustrated in Figure 4.3.

The *structure of a decision-making process*—the rules for who is involved in making the decision, how voting is conducted, and so forth—can affect the outcome, especially when no

WISHFUL THINKING

Both individual misperception and group psychology encourage overconfidence and excessive optimism among decision makers. This general tendency in every government especially marked the period of the U.S. invasion of Iraq. Here, President Bush declares victory on an aircraft carrier, May 2003.

single alternative appeals to a majority of participants. Experienced participants in foreign policy formation are familiar with the techniques for manipulating decision-making processes to favor outcomes they prefer. A common technique is to control a group's formal *decision rules*. These rules include the items of business the group discusses and the order in which proposals are considered (especially important when participants are satisficing). Probably most important is the ability to *control the agenda* and thereby structure the terms of debate.

State leaders often rely on an inner circle of advisors in making foreign policy decisions. The composition and operation of the inner circle vary across governments. For instance, President Lyndon Johnson had "Tuesday lunches" to discuss national security policy with top national security officials. Some groups depend heavily on *informal* consultations in addition to formal meetings. Some leaders create a "kitchen cabinet"—a trusted group of friends who discuss policy issues with the leader even though they have no formal positions in government. For instance, Israel's Golda Meir held many such discussions at her home, sometimes literally in the kitchen. Russian president Boris Yeltsin relied on the advice of his bodyguard, who was a trusted friend.

---

[16] Woodward, Bob. *State of Denial: Bush at War III*. Simon & Schuster, 2006.

FIGURE 4.3 Some Psychological Pitfalls of Decision Making

Note: Conflictland could be Vietnam in 1968, Bosnia in 1994, or Iraq in 2006.

Crisis Management

The difficulties in reaching rational decisions, both for individuals and for groups, are heightened during a crisis.[17] *Crises* are foreign policy situations in which outcomes are very important and time frames are compressed. Crisis decision making is harder to understand and predict than is normal foreign policy making.

In a crisis, decision makers operate under tremendous time constraints. The normal checks on unwise decisions may not operate. Communications become shorter and more stereotyped, and information that does not fit a decision maker's expectations is more likely to be discarded, simply because there is no time to consider it. In framing options decision makers tend to restrict the choices, again to save time, and tend to overlook creative options while focusing on the most obvious ones. (In the United States, shifting time constraints are measurable in a doubling or tripling in pizza deliveries to government agencies, as decision makers work through mealtimes.)

Groupthink occurs easily during crises. During the 1962 Cuban Missile Crisis, President John F. Kennedy created a small, closed group of advisors who worked together intensively for days on end, cut off from outside contact and discussion. Even the president's communication with Soviet leader Nikita Khrushchev was rerouted through Kennedy's brother Robert and the Soviet ambassador, cutting out the State Department. Recognizing the danger of groupthink, Kennedy left the room from time to time—removing the authority figure from the group—to encourage free discussion. Through this and other means, the group managed to identify an option (a naval blockade) between their first two choices (bombing the missile sites or doing nothing). Sometimes leaders purposefully designate someone in the group (known as a *devil's advocate*) to object to ideas.

Participants in crisis decision making not only are rushed, but experience severe psychological *stress,* amplifying the biases just discussed. Decision makers tend to

[17] Brecher, Michael, and Jonathan Wilkenfeld. *A Study of Crisis.* Michigan, 2000. Houghton, David. *U.S. Foreign Policy and the Iran Hostage Crisis.* Cambridge, 2001. Gelpi, Christopher. *The Power of Legitimacy: Assessing the Role of Norms in International Crisis Bargaining.* Princeton, 2003.

overestimate the hostility of adversaries and to underestimate their own hostility toward those adversaries. Dislike easily turns to hatred, and anxiety to fear. More and more information is screened out in order to come to terms with decisions being made and to restore cognitive balance. Crisis decision making also leads to physical exhaustion. *Sleep deprivation* sets in within days as decision makers use every hour to stay on top of the crisis. Unless decision makers are careful about getting enough sleep, they may make vital foreign policy decisions under shifting perceptual and mood changes.

Because of the importance of sound decision making during crises, voters pay great attention to the psychological stability of their leaders. Before Israeli prime minister Yitzhak Rabin won election in 1992, he faced charges that he had suffered a one-day nervous breakdown when he headed the armed forces just before the 1967 war. Not so, he responded; he was just smart enough to realize that the crisis had caused both exhaustion and acute nicotine poisoning, and he needed to rest up for a day in order to go on and make good decisions.

Whether in crisis mode or normal routines, individual decision makers do not operate alone. Their decisions are shaped by the government and society in which they work. Foreign policy is constrained and shaped by substate actors such as government agencies, political interest groups, and industries.

WORKING UNDER STRESS

Crisis management takes a high toll psychologically and physiologically. President Eduard Shevardnadze of Georgia seems to show this strain in 1992—just the beginning of years of civil war and perpetual crisis in that country. Shevardnadze, formerly a Soviet foreign minister, had returned to lead his native Georgia when the Soviet Union dissolved. He left office in 2003 after a popular uprising against corruption.

Domestic Influences

◉━┐Watch
the **Video**
"David Cameron
on Corporate Social
Responsibility"
on **mypoliscilab.com**

The remainder of this chapter considers other liberal theoretical approaches that, like the democratic peace, operate at the domestic level of analysis. These approaches, in contrast to realism, see international outcomes as the result of processes within states rather than just those among states. The actions of a state in the international arena result from individual human choices—by citizenry, political leaders, diplomats, and bureaucrats—aggregated through the state's internal structures. The rest of this chapter looks at the state from the inside out, trying to understand the processes and structures *within* states that make them behave as they do.

Bureaucracies

Of the many substate actors that influence states' actions in the international arena, those closest to the action are the bureaucratic agencies that states maintain for developing and carrying out foreign policy. Different states maintain different foreign policy bureaucracies but share some common elements.

Diplomats   Virtually all states maintain a *diplomatic corps*, or *foreign service*, of diplomats working in *embassies* in foreign capitals (and in *consulates* located in noncapital foreign cities), as well as diplomats who remain at home to help coordinate foreign policy. States appoint *ambassadors* as their official representatives to other states and to international organizations. Diplomatic activities are organized through a *foreign ministry* or the equivalent (for example, the U.S. State Department).

In many democracies, some diplomats are *political appointees* who come and go with changes in government leaders (often as patronage for past political support). Others are *career diplomats* who come up through the ranks of the foreign service and tend to outlast changes in administration.

Diplomats provide much of the information that goes into making foreign policies, but their main role is to carry out rather than create policies. Nonetheless, foreign ministry bureaucrats often make foreign relations so routine that top leaders and political appointees can come and go without greatly altering the country's relations. The national interest is served, the bureaucrats believe, by the stability of overall national goals and positions in international affairs.

Tension is common between state leaders and foreign policy bureaucrats. Career diplomats try to orient new leaders and their appointees, and to control the flow of information they receive (creating information screens). Politicians struggle to exercise power over the formal bureaucratic agencies because the latter can be too "bureaucratic" (cumbersome, routinized, conservative) to easily control. Also, these agencies are often staffed (at lower levels) mostly by career officials who may not owe loyalty to political leaders.

Size alone does not guarantee power for a bureaucracy. For example, the U.S. Trade Representative (USTR) and the National Security Council (NSC) each have staffs of only about 200 people, compared with 5,000 people with responsibilities for similar matters in the Commerce and State Departments. The power of these agencies is their proximity to the U.S. president. The NSC chief traditionally briefs the president every morning on international security issues.

Sometimes state leaders appoint a close friend or key advisor to manage the foreign policy bureaucracy. President George W. Bush did this in his second term with his former NSC chief and confidante Condoleezza Rice. Chinese leader Mao Zedong put his loyal ally Zhou Enlai in charge of foreign policy. At other times, state leaders may appoint rivals with differing views of foreign policy—as President Barack Obama did with his former political rival Hillary Clinton.

At times, frustration with the bureaucracy leads politicians to bypass normal channels of diplomacy. For example, during the 1962 Cuban Missile Crisis, President Kennedy demanded to be put in direct contact with military personnel in the Caribbean overseeing the blockade of Cuba, bypassing the secretary of defense and high-ranking officers.

Interagency Tensions   *Interagency* tension also affects the formulation of foreign policy. Certain agencies traditionally clash, and an endless tug-of-war shapes the foreign policies that emerge. In an extreme example of interagency rivalry, the U.S. State Department and the CIA backed opposite sides in a civil war in Laos in 1960. In the United States and the Soviet Union during the Cold War, the defense ministry was usually more hawkish (favoring military strength) and the foreign ministry or State Department more dovish (favoring diplomacy), with the president or premier holding the balance.

In general, bureaucracies promote policies under which their own capabilities will be effective and their power will increase. There is a saying that "where you stand" on an issue "depends on where you sit" (in the bureaucratic structure). One can often predict just from the job titles of participants how they will argue on a policy issue. The government bargaining model (see p. 128) pays special attention to the interagency negotiations that result from conflicts of interest between agencies of the same government. For example, after Americans were taken hostage in Iran in 1979, military and CIA officials pushed President Carter to attempt a military rescue, while the State Department vehemently opposed such a mission. After days of debate, the president decided to go ahead with the rescue mission (which proved disastrous), but did not invite the secretary of state to the meeting where the final decisions were made.

Although representatives of bureaucratic agencies usually promote the interests of their own bureaucracies, sometimes heads of agencies try to appear loyal to the state leader by forgoing the interests of their own agencies. Also, the preferences of leaders of bureaucratic agencies cannot always be predicted given the goal of their institution. For example, in the Cuban Missile Crisis, defense officials were hesitant to commit to a military solution to the crisis, while some diplomatic officials favored a preemptive military strike.

Units within agencies have similar tensions. In many countries, the different military services (army, navy, air force) pull in somewhat different directions, even if they ultimately unite to battle the foreign ministry. Bureaucrats working in particular units or projects become attached to them. Officials responsible for a new weapon system lose bureaucratic turf, and perhaps their jobs, if the weapon's development is canceled.

Of special concern in many poor states is the institutional interest that military officers have in maintaining a strong military. If civilian state leaders allow officers' salaries to fall or the size of the military forces to be cut, they may well face institutional resistance from the military—in the extreme case, a military takeover of the government (see pp. 224–225). These issues were factors in attempted military coups in the Philippines, Venezuela, and Paraguay in the 1990s.[18]

In general, bureaucratic rivalry as an influence on foreign policy challenges the notion of states as unitary actors in the international system. Such rivalries suggest that a state does not have any single set of goals—a national interest—but that its actions may result from the bargaining of subunits, each with its own set of goals.[19] Furthermore, such a perspective extends far beyond bureaucratic agencies because other substate actors have their own goals, which they seek to advance by influencing foreign policy.

---

[18] Feaver, Peter D., and Christopher Gelpi. *Choosing Your Battles: American Civil-Military Relations and the Use of Force*. Princeton, 2004.

[19] Kaarbo, Juliet. Power Politics in Foreign Policy: The Influence of Bureaucratic Minorities. *European Journal of International Relations* 4 (1), 1998: 67–97.

Interest Groups

Foreign policy makers operate not in a political vacuum but in the context of the political debates in their society. In all states, societal pressures influence foreign policy, although these are aggregated and made effective through different channels in different societies. In pluralistic democracies, interested parties influence foreign policy through interest groups and political parties. In dictatorships, similar influences occur but less visibly. Thus foreign policies adopted by states generally reflect some kind of process of domestic coalition formation.[20] Of course, international factors also have strong effects on domestic politics.[21]

Interest groups are coalitions of people who share a common interest in the outcome of some political issue and who organize themselves to try to influence the outcome. For instance, French farmers have a big stake in international negotiations in the European Community (which subsidizes agriculture) and in world trade talks (which set agricultural tariffs). The farmers exert political pressure on the French government through long-established and politically sophisticated associations and organizations. They lobby for desired legislation and contribute to politicians' campaigns. More dramatically, when their interests have been threatened—as during a U.S.-European trade dispute in 1992—French farmers have turned out in large numbers across the country to block roads, stage violent street demonstrations, and threaten to grind the national economy to a halt unless the government adopts their position. Similarly (but often less dramatically), interest groups form around businesses, labor unions, churches, veterans, senior citizens, members of an occupation, or citizens concerned about an issue such as the environment.

Lobbying is the process of talking with legislators or officials to influence their decisions on some set of issues. Three important elements that go into successful lobbying are the ability to gain a hearing with busy officials, the ability to present cogent arguments for one's case, and the ability to trade favors in return for positive action on an issue. These favors—legal and illegal—range from campaign contributions to dinners at nice restaurants, trips to golf resorts, securing illicit sexual liaisons, and paying bribes. In many states, corruption is a major problem in governmental decision making (see pp. 475–476), and interest groups may induce government officials by illegal means to take certain actions.

Ethnic groups within one state often become interest groups concerned about their ancestral nation outside that state. Many members of ethnic groups feel strong emotional ties to their relatives in other countries; because the rest of the population generally does not care about such issues one way or the other, even a small ethnic group can have considerable influence on policy toward a particular country. Such ethnic ties are emerging as a powerful foreign policy influence in various ethnic conflicts in poor regions. The effect is especially strong in the United States, which is ethnically mixed and has a pluralistic form of democracy. For example, Cuban Americans organize to influence U.S. policy toward Cuba, as do Greek Americans on Greece, Jewish Americans on Israel, and African Americans on Africa. In a 1996 U.S. Senate election in South Dakota, one candidate raised large contributions from the Pakistani-American community and the other candidate from the rival Indian-American community. But whether or not a foreign country has a large constituency of ethnic nationals within another country, it can lobby that country's government.[22]

---

[20] Solingen, Etel. *Regional Orders at Century's Dawn: Global and Domestic Influences on Grand Strategy.* Princeton, 1998. Snyder, Jack. *Myths of Empire: Domestic Politics and International Ambition.* Cornell, 1991.
[21] Gourevitch, Peter. The Second Image Reversed: International Sources of Domestic Politics. *International Organization* 32 (4), 1978: 881–911. Rogowski, Ronald. *Commerce and Coalitions: How Trade Affects Domestic Political Alignments.* Princeton, 1989.
[22] Smith, Tony. *Foreign Attachments: The Power of Ethnic Groups in the Making of American Foreign Policy.* Harvard, 2000. Paul, David M., and Rachel A. Paul. *Ethnic Lobbies and U.S. Foreign Policy.* Rienner, 2008.

Clearly, interest groups have goals and interests that may or may not coincide with the national interest as a whole (if indeed such an interest can be identified). As with bureaucratic agencies, the view of the state as a unitary actor can be questioned. Defenders of interest-group politics argue that various interest groups tend to push and pull in different directions, with the ultimate decisions generally reflecting the interests of society as a whole. But according to *Marxist* theories of international relations, the key domestic influences on foreign policy in capitalist countries are rich owners of big businesses. For instance, European imperialism benefited banks and big business, which made huge profits from exploiting cheap labor and resources in overseas colonies. This is the official view (if not always the operative one) of the Chinese government toward Western industrialized states. During the Cold War, Marxists argued that Western foreign policies were driven by the profit motive of arms manufacturers.[23]

DOMESTIC BREW

Foreign policies are affected by the pulling and tugging of various domestic interest groups. Legislatures respond to these groups, constituencies, lobbyists, and media. These interested parties pack a U.S. Senate hearing as an administration official argues that the War Powers Act does not apply to Libyan bombing, 2011.

The Military-Industrial Complex

A **military-industrial complex** refers to a huge interlocking network of governmental agencies, industrial corporations, and research institutes, working together to supply a nation's military forces. The military-industrial complex was a response to the growing importance of technology (nuclear weapons, electronics, and others) and of logistics in Cold War military planning. Because of the domestic political clout of these actors, the complex was a powerful influence on foreign policy in both the United States and the Soviet Union during the Cold War.

States at war have long harnessed their economic and technological might for the war effort. But during the Cold War, military procurement occurred on a massive scale in "peacetime," as the superpowers raced to develop new high-technology weapons. This race created a special role for scientists and engineers in addition to the more traditional role of industries that produce war materials. In response to the Soviet satellite *Sputnik* in 1957, the United States increased spending on research and development and created new science education programs. By 1961, President Dwight Eisenhower warned in

---

[23] Konobeyev, V. The Capitalist Economy and the Arms Race. *International Affairs* [Moscow] 8, 1982: 28–48.

his farewell speech that the military-industrial complex (a term he coined) was gaining "unwarranted influence" in U.S. society and that militarization could erode democracy in the United States. The size of the complex gave it more political clout than ordinary citizens could muster. Yet its interest in the arms race conflicted with the interest of ordinary citizens in peace.

The complex encompasses a variety of constituencies, each of which has an interest in military spending. *Corporations* that produce goods for the military profit from government contracts. So do military *officers* whose careers advance by building bureaucratic empires around new weapons systems. And so do universities and scientific institutes that receive military research contracts—a major source of funding for scientists in Russia and the United States.

Subcontractors and parts suppliers for big U.S. weapons projects are usually spread around many states and congressional districts, so that local citizens and politicians join the list of constituents benefiting from military spending. Early funding for the Strategic Defense Initiative (or Star Wars) was given to each military service branch, the Department of Energy, NASA, and hundreds of private contractors. Recently, a similar phenomenon has emerged in the European Community, where weapons development programs have been parceled out to several European states. A new fighter jet is less likely to be canceled if one country gets the contract for the wings, another for the engines, and so forth.

Executives in military industries, who best understand their industries, are often appointed as government officials responsible for military procurement decisions and then return to their companies again—a practice called the *revolving door*. In democracies, military industries also influence public opinion through advertising that ties their products to patriotic themes. U.S. military industries also give generous campaign contributions to

SEEKING THE COLLECTIVE GOOD

Israeli-Palestinian Peace Talks
COLLECTIVE GOOD: An End to 60+ Years of Violent Conflict

BACKGROUND: Since the founding of Israel in 1948 in the wake of World War II, Jews and Arab Palestinians have been fighting over the land. After several destructive wars, Israel and its main neighbors, Egypt and Jordan, arrived at a durable (though cold) peace. The Israelis and Palestinians, however, have yet to reach a peace agreement based on a Palestinian state in lands occupied by Israel in the 1967 war—the West Bank and the Gaza Strip—and Palestinian recognition of Israel's right to exist.

In many rounds of negotiations over the years, the two sides have gotten closer. At the end of 2000, negotiators nearly reached agreement on the parameters for a Palestinian state side by side with Israel. The effort fell short, however; new governments took power in both Israel and America, and a new wave of violence ensued. Israeli-Palestinian peace is a collective good that would benefit each side regardless of whether it or the other side made the concessions that led to an agreement.

CHALLENGE: In 2010, the U.S. administration launched a new round of Israeli-Palestinian talks to try to reach a comprehensive agreement within a year. These talks faced great challenges as a result of the domestic politics on each side. In Israel, the parliamentary ruling coalition included parties opposed to concessions toward Palestine, so the Israeli government lacked maneuvering room to make concessions even if it wanted to. In

DOMINANCE

RECIPROCITY

national politicians who vote on military budgets, and sometimes bribes to Pentagon officials as well.[24]

Public Opinion

Many domestic actors seek to influence **public opinion**—the range of views on foreign policy issues held by the citizens of a state. Public opinion has greater influence on foreign policy in democracies than in authoritarian governments. But even dictators must pay attention to what citizens think. No government can rule by force alone: it needs legitimacy to survive. It must persuade people to accept (if not to like) its policies, because in the end, policies are carried out by ordinary people—soldiers, workers, and bureaucrats.

Because of the need for public support, even authoritarian governments spend great effort on *propaganda*—the public promotion of their official line—to win support for foreign policies. States use television, newspapers, and other information media in this effort. In many countries, the state owns or controls major mass media such as television and newspapers, mediating the flow of information to its citizens; however, new information technologies with multiple channels make this harder to do.

Journalists serve as the gatekeepers of information passing from foreign policy elites to the public. The media and government often conflict because of the traditional role of the

---

[24] Der Derian, James. *Virtuous War: Mapping the Military-Industrial-Media-Entertainment Network.* Westview, 2001. Jones, Christopher M. Roles, Politics, and the Survival of the V-22 Osprey. *Journal of Political and Military Sociology* 29 (1), 2001: 46–72.

Palestine, the militant armed group Hamas controlled Gaza, leaving the Israelis negotiating with a Palestinian Authority that did not fully control the territory it hoped to claim as a state. In these ways, foreign policy processes even in democracies can constrain each side's ability to make peace.

SOLUTION: Reciprocity, a strong norm in Israeli-Palestinian relations over the decades, is basic to the negotiation of peace agreements. Yet it has not sufficed, in part because domestic constraints make it harder for governments to have cooperation based on reciprocity.

To get around these domestic constraints, the dominance principle helps. Most analysts agree that the peace talks can succeed only if the United States applies strong leadership (including pressure and inducements) to get the two parties to make concessions. Opponents on each side can then blame the United States rather than their own leaders, who thus gain maneuvering room to compromise. If an

Israeli and Palestinian leaders with U.S. Secretary of State in Washington, 2010.

Israeli-Palestinian peace agreement is ever to occur, American leadership of the process will likely play a key role in reaching it.

press as a watchdog and critic of government actions and powers. The media try to uncover and publicize what the government wants to hide. Foreign policy decision makers also rely on the media for information about foreign affairs.

Yet the media also depend on government for information; the size and resources of the foreign policy bureaucracies dwarf those of the press. These advantages give the government great power to *manipulate* journalists by feeding them information in order to shape the news and influence public opinion. Government decision makers can create dramatic stories in foreign relations—through summit meetings, crises, actions, and so forth. Bureaucrats can also *leak* secret information to the press in order to support their own point of view and win bureaucratic battles. Finally, the military and the press have a running battle about journalists' access to military operations, but both sides gained from the open access given to journalists "embedded" with U.S. forces in Iraq in 2003.

In democracies, where governments must stand for election, an unpopular war can force a leader or party from office, as happened to U.S. president Lyndon Johnson in 1968 during the Vietnam War. Or a popular war can help secure a government's mandate to continue in power, as happened to Margaret Thatcher in Britain after the 1982 Falkland Islands War. A key influence on public opinion is the content of scenes appearing on television: U.S. soldiers were sent to Somalia to assist in relief efforts in 1992 after TV news showed the heartrending results of civil war and famine there. But after TV news showed an American soldier's body being dragged through the streets by members of a Somali faction after a deadly firefight that killed 18 U.S. soldiers, public opinion shifted quickly against the Somalia operation. During the war in Bosnia, officials in the U.S. State Department said privately that the main goal of U.S. policy was often just to keep the conflict there off of the front pages of U.S. newspapers (an elusive goal, as it turned out).

Occasionally a foreign policy issue is decided directly by a referendum of the entire citizenry (the United States lacks such a tradition, which is strong in Switzerland and Denmark, for example).[25] In 2005, referendums in France and the Netherlands rejected a proposed constitution for the European Union, despite the support of major political leaders for the change (see pp. 368–369).

Even in the most open democracies, states do not merely *respond* to public opinion. Decision makers enjoy some autonomy to make their own choices, and they are pulled in various directions by bureaucracies and interest groups, whose views often conflict with the direction favored by public opinion at large. Furthermore, public opinion is seldom unified on any policy, and sophisticated polling can show that particular segments of the population (regions of the country, genders, income groups, races, etc.) often differ in their perceptions of foreign policy issues. So a politician may respond to the opinion of one constituency rather than the whole population. Public opinion varies considerably over time on many foreign policy issues. States use propaganda (in dictatorships) or try to manipulate the media (in democracies) to keep public opinion from diverging too much from state policies.

In democracies, public opinion generally has less effect on foreign policy than on domestic policy. National leaders traditionally have additional latitude to make decisions in the international realm. This derives from the special need of states to act in a unified way to function effectively in the international system, as well as from the traditions of secrecy and diplomacy that remove IR from the realm of ordinary domestic politics.

---

[25] Rourke, John T., Richard P. Hiskes, and Cyrus Ernesto Zirakzadeh. *Direct Democracy and International Politics: Deciding International Issues through Referendums.* Rienner, 1992.

POLICY PERSPECTIVES

Prime Minister of Japan, Yoshihiko Noda

PROBLEM *How do you decide what foreign policy tools best balance domestic and international concerns?*

BACKGROUND Imagine that you are the prime minister of Japan. Since the end of the Korean War in 1953, relations with your neighbor to the west, North Korea, have been tense. Military tensions have persisted as North Korea has made and then broken several agreements regarding its nuclear program. North Korea tested a nuclear weapon in 2006 and 2009, and it has also test-fired its short-range and long-range ballistic missiles directly over Japan in an effort to intimidate your country. Most analysts believe North Korea does possess the ability to produce at least a few nuclear weapons.

For its part, North Korea has long demanded reparations for Japan's 35-year colonization of the Korean peninsula and for actions taken by Japan in Korea during World War II. Japan has refused such reparations in the past, but has provided limited aid in an attempt to encourage North Korea to denuclearize. You have held talks with North Korea in the past two years, but no agreements on any political or economic issues have been reached.

In the summer of 2008, the United States removed North Korea from its list of states that sponsor terrorism. This angered many in your country, who saw this removal as giving in to North Korean demands for more aid in exchange for giving up its nuclear program. Your government vehemently protested this move by the United States, which the Japanese finance minister called "extremely regrettable."

DOMESTIC CONSIDERATIONS Public opinion in Japan is very sensitive to relations with North Korea. In 2002, North Korea admitted to secretly abducting Japanese citizens in the 1970s and 1980s, transporting them to North Korea, and using them to train North Korean spies. North Korea claims that all 13 abductees have either returned to Japan or died, but many in Japan are skeptical of this claim. Many in Japan suspect more than 13 were abducted and

have even demanded that North Korea return the bodies of the deceased. These abductions are an extremely sensitive issue in Japanese public opinion, and past Japanese governments have demanded a resolution to the abduction issue before opening formal diplomatic relations with North Korea.

SCENARIO Now imagine that the United States is negotiating a new nuclear weapons agreement with North Korea. The United States asks that Japan contribute extensive foreign aid to North Korea to help ensure that a deal is reached. In return, North Korea will agree to allow increased inspections of all key nuclear sites and will rejoin the Non-Proliferation Treaty (see p. 217). The United States is placing extensive pressure on your government to provide what it feels is critical aid.

CHOOSE YOUR POLICY How do you respond to U.S. pressure for more foreign aid? Do you risk a backlash from your public by increasing aid without having the abduction issue resolved? Do you resist pressure from the United States, your most important ally, and withhold the requested aid? Can you trust the North Korean government to hold up its end of the bargain after you give the economic aid? How do you balance a sensitive domestic political issue with a delicate set of international negotiations?

However, In the case of Japan, public opinion is a major political force restraining the military spending of the government, its commitment of military forces beyond Japan's borders, and especially the development of nuclear weapons (which is within Japan's technical abilities). The ruling party—under pressure from the United States to share the burden of defense and to shoulder its responsibilities as a great power—has slowly but steadily pushed to increase Japan's military spending and allow Japanese military forces to expand their role modestly (in the 1980s, to patrol Asian sea lanes vital to Japanese trade; in the 1990s, to participate in UN peacekeeping operations). Repeatedly, these efforts have been slowed or rebuffed by strong public opinion against the military. In Japan, people remember the horrible consequences of militarism in the 1930s and World War II, culminating in the nuclear bombings of 1945. They are thus suspicious of any increase in the size or role of military forces, and are set against Japan's having nuclear weapons. In this case, public opinion constrains the state's conduct of foreign policy and has slowed the pace of change.

The *attentive public* in a democracy is the minority of the population that stays informed about international issues. This segment varies somewhat from one issue to another, but there is also a core of people who care in general about foreign affairs and follow them closely. The most active members of the attentive public on foreign affairs constitute a foreign policy *elite*—people with power and influence who affect foreign policy. This elite includes people within governments as well as outsiders such as businesspeople, journalists, lobbyists, and professors of political science. Public opinion polls show that elite opinions sometimes (but not always) differ considerably from those of the general population, and sometimes from those of the government as well.[26]

Governments sometimes adopt foreign policies for the specific purpose of generating public approval and hence gaining domestic legitimacy.[27] This is the case when a government undertakes a war or foreign military intervention at a time of domestic difficulty, to distract attention and gain public support—taking advantage of the **"rally 'round the flag" syndrome** (the public's increased support for government leaders during wartime, at least in the short term). Citizens who would readily criticize their government's policies on education or health care often refrain from criticism when the government is at war and the lives of the nation's soldiers are on the line. Policies of this sort are often labeled **diversionary foreign policy**. Unfortunately, it is always difficult to tell whether a state adopts a foreign policy to distract the public, because leaders would never admit to trying to divert public attention.

However, wars that go on too long or are not successful can turn public opinion against the government and even lead to a popular uprising to overthrow the government. In Argentina, the military government in 1982 led the country into war with Britain over the Falkland Islands. At first Argentineans rallied around the flag, but after losing the war they rallied around the cause of getting rid of the military government, and they replaced it with a new civilian government that prosecuted the former leaders. In 2006, President Bush's popularity, which had soared early in the Iraq War, deflated as the war dragged on (see Figure 4.4), and voters threw his party out of

---

[26] Page, Benjamin I., and Marshall M. Bouton. *The Foreign Policy Disconnect*. Chicago, 2006. Jacobs, Lawrence R., and Benjamin I. Page. Who Influences U.S. Foreign Policy? *American Political Science Review* 99 (1), 2005: 107–23. Sobel, Richard. *The Impact of Public Opinion on U.S. Foreign Policy Since Vietnam*. Oxford, 2001. Holsti, Ole R. *Public Opinion and American Foreign Policy*. Rev. ed. Michigan, 2004.

[27] Baum, Matthew. The Constituent Foundations of the Rally-Round-the-Flag Phenomenon. *International Studies Quarterly* 46 (2), 2002: 263–98. Eichenberg, Richard C. Victory Has Many Friends: U.S. Public Opinion and the Use of Military Force, 1981–2005. *International Security* 30 (1), 2005: 140–77.

FIGURE 4.4 The "Rally 'Round the Flag" Syndrome

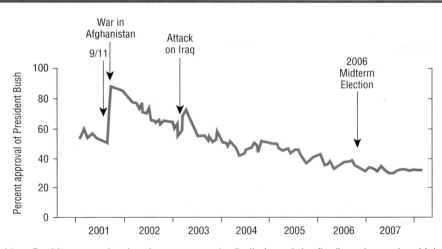

President Bush's approval rating demonstrates the "rally 'round the flag" syndrome, in which war triggers a short-term boost in public approval.

Source: Gallup Poll.

power in Congress. By the 2008 elections, his party had lost control of the Senate, House, and presidency—all of which the Republicans had held at the beginning of the Iraq War in 2003.

Legislatures

One conduit through which interest groups and public opinion may wield influence is legislatures. Some democracies, such as the United States, have presidential systems, in which legislative bodies are elected apart from the president (also referred to as *executives*). In these systems, legislatures play a direct role in making foreign policy by passing budgets, regulating bureaucratic rules, creating trade law, even controlling immigration policy. Although executives may attend summits and talks, any agreement they sign must be approved by their domestic legislature.[28]

Although few would argue that legislatures in presidential democracies do not influence foreign policy generally, different rules may apply to the use of military force. Some contend that legislatures, like public opinion, rally around the flag during times of international crises. For example, three days after the September 11, 2001, attacks, the U.S. Congress voted to give President Bush full authority to prosecute a war in Afghanistan. In October 2002, Congress passed a resolution authorizing the use of force in Iraq. Thus, legislatures rarely if ever challenge an executive on important military matters.

Others point to a different dynamic in which legislatures do stand up to executive power regarding military force. For example, because legislatures hold the "purse strings" (the ability to approve or reject new spending), they have the ability to stop a war in its tracks. In

---

[28] Milner, Helen. *Interests, Institutions, and Information: Domestic Politics and International Relations*. Princeton, 1997. Evans, Peter B., Harold K. Jacobson, and Robert D. Putnam, eds. *Double-Edged Diplomacy: International Bargaining and Domestic Politics*. California, 1993.

the United States, the War Powers Act, enacted during the close of the Vietnam War, requires the president to notify Congress when U.S. troops are deployed for combat. After this notification, the president has 60 days (plus a possible 30-day extension) to recall the troops unless Congress explicitly approves the military action. During the 2011 Libya air campaign, the Obama administration claimed that the War Powers Act did not apply because the action was not a war. Some in Congress disputed this claim but could not prevail. Finally, some evidence from the United States suggests that presidents are more likely to use military force when their own political party is in power in Congress, suggesting that politics does not stop "at the water's edge."[29]

In parliamentary systems, such as Great Britain, executives (for example, prime ministers) are chosen by the political parties that hold a dominant position in the legislative bodies. Often parliamentary executives do not need to submit treaties or policies for formal approval by the legislature. Yet legislatures in parliamentary systems still hold power regarding foreign policy. In Great Britain, for example, Parliament is not required to vote on international agreements negotiated by the prime minister, but it must approve any change to British laws that such agreements entail. Because most international agreements do involve these types of changes, Parliament effectively exercises a right of ratification over international agreements.

In many parliamentary systems, if a policy is particularly controversial, parties that do not have a majority in the legislature can attempt to call elections—meaning that the country votes again on which parties will hold seats in the legislature. If a different group of parties wins a majority of seats, a new executive is appointed. Thus, in parliamentary systems, legislatures play a key role in designing and implementing foreign policy.

Making Foreign Policy

Foreign policies are the strategies governments use to guide their actions in the international arena. Foreign policies spell out the objectives state leaders have decided to pursue in a given relationship or situation. But in general, IR scholars are less interested in specific policies than in the **foreign policy process**—how policies are arrived at and implemented.[30]

States establish various organizational structures and functional relationships to create and carry out foreign policies. IR scholars are especially interested in exploring whether certain kinds of policy processes lead to certain kinds of decisions—whether certain processes produce better outcomes (for the state's self-defined interests) than do others.

Comparative foreign policy is the study of foreign policy in various states in order to discover whether similar types of societies or governments consistently have similar types of foreign policies (comparing across states or across different time periods for a single state). Such studies have focused on three characteristics: size, wealth, and extent of democratic participation in government.[31] Unfortunately, no simple rule has been found to predict a state's warlike tendencies based on these attributes. States vary greatly among each other and even within a single state over time. For example, both

---

[29] Howell, Will, and Jon C. Pevehouse. *While Dangers Gather: Congressional Checks on Presidential War Powers.* Princeton, 2007.

[30] Neack, Laura. *The New Foreign Policy: U.S. and Comparative Foreign Policy in the 21st Century.* Rowman & Littlefield, 2003. Snow, Donald M. *United States Foreign Policy: Politics Beyond the Water's Edge.* Longman, 2003.

[31] Hook, Steven W. *Comparative Foreign Policy.* Prentice Hall, 2002. Beasley, Ryan K., et al., eds. *Foreign Policy in Comparative Perspective: Domestic and International Influences on State Behavior.* CQ Press, 2002.

capitalist and communist states have proven capable of naked aggression or peaceful behavior, depending on circumstances.

Some political scientists have tried to interpret particular states' foreign policies in terms of each one's *political culture and history*. For example, the Soviet Union (Russia) experienced repeated, devastating land invasions over the centuries (culminating in World War II) while the United States experienced two centuries of safety behind great oceans. Thus the military might of the Soviet Union, and its control of buffer states in Eastern Europe, seemed defensive in nature to Soviet leaders but appeared aggressive to U.S. leaders.

Foreign policy outcomes result from multiple forces at various levels of analysis. The outcomes depend on individual decision makers, on the type of society and government they are working within, and on the international and global context of their actions. The study of foreign policy processes runs counter to realism's assumption of a unitary state actor. Because the study of foreign policy concentrates on forces within the state, its main emphasis is on the individual and domestic levels of analysis.

FOREIGN POLICY STATEMENT

Foreign policy outcomes result from processes at several levels of analysis, including the roles of individuals. All these levels were in play in 2011 as Greek leaders sought an outside bailout to deal with massive debt. The Greek government's negotiations with European officials played out as domestic protesters vented their rage at spending cuts demanded by the EU.

The differences in the foreign policy process from one state to another are also influenced by a state's type of government, such as military dictatorship, communist party rule, one-party (noncommunist) rule, and various forms of multiparty democracy. Relatively democratic states tend to share values and interests, and hence to get along better with each other than with nondemocracies (see "The Democratic Peace," pp. 94–96). In practice, most states lie along a spectrum with some mix of democratic and authoritarian elements.

The attempt to explain foreign policy in a general and *theoretical* way has met only limited success. This is one reason why realists continue to find simple unitary-actor models of the state useful; the domestic and individual elements of the foreign policy process add much complexity and unpredictability. One area of foreign policy in which knowledge stands on a somewhat firmer basis is the *descriptive* effort to understand how particular mechanisms of foreign policy formation operate in various states. Such approaches belong to the field of comparative politics.

To summarize, foreign policy is a complex outcome of a complex process. It results from the struggle of competing themes, competing domestic interests, and competing government agencies. No single individual, agency, or guiding principle determines the outcome. Yet foreign policy does achieve a certain overall coherence. States form foreign policy on an issue or toward a region; it is not just an incoherent collection of decisions and actions taken from time to time. Out of the turbulent internal processes of foreign policy formation come relatively coherent interests and policies that states pursue.

✓•⌐**Study**
and **Review**
the **Post-Test &
Chapter Exam**
at **mypoliscilab.com**

CHAPTER REVIEW

SUMMARY

- Foreign policies are strategies governments use to guide their actions toward other states. The foreign policy process is the set of procedures and structures that states use to arrive at foreign policy decisions and to implement them.

- In the rational model of decision making, officials choose the action whose consequences best help meet the state's established goals. By contrast, in the organizational process model, decisions result from routine administrative procedures; in the government bargaining (or bureaucratic politics) model, decisions result from negotiations among governmental agencies with different interests in the outcome.

- The actions of individual decision makers are influenced by their personalities, values, and beliefs as well as by common psychological factors that diverge from rationality. These factors include misperception, selective perception, emotional biases, and cognitive biases (including the effort to reduce cognitive dissonance).

- Foreign policy decisions are also influenced by the psychology of groups (including *groupthink*), the procedures used to reach decisions, and the roles of participants. During crises, the potentials for misperception and error are amplified.

- Struggles over the direction of foreign policy are common between professional bureaucrats and politicians, as well as between different government agencies.

- Domestic constituencies (interest groups) have distinct interests in foreign policies and often organize politically to promote those interests.

- Prominent among domestic constituencies—especially in the United States and Russia, and especially during the Cold War—have been military-industrial complexes consisting of military industries and others with an interest in high military spending.

- Public opinion influences governments' foreign policy decisions (more so in democracies than in authoritarian states), but governments also manipulate public opinion.

- Legislatures can provide a conduit for public opinion and interests groups to influence foreign policy. Executives and legislators may differ on how to best achieve a state's national interest.

KEY TERMS

rational model   127
organizational process
   model   128
government bargaining
   model   128
misperceptions,
   selective
   perceptions   129

information screens   129
optimizing   131
satisficing   131
prospect theory   132
groupthink   132
interest groups   138
military-industrial
   complex   139

public opinion   141
"rally 'round the flag"
   syndrome   144
diversionary foreign
   policy   144
foreign policy
   process   146

CRITICAL THINKING QUESTIONS

1. Uncertainty about costs and benefits of an action can complicate foreign policy decision making. What are the sources of uncertainty in IR? Can decision makers take steps to reduce that uncertainty?

2. Consider an event in IR that you are familiar with. Thinking about the actors involved in making a decision concerning that event, how would that event be explained by the rational-actor model? Might it be better explained by considering standard operating procedures or bureaucratic politics?

3. Sometimes aggressive international actions are attributed to a "madman" such as Iraq's Saddam Hussein or Nazi Germany's Adolf Hitler. Do you agree that such leaders (each of whose actions severely damaged his state's well-being) must be "mad"? What other factors could account for their actions? How do you think such people achieve and maintain national leadership?

4. India and Pakistan are neighbors and enemies. Given the problems of misperception and bias in foreign policy decision making, what steps could you propose that each government adopt to keep these problems from interfering in the rational pursuit of national interests?

5. Traditionally, foreign policy elites have faced only sporadic pressure from mass public opinion. Is the role of television and the Internet changing this relationship? If you were a top foreign policy maker, what steps could you take to keep TV news and blogs from shaping the foreign policy agenda before you could define your own goals and directions?

Should Legislatures Play a Role in Deciding Whether to Use Military Force?

Overview

In nearly all democracies, there are debates about the best way to conduct foreign policy. One particularly controversial issue involves using military force—for example, initiating a war. Executives (presidents or prime ministers) usually claim the right to initiate the use of force as commanders of their militaries. Yet legislatures (Congress or parliaments) may object that they should have a say in whether a country goes to war.

In the United States, the president is the Commander in Chief of the military and thus has the power to order the deployment of American military forces. Yet Congress has the exclusive power to declare war. This has led to extensive debates in the United States about who has the ultimate authority to undertake military action. While the president has extensive advantages in terms of military intelligence and analysis (because the foreign policy bureaucracy reports to the president, not Congress), Congress must authorize funds to pay for military action. And although American presidents often seek congressional approval before taking military action, there have been important exceptions (for example, the U.S. invasion of Panama in 1989).

What is the proper relationship between a legislature and the executive regarding the use of military force? Should initiating military force be invested only in the executive, or should legislatures also have a say in when and where a country's military is put in harm's way?

Legislatures Should Not Play a Role in Deciding Whether to Use Military Force

Legislatures are slow to act in times of crisis. Because legislatures are made up of hundreds of members, it is difficult to get agreement among all members on what constitutes a threat to national security. Discussions over whether to use military force can thus be long, drawn-out affairs, which can limit the ability of a country to respond to dangers. Executives also have faster access to information at their disposal.

Internal debates can show division to enemies. Debates over the appropriateness of military force show open divisions within a country that can encourage adversaries to remain stubborn in bargaining. If an adversary feels a country is too divided to use military force against it, it will not treat threats to use force as credible.

Most legislators know little about foreign affairs. Most legislators are elected to serve local constituent interests rather than invest their time and energy in foreign affairs. Legislators have little incentive to become highly knowledgeable about foreign affairs, thus making their decisions about whether to engage in military force less informed.

Legislatures Should Play a Role in Deciding Whether to Use Military Force

More input regarding military force leads to more careful policy. Having an effective legislative debate over the potential use of military force can lead to better policy, avoiding some of the psychological pitfalls associated with small-group decision making such as groupthink.

Legislators are more directly accountable to constituents. Because a state's citizens will bear the brunt of the costs of war, it is appropriate that their representative bodies have a say in whether the country's men and women should be sent to fight. Open debates in a legislature better allow the public's voice to be heard.

Executives need checks and balances, especially with regard to decisions about war. Because of the weight of a decision to initiate military conflict, it is important to have a checks and balances system to stop hasty wars. In the United States, the Constitution specifically grants Congress the power to declare war for this reason.

Questions

- Should legislatures play a role in the decision to use military force? Are there some circumstances that are better or worse for a society to have open debates about potential military action?

- Short of military action, should legislatures play a significant role in other foreign policy areas such as economic sanctions, immigration, or military alliances? How are these foreign policy issues similar to or different from questions of using military force?

- Do you think potential adversaries pay attention to debates within a country contemplating military force? Do potential adversaries use this information to their advantage? Should this be a concern for a country contemplating the use of military force?

For Further Reading

Hamilton, Lee H., and Jordan Tama. *A Creative Tension: The Foreign Policy Roles of the President and Congress.* Woodrow Wilson Center, 2002.

Howell, William G., and Jon C. Pevehouse. *While Dangers Gather: Congressional Checks on Presidential War Powers.* Princeton, 2007.

Feaver, Peter D., and Christopher Gelpi. *Choosing Your Battles: American Civil-Military Relations and the Use of Force.* Princeton, 2003.

Fisher, Louis. *Presidential War Power.* 2nd ed. Rev. Kansas, 2004.

CHAPTER 5

International Conflict

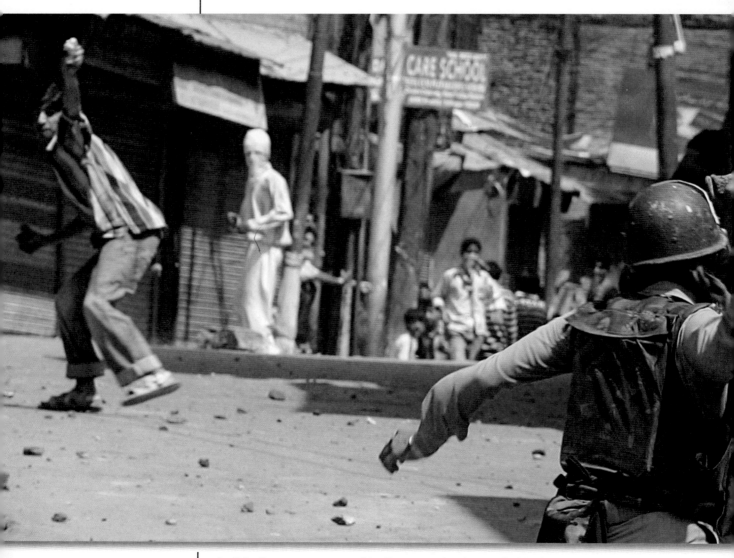

Anti-Indian protester and Indian security forces in Kashmir, 2010.

The Wars of the World

Chapters 3 (in the section "The Waning of War") discussed the decreasing number and size of wars in the world. This chapter will focus on the remaining wars, and historical cases, to explain the causes of international conflicts.

Figure 5.1 shows the 13 wars in progress in January 2012. The largest are in Afghanistan and Somalia. All 13 wars are in the global South. All but Colombia and the Philippines are in a zone of active fighting (outlined on the map) spanning parts of Africa, South Asia, and the Middle East.

In five smaller zones (dotted lines on the map), dozens of wars of recent decades have ended. Some of the countries in these zones still face difficult postwar years with the possibility of sliding back into violence, as Yemen did in 2009 after a 1999 cease-fire. But most peace agreements in the world's postwar zones are holding up.[1]

Types of War

Many different activities are covered by the general term *war*. Consequently, it is not easy to say how many wars are going on in the world at the moment. But most lists of wars set some minimum criteria—for instance, a minimum of a thousand battle deaths—to distinguish war from lower-level violence such as violent strikes or riots.

Wars are very diverse. Wars arise from different situations and play different roles in bargaining over conflicts. Starting from the largest wars, we may distinguish the following main categories.

Hegemonic war is a war over control of the entire *world order*—the rules of the international system as a whole, including the role of world hegemony (see "Hegemony," pp. 57–60). This class of wars (with variations in definition and conception) is also known as *world war*, *global war*, *general war*, or *systemic war*.[2] The last hegemonic war was World War II. Largely because of the power of modern weaponry, this kind of war probably cannot occur any longer without destroying civilization.

Total war is warfare by one state waged to conquer and occupy another. The goal is to reach the capital city and force the surrender of the government, which can then be replaced with one of the victor's choosing (see p. 185). Total war began with the massively destructive Napoleonic Wars, which introduced large-scale conscription and geared the entire French national economy toward the war effort. The practice of total war evolved with industrialization, which further integrated all of society and economy into the practice of war. The last total war between great powers was World War II.

In total war, with the entire society mobilized for the struggle, the entire society of the enemy is considered a legitimate target. For instance, in World War II Germany attacked British civilians with V-2 rockets, while British and U.S. strategic bombing killed 600,000 German civilians and hundreds of thousands of Japanese.

Limited war includes military actions carried out to gain some objective short of the surrender and occupation of the enemy. For instance, the U.S.-led war against Iraq in 1991 retook the territory of Kuwait but did not go on to Baghdad to topple Saddam Hussein's government. Many border wars have this character: after occupying the land

Read and Listen to **Chapter 5** at **mypoliscilab.com**

Study and **Review** the **Pre-Test & Flashcards** at **mypoliscilab.com**

---

[1] Fortna, Virginia Page. *Peace Time: Cease-Fire Agreements and the Durability of Peace*. Princeton, 2004.
[2] Levy, Jack S. Theories of General War. *World Politics* 37 (3), 1985: 344–74. Thompson, William R. *On Global War: Historical-Structural Approaches to World Politics*. South Carolina, 1988.

FIGURE 5.1 Wars in Progress, January 2011

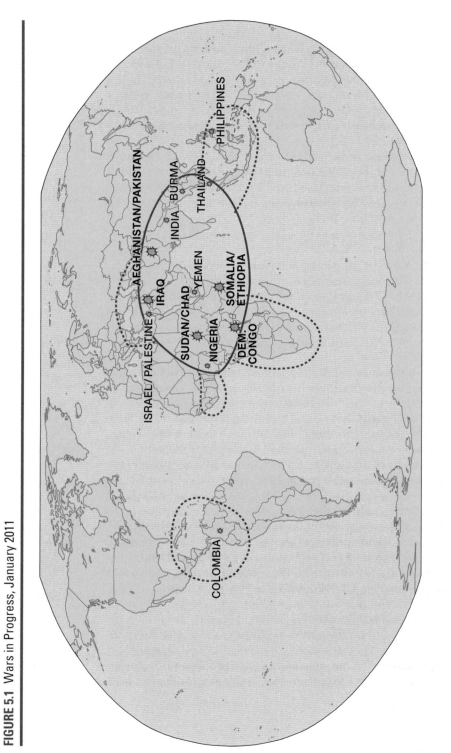

✳ Estimated deaths to date over 100,000

✳ Estimated deaths to date under 100,000

— Zone of active wars

···· Zones of transition from wars in recent decades

it wants, a state may stop short and defend its gains, as Russia did after expelling Georgian troops from disputed Georgian provinces in 2008, for example.

Raids are limited wars that consist of a single action—a bombing run or a quick incursion by land. In 2007, Israeli warplanes bombed a facility in Syria that Israel believed to be a nuclear research facility in order to stop Syria from making progress on nuclear weapons. Raids fall into the gray area between wars and nonwars because their destruction is limited and they are over quickly. Raiding that is repeated or fuels a cycle of retaliation usually becomes a limited war or what is sometimes called *low-intensity conflict.*

Civil war refers to war between factions within a state trying to create, or prevent, a new government for the entire state or some territorial part of it.[3] (The aim may be to change the entire system of government, to merely replace the people in it, or to split a region off as a new state.) The U.S. Civil War of the 1860s is a good example of a secessionist civil war, as is the war of Eritrea province in Ethiopia (now the internationally recognized state of Eritrea) in the 1980s. The war in El Salvador in the 1980s is an example of a civil war for control of the entire state (not secessionist). Civil wars often seem to be among the most brutal wars. People fighting their fellow citizens act no less cruelly than those fighting people from another state. The 50,000 or more deaths in the civil war in El Salvador, including many from massacres and death squads, were not based on ethnic differences. Of course, many of today's civil wars emerge from ethnic or clan conflicts as well. In Chad, for example, a rebel group composed of rival clans to the president's nearly overthrew the government in 2007. Sustaining a civil war usually requires a source of support for rebels, from neighboring states, diaspora ethnic communities, or revenue from natural resources or illegal drugs.

Guerrilla war, which includes certain kinds of civil wars, is warfare without front lines. Irregular forces operate in the midst of, and often hidden or protected by, civilian populations. The purpose is not to directly confront an enemy army but rather to harass and punish it so as to gradually limit its operation and effectively liberate territory from its control. Rebels in most civil wars use such methods. U.S. military forces in South Vietnam fought against Vietcong guerrillas in the 1960s and 1970s, with rising frustration. Efforts to combat a guerrilla army—counterinsurgency—are discussed in Chapter 6. In guerrilla war, without a fixed front line, there is much territory that neither side controls; both sides thus exert military leverage over the same places at the same time. Often the government controls a town by day and the guerrillas by night. Thus, guerrilla wars are extremely painful for civilians, who suffer most when no military force firmly controls a location, opening the door to banditry, personal vendettas, sexual violence, and other such lawless behavior.[4] The situation is doubly painful because conventional armies fighting against guerrillas often cannot distinguish them from civilians and punish both together. In one famous case in South Vietnam, a U.S. officer who had ordered an entire village burned to deny its use as a sanctuary by the Vietcong commented, "We had to destroy the village to save it." Warfare increasingly is irregular and guerrilla-style; it is less and less often an open, conventional clash of large state armies, although the latter still occurs occasionally.

In all types of war, the abstractions and theories of IR scholars hardly capture the horrors experienced by those on the scene, both soldiers and civilians. War suspends basic norms of behavior and, especially over time, traumatizes participants and bystanders. Soldiers see their best friends blown apart before their eyes, and they must kill and maim

Watch
the **Video**
"**The South
Ossetia Crisis**"
on **mypoliscilab.com**

Explore
the **Simulation**
"**Conflict: You Are
a Strategic Analyst**"
on **mypoliscilab.com**

---

[3] Collier, Paul, and Nicholas Sambanis, eds. *Understanding Civil War: Evidence and Analysis. Vol. 1: Africa. Vol. 2: Europe, Central Asia, and Other Regions.* World Bank, 2005. Walter, Barbara F., and Jack Snyder, eds. *Civil Wars, Insecurity, and Intervention.* Columbia, 1999.

[4] Kalyvas, Stathis N. *The Logic of Violence in Civil War.* Cambridge, 2006.

GIVING UP THE GUNS

Once armed groups stop shooting, a long process of postwar transition ensues. Disarming and demobilizing militias is the most critical aspect of this transition, but also the most difficult because it leaves disarmed groups vulnerable. Here, a major armed group turns in weapons under an amnesty in the Niger Delta region of Nigeria, 2009.

their fellow human beings; some experience lifelong psychological traumatic stress as a result. Civilians experience terror, violence, and rape; they lose loved ones and homes; they too often live with trauma afterward. The violence of war does not resemble war movies, but instead creates a nearly psychotic experience of overwhelming confusion, noise, terror, and adrenaline. Soldiers in professional armies train to keep functioning in these conditions—but still have an incredibly difficult job—whereas those in irregular forces and civilian populations caught in civil wars have little hope of coping. The horrors of all wars are magnified in cases of genocide and massacre, of child soldiers, and of brutal warfare that continues over years.

Scholars and policy makers are paying more attention in recent years to the difficult transitions from war to peace around the world—postwar reconciliation, conflict resolution, transitional governments representing opposing factions, economic reconstruction, and so forth. These efforts often address collective goods problems among the parties, as when Somali clan elders in 2007 agreed that all would be better off by giving up their guns to the new central government but none wanted to go first.[5] After the shooting stops, international peacekeepers and NGOs focus on Security Sector Reform (SSR) to create professional military and police forces instead of warlord militias. The process of Disarmament, Demobilization, and Reintegration (DDR) deals with the common problem of what to do with irregular forces after civil wars end.[6]

In several countries where long internal wars in the 1990s had led to dehumanization and atrocities—notably in South Africa—new governments used **truth commissions** to help the society heal and move forward. The commission's role was to hear honest testimony from the period, to bring to light what really happened during these wars, and in exchange to offer most of the participants asylum from punishment. Sometimes international NGOs helped facilitate the process. However, human rights groups objected to a settlement in Sierra Leone in 1999 that brought into the government a faction that had routinely cut off civilians' fingers as a terror tactic. (Hostilities did end, however, in 2001.) In 2006, Colombian right-wing militia leaders called from jail for the creation of a Truth Commission before which they could confess their role in a long civil war (and receive amnesty). Thus, after brutal ethnic conflicts give way to complex political settlements, most governments try to balance the need for justice and truth with the need to keep all groups on board.

Experts have debated how much truth and reconciliation are necessary after long conflicts. Some now argue that in some circumstances, tribunals and government-sponsored panels to investigate past crimes could lead to political instability in transitional states. Other experts disagree, noting that the work of such panels can be essential to building trust that is important for democracy.[7]

[5] Gettleman, Jeffrey. Islamists Out, Somalia Tries to Rise from Chaos. *The New York Times*, January 8, 2007: A5.
[6] Schnabel, Albert, and Hans-Georg Ehrhart, eds. *Security Sector Reform and Post-Conflict Peacebuilding.* UN University, 2006.
[7] Payne, Leigh. *Unsettling Accounts: Neither Truth Nor Reconciliation in Confessions of State Violence.* Duke. 2008. Subotic, Jelena. *Hijacked Justice: Dealing with the Past in the Balkans.* Cornell. 2009.

Theories of the Causes of War

The Roman writer Seneca said nearly 2,000 years ago: "Of war men ask the outcome, not the cause."[8] This is not true of political scientists. They want to know why countries fight.

The term **conflict** in IR generally refers to armed conflict. Conflict itself is ever present in the international system—the condition against which bargaining takes place. In conflict bargaining, states develop capabilities that give them leverage to obtain more favorable outcomes than they otherwise would achieve. Whether fair or unfair, the ultimate outcome of the bargaining process is a settlement of the particular conflict. Rarely do conflicts lead to violence, however.

The question of when conflict becomes violent can be approached in different ways. Descriptive approaches, favored by historians, tend to focus narrowly on specific direct causes of the outbreak of war, which vary from one war to another.[9] For example, one could say that the assassination of Archduke Franz Ferdinand in 1914 "caused" World War I. More theoretical approaches, favored by many political scientists, tend to focus on the search for general explanations, applicable to a variety of contexts, about why wars break out.[10] For example, one can see World War I as caused by shifts in the balance of power among European states, with the assassination being only a catalyst.

One way to organize the many theories offered by political scientists to explain why wars begin is to use the levels of analysis concept from Chapter 1. Using this framework reminds us that most important events in IR have multiple causes at different levels of analysis.[11]

The Individual Level   On the *individual* level of analysis, theories about war center on rationality. One theory, consistent with realism, holds that the use of war and other violent means of leverage in international conflicts is normal and reflects *rational* decisions of national leaders. "Wars begin with conscious and reasoned decisions based on the calculation, made by *both* parties, that they can achieve more by going to war than by remaining at peace."[12]

An opposite theory holds that conflicts often escalate to war because of *deviations* from rationality in the individual decision-making processes of national leaders. These potentials were discussed in Chapter 4—information screens, cognitive biases, groupthink, and so forth. A related theory holds that the education and mentality of whole populations of individuals determine whether conflicts become violent. In this view, public nationalism or ethnic hatred—or even an innate tendency toward violence in human nature—may pressure leaders to solve conflicts violently.

Unfortunately, None of these theories holds up very well. Some wars clearly reflect rational calculations of national leaders, whereas others clearly were mistakes and cannot

[8] Seneca, Hercules Furens. In *Seneca's Tragedies*. Vol. 1. Translated by Frank Justus Miller. Heinemann, 1917.

[9] Howard, Michael. *The Invention of Peace: Reflections on War and the International Order*. Yale, 2001. Rotberg, Robert I., and Theodore K. Rabb, eds. *The Origin and Prevention of Major Wars*. Cambridge, 1989. Blainey, Geoffrey. *Causes of War*. 3rd ed. Free Press, 1988.

[10] Vasquez, John A., ed. *What Do We Know about War?* Rowman & Littlefield, 2000. Maoz, Zeev, and Azar Gat, eds. *War in a Changing World*. Michigan, 2001. Copeland, Dale C. *The Origins of Major War*. Cornell, 2001. Van Evera, Stephen. *Causes of War: Power and the Roots of Conflict*. Cornell, 1999.

[11] Levy, Jack S. The Causes of War: A Review of Theories and Evidence. In Tetlock, P. E., et al., eds. *Behavior, Society, and Nuclear War*. Vol. 1. Oxford, 1989, pp. 209–333. Waltz, Kenneth N. *Man, the State, and War: A Theoretical Analysis*. Columbia, 2001.

[12] Howard, Michael. *The Causes of Wars, and Other Essays*. Harvard, 1983, p. 22. Emphasis in original. For a related argument, see Fearon, James. Rationalist Explanations for War. *International Organization* 49 (3), 1995: 379–414.

be considered rational. Certainly some individual leaders seem prone to turn to military force to try to settle conflicts on favorable terms. But a maker of war can become a maker of peace, as did Egypt's Anwar Sadat, for example. Individuals of many cultural backgrounds and religions lead their states into war, as do both male and female leaders.

The Domestic Level   The *domestic* level of analysis draws attention to the characteristics of states or societies that may make them more or less prone to use violence in resolving conflicts. During the Cold War, Marxists frequently said that the aggressive and greedy *capitalist* states were prone to use violence in international conflicts, whereas Western leaders claimed that the expansionist, ideological, and totalitarian nature of *communist* states made them especially prone to using violence. In truth, both types of society fought wars regularly.

Likewise, rich industrialized states and poor agrarian ones both use war at times. In fact, anthropologists have found that a wide range of *preagricultural* hunter-gatherer societies were much more prone to warfare than today's societies.[13] Thus the potential for warfare seems to be universal across cultures, types of society, and time periods—although the importance and frequency of war vary greatly from case to case.

Some argue that domestic political factors shape a state's outlook on war and peace. For example, the democratic peace suggests that democracies almost never fight other democracies (see Chapter 3), although both democracies and authoritarian states fight wars. Others claim that domestic political parties, interest groups, and legislatures play an important role in whether international conflicts become international wars.[14]

Few useful generalizations can tell us which societies are more prone or less prone to war. The same society may change greatly over time. For example, Japan was prone to using

WHY WAR?

Political scientists do not agree on a theory of why great wars like World War II occur and cannot predict whether they could happen again. The city of Stalingrad (Volgograd) was decimated during Germany's invasion of the Soviet Union, 1943.

---

[13] Keeley, Lawrence H. *War before Civilization: The Myth of the Peaceful Savage*. Oxford, 1996. O'Connell, Robert L. *Ride of the Second Horseman: The Birth and Death of War*. Oxford, 1995. Ehrenreich, Barbara. *Blood Rites: Origins and History of the Passions of War*. Metropolitan/Henry Holt, 1997. Ember, Carol R., and Melvin Ember. Resource Unpredictability, Mistrust, and War: A Cross-Cultural Study. *Journal of Conflict Resolution* 36 (2), 1992: 242–62.

[14] Shultz, Kenneth. Domestic Opposition and Signaling in International Crises. *American Political Science Review* 92 (4), 1998: 829–44. Fearon, James. Domestic Political Audiences and the Escalation of International Disputes. *American Political Science Review* 88 (3), 1994: 577–92.

violence in international conflicts before World War II, but averse to such violence since then. The !Kung bush people in Angola and Namibia—a hunter-gatherer society—were observed by anthropologists in the 1960s to be extremely peaceful. Yet anthropologists in the 1920s had observed them engaging in murderous intergroup violence.[15] If there are general principles to explain why some societies at some times are more peaceful than others and why they change, political scientists have not yet identified them.

The Interstate Level Theories at the *interstate* level explain wars in terms of power relations among major actors in the international system. Some of these theories are discussed in Chapter 2. For example, power transition theory holds that conflicts generate large wars at times when power is relatively equally distributed and a rising power is threatening to overtake a declining hegemon in overall position. At this level, too, competing theories exist that seem incompatible. Deterrence, as we have seen, is supposed to stop wars by building up power and threatening its use. But the theory of arms races holds that wars are caused, not prevented, by such actions. No general formula has been discovered to tell us in what circumstances each of these principles holds true.

Some political scientists study war from a statistical perspective, analyzing data on types of wars and the circumstances under which they occurred.[16] Current research focuses on the effects of democracy, government structure, trade, international organizations, and related factors in explaining the escalation or settlement of "militarized interstate disputes."[17]

The Global Level At the *global* level of analysis, a number of theories of war have been proposed. Of the several variations on the idea that major warfare in the international system is *cyclical*, one approach links large wars with *long economic waves* (also called *Kondratieff cycles*) in the world economy, of about 50 years' duration. Another approach links the largest wars with a 100-year cycle based on the creation and decay of world orders (see "Hegemony" on pp. 57–60). These **cycle theories** at best can explain only general tendencies toward war in the international system over time.[18]

An opposite approach in some ways is the theory of linear long-term change—that war as an outcome of conflict is becoming less likely over time due to the worldwide development of both technology and international norms. Some IR scholars argue that war and military force are becoming *obsolete* as leverage in international conflicts because these means of influence are not very effective in today's highly complex, interdependent world. A parallel line of argument holds that today's military technology is too powerful to use in most conflicts; this is especially applicable to nuclear weapons. Advocates of these theories make historical analogies to the decline of the practices of slavery, dueling, and cannibalism—once considered normal but now obsolete.[19] These approaches have a strong empirical basis (see "The Waning of War" in Chapter 3) but no consensus has emerged regarding the best explanation for this trend.

---

[15] Eibl-Eibesfeldt, Irenaus. *The Biology of Peace and War: Men, Animals, and Aggression*. Viking, 1979.

[16] Wright, Quincy. *A Study of War*. Chicago, 1965 [1942]. Richardson, Lewis F. *Arms and Insecurity*. Boxwood, 1960. Geller, Daniel S., and J. David Singer. *Nations at War: A Scientific Study of International Conflict*. Cambridge, 1998. Midlarsky, Manus I., ed. *Handbook of War Studies II*. Michigan, 2000. Diehl, Paul F., ed. *The Scourge of War: New Extensions of an Old Problem*. Michigan, 2004.

[17] Singer, J. David, and Paul F. Diehl, eds. *Measuring the Correlates of War*. Michigan, 1990. Ghosn, Faten, Glenn Palmer, and Stuart Bremer. The Militarized Interstate Dispute 3 Data Set, 1993–2001: Procedures, Coding Rules, and Description. *Conflict Management and Peace Science* 21 (2), 2004: 133–54.

[18] Goldstein, Joshua S. *Long Cycles: Prosperity and War in the Modern Age*. Yale, 1988. Modelski, George. *Long Cycles in World Politics*. Washington, 1987.

[19] Mueller, John. *Retreat from Doomsday: The Obsolescence of Major War*. Basic Books, 1989.

Thus, on all the levels of analysis, competing theories offer different explanations for why some conflicts become violent and others do not. For these reasons, political scientists cannot yet predict with any confidence which of the world's many international conflicts will lead to war. We can gain insight, however, by studying various types of conflicts to understand better what states are fighting about.

Conflicts of Ideas

👁— **Watch**
the **Video**
"The Iran-Iraq War"
on **mypoliscilab.com**

The following sections discuss six types of international conflict: ethnic, religious, ideological, territorial, governmental, and economic. The first three are conflicts over ideas, the last three conflicts over interests. These six types of conflict are not mutually exclusive, and they overlap considerably in practice. For example, the conflicts between Russia and Ukraine after the 1991 Soviet breakup were complex. *Ethnic* Russians living in Ukraine, and ethnic Ukrainians in Russia, experienced conflict. There are also *religious* differences between Ukrainian and Russian forms of Christianity. In addition, the two new states had a *territorial* dispute over the Crimean peninsula, which Soviet leader Nikita Khrushchev had transferred to Ukraine in the 1950s. The two states also had *economic* conflicts over trade and money after the Soviet breakup, which created new borders and currencies. These multiple conflicts did not lead to the use of military force, however. In 2005, the opposition took control of Ukraine's government (after a flawed election was rerun in response to weeks of mass street protests). Then-Russian president Vladimir Putin, who had campaigned for the incumbent party in Ukraine, protested vigorously but did not seriously consider military force. So the types of conflict discussed here come into play in combination rather than separately.

We will look first at the most difficult types of conflict, in which intangible elements such as ethnic hatred, religious fervor, or ideology come into play—conflicts of ideas. These identity-based sources of international conflict today have been shaped historically by nationalism as the link between identity and internationally recognized statehood. Therefore we will briefly review the development of nationalism before examining the three types of conflicts of ideas.

Nationalism

Nationalism—devotion to the interests of one's own nation over the interests of other states—may be the most important force in world politics in the past two centuries. A nation is a population that shares an identity, usually including a language and culture. But nationality is a difficult concept to define precisely. To some degree, the extension of political control over large territories such as France created the commonality necessary for nationhood—states created nations. At the same time, however, the perceived existence of a nation has often led to the creation of a corresponding state as a people win sovereignty over their own affairs—nations created states.[20]

Around A.D. 1500, countries such as France and Austria began to bring entire nations together into single states. These new nation-states were very large and powerful and overran smaller neighbors. Over time, they conquered and incorporated many small territorial units. Eventually the idea of nationalism itself became a powerful force

---

[20] Gellner, Ernest. *Nations and Nationalism.* Cornell, 1983. Tilly, Charles. *Coercion, Capital and European States, a.d. 990–1990.* Blackwell, 1990. Hobsbawm, E. J. *Nations and Nationalism Since 1780: Programme, Myth, Reality.* Cambridge, 1990. Mayall, James. *Nationalism and International Society.* Cambridge, 1990.

and ultimately contributed to the disintegration of large multinational states such as Austria-Hungary (in World War I), the Soviet Union, and Yugoslavia.

The principle of *self-determination* implies that people who identify as a nation should have the right to form a state and exercise sovereignty over their affairs. Self-determination is a widely praised principle in international affairs today (although not historically). But it is generally secondary to the principles of sovereignty (noninterference in other states' internal affairs) and territorial integrity, with which it frequently conflicts. Self-determination does not give groups the right to change international borders, even those imposed arbitrarily by colonialism, in order to unify a group with a common national identity. Generally, though not always, self-determination has been achieved by violence. When the borders of (perceived) nations do not match those of states, conflicts almost inevitably arise. Today such conflicts are widespread—in Northern Ireland, Quebec, Israel-Palestine, India-Pakistan, Sri Lanka, Tibet, Sudan, and many other places.[21]

The Netherlands helped establish the principle of self-determination when it broke free of Spanish ownership around 1600 and set up a self-governing Dutch republic. The struggle over control of the Netherlands was a leading cause of the Thirty Years' War (1618–1648), and in that war states mobilized their populations for war in new ways. For instance, Sweden drafted one man out of ten for long-term military service, while the Netherlands used the wealth derived from global trade to finance a standing professional army.

This process of popular mobilization intensified greatly in the French Revolution and the subsequent Napoleonic Wars, when France instituted a universal draft and a centrally run "command" economy. Its motivated citizen armies, composed for the first time of Frenchmen rather than mercenaries, marched longer and faster. People participated in part because they were patriotic. Their nation-state embodied their aspirations and brought them together in a common national identity.

The United States meanwhile had followed the example of the Netherlands by declaring independence from Britain in 1776. Latin American states gained independence early in the 19th century, and Germany and Italy unified their nations out of multiple political units (through war) later in that century.

Before World War I, socialist workers from different European countries had banded together as workers to fight for workers' rights. In that war, however, most abandoned such solidarity and instead fought for their own nation; nationalism thus proved a stronger force than socialism. Before World War II, nationalism helped Germany, Italy, and Japan build political orders based on *fascism*—an extreme authoritarianism girded by national chauvinism. And in World War II it was nationalism and patriotism (not communism) that rallied the Soviet people in order to sacrifice by the millions to turn back Germany's invasion.

In the past 50 years, nations by the dozens have gained independence and statehood. Jews worked persistently in the first half of the 20th century to create the state of Israel, and Palestinians aspired in the second half to create a Palestinian state. While multinational states such as the Soviet Union and Yugoslavia have fragmented in recent years, ethnic and territorial units such as Ukraine, Slovenia, and East Timor have established themselves as independent nation-states. Others, such as Montenegro and Kurdistan, seek to do so and already run their own affairs. The continuing influence of nationalism in today's world is evident. It affects several of the main types of conflict that occupy the rest of this chapter.

---

[21] Horowitz, Donald L. *Ethnic Groups in Conflict*. 2nd ed. California, 2000.

DRIVING OUT THE OUT-GROUP

Ethnic conflicts play a role in many international conflicts. Ethnocentrism based on an in-group bias can promote intolerance and ultimately dehumanization of an out-group, as in genocides in Darfur (Sudan), Rwanda, and Bosnia; South African apartheid; the persecution of Jews and other minorities in Nazi Germany; and slavery in the United States. In 2008, after decades of peace and tolerance, Kenya erupted in bloody ethnic violence after a disputed presidential election. Here, a mob from one ethnic group attacks and drives away all members of a rival ethnic group from a formerly mixed town.

Ethnic Conflict

Ethnic conflict is quite possibly the most important source of conflict in the numerous wars now occurring throughout the world.[22] **Ethnic groups** are large groups of people who share ancestral, language, cultural, or religious ties and a common *identity* (individuals identify with the group). Although conflicts between ethnic groups often have material aspects—notably over territory and government control—ethnic conflict itself stems from a dislike or hatred that members of one ethnic group systematically feel toward another ethnic group. Ethnic conflict is thus not based on tangible causes (what someone does) but on intangible ones (who someone is).

Ethnic groups often form the basis for nationalist sentiments. Not all ethnic groups identify as nations; for instance, within the United States various ethnic groups coexist (sometimes uneasily) with a common *national* identity as Americans. But in locations where millions of members of a single ethnic group live as the majority population in their ancestors' land, they usually think of themselves as a nation. In most such cases they aspire to have their own state with its formal international status and territorial boundaries.[23]

Territorial control is closely tied to the aspirations of ethnic groups for statehood. Any state's borders deviate to some extent (sometimes substantially) from the actual location of ethnic communities. Members of the ethnic group are left outside its state's borders, and members of other ethnic groups are located within the state's borders. The resulting situation can be dangerous, with part of an ethnic group controlling a state and another part living as a minority within another state controlled by a rival ethnic group. Frequently the minority group suffers discrimination in the other state, and the "home" state tries to rescue or avenge them.

Other ethnic groups lack any home state. Kurds share a culture, and many of them aspire to create a state of Kurdistan. But Kurds reside in four states—Turkey, Iraq, Iran, and Syria—all of which strongly oppose giving up control of part of their own territory to create a Kurdish state (see Figure 5.2). In the 1990s, rival Kurdish guerrilla armies fought both

---

[22] Gurr, Ted Robert. *Peoples versus States: Minorities at Risk in the New Century.* U.S. Institute of Peace Press, 2000. Saideman, Stephen M. *The Ties That Divide.* Columbia, 2001. Horowitz, Donald L. *Ethnic Groups in Conflict.* California, 1985. Williams, Robin M. *The Wars Within: Peoples and States in Conflict.* Cornell, 2003.
[23] Cederman, Lars-Erik. *Emergent Actors in World Politics: How States and Nations Develop and Dissolve.* Princeton, 1997. Shelef, Nadav. *Evolving Nationalism: Homeland, Identity, and Religion in Israel, 1925-2005.* Cornell, 2010.

FIGURE 5.2 Kurdish Areas

Ethnic populations often span international borders. The shaded region shows the approximate area of Kurdish settlements.

Iraqi and Turkish military forces and each other. Repeatedly in the late 1990s, Turkey sent large military forces into northern Iraq to attack Kurdish guerrilla bases. Kurds enjoyed autonomy in part of northern Iraq under U.S. protection in the 1990s and maintained a quasi-autonomous status in post-Saddam Iraq. The Kurds' success in the 2010 Iraqi elections gave them a strong position to retain this status.[24]

A bloody ethnic conflict broke out in 2010 in Kyrgyzstan after that country's president was overthrown. In an attempt to unseat the transitional government, supporters of the overthrown president promoted ethnic tensions between majority Kyrgyz and minority Uzbeks. The resulting violence claimed hundreds of lives and displaced as many as 400,000, creating a refugee crisis in Central Asia.

Ethnic conflicts often create pressures to redraw borders by force. When ethnic populations are minorities in territories controlled by rival ethnic groups, they may even be driven from their land or (in rare cases) systematically exterminated. By driving out the minority ethnic group, a majority group can assemble a more unified, more contiguous, and larger territory for its nation-state, as ethnic Serbs did through "ethnic cleansing" after the breakup of Yugoslavia.

Outside states often worry about the fate of "their people" living as minorities in neighboring states. For instance, Albania is concerned about ethnic Albanians who are the majority population in the Serbian province of Kosovo (but a minority of the population in Serbia). But as Kosovo moved toward independence from Serbia, Serbia worried about the minority of ethnic Serbs living in Kosovo. Similar problems have fueled wars between Armenia and Azerbaijan and between India and Pakistan. The dangerous combination of ethnic conflict and territorial disputes could lead to more wars in the future.

Causes of Ethnic Hostility   Why do ethnic groups frequently dislike each other? Often there are long-standing historical conflicts over specific territories or natural resources, or over one ethnic group's economic exploitation or political domination of another. They

---

[24] McDowall, David. *A Modern History of the Kurds*. 3rd ed. Tauris, 2004. Barkey, Henri J., and Graham E. Fuller. *Turkey's Kurdish Question*. Rowman & Littlefield, 1998.

become driven not by tangible grievances (though these may well persist as irritants) but by the kinds of processes described by social psychology that are set in motion when one group of people has a prolonged conflict with another and experiences violence at the hands of the other group.[25] The ethnic group is a kind of extended *kinship* group—a group of related individuals sharing some ancestors. Even when kinship relations are not very close, a *group identity* makes a person act as though the other members of the ethnic group were family. For instance, African American men who call each other "brother" express group identity as kinship. Likewise, Jews around the world treat each other as family even though each community has intermarried over time and shares more ancestors with local non-Jews than with distant Jews. Perhaps as technology allows far-flung groups to congregate in cyberspace, there will be less psychological pressure to collect ethnic groups physically in a territorial nation-state.

Ethnocentrism, or *in-group bias,* is the tendency to see one's own group in favorable terms and an *out-group* in unfavorable terms. Some scholars believe that ethnocentrism has roots in a biological propensity to protect closely related individuals, though this idea is controversial.[26] More often, in-group bias is understood in terms of social psychology. In either case, the ties that bind ethnic groups together, and divide them from other groups, are based on the identity principle (see pp. 6–7). Just as the reciprocity principle has its negative side (see pp. 5–6), so does the identity principle. The same forces that allow sacrifice for a group identity, as in the European Union, also allow the formation of in-group bias.

No *minimum criterion* of similarity or kin relationship is needed to evoke the group identity process, including in-group bias. In psychological experiments, even trivial differentiations can evoke these processes. If people are assigned to groups based on a known but unimportant characteristic (such as preferring, say, circles to triangles), before long the people in each group show in-group bias and find they don't much care for the other group's members.[27]

In-group biases are far stronger when the other group looks different, speaks a different language, or worships in a different way (or all three). All too easily, an out-group can be dehumanized and stripped of all human rights. This **dehumanization** includes the common use of animal names—"pigs," "dogs," and so forth—for members of the out-group. U.S. propaganda in World War II depicted Japanese people as apes. Especially in wartime, dehumanization can be extreme. The restraints on war that have evolved in regular interstate warfare, such as not massacring civilians (see "War Crimes" on pp. 270–274), are easily discarded in interethnic warfare.

Experience in Western Europe shows that over time, education can overcome ethnic animosities between traditionally hostile nations, such as France and Germany. After World War II, these states' governments rewrote the textbooks that a new generation would use to learn its people's histories. Previously, each state's textbooks had glorified its own past deeds, played down its misdeeds, and portrayed its traditional enemies in unflattering terms. In a continent-wide project, new textbooks that gave a more objective and fair rendition were created. By contrast, present-day Japanese textbooks that gloss over Japan's crimes in World War II continue to inflame relations with both China and Korea.

The existence of a threat from an out-group promotes the cohesion of an in-group, thereby creating a somewhat self-reinforcing process of ethnic division. However, ethnocentrism also often causes members of a group to view themselves as disunited (because

---

[25] Glad, Betty, ed. *Psychological Dimensions of War.* Sage, 1990.
[26] Shaw, Paul, and Yuwa Wong. *Genetic Seeds of Warfare: Evolution, Nationalism, and Patriotism.* Unwin Hyman, 1989.
[27] Tajfel, H., and J. C. Turner. The Social Identity Theory of Intergroup Behavior. In Worchel, S., and W. Austin, eds. *Psychology of Intergroup Relations.* 2nd ed. Nelson-Hall, 1986, pp. 7–24.

POLICY PERSPECTIVES

President of Liberia, Ellen Johnson-Sirleaf

PROBLEM *How do you prevent civil war while retaining control of your government?*

BACKGROUND Imagine you are the president of Liberia. Your election in the spring of 2006 as the first woman president in Africa was hailed as a breakthrough for Liberia. The election ended decades of political violence that devastated your own country as well as your neighbors Ivory Coast and Sierra Leone. Most recently, the violence ended when former Liberian president Charles Taylor went into exile in Nigeria. Tens of thousands of people lost their lives or were subject to human rights abuses, including torture and mutilation, in the wars begun under Taylor's rule.

Recently, however, there is optimism within your country and from the international community. Rebel groups have remained quiet, and Charles Taylor was arrested in 2006 and faces trial in a war crimes tribunal established by the UN for the brutal war in Sierra Leone. Economic aid has begun to stream into your country to assist in development. Your country is resource rich and has the potential to become a middle-income country owing to its vast natural agricultural and mineral resources. And you won the 2011 Nobel Peace Prize for helping end the war.

DOMESTIC CONSIDERATIONS Tremendous challenges, however, lie ahead. Economically, your country is underdeveloped, with years of civil war leading to increases in corruption and economic stagnation. Many of the powerful economic actors in your country benefit from the corruption and graft, which you have pledged to end. Unemployment is very high, with hundreds of thousands of young men unemployed. Until recently, roving bands of fighters controlled pockets of territory. Armed police have occasionally returned to the streets to restore order, and in late 2008 a mass breakout from the country's only maximum security prison allowed over 100 criminals to escape.

SCENARIO Now imagine that a group that was involved in the civil war begins to reopen the war. The group has taken refuge in Sierra Leone and now begins to make cross-border raids against your country. You also suspect they are sending weapons and funds to rebels within Liberia. Although Sierra Leone does not support the group, its government is experiencing its own political instability and has limited resources to devote to the issue.

One option is to negotiate directly with the group. Negotiations could lead to peace, but might require power sharing in your government that could derail your attempts to lessen corruption.

Another option is to use military force against the rebels. But international donors would discourage you from endangering the fragile peace in Liberia, with the implicit threat of an aid cutoff if you are perceived to be too hard-line. Thus, a military offensive against the rebels would have financial risks. In addition, the reemergence of a civil war would make your proposed democratic and economic reforms more difficult to implement. Your military is not well trained and you are very uncertain about the possibility of success against the rebels. A strong military response to the rebels, however, could discourage future aggression and establish that you are a tough leader who is serious about enforcing the peace.

CHOOSE YOUR POLICY How do you handle this new threat from the rebels? Do you adopt a hard-line policy against them in hopes of defeating them? Or do you attempt reconciliation in hopes of minimizing the prospect of further bloodshed, albeit at the price of bringing your enemies into the government and thus undermining some of your goals?

they see their own divisions up close) and the out-group as monolithic (because they see it only from the outside). This usually reflects a group's sense of vulnerability. In the Arab-Israeli conflict, Israelis tend to see themselves as fragmented into dozens of political parties and diverse immigrant communities pulling in different directions, while they see "the Arabs" as a monolithic bloc united against them. Meanwhile, Arab Palestinians see themselves as fragmented into factions and weakened by divisions among the Arab states, while "the Israelis" appear monolithic to them.

Ethnic groups are only one point along a spectrum of kinship relations—from nuclear families through extended families, villages, provinces, and nations, up to the entire human race. Loyalties fall at different points along the spectrum. Again, there is no minimum criterion for in-group identity. For instance, experts said that of all the African countries, Somalia was surely immune from ethnic conflicts because Somalis were all from the same ethnic group, spoke the same language, and shared the same religion. Then in 1991–1992 a ruinous civil war erupted between members of different clans (based on extended families), leading to mass starvation, the intervention of foreign military forces, and two decades of near-anarchy and nonstop violence.

It is unclear why people identify most strongly at one level of group identity.[28] In Somalia, loyalties are to clans; in Serbia, they are to the ethnic group; in the United States and elsewhere, multiethnic nations command people's primary loyalty. States reinforce their citizens' identification with the state through flags, anthems, pledges of allegiance, patriotic speeches, and so forth. Perhaps someday people will shift loyalties even further, developing a *global identity* as humans first and members of states and ethnic groups second.

Genocide

In extreme cases, governments use **genocide**—systematic extermination of ethnic or religious groups in whole or in part—to try to destroy scapegoated groups or political rivals. Under its fanatical policies of racial purity, Nazi Germany exterminated 6 million Jews and millions of others, including homosexuals, Roma, and communists. The mass murders, now known as the Holocaust, along with the sheer scale of war unleashed by Nazi aggression, are considered among the greatest *crimes against humanity* in history. Responsible German officials faced justice in the *Nuremberg Tribunal* after World War II (see p. 270). The pledges of world leaders after that experience to "never again" allow genocide have been found wanting as genocide recurred in the 1990s in Bosnia and Rwanda, and most recently in Darfur, Sudan.

In 1994 in Rwanda, where the Hutu group is the majority and the Tutsi group the minority, a Hutu-nationalist government carried out the most deadly genocide of recent decades. The minority Tutsis had earlier held power over the Hutus, and Belgian colonialism had exploited local rivalries. In 1994, ethnic Hutu extremists in the government gave orders throughout the country to kill ethnic Tutsis and those Hutus who had opposed the government. In short order, an estimated 800,000 men, women, and children were massacred, mostly by machete, and their bodies dumped into rivers; thousands at a time washed up on lakeshores in neighboring Uganda.

It might be tempting to view Hutu-Tutsi hatred as part of a pattern of age-old ethnic hatreds that cropped up in the post–Cold War era, especially in "backward" areas such as Africa. (This age-old-hatreds theory was often articulated by Western politicians in the Bosnia case, portraying the Balkans, like Africa, as "backward" and conflict-prone.) If killings based on age-old hatreds are inevitable, then inaction by the rest of the world

---

[28] Krause, Jill, and Neil Renwick, eds. *Identities in International Relations*. St. Martin's, 1996.

might be justifiable. However, explaining genocide as a result of backwardness does not work well, because one of the world's most civilized, "advanced" states, Germany, exterminated its Jews even more efficiently than Rwanda did its Tutsis—the difference being that the "advanced" society could kill with industrial chemicals instead of at knifepoint.

Social psychology theories treat the Rwandan genocide as pathological—a deviation from both rationality and social norms. In-group biases based on fairly arbitrary group characteristics become amplified by a perceived threat from an out-group, and exaggerated by history, myth, and propaganda (including schooling). Such feelings can be whipped up by politicians pursuing their own power. A key threshold is crossed when the out-group is dehumanized; norms of social interaction, such as not slitting children's throats, can then be disregarded.

As the genocide in Rwanda unfolded, the international community stood by. A weak UN force there had to withdraw, although its commander later estimated that with 5,000 more troops he could have changed the outcome. The weak international response to this atrocity reveals how frail international norms of human rights are compared to norms of noninterference in other states' internal affairs—at least when no strategic interests are at stake. The Hutu ultranationalists quickly lost power when Tutsi rebels defeated the government militarily, but the war spread into Democratic Congo, where the ultranationalists took refuge and where sporadic fighting continues 18 years later.[29] Top U.S. officials, including President Clinton, later apologized for their inadequate response, but the damage was done. Worse yet, renewed vows of "never again" proved wanting once more in the next case, Darfur.

In Sudan, the warring sides (largely northern Muslims versus southern Christians) in a decades-long civil war signed a peace agreement in 2003, ending a war that had killed more than a million people. The agreement called for withdrawing government forces from the south of the country, establishing a power-sharing transitional government and army, and holding a referendum in the rebel areas in six years. These proccesses led to the successful independence of South Sudan in 2011. But following this peace agreement, rebels in the western Darfur region began to protest their exclusion from the peace agreement. In response, the government helped Arab (Muslim) militias raid black African (also Muslim) Darfur villages, wantonly killing, raping, and burning. In late 2004, the government and some of the Darfur rebels reached a tentative peace agreement, and the African Union and United Nations sent in a joint peacekeeping mission in 2007. After years of Sudanese government delays and other frustrations, the force had 23,000 uniformed personnel on the ground by 2011. The international community's ineffective response to the mass murders in Darfur, like that in Rwanda in 1994, shows the limited reach of international norms in today's state-based international system.[30]

In cases of both genocide and less extreme scapegoating, ethnic hatreds do not merely bubble up naturally. Rather, politicians provoke and channel hatred to strengthen their own power. Often, in ethnically divided countries, political parties form along ethnic lines, and party leaders consolidate their positions in their own populations by exaggerating the dangers from the other side.

The Cold War, with its tight system of alliances and authoritarian communist governments, seems to have helped keep ethnic conflicts in check. In the Soviet Union and Yugoslavia—multinational states—the existence of a single strong state (willing to op-

---

[29] Power, Samantha. *The Problem from Hell: America and the Age of Genocide*. Basic Books, 2002. Barnett, Michael. *Eyewitness to a Genocide: The United Nations and Rwanda*. Cornell, 2003. Straus, Scott. *The Order of Genocide: Race, Power, and War in Rwanda*. Cornell, 2006. Des Forges, Alison. *Leave None to Tell the Story: Genocide in Rwanda*. Human Rights Watch, 1999.
[30] Hamburg, David A., M.D. *Preventing Genocide: Practical Steps Toward Early Detection and Effective Action*. Paradigm, 2008.

press local communities) kept the lid on ethnic tensions and enforced peace between neighboring communities. The breakup of these states allowed ethnic and regional conflicts to take center stage, sometimes bringing violence and war. These cases may indicate a dilemma in that freedom comes at the expense of order and vice versa. Of course, not all ethnic groups get along so poorly. After the fall of communism, most of the numerous ethnic rivalries in the former Soviet Union did not lead to warfare, and in Czechoslovakia and elsewhere, ethnic relations were relatively peaceful after the fall of communism.

Religious Conflict

One reason ethnic conflicts often transcend material grievances is that they find expression as *religious* conflicts. Because religion is the core of a community's value system in much of the world, people whose religious practices differ are easily disdained and treated as unworthy or even inhuman. When overlaid on ethnic and territorial conflicts, religion often surfaces as the central and most visible division between groups. For instance, most people in Azerbaijan are Muslims; most Armenians are Christians. This is a very common pattern in ethnic conflicts.

Nothing inherent in religion mandates conflicts—in many places members of different religious groups coexist peacefully. But religious differences hold the potential to make existing conflicts more intractable, because religions involve core values, which are held as absolute truth.[31]

This is increasingly true as *fundamentalist* movements have gained strength in recent decades. (The reasons for fundamentalism are disputed, but it is clearly a global-level phenomenon.) Members of these movements organize their lives and communities around their religious beliefs; many are willing to sacrifice, kill, and die for those beliefs. Fundamentalist movements have become larger and more powerful in recent decades in Christianity, Islam, Judaism, Hinduism, and other religions. In India, for example, Hindu fundamentalists have provoked violent clashes and massacres that have reverberated internationally. In 2002, a frenzy of burning, torturing, and raping by Hindu nationalist extremists killed nearly a thousand Muslims in India's Gujarat state, where the Hindu nationalist party controls the state government. In Israel, Jewish fundamentalists have used violence, including the assassination of Israel's own prime minister in 1995, to derail Palestinian-Israeli peace negotiations.

Fundamentalist movements challenge the values and practices of **secular** political organizations—those created apart from religious establishments. The secular practices threatened by fundamentalist movements include the rules of the international system, which treat states as formally equal and sovereign whether they are "believers" or "infidels." As transnational belief systems, religions often are taken as a higher law than state laws and international treaties. Iranian Islamist fundamentalists train and support militias in other states such as Iraq and Lebanon. Jewish fundamentalists build settlements in Israeli-occupied territories and vow to cling to the land even if their government evacuates it. Christian fundamentalists in the United States persuade their government to withdraw from the UN Population Fund because of that organization's views on family planning and abortion. Each of these actions runs counter to the norms of the international system and to the assumptions of realism.[32]

Some have suggested that international conflicts in the coming years may be generated by a "clash of civilizations"—based on the differences among the world's major cultural

---

[31] Appleby, R. Scott. *The Ambivalence of the Sacred: Religion, Violence, and Reconciliation.* Rowman & Littlefield, 2000.

[32] Juergensmeyer, Mark. *The New Cold War? Religious Nationalism Confronts the Secular State.* California, 1993.

groupings, which overlap quite a bit with religious communities.[33] The idea has been criticized for being overly general, and for assuming that cultural differences naturally create conflict. In fact, although religious and ethnic conflicts receive tremendous attention in the media, *most* ethnic and religious groups living together in states do not fight.[34]

Islamist Movements Currently, violent conflicts are being prosecuted in the name of all the world's major religions. But special attention is due to conflicts involving Islamic groups and states. Islamist actors are active participants in 9 of the world's 13 wars in progress (see p. 154). In addition, the U.S. "war on terror" is directed against a network of Islamic terror groups.However, most Islamist movements are not violent.

Islam, the religion practiced by **Muslims**, is broad and diverse. Its divergent populations include Sunni Muslims (the majority), Shi'ite Muslims (concentrated in Iran, southern Iraq, southern Lebanon, and Bahrain), and many smaller branches and sects. Most countries with mainly Muslim populations belong to the Islamic Conference, an IGO. The world's predominantly Islamic countries stretch from Nigeria to Indonesia, centered historically in the Middle East (see Figure 5.3) but with the largest populations in South and Southeast Asia. Many international conflicts around this zone involve Muslims on one side and non-Muslims on the other, as a result of geographical and historical circumstances including colonialism and oil.

Islamist groups advocate basing government and society on Islamic law. These groups vary greatly in the means they employ to pursue this goal. Most are nonviolent—charities and political parties. Some are violent—militias and terrorist networks.[35] In Jordan, Islamic parties won the largest bloc of seats in parliament without violence. In the 1990s Islamic parties gained ground in Turkey—a secular state in which the military has intervened repeatedly to prevent religious politics—and a former Islamist leader has been prime minister since 2003, making Turkay an important model of moderate Islam in the region. Islamist parties have also played leading roles in Iraq's government since 2003 and played central roles in the Arab Spring countries, winning elections in Tunisia and Egypt.

If Islamist movements seek changes primarily in domestic policies, why do they matter for IR? Islamist politics may lead to different foreign policies, but the more important answer is that some Islamist movements have become a transnational force shaping world order and global North-South relations in important ways.

MESSAGE OF HATE

Religious intolerance can exacerbate tensions between groups, sometimes crossing the line to violence, with international implications. Osama bin Laden tried to use differences between Muslims and non-Muslims to incite violent conflict. Here, in a video seized in the raid that killed him in 2011, bin Laden watches one of his own propaganda tapes on TV.

[33] Huntington, Samuel P. *The Clash of Civilizations and the Remaking of World Order*. Simon & Schuster, 1996.
[34] Fearon, James D., and David D. Laitin. Explaining Interethnic Cooperation. *American Political Science Review* 90 (4), 1996: 715–35.
[35] Husain, Mir Zohair. *Global Islamic Politics*. 2nd ed. Longman, 2003. Esposito, John L. *Unholy War: Terror in the Name of Islam*. Oxford, 2002.

FIGURE 5.3 Members of the Islamic Conference and Areas of Conflict

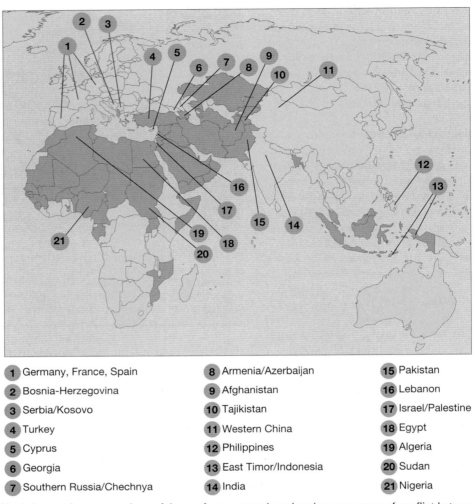

1 Germany, France, Spain	**8** Armenia/Azerbaijan	**15** Pakistan
2 Bosnia-Herzegovina	**9** Afghanistan	**16** Lebanon
3 Serbia/Kosovo	**10** Tajikistan	**17** Israel/Palestine
4 Turkey	**11** Western China	**18** Egypt
5 Cyprus	**12** Philippines	**19** Algeria
6 Georgia	**13** East Timor/Indonesia	**20** Sudan
7 Southern Russia/Chechnya	**14** India	**21** Nigeria

Shaded countries are members of the conference; numbered regions are areas of conflict between Muslims and non-Muslims or secular authorities.

In several countries, Islamists reject Western-oriented secular states in favor of governments more explicitly oriented to Islamic values.[36] These movements reflect long-standing *anti-Western* sentiment in these countries—against the old European colonizers who were Christian—and are in some ways *nationalist* movements expressed through religious channels. In some Middle Eastern countries with authoritarian governments, religious institutions (mosques) have been the only available avenue for political opposition. Religion has therefore become a means to express opposition to the status quo in politics and culture. These anti-Western feelings in Islamic countries

---

[36] Binder, Leonard. *Islamic Liberalism: A Critique of Development Ideologies.* Chicago, 1988. Davidson, Lawrence. *Islamic Fundamentalism: An Introduction.* Greenwood Press, 2003.

came to a boil in 2006 after a Danish newspaper published offensive cartoons depicting the prophet Muhammad. Across the world, Muslims protested, set fire to several Danish embassies, rioted (with dozens of deaths resulting), and boycotted Danish goods.

Public opinion in both Muslim and non-Muslim countries shows some misconceptions and differences in opinion (see Figure 5.4). Support for Islamist radicals varies greatly among countries, from a majority in Jordan down to 14 percent in Turkey and 13 percent in Morocco. A 2005 poll recalls "mirror image" perceptions (see p. 131). In five Western industrialized countries, about 40 to 80 percent thought Muslims were "fanatical," and 60 to 80 percent thought they did not respect women. But in three of five Muslim countries, more than 60 percent thought non-Muslims were "fanatical," and in four of those five countries, a majority thought non-Muslims did not respect women.

FIGURE 5.4 Public Opinion in Muslim and Non-Muslim Countries

How often is suicide bombing or violence against civilians justified in order to defend Islam?

Percent responding
often or sometimes in 2010

Lebanon	39%
Indonesia	15%
Pakistan	8%
Turkey	6%
Jordan	20%
Egypt	20%

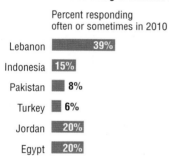

Non-Muslims think Muslims are:

Fanatical

Spain	83%
Germany	78%
France	50%
Great Britain	48%
U.S.	43%

Not respectful of women

Spain	83%
Germany	80%
France	77%
Great Britain	59%
U.S.	69%

Muslims think non-Muslims are:

Fanatical

Jordan	68%
Turkey	67%
Egypt	61%
Indonesia	41%
Pakistan	24%

Not respectful of women

Jordan	53%
Turkey	39%
Egypt	52%
Indonesia	50%
Pakistan	52%

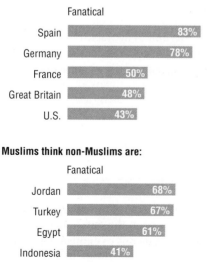
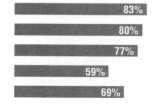
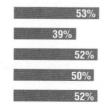

Source: Pew Global Attitudes Survey, 2005 and 2010.

The more radical Islamist movements not only threaten some existing governments—especially those tied to the West—but also undermine traditional norms of state sovereignty. They reject Western political conceptions of the state (based on individual autonomy) in favor of a more traditional Islamic orientation based on community. Some aspire to create a single political state encompassing most of the Middle East, as existed in the *caliphate* of A.D. 600–1200. Such a development would create a profound challenge to the present international system—particularly to its current status quo powers—and would therefore be opposed at every turn by the world's most powerful states.

Islamists in Middle Eastern countries, like revolutionaries elsewhere, derive their main base of strength from championing the cause of the poor masses against rich elites. Like other revolutionaries throughout the global South, Islamist movements in countries such as Turkey, Egypt, and Lebanon draw their base of support from poor slums, where the Islamists sometimes provide basic services unmet by the government.

In a public opinion poll in 2006 in Egypt, Morocco, Saudi Arabia, and Jordan, a plurality of respondents identified primarily as Muslims, more than identified primarily as citizens of their states or as Arabs. But in Lebanon and the UAE, the pattern was reversed, with large majorities identifying primarily as citizens of their states. Islamist movements tap into the public's identification with issues that may not materially affect them but affect their identities as Muslims, across national borders—especially the Arab-Israeli conflict. The public in Muslim countries also cared about wars in the 1990s in Bosnia, Azerbaijan, and Chechnya, where Christian armed forces attacked Muslim civilians. Islamists see all these conflicts as part of a broad regional (or even global) struggle of Islam against Western, Christian imperialism—a struggle dating back to the Crusades almost a thousand years ago. From the perspective of some outsiders, the religious conflicts boiling and simmering at the edges of the Islamic world look like an expansionist threat to be contained. The view from within looks more like being surrounded and repressed from several directions.

The Iraq War since 2003 greatly inflamed anti-American feeling and helped radicalize politics across the Muslim world, especially in Arab countries that saw the U.S. invasion as a humiliation to Arab dignity. Initially, the presidency of Barack Hussein Obama, whose middle name reflects Muslim family roots in Kenya and who grew up partly in Muslim Indonesia, began to alter this anti-American dynamic. Favorability ratings of America climbed in Bahrain, Jordan, and Egypt, in part due to President Obama's speech on America's relations with Muslim states in Cairo in June 2009, where Obama called for a "new beginning" to those relationships. By 2010, though, many of those numbers had begun to fall again as the Arab world began to express frustration in the Middle East peace process and the U.S. decision to stay in Afghanistan.

Armed Islamist Groups   Anti-American and anti-Western sentiments in predominantly Islamic countries have accelerated the growth of violent Islamist groups as well. Although they are in the minority, they have disproportionate effects on IR and receive the most public attention.

Armed Islamist groups vary tremendously, and in some cases violently disagree with each other (see Table 5.1). In particular, divisions between the Sunni and Shi'ite wings of Islam have led to violence, especially in and around Iraq—a Shi'ite-majority country ruled by Sunnis under Saddam Hussein. Iraq's war against Shi'ite Iran killed a million people, and Saddam's repression of a Shi'ite uprising after the 1991 Gulf War killed tens of thousands at the least. Under the U.S. occupation of Iraq since 2003, Shi'ite parties took power and Shi'ite militias exacted revenge, while some Sunnis waged a relentless and brutal insurgency.

TABLE 5.1 Major Armed Islamist Groups

Group	Country	Branch of Islam	Actions
Islamic Republic of Iran	Iran	Shi'ite	Only Islamic revolution to successfully control a state (since 1979); held off secular Iraq in 1980s war; now attempting to build nuclear weapons.
Hezbollah	Lebanon	Shi'ite	Fought well against Israeli army in 2006 war. Previously claimed credit for driving Israel from southern Lebanon in 2000. Popular even with Sunnis.
Mahdi Army	Iraq	Shi'ite	Clashed with U.S. forces in Iraq; major faction in Iraqi government.
Various	Iraq	Sunni	Insurgent forces inflicted many casualties on U.S. forces in Iraq. Foreign fighters also active in Iraq.
Hamas	Palestine (Gaza)	Sunni	Forces have killed hundreds of Israeli civilians and fought a war against Israel in 2008. Won Palestinian elections in 2006. Controls Gaza Strip.
al Shabab	Somalia	Sunni	Controls part of the country. Has allied itself with al Qaeda. Weakened in 2011.
Moro Islamic Liberation Front	Philippines	Sunni	Forces have fought for independence of certain regions in the Muslim-populated southern Philippine Islands.
al Qaeda	World (Pakistan?)	Sunni	9/11 attacks and European bombings. Weakened by deaths of top leaders.
Taliban	Afghanistan	Sunni	Controlled Afghanistan and gave sanctuary to al Qaeda until ousted after 9/11. Regrouped in remote Pakistan and staged many attacks since 2006.

Islamist guerrilla fighters/terrorists are also active in Chechnya (Russia), Kashmir (India), Central Asia, Indonesia, and Europe.

In 2006, after the bombing of a revered Shi'ite mosque in Iraq, a wave of sectarian violence killed tens of thousands of Iraqis. In the subsequent years, violence among rival factions in Iraq increased and then lessened, but the long-term relationship of Iraqi Sunnis and Shi'ites remains unsettled.

In the worldwide picture as well, armed Islamist groups divide into Sunni and Shi'ite wings that do not cooperate much. On the Shi'ite side, the most important groups are Iran's Revolutionary Guards, the Mahdi Army in Iraq (and other Shi'ite militias there), and Hezbollah (or Hizbollah) in southern Lebanon. These groups are all relatively success-ful—in Iran, the religious leadership controls the state, and in Lebanon, Hezbollah controls territory and holds seats in the national legislature.

In Iran, a popular uprising in 1979 overthrew the U.S.-backed shah and installed an Islamic government in which the top religious leaders (ayatollahs) can overturn the laws passed by the parliament. The rejection of international norms by some Islamists was dramatically illustrated when Iran refused to protect U.S. diplomats and the U.S. embassy in Iran (see "Laws of Diplomacy" on pp. 261–263). Defying the UN Security Council, Iran is currently developing nuclear technology that could produce nuclear weapons within about five years. In 2009, divisions emerged in Iran over a disputed presidential election. Moderate political elements accused Islamic extremists of hijack-ing the elections and the country, while hurting Iran's relations with the West. Protests were suppressed with force.

Iran strongly supports—with money, arms, and training—the Hezbollah militia in Lebanon. Hezbollah runs hundreds of schools, hospitals, and other charities, but is also included on the U.S. list of terrorist organizations. Hezbollah claimed that its attacks induced Israel to withdraw from southern Lebanon in 2000. Then in 2006, Hezbollah showed itself to be a competent military force, putting up a stiff fight in a brief but destructive war with Israel. Hezbollah's success in "standing up to Israel" won it popular support throughout the Arab world, even among Sunnis. But it raised old divisions within Lebanon, leading to more political instability there. Hezbollah took a leading role in Lebanon's government in 2011, despite a UN tribunal's indictment of its members for the 2005 assassination of Lebanon's prime minister.

Iran also supports Shi'ite militias in southern Iraq, but they operate independently. (Although both Iranians and southern Iraqis are Shi'ites, the first are Persians and the latter Arabs.) Two of the largest such militias are the virulently anti-American Mahdi Army, led by Moqtada al-Sadr, and the Supreme Islamic Iraqi Council (SIIC), which is less anti-American. The Mahdi Army's influence has diminished since the Iraqi government fought for and won military control of the main southern Iraqi city and the U.S. army cleared Mahdi fighters in Baghdad.

On the Sunni side, the major radical Islamist groups adhere to some version of Wahhabism, a fundamentalist interpretation of Islamic law with roots in Saudi Arabia. The most important center of this fundamentalist movement currently is in Afghanistan and the next-door tribal areas of western Pakistan.

An Islamic government was established in Afghanistan in 1992 after a civil war (and following a decade of ill-fated Soviet occupation). Rival Islamic factions then continued the war with even greater intensity for several years. By 1997, a faction called Taliban had taken control of most of Afghanistan and imposed an extreme interpretation of Islamic law. With beatings and executions, the regime forced women to wear head-to-toe coverings, girls to stay out of school, and men to grow beards, among other repressive policies.

The incendiary mixture in Afghanistan in the 1990s—unending war, grinding poverty, Islamic fundamentalism, and an ideologically driven government—allowed Afghanistan to become a base for worldwide terrorist operations, culminating in the September 11, 2001, attacks. In response, the United States exerted its power to remove the Taliban from power in Afghanistan and disrupt the al Qaeda terrorist network headquartered there. Despite U.S. successes in the 2001 war, the Taliban continues daily attacks on NATO forces. Attacks on civilians also continue in Afghanistan.

The defeat of fundamentalists in Afghanistan in 2001 put pressure on its much larger next-door neighbor, nuclear-armed Pakistan, whose military ruler tried, after 2001, to smother Islamic extremists and hold together a stable, relatively secular government. Radically anti-American Islamists have since gained control of Pakistan's autonomous "tribal areas" bordering Afghanistan, using them to launch attacks on Afghanistan, on Pakistan's cities, and, in late 2008, on Mumbai, India. Pro-democracy forces in Pakistan ousted the military ruler and installed an elected government in 2008, though not until after the movement's leader, Benazir Bhutto, had been assassinated.

The war in Afghanistan has strained relations between Pakistan and the United States and its NATO allies. American officials have accused some Pakistani officials of aiding anti-NATO Islamist forces. In 2010, a leak of over 90,000 documents on the Internet further strained Pakistani-American relations as many of those documents revealed frustrations among U.S. commanders at the cooperation between Taliban forces and some members of the Pakistani intelligence agency. These strains worsened in 2011 when U.S. forces found and killed Osama bin Laden in a Pakistani city.

Al Qaeda is an international group—more a network or movement than a central organization in recent years—that recruits fighters from various countries, possibly trains them in other countries, and perhaps sends them on missions to fight in foreign conflicts (such as in Afghanistan in the 1980s or Iraq today).[37]

Elsewhere in Asia, Islamic extremist groups connected with al Qaeda continue to operate. In 2002 terrorists killed hundreds—mostly Australians—in a nightclub bombing in Bali, Indonesia. In 2003, al Qaeda and related groups carried out terror bombings worldwide—in Morocco, Saudi Arabia, Russia, the Philippines, Indonesia, Iraq, and Turkey. In 2004, they bombed trains in Madrid, killing hundreds and apparently tipping an election against the pro-American Spanish government—and thus inducing Spain to pull its troops out of Iraq. In 2005, their followers—Muslims who had grown up in Britain—bombed the London subway and bus system. In 2008, armed attackers

THE POLITICS OF ISLAM

In some Muslim-populated countries, Islam is a political rallying point—especially in authoritarian countries in which the mosque is a rare permitted gathering point. Islamist politicians are developing new models of government, mixing democracy and Islamic tradition, especially in the countries most affected by the Arab Spring protests, which frequently peaked after Friday prayers. Here, Egyptians pray during a Friday protest against the authoritarian president early in 2011.

from Pakistan stormed hotels and public places in Mumbai, India, and killed about 150 people, mostly in random shootings. The attack heightened tensions between India and Pakistan, but cooler heads prevailed, and the nuclear-armed rivals did not move toward war.

In Saudi Arabia—home to the world's largest oil reserves, Islam's holiest sites, and the roots of Wahhabism—al Qaeda has long sought to overthrow the monarchy, which stays in power through a combination of repression, cooptation, and oil-funded economic development. In 1979, Islamist militants briefly seized control of the Grand Mosque in Mecca, and in 2003 al Qaeda suicide bombers attacked several residential compounds in the kingdom.

Saudi Arabia's neighbor to the south, Yemen, has also become a training ground for al Qaeda fighters and operatives. Yemen is the poorest country in the Middle East and has suffered from decades of civil conflict. A weak central government has tried to clamp down on al Qaeda cells (with U.S. help), but with limited success. In the fall of 2010, multiple bombs destined for the United States were traced to al Qaeda groups Yemen.

In Palestine, the radical Islamist faction Hamas is another important Sunni Islamist militia, not closely connected with al Qaeda or Taliban. Centered in the Gaza Strip,

---

[37] Wright, Lawrence. *The Looming Tower: Al Qaeda and the Road to 9/11.* Knopf, 2006.

Hamas sent suicide bombers that killed hundreds of Israelis after 2000, then won free parliamentary elections in 2006 because it was seen as less corrupt than the dominant secular Fatah party. However, the Palestinian presidency remains in Fatah control, and rival security organizations have occasionally fought street battles. Today, Palestine remains divided, with Fatah controlling the West Bank and Hamas controlling the Gaza Strip.

Sudan's civil war between the mainly Muslim north (government-run) and the mainly Christian and animist south dragged on for two decades and killed millions. A 2005 peace agreement ended the war, and led ultimately to South Sudan's independence in 2011.

Somalia has become the most recent location for Sunni Islamist activists. One important group in Somalia is known as al Shabab. It was formed from the remains of the conservative Islamic Courts Union, which was ousted from power by an invasion by Ethiopia in 2006. Al Shabab began in southern Somalia as a small, independent Islamist group, but seized control of large parts of Somalia and claims ties to al Qaeda. The group claimed credit for deadly bombings in Uganda during the 2010 World Cup finals. The African Union maintains a 6,000-strong force in Somalia, and in 2011 it managed to push al Shabab out of the capital. A terrible famine, caused by drought and war, gripped the Shabab-held areas of the country and forced refugees into Kenya. In late 2011, Kenya sent military forces into southern Somalia to attack al Shabab, trying to create a more stable border and open up famine areas to international assistance.

The predominantly Sunni Muslim republic of Chechnya, a Russian province, tried to split away from Russia in the early 1990s after the Soviet Union collapsed. In 1994–1995, Russia sent in a huge military force that destroyed the Chechen capital but faced fierce resistance from Chechen nationalist guerrillas and withdrew in defeat. In 1999–2000, another destructive Russian campaign won power in the province. But Chechen guerrillas continued to fight Russian control and took their fight to Russian territory, including airline hijackings, hostage taking, and suicide bombings. In 2004, hundreds of children died after Chechen terrorists took over a school and held them hostage. In 2005, Russian forces killed the Chechen separatist leader they held responsible, and the war in Chechnya has now all but ended.

Overall, conflicts involving Islamist movements are more complex than simply religious conflicts; they concern power, economic relations, ethnic chauvinism, and historical empires as well.

Ideological Conflict

To a large extent, ideology is like religion: it symbolizes and intensifies conflicts between groups and states more than it causes them. Ideologies have a somewhat weaker hold on core values and absolute truth than religions do, so they pose somewhat fewer problems for the international system.

For realists, ideological differences among states do not matter much, because all members of the international system pursue their national interests in the context of relatively fluid alliances. For example, the Cold War was a global ideological struggle between capitalist democracy and communism. But the alliances and military competitions in that struggle were fairly detached from ideological factors. The two communist giants—the Soviet Union and China—did not stay together very long. India, a democracy and capitalist country, chose not to ally with the United States. And even the two great rival superpowers managed to live within the rules of the international system for the most part (such as both remaining UN members).

Over the long run, even countries that experience revolutions based on strong ideologies tend to lose their ideological fervor—be it Iran's Islamic fundamentalism in 1979, China's Maoist communism in 1949, Russia's Leninist communism in 1917, or even U.S. democracy in 1776. In each case, the revolutionaries expected that their assumption of power would dramatically alter their state's foreign policy, because in each case their ideology had profound international implications. Yet within a few decades, each of these revolutionary governments turned to the pursuit of national interests above ideological ones.

Sometimes even self-proclaimed ideological struggles are not really ideological. In Angola in the 1980s, the United States backed a rebel army called UNITA against a Soviet-aligned government—supposedly a struggle of democracy against Marxism. In truth, the ideological differences were quite arbitrary. The government mouthed Marxist rhetoric to get the Soviet Union to give it aid (a policy it reversed as soon as Soviet aid dried up). The rebels who used democratic rhetoric to get U.S. support had earlier received Chinese support and mouthed Maoist rhetoric. When the government won UN-sponsored elections, the "democratic" UNITA refused to accept the results and resumed fighting. This conflict, which finally ended in 2002, really had nothing to do with ideology. It was a power struggle between two armed, ethnically based factions fighting to control Angola's oil, diamonds, and other wealth.

IDEOLOGICAL SPLIT

Ideology plays only a limited role in most international conflicts. After revolutions, ideologies such as Marxism may affect foreign policy, but over the following decades, countries such as China or the Soviet Union typically revert to a foreign policy based more on national interests than ideology. Nonetheless, ideological clashes still occur, as between the United States and Venezuela today, which have a strong trading relationship but suffer from political antagonism. Here the leftist Venezuelan president, Hugo Chavez, addresses Venezuelans while visiting Cuba, in front of a poster of communist icon Che Guevara, 2007.

In the short term, revolutions *do* change international relations—they make wars more likely—but not because of ideology. Rather, the sudden change of governments can alter alliances and change the balance of power. With calculations of power being revised by all parties, it is easy to miscalculate or to exaggerate threats on both sides. But ideology itself plays little role in this postrevolutionary propensity for wars: revolutions are seldom exported to other states.[38]

Conflicts of Interest

If conflicts of ideas can be intractable because of psychological and emotional factors, conflicts about material interests are somewhat easier to settle based on the reciprocity principle. In theory, given enough positive leverage—a payment in some form—any state should agree to another state's terms on a disputed issue.

---

[38] Walt, Stephen M. *Revolution and War*. Cornell, 1996.

Territorial Disputes

Watch
the **Video**
**"The Cuban
Missile Crisis"**
on **mypoliscilab.com**

Among the international conflicts that concern tangible "goods," those about territory have special importance because of the territorial nature of the state (see "Anarchy and Sovereignty" on pp. 49–52). Conflicts over control of territory are really of two varieties: territorial disputes (about where borders are drawn) and conflicts over control of entire states within existing borders (discussed next under "Control of Governments"). Consider first differences over where borders between two states should be drawn—that is, who controls a disputed piece of land.

Because states value home territory with an almost fanatical devotion, border disputes tend to be among the most intractable in IR. States seldom yield territory in exchange for money or any other positive reward. Nor do states quickly forget territory that they lose involuntarily. For example, in 2002, Bolivian public opinion opposed a gas export pipeline through Chile to the sea because Chile had seized the coastline from Bolivia in 1879. The goal of regaining territory lost to another state is called **irredentism**. This form of nationalism often leads directly to serious interstate conflicts.[39] Because of their association with the integrity of states, territories are valued far beyond any inherent economic or strategic value they hold. For example, after Israel and Egypt made peace in 1978, it took them a decade to settle a border dispute at Taba, a tiny plot of beachfront on which Israeli developers had built a hotel just slightly across the old border. The two states finally submitted the issue for binding arbitration, and Egypt ended up in possession. For Egypt, regaining every inch of territory was a matter of national honor and a symbol of the sovereignty and territorial integrity that defined Egyptian statehood.

The value states place on home territory seems undiminished despite the apparent reduction in the inherent value of territory as technology has developed. Historically, territory

[39] Diehl, Paul F., ed. *A Road Map to War: Territorial Dimensions of International Conflict.* Vanderbilt, 1999. Ambrosio, Thomas. *Irredentism: Ethnic Conflict and International Politics.* Praeger, 2001.

SEEKING THE COLLECTIVE GOOD

Peace in Latin America

COLLECTIVE GOOD: Peaceful Relations Among Latin American States

BACKGROUND: Of all the world regions, Latin America is one of the most peaceful. Some scholars have gone so far as to describe Latin America as a security community given the very low incidence of interstate war in the region for the past 100 years. This is despite civil wars and numerous border disagreements between states in the region. The stable peace is a collective good enjoyed by all countries in the region, even though countries that violate it might gain territory or wealth by using military force.

CHALLENGE: Despite years of relatively peaceful interstate relations in the region, persistent conflicts still exist between some states. In 1995, Peru and Ecuador fought a border skirmish. Since 2000, other

disputes have escalated. Bolivia wants to reclaim a corridor to the sea that it lost to Chile more than 100 years ago. Colombia and Venezuela trade accusations over Venezuela's support of rebels fighting in Colombia. Rival countries have linguistic differences, ideological differences, territorial disputes, economic competition, and a range of other conflicts. With the countries having sizable armies and navies at the ready, the potential for war is always present.

SOLUTION: How has Latin America avoided more large-scale interstate war? The solution can be found in both the

RECIPROCITY

IDENTITY

was the basis of economic production—agriculture and the extraction of raw materials. Winning and losing wars meant gaining or losing territory, which meant increasing or decreasing wealth. Today, however, much more wealth derives from trade and technology than from agriculture. The costs of most territorial disputes appear to outweigh any economic benefits that the territory in question could provide. Exceptions exist, however, such as the capture of diamond-mining areas in several African countries by rebels who use the diamond revenues to finance war. (In 2002, 40 states created a program of UN certification for legitimate diamonds, trying to keep the "conflict diamonds" off the international market.)

Secession   Efforts by a province or region to secede from an existing state are a special type of conflict over borders—not the borders of two existing states but the efforts to draw international borders around a new state. Dozens of secession movements exist around the world, of varying sizes and political effectiveness, but they succeed in seceding only rarely. The existing state almost always tries to hold on to the area in question. For example, in the 1990s, the predominantly Albanian population of the Serbian province of Kosovo fought a war to secede from Serbia. NATO intervention, including sustained bombing of Serbia (not approved by the UN), led to the withdrawal of Serbia's army from Kosovo and its replacement with European and American peacekeeping troops who have been there ever since. Most of the Kosovo population wants to secede and become an internationally recognized state, but Serbians argue that Kosovo is historically and presently under Serbian sovereignty. While the UN and the great powers negotiated over the future of Kosovo, with Russia insisting there be no promise of independence, Kosovars took matters into their own hands. In 2008, Kosovo declared independence without UN approval. Several countries, including the United States and the largest EU states, recognized Kosovo's independence, angering Serbia, Russia, and China. In 2011, South Sudan successfully gained independence with UN membership and the support of Sudan.

Wars of secession can be large and deadly, and they can easily spill over international borders or draw in other countries. This spillover is particularly likely if members

reciprocity and identity principles. All states are members of the Organization of American States, which promotes reciprocity and negotiation when political disputes arise. In this way, even when some fighting occurs, conflicts do not escalate and become long, large-scale military conflicts. This negotiation process has succeeded in settling many of the existing disputes, even the Peru-Ecuador dispute, three years after their border war.

The identity principle is also at work. Latin America has developed a shared norm of conflict resolution. A dispute between any two states is perceived as a threat to all states in the region. Each state thinks broadly about its own interests to include the continuation of peace in the region. In this way, threats to peace are actively dealt with by the community as a whole.

South American leaders discuss trade, not war, in Argentina, 2010.

NEW NATION

Efforts by a region to secede from a state are a frequent source of international conflict, but international norms generally treat such conflicts as internal matters unless they spill over borders. Increasingly, autonomy agreements are resolving secession conflicts. Here, however, in 2011 a citizen celebrates the independence of South Sudan, which successfully split off from Sudan in 2011, following decades of war and years of preparation under a peace agreement.

of an ethnic or a religious group span two sides of a border, constituting the majority group in one state and a majority in a nearby region of another state, but a minority in the other state as a whole. In the Kosovo case, Albanian Muslims are the majority in Albania and in Kosovo but the minority in Serbia. The same pattern occurs in Bosnia-Serbia, Moldova-Russia, and India-Pakistan. In some cases, secessionists want to merge their territories with the neighboring state, which amounts to redrawing the international border. International norms frown on such an outcome.

The strong international norms of sovereignty and territorial integrity treat secession movements as domestic problems of little concern to other states. The general principle seems to be this: "We existing states all have our own domestic problems and disaffected groups or regions, so we must stick together behind sovereignty and territorial integrity." Thus, Russia and China opposed the secession of Kosovo from Serbia because of its implications for Chechnya and Taiwan, respectively.

This principle does have limits, however. In August of 2008, after fighting broke out between the Georgian military and the Georgian province of South Ossetia, Russia intervened militarily on behalf of South Ossetia and Abkhazia, resulting in a brief war between Russia and Georgia. Russia then recognized both Georgian provinces as independent, a move denounced by the United States and the EU and not accepted by the UN.

Messy border problems can result when multinational states break up into pieces. In such cases, borders that had been internal become international; because these borders are new, they may be more vulnerable to challenge. In the former Yugoslavia, ethnic groups had intermingled and intermarried, leaving mixed populations in most of the Yugoslav republics. When Yugoslavia broke up in 1991–1992, several republics declared their independence as separate states. Two of these, Croatia and Bosnia, contained minority populations of ethnic Serbs. Serbia seized effective control of significant areas of Croatia and Bosnia that contained Serbian communities or linked such populations geographically. Non-Serbian populations in these areas were driven out or massacred—euphemistically called **"ethnic cleansing."** Then, when Croatia reconquered most of its territory in 1995, Serbian populations in turn fled. Ethnic nationalism, whipped up by opportunistic politicians, proved stronger than multiethnic tolerance in both Serbia and Croatia.

The breakup of a state need not lead to violence, however. Serbia split peacefully from Montenegro (another of the former Yugoslav republics) in 2006. Czechoslovakia split into the Czech Republic and Slovakia in a cooperative manner. And the breakup of the Soviet Union did not lead to violent territorial disputes between republics in *most* cases, even when ethnic groups spanned new international borders (such as Ukraine-Russia).

The norm against forceful redrawing of borders does not apply to cases of decolonization. Only the territorial integrity of existing, recognized states is protected by international norms. Colonies and other territorial possessions historically had value only as property to be won, lost, sold, or traded in political deals and wars. The transfer of Hong Kong from British to Chinese control in 1997 also illustrates how colonial territory is dispensable (Britain's perspective) while home territory is nearly sacred (China's perspective). From neither perspective do the views of the inhabitants carry much weight.

Increasingly, autonomy for a region has become a realistic compromise between secession and full control by a central government. In 2005, spurred partly by the devastating tsunami a year earlier, separatists in Aceh province, Indonesia, disbanded, giving up on independence and instead participating in regional elections in 2006. The Indonesian government withdrew its 24,000 troops from Aceh and offered the province limited self-rule along with 70 percent of the oil, gas, and mineral wealth earned there.

Interstate Borders   Border disputes between existing states are taken more seriously by the international community, but are less common than secessionist conflicts. Because of the norm of territorial integrity, few important border conflicts remain among long-established states.[40] At one time, huge chunks of territory passed between states at the stroke of a pen (on a peace treaty or marriage contract). However, this kind of wholesale redrawing of borders has not occurred among established states for 50 years. Since the end of World War II, only a minuscule amount of territory has changed hands between established states through force (this does not apply to the formation of new states and the fragmenting of old ones). Such efforts have been made, but have failed. For instance, when Iraq attacked Iran in 1980, one objective was to control the Shatt-al-Arab waterway (with access to the Persian Gulf) because of its commercial and strategic value. But ten years and a million deaths later, the Iran-Iraq border was back where it started.

Furthermore, when territorial disputes do occur between established states, they *can* be settled peacefully, especially when the disputed territory is small compared with the states disputing it. In 1994 a panel of Latin American judges settled a century-long border dispute between Argentina and Chile over some mountainous terrain that both claimed. The 3-to-2 ruling, after the countries submitted the dispute for judicial arbitration, awarded the territory to Argentina and provoked howls of protest from Chile—and even a hair-pulling fight between the Chilean and Argentine contestants in the Miss World beauty contest two months later. But despite the strong feelings evoked by the loss of territory, Argentina and Chile settled 22 of 24 remaining border disputes peacefully after nearly going to war in 1978 over disputed islands.

The possibility of peaceful resolution of territorial disputes was highlighted in 2006 with the withdrawal of Nigerian troops from the potentially oil-rich Bakassi Peninsula, which Nigeria ceded to Cameroon's sovereignty. The resolution of the dispute, dating from colonial times, followed more than a decade of painstaking progress through the World Court, the personal mediation of the UN secretary-general when Nigeria initially rejected the Court's decision, and the promise of outside powers to monitor implementation of the agreement. Why would Nigeria—a country with nine times Cameroon's population, more than triple its GDP, and a much stronger military—voluntarily cede territory? Doing so would seem to run counter to the predictions of realism in particular

---

[40] The CIA's *World Factbook* provides a comprehensive list of minor border and other international disputes. See http://www.cia.gov/library/publications/the-world-factbook/fields/2070.html.

and the dominance principle in general. Liberal theories would do better at explaining this outcome: Nigeria acted in its own self-interest, because turning the dispute over to the World Court and bringing in the UN to assist with implementation brought the kind of stability needed for foreign investment to develop Nigeria's own resources, primarily oil.

Lingering Disputes   Today, the few remaining interstate border disputes generate important international conflicts. Among the most difficult are the borders of *Israel*, which have never been firmly defined nor recognized by its neighbors. The 1948 cease-fire lines resulting from Israel's war of independence expanded in the 1967 war, then contracted again on the Egyptian border after the Camp David peace treaty of 1978. The remaining territories occupied in 1967—the *West Bank* near Jordan, the *Gaza Strip* near Egypt, and the *Golan Heights* of Syria—are central to the Arab-Israeli conflict. Israeli-Palestinian agreements since 1993 tried to move toward Palestinian autonomy in parts of the West Bank and the Gaza Strip, and negotiations seemed headed toward creation of a state of Palestine in all or most of the occupied territories. However, the U.S. effort to craft a final settlement at the 2000 "Camp David II" summit failed—over how to divide Jerusalem and other emotional issues—and a new phase of violence and hate began, with each side blaming the other for failing to make peace. In 2011, Palestine unsuccessfully applied for UN membership, and peace talks remained stalled.

Another serious border dispute is in the *Kashmir* area where India, Pakistan, and China intersect. The Indian-held part of Kashmir is predominantly inhabited by Muslims, a group that is the majority in Pakistan but a minority in India. A *Line of Control* divides the disputed province. Pakistan accuses India of oppressing Kashmiris and thwarting an international agreement to decide Kashmir's future by a popular referendum. India accuses Pakistan of aiding and infiltrating Islamic radicals who carry out attacks in Indian-occupied Kashmir. The two countries went to war twice over the issue, and nearly did so again in 2002—but that time with both sides holding dozens of nuclear-armed missiles that some experts estimated would kill more than 10 million people in an India-Pakistan war. Perhaps chastened by this experience, the two countries improved relations in 2003 and began a cease-fire that stopped most of the incessant low-level fighting along the Line of Control, although not the fighting between Indian authorities and insurgents. In 2004, India agreed to begin a slow withdrawal of troops. In 2008 Indian-administered elections were held, and despite separatists' calls for a boycott, turnout was high.

Many of the world's other remaining interstate territorial disputes—and often the most serious ones—concern the control of small islands, which often provide strategic advantages, natural resources (such as offshore oil), or fishing rights. International law now gives an island's owner fishing and mineral rights in surrounding seas for 200 miles in each direction. The tiny disputed *Spratly Islands* in the South China Sea, whose surrounding waters may hold substantial oil reserves, are claimed in part or in full by China, Taiwan, Vietnam, the Philippines, Malaysia, and Brunei (see Figure 5.5). All of those states except Brunei have resorted to military actions at times to stake their claims. Recently, multiple encounters between the U.S. and Chinese navies as well as Chinese pressures on Vietnamese petroleum interests have raised tensions over the controversial territory. About half of the world's trade tonnage passes near the Spratly Islands, including Persian Gulf oil and other key resources headed for Japan, China, South Korea, and Taiwan.

Japan and China also dispute tiny islands elsewhere, as do Japan and South Korea. These disputes involve low economic stakes, but have become a focus of nationalist sentiments on both sides, fueled partly by memories of World War II, when Japan occupied China and Korea. In 2005, after Japan spent half a billion dollars preserving Okinotori—an

FIGURE 5.5 Disputed Islands

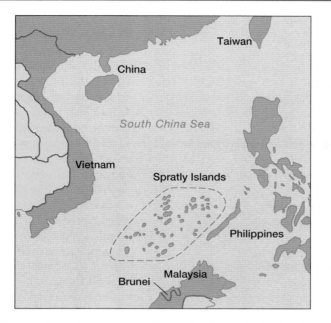

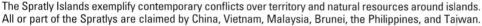

The Spratly Islands exemplify contemporary conflicts over territory and natural resources around islands. All or part of the Spratlys are claimed by China, Vietnam, Malaysia, Brunei, the Philippines, and Taiwan.

uninhabited coral reef with two tiny protrusions smaller than a house and just inches above sea level—China declared it not an "island" (with a surrounding economic zone) but just a "rock" (which, without economic activity, does not quality for such a zone).

A number of smaller conflicts exist around the globe. In the Middle East, Iran and the United Arab Emirates dispute ownership of small islands near the mouth of the Persian Gulf. In 2002, Spain sent soldiers to oust a handful of Moroccan troops from islands off Morocco's coast. In South America, Argentina and Britain still dispute control of the *Falkland Islands (Islas Malvinas)*, over which they fought a war in 1982. And the major bone of contention in Russian-Japanese relations is the ownership of the small but strategically located *Kuril Islands*, occupied by the Soviet Union in 1945. With islands now bringing control of surrounding economic zones, international conflicts over islands will undoubtedly continue in the coming years.

Territorial Waters   States treat **territorial waters** near their shores as part of their national territory. Definitions of such waters are not universally agreed upon, but norms have developed in recent years, especially since the *UN Convention on the Law of the Sea (UNCLOS)* (see p. 399). Waters within three miles of shore have traditionally been recognized as territorial, but beyond that there are disputes about how far out national sovereignty extends and for what purposes. UNCLOS generally allows a 12-mile limit for shipping and a 200-mile *exclusive economic zone (EEZ)* covering fishing and mineral rights (but allowing for free navigation by all). The EEZs together cover a third of the world's oceans. In 2010, Russia and Norway agreed to divide portions of the Arctic Ocean into EEZs for the purposes of oil and gas extraction, ending a 40-year dispute between those states.

LOCATION, LOCATION, LOCATION

Control of islands, and of the large exclusive economic zone (EEZ) that surrounds them under the law of the sea, has created a number of complicated interstate conflicts. Japan claims Okinotori, shown here in 2005, as an island with an EEZ, but China calls it merely a "rock" without surrounding economic rights.

Because of the EEZs, sovereignty over a single tiny island can now bring with it rights to as much as 100,000 square miles of surrounding ocean. But these zones overlap greatly, and shorelines do not run in straight lines; thus numerous questions of interpretation arise about how to delineate territorial and economic waters. For example, Libya claims ownership of the entire Gulf of Sidra, treating it as a bay; the United States treats it as a curvature in the shoreline and insists that most of it is international waters. In 1986, the United States sent warships into the Gulf of Sidra to make its point. U.S. planes shot down two Libyan jets that challenged the U.S. maneuvers.

Canada in 1994–1995 sent its navy to harass Spanish fishing boats just *beyond* the 200-mile zone (but affecting fish stocks within the zone). In the Sea of Okhotsk, which is a little more than 400 miles across, Russia's EEZ includes all but a small "doughnut hole" of international waters in the middle. Non-Russian boats have fished intensively in the "hole," which of course depletes fish stocks in Russia's EEZ.

A dangerous maritime dispute flared in 2010 when a South Korean warship sank in disputed waters in the Yellow Sea. International investigators concluded that a North Korean torpedo sank the vessel, although North Korea denied involvement. South Korea continues to conduct military operations in the disputed waters, while North Korea continues to fire artillery shells in the area, including an attack that killled several civilians in 2010. The two countries have never formally ended the Korean War by signing a peace treaty.

Airspace   Airspace above a state is considered the territory of the state. To fly over a state's territory, an airplane must have that state's permission. For example, in a 1986 raid on Libya, U.S. bombers based in Britain had to fly a long detour over the Atlantic Ocean because France (between Britain and Libya) would not grant permission for U.S. planes to use its airspace during the mission.

Outer space, by contrast, is considered international territory like the oceans. International law does not define exactly where airspace ends and outer space begins. However, orbiting satellites fly higher than airplanes, move very fast, and cannot easily change direction to avoid overflying a country. Also, very few states can shoot down satellites. Because satellites have become useful to all the great powers as intelligence-gathering tools, and because all satellites are extremely vulnerable to attack, a norm of demilitarization of outer space has developed. No state has ever attacked the satellite of another. In 2007, however, China rattled nerves by successfully destroying one of its own satellites with an antisatellite missile, strewing high-speed debris around orbital space.

Control of Governments

Despite the many minor border disputes that continue to plague the world, most struggles to control territory do not involve changing borders. Rather, they are conflicts over which governments will control entire states.

In theory, states do not interfere in each other's governance, because of the norm of sovereignty. In practice, however, states often have strong interests in the governments of other states and use a variety of means of leverage to influence who holds power in those states. These conflicts over governments take many forms, some mild and some severe, some deeply entwined with third parties, and some more or less bilateral. Sometimes a state merely exerts subtle influences on another state's elections; at other times, a state supports rebel elements seeking to overthrow the second state's government.

During the Cold War, both superpowers actively promoted changes of government in countries of the global South through covert operations and support of rebel armies. The civil wars in Angola, Afghanistan, and Nicaragua are good examples. Both superpowers poured in weapons, money, military advisors, and so forth—all in hopes of influencing who controlled the country's government.[41]

In 2004–2005, shadows of these old Cold War rivalries fell over Ukraine, as Russia and the West backed opposite sides in a disputed election. The election divided the largely Russian-speaking, Eastern Orthodox part of Ukraine to the east from the Ukrainian-speaking, Catholic, western part of the country. The pro-Russian incumbent carried the eastern region and was declared the winner after an election that international monitors declared unsound. Russian president Vladimir Putin had personally campaigned with him, and strongly opposed letting Ukraine—a former part of the Soviet Union—come under the influence of the West. Meanwhile the pro-Western candidate was poisoned during the campaign, but survived. His supporters took to the streets in late 2004 demanding new elections, which the top Ukrainian court eventually ordered and which the opposition won.

Occasionally, one state invades another in order to change its government. The Soviet Union did this in Czechoslovakia in 1968; the United States did so in Iraq in 2003. People generally resent having foreigners choose their government for them—even if they did not like the old government—and the international community frowns on such overt violations of national sovereignty.

International conflicts over the control of governments—along with territorial disputes—are likely to lead to the use of violence. They involve core issues of the status and integrity of states, the stakes tend to be high, and the interests of involved actors are often diametrically opposed. By contrast, economic conflicts among states are more common but far less likely to lead to violence.

Economic Conflict

Economic competition is the most pervasive form of conflict in international relations because economic transactions are pervasive. Every sale made and every deal reached across international borders entails a resolution of conflicting interests. Costa Rica wants the price of coffee, which it exports, to go up; Canada, which imports coffee, wants the

---

[41] Owen, John M. The Foreign Imposition of Domestic Institutions. *International Organization* 56 (2), 2002: 375–409.

price to go down. Angola wants foreign producers of Angolan oil to receive fewer profits from oil sales; those companies' home states want them to take home more profits. In a global capitalist market, all economic exchanges involve some conflict of interest.

However, such economic transactions also contain a strong element of mutual economic gain in addition to the element of conflicting interests (see Chapters 3 and 8). These mutual gains provide the most useful leverage in bargaining over economic exchanges: states and companies enter into economic transactions because they profit from doing so. The use of violence would for the most part interrupt and diminish such profit by more than could be gained as a result of the use of violence. Thus, economic conflicts do not usually lead to military force and war.

Economic conflict seldom leads to violence today because military forms of leverage are no longer very effective in economic conflicts. With the tight integration of the world economy and the high cost of military actions, the use of force is seldom justified to solve an economic issue. Even if an agreement is not ideal for one side in an economic conflict, rarely is what can be gained by military force worth the cost of war. Thus, most economic conflicts are not issues in international security; they are discussed in Chapters 8 through 13 (on international political economy). But economic conflicts do still bear on international security in some ways.

First, many states' foreign policies are influenced by *mercantilism*—a practice of centuries past in which trade and foreign economic policies were manipulated to build up a monetary surplus that could be used to finance war (see "Liberalism and Mercantilism" on pp. 283–288). Because a trade surplus confers an advantage in international security affairs over the long run, trade conflicts have implications for international security relations.

Second, the theory of *lateral pressure* also connects economic competition with security concerns. This theory holds that the economic growth of states leads to geographic expansion as they seek natural resources beyond their borders (by various means, peaceful and violent). As great powers expand their economic activities outward, their competition leads to conflicts and sometimes to war. The theory has been used to help explain both World War I and the expansion of Japan prior to World War II.[42]

Another kind of economic conflict that affects international security concerns *military industry*—the capacity to produce military equipment, especially high-technology weapons such as fighter aircraft or missiles. There is a world trade in such items, but national governments try (not always successfully) to keep control of such production—to try to ensure that national interests take priority over those of manufacturers and that the state is militarily self-sufficient in case of war. Economic competition (over who profits from such sales) is interwoven with security concerns (over who gets access to the weapons). In 2009, proponents of a bailout for the U.S. automobile industry argued that the industry could provide vital production capacity in a time of war, as it had during World War II. The transfer of knowledge about high-tech weaponry and military technologies to potentially hostile states is a related concern.

A different kind of economic conflict revolves around the distribution of wealth within and among states. As discussed in Chapter 12, the tremendous disparities in wealth in our world create a variety of international security problems with the potential for violence—including terrorist attacks on rich countries by groups in poor countries. Revolutions in poor countries are often fueled by disparities of wealth within the country as well as its poverty relative to other countries. These revolutions in turn frequently draw in other states as supporters of one side or the other in a civil war.

Marxist approaches to international relations, discussed in Chapters 4 and 12, treat class struggle between rich and poor people as the basis of interstate relations. According to

---

[42] Choucri, Nazli, and Robert C. North. *Nations in Conflict: National Growth and International Violence.* Freeman, 1975. Ashley, Richard K. *The Political Economy of War and Peace: The Sino-Soviet-American Triangle and the Modern Security Problematique.* Pinter, 1980. Choucri, Nazli, Robert C. North, and Susumu Yamakage. *The Challenge of Japan: Before World War II and After.* Routledge, 1993.

these approaches, capitalist states adopt foreign policies that serve the interests of the rich owners of companies. Conflicts and wars between the global North and South—rich states versus poor states—are seen as reflections of the domination and exploitation of the poor by the rich—imperialism in direct or indirect form. For example, most Marxists saw the Vietnam War as a U.S. effort to suppress revolution in order to secure continued U.S. access to cheap labor and raw materials in Southeast Asia. Many Marxists portray conflicts among capitalist states as competition over the right to exploit poor areas. Soviet founder V. I. Lenin portrayed World War I as a fight over the imperialists' division of the world.

Drug Trafficking   As a form of illegal trade across international borders, drug trafficking is smuggling, which deprives states of revenue and violates states' legal control of their borders.[43] But smuggling in general is an economic issue rather than a security one (see Illicit Trade on p. 307). Unlike other smuggling operations, however, drug trafficking supplies illegal products that are treated as a security threat because of their effect on national (and military) morale and efficiency. Drug trafficking also has become linked with security concerns because military forces participate regularly in operations against the heavily armed drug traffickers.[44] Conflicts over drugs generally concern states on one side and nonstate actors on the other. But other states can be drawn in because the activities in question cross national borders and may involve corrupt state officials.

These international ramifications are evident in the efforts of the U.S. government to prevent *cocaine cartels* based in Colombia from supplying cocaine to U.S. cities. Such cocaine derives mostly from coca plants grown by peasants in mountainous areas of Peru, Bolivia, and Colombia itself. Processed in simple laboratories in the jungle, the cocaine moves from Colombia through other countries such as Panama before arriving in the United States. In each of these countries (even the United States), the drug smugglers have bribed some corrupt officials, including military or police officers, to stay clear. But other state officials in each country are working with U.S. law enforcement agencies and the U.S. military to crack down on the cocaine trade. In 2005, Bolivians elected as president an anti-American former coca farmer who supports farming coca though not the production of cocaine.

Segments of the populations in several of these countries, especially in

DRUG WARS

Because drug trafficking crosses national borders and involves lots of guns and money, it is a source of interstate conflict. Afghanistan supplies most of the opium used to make heroin worldwide, and this illicit trade funds the Taliban in its fight against NATO and the Afghan government. Here, a poor Afghan farmer, dependent on opium poppies to make a living, checks his crop, 2007.

---

[43] Gavrilis, George. *The Dynamics of Interstate Boundaries.* Oxford, 2008.
[44] Tullis, LaMond. *Unintended Consequences: Illegal Drugs and Drug Policies in Nine Countries.* Rienner, 1995.
Kopp, Pierre. *Political Economy of Illegal Drugs.* Routledge, 2004.

cocaine-producing regions, benefit substantially from the drug trade. For poor peasants, the cocaine trade may be their only access to a decent income. More importantly for international security, rebel armies in 2 of the world's 13 active wars—Afghanistan and Colombia—fund their operations primarily through control of the trade in illicit drugs. Afghanistan, the central front in the West's struggle against Islamist extremism (specifically the Taliban), supplies most of the raw material for heroin in the world.

In Latin America, the long history of U.S. military intervention makes state cooperation with U.S. military forces a sensitive political issue. In some countries, governments have faced popular criticism for allowing the "Yankees" to "invade" in the drug war. In one case, the U.S. military literally invaded. In 1989, U.S. forces invaded Panama; arrested its leader, dictator Manuel Noriega; and convicted him in U.S. courts of complicity in drug trafficking through Panama.

Just as there are many possible outcomes of conflict, many types of war, and varied propensities for violence among different states, so too is there great diversity in how force is used if conflict leads to violence. States develop a wide array of military forces, which vary tremendously in their purposes and capabilities. These military forces occupy the next chapter.

✓•⌐**Study**
and **Review**
the **Post-Test &**
Chapter Exam
at **mypoliscilab.com**

CHAPTER REVIEW

SUMMARY

- When violent means are used as leverage in international conflicts, a variety of types of war result. These vary greatly in size and character, from guerrilla wars and raids to hegemonic war for leadership of the international system. Along this spectrum of uses of violence, the exact definition of war is uncertain.

- Many theories have been offered as general explanations about when such forms of leverage come into play—the causes of war. Contradictory theories have been proposed at each level of analysis and, with two exceptions, none has strong empirical support. Thus, political scientists cannot reliably predict the outbreak of war.

- Nationalism strongly influences IR; conflict often results from the perception of nationhood leading to demands for statehood or for the adjustment of state borders.

- Ethnic conflicts, especially when linked with territorial disputes, are very difficult to resolve because of psychological biases. It is hard to explain why people's loyalties are sometimes to their ethnic group and sometimes to a multiethnic nation.

- Fundamentalist religious movements pose a broad challenge to the rules of the international system in general and state sovereignty in particular.

- Ideologies do not matter very much in international relations, with the possible exception of democracy as an ideology. State leaders can use ideologies to justify whatever actions are in their interests.

- Territorial disputes are among the most serious international conflicts because states place great value on territorial integrity. With a few exceptions, however, almost all the world's borders are now firmly fixed and internationally recognized.

- Conflicts over the control of entire states (through control of governments) are also serious and are relatively likely to lead to the use of force.

- Economic conflicts lead to violence much less often, because positive gains from economic activities are more effective inducements than negative threats of violence.

KEY TERMS

hegemonic war   153

total war   153

limited war   153

civil war   155

guerrilla war   155

truth commissions   156

conflict   157

cycle theories   159

nationalism   160

ethnic groups   162

ethnocentrism   164

dehumanization   164

genocide   166

secular (state)   168

Islam/Muslims   169

Islamist   169

irredentism   178

"ethnic cleansing"   180

territorial waters   183

airspace   184

CRITICAL THINKING QUESTIONS

1. Given the definitions of war provided on pp. 153–155, name two current international situations that clearly fit the definition of war and two that are ambiguous "quasi-wars" (almost but not quite fitting the definition). Which do you think are more serious, the wars or the quasi-wars? Do they involve different types of actors? Different kinds of conflicts? Different capabilities?

2. European textbooks were revised after World War II to reduce ethnic and national stereotypes and to give a fairer portrayal of Europe's various nations. What about the textbooks you used to learn your country's history? Did they give an accurate picture, or did they overstate the virtues of your own ethnic group or nation at the expense of others? How?

3. The rise of fundamentalism among the world's major religions challenges traditional notions of state sovereignty. How might this trend strengthen, or weaken, the United Nations and other attempts to create supranational authority (which also challenges state sovereignty)?

4. Suppose that you were the mediator in negotiations between two states, each claiming the same piece of land. What principles could you follow in developing a mutually acceptable plan for ownership of the territory? What means could you use to persuade the two states to accept your plan?

5. How many of the six types of international conflicts discussed in this chapter can you connect with the phenomenon of nationalism discussed on pp. 160–161? What are the connections in each case?

The United States and Russia: A New Cold War?

ARGUMENT 1

Overview

When the Cold War ended in the years between 1989 and 1991, observers hoped for a new age of U.S.-Russian cooperation. Initially, all signs pointed to a healthy relationship between these superpowers: they worked together to secure Russian nuclear weapons, cooperated to stabilize the Russian economy, and reached an understanding to allow NATO expansion to some former Warsaw Pact members.

Lately, however, relations have taken a turn for the worse. As NATO has enlarged, Russia has objected to further expansion. Russia threatened to veto UN Security Council resolutions concerning Iraq in the 1990s and 2000s. The United States arrested several high-profile spies who were continuing to operate in America long after the end of the Cold War. American withdrawal from the Anti-Ballistic Missile Treaty in 2001 spurred Russian fears that the United States would engage in another arms race. During the lead-up to the 2003 Iraq War, Russia consistently opposed American efforts to gain UN Security Council approval, threatening to veto any resolution proposed by the United States. In 2008, Russia fought a war against Georgia, a U.S. ally. While relations remain civil, the friendship has cooled considerably. Although no one believes Russia and the United States will engage in war with one another, many do wonder if a new Cold War will emerge between these former rivals. What are the prospects for a new Cold War emerging between these great powers?

A New Cold War Will Emerge Between the United States and Russia

Russia and the United States have major differences in key policy areas. On several important issues, Russia and the United States do not see eye-to-eye. In particular, the United States is committed to NATO expansion, which Russia considers a direct threat to its security. In addition, the United States is committed to deploying antiballistic missiles in Europe, which Russia opposes.

Russian democracy is weak. Democracy in Russia is imperfect at best, creating additional tensions with the United States. Opposition leaders are jailed, corruption is extensive, and the press is threatened when it investigates wrongdoing. The United States has hinted that future aid will be based on Russia's improving these weak democratic institutions, angering Russian leaders.

Russia reaches out to U.S. enemies and confronts U.S. allies. Russia has recently conducted joint military exercises with Venezuela and has a cordial relationship with Iran. Russia has recently gone to war with Georgia over disputed territory and continues to threaten Ukraine over natural gas prices. Both Georgia and Ukraine are strong American allies.

No New Cold War Will Emerge Between the United States and Russia

Russia depends on Western aid and acceptance. Russia greatly values its membership in key IGOs such as the World Bank and the International Monetary Fund. It also covets membership in the World Trade Organization, which it hopes to join. Russia will not pursue - policies that threaten these relationships.

There are no major ideological differences between the United States and Russia. Unlike during the Cold War, there are no major ideological divides between these two great powers. While Russian democracy may be imperfect, Russia is unlikely to re-embrace communism or abandon its experiment with capitalism. Where their interests converge, as in the war against Islamic extremists in Afghanistan, U.S.-Russian cooperation works smoothly.

Europe will help keep tensions low. During the Cold War, Europe was divided into two camps, each supported by one of the superpowers. Now, Europe is united and can serve as a mediator between the United States and Russia. Europe has strong economic and political interests in continued cooperation with both sides and will work to ensure tensions do not spiral out of hand.

Questions

- Are Russia and the United States headed for a second Cold War? What issues are likely to continue to exacerbate tensions between these two states? Are there issues of common interest that may unite them?

- Would steps to better relations with Russia, such as ending efforts to deploy a missile shield, make relations with some European allies (for example, Poland or Ukraine) more difficult? Will the United States have to choose between improving relations with Russia and honoring its promises to European allies?

- How important is it for Russia to remain democratic to keep tensions low between it and the United States? How would the different IR theories answer this question? Do Russia's attempts at democracy explain differences in American perceptions of the danger from Russia as opposed to the danger from China?

For Further Reading

Lucas, Edward. *The New Cold War: Putin's Russia and the Threat to the West.* Palgrave Macmillan, 2009.

MacKinnon, Mark. *The New Cold War: Revolutions, Rigged Elections, and Pipeline Politics in the Former Soviet Union.* Basic Books, 2007.

Goldman, Marshall I. *Petrostate: Putin, Power, and the New Russia.* Oxford, 2008.

Levine, Steve. *Putin's Labyrinth: Spies, Murder, and the Dark Heart of the New Russia.* Random House, 2008.

CHAPTER **6** | # Military Force and Terrorism

Refugees flee new fighting near Goma, Democratic Congo, 2008.

Conventional Forces

A state leader in a conflict can apply various kinds of leverage to influence the outcome (see Figure 6.1). One set of levers represents nonviolent means of influencing other states, such as foreign aid, economic sanctions, and personal diplomacy (less tangible means include the use of norms, morality, and other ideas). A second set of levers—the subject of this chapter—represents violent actions. These levers set armies marching, suicide bombers blowing up, or missiles flying. They tend to be costly to both the attacker and the attacked. Military force tends to be a last resort. Evidence also shows that the utility of military force relative to nonmilitary means is slowly declining over time.

Yet most states still devote vast resources to military capabilities compared to other means of influence. For example, the United States has about 20,000 diplomatic personnel but 2 million soldiers; it spends about $30 billion a year on foreign aid but about $700 billion on military forces and war (equaling the rest of the world combined). Because of the security dilemma (see p. 51), states believe they must devote large resources to military capabilities if other states are doing so.[1]

Beyond defending their territories, states develop military capabilities for several other purposes. They often hope to *deter* attack by having the means to retaliate. They may also hope to *compel* other states to behave in certain ways, by threatening an attack if the state does not comply.[2] States also use military forces for humanitarian assistance

Read and Listen to **Chapter 6** at **mypoliscilab.com**

✓ Study and **Review** the **Pre-Test & Flashcards** at **mypoliscilab.com**

FIGURE 6.1 Military and Nonmilitary Means of Leverage

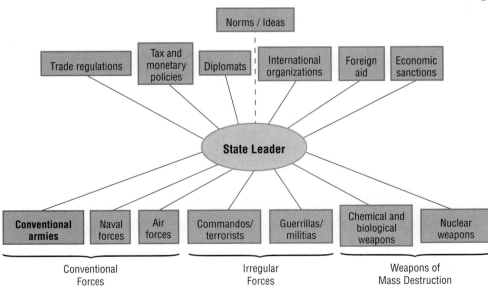

Conventional armed force is the most commonly used military form of leverage.

---

[1] Art, Robert J., and Kenneth N. Waltz, eds. *The Use of Force: Military Power and International Politics*. 7th ed. Rowman & Littlefield, 2008.

[2] Gat, Azar. *War in Human Civilization*. Oxford, 2006. Keegan, John. *A History of Warfare*. Random House, 1993. Van Creveld, Martin. *Technology and War: From 2000 b.c. to the Present*. Free Press, 1989. Luttwak, Edward, and Stuart L. Koehl. *The Dictionary of Modern War*. HarperCollins, 1991.

Watch
the **Video**
"Western Arms Sales
and the Rwandan
Genocide"
on **mypoliscilab.com**

Explore
the **Simulation**
"Military Force:
You Are a Military
Commander"
on **mypoliscilab.com**

after disasters, for peacekeeping, for surveillance of drug trafficking, and for repression of domestic political dissent, among other missions. The sizes and types of military forces reflect these missions.[3]

Great powers continue to dominate the makeup of world military forces. Table 6.1 summarizes the most important forces of the great powers. Together, they account for about two-thirds of world military spending, a third of the world's soldiers, a third of the weapons, 99 percent of nuclear weapons, and 85 percent of arms exports. (The table also indicates the sizable military forces maintained by Germany and Japan despite their non-traditional roles in international security since World War II.)

Military capabilities divide into three types: conventional forces, irregular forces (terrorism, militias), and weapons of mass destruction (nuclear, chemical, and biological weapons).

Land Forces: Controlling Territory

Whatever their ultimate causes and objectives, most wars involve a struggle to *control territory*. Territory holds a central place in warfare because of its importance in the international system, and vice versa. Borders define where a state's own military forces and rival states' military forces are free to move. Military logistics makes territoriality all the more important because of the need to control territories connecting military forces with each other. An army's supplies must flow from home territory along *supply lines* to the field. Thus the most fundamental purpose of conventional forces is to take, hold, or defend territory.

Armies are adapted to this purpose. Military forces with armed foot soldiers can *occupy* a territory militarily. Although inhabitants may make the soldiers' lives unhappy through violent or nonviolent resistance, generally only another organized, armed military force can displace occupiers.

Foot soldiers are called the **infantry**. They use assault rifles and other light weapons (such as mines and machine guns) as well as heavy artillery of various types. Artillery is extremely destructive and not very discriminating: it usually causes the most damage and casualties in wars. *Armor* refers to tanks and armored vehicles. In open terrain, such as desert, mechanized ground forces typically combine armor, artillery, and infantry. In close terrain, such as jungles and cities, however, foot soldiers are more important. For this reason, the armies of industrialized states have a greater advantage over poor armies in open conventional warfare, such as in the Kuwaiti desert. In jungle, mountain, or urban warfare, however—as in Afghan mountains and Iraqi cities—such advantages are eroded, and a cheaper and more lightly armed force of motivated foot soldiers or guerrillas may ultimately prevail over an expensive conventional army.

The superiority of conventional armed forces to irregular forces in open battle was graphically demonstrated in Somalia at the end of 2006. An Islamist militia had taken control of most of the country and the capital, leaving a transitional government near Ethiopia's border, backed by Ethiopia's large conventional military. The Islamists closed schools and sent teenagers with rifles in pickup trucks to attack the provisional government. They were no match for the Ethiopian army, which then ousted them from the whole country in two weeks. The Islamists, like most irregular forces, then had to fall back to guerrilla attacks rather than taking and holding territory. Here, in turn, the conventional Ethiopian military proved no match, and the Islamists gained ground steadily until the Ethiopian army gave up and left in January 2009. After their departure, Somali Islamist groups captured most of the country's territory, overpowering Somali government forces

---

[3] Worley, D. Robert. *Shaping U.S. Military Forces: Revolution or Relevance in a Post–Cold War World.* Praeger, 2006.

TABLE 6.1 Estimated Great Power Military Capabilities, 2010

| | Military Expenditures[a] (Billions of US $) | Active Duty Soldiers[a] (Millions) | Heavy Weapons[a] | | | Nuclear Weapons[b] | Arms Exported[a] (Billions of US $) |
			Tanks	Carriers/ Warships/ Submarines	Combat Airplanes		
United States	690	1.5	6,000	11 / 110 / 71	4,000	9,600	35
Russia	80	1.0	23,000	0 / 50 / 66	1,700	12,000	4
China	140	2.2	7,000	0 / 60 / 6	2,100	240	1
France	65	0.4	1,000	0 / 19 / 12	300	300	3
Britain	60	0.2	1,000	0 / 35 / 16	300	225	0
Germany	45	0.2	3,000	0 / 14 / 0	400	0	1
Japan	45	0.2	1,000	0 / 50 / 18	300	0	0
Approximate % of world total	75%	30%	25%	100 / 60 / 50%	40%	99%	85%

Problematic data: Russian and Chinese military expenditure estimates vary. Many Chinese aircraft and Russian tanks are old and of limited military use. U.S. and Russian nuclear warheads include deployed strategic weapons (2,500 U.S., 4,600 Russian) with the remainder held in reserve or retired (awaiting destruction).

Data on soldiers exclude reserves. Tanks include only main battle tanks. Carriers include only supercarriers. Warships are major surface combat ships over 3,000 tons. Nuclear warheads include both strategic and tactical weapons. Arms exports are for orders placed, 2008.

Sources: Author's estimates based on data provided by the following sources:
[a] 2010 data from Institute for International and Strategic Studies. *The Military Balance 2010.* [b] Carnegie Endowment for International Peace (www.ceip.org).

WINNING HEARTS AND MINDS

Counterinsurgency warfare has become central to the missions of uniformed military forces worldwide. The U.S. military rewrote its counterinsurgency manual and changed its tactics in Iraq to emphasize political and economic activities and positive relations with civilian populations. In Afghanistan, U.S. forces scaled back airstrikes, sought to minimize civilian casualties, and fanned out to work with the local population. This foreign soldier in 2010 has little way to tell if these smiling Afghans are friend or foe.

and fighting peacekeepers from the African Union. Somalia's government incorporated moderate Islamist factions but continued to fight more radical Islamist groups. By 2010, the African Union had voted to send reinforcements to battle the Islamist forces.

Counterinsurgency has received growing attention in recent years because of Iraq and Afghanistan, but it is central to all 13 wars currently in progress worldwide. Counterinsurgency warfare often includes programs to try to "win the hearts and minds" of populations so that they stop sheltering the guerrillas. In some ways, because counterinsurgency warfare is as much about political gains as military strategy, it is the most complex type of warfare. While battling armed factions of an insurgency, a government must essentially conduct a public relations campaign to persuade the population to abandon the movement, while providing public services (such as education and welfare programs) to show a government's responsiveness to the population. A government must be strong militarily, but cannot be too brutal in the application of force, lest more of the population begin to support the guerrillas.

Israel found itself in this position as it carried out strikes against Hamas in Gaza in 2009. This asymmetrical war resulted in far more Palestinian than Israeli casualties. Israel quickly found itself on the offensive militarily—initiating a ground war to eliminate Hamas's ability to fire rockets and import weapons through secret tunnels. But just as quickly it found itself on the defensive in the area of world public opinion, as many international actors condemned the attacks, warning Israel that Hamas could emerge from the war more popular with Palestinians.

U.S. military forces have conducted counterinsurgency campaigns in Iraq and Afghanistan for several years. The campaigns have included the use of lethal military force, payments to key tribal leaders to support American efforts, assisting the formation of local government, and training new police and military forces to combat the insurgency. These types of activities place tremendous stress on militaries, which are usually trained only to fight wars, not undertake rebuilding distant governments.

Counterinsurgency campaigns are costly and labor-intensive. For example, the U.S. Army's counterinsurgency manual suggests that 20 troops should be deployed for every 1,000 citizens to be protected from insurgents. Few states can afford such campaigns for long periods of time. Indeed, even including allied forces, the United States never reached such a ratio of troops-to-population in Iraq or Afghanistan. Such a ratio would require 580,000 troops for Afghanistan, compared with the 100,000 actually deployed there in 2010.

A common tool of guerrillas, insurgents, and the governments fighting them are **land mines**, which are simple, small, and cheap containers of explosives with a trigger activated by contact or sensor. These mines were a particular focus of public attention in the 1990s because in places such as Angola, Afghanistan, Cambodia, and Bosnia, they were used extensively by irregular military forces that never disarmed them. Long after such a war ends, land mines continue to maim and kill civilians who try to reestablish their lives in former war zones. As many as 100 million land mines remain from recent wars; they injure about 25,000 people a year (a third of whom are children); although they are cheap to deploy, it costs about $1,000 per mine to find and disarm them.

Public opinion and NGOs have pressured governments to restrict the use of land mines. A treaty to ban land mines was signed by more than 100 countries at a 1997 conference organized by Canada. Russia and Japan signed on shortly afterward, but not China or the United States (which said mines would be needed to slow any North Korean invasion of South Korea). By 2009, more than 44 million land mines had been destroyed under the treaty, with 86 countries eliminating their stockpiles. A new norm seems to be emerging, but its effect on actual military practice is not yet clear.

Naval Forces: Controlling the Seas

Navies are adapted primarily to control passage through the seas and to attack land near coastlines.[4] Controlling the seas in wartime allows states to move their own goods and military forces by sea while preventing enemies from doing so. In particular, navies protect sealift logistical support. Navies can also blockade enemy ports. For most of the 1990s, Western navies enforced a naval blockade against Iraq.

In 2008, navies of the Western powers faced a new mission, responding to the rapid growth of piracy in two of the world's vital shipping lanes—the waters off Somalia south of the Suez Canal, and the Straits of Malacca in Indonesia connecting the Indian Ocean with East Asia. The Somali pirates, taking advantage of near-anarchy in that country (see Chapter 5, p. 176), established safe havens onshore and ventured out to capture dozens of ships, holding the vessels, cargoes, and crews for ransom. Shipping companies generally paid up, first hundreds of thousands and eventually millions of dollars per ship, rather than lose valuable goods and people. The pirates pushed the limits by capturing first a Ukrainian freighter loaded with tanks and weapons and then a huge Saudi oil tanker with $100 million of oil.

The pirates' methods are simple but effective. Racing to ships in very small, fast boats, armed with automatic rifles and grenade launchers, they toss up grappling hooks, climb the sides, and subdue the crew, typically within about ten minutes. Western navies organized patrols in the area to deter piracy, but with limited success because of the huge stretches of sea in which the pirates could operate (more than a million square miles) and the tens of thousands of commercial ships passing through the area each year (see Figure 6.2). The problem illustrates a main challenge facing navies, namely, the sheer size of the oceans and the inability of ships to be everywhere, even in the relative confines of major shipping lanes.

In 2008, the UN Security Council unanimously passed several resolutions to deal with the problem of piracy, each calling for international cooperation in fighting the surge in hijackings. Many states have now begun to police the coast of Somalia with their navies, including the five permanent members of the Security Council. In 2010, China agreed to join U.S. and NATO forces in combating pirate attacks in the western part of the Indian Ocean.

Aircraft carriers—mobile platforms for attack aircraft—are instruments of **power projection** that can attack virtually any state in the world. Merely sending an aircraft carrier sailing to the vicinity of an international conflict implies a threat to use force—a modern version of what was known in the 19th century as "gunboat diplomacy." For example, in 1996 the United States dispatched two carriers to the Taiwan area when Chinese war games there threatened to escalate. Aircraft carriers are extremely expensive and typically require 20 to 25 supporting ships for protection and supply. Few states can afford even one. Only the United States operates large carriers, known as supercarriers. Currently, the United States maintains 11 supercarriers, costing

---

[4] Keegan, John. *The Price of Admiralty: The Evolution of Naval Warfare.* Viking, 1988.

FIGURE 6.2 Pirate Attacks Near Somalia, January to September 2008

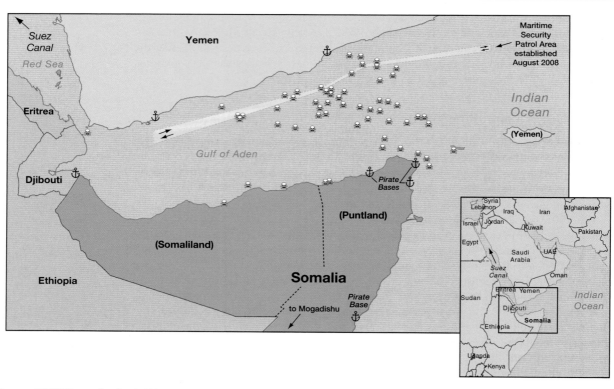

Source: UNOSAT map, October 2, 2008.

more than $5 billion each and $250 million a year to operate. In 2015, the U.S. Navy plans to launch a newly designed supercarrier, costing upward of $9 billion to build. Eight other countries (France, India, Russia, Spain, Brazil, Italy, Thailand, and the United Kingdom) maintain smaller carriers that use helicopters or small airplanes.

Surface ships, which account for the majority of warships, rely increasingly on guided missiles and are in turn vulnerable to attack by missiles (fired from ships, planes, submarines, or land). Because the ranges of small missiles now reach from dozens to hundreds of miles, naval warfare emphasizes detection at great distances without being detected oneself—a cat-and-mouse game of radar surveillance and electronic countermeasures.

Marines (part of the navy in the United States, Britain, and Russia) move to battle in ships but fight on land—amphibious warfare. Marines are also useful for great power intervention in distant conflicts where they can insert themselves quickly and establish local control.

Air Forces: Controlling the Skies

Air forces serve several purposes—strategic bombing of land or sea targets; "close air support" (battlefield bombing); interception of other aircraft; reconnaissance; and airlift of supplies, weapons, and troops. Missiles—whether fired from air, land, or sea—are increasingly important. Air forces have developed various means to try to fool such missiles, with mixed results. In the Soviet war in Afghanistan, the U.S.-made portable Stinger missiles used by guerrillas took a heavy toll on the Soviet air force. In 2003, the threat from shoulder-fired missiles kept the Baghdad airport closed to commercial traffic for more than a year after U.S. forces arrived.

Traditionally, and still to some extent, aerial bombing resembles artillery shelling in that it causes great destruction with little discrimination. This has changed somewhat as smart bombs improve accuracy. For instance, laser-guided bombs follow a sensor pointed at the target from the air or ground. Other bombs use GPS navigation (see p. 201) to hit targets through clouds, smoke, or sandstorms. Most of the bombing in the 1991 Gulf War was high-altitude saturation bombing using large numbers of dumb bombs. In typical wars, such as Russia's 1995 Chechnya War, bombing of cities causes high civilian casualties. But in the 2003 Iraq War, the massive air campaign early in the war entirely used smart bombs, hitting far more targets with fewer bombs. Even so, thousands of civilians have apparently died in U.S. airstrikes in Iraq since 2003.[5]

PROJECTING POWER

Different types of military forces are adapted to different purposes. Aircraft carriers are used for power projection in distant regions, such as in the Afghanistan and Iraq campaigns.

In cases of low-intensity conflicts and guerrilla wars, especially where forces intermingle with civilians in closed terrain such as Vietnamese jungles or Iraqi cities, bombing is of limited utility—although it was extremely effective in Afghanistan in 2001. Israel also used extensive bombing in its 2006 invasion of Lebanon. Israel found, however, that Lebanese guerrillas were able to jam some of its radar systems with rudimentary electronic devices, creating difficulties for the Israeli military.

The increasing sophistication of electronic equipment and the high-performance requirements of attack aircraft make air forces expensive—totally out of reach for some states. Thus, rich states have huge advantages over poor ones in air warfare. Despite the expense, air superiority is often the key to the success of ground operations, especially in open terrain. The U.S. bombings of Iraq (1991 and 2003), Serbia (1999), and Afghanistan (2001) demonstrated a new effectiveness of air power, applied not against the morale of enemy populations (as in World War II), but directly targeted from afar at battlefield positions. The U.S. ability to decimate distant military forces while taking only very light casualties is historically unprecedented. The 2003 attack on Iraq demonstrated the usefulness of air power, but also its limits. A massive precision bombing raid on Baghdad a few days into the war destroyed hundreds of targets of value to Saddam Hussein's government. It was designed to "shock and awe" enemy commanders into giving up. However, U.S. forces still had to fight it

[5] Roberts, Les, et al. Mortality before and after the 2003 Invasion of Iraq: Cluster Sample Survey. *The Lancet* 364, November 20, 2004: 1857–64.

out on the ground to get to Baghdad. Clearly this war could not have been won from the air. As ground soldiers have pointed out, "Nobody ever surrendered to an airplane."[6]

Air forces are a likely area for attention in any future U.S.-China arms race. China has spent large sums in the past ten years rejuvenating its aging air force capabilities. The United States continues to invest heavily in its own air force, creating new technologies to stay ahead of Chinese advances. And while air power may be less useful in small-scale warfare, states continue to build their air forces in the event of more large-scale conflicts.

Coordinating Forces: Logistics and Intelligence

All military operations rely heavily on logistical support such as food, fuel, and ordnance (weapons and ammunition). Military logistics is a huge operation, and in most armed forces the majority of soldiers are not combat troops. Global-reach capabilities combine long-distance logistical support with various power-projection forces.[7] These capabilities allow a great power to project military power to distant corners of the world and to maintain a military presence in most of the world's regions simultaneously. Only the United States today fully possesses such a capability—with worldwide military alliances, air and naval bases, troops stationed overseas, and aircraft carriers plying the world's oceans (see Table 6.2). Britain and France are in a distant second place, able to mount occasional distant operations of modest size such as the Falklands War. Russia is preoccupied with internal conflicts and its near neighbors, and China's military forces are oriented toward regional conflicts and not global in scope (although they are currently attempting to build a navy capable of better power projection).

Space forces are military forces designed to attack in or from outer space.[8] Ballistic missiles, which travel through space briefly, are not generally included in this category. Only the United States and Russia have substantial military capabilities in space. China put an astronaut in orbit in 2003, successfully tested an antisatellite missile, and launched

TABLE 6.2 Location of U.S. Military Forces, September 31, 2010

Region	Personnel	Distribution of Forces Abroad
United States	1,130,000	—
Europe	80,000	22%
Japan/Pacific	65,000	18%
Russia/CIS	130	0%
Middle East	110,000	30%
Latin America	1,900	1%
Africa	1,700	0%
South Asia	110,000	30%
Total abroad	368,730	100%

Note: Totals do not include personnel afloat in the region.
Data source: U.S. Department of Defense.

---

[6] Pape, Robert A. The True Worth of Air Power. *Foreign Affairs* 83 (2), 2004: 116–31.
[7] Harkavy, Robert E. *Bases Abroad: The Global Foreign Military Presence*. Oxford, 1989.
[8] Preston, Bob, ed. *Space Weapons: Earth Wars*. Rand, 2002.

a lunar orbiter in 2007, but it has fewer space capabilities overall. The development of space weapons has been constrained by the technical challenges and expenses of space operations, and by norms against militarizing space.

The far more common uses of space by the military are for command and coordination purposes. Satellites are used extensively for military purposes, but these purposes thus far do not include attack. Satellites perform military surveillance and mapping, communications, weather assessment, and early warning of ballistic missile launches. Satellites also provide navigational information to military forces—army units, ships, planes, and even guided missiles in flight. Locations are calculated to within about 50 feet by small receivers, which pick up beacons transmitted from a network of 18 U.S. satellites known as a *Global Positioning System (GPS)*. Handheld receivers are available commercially, so the military forces of other countries can free-ride on these satellite navigation beacons. Poorer states can buy satellite photos—including high-resolution pictures that Russia sells for hard currency. In fact, access to such information has diffused to the point that the terrorists who attacked Mumbai, India, in 2008 planned their attack using satellite images available through Google Earth, and coordinated it in real time from Pakistan using satellite phones. In the 2006 war between Hezbollah and Israel in Lebanon, Hezbollah forces used GPS jammers to complicate Israeli air support and targeting operations. But generally, in outer space great powers have advantages over smaller or poorer states.

Intelligence gathering also relies on various other means such as electronic monitoring of telephone lines and other communications, reports from embassies, and information in the open press. Some kinds of information are obtained by sending agents into foreign countries as spies. They use ingenuity (plus money and technology) to penetrate walls of secrecy that foreign governments have constructed around their plans and capabilities. For example, in 1999 a Russian spy taped conversations from a listening device planted in a high-level conference room at the U.S. State Department. The 2001 terrorist attacks showed a weakness in U.S. "human intelligence" capabilities, in that the United States had not penetrated a large terrorist network based in Afghanistan and operating globally.[9] U.S. "signal intelligence" capabilities are more impressive. The largest U.S. military intelligence agency is the National Security Agency (NSA), whose mission is encoding U.S. communications and breaking the codes of foreign communications. The NSA intercepts truly massive amounts of information from such sources as undersea phone cables, then sifts through it to find significant conversations. The NSA employs more mathematics Ph.D.s than anyone in the world, is the second largest electricity consumer in the state of Maryland, has a budget larger than the CIA's, and is believed to have the most powerful computer facility in the world. Altogether, the budgets of U.S. intelligence agencies, although officially secret, were revealed in 2005 to be around $44 billion a year. Clearly these operations taken together are very large and are growing in importance as the information revolution proceeds and as the war on terror makes their mission more central.

Evolving Technologies

Technological developments have changed the nature of military force in several ways. First, the resort to force in international conflicts now has more profound costs and consequences. Great powers in particular can no longer use force to settle disputes among themselves without risking massive destruction and economic ruin. Also, military engagements

---

[9] Gerdes, Louise I., ed. *Espionage and Intelligence Gathering*. Greenhaven, 2004. Howard, Russell D., and Reid L. Sawyer, eds. *Terrorism and Counterterrorism: Understanding the New Security Environment*. McGraw-Hill/Dushkin, 2003.

POLICY PERSPECTIVES

President of the United States, Barack Obama

PROBLEM *How do you balance the trade-offs in the use of force to combat terrorism?*

BACKGROUND   As a presidential candidate in 2008, you publicly promised to pursue members of al Qaeda and the Taliban from Afghanistan into neighboring Pakistan, even if it meant violating Pakistani sovereignty. You fulfilled the promise in 2011, when American military forces entered Pakistan to kill Osama bin Laden, the head of al Qaeda and mastermind of the 9/11 attacks of the United States. This raid was popular in the United States but caused tensions with the government of Pakistan.

The war in Afghanistan in now well over ten years old. Progress is slow and uneven. Recently, a significant source of violence against American troops in that country has been the Haqqani network—a group of anti-U.S. fighters allied to the Taliban and al Qaeda. The Haqqani network has significant ties to security forces in Pakistan, specifically the Inter-Services Intelligence (ISI). Moreover, elements of the Haqqani network take refuge in Pakistan to escape American raids. Pakistan's government would like to keep these fighters under control but fears an all-out conflict against them would be costly and unpopular.

DOMESTIC CONSIDERATIONS   Although the economy is an important issue for your administration, terrorism and the war in Afghanistan are still important issues. The American public still generally supports the war on terror, but has grown tired of the war in Afghanistan. After the death of Osama bin Laden, a growing number of Americans would like to speed the pull-out of U.S. troops from Afghanistan. Your own military advisors suggest that additional stability is needed before a significant drawdown of American forces can begin.

SCENARIO   Imagine that there is a deadly attack on American forces in Afghanistan. The Haqqani network takes credit for the attack and threatens more on military and civilian targets in Afghanistan. Your own intelligence officials suggest the attack was supported by elements within Pakistan. The attack has refocused American public opinion on the war in Afghanistan. There are increasing calls to quickly leave the country to its fate by withdrawing U.S. troops. Your advisors are divided: one group suggests that American forces have been in Afghanistan long enough and it is time to come home. The other group argues that leaving now is giving into terrorism and that U.S. forces should stay to try to bring more stability to the country before leaving.

CHOOSE YOUR POLICY   How do you respond to these domestic and international pressures? Do you pressure the government of Pakistan to be more aggressive in attacking the Haqqani network, risking instability in Pakistan? Do you immediately speed up the withdrawal of American forces, leaving the Afghani government to fend for itself? Do you open a new offensive against the insurgents, risking increasing American fatalities and a widening of the Afghanistan war, which would be unpopular at home?

now occur across greater standoff distances between opposing forces. Missiles of all types are accelerating this trend. These technological advances undermine the territorial basis of war and of the state itself. The state once had a hard shell of militarily protected borders, but today borders offer far less protection.[10] In recent years, this trend has accelerated with the use of unmanned drone aircraft, including drones armed with missiles, in U.S. military efforts in Pakistan, Yemen, and Libya.

In recent decades, the technological revolution in electronics has profoundly affected military forces, especially their command and control. **Electronic warfare** (now broadened to *information warfare*) refers to the uses of the electromagnetic spectrum (radio waves, radar, infrared, etc.) in war—employing electromagnetic signals for one's own benefit while denying their use to an enemy. Electromagnetic signals are used for sensing beyond the normal visual range through radar, infrared, and imaging equipment to see in darkness, through fog, or at great distances. These and other technologies have illuminated the battlefield so that forces cannot be easily hidden. Electronic countermeasures try to counteract enemy electronic system.

Strategies for *cyberwar*—disrupting enemy computer networks to degrade command and control, or even hacking into bank accounts electronically—were developed by NATO forces during the 1999 Kosovo war. Though mostly not implemented, these strategies will probably figure in future wars. Some experts fear that terrorist attacks also could target computer networks, including the Internet.[11]

Cyberattacks are an issue of growing importance in international relations. U.S. officials have accused Chinese hackers of thousands of attacks on Department of Defense computers. In 2010, China announced a military unit dedicated to the investigation and prevention of cyberattacks on its own computer systems. Also in 2010, the UN announced an agreement among 15 states (including Russia, China, and the United States) to begin negotiations on an international treaty concerning Internet security. Although the U.S.-Israeli Stuxnet computer worm targeted Iran's nuclear program in 2010, the United States decided against using cyberattacks to disable Libya's air defenses in 2011, out of fear of the precedent such an action could set.

Stealth technology uses special radar-absorbent materials and unusual shapes in the design of aircraft, missiles, and ships to scatter enemy radar. However, stealth is extremely expensive (the B-2 stealth bomber costs about $2 billion per plane) and is prone to technical problems.

Military historians refer to a period of rapid change in the conduct of war as a "revolution in military affairs." These periods usually combine innovative applications of new technology with changes in military doctrine, organization, or operations. Such revolutions may arise from innovations in organization, as when revolutionary France first mobilized an entire nation into a war machine two centuries ago. Or they may arise from new military doctrine as when Germany used the "blitzkrieg" to overwhelm Poland and France at the outset of World War II, or from technology alone as with the invention of nuclear weapons. Many military analysts consider the present period, starting with the 1991 Gulf War, a revolution in military affairs, especially in U.S. forces. Management of information is central to this revolution. Two centuries ago, the German military strategist Carl von Clausewitz described as a "fog of war" the confusion and uncertainty that greatly reduces the effectiveness of armies in battle. Today's U.S. forces are piercing that fog for themselves while thickening it for their

[10] Herz, John H. *International Politics in the Atomic Age*. Columbia, 1959.
[11] Rattray, Gregory J. *Strategic Warfare in Cyberspace*. MIT, 2001. Hall, Wayne M. *Stray Voltage: War in the Information Age*. Naval Institute Press, 2003.

SMALL IS BEAUTIFUL

The information revolution is making smaller weapons and smaller dispersed units more potent. A "revolution in military affairs" is driving changes in U.S. military strategy, including the expanding use of unmanned drones. This insect-sized drone shown in 2011 could collect real-time intelligence in complex urban environments.

enemies. As the fog of war becomes transparent, U.S. forces can also disperse light forces widely, rather than massing concentrations of heavy units as Clausewitz emphasized. The ability to conduct precision strikes, and the increasing use of space in warfare, are two other aspects of the present revolution.

The revolutionary potentials were first apparent in the lopsided 1991 victory over Iraq's large but not technologically advanced army, and the 1999 Kosovo campaign was notable in achieving its war aims without loss of a single U.S. life to hostile fire. But the 2001 Afghanistan campaign best exemplified the revolution. Small groups of lightly armed U.S. special forces, inserted across the country, used lasers to illuminate targets for smart bombs dropped by high-flying aircraft. The integration of these diverse forces using information-rich battle management systems resulted in a stunningly effective bombing campaign that destroyed the Taliban as an effective army and handed victory to the smaller anti-Taliban armies, all with just a handful of U.S. casualties. The 2003 invasion of Iraq seemed to continue this success, but then the postinvasion security situation in Iraq unraveled over several years despite the revolutionary technologies of U.S. forces. A more unsettling thought is that the revolution in military affairs may work for terrorists as well as states. The September 2001 attackers used information technology, such as encrypted Internet communications, to coordinate forces while keeping U.S. authorities in the dark. They carried out precision strikes over long distances with very small, dispersed units. As a result, 19 attackers killed nearly 3,000 people, and an expenditure of under $1 million caused tens of *billions* of dollars in damage.

Terrorism

● ‖ Watch
the **Video**
"Bin Laden
Killed in Pakistan"
on mypoliscilab.com

The U.S. State Department listed 45 foreign terrorist organizations in 2010. Some are motivated by religion (for example, al Qaeda) but others by class ideology (for example, Shining Path in Peru) or by ethnic conflict and nationalism (for example, Basque Fatherland and Liberty). In Chapter 5 (pp. 169–172) we discussed conflicts involving armed Islamist militias and terrorist networks. Here we discuss terrorism itself as a tactic. Since September 2001, governments and ordinary people have paid much more attention to terrorism than ever before. But terrorism itself is not new.

Terrorism refers to political violence that targets civilians deliberately and indiscriminately. Beyond this basic definition other criteria can be applied, but the definitions become politically motivated: one person's freedom fighter is another's terrorist. More than guerrilla warfare, terrorism is a shadowy world of faceless enemies and irregular tactics marked by extreme brutality.[12]

Traditionally, the purpose of terrorism is to demoralize a civilian population in order to use its discontent as leverage on national governments or other parties to a conflict. Related to this is the aim of creating drama in order to gain media attention for a cause. When the IRA planted bombs in London in the 1960s and 1970s, it hoped to make life miserable enough for Londoners that they would insist their government settle the Northern Ireland issue. The bombing also sought to keep the issue of Northern Ireland in the news, in the hope that the British government would then be pressured to concede terms more favorable to the IRA than would otherwise be the case. Terrorism is seldom mindless; rather, it is usually a calculated use of violence as leverage. However, motives and means of terrorism vary widely, having in common only that some actor is using violence to influence other actors.

The primary effect of terrorism is psychological. In part the effectiveness of terrorism in capturing attention is due to the dramatic nature of the incidents, especially as shown on television news. Terrorism also gains attention because of the randomness of victims. Although only a few dozen people may be injured by a bomb left in a market, millions of people realize "it could have been me," because they, too, shop in markets. Attacks on airplanes augment this fear because many people already fear flying. Terrorism thus amplifies a small amount of power by its psychological effect on large populations; this is why it is usually a tool of the weak.

However, al Qaeda's attacks follow a somewhat different pattern, planned less to create fear than simply to kill as many Americans and their allies as possible—and ultimately to touch off apocalyptic violence that al Qaeda's followers believe will bring about God's intervention. Indeed, terrorist attacks in general have become more deadly over the past 50 years as terrorist tactics have increasingly employed more violent means to injure or kill civilians.[13] The psychological effect is aimed at Muslim populations worldwide rather than at Americans.

In the shockingly destructive attack on the World Trade Center, tangible damage was far greater than in previous terrorist attacks—reaching into thousands of lives and tens of billions of dollars. The psychological impact was even stronger than the physical damage—changing the U.S. political and cultural landscape instantly. And the same terrorist network was trying to obtain nuclear weapons (see pp. 209–211) with which to kill not thousands but hundreds of thousands of Americans.[14]

The classic cases of terrorism—from the 1970s to the 2001 attacks—are those in which a *nonstate* actor uses attacks against *civilians* by secret *nonuniformed* forces, operating *across international borders,* as a leverage against *state* actors. Radical political factions or separatist groups hijack or blow up airplanes or plant bombs in cafés, clubs, or other crowded places. For example, Chechen radicals seized a school in Beslan, a small city in the Caucasus region in 2004. For three days, they held nearly 1,200 children, parents, and teachers without food or water. When Russian troops stormed the school, more than 300 people died, including 172 children.

---

[12] Lutz, James M. *Global Terrorism*. Routledge, 2004. Benjamin, Daniel, and Steven Simon. *The Age of Sacred Terror*. Random, 2002. Kushner, Harvey W. *Encyclopedia of Terrorism*. Sage, 2003.

[13] Cronin, Audrey Kurth. Behind the Curve: Globalization and International Terrorism. *International Security* 27 (3), 2002/03: 30–58.

[14] Young, Mitchell, ed. *The War on Terrorism*. Greenhaven, 2003. Cortright, David, and George A. Lopez. *Uniting Against Terror*. MIT, 2007.

Such tactics create spectacular incidents that draw attention to the terrorists' cause. Often terrorism is used by radical factions of movements that have not been able to get attention or develop other effective means of leverage. It is often a tactic of desperation, and it almost always reflects weakness in the power position of the attacker. For instance, Palestinian radicals in 1972 had seen Arab states defeated by Israel in war and could not see a way to gain even a hearing for their cause. By capturing media attention worldwide with dramatic incidents of violence—even at the cost of rallying world public opinion against their cause—the radicals hoped to make Palestinian aspirations an issue that Western governments could not ignore when deciding on policies toward the Middle East.

Yet, the persistence of terrorism is in some ways puzzling because the tactic has a mixed record of success. Suicide bombers were arguably effective at convincing the United States to leave Lebanon in 1983, but the Chechen terrorists' 2004 school attack marked their end as a serious force in Chechnya. The Palestinians did not win a state through terrorism. Al Qaeda affiliates in Iraq so alienated the Sunni tribes that had sheltered them that the tribes turned against them. In addition, even large numbers of suicide bombers have yet to be effective at gaining a state for the Tamils in Sri Lanka or providing leverage for Hamas or Islamic Jihad against Israel. Clearly, terrorist activities do not reliably achieve political ends.

Some research has attempted to systematically analyze when particular types of terrorism, such as suicide bombings, are effective at achieving the goals of terrorist organizations. According to one study, suicide bombings, rather than an irrational use of violence by terrorist groups, seem to follow strategic patterns (see Figure 6.3). In particular, they occur most frequently against democracies rather than autocracies, presumably because democracies are thought to strongly influence public opinion. Still, this same study concludes that this terror tactic has not been particularly successful at achieving significant goals.[15]

Terrorists are more willing than states are to violate the norms of the international system because, unlike states, they do not have a stake in that system. Conversely, when a political group gains some power or legitimacy, its use of terrorism usually diminishes. This was true of the Palestine Liberation Organization during the peace process in 1993–2000 as well as the Irish Republican Army starting in 1995.

States themselves carry out acts designed to terrorize their own populations or those of other states, but scholars tend to avoid the label "terrorism" for such acts, preferring to call it repression or war. In fact, no violent act taken during a civil or international war—by or toward a warring party—can necessarily fit neatly into the category of terrorism. Of course, because war is hard to define, so is terrorism; warring parties often call each other terrorists. In the Central American civil wars of the 1980s, both the states and the guerrillas employed tactics that, if taken in peacetime, would easily qualify as terrorism. The narrowest definition of terrorism would exclude acts either by or against *uniformed military forces* rather than civilians. This definition would exclude the killing of 243 U.S. Marines by a car bomb in Lebanon in 1983 and the 2001 attack on the Pentagon, because they were directed at military targets. It would also exclude the bombing of German cities in World War II although the purpose was to terrorize civilians. But in today's world of undeclared war, guerrilla war, civil war, and ethnic violence, a large gray zone surrounds clear cases of terrorism.[16]

[15] Pape, Robert. *Dying to Win: The Strategic Logic of Suicide Terrorism*. Random House, 2005. Bloom, Mia. *Dying to Kill: The Allure of Suicide Terror*. Columbia, 2005.

[16] Stern, Jessica. *Terror in the Name of God: Why Religious Militants Kill*. HarperCollins, 2003. Laqueur, Walter. *A History of Terrorism*. Transaction, 2001. Pilar, Paul R. *Terrorism and U.S. Foreign Policy*. Brookings, 2001. Ross, Jeffrey Ian. *Political Terrorism: An Interdisciplinary Approach*. Lang, 2006.

FIGURE 6.3 Location of Suicide Attacks, 1980-2008

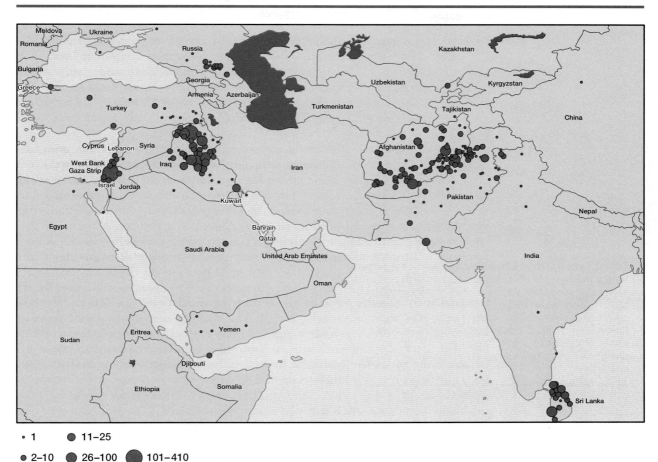

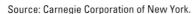

- 1
- 2–10
- 11–25
- 26–100
- 101–410

Source: Carnegie Corporation of New York.

Disagreements about whether terrorism included Palestinian attacks on Israel, and Pakistani attacks in Kashmir, scuttled efforts to pass a UN treaty on terrorism in late 2001.

State-sponsored terrorism refers to the use of terrorist groups by states—usually under control of the state's intelligence agency—to achieve political aims. In 1988, a bomb scattered pieces of Pan Am flight 103 over the Scottish countryside. Combing the fields for debris, investigators found fragments of a tape recorder that had contained a sophisticated plastic explosive bomb. The U.S. and British governments identified the Libyan intelligence agents responsible, and in 1992, backed by the UN Security Council, they demanded that Libya turn over the agents for trial. When Libya refused, the UN imposed sanctions including a ban on international flights to or from Libya. In 1999, Libya turned over the suspects for trial—two received life in prison while a third was acquitted—and the UN suspended its sanctions. In 2003, Libya formally took responsibility for the bombing, struck a multibillion-dollar compensation deal with the victims' families, and regained a normal place in the international community.

ASYMMETRICAL CONFLICT

Terrorist attacks often reflect the weakness of the perpetrators and their lack of access to other means of leverage. Terror can sometimes amplify a small group's power and affect outcomes. Al Qaeda's September 11, 2001, attacks, staged by a relatively small nonstate actor, ultimately led to the withdrawal of U.S. troops from Saudi Arabia, drew the United States into a counterinsurgency war in Iraq, and brought al Qaeda itself a surge of recruits for new attacks worldwide.

As of 2011, the United States has accused four states of supporting international terrorism—Iran, Syria, Sudan, and Cuba. All have been on the list for more than a decade. The U.S. government has barred U.S. companies from doing business in those states. However, these kinds of unilateral U.S. sanctions are of limited effect. Cuba can do business with Canada, as can Iran with Russia. North Korea was removed from the list in 2008 in exchange for promises to halt its nuclear weapons program.

Counterterrorism   Just as the methods used by terrorists have become more diverse over the past decades, so have the policies implemented to prevent terrorist incidents. Debates over how to best prevent terrorist attacks are often heated since there are also debates about why individuals engage in terrorist attacks in the first place.

Policies to combat terrorism can be placed along a spectrum involving more or less force in confronting terrorism and terrorist organizations. On the nonviolent end of the spectrum are calls for economic development. Advocates of these programs point out that in very poor states, people will be especially vulnerable to recruitment by terrorist organizations. With no bright future ahead of them and little opportunities to better themselves, people will naturally lose hope, become angry, and undertake seemingly irrational acts since they feel they have nothing to lose. And although there is little direct evidence that factors like poverty correlate directly with terrorist activities, it is clear that very poor states with weak central governments have served as recruiting grounds for international terrorist organizations.

In the middle of the spectrum are policing activities. These involve efforts by domestic police, usually in cooperation with other countries' police forces, to apprehend or kill terrorists while breaking up terrorist organizations. In one famous example of effective counterterrorist policing, the government of Peru, using an elite investigative team of the national police force, arrested the leader of the Shining Path movement, which at one point controlled over 20,000 well-armed militia members and had assassinated several Peruvian political leaders. The police arrested the movement's leader after staking out a dance studio (which he lived above) and digging through trash from the studio to find clues. After his capture, the Shining Path movement largely collapsed.

At the other end of the counterterrorism spectrum is organized military conflict. States may undertake small- or large-scale conflicts to counter terrorist organizations. In 1998, the United States launched cruise missile strikes against a plant in Sudan believed to be producing chemical weapons for al Qaeda, but turned out to be making infant formula. In addition, the U.S.-led war in Afghanistan was a response to the 9/11 attacks on the United States.

Of course, nearly every state that undertakes counterterrorism policies uses some combination of these methods. In the United States, for example, foreign aid is often justified in terms of assisting development and economic growth to decrease the possibility that the poor and uneducated can be easily drafted into terrorist organizations. The FBI and local law enforcement cooperate with many international partners to track and detain suspected terrorists, while U.S. soldiers assist other states with training and weapons in their fight against terrorists. Finally, the war in Afghanistan was a large war undertaken against the Taliban government that had protected al Qaeda.

Weapons of Mass Destruction

Weapons of mass destruction comprise three general types: nuclear, chemical, and biological weapons. They are distinguished from conventional weapons by their enormous potential lethality, given their small size and modest costs, and by their relative lack of discrimination in whom they kill. When deployed on ballistic missiles, they can potentially be fired from the home territory of one state and wreak great destruction on the home territory of another state.[17] Until now this has never happened. But the mere threat of such an action undermines the territorial integrity and security of states in the international system. Of central concern today are the potentials for proliferation—the possession of weapons of mass destruction by more and more states.

Weapons of mass destruction serve different purposes from conventional weapons. With a few exceptions, their purpose is to deter attack (especially by other weapons of mass destruction) by giving state leaders the means to inflict great pain against a would-be conqueror or destroyer. For middle powers, these weapons also provide destructive power more in line with that of the great powers, thus serving as symbolic equalizers. For terrorists, potentially, their purpose is to kill a great many people.

Nuclear Weapons

Nuclear weapons are, in sheer power, the world's most destructive weapons. A single weapon the size of a refrigerator can destroy a city. Defending against nuclear weapons is extremely difficult at best. To understand the potentials for nuclear proliferation, one has to know something about how nuclear weapons work. There are two types. *Fission weapons* (atomic bombs or A-bombs) are simpler and less expensive than *fusion weapons* (also called thermonuclear bombs, hydrogen bombs, or H-bombs).

When a fission weapon explodes, one type of atom (element) is split, or *fissioned*, into new types with less total mass. The lost mass is transformed into energy according to Albert Einstein's famous formula, $E = mc^2$, which shows that a little bit of mass is equivalent to a great deal of energy. In fact, the fission bomb that destroyed Nagasaki, Japan, in 1945 converted to energy roughly the amount of mass in a single penny. Two elements can be split in this way, and each has been used to make fission weapons. These elements— known as **fissionable material**—are uranium-235 (or U-235) and plutonium. Fission weapons were invented 60 years ago by U.S. scientists in a secret World War II science program known as the *Manhattan Project*. In 1945, one uranium bomb and one plutonium bomb were used to destroy Hiroshima and Nagasaki, killing 100,000 civilians in each city and inducing Japan to surrender unconditionally. By today's standards, those bombs were crude, low-yield weapons. But they are the kind of weapon that might be built by a poor state or a nonstate actor.[18]

Watch the **Video** "Iran's Nuclear Ambitions" on **mypoliscilab.com**

---

[17] Hutchinson, Robert. *Weapons of Mass Destruction: The No-Nonsense Guide to Nuclear, Chemical and Biological Weapons Today.* Cassell PLC, 2004. Eden, Lynn. *Whole World on Fire: Organizations, Knowledge, and Nuclear Weapons Devastation.* Cornell, 2003.

[18] Cirincione, Joseph. *Bomb Scare: The History and Future of Nuclear Weapons.* Columbia, 2007.

Fission weapons work by taking subcritical masses of the fissionable material—amounts not dense enough to start a chain reaction—and compressing them into a critical mass, which explodes as the splitting atoms release neutrons that split more atoms in a chain reaction. In the simplest design, one piece of uranium is propelled down a tube (by conventional explosives) into another piece of uranium. A more efficient but technically demanding design arranges high explosives precisely around a hollow sphere of plutonium so as to implode the sphere and create a critical mass.

Although these designs require sophisticated engineering, they are well within the capabilities of many states and some private groups. The obstacle is obtaining fissionable material. Only 10 to 100 pounds are required for each bomb, but even these small amounts are not easily obtained. U-235, which can be used in the simplest bomb designs, is especially difficult to obtain. Natural uranium (mined in various countries) has less than 1 percent U-235, mixed with nonfissionable uranium. Extracting the fissionable U-235, referred to as enriching the uranium up to weapons grade (or high grade), is slow, expensive, and technically complex—a major obstacle to proliferation. But North Korea, Iran, Iraq, and Libya all built the infrastructure to do so in recent years. North Korea promised to end its uranium program and dismantle its nuclear complex (after testing a bomb in 2006 and 2009). It made progress in this direction in 2007–2008, albeit behind schedule. But Iran defied several UN Security Council demands to stop enriching uranium in 2006–2009, insisting on its sovereign right to enrich uranium for what it calls "peaceful purposes." Talks on Iran's program continued into 2011.

Plutonium is more easily produced from low-grade uranium in nuclear power reactors—although extracting the plutonium requires a separation plant. But a plutonium bomb is more difficult to build than a uranium one—another obstacle to proliferation. Plutonium is also used in commercial breeder reactors, which Japan and other countries have built recently—another source of fissionable material. (Thus, if it decided to do so in the future, which is unlikely, Japan could quickly build a formidable nuclear arsenal.) North Korea tested a plutonium bomb in 2006, achieving fission although with a low yield.

Fusion weapons are extremely expensive and technically demanding;

NUKE IN A BOX

Nuclear weapons were invented during World War II and used on two Japanese cities in 1945. Tens of thousands have been built, and nine states now possess them. Obtaining fissionable materials is the main difficulty in making nuclear weapons. Terrorists' efforts to obtain them pose a grave threat. Here, in 1999, a U.S. congressman displays a mock-up of the Soviet-built nuclear "suitcase bomb" that, in the wrong hands, could kill hundreds of thousands of people.

they are for only the richest, largest, most technologically capable states. Here two small atoms (variants of hydrogen) fuse together into a larger atom, releasing energy. This reaction occurs only at very high temperatures (the sun "burns" hydrogen through fusion). Weapons designers use fission weapons to create these high energies and trigger an explosive fusion reaction. The explosive power of most fission weapons is between 1 and 200 kilotons (each kiloton is the equivalent of 1,000 tons of conventional explosive). The power of fusion weapons can reach 20 megatons (a megaton is 1,000 kilotons). In the post–Cold War era, megaton weapons have become irrelevant, since they are too powerful for any actor to use productively and too difficult for terrorists or small states to build.

The effects of nuclear weapons include not only the blast of the explosion, but also heat and radiation. Heat can potentially create a self-sustaining firestorm in a city. Radiation creates radiation sickness, which at high doses kills people in a few days and at low doses creates long-term health problems, especially cancers. Radiation is most intense in the local vicinity of (and downwind from) a nuclear explosion, but some is carried up into the atmosphere and falls in more distant locations as nuclear fallout. Nuclear weapons also create an electromagnetic pulse (EMP) that can disrupt and destroy electronic equipment.

Ballistic Missiles and Other Delivery Systems

Delivery systems for getting nuclear weapons to their targets—much more than the weapons themselves—are the basis of states' nuclear arsenals and strategies (discussed shortly). Inasmuch as nuclear warheads can be made quite small—weighing a few hundred pounds or even less—they are adaptable to a wide variety of delivery systems.

During the Cold War, nuclear delivery systems were divided into two categories. *Strategic* weapons could hit an enemy's homeland, usually at long range (for instance, Moscow from Nebraska). *Tactical* nuclear weapons were designed for battlefield use. In the Cold War years, both superpowers integrated tactical nuclear weapons into their conventional air, sea, and land forces using a variety of delivery systems—gravity bombs, artillery shells, short-range missiles, land mines, depth charges, and so forth. However, the tens of thousands of nuclear warheads integrated into superpower conventional forces posed dangers such as theft or accident. Their actual use would have entailed grave risks of escalation to strategic nuclear war, putting home cities at risk. Thus, both superpowers phased out tactical nuclear weapons almost entirely when the Cold War ended.

The main strategic delivery vehicles are **ballistic missiles**; unlike airplanes, they are extremely difficult to defend against. Ballistic missiles carry a warhead up along a trajectory and let it drop on the target. A trajectory typically rises out of the atmosphere—at least 50 miles high—before descending. In addition, some missiles fire from fixed sites (silos), whereas others are mobile, firing from railroads or large trailer trucks (making them hard to target). The longest-range missiles are **intercontinental ballistic missiles (ICBMs)**, with ranges of more than 5,000 miles.

Of special interest today are short-range ballistic missiles (SRBMs), with ranges of well under 1,000 miles. The modified Scud missiles fired by Iraq at Saudi Arabia and Israel during the Gulf War were (conventionally armed) SRBMs. In regional conflicts, the long range of more powerful missiles may not be necessary. The largest cities of Syria and Israel are only 133 miles from each other; the capital cities of Iraq and Iran are less than 500 miles apart, as are those of India and Pakistan (see Figure 6.4). All of these states own ballistic missiles. Short-range and some medium-range ballistic missiles are cheap enough to be obtained and even home-produced by small middle-income states. Table 6.3 lists the capabilities of the 30 states with ballistic missiles.

FIGURE 6.4 Expanding Ranges of Indian and Pakistani Missiles, 1998–2003

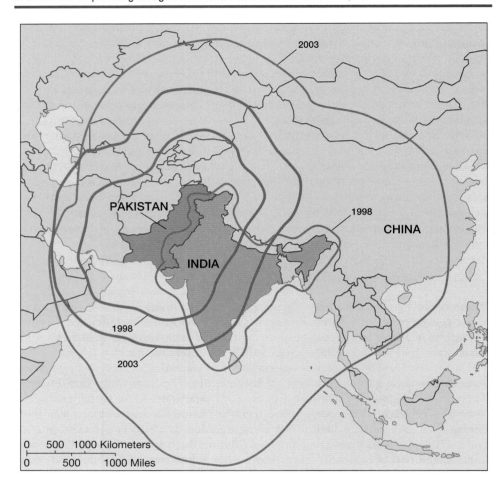

Source: *The Washington Post,* May 29, 1999: A32, Table 6.3.

Many short-range ballistic missiles, including those used by Iraq during the Gulf War, are highly inaccurate but still very difficult to defend against.[19] With conventional warheads they have more psychological than military utility (demoralizing an enemy population by attacking cities indiscriminately). With nuclear, chemical, or biological warheads, however, these missiles could be deadlier. The accuracy of delivery systems of all ranges improves as one moves to great powers, especially the United States. After traveling thousands of miles, the best U.S. missiles can land within 50 feet of a target half of the time. The trend in the U.S. nuclear arsenal has been toward less powerful warheads but more accurate missiles, for flexibility.

The **cruise missile** is a small winged missile that can navigate across thousands of miles of previously mapped terrain to reach a target, with the help of satellite guidance. Cruise missiles can be launched from ships, submarines, airplanes, or land. The United

[19] Postol, Theodore A. Lessons of the Gulf War Experience with Patriot. *International Security* 16 (3), 1991/1992: 119–71.

TABLE 6.3 Ballistic Missile Capabilities, 2010

Country	Range (Miles)	Potential Targets
United States[a]	13,000	(World)
Russia[a]	13,000	(World)
China[a]	13,000	(World)
Britain[a]	4,600	(World; submarine-launched)
France[a]	3,700 [4,600]	(World; submarine-launched)
North Korea[a]	800 [3,500]	South Korea, Russia, China [All Asia]
Iran[b,c]	900 [3,500]	Iraq, Kuwait, Afghanistan, Israel [Europe to Asia]
Israel[a,c]	900 [3,500]	Syria, Iraq, Saudi Arabia, Egypt [Iran]
India[a,c]	1,500 [2,000]	Pakistan, China, Afghanistan, Iran, Turkey
Pakistan[a]	800 [2,000]	India [Russia, Turkey, Israel]
Saudi Arabia	1,700	Iran, Iraq, Syria, Israel, Turkey, Yemen, Egypt, Libya, Sudan
Syria	300 [400]	Israel, Jordan, Iraq, Turkey
Egypt	400	Libya, Sudan, Israel
Libya	200	Egypt, Tunisia, Algeria
Yemen	200	Saudi Arabia
United Arab Emirates	200	Saudi Arabia, Iran
Afghanistan	200	Pakistan, Tajikistan, Uzbekistan
Kazakhstan	200	Uzbekistan, Tajikistan, Kyrgyzstan, Russia
Turkmenistan	200	Iran, Afghanistan, Uzbekistan, Tajikistan
Armenia	200	Azerbaijan
Belarus	200	Russia, Ukraine, Poland
Ukraine	200	Russia, Belarus, Poland, Hungary, Romania
South Korea	200	North Korea
Vietnam	200	China, Cambodia
Taiwan	80 [200]	China
Greece	100	Turkey
Turkey	100	Greece
Bahrain	100	Saudi Arabia, Qatar
Slovakia	80	Czech Rep., Hungary, Poland
Japan[c]	—	

Number of states with ballistic missiles: 30

[a]States that have nuclear weapons.

[b]States believed to be trying to build nuclear weapons.

[c]States developing space-launch missiles adaptable as long-range ballistic missiles.

Notes: Bracketed range numbers indicate missiles under development. List of potential targets includes both hostile and friendly states, and is suggestive rather than comprehensive. Missile ranges increase with smaller payloads. 200-mile ranges (Scud-B) and 300-mile ranges (Scud Mod-C) are approximate for a three-quarter-ton payload. Saudi range is for a two-ton payload; South Korean range is for a half-ton payload.

Source: Carnegie Endowment for International Peace.

States used cruise missiles extensively against Iraq in 1993, Serbian forces in Bosnia in 1995, Serbia in 1999, and Iraq in 2003.

The spread of ballistic missiles has been difficult to control.[20] Through the **Missile Technology Control Regime**, industrialized states try to limit the flow of missile-relevant technology to states in the global South, but with limited success. Short- and medium-range missiles (with ranges of up to about 2,000 miles) apparently are being developed by Iran, Israel, Saudi Arabia, Pakistan, India, North Korea, and possibly Argentina and Brazil. In 2009, Iran alarmed the West by testing a missile that could reach Egypt, Israel, and parts of Europe.

Small states or terrorists that may acquire nuclear weapons in the future could deliver them through innovative means. Because nuclear weapons are small, one could be smuggled into a target state by car, by speedboat, or in diplomatic pouches.

Since 2001, the United States has begun a container security initiative aimed at preventing weapons of mass destruction from reaching U.S. shores in seaborne shipping containers. But doing so without impeding the prosperity-inducing flow of international trade is a daunting challenge—nearly 8 million shipping containers pass through U.S. ports every year. In 2006, a bipartisan revolt in the U.S. Congress scuttled a deal, approved by the Bush administration, that would have let a company based in Dubai, an Arab country, control some operations at several U.S. ports (as other foreign companies already do). While the war on terrorism continues, U.S. cities remain at grave risk of destruction by nuclear weapons smuggled into the United States.

Chemical and Biological Weapons

A *chemical weapon* releases chemicals that disable and kill people.[21] The chemicals vary from lethal ones such as nerve gas to merely irritating ones such as tear gas. Different chemicals interfere with the nervous system, blood, breathing, or other body functions. Some can be absorbed through the skin; others must be inhaled. Some persist in the target area long after their use; others disperse quickly.

It is possible to defend against most chemical weapons by dressing troops in protective clothing and gas masks and following elaborate procedures to decontaminate equipment. But protective suits are hot, and antichemical measures reduce the efficiency of armies. In addition, Civilians are much less likely to have protection against chemicals than are military forces. Chemical weapons are by nature indiscriminate about whom they kill. Several times, chemical weapons have been deliberately used against civilians (notably by the Iraqi government against Iraqi Kurds in the 1980s).

Use of chemical weapons in war has been rare. Mustard gas, which produces skin blisters and lung damage, was widely used in artillery shells in World War I. After the horrors of that war, the use of chemical weapons was banned in the 1925 Geneva protocol, still in effect today. In World War II, both sides were armed with chemical weapons but neither used them, for fear of retaliation. Since then (with possibly a few unclear exceptions), only Iraq has violated the treaty—against Iran in the 1980s. Unfortunately, Iraq's actions not only breached a psychological barrier against using chemical weapons, but showed such weapons to be cheap and effective against human waves of attackers without protective gear. This example stimulated dozens more poor states to begin acquiring chemical weapons. Chemical weapons are a cheap way for states to gain weapons of mass destruction. Chemical weapons can be produced using processes and facilities similar to

[20] Mistry, Dinshaw. *Containing Missile Proliferation: Strategic Technology, Security Regimes, and International Cooperation in Arms Control.* Washington, 2003.

[21] Price, Richard M. *The Chemical Weapons Taboo.* Cornell, 1997.

those for pesticides, pharmaceuticals, and other civilian products, which makes it difficult to find chemical weapons facilities in suspect countries or to deny those states access to the needed chemicals and equipment.

The 1925 treaty did not ban the production or possession of chemical weapons, only their use, and several dozen states built stockpiles of them. The United States and the Soviet Union maintained large arsenals of chemical weapons during the Cold War but have reduced them greatly in the past decade. The 1992 **Chemical Weapons Convention** to ban the production and possession of chemical weapons has been signed by all the great powers and nearly all other states, with a few exceptions including Egypt, Syria, and North Korea. The new treaty includes strict verification provisions and the threat of sanctions against violators including (an important extension) nonparticipants in the treaty. Several states (including India, China, South Korea, France, and Britain) admitted to having secret

VULNERABLE

Civilians are more vulnerable to chemical weapons than soldiers are. A treaty aims to ban chemical weapons worldwide. Here, Israeli kindergarteners prepare against a chemical warfare threat from Iraqi Scud missiles during the Gulf War, 1991.

chemical weapons programs, which are now being dismantled under international oversight. Russia still faces very costly and long-term work to destroy a 44,000-ton arsenal of chemical weapons built during the Cold War. From 1997 to 2010, the treaty organization oversaw the elimination of more than half of the world's chemical weapons (over 40,000 metric tons).

Biological weapons resemble chemical ones, but use deadly microorganisms or biologically derived toxins. Some use viruses or bacteria that cause fatal diseases, such as smallpox, bubonic plague, and anthrax. Others cause nonfatal, but incapacitating, diseases or diseases that kill livestock. Theoretically, a single weapon could spark an epidemic in an entire population, but this would pose too great a danger, so less contagious microorganisms are preferred. Biological weapons have virtually never been used in war (Japan tried some on a few Chinese villages in World War II). Their potential strikes many political leaders as a Pandora's box that could let loose uncontrollable forces if opened.

For this reason, the development, production, and possession of biological weapons are banned under the 1972 **Biological Weapons Convention**, signed by more than 100 countries including the great powers. The superpowers destroyed their stocks of biological weapons and had to restrict their biological weapons complexes to defensive research rather than the development of weapons. However, because the treaty makes no provision for inspection and because biological weapons programs are, like chemical ones, relatively easy to hide, several states remain under suspicion of having biological weapons. UN inspections of Iraq in the mid-1990s uncovered an active biological weapons program. Evidence surfaced after the collapse of the Soviet Union that a secret biological weapons program had been under way there as well. In 2001, the United States pulled out of talks to strengthen the 1972 treaty, declaring the proposed modifications unworkable.

Today the United States and perhaps a dozen other countries maintain biological weapons research (not banned by the treaty). Researchers try to ascertain the military implications of advances in biotechnology.[22]

Proliferation

Proliferation is the spread of weapons of mass destruction—nuclear weapons, ballistic missiles, and chemical or biological weapons—into the hands of more actors. The implications of proliferation for international relations are difficult to predict but profound. Ballistic missiles with weapons of mass destruction remove the territorial protection offered by state borders and make each state vulnerable to others. Some realists, who believe in the rationality of state actions, are not so upset by this prospect, and some even welcome it. They reason that in a world where the use of military force could lead to mutual annihilation, there would be fewer wars—just as during the arms race of the Cold War the superpowers did not blow each other up. Other IR scholars who put less faith in the rationality of state leaders are much more alarmed by proliferation. They fear that with more and more nuclear (or chemical/biological) actors, miscalculation or accident—or fanatical terrorism—could lead to the use of weapons of mass destruction on a scale unseen since 1945.[23]

The leaders of the great powers tend to side with the second group.[24] They have tried to restrict the most destructive weapons to the great powers. Proliferation erodes the great powers' advantage relative to middle powers. There is also a widespread fear that these weapons may fall into the hands of terrorists or other nonstate actors who would be immune from threats of retaliation (with no territory or cities to defend). Evidence captured during the 2001 war in Afghanistan showed that the al Qaeda organization was trying to obtain weapons of mass destruction and would be willing to use them. Lax security at the vast, far-flung former Soviet nuclear complex increased fears that fissionable materials could reach terrorists.[25]

Nuclear proliferation could occur simply by a state or nonstate actor's buying (or stealing) one or more nuclear weapons or the components to build one. The means to prevent this include covert intelligence, tight security measures, and safeguards to prevent a stolen weapon from being used. In 2007, two teams of armed assailants broke into the South African nuclear facility where atomic bombs had once been designed and produced. After reaching the control room and shooting one guard, they were repelled, leaving a mystery along with doubts about the security of such nuclear facilities. As broader political unrest occurs in other nuclear states, notably Pakistan, thoughts often turn toward the safety of nuclear weapons and materials.[26]

---

[22] Lederberg, Joshua, ed. *Biological Weapons: Limiting the Threat.* MIT, 1999. Tucker, Jonathan B., ed. *Toxic Terror: Assessing Terrorist Use of Chemical and Biological Weapons.* MIT, 2000. Price-Smith, Andrew T., ed. *Plagues and Politics: Infectious Diseases and International Policy.* Palgrave, 2001.

[23] Paul, T. V., Richard J. Harknett, and James J. Wirtz, eds. *The Absolute Weapon Revisited.* Michigan, 1998. Sagan, Scott D., and Kenneth N. Waltz. *The Spread of Nuclear Weapons: A Debate.* Norton, 1995.

[24] Utgoff, Victor, ed. *The Coming Crisis: Nuclear Proliferation, U.S. Interests, and World Order.* MIT, 1999.

[25] Allison, Graham. *Nuclear Terrorism: The Ultimate Preventable Catastrophe.* Times, 2004. Finn, Peter. Experts Discuss Chances of Nuclear Terrorism. *The Washington Post,* November 3, 2001: A19. Erlanger, Steven. Lax Nuclear Security in Russia Is Cited as Way for bin Laden to Get Arms. *The New York Times,* November 12, 2001: B1. Gur, Nadine, and Benjamin Cole. *The New Face of Terrorism: Threats from Weapons of Mass Destruction.* Tauris, 2000. Falkenrath, Richard A., Robert D. Newman, and Bradley A. Thayer. *America's Achilles' Heel: Nuclear, Biological, and Chemical Terrorism and Covert Attack.* MIT, 1998.

[26] Bunn, Matthew. *Securing the Bomb 2008.* Harvard University, 2008.

A stronger form of nuclear proliferation is the development by states of nuclear complexes to produce their own nuclear weapons on an ongoing basis.[27] Here, larger numbers of weapons are involved and strong potentials exist for arms races in regional conflicts and rivalries. The relevant regional conflicts are those between Israel and the Arab states, Iran and its Arab neighbors, India and Pakistan,[28] the two Koreas, and possibly Taiwan and China. India and Pakistan each have dozens of nuclear weapons and the missiles to deliver them. North Korea tested weapons in 2006 and 2009, and negotiations over its program continue. South Africa reported after the fact that it had built several nuclear weapons but then dismantled them in the 1980s before white minority rule ended.

In the 1990s, Pakistan's top nuclear scientist sold bomb kits with low-grade uranium, enrichment centrifuges, and bomb designs to Libya, Iran, and North Korea. Libya gave its up, North Korea negotiated but remained coy about its uranium program (while giving up its plutonium program), and Iran continues to enrich uranium. Israel has never officially admitted it has nuclear weapons but is widely believed to have a hundred or more. Israel wants these capabilities to convince Arab leaders that military conquest of Israel is impossible.[29] To prevent Iraq from developing nuclear weapons, Israel carried out a bombing raid on the main facility of the Iraqi nuclear complex in 1981. In 2007, Israeli warplanes destroyed a site in Syria thought to be a nuclear reactor of North Korean design. Syria quickly cleared all traces of the building after the attack.

The **Non-Proliferation Treaty (NPT)** of 1968 created a framework for controlling the spread of nuclear materials and expertise.[30] The International Atomic Energy Agency (IAEA), a UN agency based in Vienna, is charged with inspecting the nuclear power industry in member states to prevent secret military diversions of nuclear materials. However, a number of potential nuclear states (such as Israel) have not signed the NPT, and even states that have signed may sneak around its provisions by keeping some facilities secret (as Iraq and Iran did). Under the terms of the Gulf War cease-fire, Iraq's nuclear program was uncovered and dismantled by the IAEA. In 2006, a deal between the United States and India to share nuclear technology led many states to question the NPT, because those benefits were supposedly reserved for only signatories. Nonetheless the deal received final U.S. and Indian approval in 2008.

North Korea withdrew from the IAEA in 1993, then bargained with Western leaders to get economic assistance, including safer reactors, in exchange for freezing its nuclear program. North Korea's leader died months later, but the compromise held up. In 1999

SOMETHING TO HIDE

The most important hurdle in making nuclear weapons is access to fissionable materials (plutonium and uranium). Iran's enrichment of uranium could give that country nuclear bombs within the decade. Fueling Western suspicions, Iran has not been forthcoming with international inspectors. Iran bulldozed this large site and removed its topsoil in 2004 before letting inspectors in. In 2006 and 2007 the UN Security Council applied mild sanctions against Iran over its refusal to stop enriching uranium.

[27] Abraham, Itty. *The Making of the Indian Atomic Bomb: Science, Secrecy, and the Post-Colonial State.* Zed/St. Martin's, 1998. Perkovich, George. *India's Nuclear Bomb: The Impact on Global Proliferation.* California, 1999. Lewis, John Wilson, and Xus Litai. *China Builds the Bomb.* Stanford, 1988.

[28] Albright, David, and Mark Hibbs. India's Silent Bomb. *Bulletin of the Atomic Scientists* 48 (7), 1992: 27–31. Albright, David, and Mark Hibbs. Pakistan's Bomb: Out of the Closet. *Bulletin of the Atomic Scientists* 48 (6), 1992: 38–43.

[29] Cohen, Avner. *Israel and the Bomb.* Columbia, 1998. Hersh, Seymour M. *The Samson Option: Israel's Nuclear Arsenal and American Foreign Policy.* Random House, 1991. Maoz, Zeev. *Defending the Holy Land: A Critical Analysis of Israel's Security and Foreign Policy.* Michigan, 2006.

[30] Kokoski, Richard. *Technology and the Proliferation of Nuclear Weapons.* Oxford/SIPRI, 1996. Chafetz, Glenn. The Political Psychology of the Nuclear Nonproliferation Regime. *Journal of Politics* 57 (3), 1995: 743–75.

North Korea allowed inspection of a disputed underground complex and agreed to suspend missile tests in exchange for aid and partial lifting of U.S. trade sanctions.[31] Then in 2002 the United States confronted North Korea with evidence of a secret uranium enrichment program, which the North Koreans then admitted to having. North Korea then pulled out of the agreement and out of the IAEA, restarted its nuclear reactor, and apparently turned its existing plutonium into a half-dozen bombs within months, one of which it tested in 2006. North Korea again agreed to give up its program in 2008, yet after another nuclear test in 2009, it began processing nuclear material again.

At present, in addition to the "big five" Security Council members, nuclear states are Israel, India and Pakistan (with dozens of warheads each, and growing), and North Korea (with perhaps a half-dozen).

Iran denies, but appears to be, working to develop nuclear weapons. Since 2003, Iran first agreed to suspend its uranium enrichment program and allow surprise IAEA inspections, then restarted enrichment, suspended it again, and restarted it again. In 2005, U.S.-backed efforts by Europe to offer Iran economic incentives to dismantle its program, and by Russia to enrich Iran's uranium on Russian soil with safeguards, both faltered. In 2006, the UN Security Council condemned Iran's actions and imposed mild sanctions. Iran insisted on its right to enrich uranium for what it called peaceful purposes. In 2008, Iran's behavior led to further UN Security Council sanctions, and in 2009, after a secret underground processing facility was discovered, Iran was engaged in talks over the program with Western powers.

A number of middle powers and two great powers (Japan and Germany) have the potential to make nuclear weapons but have chosen not to do so. The reasons for deciding against "going nuclear" include norms against using nuclear weapons, fears of retaliation, and practical constraints including cost. Brazil and Argentina seemed to be headed for a nuclear arms race in the 1980s but then called it off as civilians replaced

---

[31] Sigal, Leon V. *Disarming Strangers: Nuclear Diplomacy with North Korea.* Princeton, 1999. Cha, Victor D., and David C. Kang. *Nuclear North Korea: A Debate on Engagement Strategies.* Columbia, 2003.

SEEKING THE COLLECTIVE GOOD

Arms Control
COLLECTIVE GOOD: Limiting Nuclear Arsenals

BACKGROUND: After the creation of nuclear weapons in World War II, the two superpowers built large arsenals of them during the decades of the Cold War. Eventually, each side had tens of thousands. These nuclear weapons posed a grave danger that miscalculation or accident could lead to truly catastrophic consequences. Limiting and controlling nuclear arms, to avoid this catastrophic outcome, is a collective good. Both sides benefited if nuclear war was avoided, regardless of which side gave up however many weapons in a negotiated agreement.

CHALLENGE: Arms races represent the dark side of the reciprocity principle, a downward spiral of relations in which each reciprocates the other's hostile actions—in this case, deploying more nuclear weapons. Ever since the 1960s, the two sides have used negotiated agreements to try to control the arms race. For decades the effort merely channeled and illuminated the steady buildup of arms on both sides.

SOLUTION: The same reciprocity that fueled the arms race also fueled its

RECIPROCITY

military governments in both countries.[32] In 2004, after years of resistance, Brazil gave IAEA inspectors access to a controversial uranium enrichment plant (not part of a nuclear weapons program, evidently).

Nuclear Strategy and Arms Control

The term *nuclear strategy* refers to decisions about how many nuclear weapons to deploy, what delivery systems to put them on, and what policies to adopt regarding the circumstances in which they would be used.[33]

The reason for possessing nuclear weapons is almost always to deter another state from a nuclear or conventional attack by threatening ruinous retaliation. This should work if state leaders are rational actors wanting to avoid the huge costs of a nuclear attack. But it will work only if other states believe that a state's threat to use nuclear weapons is credible. The search for a credible deterrent by two or more hostile states tends to lead to an ever-growing arsenal of nuclear weapons. To follow this logic, start with Pakistan's deployment of its first nuclear missile aimed at India (the example also works with the countries reversed). Then India would not attack—that is, unless it could prevent Pakistan from using its missile. India could do this by building offensive forces capable of wiping out the Pakistani missile (probably using nuclear weapons, but that is not the key point here). Then the Pakistani missile, rather than deter India, would merely spur India to destroy the missile before any other attack. An attack intended to destroy—largely or entirely—a state's nuclear weapons before they can be used is called a *first strike*.

[32] Leventhal, Paul L., and Sharon Tanzer, eds. *Averting a Latin American Nuclear Arms Race: New Prospects and Challenges for Argentine-Brazil Nuclear Cooperation*. St. Martin's, 1992.

[33] Glaser, Charles L. *Analyzing Strategic Nuclear Policy*. Princeton, 1990. Sagan, Scott D. *Moving Targets: Nuclear Strategy and National Security*. Princeton, 1989. Jervis, Robert. *The Meaning of the Nuclear Revolution: Statecraft and the Prospect of Armageddon*. Cornell, 1989. Talbott, Strobe. *The Master of the Game: Paul Nitze and the Nuclear Peace*. Knopf, 1988.

reversal after the Cold War ended. Each side has matched the other's reductions in weapons, governed by a series of formal, verifiable treaties. The arsenals have shrunk dramatically as a result.

In 2010, the U.S. and Russian presidents signed a new nuclear arms control treaty. Over seven years it will cut strategic nuclear warheads by almost one-third, from 2,200 to 1,550 for each side. Each side also agrees to extensive monitoring to ensure that the other side is living up to its bargain. Using the reciprocity principle, the former superpowers have used step-by-step measures, each side matching the other, to first limit and then to greatly reduce their stockpiles of nuclear weapons.

The U.S. and Russian presidents sign thick arms control treaty, 2010.

THE RACE IS ON

India and Pakistan are building arsenals of nuclear-tipped missiles that could devastate each other's main cities. Their current arms race follows that of the superpowers during the Cold War. Superpower arms control agreements helped develop norms and expectations about the role of nuclear weapons, but did not stop a buildup of tens of thousands of nuclear weapons—the downside of the reciprocity principle. Here, Pakistan tests its nuclear-capable intermediate-range ballistic missile, 2008.

Pakistan could make its missile survivable (probably by making it mobile). It could also build more nuclear missiles so that even if some were destroyed in an Indian first strike, some would survive with which to retaliate. Weapons that can take a first strike and still strike back give a state *second-strike* capabilities. Possession of second-strike capabilities by both sides is called **mutually assured destruction (MAD)** because neither side can prevent the other from destroying it. The term implies that the strategy, though reflecting "rationality," is actually insane (mad) because deviations from rationality could destroy both sides.

If India could not assuredly *destroy* Pakistan's missile, it would undoubtedly deploy its own nuclear missile(s) to *deter* Pakistan from using its missile. India, too, could achieve a second-strike capability. Now the question of credibility becomes important. In theory, India could launch a nonnuclear attack on Pakistan, knowing that rational Pakistani leaders would rather lose such a war than use their nuclear weapons and bring on an Indian nuclear response. The nuclear missiles in effect cancel each other out.

Defense has played little role in nuclear strategy because no effective defense against missile attack has been devised. However, the United States is spending billions of dollars a year to try to develop defenses that could shoot down incoming ballistic missiles. The program is called the **Strategic Defense Initiative (SDI)**, "Star Wars," or Ballistic Missile Defense (BMD). It originated in President Ronald Reagan's 1983 call for a comprehensive shield that would make nuclear missiles obsolete.[34] However, the mission soon shifted to defending some U.S. missiles in a massive Soviet attack. After the Cold War the mission shifted again, to protecting U.S. territory from a very limited missile attack (at most a few missiles), such as might occur in an unauthorized launch, an accident, or an attack by a small state. Japan is spending $1 billion a year to build a U.S.-designed missile defense system, which it tested successfully in late 2007. North Korea has more than 600 ballistic missiles capable of hitting Japan, however.

As of 2010, the United States is deploying a multilayer system with 24 ground-based interceptor missiles in Alaska and California (directed toward the North Korean

---

[34] Lindsay, James M., and Michael O'Hanlon. *Defending America: The Case for Limited National Missile Defense.* Brookings, 2001. Wirtz, James J., and Jeffrey A. Larsen. *Rocket's Red Glare: Missile Defenses and the Future of World Politics.* Westview, 2001.

threat), 21 ship-based interceptors, about 500 Patriot missiles for short-range ballistic missile threats, and a series of radars and control centers. It had begun testing an airplane-based laser system and had concluded agreements with Poland and the Czech Republic to build missile defenses in those countries. The Obama administration reversed these plans, however, opting for a sea-based system to guard against any Iranian threat, with a radar system based in Turkey.

In addition to the technical challenges of stopping incoming ballistic missile warheads, such as distinguishing warheads from decoys, a true strategic defense would also have to stop cruise missiles (possibly launched from submarines), airplanes, and more innovative delivery systems. If a rogue state or terrorist group struck the United States with a nuclear weapon, it would probably not use an ICBM to do so. Nobody has an answer to this problem.

During the Cold War, the superpowers' nuclear forces grew and technologies developed. Those evolving force structures were codified (more than constrained) by a series of arms control agreements. *Arms control* is an effort by two or more states to regulate by formal agreement their acquisition of weapons,[35] using the reciprocity principle to solve the collective goods problem of expensive arms races that ultimately benefit neither side (see p. 6). Arms control is broader than just nuclear weapons—for instance, after World War I the great powers negotiated limits on sizes of navies—but in the Cold War nuclear weapons were the main focus of arms control. Arms control agreements typically require long, formal negotiations with many technical discussions, culminating in a treaty. Some arms control treaties are multilateral, but during the Cold War most were bilateral (U.S.-Soviet). Some stay in effect indefinitely; others have a limited term.

Several treaties in the 1970s locked in the superpowers' basic parity in nuclear capabilities under MAD. The 1972 **Anti-Ballistic Missile (ABM) Treaty** prevented either side from using a ballistic missile defense as a shield from which to launch a first strike. However, to allow full-scale testing of missile-defense technologies, the United States withdrew from the ABM Treaty with six months' notice (as provided in the treaty) in 2002. President Bush called the treaty a relic of the Cold War, but critics called U.S. missile defense a costly blunder that could induce China to greatly enlarge its minimal nuclear arsenal (which in turn could accelerate India's nuclear weapons production, and thus Pakistan's as well).

The Strategic Arms Limitation Treaties (SALT) in the 1970s put formal ceilings on the growth of both sides' strategic weapons. More recent arms control agreements regulated the substantial reduction of nuclear forces after the end of the Cold War.[36] The U.S. arsenal peaked in the 1960s at more than 30,000 warheads; the Soviet arsenal peaked in the 1980s at more than 40,000. The 1991 START treaty limited warheads to 6,000 on each side. Meanwhile the 2002 SORT treaty called for further reductions to 2,200 each by 2012, but relies on START mechanisms for verification. In March 2010, the sides signed a treaty (referred to as New START) that will lower the number of warheads to 1,550 and also creates additional verification mechanisms for both sides. The reciprocity principle that helped fuel the arms race also enables its step-by-step reversal.

China, France, and Britain each have several hundred weapons—France's and Britain's mostly on submarine-launched missiles and China's mostly on long-range bombers and intermediate-range missiles.

A **Comprehensive Test Ban Treaty (CTBT)** to halt all nuclear test explosions was signed in 1996 after decades of stalemate. It aims to impede the development of

---

[35] Adler, Emanuel, ed. *The International Practice of Arms Control.* Johns Hopkins, 1992.

[36] Larsen, Jeffrey A. *Arms Control: Cooperative Security in a Changing Environment.* Rienner, 2002.

THE WAR IS OVER

U.S. and Russian nuclear forces were greatly reduced in the 1990s. Here, U.S. B-52 bombers are being chopped up, under the eye of Russian satellites, to bring force levels down.

new types of nuclear weapons. However, the treaty does not take effect until signed and ratified by all 44 states believed capable of building at least a crude nuclear weapon. India did not sign the CTBT and defied it in 1998 with five nuclear tests. Pakistan followed suit with its own tests. The U.S. Senate voted in 1999 against ratifying the CTBT. Russia ratified it in 2000. Although no nuclear tests occurred worldwide in 1999–2005, North Korea's nuclear tests in 2006 and 2009 dealt more setbacks to the CTBT.

All the weapons of mass destruction are relatively difficult and expensive to build, yet provide only specialized capabilities that are rarely if ever actually used. This is why most states that could technically acquire them have decided not to do so. Such cost-benefit thinking also applies more broadly to states' decisions about the acquisition of all kinds of military forces.

States and Militaries

Given the range of military capabilities available to states (at various costs), how much and what types should state leaders choose to acquire? This question confronts all states but they answer it in different ways.

Military Economics

Watch the **Video** "Civil-Military Relations and Revolution in Egypt" on **mypoliscilab.com**

Choices about military forces depend on the connection between a state's military spending and its economic health. People once believed in the United States that "war is good for the economy" because, seemingly, military spending had helped end the Great Depression in the late 1930s. If this were true, state leaders would not face difficult choices in setting military budgets. High military spending would give them both more military capabilities for use in international conflicts *and* more economic growth for domestic needs (buying popular and political support in various ways). Unfortunately for state leaders, allocating economic resources for military purposes deprives the rest of the economy and reduces its long-term growth.

Both the long- and short-term effects of military spending are magnified by actual warfare. War not only stimulates high military spending, it destroys capital (people, cities, farms, and factories in battle areas) and causes inflation (reducing the supply of various goods while increasing demand for them). Governments must pay for war goods by borrowing money (increasing government debt), by printing more currency (fueling inflation), or by raising taxes (reducing spending and investment). U.S. revolutionary Thomas Paine warned in 1787 that "war . . . has but one thing certain, and that is to increase taxes."[37]

---

[37] Paine, Thomas. *The Writings of Thomas Paine*. Vol. 2. Knickerbocker, 1894.

Nonetheless, war and high military spending can have certain economic benefits. Short-term stimulation can result from a boost in military spending. Another potential benefit is the acquisition of territory (containing resources and capital).[38] Serbian ultranationalists made fortunes off the plunder of Bosnians whom they "ethnically cleansed," and Congolese militia leaders enriched themselves with minerals exported during the civil war. Another potential economic benefit of war is to stir up a population's patriotism so that it will work harder for less pay. But overall, the economic costs of war usually far surpass any benefits.

States vary widely in military spending, from Costa Rica, with virtually no military spending at all, to North Korea, which devotes 20 percent or more of all economic activity to military purposes. If military budgets are too low, states may be unprepared to meet a security threat; in the worst case, they may even be overrun and conquered militarily. But if leaders set military budgets too high, they will overburden and stifle the national economy.

World military spending is about 2 percent of the total goods and services in the world economy—about $1.2 trillion every year, or roughly $1 million every 30 seconds. Most is spent by a few big states, nearly half by the United States alone. World military spending is a vast flow of money that could, if redirected to other purposes, change the world profoundly and improve major world problems.[39] Of course, "the world" does not spend this money or choose how to direct it; states do.

In the global South, military spending varies greatly across countries, depending in part on the government in power (military or civilian).[40] Spending also depends heavily on available hard currency, from exports of oil or other products, to pay for arms purchases.

Arms imports by states of the global South make up more than half of all arms sales. In recent decades, about half of the South's arms imports have been in the Middle East, but lately India and China have taken a growing share. Of all international arms exports, about half come from the United States, with Russia, France, and Britain ranked next. Worldwide, these four countries together account for the vast majority of international arms sales. In the immediate post–Cold War era, global arms sales fell, but have since climbed back to near–Cold War levels.[41]

Activists have called attention to the sales of small arms, especially assault rifles, to unstable conflict zones where irregular armies commit brutalities. In 2001, 140 states agreed to a voluntary pact to curb small-arms sales to conflict zones. The United States, by far the largest exporter of small arms, blocked proposals to restrict sales of military weapons to rebel movements and to civilians. In the fall of 2009, the UN General Assembly voted nearly unanimously to begin work on an Arms Trade Treaty in hopes of completing work by 2012. Previously, the United States had opposed this effort, but the Obama administration reversed course, voting in favor of treaty negotiations.[42]

---

[38] Liberman, Peter. *Does Conquest Pay? The Exploitation of Occupied Industrial Societies*. Princeton, 1996.

[39] Forsberg, Randall, Robert Elias, and Matthew Goodman. Peace Issues and Strategies. In *Institute for Defense and Disarmament Studies. Peace Resource Book 1986*. Ballinger, 1985, pp. 5–13.

[40] Singh, Ravinder Pal, ed. *Arms Procurement Decision-Making Processes: China, India, Israel, Japan, and South Korea*. Oxford/SIPRI, 1997. Gill, Bates, and J. N. Mak, eds. *Arms Trade, Transparency, and Security in South-East Asia*. Oxford/SIPRI, 1997.

[41] Craft, Cassady. *Weapons for Peace, Weapons for War: The Effect of Arms Transfers in War Outbreak, Involvement, and Outcomes*. Routledge, 1999. Forsberg, Randall, ed. *The Arms Production Dilemma: Contraction and Restraint in the World Combat Aircraft Industry*. MIT, 1994.

[42] See http://www.controlarms.org. Boutwell, Jeffrey, and Michael T. Klare. *Light Weapons and Civil Conflict: Controlling the Tools of Violence*. Rowman & Littlefield, 1999.

Beyond these considerations about the size of military forces, the configuration of a state's military forces also presents difficult choices. Different missions require different forces. During the Cold War, about half of all military spending in the U.S. budget—and of world military spending—was directed toward the East-West conflict in Europe. Now other missions such as intervention in regional conflicts and counterinsurgency are more important.[43] And other new missions for military forces include humanitarian assistance, drug interdiction, and aid to other nations in building roads and schools.

Control of Military Forces

One cannot take for granted the ability of a state leader to make military forces take desired actions. At best, military forces are large and complex institutions, operating in especially difficult conditions during wartime. At worst, military forces have a mind of their own. Sometimes, the state leader appears to exert only incomplete control over the military.

States control military forces through a **chain of command** running from the highest authority through a hierarchy spreading out to the lowest-level soldiers. The highest authority, or commander in chief, is usually the top political leader. The importance of this military hierarchy is illustrated by a story from ancient China in which a king was thinking of hiring Sun Tzu (see p. 43) as an advisor. As a test, the king asked Sun Tzu to turn his harem of 200 concubines into troops. Sun Tzu divided them into two units, commanded by the king's two favorites. He explained the signals to face forward, backward, right, and left. But when he gave the signals, the women just laughed. Sun Tzu then had the two "officers" executed on the spot and put the next most senior concubines in their places. When he gave the signals again, the women obeyed flawlessly. Sun Tzu declared that "the troops are in good order and may be deployed as the King desires." Thus, military hierarchy and discipline make armed forces function as instruments of state power—at the price of brutality and loss of individual freedom.

In actual battle conditions, controlling armed forces is especially difficult because of complex operations, rapid change, and the fog of war created by the gap between battlefield activity and command-level information. Participants are pumped up with adrenaline, deafened by noise, and confused by a mass of activity that—from the middle of it—may seem to make no sense. They are called on to perform actions that may run against basic instincts as well as moral norms—killing people and risking death. It is difficult to coordinate forces effectively in order to carry out overall plans of action. Military forces counteract these problems through military discipline. Insubordination, mutiny, or deserting are serious offenses punishable by prison or death. But discipline depends not only on punishment but also on patriotism and professionalism on the part of soldiers. Officers play to nationalist sentiments, reminding soldiers

CHAIN OF COMMAND?

Through a hierarchical chain of command, states control the actions of millions of individual soldiers, creating effective leverage in the hands of state leaders. But many armed militias and warlord armies do not answer to state leaders. Egyptian protesters in 2011, like these celebrating on a tank, won the day when the army refused to fire on them.

[43] Hoffman, Peter J., and Thomas G. Weiss. *Sword and Salve: Confronting New Wars and Humanitarian Crises.* Rowman & Littlefield, 2006. Feste, Karen A. *Intervention: Shaping the Global Order.* Praeger, 2003. MacFarlane, S. Neil. *Intervention in Contemporary World Politics.* Oxford, 2002.

that they fight for their nation and family. Combat, logistics, communication, and command all depend on individual performance; motivation matters.

Military units also rely on soldiers' sense of group solidarity. Soldiers risk their lives because their "buddies" depend on them.[44] Abstractions such as nationalism, patriotism, and religious fervor are important, but loyalty to the immediate group (along with a survival instinct) is a stronger motivator. Recent debates about participation of women in the U.S. armed forces revolve around whether their presence disrupts group solidarity. (Evidence suggests that it need not, and in 2011 the ban on U.S. gay soldiers was lifted for simlar reasons.)

Finally, officers and political leaders need accurate intelligence to make good decisions.[45] Of course, even the most advanced intelligence systems cannot stop human error. "Friendly fire" incidents account for a substantial fraction of U.S. military fatalities. In late 2001, U.S. special forces were traveling with Hamid Karzai, believed at the time to be the only person who could lead a united, U.S.-allied Afghan government. As a U.S. soldier called in airstrikes on an enemy position, the battery in his GPS unit needed changing, and the unit's coordinates defaulted to its own position. A U.S. warplane dropped a bomb right on that target, killing three U.S. soldiers and five Afghan allies and nearly killing Karzai himself.

Civil-Military Relations

Beyond overcoming chaos and complexity, state leaders sometimes must confront challenges from within their own military ranks as well. Many states, especially democratic states, adhere to a principle of *civilian supremacy*. This is the idea that civilian leaders (who are either elected or appointed) are at the top of the chain of command. Civilians, not military officers, decide when and where the military fights. The officers, by contrast, are supposed to control how the military fights.

This division of labor between civilians and militaries inevitably leads to tensions. The interaction of civilian with military leaders—called **civil-military relations**—is an important factor in how states use force.[46] Military leaders may undermine the authority of civilian leaders in carrying out foreign policies, or they may even threaten civilian supremacy if certain actions are taken in international conflicts. Military officers also want autonomy of decision once force is committed, in order to avoid the problems created in the Vietnam War when President Johnson sat in the White House situation room daily picking targets for bombing raids. Worse yet, in NATO's 1999 bombing of Serbia, specific targets had to be approved by politicians in multiple countries. In 2010, the commanding American general in Afghanistan lost his job after publicly questioning President Obama's Afghanistan policies.

Even outside of the context of ongoing warfare, differences between civilian and military leaders can lead to tensions. In the United States, opinion surveys consistently show that military officers, on average, maintain different opinions than civilians on issues such as the use of force as a tool of leverage. Scholars have begun to study why

---

[44] Bourke, Joanna. *An Intimate History of Killing: Face-to-Face Killing in Twentieth-Century Warfare*. Basic, 1999. Grossman, Dave. *On Killing: The Psychological Cost of Learning to Kill in War and Society*. Little, Brown, 1995. Gray, J. Glenn. *The Warriors: Reflections on Men in Battle*. Harper & Row, 1967 [1959].

[45] Lowenthal, Mark M. *Intelligence: From Secrets to Policy*. CQ Press, 2000. Richelson, Jeffery T. *A Century of Spies: Intelligence in the Twentieth Century*. Oxford, 1995.

[46] Feaver, Peter D., and Richard D. Kohn, eds. *Soldiers and Civilians*. MIT, 2001. Choi, Seung-Whan, and Patrick James. *Civil-Military Dynamics, Democracy, and International Conflict: A New Quest for International Peace*. Palgrave, 2005.

this gap between civilians and the military has developed and its implications for American foreign policy.[47]

Similar tensions exist in other democracies. In Turkey, tensions have grown between the Islamic government and its military. Historically, Turkey's military has intervened numerous times to take control from elected leaders when military officers felt the government was threatening the secular nature of Turkey. Recently, however, the civilian government has been aggressive at arresting officers who they believe were plotting a coup. These actions have led to a fragile situation in that country. In the 2011 Arab Spring, the Egyptian military refused to fire on protesters, whereas Syrian forces did use lethal fire.

If tensions become too sharp between a civilian leadership and their military forces, a **coup d'état** (French for "blow against the state") can result. A coup is the seizure of political power by domestic military forces—a change of political power outside the state's constitutional order.[48] The outcome of a coup attempt is hard to predict. If most or all of the military go along with the coup, civilian leaders are generally helpless to stop it. But if most of the military officers follow the existing chain of command, the coup is doomed. In the Philippines in the late 1980s, the top general, Fidel Ramos, remained loyal to the civilian president, Corazón Aquino, in seven coup attempts by subordinate officers. In each case, the bulk of the Philippine military forces stayed loyal to Ramos, and the coups failed.

International pressures, such as sanctions, may also convince military leaders to step down. In late 2009, military leaders took power in Honduras after deposing its president. The international community, including the Organization of American States, pressured Honduras after the 2009 coup. Elections were held in the fall of 2009, restoring a democratic government, but Hondurans remains divided over the legitimacy of the new government.

If a coup is successful, military forces themselves control the government. These **military governments** tend to be the most common in poor countries, where the military may be the only large modern institution in the country. Ironically, the disciplined central command of military forces, which makes them effective as tools of state influence, also lets the state lose control of them to military officers. Soldiers are trained to follow the orders of their commanding officers, not to think about politics.

Covert operations can also get out of the control of governments. Several thousand such operations were mounted during the Cold War, when the CIA and its Soviet counterpart, the KGB, waged an ongoing worldwide secret war. CIA covert operations in the 1950s overthrew unfriendly foreign governments—in Iran and Guatemala—by organizing coups against them. The CIA-organized Bay of Pigs invasion in Cuba, in 1961, was its first big failure, followed by other failed efforts against the Castro government (including eight assassination attempts). CIA covert activities were sharply scaled back after congressional hearings in the 1970s revealed scandals. After September 2001, the executive branch enjoyed greater authority in conducting covert operations with less congressional scrutiny.

Overall, states face complex choices regarding the configuration of their military forces in the post–Cold War era. Not only have the immediate contingencies and threats changed drastically, but the nature of threats in the new era is unclear. Perhaps most important, world order itself is evolving even as military technologies do. The next chapter discusses the evolving structures and norms governing international political relations and how they are changing the nature of world order.

✓•–**Study** and **Review** the **Post-Test & Chapter Exam** at **mypoliscilab.com**

---

[47] Feaver, Peter D. and Christopher Gelpi. *Choosing Your Battles: American Civil-Military Relations and the Use of Force*. Princeton, 2005.

[48] Carlton, Eric. *The State against the State: The Theory and Practice of the Coup d'Etat*. Ashgate, 1997.

CHAPTER REVIEW

SUMMARY

- Military forces include a wide variety of capabilities suited to different purposes. Conventional warfare requires different kinds of forces than those needed to threaten the use of nuclear, chemical, or biological weapons.

- Control of territory is fundamental to state sovereignty and is accomplished primarily with ground forces.

- Air war, using precision-guided bombs against battlefield targets, proved extremely effective in the U.S. campaigns in Iraq in 1991, Serbia in 1999, Afghanistan in 2001, and Iraq in 2003.

- Small missiles and electronic warfare are increasingly important, especially for naval and air forces. The role of satellites is expanding in communications, navigation, and reconnaissance.

- Terrorism is effective if it damages morale in a population and gains media exposure for the cause.

- The September 2001 attacks differed from earlier terrorism both in their scale of destruction and in the long reach of the global al Qaeda terrorist network. The attacks forced dramatic changes in U.S. and worldwide security arrangements and sparked U.S. military intervention in Afghanistan to overthrow the Taliban regime and destroy the al Qaeda bases there.

- Weapons of mass destruction—nuclear, chemical, and biological—have rarely been used in war.

- The production of nuclear weapons is technically within the means of many states and some nonstate actors, but the necessary fissionable material (uranium-235 or plutonium) is very difficult to obtain.

- Most industrialized states, and many poor ones, have refrained voluntarily from acquiring nuclear weapons. These states include two great powers, Germany and Japan.

- More states are acquiring ballistic missiles capable of striking other states from hundreds of miles away (or farther, depending on the missile's range). But no state has ever attacked another with weapons of mass destruction mounted on ballistic missiles.

- Chemical weapons are cheaper to build than nuclear weapons, they have similar threat value, and their production is harder to detect. More middle powers have chemical weapons than nuclear ones. A new treaty bans the possession and use of chemical weapons.

- Several states conduct research into biological warfare, but by treaty the possession of such weapons is banned.

- Slowing the proliferation of ballistic missiles and weapons of mass destruction in the global South is a central concern of the great powers.

- The United States is testing systems to defend against ballistic missile attack, although none has yet proven feasible, and withdrew from the ABM Treaty with Russia to pursue this program.

- The United States and Russia have arsenals of thousands of nuclear weapons; China, Britain, and France have hundreds. Israel, India, and Pakistan each have scores. Weapons deployments are guided by nuclear strategy based on the concept of deterrence.

- Arms control agreements formally define the contours of an arms race or mutual disarmament process. Arms control helped build confidence between the superpowers during the Cold War.

- Political leaders face difficult choices in configuring military forces and paying for them. Military spending tends to stimulate economic growth in the short term but reduce growth over the long term.

- In the 1990s, military forces and expenditures of the great powers—especially Russia—were reduced and restructured.

- Except in times of civil war, state leaders—whether civilian or military—control military forces through a single hierarchical chain of command.

- Military forces can threaten the domestic power of state leaders, who are vulnerable to being overthrown by coups d'état.

KEY TERMS

infantry 194
counterinsurgency 196
land mines 196
power projection 198
electronic warfare 203
stealth technology 203
state-sponsored
  terrorism 207
weapons of mass
  destruction 209
fissionable
  material 209
ballistic missile 211
intercontinental ballistic
  missile (ICBM) 211

cruise missile 212
Missile Technology
  Control Regime 214
Chemical Weapons
  Convention 215
Biological Weapons
  Convention 215
proliferation 216
Non-Proliferation Treaty
  (NPT) 217
mutually assured
  destruction
  (MAD) 220
Strategic Defense
  Initiative (SDI) 220

Anti-Ballistic
  Missile (ABM)
  Treaty 221
Comprehensive
  Test Ban Treaty
  (CTBT) 221
chain of command 224
civil-military
  relations 225
coup d'état 226
military
  governments 226

CRITICAL THINKING QUESTIONS

1. If you were the leader of, say, Vietnam, what size and kinds of military forces would you want your country to have? To meet what kinds of threats would you choose each type of capability?

2. Suppose that Iran turned out to have obtained three tactical nuclear warheads from the former Soviet arsenal and was keeping them in unknown locations. What, if anything, should the great powers do about this? What consequences might follow from their actions?

3. Imagine a world in which most of the states, rather than just a few, had nuclear weapons and long-range ballistic missiles. Would it be more peaceful or more war-prone? Why?

4. Most of the great powers are reconfiguring their military forces in the post–Cold War era. What kinds of capabilities do you think your own country needs in this period? Why?

5. World military spending is more than a trillion dollars every year. If you could redirect these funds, how would you use them? Would such uses be better or worse for the states involved? Do you think there is a realistic chance of redirecting military spending in the way you suggest?

Negotiations with North Korea: Progress Toward Disarmament or Fool's Errand?

Overview

For over a decade, North Korea has defied the international community and proceeded with its nuclear program. Several times, North Korea has agreed to give up its nuclear program, only to renege on that promise. In 2006, North Korea tested a nuclear weapon. Although the test had only a small yield, North Korea clearly possesses the knowledge, resources, and ability to produce nuclear weapons.

In 2007, an agreement was reached in which North Korea promised to halt its nuclear program in exchange for international assistance including fuel and food aid. It then destroyed part of its nuclear processing facilities, but restarted its program when the United States delayed removing North Korea from its list of terror-supporting states. Once North Korea was removed from the list in the fall of 2008, it promised to allow nuclear inspectors to verify the stopping of its program. When the time came to formalize the agreement in writing, however, North Korea refused. Then, in 2010, North Korea sank a South Korean warship and shelled an island, killing four people, greatly increasing tensions between the two countries.

Based on this history of failed agreements and tense negotiations, some have suggested ending negotiations with North Korea over its nuclear program. Others point to the potential danger posed by a North Korean nuclear program and urge continuation of the talks. Should the United States continue the multilateral talks aimed at disarming North Korea?

The United States Should Continue to Pursue North Korean Talks

U.S. allies favor negotiations. Although they are concerned that North Korea not be rewarded for its bad behavior, South Korea and Japan both would like negotiations to continue. While these U.S. allies do not want to reach an agreement at any cost, because any conflict with North Korea would be exceedingly costly to one or both of them, they would prefer a diplomatic solution to this problem.

North Korea is interested in trading its program for aid. North Korea's economy is crumbling, and it can no longer count on Russia or China for assistance. To preserve its bargaining position, North Korea uses its nuclear weapons development program as leverage to get U.S., Japanese, and South Korean aid. In exchange for an attractive aid package, North Korea may well give up its program.

Isolating North Korea could be the most dangerous policy of all. The most likely scenario for North Korean leadership to actually use their nuclear arsenal would be a time when they feel backed into a corner. Walking away from negotiations to leave them in isolation would accomplish exactly that goal. They could lash out militarily at South Korea or Japan, two important U.S. allies.

The United States Should Give Up Its Quest for a North Korean Deal

North Korea has never kept its promises. After its rejection of the NPT in the 1990s, North Korea has not only refused to honor many of the commitments but actively cheated on them to continue its nuclear weapons program. Even if an agreement were reached, there would be no guarantee North Korea would not cheat.

The North Korean regime is untrustworthy. North Korean leaders do not care about the welfare of citizens and care even less about international reputation. While North Korea may rely on international aid to stay afloat, it could extract even more aid if it had a more successful nuclear program.

Only a collapse of the North Korean regime will bring true change. As long as the current regime is in power, nothing will change in North Korea. The faster international isolation undermines the regime, the better. Without fuel and food aid from the United States or nearby countries, the regime may collapse more quickly.

Questions

- Do you think North Korea is a trustworthy negotiating partner? How many chances should it be given to live up to its agreements? What realistic alternatives are there to negotiations?

- How much say should U.S. allies have in the negotiations? Does the proximity of South Korea and Japan to North Korea make their negotiating interests more important than those of the United States?

- What might be some of the potential problems if the United States took unilateral steps for the permanent disarmament of North Korea? Those unilateral steps could include more sanctions, war, or, on the other extreme, massive flows of financial aid to pay North Korea for giving up its nuclear arsenal.

For Further Reading

O'Hanlon, Michael, and Mike Mochizuiki. *Crisis on the Korean Peninsula: How to Deal with a Nuclear North Korea.* McGraw-Hill, 2003.

Cha, Victor, and David Kang. *Nuclear North Korea: A Debate on Engagement Strategies.* Columbia, 2005.

Rozman, Gilbert. *Strategic Thinking about the Korean Nuclear Crisis: Four Parties Caught between North Korea and the United States.* Palgrave Macmillan, 2007.

Wit, Joel S. *Going Critical: The First North Korean Nuclear Crisis.* Brookings, 2005.

CHAPTER 7

International Organization, Law, and Human Rights

Southern Sudan rebels arrive for joint exercise with government, 2008.

Roles of International Organizations

Most international conflicts are not settled by military force. Despite the anarchic nature of the international system based on state sovereignty, the security dilemma does not usually lead to a breakdown in basic cooperation among states. States generally refrain from taking maximum short-term advantage of each other (such as by invading and conquering). Rather, states work *with* other states for mutual gain and take advantage of each other only "at the margin." Unfortunately, the day-to-day cooperative activities of international actors often are less newsworthy than their conflicts.

States work together by following rules they develop to govern their interactions. States usually *do* follow the rules. Over time, the rules become more firmly established and institutions grow up around them. States then develop the habit of working through those institutions and within the rules. They do so because of self-interest. Great gains can be realized by regulating international interactions through institutions and rules, thereby avoiding the costly outcomes associated with a breakdown of cooperation (see p. 6).

The rules that govern most interactions in IR are rooted in norms. **International norms** are the expectations actors hold about normal international relations. The invasion of Kuwait by Iraq not only was illegal, but was widely viewed as immoral—beyond the acceptable range of behavior of states. Political leaders in the United States and around the world drew on moral norms to generate support for a collective response to Iraq. Thus morality is an element of power (see "Elements of Power" on pp. 47–49) drawing on the core principle of identity (most state leaders want to be seen by their publics and other leaders as upholding high morals).

Some norms, such as sovereignty and respect for treaties, are widely held; they shape expectations about state behavior and set standards that make deviations stand out. Constructivist scholars in IR (see Chapter 4) emphasize the importance of these global norms and standards. The attempt to define international norms follows a centuries-long philosophical tradition. Philosophers such as Kant argued that it was natural for autonomous individuals (or states) to cooperate for mutual benefit because they could see that pursuing their narrow individual interests would end up hurting all. Thus, sovereign states could work together through structures and organizations (such as Kant's proposed world federation) that would respect each member's autonomy, and not create a world government over them. In the 19th century, such ideas were embodied in practical organizations in which states participated to manage specific issues such as international postal service and control of traffic on European rivers.

Agreed norms of behavior, institutionalized through such organizations, become *habitual* over time and gain *legitimacy*. State leaders become used to behaving in a normal way and stop calculating, for each action, whether violating norms would pay off. For example, at the turn of the 19th century, U.S. war planners had active war plans for the possibility of a major naval conflict between the United States and Great Britain. Today, such plans would seem ridiculous. Over time, states refrain from behavior not just for cost-benefit reasons (as emphasized by realists and liberals) but for normative reasons having little to do with material calculations (as emphasized by constructivists). Legitimacy and habit explain why international norms can be effective even when they are not codified and enforced.

The power of international norms and standards of morality, however, may vary when different states or world regions hold different expectations of what is normal. To the United States, it was a moral imperative to remove Saddam Hussein from power. But

Read and **Listen** to **Chapter 7** at **mypoliscilab.com**

Study and **Review** the **Pre-Test & Flashcards** at **mypoliscilab.com**

NOT THE NORM

International norms are evolving in such areas as humanitarian intervention and human rights. These norms help define the roles of international organizations. One of their areas of concern is the use of child soldiers, like this ten-year-old Libyan rebel in 2011. Another concern, the protection of civilians from slaughter, inspired NATO intervention in the Libya conflict.

from the perspective of Arab populations, the U.S. invasion was an unjust violation of territorial sovereignty. In cases of diverging norms, morality can be a factor for misunderstanding and conflict rather than a force of stability. Realists point to examples such as these to suggest that international norms do not hold much sway on important matters of IR. Rather, realists point out, many of the accepted norms were shaped by the powerful states in the system (the dominance principle), and these same powerful states are often responsible for their interpretation. Yet constructivist scholars point out that even if international norms are violated, states (even the United States) go to tremendous lengths to justify behaviors that violate the norms. This suggests that strong norms do exist and are recognized by even the most powerful states.

Especially in times of change, when shared norms and habits may not suffice to solve international dilemmas and achieve mutual cooperation, institutions play a key role. They are concrete, tangible structures with specific functions and missions. These institutions have proliferated rapidly in recent decades, and continue to play an increasing role in international affairs. **International organizations (IOs)** include *intergovernmental organizations (IGOs)* such as the UN, and *nongovernmental organizations (NGOs)* such as the International Committee of the Red Cross.

Liberals point out that, contrary to realists or constructivists, it is the codification of international norms in institutions that gives norms their power. As discussed in Chapter 3, these institutions create incentives to reciprocate behavior encouraged by a norm (the reciprocity principle), while also constraining the behavior of powerful states through rules that govern behavior. Liberals point to the large and growing number of international institutions as evidence of their power and importance.

The number of IOs has grown more than fivefold since 1945, to about 400 independent IGOs and tens of thousands of NGOs (depending somewhat on definitions).[1] Figure 7.1 illustrates this growth. New NGOs are created around the world daily. This weaving together of people across national boundaries through specialized groups reflects interdependence (see p. 87).[2]

[1] Pevehouse, Jon C., Timothy Nordstrom, and Kevin Warnke. The Correlates of War 2 International Governmental Organizations Data Version 2.0. *Conflict Management and Peace Science* 21 (2), 2004: 101–20.
[2] Barnett, Michael N., and Martha Finnemore. *Rules for the World: International Organizations and Global Politics.* Cornell, 2004. Boli, John, and George M. Thomas, eds. *Constructing World Culture: International Nongovernmental Organizations Since 1875.* Stanford, 1999.

FIGURE 7.1 States and IGOs in the World, 1815–2005

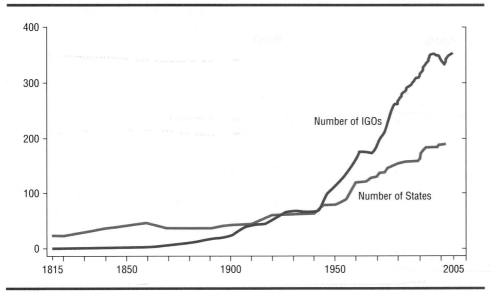

Some IGOs are global in scope; others are regional or just bilateral (having only two states as members). Some are general in their purposes; others have specific functional purposes. Overall, the success of these IGOs has been mixed; the regional ones have had more success than the global ones, and those with specific functional or technical purposes have worked better than those with broad purposes (see pp. 355–358). IGOs hold together because they promote the national interests (or enhance the leverage) of their member states—not because of vague ideals.

Among *regional* IGOs, the European Union encompasses some of the most important organizations (see Chapter 10), but it is not the only example. Other important regional IGOs are the Association of South East Asian Nations (ASEAN), the Southern Cone Common Market (MERCOSUR), and the African Union. The functional roles of IOs are important to their overall effect on international relations, but those roles are taken up in Chapter 10 on international integration. Here we will rely on the more general theoretical discussion of international institutions begun in Chapter 3.

Global IGOs (aside from the UN) usually have functional purposes involving coordinating actions of some set of states around the world. The IGO called Intelsat, for example, is a consortium of governments and private businesses that operates communications satellites. Members of the Organization of the Petroleum Exporting Countries (OPEC) are major oil producers who meet periodically in Vienna to set production quotas for members in an effort to keep world oil prices high and stable. Note that although the key members of IGOs are states, NGOs, businesses, or individuals can have important advisory and consulting roles in IGOs.

NGOs tend to be more specialized in function than IGOs. For instance, someone wanting to meet political scientists from other countries can join the International Political Science Association. Many NGOs have economic or business-related functions. The International Air Transport Association coordinates the work of airline companies. Other NGOs have global political purposes—for example, Amnesty International for human rights and Planned Parenthood for reproductive rights and family planning. Still others have cultural purposes—for example, the International Olympic Committee.

Religious groups are among the largest NGOs—their memberships often span many countries. Both in today's world and historically, sects of Christianity, Islam, Buddhism, Judaism, Hinduism, and other world religions have organized themselves across state borders, often in the face of hostility from one or more national governments. Missionaries have deliberately built and nurtured these transnational links. The Catholic Church historically held a special position in the European international system, especially before the 17th century. NGOs with broad purposes and geographical scope often maintain observer status in the UN so that they can participate in UN meetings about issues of concern. For example, Greenpeace attends UN meetings about the global environment.

A web of international organizations of various sizes and types now connects people in all countries. The rapid growth of this network, and the increasingly intense communications and interactions that occur within it, indicate rising international interdependence. These organizations in turn provide the institutional mesh to hold together some kind of world order even when leaders and contexts come and go, and even when norms are undermined by sudden changes in power relations. At the center of that web of connection stands the most important international organization today, the United Nations.

The United Nations

**◉─⌐ Watch
the Video
"UN Aid in Somalia"
on mypoliscilab.com**

The UN and other international organizations have both strengths and weaknesses in the anarchic international system. State sovereignty creates a real need for such organizations on a practical level, because no central world government performs the function of coordinating the actions of states for mutual benefit. However, state sovereignty also severely limits the power of the UN and other IOs, because governments reserve power to themselves and are stingy in delegating it to the UN or anyone else. The UN has had a mixed record with these strengths and weaknesses—in some ways providing remarkable global-level management and in other ways appearing helpless against the sovereignty of even modest-sized states (not to mention great powers).

The UN System

The UN is a relatively new institution, just over 60 years old. Even newer is the more prominent role that the UN has played in international security affairs since the end of the Cold War. Despite this new prominence, the main purposes of the UN are the same now as when it was founded after World War II.[3]

Purposes of the UN   The UN is the closest thing to a world government that has ever existed, but it is not a world government. Its members are sovereign states that have not empowered the UN to enforce its will within states' territories except with the consent of those states' governments. Thus, although the UN strengthens world order, its design acknowledges the realities of international anarchy and the unwillingness of states to surrender their sovereignty. Within these limits, the basic purpose of the UN is to provide a global institutional structure through which states can sometimes settle conflicts with less reliance on the use of force.

---

[3] Weiss, Thomas G., and Sam Daws, eds. *The Oxford Handbook on the United Nations.* Oxford, 2007. Kennedy, Paul. *The Parliament of Man: The Past, Present, and Future of the United Nations.* Random House, 2006. Krasno, Jean E. *The United Nations: Confronting the Challenges of a Global Society.* Rienner, 2004.

The **UN Charter** is based on the principles that states are *equal* under international law; that states have full *sovereignty* over their own affairs; that states should have full *independence* and *territorial integrity*; and that states should carry out their international *obligations*—such as respecting diplomatic privileges, refraining from committing aggression, and observing the terms of treaties they sign. The Charter also lays out the structure of the UN and the methods by which it operates.

The UN does not exist because it has power to force its will on the world's states; it exists because states have created it to serve their needs. A state's membership in the UN is essentially a form of indirect leverage. States gain leverage by using the UN to seek more beneficial outcomes in conflicts (especially on general multilateral issues for which a global forum brings all parties together). The cost of this leverage is modest—UN dues and the expenses of diplomatic representatives, in addition to the agreement to behave in accordance with the Charter (most of the time).

States get several benefits from the UN. Foremost among these is the international stability (especially in security affairs) that the UN tries to safeguard; this allows states to realize gains from trade and other forms of exchange (see Chapter 8). The UN is a *symbol* of international order and even of global identity. It is also a *forum* where states promote their views and bring their disputes. And it is a *mechanism* for conflict resolution in international security affairs. The UN also promotes and coordinates development assistance (see Chapter 13) and other programs of economic and social development in the global South. These programs reflect the belief that economic and social problems—above all, poverty—are an important source of international conflict and war. Finally, the UN is a *coordinating system for information* and planning by hundreds of internal and external agencies and programs, and for the publication of international data.

Despite its heavy tasks, the UN is still a small and fragile institution. Compare, for instance, what states spend on two types of leverage for settling conflicts: military forces and the UN. Every year, the world spends about $1.2 trillion on the military, and less than $2 billion on the UN regular budget. The whole budget of UN operations, peacekeeping, programs, and agencies combined is less than $30 billion, or less than 3 percent of world military spending. That proportion is even more extreme in the United States: more than 100 to 1. Each U.S. citizen pays (on average) nearly $2,000 a year for U.S. military spending but only about $15 a year for U.S. payments of UN dues, assessments, and voluntary contributions to UN programs and agencies combined.

Sometimes the UN succeeds and sometimes it fails. The UN deals with the issues that are perhaps the most difficult in the world. If groups of states could easily solve problems such as ethnic conflicts, human rights, refugees, and world hunger themselves, they most likely would have done so. Instead, states turn many of these difficult problems over to the UN and hope it can take care of them.

Structure of the UN   The UN's structure, shown in Figure 7.2, centers on the **UN General Assembly**, where representatives of all states sit together in a huge room, listen to speeches, and pass resolutions. The General Assembly coordinates a variety of development programs and other autonomous agencies through the *Economic and Social*

MAKING PROGRESS

The United Nations has very limited powers and resources, yet the world places great hopes in the UN when national governments cannot solve problems. Sometimes the UN seems to need an assist, like this vehicle in 2010 in Western Sahara, where the peace process itself has been stuck for many years.

FIGURE 7.2 The United Nations

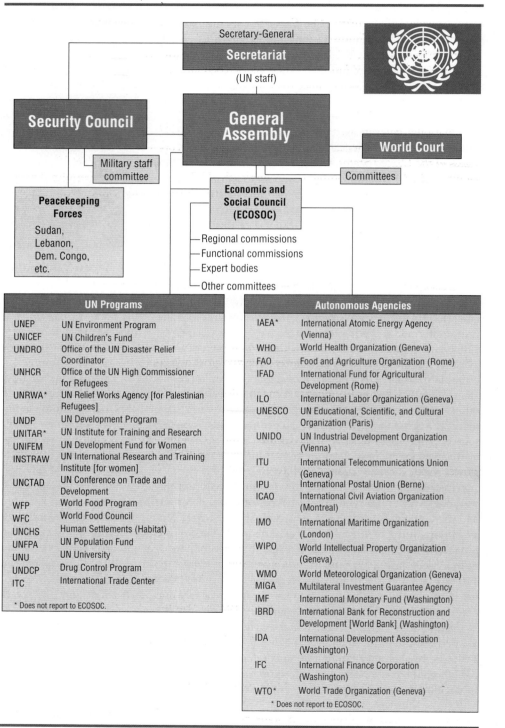

UN Programs	
UNEP	UN Environment Program
UNICEF	UN Children's Fund
UNDRO	Office of the UN Disaster Relief Coordinator
UNHCR	Office of the UN High Commissioner for Refugees
UNRWA*	UN Relief Works Agency [for Palestinian Refugees]
UNDP	UN Development Program
UNITAR*	UN Institute for Training and Research
UNIFEM	UN Development Fund for Women
INSTRAW	UN International Research and Training Institute [for women]
UNCTAD	UN Conference on Trade and Development
WFP	World Food Program
WFC	World Food Council
UNCHS	Human Settlements (Habitat)
UNFPA	UN Population Fund
UNU	UN University
UNDCP	Drug Control Program
ITC	International Trade Center

* Does not report to ECOSOC.

Autonomous Agencies	
IAEA*	International Atomic Energy Agency (Vienna)
WHO	World Health Organization (Geneva)
FAO	Food and Agriculture Organization (Rome)
IFAD	International Fund for Agricultural Development (Rome)
ILO	International Labor Organization (Geneva)
UNESCO	UN Educational, Scientific, and Cultural Organization (Paris)
UNIDO	UN Industrial Development Organization (Vienna)
ITU	International Telecommunications Union (Geneva)
IPU	International Postal Union (Berne)
ICAO	International Civil Aviation Organization (Montreal)
IMO	International Maritime Organization (London)
WIPO	World Intellectual Property Organization (Geneva)
WMO	World Meteorological Organization (Geneva)
MIGA	Multilateral Investment Guarantee Agency
IMF	International Monetary Fund (Washington)
IBRD	International Bank for Reconstruction and Development [World Bank] (Washington)
IDA	International Development Association (Washington)
IFC	International Finance Corporation (Washington)
WTO*	World Trade Organization (Geneva)

* Does not report to ECOSOC.

Council (ECOSOC). Parallel to the General Assembly is the **UN Security Council**, in which five great powers and ten rotating member states make decisions about international peace and security. The Security Council dispatches peacekeeping forces to trouble spots. The administration of the UN takes place through the **UN Secretariat** (executive branch), led by the secretary-general of the UN. The *World Court* (International Court of Justice), which is discussed later in the chapter, is a judicial arm of the UN. (A *Trusteeship Council* oversaw the transition of a handful of former colonial territories to full independence, but with the last trust territory's independence in 1994, the Council suspended operations.)

National delegations to the UN, headed by ambassadors from each member state, work and meet together at UN headquarters in New York City. They have diplomatic status in the United States, which as host country also assumes certain other obligations to facilitate the UN's functioning. For example, the U.S. government has permitted people such as Fidel Castro—normally barred from entry to the United States—to visit New York long enough to address the UN.

A major strength of the UN structure is the *universality of its membership*. The UN had 193 members in 2011. Virtually every territory in the world is either a UN member or formally a province or colony of a UN member. (Switzerland, which traditionally maintains strict neutrality in the international system, joined only in 2003 and Palestine applied, unsuccessfully, for membership in 2011.) Formal agreement on the Charter, even if sometimes breached, commits all states to a set of basic rules governing their relations. The old League of Nations, by contrast, was flawed by the absence of several important actors.

One way the UN induced all the great powers to join was to reassure them that their participation in the UN would not harm their national interests. Recognizing the role of power in world order, the UN Charter gave five great powers each a veto over substantive decisions of the Security Council.

The UN Charter establishes a mechanism for *collective security*—the banding together of the world's states to stop an aggressor. Chapter 7 of the Charter explicitly authorizes the Security Council to use military force against aggression if the nonviolent means called for in Chapter 6 have failed. Under Chapter 7, the UN authorized the use of force to reverse Iraqi aggression against Kuwait in 1990. However, because of the great power veto, the UN cannot effectively stop aggression by (or supported by) a great power. As often happens with the dominance principle, this structure creates resentments by smaller powers. In 2006, Iran's president asked the General Assembly, "If the governments of the United States or the United Kingdom commit atrocities or violate international law, which of the organizations in the United Nations can take them to account?" (None of them, of course, is the answer.) Chapter 7 was used only once during the Cold War—in the Korean War when the Soviet delegation unwisely boycotted the proceedings (and when China's seat was held by the nationalists on Taiwan).

History of the UN   The UN was founded in 1945 in San Francisco by 51 states. It was the successor to the League of Nations, which had failed to effectively counter aggression in the 1930s. Like the League, the UN was founded to increase international order and the rule of law to prevent another world war.

A certain tension has long existed between the UN and the United States as the world's most powerful state. (The United States had not joined the League, and it was partly to ensure U.S. interest that the UN headquarters was placed in New York.) The UN in some ways constrains the United States by creating the one coalition that can rival U.S. power—that of all the states. A certain isolationist streak in U.S. foreign policy runs counter to the UN concept. However, the UN *amplifies U.S. power* when the United States leads the global UN coalition. The United States is not rich or strong enough to keep order in the world by itself. And, as a great trading nation, the United States benefits from the stability and order that the UN helps create.

In the 1950s and 1960s, the UN's membership more than doubled as colonies in Asia and Africa won independence. This expansion changed the character of the General Assembly, in which each state has one vote regardless of size. The new members had different concerns from those of the Western industrialized countries and in many cases resented having been colonized by Westerners. Many states in the global South believed that the United States enjoyed too much power in the UN. They noticed that the UN is usually effective in international security affairs only when the United States leads the effort (which happens when U.S. interests are at stake).

The growth in membership thus affected voting patterns in the UN. During the UN's first two decades, the General Assembly had regularly sided with the United States, and the Soviet Union was the main power to use its veto in the Security Council to counterbalance that tendency. But as newly independent states began to predominate, the United States found itself in the minority on many issues, and by the 1970s and 1980s it had become the main user of the veto.[4]

Until 1971, China's seat on the Security Council (and in the General Assembly) was occupied by the nationalist government on the island of Taiwan, which had lost power in mainland China in 1949. The exclusion of communist China was an exception to the UN principle of universal membership, and in 1971 the Chinese seat was taken from the nationalists and given to the communist government. Today, the government of Taiwan—which functions autonomously in many international matters despite its formal status as a Chinese province—is not a member of the UN. But it is the only important such case.

Throughout the Cold War, the UN had few successes in international security because the U.S.-Soviet conflict prevented consensus. The UN appeared somewhat irrelevant in a world order structured by two opposing alliance blocs. A few notable exceptions exist, such as defending South Korea during the Korean War and agreeing to station peacekeeping forces in the Middle East, but the UN did not play a central role in solving international conflicts. The General Assembly, with its predominantly third world membership, concentrated on the economic and social problems of poor countries, and these became the main work of the UN.

States in the global South also used the UN as a forum to criticize rich countries in general and the United States in particular. By the 1980s, the U.S. government showed its displeasure with this trend by withholding U.S. dues to the UN (eventually more than $1 billion), paying up only years later after UN reforms.

After the Cold War, the great powers could finally agree on measures regarding international security. In this context the UN moved to center stage in international security affairs.[5] The UN had several major successes in the late 1980s in ending violent regional conflicts (in Central America and the Iran-Iraq War) while introducing peacekeepers to monitor the cease-fires. In Namibia, a UN force oversaw independence from South Africa and the nation's first free elections. By the 1990s, the UN had emerged as the world's most important tool for settling international conflicts. Between 1987 and 1993, Security Council resolutions increased from 15 to 78, peacekeeping missions from 5 to 17, peacekeepers from 12,000 to 78,000, and countries sending troops from 26 to 76.

---

[4] Weiss, Thomas G. *What's Wrong with the United Nations and How to Fix It*. Polity, 2009.
[5] Price, Richard M., and Mark W. Zacher. *The United Nations and Global Security*. Palgrave Macmillan, 2004. Newman, Edward, and Oliver P. Richmond. *The United Nations and Human Security*. Palgrave, 2001.

The new missions ran into serious problems, however. Inadequate funding and management problems undermined peacekeeping efforts in Angola, Somalia, and Cambodia. In the former Yugoslavia in 1993–1995, the UN undertook a large peacekeeping mission before a cease-fire was in place—"peacekeeping where there is no peace to keep." In response to these problems (and to the unpaid U.S. dues), the UN scaled back peacekeeping operations in 1995–1997 (from 78,000 to 19,000 troops) and carried out reductions and reforms in the UN Secretariat and UN programs.

For years the United States failed to pay its bills, even though a new secretary-general shrank budgets and jobs as the United States had demanded. This U.S. free riding shows that support of intergovernmental organizations presents a difficult collective goods problem (see pp. 56–57). Finally, after criticism from allies, the United States agreed to pay up, but under renegotiated terms for the future.

The 2003 Iraq War, however, triggered serious divisions among the great powers that sidelined the UN. After reaching consensus to insist on Iraqi disarmament and send back UN weapons inspectors, the Security Council split on whether to authorize force against Iraq—the United States and Britain in favor; France, Russia, and China against. When France threatened to veto a UN resolution authorizing war, a U.S.-British coalition toppled the Iraqi government without explicit UN backing. UN secretary-general Kofi Annan later called the war "illegal." The UN sent a team to Iraq to help with reconstruction, but suicide truck bombers destroyed it, killing the chief of the mission and dozens of others. The UN withdrew its staff from Iraq in 2003 and found itself largely sidelined in the world's most prominent international conflict.

To further aggravate U.S.-UN tensions, documents recovered during the Iraq War showed that high-ranking UN, French, Chinese, and Russian officials (and American oil companies) illegally profited from the UN's $64 billion oil-for-food program for Iraq, which was supposed to ease the civilian suffering caused by economic sanctions in the 1990s. A Swiss company under investigation for suspected fraud in the Iraq program turned out to be paying Annan's son thousands of dollars a month, creating what Annan admitted was a "perception problem." In 2005, an independent investigation cleared Annan of personal wrongdoing, but found the program corrupt and heavily criticized the UN for mismanagement and poor oversight of the program.[6]

Currently, the UN follows a principle of "three pillars"—security, economic development, and human rights—which are considered mutually necessary for any of them to succeed. At the end of 2006, the outgoing and incoming secretaries-general both referred to this principle. In a postwar conflict situation, in particular, the three reinforce each other.

The UN is in some ways just beginning to work as it was originally intended to, through a concert of great powers and universal recognition of the Charter. However, as states turned increasingly to the UN after the Cold War, its modest size and resources became seriously overburdened, leading to contraction of missions and funding. Today, the UN is more important than ever, yet still in danger of failing. In the coming few years the UN must continue to grapple with the challenges of its evolving role in a unipolar world, the limitations of its budget, and the continuing strength of state sovereignty.

---

[6] Traub, James. *The Best Intentions: Kofi Annan and the UN in the Era of American World Power.* Farrar, Straus & Giroux, 2006.

The Security Council

The Security Council is responsible for maintaining international peace and security and for restoring peace when it breaks down. Its decisions are *binding* on all UN member states. The Security Council has tremendous power to *define* the existence and nature of a security threat, to *structure* the response to such a threat, and to *enforce* its decisions through mandatory directives to UN members (such as to halt trade with an aggressor).

In six decades, the Council has passed more than 1,700 resolutions, with new ones added every week. These resolutions represent the great powers' blueprints for resolving the world's various security disputes, especially in regional conflicts. (Because of the veto system, the Council avoids conflicts among great powers themselves, such as on arms control.)

The five *permanent members* of the Council—the United States, Britain, France, Russia, and China—are the most important. What they can agree on, generally the world must go along with. Issues on which they disagree can quickly become contentious. In 2008, after the Security Council failed to decide whether the Serbian province of Kosovo should be independent, Kosovars unilaterally declared their independence from Serbia. Kosovo was quickly recognized by some Security Council members (the United States, France, and Britain), but not by others (China and Russia). Angry Serbians rejected Kosovo's declaration and blamed the Western powers for encouraging Kosovo's declaration. In 2010, the International Court of Justice held Kosovo's declaration to be legal, potentially opening the way for wider recognition of Kosovo's independent status.

Security Council resolutions require 9 votes from among the 15 members. But a "no" vote by any permanent member defeats the resolution—the *veto* power. Many resolutions have been vetoed by the permanent members, and many more have never been proposed because they would have faced certain veto. However, since the early 1990s the use of the veto has dropped abruptly, to just 23 vetoes in the last 20 years—14 of them by the United States, and 9 by Russia, China, or both.

The Council's ten *nonpermanent members* rotate onto the Council for two-year terms. Nonpermanent members are elected (five each year) by the General Assembly from a list prepared by informal regional caucuses. Usually there is a mix of regions and country sizes, though not by any strict formula. Often, countries lobby vigorously for a seat on the Council, producing books, advertisements, and memos to gain votes from other members of the regional caucuses. In 2006, Venezuela campaigned for the upcoming Latin American seat on the Council, seeking a platform to lead a growing, virulently anti-American coalition. Its president, in his speech to the General Assembly, called the U.S. president "the devil" and said the room still smelled of sulfur from his speech the previous day. Guatemala, with U.S. support, also campaigned for the seat. In the General Assembly, neither country could achieve the required two-thirds majority for election to the Council. After voting 47 times, the Assembly finally gave the seat to Panama as a compromise. In 2008, Iran campaigned for a seat, but gained only a handful of votes, while Turkey was voted onto the Council for the first time in more than 45 years.

Table 7.1 shows the recent rotations of members onto the Security Council. The system of nomination by regional caucuses has worked to keep the regional balance on the Council fairly constant as individual states come and go. Major regional actors tend to rotate onto the Council more often than do less important states.

Members can *abstain* on resolutions, an option that some permanent members use to register misgivings about a resolution without vetoing. China regularly abstains when its own security is not directly affected, and the United States has abstained several times to register a middle position on resolutions critical of Israel.

TABLE 7.1 Regional Representation on the UN Security Council

Region	Permanent Members[a]	Nonpermanent Members[b]			Possible Contenders for New Permanent Seats[c]
		2012	2011	2010	
North America	United States				
W. Europe	Britain France	Germany Portugal	Germany Portugal Bosnia	Austria Bosnia	Germany
Japan/Pacific				Japan	Japan
Russia/CIS	Russia	Azerbaijan			
China	China				
Middle East		Morocco	Lebanon	Lebanon Turkey	Egypt?
Latin America		Guatemala Colombia	Brazil Colombia	Brazil Mexico	Brazil, Mexico?
South Asia		India Pakistan	India		India, Indonesia?
Africa		South Africa Togo	South Africa Nigeria Gabon	Uganda Nigeria Gabon	Nigeria? South Africa?

[a]The five permanent members hold veto power.
[b]Nonpermanent members are elected for two-year terms by the General Assembly, based on nominations by regional caucuses.
[c]Possible new permanent seats might have fewer if any veto powers.

The Security Council *meets irregularly* (in the New York UN headquarters) upon request of a UN member—often a state with a grievance regarding another state's actions. When Kuwait was invaded, and when Bosnia was being overrun, the victims called on the Security Council—a kind of 911 phone number for the world (but one without a standing police force). Because international security continues to be troublesome in many regions and because these troubles often drag on for months or years, meetings of the Council are frequent.

The Security Council's power is limited in two major ways; both reflect the strength of state sovereignty in the international system. First, the Council's decisions depend entirely on the interests of its member states (see Figure 7.3). The ambassadors who represent those states cannot change a Council resolution without authorization from their governments. Second, although Security Council resolutions in theory bind all UN members, member states in practice often try to evade or soften their effect. For instance, trade sanctions are difficult to enforce. A Security Council resolution can be enforced in practice only if enough powerful states care about it.

Military forces responding to aggression under the auspices of Security Council resolutions remain under national command. For example, neither U.S. forces in the Gulf War charged with enforcing UN resolutions, nor U.S. soldiers sent to Somalia in late 1992 to restore humanitarian relief efforts disrupted by civil war, displayed UN insignia or flags. Similarly, NATO forces in the former Yugoslavia, and the Australian-led force in East

COUNCIL OF POWER

Collective security rests with the UN Security Council, which has authorized such military interventions as the Gulf War and the 2001 campaign in Afghanistan. Military actions not approved by the Council—such as the 1999 bombing of Serbia and the 2003 U.S.-British invasion of Iraq—tend to be controversial. Here, Serbia's president (left end of table) objects to Kosovo's claim of independence from Serbia, 2008. With the permanent members split on the issue—Russia and China backed Serbia while the United States, Britain, and France recognized Kosovo—the Council did not take action.

Timor, operate under their national flags but their missions are authorized by UN resolution. (Peacekeeping operations are different, and are discussed shortly.)

Even when the Security Council cannot agree on means of enforcement, its resolutions shape the way disputes are seen and ultimately how they are resolved. Security Council Resolution 242 after the Arab-Israeli war of 1967 laid out the principles for a just peace in that conflict—primarily the right of all states in the region to live within secure and well-defined borders and the return by Israel of territories captured in the 1967 war. (The parties are still arguing about whether territories to be returned by Israel means "all" territories.) Reaffirmed in Resolution 338 after the 1973 war, these resolutions helped shape the 1978 Camp David agreement and later formed the basis for peace negotiations between Israel and its Arab neighbors that began in 1991. If a Palestinian-Israeli settlement is ever reached, it surely will follow the outlines of Resolutions 242 and 338.

Proposed Changes   The structure of the Security Council is not without problems. Japan and Germany are great powers that contribute substantial UN dues (based on economic size) and make large contributions to UN programs and peacekeeping operations. Yet they have exactly the same formal representation in the UN as tiny states with less than one-hundredth of their populations: one vote in the General Assembly and the chance to rotate onto the Security Council (in practice they rotate onto the Council more often than the tiny states). As global trading powers, Japan and Germany have huge stakes in the ground rules for international security affairs and would like seats at the table.

But including Japan and Germany as permanent Security Council members would not be simple. If Germany joined, three of the seven permanent members would be European, giving that region unfair weight. The three European seats could be combined into one (a rotating seat or one representing the European Union), but this would water down the power of Britain and France, which can veto any such change in the Charter. Japan's bid for a seat faces Chinese opposition. Also, if Japan or Germany got a seat, then what about India, with 20 percent of the world's population? And what about an Islamic country such as Indonesia? Finally, what about Latin America and Africa? Possible new permanent members could include Germany, Japan, India, Brazil, Egypt, and either Nigeria or South Africa. None of these plans has made much progress. Any overhaul of the Security Council would require a change in the UN Charter, and a change in membership would reduce the power of the current five permanent members, any of which could veto the change, making any change very difficult. In late 2004, an expert panel appointed by Annan recommended expanding the Security

FIGURE 7.3 Divergent Interests on the UN Security Council

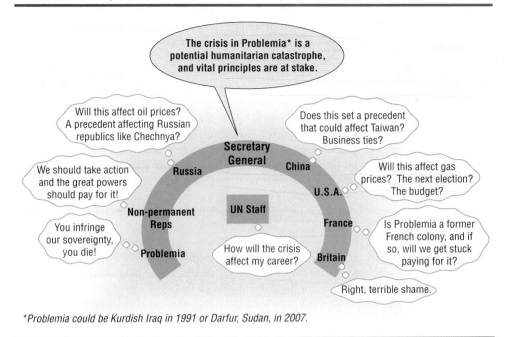

*Problemia could be Kurdish Iraq in 1991 or Darfur, Sudan, in 2007.

Council to 24 members under either of two formulas, neither changing veto powers. These proposals were debated in 2005 but no agreement was reached and the issue was put on hold. During the debate, 42 million people in China and 40 other countries signed a petition against Japan's getting a Council seat until it recognizes and sincerely apologizes for its war crimes in World War II.

Peacekeeping Forces

Peacekeeping forces are not mentioned in the UN Charter. Secretary-General Dag Hammarskjöld in the 1960s joked that they were allowed under "Chapter Six and a Half"—somewhere between the nonviolent dispute resolution called for in Chapter 6 of the Charter and the authorization of force provided for in Chapter 7. The Charter requires member states to place military forces at the disposal of the UN, but such forces were envisioned as being used in response to aggression (under collective security). In practice, when the UN has authorized force to reverse aggression—as in the Gulf War in 1990—the forces involved have been *national* forces not under UN command.

The UN's *own* forces—borrowed from armies of member states but under the flag and command of the UN—have been *peacekeeping* forces to calm regional conflicts, playing a neutral role between warring forces.[7] These forces won the Nobel Peace Prize in 1988 in recognition of their growing importance and success. As was learned in Bosnia, however, such neutral forces do not succeed well in a situation in which the Security Council has identified one side as the aggressor.

---

[7] Fortna, Virginia Page. *Does Peacekeeping Work? Shaping Belligerents' Choices after Civil War*. Princeton, 2008. Doyle, Michael W., and Nicholas Sambanis. *Making War and Building Peace: United Nations Peace Operations*. Princeton, 2006. Durch, William J., ed. *Twenty-First-Century Peace Operations*. U.S. Institute of Peace, 2006. Findlay, Trevor. *The Use of Force in UN Peace Operations*. Oxford, 2002.

Peacekeeping Missions The secretary-general assembles a peacekeeping force for each mission, usually from a few states totally uninvolved in the conflict, and puts it under a single commander. The soldiers are commonly called *blue helmets*. Peacekeeping forces serve at the invitation of a host government and must leave if that government orders them out.

Authority for peacekeeping forces is granted by the Security Council, usually for a period of three to six months that may be renewed—in some cases for decades. In one early case, the Suez crisis in 1956, the General Assembly authorized the forces under the "Uniting for Peace" resolution, which allowed the General Assembly to take up security matters when the Security Council was deadlocked. In the Congo in 1960, the secretary-general took the initiative. But today the Security Council firmly controls peacekeeping operations.

Funds must be voted on by the General Assembly, and lack of funds is today the single greatest constraint on the use of peacekeeping forces. Special assessments against member states pay for peacekeeping operations. With the expansion of peacekeeping since 1988, the expenses of these forces (over $7 billion in 2012) are several times larger than the regular UN budget.

Recent Missions In early 2012, the UN maintained over 100,000 troops (including police and military observers) in 15 peacekeeping or observing missions, using military personnel from 114 countries, spanning five world regions (see Table 7.2).

The two largest peacekeeping missions in 2012 were in the Democratic Congo (DRC) and the Darfur region of Sudan. In the DRC mission, 20,000 peacekeepers monitored a cease-fire and protected civilians after a civil war. In 2008, these UN peacekeepers were criticized for not doing enough to protect civilians in refugee camps as the

TABLE 7.2 UN Peacekeeping Missions as of September 2011

Location	Region	Personnel	Annual Cost (million $)	Role	Since
Sudan/Darfur	Africa	24,000	$1,700	Protect civilians	2007
Democratic Congo	Africa	20,000	1,400	Enforce cease-fire; protect civilians	1999
Lebanon	Middle East	12,400	550	Monitor cease-fire on Israeli border	1978
Haiti	Latin America	12,000	800	Assist transitional govt.	2004
Sudan/South Sudan	Africa	11,000	950	Support peace agreement	2011
Ivory Coast	Africa	11,000	500	Help implement peace agreement	2004
Liberia	Africa	9,500	525	Assist transitional govt.	2003
Sudan/Abyei	Africa	2,000	?	Monitor disputed town on border	2011
East Timor	Japan/Pacific	1,600	200	Observe cease-fire; policing	2006
Syria (Golan Heights)	Middle East	1,000	80	Monitor Israel-Syria cease-fire	1974
Cyprus	Middle East	900	55	Monitor Greek-Turkish cease-fire	1964
Western Sahara	Africa	300	60	Organize referendum in territory	1991
Israel	Middle East	150	60	Observe Arab-Israeli truce	1948
Kosovo	Europe	150	45	Civil administration; relief	1999
India/Pakistan	South Asia	40	15	Observe India-Pakistan cease-fire	1949
Total		106,000	7,000		

Note: Size indicates total international personnel (mostly troops but some civilian administrators and police).

civil war in the eastern portion of the DRC reignited. UN forces occasionally were attacked by rebels and even local civilians angry at the UN's failure to protect them. The secretary-general called for thousands of additional troops for the DRC, but member states were reluctant to bear the cost of providing them. This problem illustrates the limits of the identity principle in solving a collective goods problem, where potential suppliers of peacekeepers face neither rewards for doing so (reciprocity) nor punishment for failing to do so (dominance).

In 2007, the Security Council approved a nearly 20,000-troop peacekeeping force (plus more than 6,000 police) for the Darfur region in Sudan, after several years of resistance from the Sudanese government. The UN troops were to join an already-deployed (but small) African Union contingent. By 2010, after years of delay, nearly all of the authorized troops had been deployed after overcoming numerous objections from Sudan. These new deployments are in addition to the 7,000 UN troops enforcing a cease-fire between Sudan and newly independent South Sudan.

The UN's other largest peacekeeping operations were in Liberia (maintaining a cease-fire after a civil war), Ivory Coast (stabilizing a peace agreement), Lebanon (following the 2006 Israeli-Hezbollah war), and Haiti (trying to maintain stability after a military coup). The largest recent missions reflect the resurgence of UN peacekeeping after a shakeout in the mid-1990s.

At its peak in the early 1990s, the UN ran several large peacekeeping operations in addition to those in the former Yugoslavia and in Lebanon. One of the most important was in Cambodia. There, 15,000 peacekeepers were coupled with a large force of UN administrators who took over substantial control of the Cambodian government under a fragile pact that ended (for the most part) a long and devastating civil war. Despite difficulty in obtaining the cooperation of the Khmer Rouge faction (which refused to disarm as it had agreed), the UN pressed forward to hold elections in 1993 that chose a Cambodian government (though not a stable one).

The lessons learned in Cambodia helped the UN accomplish a similar mission more easily in Mozambique. A peace agreement ended a long and devastating civil war there, setting up mechanisms for disarmament, the integration of military forces, and the holding of internationally supervised elections for a new government. In 1992, the UN had tried to accomplish a similar mission in Angola with only 500 personnel. The peace process was on track until the government won the elections; the rebels refused to accept the results and resumed an even more destructive civil war. At the next opportunity, the UN sent a force to Angola ten times as large as before. Results improved, but the war started again and the UN Security Council ended the mission in 1999. These experiences helped the UN respond more effectively after civil wars in Sierra Leone, Ivory Coast, and Liberia in 2002–2003. Because of problems with sex-related crimes in UN peacekeeping operations, and the importance of women in postwar societies, the Security Council passed Resolution 1325 in 2000 to focus attention on gender issues in UN peacekeeping and reconstruction (see p. 115).[8]

As UN peacekeeping has become more intensive in recent years, new missions have expanded the range of what are now called broadly *peace operations*. These operations include not only traditional peacekeeping but also the use of force to protect civilians (as in Democratic Congo), the supervision of elections (as in Liberia), and even running the government while a society gets back on its feet (as in Cambodia, East Timor, and Kosovo). These expanded operations after conflicts are called **peacebuilding**. In an effort to provide

---

[8] Whitworth, Sandra. *Men, Militarism and UN Peacekeeping: A Gendered Analysis*. Rienner, 2007.

longer-term support after wars, in 2005 the UN created a Peacebuilding Commission to co-ordinate reconstruction, institution building, and economic recovery efforts after peace-keeping missions end.[9]

Observing and Peacekeeping   "Peacekeepers" actually perform two different functions—observing and peacekeeping. *Observers* are unarmed military officers sent to a conflict area in small numbers simply to watch what happens and report back to the UN. With the UN watching, the parties to a conflict are often less likely to break a cease-fire. Observers can monitor various aspects of a country's situation—cease-fires, elections, respect for human rights, and other areas.[10]

The function of *peacekeeping* is carried out by lightly armed soldiers (in armored vehicles with automatic rifles but without artillery, tanks, and other heavy weapons). Such forces play several roles. They can *interpose* themselves physically between warring parties to keep them apart (more accurately, to make them attack the UN forces in order to get to their enemy). UN peacekeepers often try to *negotiate* with military officers on both sides. This channel of communication can bring about tactical actions and understandings that support a cease-fire. But the UN forces in a war zone cannot easily get from one side's positions to those of the other to conduct negotiations.

Peacekeeping is much more difficult if one side sees the UN forces as being biased toward the other side. Israel feels this way about UN forces in southern Lebanon, for example. On occasion, Israeli forces have broken through UN lines to attack enemies, and they allegedly have targeted UN outposts on occasion. In Cambodia and the former Yugoslavia in the early 1990s, one party deliberately attacked UN forces many times, causing a number of deaths. In general, when cease-fires break down, UN troops get caught in the middle. More than 2,800 have been killed over the years.

Many countries contribute their national military forces to UN peacekeeping missions. In 2010, the five leading contributors (with troop numbers) are Bangladesh (11,000), Pakistan (9,000), India (8,000), Nigeria (6,000), and Nepal (4,000). Reasons for troop contributions to UN peacekeeping vary. Some states feel that by contributing to a common good, they are advancing the interest of peace, while simultaneously projecting the image of a strong military power. In this way, states may serve to increase their soft power. Alternatively, some states find contributing to these missions financially beneficial, since peacekeeping forces are paid by UN contributions. In a few countries such as Nepal and Sierra Leone, sending military forces out of the country for peacekeeping is useful for domestic political stability after a civil war.

In some conflicts, peacekeepers organized outside the UN framework have been used instead of UN-commanded forces. Some 3,500 French peacekeepers—not under UN command—serve in Ivory Coast alongside 11,000 UN peacekeepers, monitoring a 2003 cease-fire. When government airstrikes killed nine French soldiers in 2004, the French forces retaliated robustly, destroying the government's air force. In 2011, after the incumbent president lost an election but refused to leave, UN and French troops helped the winner dislodge him by force.

Peacekeeping forces have generally been unable to make peace, only to keep it. To go into a shooting war and suppress hostilities requires military forces far beyond those of past UN peacekeeping missions. Thus, peacekeepers are usually not sent until a cease-fire has been arranged, has taken effect, and has held up for some time. Often dozens of cease-fires are broken before one sticks. Wars may simmer along for years, taking a terrible toll, before the UN gets its chance.

---

[9] Howard, Lise Morjé. *UN Peacekeeping in Civil Wars*. Cambridge, 2008.
[10] Lindley, Dan. *Promoting Peace with Information: Transparency as a Tool of Security Regimes*. Princeton, 2007.

To address this problem, the secretary-general in 1992 proposed the creation of UN *peace-making* (or *peace enforcement*) units that would not only monitor a cease-fire but enforce it if it broke down.[11] The secretary-general called for member states to make available, on a rapid deployment basis, 1,000 soldiers each—specially trained volunteers—to create a standby UN army that could respond quickly to crises. Not only did the member states refuse the request for soldiers, they shot down the idea of peacemaking altogether. Since then, the UN has authorized member states to provide real military forces, not peacekeepers, when fighting may be required. In an exception that may or may not indicate a trend, the Security Council broadened the mandate of UN peacekeepers in Democratic Congo to let them protect civilians (which UN forces have been criticized for not doing). In 2005, Pakistani peacekeepers killed 50 militia fighters after nine peacekeepers from Bangladesh were killed in an ambush.

In the late 1990s, seven countries—Denmark, Norway, Sweden, Poland, the Netherlands, Austria, and Canada—formed a 4,000-troop UN Standby High Readiness Brigade. Headquartered in Denmark and available to deploy to conflict areas in two to four weeks rather than months, the brigade is controlled by the Security Council. It participated in the UN mission to Ethiopia-Eritrea in 2000–2001. In early 2005, the brigade deployed to Sudan to support a peace agreement between northern and southern regions after a long civil war.

The Secretariat

The secretary-general of the UN is the closest thing to a "president of the world" that exists. But the secretary-general represents member states—not the world's 7 billion people. Where the great powers do not have consensus, it is hard for the secretary-general to make anything happen.

The secretary-general is nominated by the Security Council—requiring the consent of all five permanent members—and must be approved by the General Assembly. The term of office is five years and may be renewed. Past secretaries-general have come from various regions of the world but never from a great power.

Secretary-General Ban Ki-moon, a former foreign minister of South Korea, began his term in 2007 focused on UN reform, economic development, human rights, terrorism, proliferation, environmental problems, and HIV/AIDS. He was elected to a second term starting in 2012. His predecessor, Kofi Annan, served ten years and helped reinvigorate the UN, winning the one-hundredth-anniversary Nobel Peace Prize for his efforts.

MAN ON THE MOVE

The UN secretary-general has a lofty mission but limited power and resources. Ban Ki-moon, here going to a meeting with a state leader at the UN, will face a daunting agenda in his second term serving multiple bosses (the member states) with a tight budget.

---

[11] Boutros-Ghali, Boutros. *An Agenda for Peace: Preventive Diplomacy, Peacemaking and Peace-keeping.* United Nations, 1992. Woodhouse, Tom, Robert Bruce, and Malcolm Dando, eds. *Peacekeeping and Peacemaking: Towards Effective Intervention in Post–Cold War Conflicts.* St. Martin's, 1998.

The Secretariat of the UN is its executive branch, headed by the secretary-general. It is a bureaucracy for administering UN policy and programs, just as the State Department is a bureaucracy for U.S. foreign policy. In security matters, the secretary-general personally works with the Security Council; development programs in poor countries are coordinated by a second-in-command, the director-general for Development and International Economic Co-operation. The Secretariat is divided into functional areas, with undersecretaries-general and assistant secretaries-general.

The UN staff in these areas includes administrative personnel as well as technical experts and economic advisors working on various programs and projects. The staff numbers about 15,000 people, and the total number of employees in the UN system (including the World Bank and IMF) is 80,000. UN-related agency offices are concentrated in Geneva, Switzerland. Geneva is a frequent site of international negotiations and is seen by some as more neutral than New York.

One purpose of the UN Secretariat is to develop an international civil service of diplomats and bureaucrats whose loyalties lie at the global level, not with their states of origin. The UN Charter sets the secretary-general and staff apart from the authority of national governments and calls on member states to respect the staff's "exclusively international character." The UN has been fairly successful in this regard; the secretary-general is most often seen as an independent diplomat thinking about the whole world's interests, not as a pawn of any state. But in the early 1990s the UN bureaucracy came under increasing criticism for both inefficiency and corruption. These criticisms, coming especially from the United States, which saw itself as bearing an unfair share of the costs, led to a reform program. By the late 1990s, UN staff was reduced by one-quarter compared to a decade earlier, and budgets were scaled back year by year. By winter 2002, a strapped UN could not keep its New York headquarters building heated. Since then, the situation has improved, but money remains extremely tight.

The secretary-general is more than a bureaucratic manager. He (it has not yet been a she) is a visible public figure whose personal attention to a regional conflict can move it toward resolution. The Charter allows the secretary-general to use the UN's "good offices" to serve as a neutral mediator in international conflicts—to bring hostile parties together in negotiations.

The secretary-general also works to bring together the great power consensus on which Security Council action depends. The secretary-general has the power under the Charter to bring to the Security Council any matter that might threaten international peace and security, and so to play a major role in setting the UN's agenda in international security affairs. Still, the secretary-general experiences tensions with the Security Council. When the secretary-general asks for authority for a peacekeeping mission for six months, the Security Council is likely to say "three months." If the secretary-general asks for $10 million, he might get $5 million. Thus the secretary-general remains, like the entire UN system, constrained by state sovereignty.

The General Assembly

The General Assembly is made up of all 193 member states of the UN, each with one vote.[12] It usually meets every year, from late September through January, in *plenary session*. State leaders or foreign ministers, including the U.S. president, generally come through one by one to address this assemblage. The Assembly sessions, like most UN deliberations,

---

[12] Peterson, M. J. *The United Nations General Assembly*. Routledge, 2005.

are simultaneously translated into dozens of languages so that delegates from around the world can carry on a single conversation. This global town hall is a unique institution and provides a powerful medium for states to put forward their ideas and arguments. Presiding over it is a president elected by the Assembly—a post without much power.

The Assembly convenes for *special sessions* every few years on general topics such as economic cooperation. The UN special session on disarmament in June 1982 provided the occasion for one of the largest political rallies in U.S. history—a peace demonstration of a million people in New York. The Assembly has met in *emergency session* in the past to deal with an immediate threat to international peace and security, but this has happened only nine times and has now become uncommon.

ASSEMBLY OF EQUALS

The universal membership of the United Nations is one of its strengths. All member states have a voice and a vote in the General Assembly, where state leaders rotate through each autumn. Here, the president of Palestine, which hopes to join the UN as soon as the Security Council allows it, addresses the Assembly in 2011.

The General Assembly has the power to accredit national delegations as members of the UN (through its Credentials Committee). For instance, in 1971 the delegation of the People's Republic of China was given China's seat in the UN (including on the Security Council) in place of the nationalists in Taiwan. For decades, neither North Korea nor South Korea became members of the UN (because both claimed the whole of Korea), but they finally took seats as separate delegations in 1991. Some political entities that fall short of state status send *permanent observer missions* to the UN. These missions participate without a vote in the General Assembly. They include the Vatican (Holy See) and the Palestinian Authority.

The General Assembly's main power lies in its control of finances for UN programs and operations, including peacekeeping. It also can pass resolutions on various matters, but these are purely advisory and at times have served largely to vent frustrations of the majority of poor countries. The Assembly also elects members of certain UN agencies and programs. Finally, the Assembly coordinates UN programs and agencies through its own system of committees, commissions, councils, and so forth.

The Assembly coordinates UN programs and agencies through the Economic and Social Council (ECOSOC), which has 54 member states elected by the General Assembly for three-year terms. ECOSOC manages the overlapping work of a large number of programs and agencies. Its *regional commissions* look at how UN programs work together in a particular region; its *functional commissions* deal with global topics such as population growth, narcotics trafficking, human rights, and the status of women; and its *expert bodies* work on technical subjects that cut across various UN programs in areas such as crime prevention and public finances. Outside ECOSOC, the General Assembly operates many other *specialized committees*. Standing committees ease the work of the Assembly in issue areas such as decolonization, legal matters, and disarmament.

Many of the activities associated with the UN do not take place under tight control of either the General Assembly or the Security Council. They occur in functional agencies and programs that have various amounts of autonomy from UN control.

UN Programs

Through the Economic and Social Council, the General Assembly oversees more than a dozen major programs to advance economic development and social stability in poor states of the global South. Through its programs, the UN helps manage global North-South relations: it organizes a flow of resources and skills from the richer parts of the world to support development in the poorer parts.

The programs are funded partly by General Assembly allocations and partly by contributions that the programs raise directly from member states, businesses, or private charitable contributors. The degree of General Assembly funding, and of operational autonomy from the Assembly, varies from one program to another. Each UN program has a staff, a headquarters, and various operations in the field, where it works with host governments in member states.

Several of these programs are of growing importance. The *UN Environment Program* *(UNEP)* became more prominent in the 1990s as the economic development of the global South and the growing economies of the industrialized world took a toll on the world environment (see Chapter 11). The UNEP grapples with global environmental strategies. It provides technical assistance to member states, monitors environmental conditions globally, develops standards, and recommends alternative energy sources.

UNICEF is the UN Children's Fund, which gives technical and financial assistance to poor countries for programs benefiting children. Unfortunately, the needs of children in many countries are still urgent, and UNICEF is kept busy. Financed by voluntary contributions, UNICEF has for decades organized U.S. children in an annual Halloween fund drive on behalf of their counterparts in poorer countries.

The *Office of the UN High Commissioner for Refugees (UNHCR)* is also busy. UNHCR coordinates efforts to protect, assist, and eventually repatriate the many refugees who flee across international borders each year to escape war and political violence. The longer-standing problem of Palestinian refugees is handled by a different program, the *UN Relief Works Agency (UNRWA)*.

The *UN Development Program (UNDP)*, funded by voluntary contributions, coordinates all UN efforts related to development in poor countries. With about 5,000 projects operating simultaneously around the world, UNDP is the world's largest international agency for technical development assistance. The UN also runs several development-related agencies for training and for promoting women's role in development.

Many poor countries depend on export revenues to finance economic development, making them vulnerable to fluctuations in commodity prices and other international trade problems. The **UN Conference on Trade and Development (UNCTAD)** negotiates international trade agreements to stabilize commodity prices and promote development. Because countries of the global South do not have much power in the international economy, however, UNCTAD has little leverage to promote their interests in trade (see p. 482). The World Trade Organization has thus become the main organization dealing with trade issues (see pp. 294–298).

In 2006, the UN created a new Human Rights Council, replacing a Human Rights Commission notorious for including human rights abusers as member states. The new council has expanded powers and more selective membership.

Other UN programs manage problems such as disaster relief, food aid, housing, and population issues. Throughout the poorer countries, the UN maintains an active presence in economic and social affairs.

Autonomous Agencies

In addition to its own programs, the UN General Assembly maintains formal ties with about 20 autonomous international agencies not under its control. Most are specialized technical organizations through which states pool their efforts to address problems such as health care and labor conditions.

The only such agency in international security affairs is the *International Atomic Energy Agency (IAEA)*, headquartered in Vienna, Austria. It was established under the UN but is formally autonomous. Although the IAEA has an economic role in helping develop civilian nuclear power plants, it mainly works to prevent nuclear proliferation (see pp. 217–219). The IAEA was responsible for inspections in Iraq in 2002–2003, which found no evidence of a secret nuclear weapons program. It is involved in monitoring Iran's nuclear program to the extent Iran allows. The IAEA won the 2005 Nobel Peace Prize.

In the area of health care, the Geneva-based **World Health Organization (WHO)** provides technical assistance to improve conditions and conduct major immunization campaigns in poor countries. In the 1960s and 1970s, WHO led one of the great public health victories of all time—the worldwide eradication of smallpox. Today WHO is a leading player in the worldwide fight to control AIDS (see pp. 414–417).

In agriculture, the *Food and Agriculture Organization (FAO)* is the lead agency. In labor standards, it is the *International Labor Organization (ILO)*. UNESCO—the *UN Educational, Scientific, and Cultural Organization*—facilitates international communication and scientific collaboration. The *UN Industrial Development Organization (UNIDO)* promotes industrialization in the global South.

The longest-established IOs, with some of the most successful records, are specialized agencies dealing with technical aspects of international coordination such as aviation and postal exchange. For instance, the *International Telecommunications Union (ITU)* allocates radio frequencies. The *Universal Postal Union (UPU)* sets standards for international mail. The *International Civil Aviation Organization (ICAO)* sets binding standards for international air traffic. The *International Maritime Organization (IMO)* facilitates international cooperation on shipping at sea. The *World Intellectual Property Organization (WIPO)* seeks world compliance with copyrights and patents and promotes development and technology transfer within a legal framework that protects such intellectual property (see pp. 305–306). Finally, the *World Meteorological Organization (WMO)* oversees a world weather watch and promotes the exchange of weather information.

HELPING WHERE NEEDED

An array of UN programs, operating under the General Assembly, aim to help countries in the global South to overcome social and economic problems. These programs play a crucial role in the international assistance after disasters and wars. This girl displaced by ethnic violence in Kyrgyzstan in 2010 receives help from UNICEF.

The major coordinating agencies of the world economy (discussed in Chapters 8, 9, and 13) are also UN-affiliated agencies. The World Bank and the International Monetary Fund (IMF) give loans, grants, and technical assistance for economic development (and the IMF manages international balance-of-payments accounting). The World Trade Organization (WTO) sets rules for international trade.

Overall, the density of connections across national borders, both in the UN system and through other IOs, is increasing year by year. In a less tangible way, people are also becoming connected across international borders through the meshing of ideas, including norms and rules. And gradually the rules are becoming international laws.

International Law

◉—⌐ **Watch**
the **Video**
"**Global Governance
and the ICC**"
on **mypoliscilab.com**

International law, unlike national laws, derives not from actions of a legislative branch or other central authority, but from tradition and agreements signed by states. It also differs in the difficulty of enforcement, which depends not on the power and authority of central government but on reciprocity, collective action, and international norms.[13]

Sources of International Law

Laws within states come from central authorities—legislatures or dictators. Because states are sovereign and recognize no central authority, international law rests on a different basis. The declarations of the UN General Assembly are not laws, and most do not bind the members. The Security Council can compel certain actions by states, but these are commands rather than laws: they are specific to a situation. No body of international law has been passed by a national legislative body. Four sources of international law are recognized: treaties, custom, general principles of law (such as equity), and legal scholarship (including past judicial decisions).

Treaties and other written conventions signed by states are the most important source.[14] International treaties now fill more than a thousand thick volumes, with tens of thousands of individual agreements. A principle in international law states that treaties, once signed and ratified, must be observed (*pacta sunt servanda*). States violate the terms of treaties they have signed only if the matter is very important or the penalties for such a violation seem very small. In the United States, treaties duly ratified by the Senate are considered the highest law of the land, equal with acts passed by Congress.

Treaties and other international obligations such as debts are binding on successor governments whether the new government takes power through an election, a coup, or a revolution. For example, after the revolutions in Eastern Europe around 1990, newly democratic governments were held responsible for debts incurred by their communist predecessors. Even when the Soviet Union broke up, Russia as the successor state had to guarantee that Soviet debts would be paid and Soviet treaties honored. Although revolution does not free a state from its obligations, some treaties have built-in escape clauses that

---

[13] Shaw, Malcolm N. *International Law*. 5th ed. Cambridge, 2003. Joyner, Christopher C. *International Law in the 21st Century: Rules for Global Governance*. Rowman, 2005. Franck, Thomas M. *Fairness in International Law and Institutions*. Oxford, 1995. Ku, Charlotte, and Paul F. Diehl. *International Law: Classic and Contemporary Readings*. 3rd ed. Rienner, 2008. Goldsmith, Jack L., and Eric A. Posner. *The Limits of International Law*. Oxford, 2006.

[14] Gardiner, Richard. *Treaty Interpretation*. Oxford, 2008. Aust, Anthony. *Modern Treaty Law and Practice*. 2nd ed. Cambridge, 2007.

let states legally withdraw from them, after giving due notice, without violating international law. For example, the United States in 2001 invoked the six-month opt-out provision of the ABM treaty.

Because of the universal commitment by all states to respect certain basic principles of international law, the UN Charter is one of the world's most important treaties. Its implications are broad and far-reaching, in contrast to more specific treaties such as a fishery management agreement. However, the specialized agreements are usually easier to interpret and more enforceable than broad treaties such as the Charter. Another key treaty in international law is the 1949 Geneva Conventions (expanding an 1864 convention) defining the laws of war regarding the protection of civilians and prisoners, among related issues.[15]

Custom is the second major source of international law. If states behave toward each other in a certain way for long enough, their behavior may become generally accepted practice with the status of law. Western international law (though not Islamic law) tends to be *positivist* in this regard—it draws on actual customs, the practical realities of self-interest, and the need for consent rather than on an abstract concept of divine or natural law.

General principles of law also serve as a source of international law. Actions such as theft and assault recognized in most national legal systems as crimes tend to have the same meaning in an international context. Iraq's invasion of Kuwait was illegal under treaties signed by Iraq (including the UN Charter and that of the Arab League) and under the custom Iraq and Kuwait had established of living in peace as sovereign states. Beyond treaty or custom, the invasion violated international law because of the general principle that one state may not overrun its neighbor's territory and annex it by force. (Of course, a state may still think it can get away with such a violation of international law.)

The fourth source of international law, recognized by the World Court as subsidiary to the others, is *legal scholarship*—the written arguments of judges and lawyers around the world on the issues in question. Only the writings of the most highly qualified and respected legal figures can be taken into account, and then only to resolve points not resolved by the first three sources of international law.

Often international law lags behind changes in norms; law is quite tradition-bound. Certain activities such as espionage are technically illegal but are so widely condoned that they cannot be said to violate international norms. Other activities are still legal but have come to be frowned upon and seen as abnormal. For example, China's shooting of student demonstrators in 1989 violated international norms but not international law.

Enforcement of International Law

Although these sources of international law distinguish it from national law, an even greater difference exists as to the *enforcement* of the two types of law. International law is much more difficult to enforce. There is no world police force. Enforcement of international law depends on the power of states themselves, individually or collectively, to punish transgressors.

Enforcement of international law depends heavily on the reciprocity principle (see pp. 5–6). States follow international law most of the time because they want other states to do so. The reason neither side in World War II used chemical weapons was not that anyone could enforce the treaty banning use of such weapons. It was that the other side would probably respond by using chemical weapons, too, and the costs would be high to both

---

[15] Kinsella, Helen M. *The Image Before the Weapon: A Critical History of the Distinction Between Combatant and Civilian.* Cornell, 2011.

sides. International law recognizes in certain circumstances the legitimacy of *reprisals*: actions that would have been illegal under international law may sometimes be legal if taken in response to the illegal actions of another state.

A state that breaks international law may face a collective response by a group of states, such as the imposition of *sanctions*—agreements among other states to stop trading with the violator, or to stop some particular commodity trade (most often military goods) as punishment for its violation. Over time, a sanctioned state can become a pariah in the community of nations, cut off from normal relations with others. This is very costly in today's world, in which economic well-being everywhere depends on trade and economic exchange in world markets. Libya suffered for decades from its isolated status in the international community, and decided in 2003 to make a clean break and regain normal status. Libya admitted responsibility for past terrorism, began to compensate victims, and agreed to disclose and dismantle its nuclear, chemical, and biological weapons programs.

Even the world's superpower constrains its behavior, at least some of the time, to adhere to international law. For example, in late 2002 a North Korean freighter was caught en route to Yemen with a hidden load of 15 Scud missiles. The United States, fighting the war on terrorism, had an evident national interest in preventing such proliferation, and had the power to prevent it. But when U.S. government lawyers determined that the shipment did not violate international law, the United States backed off and let the delivery continue.

International law enforcement through reciprocity and collective response has one great weakness—it depends entirely on national power. Reciprocity works only if the aggrieved state has the power to inflict costs on the violator. Collective response works only if the collective cares enough about an issue to respond. Thus, it is relatively easy to cheat on small issues (or to get away with major violations if one has enough power).

If international law extends only as far as power reaches, what good is it? The answer lies in the uncertainties of power (see Chapter 2). Without common expectations regarding the rules of the game and adherence to those rules most of the time by most actors, power alone would create great instability in the anarchic international system. International law, even without perfect enforcement, creates expectations about what constitutes legal behavior by states. Because violations or divergences from those expectations stand out, it is easier to identify and punish states that deviate from accepted rules. When states agree to the rules by signing treaties (such as the UN Charter), violations become more visible and clearly illegitimate. In most cases, although power continues to reside in states, international law establishes workable rules for those states to follow. The resulting stability is so beneficial that usually the costs of breaking the rules outweigh the short-term benefits that could be gained from such violations.

The World Court

As international law has developed, a general world legal framework in which states can pursue grievances against each other has begun to take shape. The rudiments of such a system now exist in the **World Court** (formally called the **International Court of Justice**), although its jurisdiction is limited and its caseload light.[16] The World Court is a branch of the UN.

Only states, not individuals or businesses, can sue or be sued in the World Court. When a state has a grievance against another, it can take the case to the World Court for an impartial hearing. The Security Council or General Assembly may also request advisory

---

[16] Meyer, Howard N. *The World Court in Action: Judging among Nations*. Rowman & Littlefield, 2002.

Court opinions on matters of international law. For example, the 2010 Court ruling declaring Kosovo's declaration of independence legal was an advisory opinion requested by the General Assembly.

The World Court is a panel of 15 judges elected for nine-year terms (5 judges every three years) by a majority of both the Security Council and General Assembly. The Court meets in The Hague, the Netherlands. It is customary for permanent members of the Security Council to have one of their nationals as a judge at all times. Ad hoc judges may be added to the 15 if a party to a case does not already have one of its nationals as a judge.

The great weakness of the World Court is that states have not agreed in a comprehensive way to subject themselves to its jurisdiction or obey its decisions. Almost all states have signed the treaty creating the Court, but only about a third have signed the *optional clause* in the treaty agreeing to give the Court jurisdiction in certain cases—and even many of those signatories have added their own stipulations reserving their rights and limiting the degree to which the Court can infringe on national sovereignty. The United States withdrew from the optional clause when it was sued by Nicaragua in 1986 (over the CIA's mining of Nicaraguan harbors).[17] Similarly, Iran refused to acknowledge the jurisdiction of the Court when sued by the United States in 1979 over its seizure of the U.S. embassy in Iran. In such a case, the Court may hear the case anyway and usually rules in favor of the participating side—but has no means to enforce the ruling. Justice can also move slowly. In 2007, the Court issued a ruling against Bosnia's case accusing Serbia of genocide, after 14 years of preliminary maneuvering.

In one of its most notable successes, the World Court in 1992 settled a complex border dispute between El Salvador and Honduras dating from 1861. In 2002, the World Court settled a long-standing and sometimes violent dispute over an oil-rich peninsula on the Cameroon-Nigeria border. It gave ownership to Cameroon, and Nigeria (which is more powerful) pulled troops out in 2006.

A main use of the World Court now is to arbitrate issues of secondary importance between countries with friendly relations overall. The United States has settled commercial disputes with Canada and with Italy through the Court. Because security interests are not at stake, and because the overall friendly relations are more important than the particular issue, states have been willing to submit to the Court's jurisdiction. In 2004, the court

ALL RISE

The World Court hears international disputes but with little power to enforce judgments. Here, in 2004, the judges rule in favor of Mexico's complaint that the U.S. death penalty against Mexican citizens violated a 1963 treaty.

---

[17] Forsythe, David P. *The Politics of International Law: U.S. Foreign Policy Reconsidered.* Rienner, 1990.

FIGURE 7.4 World Court Case of Argentina v. Uruguay

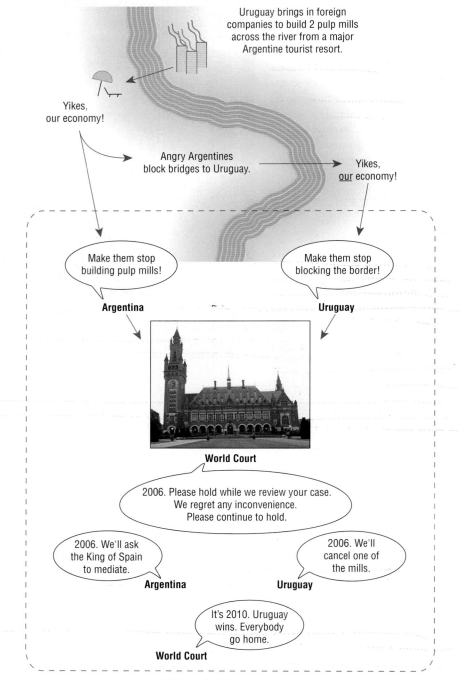

ordered the United States to review death sentences of Mexican nationals to see if their lack of access to Mexican officials had harmed their legal case. Under the 1963 Vienna Convention on Consular Relations, citizens arrested in a foreign country must be advised of their right to meet with their home country's representatives. The United States had often failed to do so despite demanding this right for Americans abroad. The World Court suggested that U.S. courts add relevant language to the Miranda warning for cases when police arrest foreign nationals. Figure 7.4 illustrates one of the Court's recent cases, a dispute between Argentina and Uruguay.

Because of the difficulty of winning enforceable agreements on major conflicts through the World Court, states have used the Court infrequently over the years—a dozen or fewer cases per year (about 140 judgments and advisory opinions since 1947).

International Cases in National Courts

Most legal cases concerning international matters—whether brought by governments or by private individuals or companies—remain entirely within the legal systems of one or more states. National courts hear cases brought under national laws and can enforce judgments by collecting damages (in civil suits) or imposing punishments (in criminal ones).

A party with a dispute that crosses national boundaries gains several advantages by pursuing the matter through the national courts of one or more of the relevant states, rather than through international channels. First, judgments are enforceable. The party that wins a lawsuit in a national court can collect from the other party's assets within the state. Second, individuals and companies can pursue legal complaints through national courts (as can subnational governmental bodies), whereas in most areas of international law, states must themselves bring suits on behalf of their citizens. (In truth, even national governments pursue most of their legal actions against each other through national courts.)

Third, there is often a choice of more than one state within which a case could legally be heard; one can pick the legal system most favorable to one's case. Each state's court system must decide whether it has *jurisdiction* in a case (the right to hear it), and courts tend to extend their own authority with a broad interpretation. Traditionally, a national court may hear cases concerning any activity on its national territory, any actions of its own citizens anywhere in the world, and actions taken toward its citizens elsewhere in the world. Noncitizens can use the national courts to enforce damages against citizens, because the national court has authority to impose fines and, if necessary, to seize bank accounts and property.

The United States is a favorite jurisdiction within which to bring cases for two reasons. First, U.S. juries have a reputation for awarding bigger settlements in lawsuits than juries elsewhere in the world (if only because the United States is a rich country). Second, because many people and governments do business in the United States, it is often possible to collect damages awarded by a U.S. court. For these reasons, U.S. courts in recent years have ruled on human rights cases brought by Chinese dissidents over the 1989 Tiananmen massacre, Cuban exiles against the Cuban government, and a Paraguayan doctor suing a Paraguayan police official for torturing the doctor's son. In 2003, U.S. courts ordered large payments by Iraq and Iran to U.S. victims of terrorism and torture. The Alien Tort Claims Act of 1789 gives federal courts jurisdiction over civil lawsuits against foreigners for "violation of the law of nations." Human rights activists have used the law against repressive governments in recent years, as when they sued U.S. oil companies ExxonMobil and Unocal for aiding abusive regimes in Indonesia and Burma, respectively. The rapid extension of U.S. legal jurisdiction may bring a reciprocal response from European (and other) states, which may seek on occasion to extend their national laws to U.S. shores.[18]

Belgium's national courts are a favorite venue for international human rights cases because a 1993 law gives them jurisdiction over any violation of the Geneva Conventions. In 2001, four people accused of war crimes in Rwanda in 1994 were sent to prison by a Belgian jury. (Rwanda is a former Belgian colony, and ten Belgian soldiers had been killed at the outset of the genocide there.) In 2005, Belgium indicted a former leader of Chad accused of 40,000 political murders in Chad in the 1980s, and Senegal (where he lived) asked the African Union to rule on whether it should extradite him. The African Union encouraged Senegal to try him domestically rather than send him to Belgium.

There are important limits to the use of national courts to resolve international disputes, however. Most important is that the authority of national courts stops at the state's borders, where sovereignty ends. A court in Zambia cannot compel a resident of Thailand to come and testify; it cannot authorize the seizure of a British bank account to pay damages; it cannot arrest a criminal suspect (Zambian or foreigner) except on Zambian soil. To take such actions beyond national borders, states must persuade other states to cooperate.

To bring a person outside a state's territory to trial, the state's government must ask a second government to arrest the person on the second state's territory and hand him or her over for trial. Called *extradition,* this is a matter of international law because it is a legal treaty arrangement between states. Hundreds of such treaties exist, many dating back hundreds of years. If no such treaty exists, the individual generally remains immune from a state's courts by staying off its territory. Some U.S. allies do not usually extradite to the United States suspects who would face the death penalty. The war on terrorism since 2001, however, has expanded international legal and law enforcement cooperation.

In one high-profile debate about extradition, the former Chilean military dictator Augusto Pinochet was arrested in England in 1999 on a Spanish warrant, based on crimes committed against Spanish citizens in Chile during Pinochet's rule. His supporters claimed that he should have immunity for acts taken as head of state, but because he was not an accredited diplomat in England (where he had gone for medical treatment) and no longer head of state, the British courts held him on Spain's request to extradite him for trial there. Once on British soil without current diplomatic immunity, Pinochet was subject to British law, including its extradition treaties. However, the British government eventually let him return to Chile, citing his medical condition, and a Chilean court suspended his case on health grounds. He died in 2006 without standing trial.

Gray areas exist in the jurisdiction of national courts over foreigners. If a government can lure a suspect onto the high seas, it can nab the person without violating another country's territoriality. More troublesome are cases in which a government obtains a foreign citizen from a foreign country for trial without going through extradition procedures. In a famous case in the 1980s, a Mexican doctor was wanted by U.S. authorities for allegedly participating in the torture and murder of a U.S. drug agent in Mexico. The U.S.

---

[18] Liptak, Adam. U.S. Courts' Role in Foreign Feuds Comes under Fire. *The New York Times,* August 3, 2003: A1.

government paid a group of bounty hunters to kidnap the doctor in Mexico, carry him forcibly across the border, and deliver him to the custody of U.S. courts. The U.S. Supreme Court gave the U.S. courts jurisdiction in the case—showing the tendency to extend state sovereignty wherever possible—although international lawyers and Mexican officials objected strongly. The U.S. government had to reassure the Mexican government that it would not kidnap Mexican citizens for trial in the United States in the future. The doctor returned home after the case was thrown out for lack of evidence. In late 2004, Colombia arranged the abduction of a leading Colombian rebel living in Venezuela, provoking Venezuelan protests about the violation of sovereignty.

The principle of territoriality also governs **immigration law**. When people cross a border into a new country, the decision about whether they can remain there, and under what conditions, is up to the new state. The state of origin cannot compel their return. National laws establish conditions for foreigners to travel and visit on a state's territory, to work there, and sometimes to become citizens (*naturalization*). Many other legal issues are raised by people traveling or living outside their own country—passports and visas, babies born in foreign countries, marriages to foreign nationals, bank accounts, businesses, taxes, and so forth. Practices vary from country to country, but the general principle is that national laws prevail on the territory of a state.

Despite the continued importance of national court systems in international legal affairs and the lack of enforcement powers of the World Court, it would be wrong to conclude that state sovereignty is supreme and international law impotent. Rather, a balance of sovereignty and law exists in international interactions.

Law and Sovereignty

The remainder of this chapter discusses particular areas of international law, from the most firmly rooted and widely respected to newer and less-established areas. In each area, the influence of law and norms runs counter to the unimpeded exercise of state sovereignty. This struggle becomes more intense as one moves from long-standing traditions of diplomatic law to recent norms governing human rights.

⊙ **Watch the Video "The Uncertain Status of Enemy Combatants"** on **mypoliscilab.com**

Laws of Diplomacy

The bedrock of international law is respect for the rights of diplomats. The standards of behavior in this area are spelled out in detail, applied universally, and taken very seriously. The ability to conduct diplomacy is necessary for all other kinds of relations among states, except perhaps all-out war. Since the rise of the international system five centuries ago, it has been considered unjustifiable to harm an emissary sent from another state as a means of influencing the other state. Such a norm has not always existed; it is natural in some ways to kill the messenger who brings an unpleasant message, or to use another state's official as a hostage or bargaining chip. But today this kind of behavior is universally condemned, though it still happens from time to time.

The status of embassies and of an ambassador as an official state representative is explicitly defined in the process of diplomatic recognition. Diplomats are *accredited* to each other's governments (they present "credentials"), and thereafter the individuals so defined enjoy certain rights and protections as foreign diplomats in the host country. Diplomats have the right to occupy an *embassy* in a host country, within which the host country's laws may not be enforced without the consent of the embassy's country. For this reason, embassies occasionally shelter dissidents who take refuge there from their own governments.

SAFE HAVEN

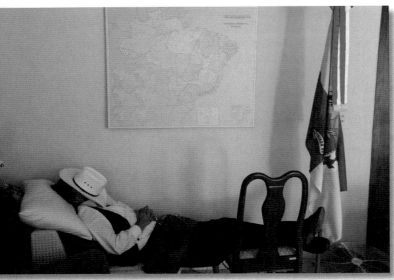

International law prohibits attacks on diplomats and embassies. This fundamental principle, like others in international law, can ultimately be enforced only by applying the power of other states (through such leverage as imposing economic sanctions, freezing relations, or threatening military force). Here, the president of Honduras, after sneaking back into the country months after being ousted in a coup, takes a siesta in the Brazilian embassy in Honduras's capital, seemingly untouchable by the government outside the embassy walls (2009).

A flagrant violation of the sanctity of embassies occurred in Iran after Islamic revolutionaries took power in 1979. Iranian students seized and occupied the U.S. embassy compound, holding the U.S. diplomats hostage for more than a year. The Iranian government did not directly commit this act but did condone it and did refuse to force the students out of the embassy. (Host countries are expected, if necessary, to use force against their own citizens to protect a foreign embassy.)

Diplomats enjoy **diplomatic immunity** even when they leave the embassy grounds. The right to travel varies from one country to another; diplomats may be restricted to one city or free to roam about the countryside. Alone among all foreign nationals, diplomats are beyond enforcement of the host country's national courts. If they commit crimes, from jaywalking to murder, they may be shielded from arrest. All the host country can do is take away a diplomat's accreditation and expel the person from the host country. However, strong countries sometimes pressure weaker ones to lift immunity so that a diplomat may face trial for a crime. This happened twice in 1997, for example, when the United States and France were allowed to prosecute diplomats from Georgia and Zaire, respectively, for reckless driving that killed children.

U.S. commitments as host country to the UN include extending diplomatic immunity to the diplomats accredited to the UN. Given this immunity, delegates simply tear up thousands of parking tickets each year, for example. It is estimated that the city of New York is owed $18 million in unpaid tickets. The parking ticket issue has become a sensitive political issue, as the State Department now reserves the right to revoke driver's licenses, license plates, and even reduce foreign aid based on outstanding parking tickets. Similarly, in London three cars driven by Sudanese diplomats received over 800 tickets tallying over $100,000 in fines.

Because of diplomatic immunity, espionage activities are commonly conducted through the diplomatic corps, out of an embassy. Spies are often posted to low-level positions in embassies, such as cultural attaché, press liaison, or military attaché. If the host country catches them spying, it cannot prosecute them, so it merely expels them. Diplomatic norms (though not law) call for politeness when expelling spies; the standard reason given is "for activities not consistent with his or her diplomatic status." If a spy operates under cover of being a businessperson or tourist, then no immunity applies; the person can be arrested and prosecuted under the host country's laws. Such was the case in 2010, when the U.S. government arrested ten Russian spies who were leading lives as ordinary citizens in America. Before the prosecution of the accused spies could proceed in New York courts, however, the United States and Russia agreed to an exchange of accused spies.

A *diplomatic pouch* is a package sent between an embassy and its home country. As the name implies, it started out historically as a small and occasional shipment, but today a large and steady volume of such shipments travel all over the world. Diplomatic pouches, too, enjoy the status of home country territoriality: they cannot be opened, searched, or confiscated by a host country. Although we do not know how much mischief goes on in diplomatic pouches (because they are secret), it is safe to assume that illicit goods such as guns and drugs regularly find their way across borders in diplomatic pouches.

To *break diplomatic relations* means to withdraw one's diplomats from a state and expel that state's diplomats from one's own state. This tactic is used to show displeasure with another government; it is a refusal to do business as usual. When a revolutionary government comes into power, some countries may withdraw recognition. Most activity regarding diplomatic recognition today occurs when small states recognize Taiwan diplomatically, are subsequently pressured by China, and occasionally withdraw recognition.

When two countries lack diplomatic relations, they often do business through a third country willing to represent a country's interests formally through its own embassy. This is called an *interests section* in the third country's embassy. Thus, the practical needs of diplomacy can overcome a formal lack of relations between states. For instance, U.S. interests are represented by the Swiss embassy in Cuba, and Cuban interests are represented by the Swiss embassy in the United States. In practice, these interests sections are located in the former U.S. and Cuban embassies and staffed with U.S. and Cuban diplomats.

States register lower levels of displeasure by *recalling their ambassadors* home for some period of time; diplomatic norms call for a trip home "for consultations" even when everyone knows the purpose is to signal annoyance. Milder still is the expression of displeasure by *a formal complaint*. Usually the complaining government does so in its own capital city, to the other's ambassador.

The law of diplomacy is repeatedly violated in one context—terrorism (see pp. 204–209). Because states care so much about the sanctity of diplomats, the diplomats make a tempting target for terrorists, and because terrorist groups do not enjoy the benefits of diplomatic law (as states do), they are willing to break diplomatic norms and laws. An attack on diplomats or embassies is an attack on the territory of the state itself—yet can be carried out far from the state's home territory. Many diplomats have been killed in recent decades. In 1998, al Qaeda terrorists bombed the U.S. embassies in Kenya and Tanzania, killing more than 200 people. In late 2004, al Qaeda forces stormed a U.S. consulate in Saudi Arabia, killing several guards.

Just War Doctrine

After the law of diplomacy, international law regarding war is one of the most developed areas of international law. Laws concerning war are divided into two areas—laws *of* war (when war is permissible) and laws *in* war (how wars are fought).

To begin with the laws of war, international law distinguishes **just wars** (which are legal) from wars of aggression (which are illegal). (We discuss laws in war later in the context of human rights.) This area of law grows out of centuries-old religious writings about just wars (which once could be enforced by threats to excommunicate individuals from the church). Today, the legality of war is defined by the UN Charter, which outlaws aggression. Above and beyond its legal standing, just war doctrine has become a strong international norm, not one that all states follow but an important part of the modern intellectual tradition governing matters of war and peace that evolved in Europe.[19]

---

[19] Walzer, Michael. *Arguing about War.* Yale, 2004. Walzer, Michael. *Just and Unjust Wars: A Moral Argument with Historical Illustrations.* 4th ed. Basic, 2006. Hensel, Howard M. *The Legitimate Use of Military Force: The Just War Tradition and the Customary Law of Armed Conflict.* Ashgate, 2008.

The idea of aggression, around which the doctrine of just war evolved, is based on a violation of the sovereignty and territorial integrity of states. *Aggression* refers to a state's use of force, or an imminent threat to do so, against another state's territory or sovereignty—unless the use of force is in response to aggression. Tanks swarming across the border constitute aggression, but so do tanks massing at the border if their state has threatened to invade. The lines are somewhat fuzzy. But for a threat to constitute aggression (and justify the use of force in response), it must be a clear threat of using force, not just a hostile policy or general rivalry.

States have the right to respond to aggression in the only manner thought to be reliable—military force. Just war doctrine is thus not based on nonviolence. Responses can include both *repelling* the attack itself and *punishing* the aggressor. Responses can be made by the victim of aggression or by other states not directly affected—as a way of maintaining the norm of nonaggression in the international system. The collective actions of UN members against Iraq after its invasion of Kuwait are a classic case of such a response.

Response to aggression is the only allowable use of military force according to just war doctrine. The just war approach thus explicitly rules out war as an instrument to change another state's government or policies, or in ethnic and religious conflicts. In fact, the UN Charter makes no provision for "war" but rather for "international police actions" against aggressors. The analogy is with law and order in a national society, enforced by police when necessary. Because only aggression justifies military force, if all states obeyed the law against aggression, there would be no international war.

For a war to be *morally* just, it must be more than a response to aggression; it must be waged for the *purpose* of responding to aggression. The *intent* must be just. A state may not take advantage of another's aggression to wage a war that is essentially aggressive. Although the U.S.-led war effort to oust Iraq from Kuwait in 1991 was certainly a response to aggression, critics found the justness of the war to be compromised by the U.S. interest in obtaining cheap oil from the Middle East—not an allowable reason for waging war.

Just war doctrine has been undermined, even more seriously than have laws of war crimes, by the changing nature of warfare.[20] In civil wars and low-intensity conflicts, the belligerents range from poorly organized militias to national armies, and the battleground is often a patchwork of enclaves and positions with no clear front lines (much less borders). It is thus harder to identify an aggressor in such situations, and harder to balance the relative merits of peace and justice.

Human Rights

One of the newest areas of international law concerns **human rights**—the rights of human beings against certain abuses of their own governments.[21]

---

[20] Johnson, James Turner. *Can Modern War Be Just?* Yale, 1984.
[21] Donnelly, Jack. *Universal Human Rights in Theory and Practice*. 2nd ed. Cornell, 2003. Donnelly, Jack. *International Human Rights*. 3rd ed. Westview, 2006. DeLaet, Debra L. *The Global Struggle for Human Rights: Universal Principles in World Politics*. Wadsworth, 2005. Thomas, Daniel. *The Helsinki Effect: International Norms, Human Rights, and the Demise of Communism*. Princeton, 2001. Risse, Thomas, Stephen C. Ropp, and Kathryn Sikkink, eds. *The Power of Human Rights: International Norms and Domestic Change*. Cambridge, 1999. Cohen, Cynthia Price, ed. *Human Rights of Indigenous Peoples*. Transnational, 1998. Cronin, Bruce. *Institutions for the Common Good: International Protection Regimes in International Society*. Cambridge, 2003.

Individual Rights versus Sovereignty

The very idea of human rights flies in the face of the sovereignty and territorial integrity of states. Sovereignty gives states the right to do as they please in their own territory: nobody can tell them how to treat their own citizens.

Thus, a consensus on what are the most important human rights is difficult to reach.[22] One approach to human rights argues that rights are *universal*. No matter where a person resides, no matter his or her ethnic nationality, and no matter his or her local religious, ethnic, or clan traditions, that person has certain rights that must be respected. The other approach to human rights is often labeled *relativism*. According to this idea, local traditions and histories should be given due respect, even if this means limiting rights that others outside that local context find important. Efforts to promote human rights are routinely criticized by governments with poor human rights records by Western standards (including China and Russia) as "interference in our internal affairs." This charge puts human rights law on shaky ground and reflects a more relativist stance.

The concept of human rights arises from at least three sources.[23] The first is religion. Nearly every major world religion has at its foundation the idea that humans were created in an image of a higher power and that therefore all humans are to be afforded the dignity and respect that are due that higher power. Nowhere is this idea more clearly spelled out than in the American Declaration of Independence, written by Thomas Jefferson, that all people are "endowed by their creator with certain unalienable rights."

Second, political and legal philosophy for centuries has discussed the idea of natural law and natural rights. From Aristotle, to John Locke, to Immanuel Kant, to Jean-Jacques Rousseau, political philosophers have developed the idea that a natural law exists that grants all humans the right to life, liberty, property, and happiness.[24]

Finally, political revolutions in the 18th century, such as the American and French Revolutions, translated the theory of natural law and natural rights into practice. In America, the Declaration of Independence, and in France, the Declaration of the Rights of

SEA OF RED

International norms concerning human rights conflict with state sovereignty, causing friction in relationships such as that of Burma (Myanmar) with the international community. Here, in 2008, Buddhist monks in Burma's capital lead huge demonstrations against the repressive military government, which cracked down harshly within days. Western powers apply economic sanctions against Burma because of its human rights record.

Watch
the **Video**
**"State Sovereignty
and the 'Responsibility
to Protect'"**
on **mypoliscilab.com**

Explore
the **Simulation**
**"Human Rights:
You Are a Refugee"**
on **mypoliscilab.com**

[22] An-Na'im, Abdullahi Ahmed, ed. *Human Rights in Cross-Cultural Perspectives: A Quest for Consensus.* Pennsylvania, 1991.

[23] Lauren, Paul Gordon. *The Evolution of International Human Rights: Visions Seen.* Pennsylvania, 2003.

[24] Hayden, Patrick, ed. *The Philosophy of Human Rights.* Paragon, 2001.

Man and Citizen, created laws that solidified the idea that humans have certain rights that no state or other individuals can take away.

Of course, criticisms of these ideas of human rights exist, on both a theoretical and a practical level. Theoretically, relativists point out that much of the origin and development of human rights ideas (at least two of the three sources discussed) are Western in origin. Non-Western societies have different philosophical traditions and may choose to emphasize group or family rights, for example, over individual ones. At a practical level, many (especially non-Western) critics are quick to point out that even after the 18th-century revolutions in Europe and America, rights were still not universal. Women, children, and usually nonwhites were not assumed to enjoy the same rights as landholding white males, making the very idea of universal rights misleading.

Partially because of this controversy, no globally agreed-upon definitions of the essential human rights exist. Rights are often divided into two broad types: civil-political and economic-social. Civil-political rights are sometimes referred to as "negative rights" and include what are considered traditional Western rights such as free speech, freedom of religion, equal protection under the law, and freedom from arbitrary imprisonment. These are rights generally thought to be best guaranteed by limiting the power of governments over their people. Economic-social rights are referred to as "positive rights" and include rights to good living conditions, food, health care, social security, and education.[25] These rights are often held to be best promoted by the expansion of governments to provide minimal standards to their people.

No state has a perfect record on any type of human rights, and states differ as to which areas they respect or violate. When the United States criticizes China for prohibiting free speech, using prison labor, and torturing political dissidents (civil-political rights), China notes that the United States has 40 million poor people, the highest ratio of prison inmates in the world, and a history of racism and violence (economic-social rights).[26] During the Cold War, the United States and its allies consistently criticized the Soviet Union and China for violations of civil-political rights, yet refused to endorse treaties championing economic-social rights. Likewise, communist states encouraged the development of the latter rights, while ignoring calls for the former. Overall, despite the poor record of the world's states on some points, progress has been made on others. For example, slavery—once considered normal worldwide—has been largely abandoned in the past 150 years.

Historically, a significant global shift in human rights occurred at the end of World War II. Horrified by Nazi Germany's attempt to exterminate the Jewish population and by Japanese abuses of Chinese citizens, many scholars and practitioners began to suggest that there were limits to state sovereignty. States could not claim to be sovereign and above interference if they attempted to massacre their own people. In the aftermath of World War II and the creation of the United Nations, some of the most significant international attempts to codify and enforce human rights began. In the next section, we examine some of these agreements and institutions.

Human Rights Institutions

In 1948, the UN General Assembly adopted what is considered the core international document concerning human rights: the **Universal Declaration of Human Rights (UDHR)**.[27]

---

[25] Forsythe, David. *Human Rights in International Relations*. Cambridge, 2000.
[26] People's Republic of China, State Council. America's "Abominable" Human Rights Conditions. *The Washington Post*, February 16, 1997: C3.
[27] Morsink, Johannes. *The Universal Declaration of Human Rights: Origins, Drafting, and Intent*. Pennsylvania, 1999.

The UDHR does not have the force of international law, but it sets forth (hoped-for) international norms regarding behavior by governments toward their own citizens and foreigners alike. The declaration roots itself in the principle that violations of human rights upset international order (causing outrage, sparking rebellion, etc.) and in the fact that the UN Charter commits states to respect fundamental freedoms. The declaration proclaims that "all human beings are born free and equal" without regard to race, sex, language, religion, political affiliation, or the status of the territory in which they were born. It goes on to promote norms in a wide variety of areas, including banning torture, guaranteeing religious and political freedom, and ensuring the right of economic well-being.

Since the adoption of the UDHR, the UN has opened seven treaties for state signature to further define protections of human rights (see Table 7.3). Unlike the UDHR, these treaties are legally binding contracts signed by states. Of course, international law is only as good as the enforcement mechanisms behind it. Yet these seven treaties are important in outlining the basic protections for individuals expected by the international community.

Two key treaties are the *International Covenant on Civil and Political Rights (CCPR)* and the *International Covenant on Economic, Social, and Cultural Rights (CESCR)*. These two treaties, both of which entered into force in 1976, codify the promises of the UDHR while dividing the list of rights in the UDHR into civil-political and economic-social rights, respectively. These two covenants, along with the UDHR, are often referred to as the International Bill of Human Rights.[28]

The remaining treaties each deal with a particular group that the international community considers vulnerable. The *International Convention on the Elimination of All Forms of Racial Discrimination (CERD)*, enacted in 1969, bans discrimination against individuals based on race, ethnicity, religion, or national origin. The CERD does not

TABLE 7.3 Ratification Status of Seven Core UN Human Rights Treaties, 2011

Treaty	Date in Force	Number of Signatories	Key Non-Members
Convention on the Elimination of All Forms of Racial Discrimination (CERD)	January 4, 1969	174	Bhutan, Burma, Malaysia, North Korea
Covenant on Economic, Social and Cultural Rights (CESCR)	January 3, 1976	160	Cuba, Saudi Arabia, South Africa, U.S.
Covenant on Civil and Political Rights (CCPR)	March 23, 1976	167	Burma, China, Cuba, Saudi Arabia
Convention on the Elimination of Discrimination Against Women (CEDAW)	September 3, 1981	187	Iran, Somalia, Sudan, U.S.
Convention Against Torture (CAT)	June 26, 1987	147	Burma, India, Iraq, Iran, Sudan
Convention on the Rights of the Child (CRC)	September 2, 1990	194	Somalia, U.S.
Convention on the Protection of the Rights of all Migrant Workers (CMW)	July 1, 2003	51	France, Great Britain, China, Russia, U.S.

---

[28] Simmons, Beth. *Mobilizing for Human Rights: International Law in Domestic Politics*. Cambridge, 2009.
Oberleitner, Gerd. *Global Human Rights Institutions*. Polity, 2007.

include language concerning gender discrimination. The Convention on the Elimination of All Forms of Discrimination against Women (CEDAW), however, fills this void by banning discrimination against women. CEDAW entered into force in 1981.

The Convention against Torture (CAT), instituted in 1987, bans dehumanizing, degrading, and inhumane treatment of individuals even in times of war.[29] The Convention on the Rights of the Child (CRC), enacted in 1990, promotes children's health, education, and physical well-being (every country in the world except Somalia and the United States has approved the CRC). Finally, the most recent UN human rights treaty is the International Convention on the Protection of the Rights of All Migrant Workers and Members of Their Families (CMW), which entered into force in 2003. The CMW attempts to protect the political, labor, and social rights of the nearly 100 million migrant workers around the globe.

Equally important as these UN treaties themselves are the *optional protocols* that are attached to several of the treaties. These protocols can be thought of as addendums to the treaties as they contain additional protections not included in the original documents. In general, far fewer states sign these optional protocols since the protections contained in them were too controversial for the original document. In addition, some of the optional protocols contain stronger enforcement mechanisms, such as giving individuals in signatory states the right to go to the UN monitoring bodies without the approval of their governments. States that are not party to the original treaty may sign them, as is the case with the United States, which has not signed the CRC, but has signed its two optional protocols.

Besides the UN-related human rights treaties, several regional IOs have promoted the protection of human rights. Nowhere is this more true than in Europe, where the European Union, the Council of Europe, and the European Court of Human Rights all work to ensure that human rights are respected by all states in the region (see Chapter 10). In Latin America as well, the *Inter-American Court of Human Rights* has had some success in promoting human rights, yet it has also been limited by state refusal to abide by its decisions. Finally, the African Union helps support the African Human Rights Commission, but the commission has been hampered by its lack of monetary and political support from African states.

In the past decade, developed states have begun to use other international organizations to pressure developing states to improve human rights conditions. Free trade agreements (see Chapter 8) frequently contain provisions that condition trade benefits on the respect for human rights, especially workers' rights.[30] Because these treaties provide policies beneficial to the developing states, they create a ready mechanism to punish countries who abuse their citizens. Others argue, however, that limiting economic benefits to countries harms their economic development, which is likely only to make the human rights situation worse.

Today, NGOs play a key role in efforts to win basic political rights in authoritarian countries—including a halt to the torture, execution, and imprisonment of those expressing political or religious beliefs.[31] The leading organization pressing this struggle is **Amnesty International**, an NGO that operates globally to monitor and try to rectify glaring abuses of human rights.[32] Amnesty International has a reputation for impartiality and has criticized abuses in many countries, including the United States. Other groups, such as

[29] Nowak, Manfred, and Elizabeth McArthur. *The United Nations Convention against Torture*. Oxford, 2008.

[30] Hafner-Burton, Emilie. *Forced to Be Good: Why Trade Agreements Boost Human Rights*. Cornell, 2009.

[31] Keck, Margaret, and Kathryn Sikkink. *Activists Beyond Borders: Advocacy Networks in International Politics*. Cornell, 1998. Risse, Ropp, and Sikkink, *The Power of Human Rights* (see footnote 21 in this chapter).

[32] Hopgood, Stephen. *Keepers of the Flame: Understanding Amnesty International*. Cornell, 2006.

Human Rights Watch, work in a similar way but often with a more regional or national focus. NGOs often provide information and advocacy for UN and other regional organizations. They essentially serve as a bridge between the global or regional organizations and efforts to promote human rights "on the ground."[33]

Enforcing norms of human rights is difficult because it involves interfering in a state's internal affairs.[34] Cutting off trade or contact with a government that violates human rights tends to hurt the citizens whose rights are being violated by further isolating them. In the case of Burma, for example, continued sanctions and trade embargoes have done little to challenge the country's military rulers. Yet, such measures keep those suffering from human rights abuses in the global spotlight, drawing more attention to their plight.

The most effective method yet discovered is a combination of *publicity* and *pressure*. Publicity entails digging up information about human rights abuses, as Amnesty International does. Through a process some scholars have dubbed "naming and shaming," supporters of human rights hope that publicity will embarrass the regime and change its behavior.[35] The publicity also serves to alert those traveling to or doing business with offending regimes to the conditions in those countries. Human rights activists hope this negative attention will convince individuals to stop their interactions with the state in question, putting further economic pressure on it.

The pressure of other governments, as well as private individuals and businesses, consists of threats to punish the offender in some way through nonviolent means. But because most governments seek to maintain normal relations with each other most of the time, this kind of intrusive punishment by one government of another's human rights violations is rare—and not reliably successful.

Also rare are humanitarian interventions using military force to overcome armed resistance by local authorities or warlords and bring help to civilian victims of wars and disasters. However, international norms have increasingly shifted against sovereignty and toward protecting endangered civilians. A major summit of world leaders in 2005 enshrined the concept of the **responsibility to protect (R2P),** which holds that governments worldwide must act to save civilians from genocide or crimes against humanity perpetrated or allowed by their own governments.[36] Three important humanitarian interventions in the 1990s were in Kurdish areas of Iraq, in Somalia, and in Kosovo (Serbia). The UN-authorized NATO campaign in Libya in 2011 followed from the R2P concept.

The U.S. State Department has actively pursued human rights since the late 1970s. An annual U.S. government report assesses human rights in states around the world. In states where abuses are severe or becoming worse, U.S. foreign aid has been withheld. (But in other cases, CIA funding has supported the abusers.)[37]

---

[33] Amnesty International. *Amnesty International Report*. London, annual. Clark, Ann Marie. *Diplomacy of Conscience: Amnesty International and Changing Human Rights Norms*. Princeton, 2000.

[34] Poe, Steven, C. Neal Tate, and Linda Camp Keith. Repression of the Human Right to Personal Integrity Revisited: A Global Cross-National Study. *International Studies Quarterly* 43 (2), 1999: 291–313. Hafner-Burton, Emilie M., and Kiyoteru Tsutsui. Human Rights in a Globalizing World: The Paradox of Empty Promises. *American Journal of Sociology* 110, 2005: 1373–1411.

[35] Keck and Sikkink, *Activists Beyond Borders: Advocacy Networks in International Politics* (see footnote 31 in this chapter).

[36] Evans, Gareth. *The Responsibility to Protect: Ending Mass Atrocity Crimes Once and for All*. Brookings, 2008. Weiss, Thomas G. *Military-Civilian Interactions: Humanitarian Crises and the Responsibility to Protect*. 2nd ed. Rowman & Littlefield, 2005. Welsh, Jennifer M., ed. *Humanitarian Intervention and International Relations*. Oxford, 2004.

[37] Liang-Fenton, Debra, ed. *Implementing U.S. Human Rights Policy: Agendas, Policies, and Practices*. U.S. Institute of Peace Press, 2004.

Currently, human rights is one of the two main areas of conflict (along with Taiwan) in China's relationship with the United States. Several practices draw criticism; these include imprisoning political opponents of the government, the use of prison labor, and a criminal justice system prone to abuses. According to Amnesty International, China executes more people than the rest of the world combined—thousands each year—sometimes within days of the crime and sometimes for relatively minor crimes.[38]

War Crimes

Large-scale abuses of human rights often occur during war. Serious violations of this kind are considered **war crimes**.[39] In wartime, international law is especially difficult to enforce, but extensive norms of legal conduct in war as well as international treaties are widely followed. After a war, losers can be punished for violations of the laws of war, as Germans were in the Nuremberg trials after World War II. Since the Nazi murders of civilians did not violate German law, the Nuremberg tribunal treated them as a new category, **crimes against humanity**, conceived as inhumane acts and persecutions against civilians on a vast scale in the pursuit of unjust ends.

---

[38] Amnesty International. *Executed "According to Law"? The Death Penalty in China*. March 17, 2004.

[39] Falk, Richard, Irene Gendzier, and Robert Jay Lifton, eds. *Crimes of War: Iraq*. Nation, 2006. Howard, Michael, George J. Andreopoulos, and Mark R. Shulman, eds. *The Laws of War: Constraints on Warfare in the Western World*. Yale, 1994. Best, Geoffrey. *War and Law Since 1945*. Oxford, 1994. Hartle, Anthony E. *Moral Issues in Military Decision Making*. Kansas, 2004.

SEEKING THE COLLECTIVE GOOD

Responsibility to Protect

COLLECTIVE GOOD: Stopping Atrocities Against Civilians

BACKGROUND: The international system based on sovereignty has historically treated serious human rights abuses as domestic problems of no concern to outside countries. Over the years, however, a norm has developed that treats the most serious atrocities as matters of concern for all of humanity. For instance, after the horrors of the Nazi Holocaust during World War II, the world's countries signed the Genocide Convention in 1948. Signatories (currently 140 states) pledge to "prevent and punish" genocide in both war and peacetime. Many scholars of international law interpret this as a commitment by states to intervene in recognized cases of genocide to stop the killing.

The concept that the international community must stop abuses by governments against their own people has gained momentum over the years since then, with various treaties and practices moving in this direction. The International Criminal Court (ICC) and several international war crimes tribunals have

tried individuals accused of war crimes, crimes against humanity, and genocide. Recently, human rights advocates proposed the overarching concept of "responsibility to protect," or R2P. The international community should try prevention and diplomacy first, but ultimately must use military intervention as a last resort if necessary to stop mass atrocities.

Everyone agrees that the world would be better off without atrocities, which degrade humanity and undermine norms of peaceful politics. These ideals, however, are a collective good, enjoyed by all countries regardless of which ones put money and lives on the line.

CHALLENGE: Mass atrocities continue to occur despite the Genocide Convention, the human rights treaties, the tribunals. and the R2P concept. In 1994 in Rwanda, ultranationalists seized

DOMINANCE

In the 1990s, for the first time since World War II, the UN Security Council authorized an international war crimes tribunal, directed against war crimes in the former Yugoslavia. Similar tribunals were later established for genocide in Rwanda and Sierra Leone.[40] The tribunal on the former Yugoslavia, headquartered in The Hague, the Netherlands, issued indictments against the top Bosnian Serb leaders and other Serbian and Croatian officers, and in 1999 against Serbian strongman Slobodan Milosevic for his expulsion of Albanians from Kosovo. The tribunal was hampered by lack of funding and by its lack of power to arrest suspects who enjoyed the sanctity of Serbia and Croatia. After Milosevic lost power in Serbia, the new Serbian government turned him over to the tribunal in 2001, and he died in custody in 2006. In 2008, the leader of the Bosnian Serbs accused of ordering his forces to kill thousands of Muslims in Bosnia was arrested after 13 years in hiding. He is currently on trial in The Hague, charged with persecuting Bosnian Muslims and Croats, shelling civilian population centers, and destroying property including places of worship. In 2011 his military commander was also arrested, leaving no Bosnia war criminals at large.

Following the civil war in Sierra Leone, the government there runs a war crimes tribunal jointly with the UN. In 2003, it indicted the sitting state leader in next-door Liberia, Charles Taylor, for his role in the war's extreme brutality. He fled to Nigeria shortly afterward but was captured there and turned over to the tribunal in 2006.

---

[40] Moghalu, Kingsley. *Global Justice: The Politics of War Crimes Trials.* Stanford, 2008. Bass, Gary Jonathan. *Stay the Hand of Vengeance: The Politics of War Crimes Tribunals.* Princeton, 2000.

power and slaughtered more than half a million ethnic minority members and political opponents. In 2004, Sudan used an armed militia to murder and displace large numbers of inhabitants of the Darfur region where rebels opposed the government. In these and other cases, no states intervened effectively to stop the atrocities. But in 2011, outsiders did halt an imminent slaughter by Libya's dictator.

SOLUTION: Human rights organizations rely on the identity principle to try to spur action by the international community. They publicize crises and goad the governments of democracies to act in the name of humanity. In the case of Darfur, a well-funded campaign with plentiful popular support called for strong action to stop the Sudanese government. These appeals, however, have brought meager results, as Western governments do not want to spend blood and treasure to intervene in messy foreign conflicts. The reciprocity principle has also come up short, as the ICC, which the world's countries are supposed to mutually support, has been unable to arrest the president of Sudan after indicting him for war crimes.

Rwandan survivor visits memorial on tenth anniversary of the 1994 genocide.

The dominance principle, then, governs the response to atrocities. When great powers see action as in their national interest, they act. Otherwise, they do not. Until the world's strong military powers decide to act against mass atrocities, the provision of the collective good embodied by R2P will continue to fall short.

REMAINS OF WAR CRIMES

War crimes include unnecessary targeting of civilians and mistreatment of prisoners of war (POWs). The most notorious war crime in Europe in recent decades was the massacre of more than 7,000 men and boys by Serbian forces who overran the UN "safe area" of Srebrenica, Bosnia, in 1995. Here, a mass grave there is excavated in 2007.

Following up on the UN tribunals for former Yugoslavia and Rwanda, in 1998 most of the world's states signed a treaty to create a permanent **International Criminal Court (ICC)**.[41] It hears cases of genocide, war crimes, and crimes against humanity from anywhere in the world. The ICC opened for business in 2003 in The Hague, with 18 judges sworn in from around the world (but not the United States). In 2008, the ICC began its first trial, of a militia leader from Democratic Congo accused of drafting children under 15 and killing civilians.

The United States has refused to ratify the ICC agreement and shows little interest in doing so. In addition, the United States has pressured many ICC member states to sign immunity agreements (known as Bilateral Immunity Agreements or BIA) to protect American soldiers serving in those countries from prosecution. In 2005, after several ICC members refused to sign a BIA, Congress voted to cut foreign aid to those states. U.S. leaders are concerned that American soldiers, serving in peacekeeping missions or in NATO allies, will fall under the jurisdiction of the ICC rather than under the American military's own justice system.

War crimes in Darfur, Sudan—which a UN commission found grave but short of "genocide"—have also been referred to the ICC after the United States dropped its objections in 2005 (when exemptions for U.S. soldiers serving in peacekeeping operations were restored).[42] The Darfur case is a difficult challenge for the ICC. In 2009, the ICC indicted the sitting Sudanese president, Omar al-Bashir, on charges of war crimes and crimes against humanity, and issued a warrant for his arrest. The indictment angered the Sudanese government, which then expelled humanitarian organizations from Darfur. In 2010, al-Bashir left Sudan for the first time, but his destination country of Chad refused to arrest him, citing bias in the ICC (all ICC prosecutions have been in Africa). The ICC faces a difficult balance in holding officials in Sudan accountable, yet being sensitive to efforts to end the violence in Darfur (see p. 167) In 2011, the ICC quickly indicted Libya's dictator and several others, but he was killed before facing justice.

What makes the ICC different (and controversial) is the idea of *universal jurisdiction*—that the court has the ability to prosecute individuals of any nation. This distinguishes the ICC from the World Court, which has only states as complainants and defendants. Under the ICC, individuals can be prosecuted for their roles in violations of human rights. Three

[41] Schiff, Benjamin N. *Building the International Criminal Court*. Cambridge, 2008. Schabas, William A. *An Introduction to the International Criminal Court*. 2nd ed. Cambridge, 2004.
[42] Prunier, Gerard. *Darfur: A 21st Century Genocide*. 3rd ed. Cornell, 2008.

mechanisms can trigger an ICC trial. First, a state can turn over an individual for trial if the state agrees to do so. Second, against the wishes of a state, a special prosecutor at the ICC can begin a trial if the crimes occurred in the territory of a signatory to the ICC. Third, the UN Security Council can begin proceedings even against individuals from nonsignatory states. It is hoped that the ICC, more than prosecuting every individual case of war crimes, will also serve to deter potential violators of these norms under the threat of potential prosecution under the ICC.[43]

The most important principle in the laws of war is the effort to limit warfare to the combatants and to protect civilians. It is illegal to target civilians in a war. It is not illegal, however, to target military forces knowing civilians will be killed. Even then, the amount of force used must be *proportional* to the military gain, and only the *necessary* amount of force can be used.

To help separate combatants from civilians, soldiers must wear uniforms and insignia, such as a shoulder patch with a national flag. This provision is frequently violated in guerrilla warfare, making that form of warfare particularly brutal and destructive of civilian life. If one cannot tell the difference between a bystander and a combatant, one is likely to kill both when in doubt. By contrast, in a large-scale conventional war it is much easier to distinguish civilians from soldiers, although the effort is never completely successful.[44] When U.S. special forces in Afghanistan made friends with local fighters by operating out of uniform and with bushy beards, humanitarian-aid agencies complained and the Pentagon ordered the soldiers back into uniform. In the Iraq War, insurgents have repeatedly targeted civilians and attacked in civilian clothes, from hospitals and schools, and after feigning surrender—all against the laws of war. And a 2007 report from Human Rights Watch accused the presidential guard unit in the Central African Republic of dozens of summary executions of civilians.

In recent years, the unprecedented rise in the use of private military forces in wars, especially in Iraq, has challenged the laws of war.[45] Because these private forces are not members of a country's military, the international laws of war do not necessarily apply to them (only states, not corporations, sign the Geneva Conventions). In Iraq, the U.S. government had granted a waiver to these companies to ensure that they could not be prosecuted for violations of international law, only local law. But because there was no formal Iraqi government, no one could enforce violations of domestic law committed by these companies. Several high-profile incidents (including abuses at the Abu Ghraib prison and several shootings of civilians) led Congress, the UN, and Iraq to hold private forces accountable. A 2008 Iraqi-U.S. agreement on the status of American military forces ended the legal waiver for private contractors beginning in 2009.

Soldiers have the right under the laws of war to surrender, which is to abandon their status as combatants and become **prisoners of war (POWs)**. They give up their weapons and their right to fight, and earn instead the right (like civilians) not to be targeted. POWs may not be killed, mistreated, or forced to disclose information beyond their name, rank, and serial number. The law of POWs is enforced through practical reciprocity. Once, late in World War II, German forces executed 80 POWs from the French partisan forces (whom Germany did not recognize as legitimate belligerents). The partisans responded by executing 80 German POWs.

---

[43] Cryer, Robert. *Prosecuting International Crimes: Selectivity and the International Criminal Law Regime.* Cambridge, 2005.

[44] Sterba, James P., ed. *Terrorism and International Justice.* Oxford, 2003.

[45] Avant, Deborah. *The Market for Force: The Consequences of Privatizing Security.* Cambridge, 2005.

The laws of war reserve a special role for the **International Committee of the Red Cross (ICRC)**. The ICRC provides practical support—such as medical care, food, and letters from home—to civilians caught in wars and to POWs. Exchanges of POWs are usually negotiated through the ICRC. Armed forces must respect the neutrality of the Red Cross, and usually do so (again, guerrilla war is problematical). In the current war on terrorism, the United States does not consider the "enemy combatants" it detains to be POWs, but has granted the ICRC access to most (though not all) of them. More controversial is the U.S. policy called "extraordinary rendition," which lets terrorist suspects captured overseas be transferred to other countries, including some that use torture, for questioning.

The laws of warfare impose moral responsibility on individuals in wartime, as well as on states. The Nuremberg Tribunal established that participants can be held accountable for war crimes they commit. German officers defended their actions as "just following orders," but this was rejected; the officers were punished, and some executed, for their war crimes.

Not all Nuremberg defendants were found guilty, however. For example, laws of war limit the use of force against civilians to what is necessary and proportional to military objectives. In World War II, the German army besieged the Russian city of Leningrad (St. Petersburg) for two years, and civilians in the city were starving. Sieges of this kind are permitted under international law if an army cannot easily capture a city.

Changing Context   The laws of warfare have been undermined by the changing nature of war. Conventional wars by defined armed forces on defined battlegrounds are giving way to irregular and "low-intensity" wars fought by guerrillas and death squads in cities or jungles. The lines between civilians and soldiers blur in these situations, and war crimes become more commonplace. In the Vietnam War, one of the largest problems faced by the United States was an enemy that seemed to be everywhere and nowhere. This led frustrated U.S. forces to attack civilian villages seen as supporting the guerrillas. In one infamous case, a U.S. officer was court-martialed for ordering his soldiers to massacre hundreds of unarmed civilians in the village of My Lai in 1968 (he was convicted but given a light sentence). In today's irregular warfare, frequently inflamed by ethnic and religious conflicts, the laws of war are increasingly difficult to uphold.[46]

Another factor undermining laws of war is that states rarely issue a *declaration of war* setting out whom they are warring against and the cause of their action. Ironically, such declarations are historically the exception, not the rule. This trend continues today because declarations of war bring little benefit to the state declaring war and incur obligations under international law. In many cases, such as revolutionary and counterrevolutionary civil wars, a declaration would not even be appropriate, because wars are declared only against states, not internal groups. In undeclared wars the distinctions between participants and nonparticipants are undermined (along with the protection of the latter). The Bush administration called the 2001 terrorist attacks acts of war, and the response a war on terror, but Congress did not formally declare war (just as it had not during the Korean and Vietnam Wars).

---

[46] Wippman, David, and Matthew Evangelista, eds. *New Wars, New Laws? Applying the Laws of War in 21st Century Conflicts.* Transnational, 2005.

POLICY PERSPECTIVES

International Criminal Court Chief Prosecutor, Fatou Bensouda

PROBLEM *How do you balance respect for international legal principles and national interests?*

BACKGROUND For six years, fighting has raged in the western Sudanese province of Darfur. This conflict has been labeled a genocide by many observers. It is estimated that 2.7 million people have been forced from their homes and perhaps 300,000 have died. While some of the violence in Darfur is between warring rebel groups, the Sudanese government has been accused of arming one set of militias and encouraging the violence.

You are the chief prosecutor for the International Criminal Court (ICC). Although Sudan is not a member of the ICC, because the Security Council referred the Darfur case to the ICC you may choose to begin a case against anyone in the Sudan. The ICC has already issued two arrest warrants for war crimes related to Darfur. In 2009, your predecessor obtained an indictment and arrest warrant against Sudan's president, Omar al-Bashir, on charges of war crimes and crimes against humanity. Such a move to prosecute a sitting president of a country in the middle of a civil war was unprecedented.

DOMESTIC CONSIDERATIONS While human rights groups applauded the decision to pursue criminal charges against the Sudanese president, many countries opposed the move. China and Russia, both of which maintain diplomatic ties with Sudan, have expressed disapproval and pressed the ICC to stop prosecutions. Many African Union (AU) countries, which currently deploy peacekeepers in Darfur, have opposed the move, warning that it could lead to a breakdown of the peace process. In fact, after the ICC announced plans to indict al-Bashir, violence did increase in Darfur, including attacks against AU peacekeepers, and after the indictment was announced, Sudan expelled humanitarian NGOs from Darfur, gravely imperiling the population there.

The AU has called for the ICC to suspend all ICC proceedings relating to Darfur, and the Arab League has condemned the indictment of al-Bashir.

The United States and the major European countries support efforts to bring members of the Sudanese government to justice. And while Russia and China have suggested revoking ICC authority to prosecute cases related to Darfur, the United States, France, or Britain could use their Security Council vetoes to stop such an effort. Supporters of the ICC have argued that Darfur represents a crucial case for the future of the legitimacy of the Court. This case will set important precedents as to the power of this relatively new body.

SCENARIO Imagine that the Chinese government approaches you and asks you to suspend the indictment of al-Bashir. In return, China agrees to press Sudan to both end violence in Darfur and allow more peacekeepers to be deployed there. China has no direct control over Sudan, however, so China's promises may bring little change in behavior on the part of Sudan. On the other hand, China does have some pull with the Sudanese leadership. The United States and its allies would be likely to support such a move if it resulted in a stable cease-fire.

CHOOSE YOUR POLICY Do you suspend the ICC's efforts to prosecute the Sudanese leadership, especially the Sudanese president, for war crimes? How do you balance the demands of competing great powers? How do you balance your desire to bring justice to the victims of the conflict in Darfur with the reality of the peace process, which hangs in the balance? Can justice be delayed to save lives in the short term? If justice is delayed, will it ever be achieved?

The Evolution of World Order

The most powerful states, especially hegemons, have great influence on the rules and values that have become embedded over time in a body of international law.[47] For example, the principle of free passage on the open seas is now formally established in international law. But at one time warships from one state did not hesitate to seize the ships of other states and make off with their cargoes. This practice was profitable to the state that pulled off such raids, but of course their own ships could be raided in return. Such behavior made long-distance trade itself more dangerous, less predictable, and less profitable. The trading states could benefit more by getting rid of the practice. So, over time, a norm developed around the concept of freedom of navigation on the high seas. It became one of the first areas of international law developed by the Dutch legal scholar Hugo Grotius in the mid-1600s—a time when the Dutch dominated world trade and could benefit most from free navigation.

Dutch power, then, provided the backbone for the international legal concept of freedom of the seas. Later, when Britain was dominant, it enforced the principle of free seas through the cannons of its warships. As the world's main trading state, Britain benefited from a worldwide norm of free shipping and trade. And with the world's most powerful navy, it was in a position to define and enforce the rules for the world's oceans.

Likewise, 20th-century world order depended heavily on the power of the United States (and, for a few decades, on the division of power between the United States and the Soviet Union). The United States at times came close to adopting the explicit role of "world police force." But in truth the world is too large for any single state—even a hegemon—to police effectively. Rather, the world's states usually go along with the rules established by the most powerful state without constant policing. Meanwhile, they try to influence the rules by working through international institutions (to which the hegemon cedes some of its power). In this way, although states do not yield their sovereignty, they vest some power and authority in international institutions and laws and generally work within that framework.

Three factors combined to shake up international norms in the post–Cold War era—the end of the Cold War, the shifts in economic position of various regions and states, and the effects of technological change in creating a "small world." Domestic and local politics now play out on a global stage. These new norms still remain unsettled. New expectations are emerging in such areas as human rights, UN peacekeeping, humanitarian interventions, Russia's and China's roles as great powers, and the U.S. role as a superpower. However, core norms and stable institutions shape international political economy—the subject of the remaining chapters of this book—with more stability than in international security. We return to the pinnacle of international organization, the EU, in Chapter 10. But first, we review key world economic arrangements.

✓•⌐**Study**
and **Review**
the **Post-Test &**
Chapter Exam
at **mypoliscilab.com**

---

[47] Ikenberry, G. John. *After Victory: Institutions, Strategic Restraint, and the Rebuilding of Order after Major Wars.* Princeton, 2001.

CHAPTER REVIEW

SUMMARY

- International anarchy is balanced by world order—rules and institutions through which states cooperate for mutual benefit.

- States follow the rules—both moral norms and formal international laws—much more often than not. These rules operate through institutions (IOs), with the UN at the center of the institutional network.

- The UN embodies a tension between state sovereignty and supranational authority. In part because of its deference to state sovereignty, the UN has attracted virtually universal membership of the world's states, including all the great powers.

- The UN particularly defers to the sovereignty of great powers, five of whom as permanent Security Council members can each block any security-related resolution binding on UN member states. The five permanent members of the Security Council are the United States, France, Great Britain, China, and Russia.

- Each of the 193 UN member states has one vote in the General Assembly, which serves mainly as a world forum and an umbrella organization for social and economic development efforts.

- The UN is administered by international civil servants in the Secretariat, headed by the secretary-general.

- The regular UN budget plus all peacekeeping missions together amount to far less than 1 percent of what the world spends on military forces.

- UN peacekeeping forces are deployed in regional conflicts in five world regions. Their main role is to monitor compliance with agreements such as cease-fires, disarmament plans, and fair election rules. They were scaled back dramatically in 1995–1997, then grew rapidly since 1998.

- UN peacekeepers operate under the UN flag and command. Sometimes national troops operate under their own flag and command to carry out UN resolutions.

- IOs include UN programs (mostly on economic and social issues), autonomous UN agencies, and organizations with no formal tie to the UN. This institutional network helps strengthen and stabilize the rules of IR.

- International law, the formal body of rules for state relations, derives from treaties (most important), custom, general principles, and legal scholarship—not from legislation passed by any government.

- International law is difficult to enforce and is enforced in practice by national power, international coalitions, and the practice of reciprocity.

- The World Court hears grievances of one state against another but cannot infringe on state sovereignty in most cases. It is an increasingly useful avenue for arbitrating relatively minor conflicts.

- A permanent International Criminal Court (ICC) began operations in 2003. Taking over from two UN tribunals, it hears cases of genocide, war crimes, and crimes against humanity.

- In international law, diplomats have long had special status. Embassies are considered the territory of their home country.

- Laws of war are also long-standing and well established. They distinguish combatants from civilians, giving each certain rights and responsibilities. Guerrilla wars and ethnic conflicts have blurred these distinctions.

- International norms concerning human rights are becoming stronger and more widely accepted. However, human rights law is problematic because it entails interference by one state in another's internal affairs.

KEY TERMS

international
    norms   233
international organizations
    (IOs)   234
UN Charter   237
UN General
    Assembly   237
UN Security
    Council   239
UN Secretariat   239
peacebuilding   247
UN Conference
    on Trade and
    Development
    (UNCTAD)   252

World Health Organization
    (WHO)   253
World Court
    (International Court
    of Justice)   256
immigration law   261
diplomatic
    recognition   261
diplomatic
    immunity   262
just wars   263
human rights   264
Universal Declaration of
    Human Rights
    (UDHR)   266

Amnesty
    International   268
responsibility to protect
    (R2P)   269
war crimes   270
crimes against
    humanity   270
International
    Criminal Court
    (ICC)   272
prisoners of war
    (POWs)   273
International Committee
    of the Red Cross
    (ICRC)   274

CRITICAL THINKING QUESTIONS

1. Suppose you were asked to recommend changes in the structure of the UN Security Council (especially in permanent membership and the veto). What changes would you recommend, if any? Based on what logic?

2. The former UN secretary-general Boutros Boutros-Ghali proposed (without success) the creation of a standby army of peacemaking forces loaned by member states (see p. 249). This would reduce state sovereignty a bit and increase supranational authority. Discuss this plan's merits and drawbacks.

3. Collective security against aggression depends on states' willingness to bear the costs of fighting wars to repel and punish aggressors. Sometimes great powers have been willing to bear such costs; at other times they have not. What considerations do you think should guide such decisions? Give examples of situations (actual or potential) that would and would not merit the intervention of great powers to reverse aggression.

4. Given the difficulty of enforcing international law, how might the role of the World Court be strengthened in future years? What obstacles might such plans encounter? How would they change the Court's role if they succeeded?

5. Although international norms concerning human rights are becoming stronger, China and many other states continue to consider human rights an internal affair over which the state has sovereignty within its territory. Do you think human rights are a legitimate subject for one state to raise with another? If so, how do you reconcile the tensions between state autonomy and universal rights? What practical steps could be taken to get sovereign states to acknowledge universal human rights?

Human Rights: A Hollow Promise to the World?

Overview

Since the adoption of the UN Universal Declaration of Human Rights over 60 years ago, states have been committed to advancing human rights. Seven different UN treaties, signed by the majority of the world's states, guarantee the protection and advancement of human rights in several areas including the rights of women, the rights of the child, the rights of migrant workers, and protection from torture. Numerous other regional treaties and protocols promote economic well-being, protect due-process rights, and endorse self-determination.

State leaders consistently tout the importance of human rights in promoting fairness, justice, and equality. This is true of both democratic and non-democratic states. In rhetoric, the importance of promoting and protecting human rights does seem universal.

Yet, violations of all of these treaties still occur and indeed, at times, seem commonplace. Violations range from small (lack of equal protection for minorities in some states, the allowing of torture of a few individuals) to large (genocide in Darfur). No matter the scale of the violations, all show a brazen disregard for the importance of human rights. This leads many to ask, is the promise of global human rights one that states will ever attempt to fulfill? Can individuals count on state governments to promote and protect human rights?

ARGUMENT 1

States Make Few Efforts to Promote and Protect Human Rights

Most UN treaties concerning human rights are not enforced. The core UN human rights treaties have little, if any, enforcement attached to them. In fact, some of the worst violators of human rights are often the first to sign these documents because they know there will be no enforcement of the rules. The treaties are only pieces of paper.

Political goals will always subvert the promotion of human rights. When push comes to shove, states will ignore human rights abuses to achieve other political goals. Whether it is the United States ignoring political repression in China, China ignoring genocide in Sudan, or South Africa ignoring a crackdown in Zimbabwe, states of all types will turn a blind eye to human rights abuses if it serves their purposes.

Human rights standards are applied unevenly. When attention is paid to human rights violations, it is done so unevenly. More often than not, violations are brought to light only against states that are considered enemies or politically unimportant. Meanwhile, similar violations are ignored in allied or politically powerful states.

States Do Help to Promote Human Rights

Emerging norms of democracy are promoting human rights. The growing number of democratic countries around the globe is serving to increase respect for human rights. Democracies are more likely to protect and promote human rights. Many Western countries have expanded their support for young democracies, which will help human rights worldwide.

NGOs continue to work with states to promote human rights. NGOs such as Amnesty International and Human Rights Watch continue to provide information to states and their citizens concerning human rights abuses. While states do not act on all of these instances, they do respond to some of these grassroots efforts to improve global respect for human rights. NGOs are thus important agents for states wanting to advance the cause of human rights.

States promote human rights through other institutions. Many states are beginning to condition foreign aid and free trade policies on human rights behavior. The European Union requires all signatories to trade agreements to abide by certain human rights standards, while the United States requires all free trade partners to acknowledge workers' and children's rights. These requirements, embedded in economically important treaties, are more likely to be enforced.

Questions

- Do states, especially Western states, effectively advance human rights? Do you think there has been more or less enforcement of human rights standards in the past decade? Are there important cases of states supporting human rights? Or ignoring violations of them?

- How can human rights standards be more effectively promoted? Is it more effective to use sticks (threats of punishment) or carrots (promises of rewards for better behavior) to improve respect for human rights?

- Is promoting human rights standards forcing a particular set of morals and norms on non-Western states? Is there such a thing as universal human rights?

For Further Reading

Donnelly, Jack. *International Human Rights.* 3rd ed. Westview, 2006.

Mahoney, Jack. *The Challenge of Human Rights: Origin, Development and Significance.* Wiley-Blackwell, 2006.

Mutua, Makau. *Human Rights: A Political and Cultural Critique.* Pennsylvania, 2008.

Farmer, Paul, and Amartya Sen. *Pathologies of Power: Health, Human Rights, and the New War on the Poor.* California, 2004.

CHAPTER 8 International Trade

Port in Valparaiso, Chile, 2005.

Theories of Trade

International trade amounts to a sixth of the total economic activity in the world. About $19 trillion of goods and services cross international borders each year.[1] This is a very large number, about 12 times the world's military spending, for example. The great volume of international trade reflects the fact that trade is profitable.

The role of trade in the economy varies somewhat from one nation to another, but overall, it is at least as important in the global South as in the industrialized North. Although the global South accounts for a relatively small part of all trade in the world economy, this is because its economic activity itself is only 40 percent of the world total (see p. 24).

Trade is not only an economic issue but a highly political one. It crosses state-defined borders, is regulated by states that are pressured by interest groups, and occurs within trade regimes maintained by and negotiated among states.

Scholars of *international political economy (IPE)* thus study the politics of international economic activities.[2] The most frequently studied of these activities are trade, monetary relations, and multinational corporations (see this chapter and Chapter 9). In addition, two topics of special interest in recent years are the economic integration of Europe and other regions (Chapter 10) and the international politics of the global environment (Chapter 11). Most scholars of IPE focus on the industrialized regions of the world, where most of the world's economic activity occurs. However, the global South has received growing attention as globalization integrates parts of the South into the world economy more intensely (Chapters 12 and 13). Although these issues overlap (to varying degrees) with international security matters, they all deal primarily with political bargaining over economic issues and thus fit within IPE broadly defined.

The core principles laid out in Chapter 1 and the concepts of power and bargaining developed initially in Chapter 2 apply to IPE. States are the most important actors in IPE, but are not as important as in international security. Actors in IPE, as in security affairs, tend to act in their own interests. As Brazil's foreign minister explained in 2001, his country shared with the United States the same guiding principle in negotiating a hemisphere-wide free trade area: "What's in it for us?"[3]

Liberalism and Mercantilism

Two major approaches within IPE differ on their views of trade.[4] One approach, called **mercantilism**, generally shares with realism the belief that each state must protect its own interests at the expense of others—not relying on international organizations to

CHAPTER OUTLINE

Theories of Trade
- Liberalism and Mercantilism
- Comparative Advantage
- Political Interference in Markets
- Protectionism

Trade Regimes
- The World Trade Organization
- Bilateral and Regional Agreements
- Cartels
- Industries and Interest Groups
- Enforcement of Trade Rules

Economic Globalization
- The Evolving World Economy
- Resistance to Trade

☐●☐ **Read** and **Listen** to **Chapter 8** at **mypoliscilab.com**

✓●☐ **Study** and **Review** the **Pre-Test & Flashcards** at **mypoliscilab.com**

---

[1] Data in this chapter are calculated from World Trade Organization statistics.

[2] Oatley, Thomas H. *International Political Economy: Interests and Institutions in the Global Economy.* 4th ed. Longman, 2009. Frieden, Jeffry A., and David A. Lake. *International Political Economy: Perspectives on Global Power and Wealth.* 4th ed. St. Martin's, 2000. Peterson, V. Spike. *A Critical Rewriting of Global Political Economy: Integrating Reproductive, Productive, and Virtual Economies.* Routledge, 2003. Chase-Dunn, Christopher, ed. *The Historical Evolution of the International Political Economy.* Elgar, 1995. Murphy, Craig N. *International Organization and Industrial Change, Global Governance Since 1850.* Polity, 1994.

[3] Rohter, Larry, with Jennifer L. Rich. Brazil Takes a Trade Stance and Offers a Warning to U.S. *The New York Times,* December 19, 2001: W1.

[4] Hellenier, Eric. Economic Liberalism and Its Critics: The Past as Prologue? *Review of International Political Economy* 10 (4), 2003: 685–96.

Explore
the Simulation
"International Trade:
You Are a Trade
Expert"
on mypoliscilab.com

create a framework for mutual gains. Mercantilists therefore emphasize relative power (as do realists): what matters is not so much a state's absolute amount of well-being as its position relative to rival states.[5]

In addition, mercantilism (like realism) holds that the importance of economic transactions lies in their implications for the military. States worry about relative wealth and trade because these can be translated directly into military power. Thus, although military power is generally not useful in economic negotiations, mercantilists believe that the outcome of economic negotiations matters for military power.

Economic liberalism, an alternative approach, generally shares with liberal internationalism a belief in the possibility of cooperation to realize common gains (see pp. 90–92 and pp. 233–235).[6] It holds that by building international organizations, institutions, and norms, states can mutually benefit from economic exchanges. It matters little to liberals whether one state gains more or less than another—just whether the state's wealth is increasing in *absolute* terms.

Liberalism and mercantilism are *theories* of economics and also *ideologies* that shape state policies. Liberalism is the dominant approach in Western economics, though more so in *microeconomics* (the study of firms and households) than in *macroeconomics* (the study of national economies). Marxism is often treated as a third theoretical/ideological approach to IPE, along with mercantilism and liberalism (see Chapter 4). Marxist approaches are attuned to economic exploitation as a force that shapes political relations. We will explore Marxist theories in depth in Chapter 12, as they find their greatest explanatory power in North-South relations.

Most international economic exchanges (as well as security relationships) contain some element of mutual interests—joint gains that can be realized through cooperation—and some element of conflicting interests. Game theorists call this a "mixed interest" game. For example, in the game of Chicken (see p. 78), the two drivers share an interest in avoiding a head-on collision, yet their interests diverge in that one can be a hero only if the other is a chicken. In international trade, even when two states both benefit from a trade (a shared interest), one or the other will benefit more (a conflicting interest).

Liberalism emphasizes the shared interests in economic exchanges, whereas mercantilism emphasizes the conflicting interests. For liberals, the most important goal of economic policy is to create a maximum of total wealth by achieving optimal *efficiency* (maximizing output, minimizing waste). For mercantilists, the most important goal is to create the most favorable possible *distribution* of wealth (see Figure 8.1).

Liberal economists believe in markets. The terms of an exchange are defined by the price at which goods are traded. Often the *bargaining space*—the difference between the lowest price a seller would accept and the highest price a buyer would pay—is quite large. For example, Saudi Arabia would be willing to sell a barrel of oil (if it had no better option) for as little as, say, $10 a barrel, and industrialized countries are willing to pay more than $100 a barrel for the oil. (In practice, oil prices have fluctuated in this broad range in recent decades.) How are prices determined within this range? That is, how do the participants decide on the distribution of benefits from the exchange?

[5] Gilpin, Robert. *Global Political Economy: Understanding the International Economic Order.* Princeton, 2001. Grieco, Joseph, and John Ikenberry. *State Power and World Markets: The International Political Economy.* Norton, 2002.

[6] Neff, Stephen C. *Friends but No Allies: Economic Liberalism and the Law of Nations.* Columbia, 1990. Ward, Benjamin. *The Ideal Worlds of Economics: Liberal, Radical, and Conservative Economic World Views.* Basic, 1979.

FIGURE 8.1 Joint and Individual Benefits

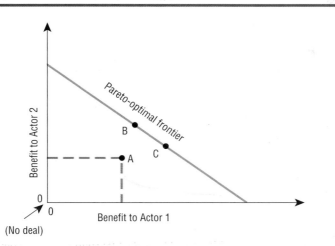

Any deal struck, such as at point A, yields certain benefits to each actor (dotted lines). Joint benefits are maximized at the Pareto-optimal frontier, but the distribution of those benefits, as between points B and C (both of which are better than A for both actors), is a matter for bargaining. Liberalism is more concerned with joint benefits, mercantilism more with the relative distribution.

When there are multiple buyers and sellers of a good (or equivalent goods that can be substituted for it), prices are determined by market competition.[7] In practice, free markets are supposed to (and sometimes do) produce stable patterns of buying and selling at a fairly uniform price. At this *market price*, sellers know that an effort to raise the price would drive the buyer to seek another seller, and buyers know that an effort to lower the price would drive the seller to seek another buyer. Thus, in liberal economics, *bilateral* relations between states are less important than they are in security affairs. The existence of world markets reduces the leverage that one state can exert over another in economic affairs (because the second state can simply find other partners). For example, U.S. sanctions on Iran, a major oil exporter, invited European companies to fill the void in recent years. In IPE, then, power is more diffuse and involves more actors at once than in international security.

Buyers vary in the value they place on an item (such as a barrel of oil); if the price rises, fewer people are willing to buy it, and if the price drops, more people are willing to buy it. This is called the *demand curve* for the item. Sellers also vary in the value they place on the item. If the price rises, more sellers are willing to supply the item to buyers; if the price drops, fewer sellers are willing to supply the item. This is called the *supply curve*. In a free market, the price at which the supply and demand curves cross is the *equilibrium price*. At this price, sellers are willing to supply the same number of units that buyers are willing to purchase. (In practice, prices reflect *expectations* about supply and demand in the near future.)

The supply and demand system does not always produce stability, however. Such a failure can be seen with oil, arguably the most important commodity in the world economy

---

[7] Lindblom, Charles E. *The Market System: What It Is, How It Works, and What to Make of It.* Yale, 2001.

and the most traded one by value. The price of a barrel of oil has fluctuated radically over recent years. Each time world economic growth accelerates, demand for oil rises and so does its price. But each time oil prices spike up, Western economies go into recession because high prices for this key commodity undermine the whole economy. These recessions in turn reduce demand, and oil prices drop.[8] The amount of economic activity may vary by only 5 or 10 percent, but the price of oil doubles or triples, then drops in half. The most recent case of this cycle, in 2007–2008, saw spectacular, unprecedented (and unsustainable) increases in oil prices from around $70 a barrel to $140 a barrel, driven by new demand in fast-growing Asian economies, among other factors. The world economy then entered a spectacular, unprecedented recession, and oil prices dropped in just a few months back to $40 a barrel. This kind of instability in the price of a key commodity is terrible for the world economy, and creates a big incentive for governments to take political actions rather than rely entirely on market forces.

Liberalism sees individual households and firms as the key actors in the economy and views government's most useful role as one of noninterference in economics, except to regulate markets in order to help them function efficiently (and to create infrastructure such as roads, which also help the economy function efficiently). Politics, in this view, should serve the interests of economic efficiency. With the hand of government removed from markets, the "invisible hand" of supply and demand can work out the most efficient patterns of production, exchange, and consumption (through the mechanism of prices). Because of the benefits of **free trade** among countries, liberals disdain realists' obsession with international borders, because borders constrain the maximum efficiency of exchange. Trade-based wealth depends on international political cooperation, and violence usually does not work well in pursuing such wealth. Thus, liberals argue that interdependence inherently promotes peace, an idea introduced earlier (pp. 90–92).[9] (Then again, some observers saw similar trends in international interdependence just before World War I, but war occurred anyway.)

For mercantilists, by contrast, economics should serve politics: the creation of wealth underlies state power. Because power is relative, trade is desirable only when the distribution of benefits favors one's own state over rivals.[10] The terms of exchange shape the relative rates at which states accumulate power and thus shape the way power distributions in the international system change over time.

Mercantilism achieved prominence several hundred years ago, and Britain used trade to rise in relative power in the international system around the 18th century. At that time mercantilism meant specifically the creation of a trade surplus in order to stockpile money in the form of precious metal (gold and silver), which could then be used to buy military capabilities (mercenary armies and weapons) in time of war.[11]

Mercantilism declined in the 19th century as Britain decided it had more to gain from free trade than from protectionism. It returned as a major approach in the period between World Wars I and II, when liberal global trading relations broke down. With the global recession in 2009, world leaders eyed each other warily to see if mercantilism would again make a comeback.

---

[8] Goldstein, Joshua S., Xiaoming Huang, and Burcu Akan. Energy in the World Economy, 1950–1992. *International Studies Quarterly* 41 (2), 1997: 241–66.
[9] Mansfield, Edward D., ed. *International Conflict and the Global Economy*. Elgar, 2004.
[10] Grieco, Joseph M. *Cooperation among Nations: Europe, America, and Non-Tariff Barriers to Trade*. Cornell, 1990. Gowa, Joanne. *Allies, Adversaries, and International Trade*. Princeton, 1993. Hirschman, Albert O. *National Power and the Structure of Foreign Trade*. California, 1945.
[11] Coulomb, Fanny. *Economic Theories of Peace and War*. Routledge, 2004.

FIGURE 8.2 China's Growing Trade Surplus

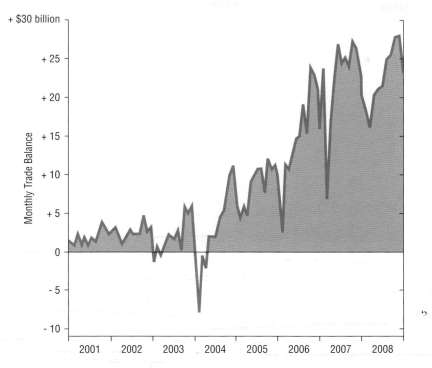

Source: *New York Times* September 12, 2006: U.S. Census, *Foreign Trade Statistics*.

Mercantilists' preferred means of making trade serve a state's political interests—even at the cost of some lost wealth that free markets might have created—is to create a favorable balance of trade. The **balance of trade** is the value of a state's imports relative to its exports. A state that exports more than it imports has a *positive balance of trade, or trade surplus.* China has run a large trade surplus for years, passing $250 billion per year. It gets more money for the many goods it exports than it pays for raw materials and other imported goods (see Figure 8.2). A state that imports more than it exports has a *negative balance of trade (trade* deficit). A trade deficit is different from a budget deficit in government spending (see pp. 336–337). Since the late 1990s, the U.S. trade deficit has grown steadily to hundreds of billions of dollars per year, approaching $1 trillion, with about a quarter accounted for by China and another quarter by oil imports.

States must ultimately reconcile the balance of trade. It is tracked financially through the system of national accounts (pp. 333–334). In the short term, a state can trade for a few years at a deficit and then a few years at a surplus. The imbalances are carried on the national accounts as a kind of loan. But a trade deficit that persists for years becomes a problem. In recent years, to balance its trade deficit, the United States has "exported" currency (dollars) to China, Japan, Europe, and other countries, which use the dollars to buy such things as shares of U.S. companies, U.S. Treasury bills, or U.S. real estate. Economists worry that if foreigners lose their taste for investments in the United States, the U.S. economy could suffer.

FIGURE 8.3 Balance of Trade

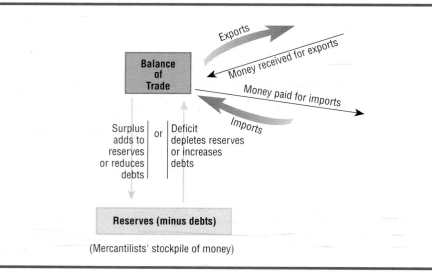

(Mercantilists' stockpile of money)

This is one reason why mercantilists favor national economic policies to create a trade surplus. Then, rather than being unable to find the money it might need to cope with a crisis or fight a war, the state sits on a pile of money representing potential power. Historically, mercantilism literally meant stockpiling gold (gained from running a trade surplus) as a fungible form of power (see Figure 8.3). Such a strategy is attuned to realism's emphasis on relative power and is an example of the dominance principle. For one state to have a trade surplus, another must have a deficit.

Comparative Advantage

The overall success of liberal economics is due to the substantial gains that can be realized through trade.[12] These gains result from the **comparative advantage** that different states enjoy in producing different goods (a concept pioneered by economists Adam Smith and David Ricardo 200 years ago). States differ in their abilities to produce certain goods because of differences in natural resources, labor force characteristics, technology, and other such factors. In order to maximize the overall creation of wealth, each state should specialize in producing the goods for which it has a comparative advantage and then trade for goods that another state produces best. Of course, the costs of transportation and of processing the information in the trade (called *transaction costs*) must be included in the costs of producing an item. But increasingly, as globalization proceeds, both of these are low relative to the differences in the cost of producing items in different locations.

Two commodities of great importance in the world are oil and cars. It is much cheaper to produce oil (or another energy source) in Saudi Arabia than in Japan, and much cheaper to produce cars in Japan than in Saudi Arabia. Japan needs oil to run its industry (including its car industry), and Saudi Arabia needs cars to travel its vast territory (including reaching its remote oil wells). Even with shipping and transaction costs, shipping Japanese

---

[12] Irwin, Douglas. *Against the Tide: An Intellectual History of Free Trade.* Princeton, 1996. Dimond, Robert. *Classical Theory of the Gains from Trade: The Origins of International Economics.* Routledge, 2004.

cars to Saudi Arabia and Saudi oil to Japan saves a huge amount of money, compared to the costs if each tried to be self-sufficient.

A state need not have an absolute advantage (that is, be the most efficient producer in the world) in producing one kind of good in order to make specialization pay. It need only specialize in producing goods that are relatively lower in cost than other goods. Imagine that Japan discovered a way to produce synthetic oil using the same mix of labor and capital that it now uses to produce cars, and that this synthetic oil could be produced a bit more cheaply than what it costs Saudi Arabia to produce oil, but that Japan could still produce cars *much* more cheaply than Saudi Arabia. It might seem intuitive that Japan should produce synthetic oil rather than pay extra for Saudi oil. But this is wrong. From a strictly economic point of view, Japan should keep producing cars (where it has a huge comparative advantage) and not divert capital and labor to make synthetic oil (where it has only a slight advantage). The extra profits Japan would make from exporting more cars would more than compensate for the slightly higher price it would pay to import oil.

Thus, international trade generally expands the Pareto-optimal frontier (see Figure 8.1 on p. 285) by increasing the overall efficiency of production. Free trade allocates global resources to states that have the greatest comparative advantage in producing each kind of commodity. As a result, prices are both lower overall and more consistent worldwide. Increasingly, production is oriented to the world market.

The economic benefits of trade, however, come with some political drawbacks. First, long-term benefits may incur short-term costs. When a state begins to import goods that it had been producing domestically, its economy may be disrupted; workers may need to retrain and find new jobs, and capital may not be easy to convert to new uses. Thus, state leaders may feel political pressure to become involved in economic policy (see "Resistance to Trade," pp. 313–314). Also, the benefits and costs of trade tend to be unevenly distributed within a state. Some industries or communities may benefit at the expense of others. For example, if a U.S. manufacturing company moves its factory to Mexico to take advantage of cheaper labor there and exports its goods back to the United States, the workers at the old U.S. factory lose their jobs, but U.S. consumers enjoy cheaper goods. The costs of such a move fall heavily on a few workers, but the benefits are spread thinly across many consumers.

By the same logic, protectionist measures benefit a few people greatly, and cost many people a bit. By one estimate, a 20 percent steel tariff enacted by the Bush administration in 2002–2003 cost consumers $7 billion and saved 7,300 U.S. jobs—a pricey $326,000 per job.[13] Yet those 7,300 workers (and their unions and companies) benefit greatly, whereas the roughly $20 cost per U.S. citizen goes unnoticed. This kind of unequal distribution of costs and benefits often creates political problems for free trade even when the *overall* economic benefits outweigh the costs. Worker or industry interest groups (see pp. 304–307) will form against the concentrated costs (losing jobs) far more often than consumer groups will form against the diffuse losses (such as a $20 increase for many).

Political Interference in Markets

A free and efficient market requires many buyers and sellers with fairly complete information about the market. Also, the willingness of participants to deal with each other should not be distorted by personal (or political) preferences but should be governed only by price and quality considerations. Deviations from these conditions, called *market imperfections*, reduce efficiency. Most political intrusions into economic transactions are market imperfections.

---

[13] Kahn, Joseph. U.S. Trade Panel Backs Putting Hefty Duties on Imported Steel. *The New York Times*, December 8, 2001: C1, C3.

International trade occurs more often at world market prices than does *domestic* economic exchange. No world government owns industries, provides subsidies, or regulates prices. Nonetheless, world markets are often affected by politics. When states are the principal actors in international economic affairs, the number of participants is often small. When there is just one supplier of an item—a *monopoly*—the supplier can set the price quite high. For example, the South African company De Beers produces 40 percent of the world supply and controls two-thirds of the world market for uncut diamonds. An *oligopoly* is a monopoly shared by just a few large sellers—often allowing for tacit or explicit coordination to force the price up. For example, OPEC members agree to limit oil production to keep prices up. To the extent that companies band together along national lines, monopolies and oligopolies are more likely.

Another common market imperfection in international trade is *corruption*; individuals may receive payoffs to trade at nonmarket prices. The government or company involved may lose some of the benefits being distributed, but the individual government official or company negotiator gets increased benefits (see pp. 475–476).

Politics provides a *legal framework* for markets—ensuring that participants keep their commitments, contracts are binding, buyers pay for goods they purchase, counterfeit money is not used, and so forth. In the international economy, lacking a central government authority, rules are less easily enforced. As in security affairs, such rules can be codified in international treaties, but enforcement depends on practical reciprocity (see pp. 273–274).

Taxation is another political influence on markets. Taxes are used both to generate revenue for the government and to regulate economic activity by incentives. For instance, a government may keep taxes low on foreign companies in hopes of attracting them to locate and invest in the country. Taxes applied to international trade itself, called *tariffs*, are a frequent source of international conflict (see "Protectionism," pp. 291–294).

Sanctions   Political interference in free markets is most explicit when governments apply *sanctions* against economic interactions of certain kinds or between certain actors. Political power then prohibits an economic exchange that would otherwise have been mutually beneficial. In 2011, the United States had trade restrictions on 15 states in response to those states' political actions, such as human rights violations.[14]

Enforcing sanctions is always a difficult task, because participants have a financial incentive to break the sanctions through black markets or other means.[15] Without broad, multilateral support for international sanctions, they generally fail. When the United States tried to punish the Soviet Union in the 1970s by applying trade sanctions against a Soviet oil pipeline to Western Europe, the move did not stop the pipeline. It just took profitable business away from a U.S. company (Caterpillar) and allowed European companies to profit instead because European states did not join in the sanctions. The difficulty of applying sanctions reflects a more general point made earlier—that power in IPE is more diffused among states than it is in security affairs. Refusing to participate in mutually profitable economic trade often harms oneself more than the target of one's actions, unless nearly all other states follow suit (note that sanctions enforcement is a form of the collective goods problem).

---

[14] See http://www.ustreas.gov/offices/enforcement/ofac/programs/index.shtml.
[15] Hufbauer, Gary Clyde, Jeffrey Schott, Kimberly Ann Elliot, and Barbara Oegg. *Economic Sanctions Reconsidered.* Peterson Institute, 2008. Drezner, Daniel W. *The Sanctions Paradox: Economic Statecraft and International Relations.* Cambridge, 1999. Lopez, George A., and David Cortwright. *Smart Sanctions: Targeting Economic Statecraft.* Rowman & Littlefield, 2002. Martin, Lisa L. *Coercive Cooperation: Explaining Multilateral Economic Sanctions.* Princeton, 1992.

Autarky One obvious way to avoid becoming dependent on other states, especially for a weak state whose trading partners would tend to be more powerful, is to avoid trading and instead to try to produce everything it needs by itself. Such a strategy is called *self-reliance* or **autarky**. But it has proven ineffective. A self-reliant state pays a very high cost to produce goods for which it does not have a comparative advantage. As other states cooperate among themselves to maximize their joint creation of wealth, the relative power of the autarkic state in the international system tends to fall.

States that have relied on a policy of autarky have indeed lagged behind others. A classic case in recent decades was the small state of Albania in southeast Europe. A communist state that split from both the Soviet Union and China, Albania for decades did not participate in world markets but relied on a centrally planned economy designed for self-sufficiency. Few foreigners could visit, little trade took place, and Albania pursued autarky to prevent outsiders from gaining power over it. When this curtain of isolation finally fell in 1991, Albania was as poor as decades earlier and had missed out on the prosperity that came to the rest of Europe.

BLAST FROM THE PAST

Economic sanctions, such as the U.S. restrictions on trade with Cuba, are among the most obvious ways that politics interferes in markets. But sanctions are hard to enforce, especially when not all countries participate, because doing business is profitable. The U.S. government has had sanctions on Cuba for decades, whereas Canada and Europe trade with Cuba. Here a vintage American car, maintained in running condition since the 1959 revolution, passes a billboard promising "socialism or death," 2006.

China's experience also illustrates the problems with autarky. China's economic isolation in the 1950s and 1960s, resulting from an economic embargo imposed by the United States and its allies, deepened during its Cultural Revolution in the late 1960s when it broke ties with the Soviet Union as well. In that period, China rejected all things foreign. When China opened up to the world economy in the 1980s, the pattern reversed. The rapid expansion of trade, along with some market-oriented reforms in its domestic economy, resulted in rapid economic growth. By contrast, North Korea maintained a policy of self-reliance and isolation even after the Cold War, and experienced mass starvation in the 1990s.

Protectionism

Although few states pursue strategies of autarky, many states try to manipulate international trade to strengthen one or more domestic industries and shelter them from world markets. Such policies are broadly known as **protectionism**—protection of domestic industries from international competition. Although this term encompasses a variety of trade policies arising from various motivations, all are contrary to liberalism in that they seek to distort free markets to gain an advantage for the state (or for substate actors within it), generally by discouraging imports of competing goods or services.[16]

---

[16] Lustzig, Michael. *The Limits of Protectionism: Building Coalitions for Free Trade*. Pittsburgh, 2004. Goldstein, Judith. The Political Economy of Trade: Institutions of Protection. *American Political Science Review* 80 (1), 1986: 161–84.

A state's *motivation* to protect domestic industry can arise from several sources. Often governments simply cater to the political demands of important domestic industries and interests, regardless of the overall national interest. An industry may lobby or give campaign contributions in order to win special tax breaks, subsidies, or restrictions on competing imports (see "Industries and Interest Groups" later in this chapter).

States often attempt to protect an *infant industry* as it starts up in the state for the first time, until it can compete on world markets. For instance, when South Korea first developed an automobile industry, it was not yet competitive with imports, so the government gave consumers incentives to buy Korean cars. Eventually the industry developed and could compete with foreign producers and even export cars profitably. In a number of poor states, the *textile* trade has been a favored infant industry (adding value without heavy capital requirements) that governments have protected.[17] Protection of infant industry is considered a relatively legitimate reason for (temporary) protectionism.

Another motivation for protection is to give a domestic industry breathing room when market conditions shift or new competitors arrive on the scene. Sometimes domestic industry requires time to adapt and can emerge a few years later in a healthy condition. When gas prices jumped in the 1970s, U.S. auto producers were slow to shift to smaller cars, and smaller Japanese cars gained a great advantage in the U.S. market. The U.S. government used a variety of measures, including import quotas and loan guarantees, to help the U.S. industry through this transition. (Yet when gas prices jumped again in 2008, the U.S. producers again were unprepared, and needed government help to stay afloat in 2009.)

Government also protects industries considered vital to national security. In the 1980s, U.S. officials sought to protect the U.S. electronics and computer industries against being driven out of business by Japanese competitors, because those industries were considered crucial to military production. The government sponsored a consortium of U.S. computer chip companies to promote the U.S. capability to produce chips cheaply (ordinarily the government would discourage such a consortium as an antitrust violation). Autarky may not pay in most economic activities, but for military goods, states will sacrifice some economic efficiency for the sake of self-sufficiency, to reduce vulnerability in the event of war.

KING COTTON

Protectionism uses various means to keep foreign imports from competing with domestic products. Agricultural producers in the global South complain that subsidies and other protectionist measures in Europe and the United States prevent poor farmers in developing countries from exporting to world markets. Here, cotton awaits processing in Mali, where low prices for cotton, the country's most important cash crop, have hurt farmers badly (2006).

---

[17] Aggarwal, Vinod K. *Liberal Protectionism: The International Politics of Organized Textile Trade.* California, 1985. English, Beth. *A Common Thread: Labor, Politics, and Capital Mobility in the Textile Industry.* Georgia, 2006.

Finally, protection may be motivated by a defensive effort to ward off predatory practices by foreign companies or states. *Predatory* generally refers to efforts to unfairly capture a large share of world markets, or even a near-monopoly, so that eventually the predator can raise prices without fearing competition. Most often these efforts entail dumping products in foreign markets at prices below the minimum level necessary to make a profit. Within a domestic economy, the government can use antitrust laws to break up an impending monopoly, but because no such mechanism exists in IR, governments try to restrict imports in such situations to protect their state's industries. Such restrictions are recognized as legitimate, although great disagreements exist about whether a given price level is predatory or merely competitive. These conflicts now generally are resolved through the WTO (see pp. 294–298).

Dumping complaints are usually lodged by particular industries that feel they have been harmed by foreign competitors. They must first convince their own governments that they have been unfairly targeted. Then, after their government places tariffs on imports of the good, the foreign government may file a complaint with the WTO. In 2007, the WTO ruled against the United States in a complaint brought by Japanese manufacturers who claimed they had been unfairly accused of dumping industrial goods on the American market. Ironically, rather than denying that Japan had dumped goods on the American market, the WTO criticized how the United States had computed the tariff on Japanese goods, ruling that it was set too high to create a level playing field. The United States was then forced to review how it proceeds with dumping complaints because of the WTO ruling.

Just as there are several motivations for protectionism, so too governments use several tools to implement this policy. The simplest is a **tariff** or *duty*—a tax imposed on certain types of imported goods (usually as a percentage of their value) as they enter the country. Tariffs not only restrict imports but also can be an important source of state revenues. If a state is to engage in protectionism, international norms favor tariffs as the preferred method of protection because they are straightforward and not hidden (see pp. 294–298). Most states maintain a long and complex schedule of tariffs based on thousands of categories and subcategories of goods organized by industry.

Other means to discourage imports are **nontariff barriers** to trade. Imports can be limited by a *quota*. Quotas are ceilings on how many goods of a certain kind can be imported; they are imposed to restrict the growth of such imports. The extreme version is a flat prohibition against importing a certain type of good (or goods from a certain country). The U.S. government used quotas to restrict the number of Japanese-made cars that could enter the United States in the 1980s, when the U.S. automobile industry was losing ground rapidly to Japanese imports. Most of those quotas were *voluntary* in that Japan and the United States negotiated a level that both could live with.

The two nontariff barriers that are the most fought about in the WTO are subsidies and regulation. *Subsidies* are payments by a government to a domestic industry that allow it to lower its prices without losing money. Such subsidies are extensive in, but not limited to, state-owned industries. Subsidies to an industry struggling to get established or facing strong foreign competition include *tax breaks, loans* (or guaranteed private loans) on favorable terms, and high *guaranteed prices* paid by governments. Subsidies to farmers have been the major sticking point between rich and poor countries in the Doha Round trade talks. In 2010, the United States and Brazil settled a WTO case over American subsidies to cotton growers. Prior to the settlement, Brazil was set to begin imposing nearly $830 million in sanctions against the United States.

Subsidies are also a frequent source of U.S.-European conflict, often involving EU policies regarding the Common Agricultural Policy (see p. 360). Subsidies outside the agricultural sector can also be sensitive politically. A European aerospace company that receives EU subsidies now actively bids on American defense department projects. American manufacturers complain that the subsidies given to the EU-based company make it difficult for them to compete since the subsidies allow the European company to place a lower bid. Thus, subsidies have moved from an issue in trade policy to the security area as well.

Imports can also be restricted by *restrictions* and *regulations* that make it hard to distribute and market a product even when it can be imported. In marketing U.S. products in Japan, U.S. manufacturers complain of complex bureaucratic regulations and a tight system of corporate alliances funneling the supply of parts from Japanese suppliers to Japanese manufacturers. Environmental and labor regulations can function as nontariff barriers as well. This has caused great controversy in the WTO (see pp. 294–298), such as when Europe banned genetically modified crops that happened to come mostly from the United States. Finally, when a state nationalizes an entire industry, such as oil production or banking, foreign competition is shut out.

Sometimes a country's culture, rather than state action, discourages imports. Citizens may (with or without government encouragement) follow a philosophy of *economic nationalism*—use of economics to influence international power and relative standing in the international system (a form of mercantilism). For example, U.S. citizens sometimes ignore the advice of liberal economists to buy the best products at the best price, and instead "buy American" even if it means paying more for an equivalent product. Although such a bias reduces the overall efficiency of world production, it does benefit U.S. workers.

Protectionism has both positive and negative effects on an economy, most often helping producers but hurting consumers. For instance, although U.S. automobile manufacturers were aided somewhat by the restrictions imposed on Japanese imports in the 1980s, U.S. automobile consumers paid more for cars as a result (several hundred dollars more per car by some estimates). Another problem with protectionism is that domestic industry may use protection to avoid needed improvements and may therefore remain inefficient and uncompetitive—especially if protection continues over many years.

Still, temporary protectionism can have a stabilizing effect under certain conditions. When U.S. motorcycle manufacturer Harley-Davidson lost half its U.S. market share in just four years, the U.S. government imposed tariffs on imported Japanese motorcycles. The tariffs started at 45 percent in 1983 and were to decline each year for five years and then be eliminated. With the clock running, Harley scrambled to improve efficiency and raise quality. As a result, Harley regained its market share, and the tariffs were lifted a year early. In the late 1980s, a reinvigorated Harley expanded its market share and began exporting to Japan. Protectionism worked in this case because it was short term and straightforward.

Trade Regimes

Watch the **Video** "IMF Conditionality and the Irish Bailout" on **mypoliscilab.com**

As technology links the world across space, a global integration process based on free trade is shaping the international economic agenda. The World Trade Organization plays the central role in this process.

The World Trade Organization

The **World Trade Organization (WTO)** is a global, multilateral IGO that promotes, monitors, and adjudicates international trade. Together with the regional and bilateral arrangements described shortly, the WTO shapes the overall expectations and practices of states regarding international trade.[18] The WTO is the successor organization to the **General Agreement on Tariffs and Trade (GATT)**, which was created in 1947 to facilitate freer trade on a multilateral basis. The GATT was more of a negotiating framework than an administrative institution. It did not actually regulate trade. Before the GATT, proposals for a stronger institutional agency had been rejected because of U.S. fears that overregulation would stifle free trade. The GATT had little institutional infrastructure until the mid-1990s, with just a small secretariat headquartered in Geneva, Switzerland (where the WTO remains). In addition to its main role as a negotiating forum, the GATT helped arbitrate trade disputes, clarifying the rules and helping states observe them.

In 1995, the GATT became the WTO, which incorporated the GATT agreements on manufactured goods and extended the agenda to include trade in services and intellectual property. The WTO has some powers of enforcement and an international bureaucracy (more than 600 people) that monitors trade policies and practices in each member state and adjudicates disputes among members. The WTO wields some power over states, but as with most international institutions, this power is limited. An ongoing public backlash against free trade (see pp. 313–314) reflects uneasiness about the potential power of a foreign and secretive organization to force changes in democratically enacted national laws. But the WTO is the central international institution governing trade and therefore one that almost all countries want to participate in and develop.

Over time, the membership of the WTO has grown. By 2012, 155 countries—including all of the world's major trading states—had joined the WTO. Russia's membership bid succeeded in 2011 after 17 years, when neighboring Georgia agreed not to block it (a consensus of all members is needed). Vietnam joined in 2007, and Ukraine in 2008. More than 25 states are seeking admission, the most important of which are Iran and Iraq. After more than a decade of negotiations, China joined in 2001. The United States and other countries usually demand, as a condition of membership, liberalization of the trading practices of would-be members. These new practices have affected China's economic and political development (see pp. 464–467).

The WTO framework rests on the principle of reciprocity—matching states' lowering of trade barriers to one another. It also uses the concept of nondiscrimination, embodied in the **most-favored nation (MFN)** concept, which says that trade restrictions imposed by a WTO member on its most-favored trading partner must be applied equally to all WTO members. If Australia applies a 20 percent tariff on auto parts imported from France, it must not apply a 40 percent tariff on auto parts imported from the United States. Thus, the WTO does not get rid of barriers to trade altogether but equalizes them in a global framework to create a level playing field for all member states. States are not prevented from protecting their own industries but cannot play favorites among their trading partners. States may also extend MFN status to others that are not WTO members, as the United States did with China before it joined the WTO.

An exception to the MFN system is the **Generalized System of Preferences (GSP)**, dating from the 1970s, by which rich states give trade concessions to poor ones to help their economic development. Preferences amount to a promise by rich states to allow imports from poor ones under lower tariffs than those imposed under MFN.[19]

The WTO continues the GATT's role as a negotiating forum for multilateral trade agreements that lower trade barriers on a fair and reciprocal basis. These detailed and complex agreements specify commitments to lower certain trade barriers by certain

[18] Hoekman, Bernard, and Michel Kostecki. *The Political Economy of the World Trading System: The WTO and Beyond.* 2nd ed. Oxford, 2001.
[19] Ozden, Caglar, and Eric Reinhardt. The Perversity of Preferences: GSP and Developing Country Trade Policies, 1976–2000. *Journal of Development Economics* (78) 1, 2005: 1–21.

amounts on fixed schedules. Almost every commitment entails domestic political costs, because domestic industries lose protection against foreign competition. Even when other states agree to make similar commitments in other areas, lowering trade barriers is often hard for national governments.

As a result, negotiations on these multilateral agreements are long and difficult, typically stretching on for years in a *round of negotiations.* Among the five rounds of GATT negotiations from 1947 to 1995, the Kennedy Round in the 1960s—so called because it started during the Kennedy administration—paid special attention to the growing role of European integration, which the United States found somewhat threatening. The Tokyo Round (begun in Tokyo) in the 1970s had to adjust rules to new conditions of world interdependence when, for instance, OPEC raised oil prices and Japan began to dominate the automobile export business.

The **Uruguay Round** started in 1986 (in Uruguay). Although the rough outlines of a new GATT agreement emerged after a few years, closure eluded five successive G7 summit meetings in 1990–1994. As the round dragged on year after year, participants said the GATT should be renamed the "General Agreement to Talk and Talk." A successful conclusion to the round would add more than $100 billion to the world economy annually. But that money was a collective good, to be enjoyed both by states that made concessions in the final negotiations and by states that did not. Agreement was finally reached in late 1994. The United States had pressured Europe to reduce agricultural subsidies and states in the global South to protect intellectual property rights. In the end, the United States got some, but not all, of what it wanted. For example, France held out adamantly and won the right to protect its film industry against U.S. films.

From 1947, the GATT encouraged states to use import tariffs rather than nontariff barriers to protect industries, and to lower those tariffs over time. The GATT concentrated on manufactured goods and succeeded in substantially reducing the average tariffs, from 40 percent of the goods' value decades ago to 3 percent by 2002 (under the Uruguay Round agreement). Tariff rates in the global South are much higher, around 15 percent (reflecting the greater protection that industry there apparently needs).

Agricultural trade is politically more sensitive than trade in manufactured goods (see p. 138) and came into play only in the Uruguay Round.[20] Trade in services, such as banking and insurance, is another current major focus of the WTO. Such trade approached one-fifth of the total value of world trade in 2007. Trade in telecommunications is a related area of interest. In 1997, 70 states negotiating through the WTO agreed on a treaty to allow telecommunications companies to enter each other's markets.

The problems in expanding into these and other sensitive areas became obvious at a 1999 Seattle WTO conference, where trade ministers had hoped to launch a new, post-Uruguay round of trade negotiations. Representatives of poor countries argued that they needed trade to raise incomes and could not meet the standards of industrialized countries (which, after all, had allowed low wages, harsh working conditions, and environmental destruction when *they* began industrializing). Environmental and labor activists, joined by window-smashing anarchists, staged street protests that delayed the conference opening by a day. The meeting ended in failure.

Recovering from Seattle, in 2001 trade ministers meeting in Doha, Qatar, agreed to launch a new round of trade negotiations, the **Doha Round**. The issues under negotiation

---

[20] Marlin-Bennett, Renee Elizabeth. *Food Fights: International Regimes and the Politics of Agricultural Trade Disputes.* Gordon & Breach, 1993. Anderson, Kym, and Will Martin. *Agricultural Trade Reform and the Doha Development Agenda.* World Bank, 2006. UNCTAD. *Roadblock to Reform: The Persistence of Agricultural Export Subsidies.* United Nations, 2006.

included agriculture, services, industrial products, intellectual property, WTO rules (including how to handle antidumping cases), dispute settlement, and some trade and environmental questions. At the 2003 meeting in Cancun, Mexico, states from the global South walked out after the industrialized countries would not agree to lift their agricultural subsidies, which were shutting out poor countries' agricultural exports. At the 2005 Hong Kong meeting, wealthy states agreed to end the export subsidies, but tough negotiations continued over tariffs on manufactured goods, protection of intellectual property, and opening financial sectors. The main obstacle remains the resistance of the industrialized West to cut agricultural subsidies as demanded by countries in the global South.

In explaining the difficulty in wrapping up a major trade agreement such as the Doha Round, game theorists might look to the game of Chicken (see p. 78) as an explanatory model. In most trade disputes, each state would rather get to a deal, even on terms that somewhat favor the other state if need be. But each would like, if possible, to get a deal on its own terms. Similarly, in a game of Chicken each player wants to avoid a head-on collision,

MAKING MAGIC

Rounds of trade negotiations, such as the current Doha Round begun in 2001, last for years as members negotiate complex deals that must be approved by consensus of all 150 member states. A conference of trade ministers in December 2005 tried to regain momentum for the stalled Doha Round, with mixed success. Here, WTO head Pascal Lamy opens the conference with the tool he hopes will bring success—a magic wand. The talks remained stalled in early 2012.

and being a hero or a chicken is a secondary consideration. In trade negotiations, both states hold out for their own terms (not swerving) for as long as possible, then come to agreement only when faced with an imminent collision—the expiration of a deadline beyond which there will be no deal at all. In Chicken, there is no incentive to give ground before the last minute.

The Doha Round of WTO negotiations stretched from 2001 to 2012 without conclusion. In 2007, participants tried to use a key deadline—expiration of the U.S. Congress's fast-track authorization, after which U.S. approval of a new WTO agreement would become difficult—to inspire a final agreement. After that deadline passed, other deadlines came and went as well. For instance, before the November 2008 summit in Washington, D.C., that grappled with a growing financial crisis, some leaders suggested just wrapping up the Doha Round over that weekend, before the change in U.S. administrations. As each such deadline passed, it became harder to believe that the next deadline was real, that the head-on collision loomed if states did not "swerve" in time. The Chicken game may help us understand such dynamics. One drawback of the model, however, is that it does not predict the outcomes, because the game is inherently unstable. What it does predict is that an agreement, if reached, will arrive suddenly, ahead of a credible deadline, and that a disastrous failure will come as an unpleasant surprise to participants ("why didn't he swerve?").

In general, states continue to participate in the WTO because the benefits, in terms of global wealth creation, outweigh the costs, in terms of harm to domestic industries and painful adjustments in national economies. States try to change the rules in their favor during negotiations and between rounds they may evade the rules in minor ways. But the overall benefits are too great to jeopardize by nonparticipation or frequent trade wars.

Bilateral and Regional Agreements

Although the WTO provides an overall framework for multilateral trade in a worldwide market, most international trade also takes place under more specific international political agreements—bilateral trade agreements and regional free trade areas.

Bilateral Agreements   Bilateral treaties covering trade are reciprocal arrangements to lower barriers to trade between two states. Usually they are very specific. For instance, one country may reduce its prohibition on imports of product X (which the second country exports at competitive prices) while the second country lowers its tariff on product Y (which the first country exports). A sweeping agreement, such as that between Canada and India in 2007, generally contains mind-numbing levels of detail concerning specific industries and products. As with most agreements based on the reciprocity principle, trade treaties involve great complexity and constant monitoring. U.S. free trade deals with South Korea, Panama, and Colombia took effect in 2011.

Part of the idea behind the GATT/WTO was to strip away the maze of bilateral agreements on trade and simplify the system of tariffs and preferences. This effort has only partially succeeded, however, as bilateral trade agreements continue to play an important

SEEKING THE COLLECTIVE GOOD

Freer Trade
COLLECTIVE GOOD: A Doha Round WTO Agreement

BACKGROUND: Over the decades the world has substantially lowered trade barriers and enjoyed rising prosperity as a result of trade. Negotiating through the World Trade Organization (WTO), countries have concluded successive "rounds" of trade agreements, in which each state reciprocates the concessions of other states. These negotiations require every single member—almost all the world's major trading powers—to agree before any can enjoy the benefits of an agreement.

A new WTO agreement is a collective good because all the member states profit from relaxing trade restrictions regardless of which of them made the concessions needed to reach a deal. For example, in the previous Uruguay Round, the entire deal was held up while France and the United States fought

about French restrictions on U.S. films. Whether France or the United States hung tough to win on this issue, both would benefit overall from the deal. But if both hung tough, the entire deal would break down and the collective good would not be provided. (In the end, France was able to free-ride, and the trade deal went forward.)

CHALLENGE: The current Doha Round has been stalled for several years. Countries want the overall freer trade that an agreement would bring—worth many billions of dollars to the world— but are fighting about agricultural subsidies and other issues. The talks have broken down and been resurrected several times. Until the participants find

RECIPROCITY

role. They have the advantages of reducing the collective goods problem inherent in multilateral negotiations and facilitating reciprocity as a means to achieve cooperation.[21] When WTO negotiations bog down, bilateral agreements can keep trade momentum going. Because most states do most of their trading with a few partners, a few bilateral agreements can go a long way in structuring a state's trade relations. The number of bilateral agreements has grown substantially in the past decade and their numbers far overwhelm all other types of agreements combined.

Free Trade Areas   Regional free trade areas also matter in the structure of world trade. In such areas, groups of neighboring states agree to remove most or all trade barriers within their area. Beyond free trade areas, states may reduce trade barriers *and* adopt a common tariff toward states that are not members of the agreement. This is known as a *customs union*. If members of a customs union decide to coordinate other policies such as monetary exchange, the customs union becomes a *common market*. The creation of a regional trade agreement (of any type) allows a group of states to cooperate in increasing their wealth without waiting for the rest of the world.

The most important free trade area is in Europe; it is connected with the European Union but has a somewhat larger membership. Because Europe contains a number of small industrialized states living close together, the creation of a single integrated market

[21] Oye, Kenneth A. *Economic Discrimination and Political Exchange: World Political Economy in the 1930s and 1980s.* Princeton, 1992.

agreement on these pesky remaining issues, nobody can enjoy the economic boost that a new WTO agreement will bring.

SOLUTION: Only reciprocity can solve this dilemma. No feel-good shared identity can compete with the dollars in the pockets of participating states and their constituents (industries, citizens, etc.). And the entire structure of world trade relies on the formal equality of all participants, so dominance does not play a major role. Certainly military force cannot resolve trade disputes as it might have done centuries ago.

Consistent with reciprocity solutions generally, trade agreements have great complexity, fine-level detail, and considerable effort to monitor compliance. When an

WTO trade ministers from 153 countries meet in Geneva, 2009.

agreement finally emerges from the Doha Round, it will result from breaking the disagreements into many tiny pieces and finding reciprocal compromises—everyone giving some ground—on each one.

allows these states to gain the economic advantages that come inherently to a large state such as the United States. The European free trade experiment has been a great success overall, contributing to Europe's accumulation of wealth since World War II (see Chapter 10).

The United States, Canada, and Mexico signed the **North American Free Trade Agreement (NAFTA)** in 1994, following a U.S.-Canadian free trade agreement in 1988.[22] In NAFTA's first decade, U.S. imports from both Mexico and Canada more than doubled, then fell back somewhat (after 1999). Canada and Mexico were the largest and third-largest U.S. trading partners, respectively (Japan was second). Initially, Mexico's currency dropped drastically relative to the dollar in 1994–1995. U.S. opponents of NAFTA, including various U.S. labor unions, criticized the low wages and poor labor laws in Mexico, which they feared would drag down U.S. labor standards. Environmentalists similarly criticized Mexico's lax environmental laws (relative to those of the United States) and saw NAFTA as giving U.S. corporations license to pollute by moving south of the border (see p. 305). But over 15 years, neither the great benefits predicted by NAFTA supporters nor the disasters predicted by opponents materialized.

Politicians in North and South America have long spoken of creating a single free trade area in the Western Hemisphere, from Alaska to Argentina—the *Free Trade Area of the Americas (FTAA)*. To empower him to do so, President Clinton asked Congress in 1997 to reinstate fast-track legislation. But Democrats in Congress defeated the measure, demanding that free trade agreements include requirements for labor and environmental standards for other countries—points on which they found NAFTA's record wanting. President Bush had more success winning fast-track authority from Congress, and FTAA negotiations began in 2003 with a target date of 2005. But by then several factors had created pressures against the FTAA. The 2001 recession and post–September 11 security measures reduced trade; China provided U.S. companies with a better source of cheap labor; and left-leaning governments, wary of liberal economic advice, came to power in most of the Latin American countries. Those countries cared most about tariff-free trade, while the U.S. position emphasized a range of other issues such as services, intellectual property, and financial openness. In late 2005, trade talks failed at a summit meeting in Argentina, where one participant, Venezuelan president Hugo Chavez, led a 25,000-person anti-American rally in the streets. Currently, the FTAA talks remain in hibernation, and the weight of trade negotiations fall to the Doha Round. Meanwhile, however, the United States reached free trade agreements with several Latin American countries.

Efforts to create a free trade area in Asia began in the late 1980s but moved slowly. Unlike the European and North American arrangements, an Asian bloc would include very different kinds of states—rich ones such as Japan; poor ones such as the Philippines; and democracies, dictatorships, and communist states. It is unclear how well such diverse states could coordinate their common interests, especially because their existing trade patterns are not focused on each other but spread out among other states including the United States (again in contrast to trade patterns existing before the creation of the European and North American free trade areas).

But despite these problems, in 2007 the ten ASEAN countries met with China, Japan, India, Australia, and New Zealand to begin negotiating an East Asian free trade area. The group, unlike some other Asia-Pacific IGOs, does not include the United States, but it does include half the world's population and some of its most dynamic economies. The

---

[22] Hakim, Peter, and Robert E. Litan, eds. *The Future of North American Integration: Beyond NAFTA.* Brookings, 2002. Andreas, Peter, and Thomas J. Biersteker, eds. *The Rebordering of North America: Integration and Exclusion in a New Security Conflict.* Routledge, 2003.

POLICY PERSPECTIVES

President of Brazil, Dilma Rousseff

PROBLEM *How do you balance the demands of key trading partners with domestic economic needs?*

BACKGROUND Imagine that you are the president of Brazil. You were recently elected and are expected to continue the policies of your predecessor. Brazil is now the tenth-largest economy in the world and in 2010, growth was around 5 percent, up from −0.5 percent in 2003. Your country's export-led growth strategy is an important piece of this economic picture. Exports to industrialized countries are at an all-time high, and in 2005 you ran a current account surplus for the first time since 1992.

The United States, Argentina, China, the Netherlands, and Germany are your key export partners. The United States alone accounts for 11 percent of your exports and about 16 percent of your imports. EU states combine to account for more than 23 percent of your exports, but far less of your imports.

You have been pressured extensively by the United States to join a Free Trade Area of the Americas (FTAA), but have refused to do so. Your goal for the FTAA is that developed countries lower their agricultural subsidies and increase their quotas for Brazilian farm products. To date, America has largely turned down your demands in the agricultural realm. Given U.S. bargaining power, this may be a difficult concession to extract in future negotiations.

DOMESTIC CONSIDERATIONS Domestically, you are being pressured to ensure continued market access for your industrial and agricultural products in international markets. Luckily, trade relations with your neighbors are relatively good. You are the largest state in the Southern Cone Common Market (Mercosur). You recently pushed to bring several other Latin American states (such as Mexico and Peru) into Mercosur as associate members to hedge your bets against a collapse in the FTAA negotiations.

Unfortunately, you cannot rely on your Mercosur partners alone to absorb your export production. For example, your three full partners in Mercosur (Argentina, Paraguay, and Uruguay) have a combined total GDP smaller than Canada's.

SCENARIO Now imagine that the EU offers a free trade agreement with better terms (especially concerning agricultural goods) than a potential FTAA agreement. Because several EU states are key trading partners, this is an attractive offer. In order for your exports to continue to grow, your market opportunities must expand. This would provide such an opportunity while satisfying those export-oriented industries.

But accepting the EU offer would likely anger the United States. If the United States then completed an FTAA without you, this would be costly to your economy because any similar goods produced by your neighbors would have preferential access to U.S. markets, making them more attractive than Brazilian goods to U.S. businesses and consumers.

CHOOSE YOUR POLICY Do you accept the EU offer? Do you attempt to bargain more with the United States in hopes of achieving a breakthrough? How do you balance the demands of competing (and important) trade partners while trying to achieve the best outcome for your public?

negotiations between ASEAN states and China were successful, and in 2010, a free trade area went into effect between these countries. The ASEAN-China FTA is the world's third-largest free trade area, after the EU and NAFTA.

During the Cold War, the Soviet bloc maintained its own trading bloc. After the Soviet Union collapsed, the members scrambled to join up with the world economy, from which they had been largely cut off. The Commonwealth of Independent States (CIS), formed by 12 former Soviet republics, remains economically integrated (although Georgia quit after its 2008 war with Russia). It was previously a free trade zone by virtue of being part of a single state with integrated transportation, communication, and other infrastructure links.

Other efforts to create free trade areas have had mixed results. The Southern Cone Common Market (Mercosur) began in the early 1990s with Brazil, Argentina, Uruguay, and Paraguay. Venezuela joined later. Chile, Bolivia, Colombia, Ecuador, and Peru have joined as associate members. Still, Mercosur members trade more with the United States than they do with each other. In 2002, the countries agreed to allow their 250 million citizens free movement and residency across countries. A Caribbean common market (CARICOM) was created in 1973, but the area is neither large nor rich enough to make regional free trade a very important accelerator of economic growth. Eleven countries created a Latin American Free Trade Association (LAFTA) in 1960 (changed in 1980 to the Latin American Integration Association), but the effort was held back by the different levels of poverty and wealth among the members and their existing patterns of trade. Colombia, Ecuador, Peru, and Bolivia created the Andean Common Market in 1969; it had modest successes but not dramatic results, because trade within the bloc was not important enough. (Venezuela joined in 1973 but left in 2006 to join Mercosur, while Chile left in 1976 but plans to rejoin.)

If regional free trade areas such as now exist in Europe and in North America gain strength and new ones arise, the WTO may be weakened. The more that states meet the political requirements of economic growth through bilateral and regional agreements, the less they may depend on the worldwide agreements developed through the WTO. Furthermore, the overlap of WTO rules and regional agreements can create confusion.[23] For example, in 2006 a WTO panel upheld U.S. duties on Canadian softwood lumber while a NAFTA panel overturned the duties and ordered refunds to Canada. (On appeal, the WTO reversed its ruling and the two countries promptly signed a new agreement, with the United States refunding more than $4 billion.) Ultimately, regional agreements might divide the world into three competing trading blocs, each internally integrated but not very open to the other two blocs. Regional free trade areas in Europe and North America, and perhaps in Asia in the future, raise the possibility of trading zones practicing liberalism inwardly and mercantilism outwardly.

Cartels

A **cartel** is an association of producers or consumers, or both, of a certain product—formed to manipulate its price on the world market. It is an unusual but interesting form of trade regime. Most often producers and not consumers form cartels, because there are usually fewer producers than consumers, and it seems possible for them to coordinate to keep prices high. Cartels can use a variety of means to affect prices; the most effective is to coordinate limits on production by each member so as to lower the supply, relative to demand, of the good.

---

[23] Davis, Christina. Overlapping Institutions in Trade Politics. *Perspectives on Politics* 7 (1), 2009: 25–31.

The most prominent cartel in the international economy is the **Organization of Petroleum Exporting Countries (OPEC)**. Its member states together control hundreds of billions of dollars in oil exports annually—about 40 percent of the world total and enough to significantly affect the price. (A cartel need not hold a monopoly on production of a good to affect its price.) At OPEC's peak of strength in the 1970s, the proportion was even higher. OPEC maintains a headquarters in Vienna, Austria, and holds negotiations several times a year to set quotas for each country's production of oil in order to keep world oil prices in a target range. Saudi Arabia is by far the largest oil exporter and therefore occupies a unique position in the world economy (see Table 8.1).

OPEC illustrates the potential that a cartel creates for collective goods problems. Individual members of OPEC can cheat by exceeding their production quotas while still enjoying the collective good of high oil prices. The collective good breaks down when too many members exceed their quotas, as has happened repeatedly to OPEC. Then world oil prices drop. (Iraq's accusations that fellow OPEC member Kuwait was exceeding production quotas and driving oil prices down was one factor in Iraq's invasion of Kuwait in 1990.)

OPEC may work as well as it does only because one member, Saudi Arabia, has enough oil to unilaterally manipulate supply enough to drive prices up or down—a form of hegemonic stability (see p. 59) within the cartel. Saudi Arabia can take up the slack from some cheating in OPEC (cutting back its own production) and keep prices up. Or if too many OPEC members are cheating on their quotas, it can punish them by flooding the market with oil and driving prices down until the other OPEC members collectively come to their senses.

TABLE 8.1 OPEC Members and Oil Production, 2011

Member State	Millions of Barrels/Day
Saudi Arabia	8.2
Iran	3.5
Venezuela	2.8
Iraq	2.4
Kuwait	2.4
United Arab Emirates	2.3
Nigeria	2.0
Angola	1.7
Libya	1.5
Algeria	1.1
Qatar	0.7
Ecuador[a]	0.5
Total OPEC	29.2
Percent of World	40%

[a]Ecuador re-joined OPEC in 2007 after suspending its membership in 1992.

Note: Major oil exporters not in OPEC include Russia, Kazakhstan, Mexico, China, Britain, and Norway. Gabon left OPEC in 1995 and indonesia left OPEC in 2008. The United States, until several decades ago a major oil exporter, is now a major importer.

Source: Data adapted from: http://www.platts.com/NewsFeature/2010/opec/prod_table.

Consumers usually do not form cartels. However, in response to OPEC, the major oil-importing states formed their own organization, the *International Energy Agency (IEA)*, which partly functions as a cartel. The IEA coordinates the energy policies of major industrialized states—such as the maintenance of oil stockpiles in case of a shortage on world markets—in order to keep world oil prices low and stable. The largest importers of oil are the members of the G8 (large industrialized states). Considering the importance of oil to the world economy, and the existence of both producer and consumer cartels, the price of oil has been surprisingly unstable, with prices fluctuating from about $20 per barrel in 1998 to over $140 and back to $40 in 2008. This shows the limits of cartels in affecting prices.

For a few commodities that are subject to large price fluctuations on world markets—detrimental to both producers and consumers—joint producer-consumer cartels have been formed. In order to keep prices stable, producing and consuming states use the cartel to coordinate the overall supply and demand globally. Such cartels exist for coffee, several minerals, and some other products. NGOs introduced Fair Trade Certified coffee, and later chocolate and other products, guaranteeing farmers a price above their production costs through the price booms and busts. More than a million farmers in 70 countries benefit from these arrangements.

In general, the idea of cartels runs counter to liberal economics because cartels deliberately distort free markets. Cartels usually are not as powerful as market forces in determining overall world price levels: too many producers and suppliers exist—and too many substitute goods can replace ones that become too expensive—for a cartel to corner the market.

Industries and Interest Groups

Industries and other domestic political actors often seek to influence a state's foreign economic policies (see "Interest Groups," pp. 138–139).[24] These pressures do not always favor protectionism. Industries that are advanced and competitive in world markets try to influence their governments to adopt free trade policies. This strategy promotes a global free trade system in which such industries can prosper. By contrast, industries that lag behind their global competitors tend to seek protection.

Means to influence foreign economic policy include lobbying, forming interest groups, paying bribes, and even encouraging coups. Actors include industry-sponsored groups, companies, labor unions, and individuals. Within an industry, such efforts usually work in a common direction because, despite competition among companies and between management and labor, all share common interests regarding the trade policies. However, a different industry may be pushing in a different direction. For instance, some U.S. industries supported the North American Free Trade Agreement (NAFTA); others opposed it.

In many countries, government not only responds to industry influence, but works actively with industries to promote their growth and tailor trade policy to their needs. Such industrial policy is especially common in states where one or two industries are crucial to the entire economy (and of course where states own industries directly).[25]

[24] Rothgeb, John M., Jr. *U.S. Trade Policy: Balancing Economic Dreams and Political Realities*. CQ Press, 2001. Hiscox, Michael. *International Trade and Political Conflict: Commerce, Coalitions, and Mobility*. Princeton, 2001.
[25] Busch, Marc L. *Trade Warriors: States, Firms, and Strategic Policy in High Technology Competition*. Cambridge, 1999. Hart, Jeffrey A. *Technology, Television, and Competition: The Politics of Digital TV*. Cambridge, 2004. McGillivray, Fiona. *Privileging Industry: The Comparative Politics of Trade and Industrial Policy*. Princeton, 2004.

Interest groups not organized along industry lines also have particular interests in state trade policies. U.S. environmentalists, for example, do not want U.S. companies to use NAFTA to avoid pollution controls by relocating to Mexico (where environmental laws are less strict). U.S. labor unions do not want companies to use NAFTA to avoid paying high wages. However, Mexican American citizens' groups in the United States tend to support NAFTA because it strengthens ties to relatives in Mexico.

Several industries are particularly important in trade negotiations currently. Atop the list is the agricultural sector. Traditionally, agriculture has been protected since self-sufficiency in food reduces national vulnerability (especially in time of war). Although such security concerns have now faded somewhat, farmers are well-organized and powerful domestic political actors in Europe, the United States, Japan, and other countries. For instance, Japanese farmers argue that Japan's rice-centered culture demands self-sufficiency in rice production. In the Doha Round of WTO negotiations, agricultural subsidies were a

COMPETING WITH BIG CORN

Agriculture is at the top of the agenda of international trade negotiations, as developing countries push richer ones to end farm subsidies. Here, Mexican farmers protest the full opening of Mexico's markets to imported U.S. corn under NAFTA, 2008.

key sticking point. The talks collapsed in 2003 in Cancun, Mexico, over the subsidies, but were revived the next year by U.S. promises to cut farm subsidies 20 percent. At the 2005 Hong Kong talks, wealthy countries agreed to end all farm export subsidies by 2013.

A second important focus in recent years has been the textile and garment sector. As of 2005, textile quotas worldwide were dropped as a part of previously negotiated WTO deals. At the same time, China began dominating world clothing exports, with whole cities specializing in one type of garment produced for mass export to giant retailers.[26] With vast pools of cheap and disciplined labor, China threatened to drive U.S. textile and clothing producers out of business and give stiff new competition to exporters such as Pakistan and Bangladesh, where textiles make up 70 percent of exports. Later in 2005, the European Union and the United States each reached bilateral agreements with China to reimpose textile quotas for a few years. Now, countries such as Vietnam have begun to take textile business away from China by providing even lower production costs.

Intellectual property rights are a third contentious area of trade negotiations. Intellectual property rights are the rights of creators of books, films, computer software, and similar products to receive royalties when their products are sold. The United States has a major conflict with some states over piracy of computer software, music, films, and other creative works—products in which the United States has a strong comparative advantage globally. It is technically easy and cheap to copy such works and sell them in violation of

[26] Barboza, David. In Roaring China, Sweaters Are West of Socks City. *The New York Times*, December 24, 2004: A1.

J'ACCUSE!

Intellectual property rights have been an important focus of recent trade negotiations. In many countries, pirated copies of videos, music, and software sell on the street with no royalty payments. Here, the U.S. Trade Representative holds a pirated DVD from China as she filed a copyright complaint against China in the World Trade Organization, 2007.

the copyright, patent, or trademark. Because U.S. laws cannot be enforced in foreign countries, the U.S. government wants foreign governments to prevent and punish such violations. Countries that reportedly pirate large amounts of computer software and music and entertainment products include China, Taiwan, India, Thailand, Brazil, and the former Soviet republics. The Russian government estimated in 2002 that more than 80 percent of films sold in Russia on video and DVD were produced illegally. The worldwide piracy rate was estimated at 40 percent in 2001. Infringement of intellectual property rights is widespread in many third world countries, on products such as DVDs and prescription drugs.

In response, the international community has developed an extensive IGO with 184 member states, the World Intellectual Property Organization (WIPO), which tries to regularize patent and copyright law across borders. Most states have signed an important 1994 patent treaty and a 1996 copyright treaty. The WTO oversees the world's most important multilateral agreement on intellectual property, called TRIPS (Trade-Related aspects of Intellectual Property Rights). Most industrialized countries prefer to use TRIPS rules because these rules are stronger than WIPO safeguards and can be relaxed only if all WTO members agree. WIPO rules require only a majority vote to change.

The 2001 WTO meeting at Doha led to a declaration that states could exempt certain drugs from TRIPS rules to deal with serious domestic health crises, such as an HIV/AIDS epidemic. (The U.S. government supported this move after it had threatened to take over production of a powerful antibiotic drug, Cipro, during the post-9/11 anthrax scare.) Although procedures were established for these exceptions, only a few developing countries have used them. For several years these disputes slowed the effective distribution of medicines to millions of Africans with AIDS, though progress picked up after 2004.

Companies trying to protect intellectual property in an international context cannot rely on the same enforcement of rules as in domestic contexts. Instead, they need to bring their own state's government to bear, as well as use their own resources. Because of state sovereignty in legal matters, private international economic conflicts easily become government-to-government issues.[27]

---

[27] Marlin-Bennett, Renée. *Knowledge Power: Intellectual Property, Information, and Privacy.* Rienner, 2004.

A fourth key trade issue is the openness of countries to trade in the service sector of the economy. This sector includes many services, especially those concerning information, but the key focus in international trade negotiations is on banking, insurance, and related financial services. U.S. companies, and some in Asia, enjoy a comparative advantage in these areas because of their information-processing technologies and experience in financial management. In general, as telecommunications becomes cheaper and more pervasive, services offered by companies in one country can be efficiently used by consumers in other countries. U.S. consumers phoning customer service at U.S. companies and connecting to India or another English-speaking developing country engage in a long-distance trade in services.

Another especially important industry in international trade is the arms trade, which operates largely outside the framework of normal commercial transactions because of its national security implications. Governments in industrialized countries want to protect their domestic arms industries rather than rely on imports to meet their weapons needs. And those domestic arms industries become stronger and more economically viable by exporting their products (as well as supplying their own governments). Governments usually participate actively in the military-industrial sector of the economy, even in countries such as the United States that lack industrial policy in other economic sectors. For example, fighter jets are a product in which the United States enjoys a global comparative advantage. In the 1990s, the U.S. arms industry, like the tobacco industry, looked overseas for new customers to offset declining demand at home. The Middle East has been the leading arms-importing region of the global South, with India and China increasing recently.

A different problem is presented by the "industry" of illicit trade, or *smuggling*. No matter what restrictions governments put on trading certain goods, someone is usually willing to risk punishment to make a profit in such trade. Illegal goods, and legal goods imported illegally, often are sold in black markets—unofficial, sometimes secret markets. This deprives governments of significant revenue. Black markets also exist for foreign currency exchange (see Chapter 9).

The extent of illicit trade varies from one country and industry to another, depending on profitability and enforcement. Drugs and weapons are most profitable, and worldwide illegal trade networks exist for both. International black markets for weapons trade, beyond government controls, are notorious. A state with enough money can buy—although at premium prices—most kinds of weapons.

Enforcement of Trade Rules

As with international law generally, economic agreements among states depend strongly on the reciprocity principle for enforcement (see pp. 5–6, 225). If one state protects its industries, or puts tariffs on the goods of other states, or violates the copyright on works produced in other countries, the main resort that other states have is to apply similar measures against the offending state. The use of reciprocity to enforce equal terms of exchange is especially important in international trade, in which states often negotiate complex agreements—commodity by commodity, industry by industry—based on reciprocity.[28] Trade disputes and retaliatory measures are common. States keep close track of the exact terms of trade. Large bureaucracies monitor international economic transactions (prices relative to world market levels, tariffs, etc.) and develop detailed policies to reciprocate any other state's deviations from cooperation.

---

[28] Bayard, Thomas O., Kimberly Ann Elliott, Amelia Porges, and Charles Iceland. *Reciprocity and Retaliation in U.S. Trade Policy*. Institute for International Economics, 1994. Bhagwati, Jagdish, ed. *Going Alone: The Case for Relaxed Reciprocity in Freeing Trade*. MIT, 2002.

Enforcement of equal terms of trade is complicated by differing interpretations of what is "fair." States generally decide which practices of other states they consider unfair (often prodded by affected domestic industries) and then take (or threaten) retaliatory actions to punish those practices. A U.S. law, the Super 301 provision, mandates retaliation against states that restrict access of U.S. goods to their markets. However, if the other state does not agree that its practices are unfair, the retaliatory actions may themselves seem unfair and call for retaliation. One disadvantage of reciprocity is that it can lead to a downward spiral of noncooperation, popularly called a trade war (the economic equivalent of an arms race; see p. 75). To prevent this, states often negotiate agreements regarding what practices they consider unfair. In some cases, third-party arbitration can also be used to resolve trade disputes. Currently, the World Trade Organization (see pp. 294–298) hears complaints and sets levels of acceptable retaliation. In addition, some regional trade agreements establish mechanisms to hear and resolve complaints as well.

Retaliation for unfair trade practices usually tries to match the violation in type and extent. Under WTO rules, a state may impose retaliatory tariffs equivalent to the losses caused by another state's unfair trade practices (as determined by WTO hearings). In 2001, the European Union threatened the United States with sanctions on an unprecedented $4 billion of goods in response to U.S. tax credits to exporters such as Microsoft and Boeing (which the WTO had ruled unfair). Usually, at the last minute, negotiators agree to avert large-scale retaliatory sanctions or trade wars, but in 2004 Europe imposed the retaliatory tariffs, and lifted them in January 2005, only after the U.S. Congress repealed the tax breaks.

In cases of dumping, retaliation aims to offset the advantage enjoyed from goods imported at prices below the world market. Retaliatory tariffs raise the price back to market levels. In 2001, the weakened U.S. steel industry pleaded for U.S. government protection from cheap foreign steel, under an antidumping rationale. The Bush administration, although usually favoring free trade, agreed to offer relief (scoring points with labor unions and swing voters in Pennsylvania and West Virginia).

Before such tariffs are imposed, a U.S. government agency, the International Trade Commission (ITC), decides whether the low-priced imports have actually hurt the U.S. industry.[29] The ITC ruled that U.S. steelmakers had indeed been hurt, and suggested tariffs of 5 to 40 percent. President Bush imposed 30 percent tariffs in 2002, and other countries challenged them in the WTO, which ruled against the United States in 2003. The WTO also gave other countries the right to impose $2 billion in retaliatory tariffs against the United States. As Europeans drew up their list of tariffs, targeting maximum damage to swing electoral states in 2004, President Bush backed down and abolished the steel tariffs (declaring them successful and no longer needed). By making the cost of tariffs higher than the benefits, the WTO effectively changed U.S. policy—an indication of the WTO's growing power.[30] This example also shows how closely international trade connects with domestic politics.

Trade cooperation is easier to achieve under hegemony (see "Hegemony" on pp. 57–60). The efficient operation of markets depends on a stable political framework such as hegemony can provide. Political power can protect economic exchange from the distorting influences of violent leverage, of unfair or fraudulent trade practices, and of uncertainties of international currency rates. A hegemon can provide a world currency in which value can be universally calculated. It can punish the use of violence and can enforce

[29] Hansen, Wendy L. The International Trade Commission and the Politics of Protectionism. *American Political Science Review* 84 (1), 1990: 21–46.

[30] Sanger, David E. A Blink from the Bush Administration: Backing Down on Tariffs, U.S. Strengthens Trade Organization. *The New York Times*, December 5, 2003: A25.

norms of fair trade. Because its economy is so large and dominating, the hegemon can threaten to break off trade ties even without resorting to military force. For example, to be denied access to U.S. markets today would seriously hurt export industries in many states. U.S. hegemony thus helped create the major norms and institutions of international trade in the post–1945 era. Now that U.S. hegemony seems to be giving way to a more multipolar world—especially in economic affairs among the great powers—institutions are even more important for the success of the world trading system.

States have found it worthwhile to expand trade steadily, using a variety of regimes and institutions to do so—the WTO, free trade areas, bilateral agreements, and cartels. Overall, despite some loss of state sovereignty as a result of growing interdependence, these efforts have benefited participating states. Stable political rules governing trade allow states to realize the great economic gains that can result from international exchange.

Economic Globalization

We introduced the process of *globalization* in Chapter 1 (see pp. 19–21) in general terms, and will now consider some specifically economic aspects of globalization. The expansion of trade is a central aspect of globalization in the international political economy, but hardly the only one. Globalization is transforming not only trade but money, business, integration, communication, environmental management, and the economic development of poor countries—the subjects of the remaining chapters of this book. Today's accelerating pace of economic activity grows out of a long history of world economic expansion, which serves as the foundation for globalization.[31]

Watch the **Video** "**Anti-Globalization Protests**" on **mypoliscilab.com**

The Evolving World Economy

In 1750, Britain, the world's most advanced economy, had a GDP of about $1,200 per capita (in today's dollars). That is less than the present level of most of the global South. However, today Britain produces more than ten times that much per person (and with a much larger population than in 1750). This accomplishment is due to **industrialization**— the use of energy to drive machinery and the accumulation of such machinery along with the products created by it. The Industrial Revolution started in Britain in the 18th century, underpinned Britain's emerging leadership role in the world economy, and spread to the other advanced economies (see Figure 8.4).[32]

By around 1850, the wooden sailing ships of earlier centuries had given way to larger and faster coal-powered iron steamships. Coal-fueled steam engines also drove factories producing textiles and other commodities. The great age of railroad building was taking off. These developments not only increased the volume of world production and trade, but also tied distant locations more closely together economically. The day trip across France by railroad contrasted with the same route a hundred years earlier, which took three weeks to complete. In this period of mechanization, however, factory conditions were extremely harsh, especially for women and children operating machines.

---

[31] Rosencrance, Richard. *The Rise of the Virtual State: Wealth and Power in the Coming Century*. Basic, 2000.
[32] North, Douglass C., and Robert Paul Thomas. *The Rise of the Western World: A New Economic History*. Cambridge, 1973. Hobsbawm, E. J. *Industry and Empire: From 1750 to the Present Day*. Penguin-Pelican, 1969. Tracy, James D., ed. *The Political Economy of Merchant Empires: State Power and World Trade, 1350–1750*. Cambridge, 1991.

FIGURE 8.4 The World Economy, 1750–2000

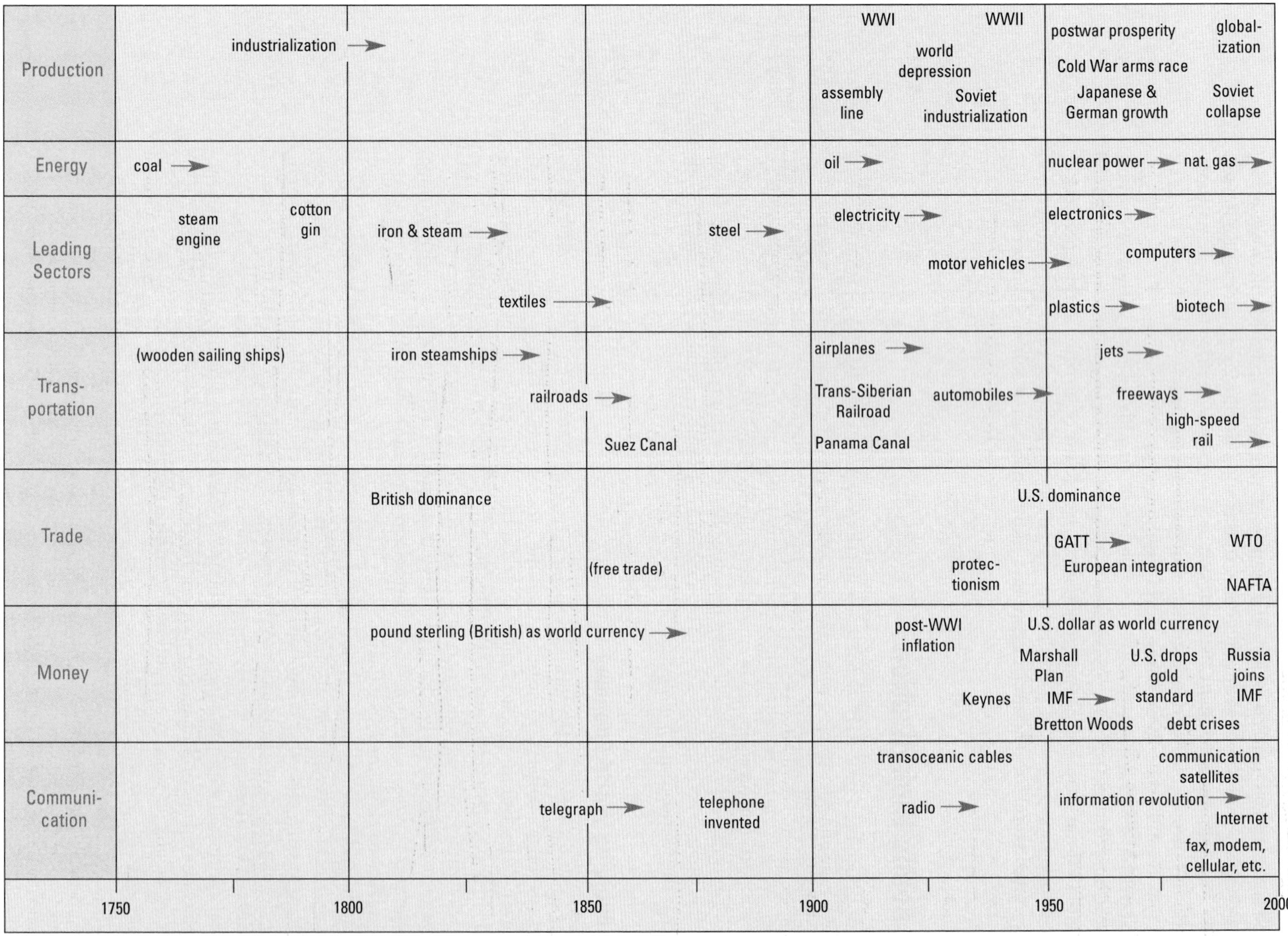

Timeline: 1750 — 1800 — 1850 — 1900 — 1950 — 2000

Category	Entries (positioned along timeline)
Production	industrialization → (c. 1800); WWI; world depression; Soviet industrialization; WWII; postwar prosperity; Cold War arms race; Japanese & German growth; globalization; Soviet collapse
Energy	coal → ; oil → ; nuclear power → ; nat gas →
Leading Sectors	steam engine; cotton gin; iron & steam → ; textiles → ; steel → ; electricity → ; motor vehicles → ; electronics → ; computers → ; plastics → ; biotech →
Transportation	(wooden sailing ships); iron steamships → ; railroads → ; Suez Canal; airplanes → ; Trans-Siberian Railroad; Panama Canal; automobiles → ; jets → ; freeways → ; high-speed rail →
Trade	British dominance; (free trade) → ; protectionism → ; U.S. dominance; GATT → ; European integration → ; WTO; NAFTA
Money	pound sterling (British) as world currency → ; post-WWI inflation → ; Bretton Woods; IMF; Keynes; Marshall Plan; U.S. dollar as world currency → ; U.S. drops gold standard; debt crises; Russia joins IMF
Communication	telegraph → ; telephone invented; transoceanic cables → ; radio → ; communication satellites; information revolution → ; Internet; fax, modem, cellular, etc.

Britain dominated world trade in this period. Because Britain's economy was the most technologically advanced in the world, its products were competitive worldwide. Thus British policy favored free trade. In addition to its central role in world trade, Britain served as the financial capital of the world, managing an increasingly complex world market in goods and services in the 19th century. The British currency, pounds sterling (silver), became the world standard. International monetary relations were still based on the value of precious metals, as they had been in the 16th century when Spain bought its armies with Mexican silver and gold.

By the outset of the 20th century, however, the world's largest and most advanced economy was no longer Britain but the United States. The industrialization of the U.S. economy was fueled by territorial expansion throughout the 19th century, adding vast natural resources. The U.S. economy attracted huge pools of immigrant labor from Europe as well. The United States led the world in converting from coal to oil and from horse-drawn transportation to motor vehicles. New technical innovations, from electricity to airplanes, also helped push the U.S. economy into a dominant world position.

In the 1930s, the U.S. and world economies suffered a severe setback in the Great Depression. The protectionist Smoot-Hawley Act adopted by the United States in 1930, which imposed tariffs on imports, contributed to the severity of the depression by provoking retaliation and reducing world trade. Adopting the principles of *Keynesian economics*, the U.S. government used deficit spending to stimulate the economy, paying itself back from new wealth generated by economic recovery.[33] The government's role in the economy intensified during World War II.

Following World War II, the capitalist world economy was restructured under U.S. leadership. Today's international economic institutions, such as the World Bank and the International Monetary Fund (IMF), date from this period. The United States provided massive assistance to resuscitate the Western European economies (through the Marshall Plan) as well as Japan's economy. World trade greatly expanded, and the world market became ever more closely woven together through air transportation and telecommunications. Electronics emerged as a new leading sector, and technological progress accelerated throughout the 20th century.

Standing apart from this world capitalist economy, the economies of the Soviet Union and Eastern Europe followed communist principles of central planning and state ownership. In a **centrally planned economy (or** *command economy***)**, political authorities set prices and decide on quotas for production and consumption of each commodity according to a long-term plan, and international trade occurs at government-controlled prices. The proponents of central planning claimed that it would make economies both more rational and more just. By controlling the economy, governments could guarantee the basic needs of citizens and could mobilize the state fully for war if necessary. Proponents of central planning also hoped that governments' long-term view of resources and needs would smooth out the "boom and bust" fluctuations of capitalist economies (known as business cycles).

The Soviet economy had some notable successes in rapidly industrializing the country in the 1930s, surviving the German assault in the 1940s, and developing world-class aerospace and military production capability in the 1950s and 1960s. The Soviet Union launched the world's first satellite (*Sputnik*) in 1957, and in the early 1960s its leaders

---

[33] Markwell, Donald. *John Maynard Keynes and International Relations: Economic Paths to War and Peace.* Oxford, 2006.

boasted that communist economies would outperform capitalist ones within decades. Instead, the Soviet-bloc economies stagnated under the weight of bureaucracy, ideological rigidity, environmental destruction, corruption, and high military spending. Centrally planned economies proved hopelessly inefficient.

Now the former Soviet republics and Eastern Europe are transitional economies, changing over to a market-based economy connected to the world capitalist economy.[34] This transition proved difficult. In the first half of the 1990s, the total GDP of the region shrank by about 35 percent—a depression worse than the Great Depression the United States experienced in the early 1930s. Living standards dropped dramatically. In Boris Yeltsin's administration (1991–1999), Russia's economy remained dysfunctional, owing to depression, corruption, tax delinquency, and the vast differences between the old communist and new capitalist models. President Vladimir Putin (2000–2008) brought new energy to economic reform, and high prices for crude oil, a major Russian export, buoyed its economy in the new century, but Putin's centralization of political power could choke off capitalist growth.

China, whose government continues to follow a Marxist *political* line (central control by the Communist party), has shifted substantially toward a market *economy*.[35] (The state still controls major industries.) This transition has dramatically increased China's economic growth ever since the 1980s. Growth reached a sustained annual rate of about 10 percent throughout the 1990s and nearly as fast in recent years (see "The Chinese Experience" on pp. 464–467).

Today, the world's economic activity follows the principles of free markets more than central planning but often falls somewhere between the extremes. Many governments control domestic prices on some goods (for instance, subsidizing certain goods to win political support). Many states *own* (all or part of) industries thought to be vital for the national economy—state-owned industries such as oil production companies or national airlines. And the government sector of the economy (military spending, road building, Social Security, and so on) makes up a substantial fraction of the industrialized countries' economies. Because they contain both some government control and some private ownership, the economies of the industrialized West are often called **mixed economies**.[36]

Today there is a single integrated world economy that almost no country can resist joining. At the same time, the imperfections and problems of that world economy are evident in periodic crises and recessions and in the sharpening of disparities between the richest and poorest world regions. At no time have these imperfections been more glaring than during the 2008–2009 global financial crisis and ensuing world recession. Starting with the sub-prime mortgage collapse in the United States, economic troubles quickly spread to Europe as major banks and investment companies lost hundreds of billions of dollars. These losses led to a global slowdown in consumer spending and production that caused large job losses in countries like the United States, China, and India. The subsequent fall in consumer demand for goods led to declines in global trade of 9 percent—the largest decline since World War II.

---

[34] Gustafson, Thane. *Capitalism Russian-Style*. Cambridge, 1999. Frye, Timothy. *Brokers and Bureaucrats: Building Market Institutions in Russia*. Michigan, 2000.

[35] Gore, Lance L. P. *Market Communism: The Institutional Foundation of China's Post-Mao Hyper-Growth*. Oxford, 1999. Wedeman, Andrew H. *From Mao to Market: Rent Seeking, Local Protectionism, and Marketization in China*. Cambridge, 2003.

[36] Meso-Lago, Carmelo. *Market, Socialist, and Mixed Economies: Comparative Policy and Performance—Chile, Cuba and Costa Rica*. Johns Hopkins, 2000. Ikeda, Sanford. *Dynamics of the Mixed Economy*. Taylor & Francis, 2007.

Resistance to Trade

The globalization of the world economy has fueled a countercurrent of growing nationalism in several world regions where people believe their identities and communities to be threatened by the penetration of foreign influences. In addition, the material dislocations caused by globalization directly affect the self-interests of certain segments of countries' populations.

Workers in industrialized countries in industries that face increasing competition from low-wage countries in the global South—such as steel, automobiles, electronics, and clothing—are among the most adversely affected by free trade. Inevitably, the competition from low-wage countries holds down wages in those industries in the industrialized countries. It also creates pressures to relax standards of labor regulation, such as those protecting worker safety, and it can lead to job losses if manufacturers close down plants in high-wage countries and move operations to the global South. Not surprisingly, labor unions have been among the strongest political opponents of unfettered trade expansion. (Although the United States stands at the center of these debates, other industrialized countries face similar issues.)

Human rights NGOs have joined labor unions in pushing for trade agreements to include requirements for improving working conditions in low-wage countries; these could include laws regarding minimum wages, child labor, and worker safety. The U.S. Congress in 1997 banned U.S. imports of goods (mostly rugs) manufactured by South Asia's 15 million indentured (slave) child laborers. Clothing manufacturers such as Nike and Reebok, meanwhile, stung by criticism of "sweatshop" conditions in their Asian factories, adopted a voluntary program to end the worst abuses. More than 200 million children under age 14 work in the global South, more than half of them in hazardous labor, according to the UN-affiliated International Labor Organization. That total represents about 5 percent of 5- to 14-year-olds in Latin America, 20 percent in Asia, and 25 percent in Africa. In Ivory Coast, the world's largest exporter of cocoa (for chocolate consumed in the global North), tens of thousands of children work for low wages, or even as slaves, on cocoa plantations.

Environmental groups also have actively opposed the unrestricted expansion of trade, which they see as undermining environmental laws in industrialized countries and promoting environmentally harmful practices worldwide (see p. 392). For example, U.S. regulations require commercial shrimp boats to use devices that prevent endangered species of sea turtles from drowning in shrimp nets. Indonesia, Malaysia, Thailand, and Pakistan, whose shrimp exports to the United States were blocked because they do not require the use of such devices, filed a complaint with the World Trade Organization, arguing that the U.S. regulation unfairly discriminated against them. In 1998, the United States lost the WTO ruling and appeal. Sea turtles became a symbol of environmentalist opposition to the WTO. (In 2001, the WTO ruled the U.S. law acceptable after changes had made application of the law more even-handed.) In 1996, Brazil and Venezuela took the United States to the WTO and forced a change in U.S. environmental rules regarding

CHEAP LABOR

Labor, environmental, and human rights organizations have all criticized unrestricted free trade. They argue that free trade agreements encourage MNCs to produce goods under unfair and unhealthy conditions, including the use of child labor. This boy in India makes soccer balls, 2002.

UNSETTLING CHANGES

Growing trade makes states more interdependent. This may make them more peaceful, but can also introduce new insecurities and sources of conflict. The worldwide economic turmoil starting in 2008 sharpened some trade conflicts, while WTO negotiations remained stalled. This ship that ran aground off New Zealand in 2011 seemed to embody the precarious state of trade relations.

imported gasoline, claiming that regulations under the Clean Air Act were functioning as nontariff barriers.

In general, unrestricted trade tends to force countries to equalize their regulations in a variety of areas not limited to labor and environmental rules. For example, the WTO ruled in 1997 that Europeans' fears about the use of growth hormones in beef were not scientifically warranted, and therefore EU regulations could not be used to exclude U.S. beef containing hormones. When the European Union persisted, the United States was allowed to retaliate by imposing high tariffs on a list of EU exports such as French cheeses. Similarly, in 2006 the WTO ruled that European restrictions on imports of genetically modified food from the United States violated trade rules.

These examples illustrate the variety of sources of backlash against free trade agreements. Labor, environmental, and consumer groups all portray the WTO as a secretive bureaucracy outside democratic control that serves the interests of big corporations at the expense of ordinary people in both the global North and South. More fundamentally, these critics distrust the corporate-driven globalization (see pp. 19–21) of which the WTO is just one aspect. Recent U.S. surveys show a drop in the belief that trade is good for the economy. According to a June 2008 survey, 34 percent believe free trade is good for the United States, while 36 percent say it is not—down from 59 percent just two years earlier. In similar surveys, Americans' support for NAFTA has also declined: 56 percent say it should be renegotiated while only 16 percent support the agreement as it currently stands.[37] Globally, however, public opinion supports trade: a 2009 poll found that majorities in all 22 countries surveyed saw international trade as a good thing, despite concerns about negative cultural and environmental effects. Support was especially high in export-dependent economies—above 90 percent in China, India, South Korea, and Lebanon, for example. The United States ranked near the bottom in the survey, with 65 percent supporting trade.[38]

The benefits of free trade, as noted earlier, are much more diffuse than the costs. U.S. consumers enjoy lower prices on goods imported from low-wage countries. The consumers may therefore spend more money on other products and services, eventually employing more U.S. workers. Cheap imports also help keep inflation low, which benefits citizens. This is small comfort, however, if you are the one who just lost your job.

Of course, international trade requires money to facilitate exchange. In the era of globalization, a significant amount of international trade is conducted through multinational corporations. The next chapter takes up these two issues in the context of the global economy.

✓•⌈**Study**
and **Review**
the **Post-Test &**
Chapter Exam
at **mypoliscilab.com**

---

[37] Rasmussen Reports. "56% Want NAFTA Renegotiated, Americans Divided on Free Trade." June 20, 2008. See http://www.rasmussenreports.com.
[38] Pew Global Attitudes Project. *Views on Trade.* Pew Research Center, 2010. http://pewglobal.org.

CHAPTER REVIEW

SUMMARY

- Liberal economics emphasizes international cooperation—especially through world-wide free trade—to increase the total creation of wealth (regardless of its distribution among states).

- Mercantilism emphasizes the use of economic policy to increase state power relative to that of other states. It mirrors realism in many ways. Mercantilists favor trade policies that produce a trade surplus for their own state. Such a positive trade balance generates money that can be used to enhance state power.

- Trade creates wealth by allowing states to specialize in producing goods and services for which they have a comparative advantage (and importing other needed goods).

- The distribution of benefits from an exchange is determined by the price of the goods exchanged. With many buyers and sellers, prices are generally determined by market equilibrium (supply and demand).

- Politics interferes in international markets in many ways, including the use of economic sanctions as political leverage on a target state. However, sanctions are difficult to enforce unless all major economic actors agree to abide by them.

- States that have reduced their dependence on others by pursuing self-sufficient autarky have failed to generate new wealth to increase their well-being. Self-reliance, like central planning, has been largely discredited as a viable economic strategy.

- Through protectionist policies, many states try to protect certain domestic industries from international competition. Such policies tend to slow down the global creation of wealth but do help the particular industry in question. Protectionism can be pursued through various means, including import tariffs (the favored method), quotas, subsidies, and other nontariff barriers.

- The volume of world trade is very large—about one-sixth of global economic activity—and is concentrated heavily in the states of the industrialized West (Western Europe, North America, and Japan/Pacific) and China.

- Over time, the rules embodied in trade regimes (and other issue areas in IR) become the basis for permanent institutions, whose administrative functions provide yet further stability and efficiency in global trade.

- The World Trade Organization (WTO), formerly the GATT, is the most important multilateral global trade agreement. The GATT was institutionalized in 1995 with the creation of the WTO, which expanded the focus on manufactured goods to consider agriculture and services. Intellectual property is another recent focus.

- In successive rounds of GATT negotiations over 50 years, states have lowered overall tariff rates (especially on manufactured goods). The Uruguay Round of the GATT, completed in 1994, added hundreds of billions of dollars to the global creation of wealth. The Doha Round began in 2003 and has yet to conclude. Meanwhile textile tariffs were dropped worldwide in January 2005.

- Although the WTO provides a global framework, states continue to operate under thousands of bilateral trade agreements specifying the rules for trade in specific products between specific countries.

- Regional free trade areas (with few if any tariffs or nontariff barriers) have been created in Europe, North America, and several other less important instances. NAFTA includes Canada, Mexico, and the United States.

- International cartels are occasionally used by leading producers (sometimes in conjunction with leading consumers) to control and stabilize prices for a commodity on world markets. The most visible example in recent decades has been the oil producers' cartel, OPEC, whose members control more than half the world's exports of a vital commodity, oil.

- Industries often lobby their own governments for protection. Governments in many states develop industrial policies to guide their efforts to strengthen domestic industries in the context of global markets.

- Certain economic sectors—especially agriculture, intellectual property, services, and military goods—tend to deviate more than others from market principles. Political conflicts among states concerning trade in these sectors are frequent.

- Because there is no world government to enforce rules of trade, such enforcement depends on reciprocity and state power. In particular, states reciprocate each other's cooperation in opening markets (or punish each other's refusal to let in foreign products). Although it leads to trade wars on occasion, reciprocity has achieved substantial cooperation in trade.

- The world economy has generated wealth at an accelerating pace in the past two centuries and is increasingly integrated on a global scale, although with huge inequalities.

- Communist states during the Cold War operated centrally planned economies in which national governments set prices and allocated resources. Almost all these states are now in transition toward market-based economies, which more efficiently generate wealth.

- Free trade agreements have led to a backlash from politically active interest groups adversely affected by globalization; these include labor unions, environmental and human rights NGOs, and certain consumers.

KEY TERMS

mercantilism 283
economic liberalism 284
free trade 286
balance of trade 286
comparative advantage 288
autarky 291
protectionism 291
dumping 293
tariff 293
nontariff barriers 293
World Trade Organization (WTO) 294
General Agreement on Tariffs and Trade (GATT) 295

most-favored nation (MFN) 295
Generalized System of Preferences (GSP) 295
Uruguay Round 296
Doha Round 296
North American Free Trade Agreement (NAFTA) 300
cartel 301
Organization of Petroleum Exporting Countries (OPEC) 303

industrial policy 304
intellectual property rights 305
service sector 307
industrialization 309
centrally planned economy 311
transitional economies 312
state-owned industries 312
mixed economies 312

CRITICAL THINKING QUESTIONS

1. Suppose your state had a chance to reach a major trade agreement by making substantial concessions. The agreement would produce $5 billion in new wealth for your state, as well as $10 billion for each of the other states involved (which are political allies but economic rivals). What advice would a mercantilist give your state's leader about making such a deal? What arguments would support the advice? How would liberal advice and arguments differ?

2. China seems to be making a successful transition to market economics and is growing rapidly. It is emerging as the world's second-largest economy. Do you think this is a good thing or a bad thing for your state? Does your reasoning reflect mercantilist or liberal assumptions?

3. Given the theory of hegemonic stability (p. 59), what effects might a resurgence of U.S. power in the post–Cold War era have on the world trading system? How might those effects show up in concrete ways?

4. Before you read this chapter, to what extent did you prefer to buy products made in your own country? Has reading this chapter changed your views on that subject? How?

5. The proposed Free Trade Area of the Americas would join Canada and the United States with Latin American countries, where wages are lower and technology is less developed. Which U.S. industries do you think would gain from such a trade area? Specifically, do you think labor-intensive industries or high-technology industries would be winners? Why?

Are Free Trade Agreements Good for the Global Economy?

Overview

In the past two decades, the number of bilateral and multilateral free trade agreements (FTAs) has skyrocketed. Today, nearly every country is a party to at least one FTA. Many countries are party to multiple FTAs, and nearly all FTAs cover states that are members of the WTO.

There are several reasons offered for the recent explosion of these arrangements. Some attribute the popularity of the neoliberal economic model and its emphasis on free trade as a source of motivation for these agreements. Others point to the near-collapse of the Doha Round of the WTO negotiations. Should the WTO cease to expand in scope, groups of states will do so on their own by signing an FTA. Finally, some point to business pressure to join these arrangements because under an FTA, an MNC with factories in multiple states can ship goods between those factories tariff free.

Despite the prevalence of these agreements, they are controversial. As discussed in this chapter, because free trade brings diffuse benefits but concentrated costs, there are always opponents to these agreements within member states. Economists are also divided on whether FTAs are beneficial, since states may be less likely to cooperate to achieve global free trade (the best outcome for economists) if they are happy with free trade among their key trading partners. Yet others contend they are acceptable "stepping stones" to a world of global free trade. Are FTAs good for the global economy, or do they bring more difficulties domestically and internationally?

FTAs Are Beneficial to the Global Economy

FTAs usually increase trade. Several studies in economics have shown that free trade areas do increase the amount of trade between countries. This trade can be beneficial to consumers and producers, and helps increase economic growth. Given the slow rate of progress at the WTO talks, other solutions are needed to increase trade.

Free trade lowers costs for consumers. Once tariffs are removed from goods, these goods may be sold at a cheaper price. Consumers benefit from these cheaper prices. In extreme cases, FTAs can lower tariffs that effectively exclude goods from entering a market, giving consumers more choice in the products they buy.

FTAs increase foreign investment. Because FTAs eliminate or lower trade barriers, they encourage companies located in states outside the FTAs to locate new factories within the FTAs in order to take advantage of lower tariffs. Some research has shown that FTAs lure increased foreign investment to member states—an important way to increase economic growth, especially in poor countries.

FTAs Are Harmful to the Global Economy

FTAs hinder the advancement of global free trade. Most economists agree that the ideal situation in the global economy is the complete elimination of trade barriers through a large agreement like the WTO. Once states have secured their best trading partners in an FTA, they have no incentive to advance the WTO process.

FTAs are exclusionary and discriminatory. By definition, FTAs provide lower tariffs for only a small number of states. They do not address tariffs levied against nonmembers, and states may have incentives to increase tariffs against nonmembers to encourage trade within the FTA and discourage imports from outside of it.

FTAs threaten jobs and general economic well-being. Because FTAs make it easier for goods to cross borders, companies can locate in other member states where labor costs or environmental standards are lower, in order to cut their production costs. This means fewer jobs in some member states and can lead to further degradation of the natural environment.

Questions

- Do you feel that FTAs are helpful or harmful to the global economy? Would the global economy be better off with no FTAs, leaving only the WTO to liberalize trade?

- When the economy emerges from its current economic downturn, will we see a move back to free trade? How much of the current opinion toward the effects of free trade is influenced by the global economic recession?

- Suppose WTO negotiations continue to be deadlocked, with no hope in sight for a more extensive global trade agreement. Does this change your opinion of whether more FTAs should exist? Or are the domestic implications (price changes versus job losses) more important in your thinking?

For Further Reading

Rodrik, Dani. *One Economics, Many Recipes: Globalization, Institutions, and Economic Growth.* Princeton, 2007.

Irwin, Douglas. *Free Trade Under Fire.* Princeton, 2002.

Stiglitz, Joseph, and Andrew Charlton. *Fair Trade for All: How Trade Can Promote Development.* Oxford, 2006.

Chang, Ha-Joon. *Bad Samaritans: The Myth of Free Trade and the Secret History of Capitalism.* Bloomsbury, 2007.

CHAPTER 9 Global Finance and Business

Tokyo brokerage, 2010.

Globalization and Finance

Globalization has led to momentous changes in many areas of international relations. So far, we have discussed how globalization has influenced global security and international trade relations. Globalization has had its most profound influence in the way states, businesses, and individuals deal with financial markets.

Today, global financial markets are as integrated as they have ever been. Investors in one country buy and sell assets or exchange currency with a few clicks of a mouse. Banks' investment portfolios often contain millions of dollars in assets (real estate, land, stocks) located in other countries. Nearly a trillion and a half dollars a day is exchanged on currency markets as investors need various currencies to do business in other countries, but also to bet on the rise and fall of currencies, which we discuss momentarily.

This financial integration has tremendous advantages. It offers investors and businesses access to overseas markets to spur economic growth. It allows for the possibility of better returns on investment for individuals investing for college tuition or retirement. But as we have witnessed in the past two years, financial integration also carries risks. An economic crisis in one state can quickly spread to another, then another. The spread of economic difficulties can quickly lead to a global economic crisis affecting small and large economies alike.

Such was the case in 2008. As an economic downturn began in the United States, many Americans who had taken out loans on their homes found themselves unable to pay these loans back. At the same time, the value of their homes began to fall, so that even if banks were to reclaim them, the banks could not recover the money they had loaned. Moreover, these loans had been resold by the banks to other businesses as investments, often in other countries. Several large U.S. banks then announced that they were on the verge of failing because they had too much money tied up in these bad home loans. This was a problem not only for the banks and the individuals who could not pay for their homes, but also for those businesses who had purchased these loans as investments.

Given the global integration of financial markets, this housing crisis led quickly to a global banking crisis. Several British banks then announced they were near bankruptcy. The U.S. government responded with a rescue package of $800 billion to help shore up failing banks. Britain also created a rescue package of nearly $450 billion. The entire banking sector of Iceland was taken over by the government, and Iceland, a prosperous country, needed a loan from the International Monetary Fund (IMF) to rescue the government from bankruptcy.

Global stock markets tumbled dramatically as a result of this financial crisis, by a third, a half, and even two-thirds in the case of China. Unemployment increased worldwide. What began as trouble in the U.S. housing market ended as a global financial meltdown.

In 2010, a global economic recovery appeared to be underway, but that recovery was challenged through the ripple effects of a debt crisis in Greece. The economic crisis there affected not only the major European economies, but the U.S. economy as well, showing once again that problems in one country can easily become the problems of other countries.

This chapter investigates two central pillars of our global financial markets: the politics of the world monetary system and the role of private companies as nonstate actors in the world economy.

Read and **Listen** to **Chapter 9** at **mypoliscilab.com**

Study and **Review** the **Pre-Test & Flashcards** at **mypoliscilab.com**

Watch the **Video** "**The Mexican Peso Crisis**" on **mypoliscilab.com**

The Currency System

Explore
the Simulation
"Business: You
Are a Foreign
Market Analyst"
on mypoliscilab.com

Nearly every state prints its own money. The ability to print one's own currency is one of the hallmarks of state sovereignty. Yet, in a globalized system of trade and finance, businesses and individuals often need other states' currencies to do business.

About Money

Because of the nature of state sovereignty, the international economy is based on national currencies, not a world currency. One of the main powers of a national government is to create its own currency as the sole legal currency in the territory it controls. The national currencies are of no inherent value in another country, but can be exchanged one for another.[1]

Traditionally, for centuries, the European state system used *precious metals* as a global currency, valued in all countries. *Gold* was most important, and *silver* second. These metals had inherent value because they looked pretty and were easily molded into jewelry or similar objects. They were relatively rare, and the mining of new gold and silver was relatively slow. These metals lasted a long time, and they were difficult to dilute or counterfeit.

Over time, gold and silver became valuable *because* they were a world currency—because other people around the world trusted that the metals could be exchanged for future goods—and this overshadowed any inherent functional value of gold or silver. Bars of gold and silver were held by states as a kind of bank account denominated in an international currency. These piles of gold (literal and figurative) were the object of mercantilist trade policies in past centuries (see Chapters 2 and 8). Gold has long been a key power resource with which states could buy armies or other means of leverage.

In recent years the world has not used such a **gold standard** but has developed an international monetary system divorced from any tangible medium such as precious metals. Even today, some private investors buy stocks of gold or silver at times of political instability, as a haven that would reliably have future value. But gold and silver have now become basically like other commodities, with unpredictable fluctuations in price. The change in the world economy away from bars of gold to purely abstract money makes international economics more efficient; the only drawback is that without tangible backing in gold, currencies may seem less worthy of people's confidence.

International Currency Exchange

Today, national currencies are valued against each other, not against gold or silver. Each state's currency can be exchanged for a different state's currency according to an **exchange rate**—defining, for instance, how many Canadian dollars are equivalent to one U.S. dollar. These exchange rates affect almost every international economic transaction—trade, investment, tourism, and so forth.[2]

Most exchange rates are expressed in terms of the world's most important currencies—the U.S. dollar, the Japanese yen, and the EU's euro. Thus, the rate for exchanging Danish kroner for Brazilian reals depends on the value of each relative to these world currencies. Exchange rates that most affect the world economy are those *within* the largest economies—U.S. dollars, euros, yen, British pounds, and Canadian dollars.

---

[1] Solomon, Robert. *Money on the Move: The Revolution in International Finance Since 1980*. Princeton, 1999. Cohen, Benjamin J. *The Future of Money*. Princeton, 2004.
[2] Aliber, Robert Z. *The New International Money Game*. Chicago, 2002.

The relative values of currencies at a given point in time are arbitrary; only the *changes* in values over time are meaningful. For instance, the euro happens to be fairly close to the U.S. dollar in value, whereas the Japanese yen is denominated in units closer to the U.S. penny. In itself this disparity says nothing about the desirability of these currencies or the financial positions of their states. However, when the value of the euro rises (or falls) *relative* to the dollar, because euros are considered more (or less) valuable than before, the euro is said to be strong (or weak). A strong currency makes imports more affordable, while a weak currency makes exports more competitive. For example, when the U.S. dollar's value fell in 2001–2006, the exports of 200 large U.S. companies with substantial foreign sales rose from 32 to 44 percent of their total sales.[3]

Some states do not have **convertible currencies**. The holder of such money has no guarantee of being able to trade it for another currency. Such is the case in states cut off from the world capitalist economy, such as the former Soviet Union. In practice, even nonconvertible currency can often be sold, in black markets or by dealing directly with the government issuing the currency, but the price may be extremely low. Some currencies are practically nonconvertible because they are inflating so rapidly that holding them for even a short period means losing money. Inflation reduces a currency's value relative to more stable (more slowly inflating) currencies.

The industrialized West has kept inflation relatively low— mostly below 5 percent annually—since 1980. (The 1970s saw inflation of more than 10 percent per year in many industrialized economies, including the United States.) Inflation in the global South is lower than a decade ago (see Table 9.1). Latin America brought inflation from 750 percent to below 15 percent, while China and South Asia got inflation rates below 5 percent. Most dramatically, in Russia and other former Soviet republics, inflation rates of more than 1,000 percent came down to less than 10 percent.

Extremely high, uncontrolled inflation—more than 50 percent per month, or 13,000 percent per year—is called **hyperinflation**. The 100-trillion-dollar notes introduced by Zimbabwe in 2009 quickly lost most of their initial value (about 30 U.S. dollars) under hyperinflation exceeding 200 million percent per year. Even at less extreme levels, currencies can lose 95 percent of their value in a year. In such conditions, money loses 5 percent of its value every week, and it becomes hard to conduct business domestically, let alone internationally.

In contrast with nonconvertible currency, **hard currency** is money that can be readily converted to leading world currencies (which now have relatively low inflation). For example, a Chinese computer producer can export its products and receive payment in dollars, euros, or another hard currency, which it can use to pay for components it needs to import from abroad. But a Chinese farmer paid in Chinese currency for rice could not simply use that currency to buy imported goods. Rather, the exchange for foreign currency would be controlled by the Chinese government at rates the government set. In a few countries, such as Cuba, two versions of currency circulate, one convertible to foreign hard currency and

WHAT'S IT WORTH TO YOU?

Money has value only because people trust its worth. Inflation erodes a currency's value if governments print too much money or if political instability erodes public confidence in the government. This Russian stands next to currency exchange rate signs as the Russian ruble became fully convertible with other world currencies, 2006.

[3] *New York Times*, November 20, 2007: A15.

TABLE 9.1 Inflation Rates by Region, 1993–2011

Region	Inflation Rate (percent per year)		
	1993	2001	2011[a]
Industrialized West	3	2	1
Russia/CIS	1,400	22	8
China	15	7	3
Middle East	27	17	5
Latin America	750	6	6
South Asia	6	6	4
Africa	112	6	6

[a]Data are estimates based on partial data for 2009.

Note: Regions are not identical to those used elsewhere in this book.

Source: Adapted from United Nations. *World Economic Situation and Prospects 2011*. United Nations, 2011.

one for internal use only. Cubans complain that needed goods are available only at stores taking the hard version (such as stores selling to tourists), whereas their salaries are paid in the soft version. Generally, as economies develop and join the global marketplace, their currencies also develop, from the shaky versions based on beer cans or prone to hyperinflation, to the much more stable versions such as China's today, and eventually to the fully convertible model.

States maintain **reserves** of hard currency. These are the equivalent of the stockpiles of gold in centuries past. National currencies are now backed by hard-currency reserves, not gold. Some states continue to maintain gold reserves as well. In 2010, Saudi Arabia disclosed that it maintained over 300 tons of gold in reserve, worth more than $10 billion. China's gold reserves were three times larger. The industrialized countries have financial reserves roughly in proportion to the size of their economies.

One form of currency exchange uses **fixed exchange rates**. Here governments decide, individually or jointly, to establish official rates of exchange for their currencies. For example, the Canadian and U.S. dollars were for many years equal in value; a fixed rate of one-to-one was maintained (this is no longer true). States have various means for trying to maintain, or modify, such fixed rates in the face of changing economic conditions (see "Why Currencies Rise or Fall" later in this chapter).

Floating exchange rates are now more commonly used for the world's major currencies. Rates are determined by global currency markets in which private investors and governments alike buy and sell currencies. There is a supply and demand for each state's currency, with prices constantly adjusting in response to market conditions. Just as investors might buy shares of Apple or Wal-Mart stock if they expected its value to rise, so they would buy a pile of Japanese yen if they expected that currency's value to rise in the future. Through short-term speculative trading in international currencies, exchange rates adjust to changes in the longer-term supply and demand for currencies.

Major international currency markets operate in a handful of cities—the most important being New York, London, Zurich (Switzerland), Tokyo, and Hong Kong—linked together by instantaneous computerized communications. These markets are driven in the short term by one question: What will a state's currency be worth in the future relative to what it is worth today? These international currency markets involve huge amounts of money—a trillion and a half dollars every day—moving around the world (of course, only the computerized information actually moves). They are private markets, not as strongly regulated by governments as are stock markets.[4]

National governments periodically *intervene* in financial markets, buying and selling currencies in order to manipulate their value. (These interventions may also involve changing interest rates paid by the government; see p. 334.) Such government intervention to manage the otherwise free-floating currency rates is called a **managed float** system. The leading industrialized states often, but not always, work together in such interventions. If the price of the U.S. dollar, for instance, goes down too much relative to other important currencies (a political judgment), governments step into the currency markets, side by side with private investors, and buy dollars. With this higher demand for dollars, the price may then stabilize and perhaps rise again. (If the price gets too high, governments step in to sell dollars, increasing supply and driving the price down.) Such interventions usually happen quickly, in one day, but may be repeated several times within a few weeks in order to have the desired effect.[5] Note that monetary intervention requires costly multilateral cooperation among states. Liberals point to such cooperation as evidence that states recognize their long-term interest in a mutually beneficial international economy.

In their interventions in international currency markets, governments are at a disadvantage because even acting together, they control only a small fraction of the money moving on such markets; most of it is privately owned. However, governments have one advantage in that they can work together to have enough impact on the market to make at least modest changes in price. Governments can also operate in secret, keeping private investors in the dark regarding how much currency governments may eventually buy or sell, and at what price. Only *after* a coordinated multinational intervention into markets does the public find out about it. (If speculators knew in advance, they could make money at the government's expense.) Note that this is an area where states have a common interest (making sure a large economy does not collapse) aligned against transnational actors, investors who are trying to make money at the expense of states.

A successful intervention can make money for governments at the expense of private speculators. If, for example, the G20 governments step in to raise the price of U.S. dollars by buying them around the world (selling other hard currencies), and if they succeed, the governments can then sell again and pocket a profit. However, if the intervention fails and the price of dollars keeps falling, the governments *lose* money and may have to keep buying and buying in order to stop the slide. In fact, if investors become aware of such moves, they may interpret this action as a signal that the currency being bought is weak, which could depress the price even further. In extreme cases, the governments may run out of their stockpiles of hard currencies before then and have to absorb a huge loss. Thus governments must be realistic about the limited effects they can have on currency prices.

These limits were well illustrated in the 2001 Argentine financial collapse. Argentina in the 1990s had pegged the value of its currency at a fixed rate to the U.S.

---

[4] Baker, Andrew. *Governing Financial Globalization: International Political Economy and Multi-Level Governance.* Routledge, 2008.

[5] Bearce, David H. *Monetary Divergence: Domestic Political Autonomy in the Post-Bretton Woods Era.* Michigan, 2007. Kirshner, Jonathan. *Currency and Coercion: The Political Economy of International Monetary Power.* Princeton, 1997.

dollar—a wonderfully effective way to stop the runaway inflation that had recently wreaked devastation on Argentina's economy. Tying the peso to the dollar, however, represented a loss of sovereignty over monetary policy, one of the key levers to control an economy. Argentina and the United States in the late 1990s had different needs. As a historic U.S. expansion brought unprecedented prosperity (allowing interest rates to be kept relatively high), Argentina suffered four years of recession, but could not lower interest rates to stimulate growth. Argentina accumulated more than $100 billion in foreign loans and could not service its debts. Assistance from the IMF in restructuring debt was contingent on a tight financial policy of tax increases and spending cuts—a mistake during a major multiyear recession, according to critics. In 2001, as the United States and IMF stood by, Argentina's economy collapsed; two presidents resigned in short order; and a populist took power, defaulted on foreign debts, and devalued the peso to create jobs—an embarrassing chapter for the IMF and a painful one for Argentina. In 2003, Argentina defaulted on a $3 billion payment to the IMF, the largest default in IMF history. Its economy turned around and it paid the IMF off in 2006, though negotiations with foreign government creditors continued.

More recently, pressures built up in a vastly more important case—China's currency. As in Argentina in 2001, the current policy of "pegging" China's currency to the dollar did not adjust to different economic conditions in China and the United States. China runs a big trade surplus (see p. 287) while the United States runs a big trade deficit—well over $200 billion with China alone in 2010 and nearly $400 billion in total. Critics charge that the dollar-yuan ratio is held artificially high, making China's exports to the United States cheaper and contributing to the trade imbalance and the loss of U.S. manufacturing jobs—an issue in U.S. domestic politics. As the economic position of the United States has worsened in the past three years, pressure on China to reform its currency has grown. Yet, China is concerned about domestic stability—for employment to stay high, China must

SEEKING THE COLLECTIVE GOOD

Currency Stability

COLLECTIVE GOOD: Stable Currency Exchange Rates for World Business

BACKGROUND: Globalization has brought great wealth to the world as business increasingly operates internationally. The ability to do business internationally depends on the stability of currency exchange rates in different countries. Whatever the exchange rate, businesspeople can plan on investments, imports, or purchases based on knowing what these things will cost if paid in a foreign currency. This stability is a collective good for the world. If the world's major countries maintain stability by coordinating their financial policies, all enjoy the benefit. That stability can be achieved even if some states free-ride by manipulating their own currency exchange rates to advantage. If too many countries do so, the collective good is not

achieved, as shown in the competitive devaluations of major currencies in the 1930s, which worsened the Great Depression.

CHALLENGE: China has kept its currency pegged to the U.S. dollar for years, even as economic conditions in the two countries have diverged and a huge trade imbalance developed. Most economists expect that if allowed to float freely like the world's other major currencies, the Chinese currency would rise substantially. This would help American exports and harm Chinese exports, reducing the trade imbalance somewhat. However, although China

DOMINANCE

export goods. China's undervalued currency keeps exports cheap and workers employed. China has only slowly allowed its currency to appreciate in value modestly, and will not allow it to float freely.

In 2006, China, Japan, and South Korea announced plans to work toward coordinating their currency policies. In 2010, South Korea agreed to further coordinate currency exchanges with China. Along with the ASEAN countries, they are also studying the creation of an Asian currency unit that would track the aggregate value of the region's currencies. Both measures are possible early steps toward the eventual creation of an Asian currency like the euro. But such a major move is in the early stages at best.

Why Currencies Rise or Fall

In the short term, exchange rates depend on speculation about the future value of currencies. But over the long term, the value of a state's currency tends to rise or fall relative to others because of changes in the long-term supply and demand for the currency. *Supply* is determined by the amount of money a government prints. Printing money is a quick way to generate revenue for the government, but the more money printed, the lower its price. Domestically, printing too much money creates inflation because the amount of goods in the economy is unchanged but more money is circulating to buy them with. *Demand* for a currency depends on the state's economic health and political stability. People do not want to own the currency of an unstable country, because political instability leads to the breakdown of economic efficiency and of trust in the currency. Conversely, political stability boosts a currency's value. For instance, in 2001, when a new Indonesian president took office after a period of political and economic turmoil, the Indonesian currency jumped 13 percent in two days because of expectations of greater stability.

says occasionally that it will let the currency rise, the actual changes have been quite modest.

SOLUTION: Unlike the trade system based on equality and reciprocity, the international financial system more closely resembles a dominance hierarchy. The IMF uses a weighted voting system that gives power to the largest economies. Until recently, major world currency decisions were taken by the Group of Seven (G7) countries. This was expanded to the larger and more inclusive G20—a flattening of the dominance hierarchy in response to the world economic crisis—but still leaves the top countries calling the shots. World currency markets are dominated by the U.S. dollar, the euro, and the Japanese yen.

By keeping its currency artificially low, China is free riding on the world currency system by boosting its own exports. However, China is not a large enough

Dollars and euros anchor the currency system, 2010.

piece of the world economy as a whole to bring down the currency system by its nonparticipation.

PRICES SUBJECT TO CHANGE

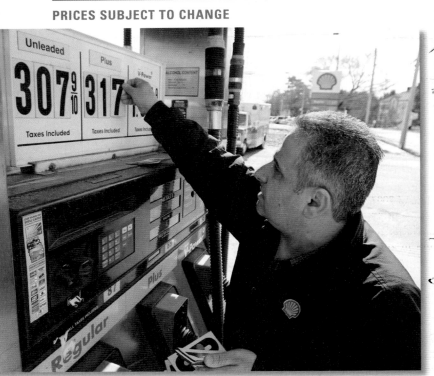

Changes in the value of the dollar—reflecting underlying trends in U.S. and foreign economies as well as governments' monetary policies—directly affect the prices of imported goods such as gasoline, here rising in 2008.

Currency stability is hard to achieve. Between 1995 and 2004 the U.S. dollar dropped from 100 Japanese yen to 80, rose to 130, and dropped back to 105. This kind of instability in exchange rates disrupts business in trade-oriented sectors because companies face sudden and unpredictable changes in their plans for income and expenses (for example, changes in the cost of computer chips from Japan needed to manufacture U.S. computers, or U.S. software needed in Japan). States also have a shared interest in currency stability because instability tends to be profitable for speculators at the expense of central banks. States also share an interest in the integrity of their currencies against counterfeiting, but "rogue" states may feel otherwise. In 2006, the United States accused North Korea of passing off tens of millions of dollars in extremely realistic counterfeit $100 bills—a direct gain for the North Korean regime at the expense of the U.S. Treasury.

Despite these shared interests in currency stability, states also experience conflicts over currency exchange. States often prefer a *low* value for their own currency relative to others, because a low value promotes exports and helps turn trade deficits into surpluses—as mercantilists especially favor (see pp. 286–287). This explains why China has kept its currency value relatively low in recent years.

To some extent, exchange rates and trade surpluses or deficits tend to adjust automatically toward equilibrium (the preferred outcome for liberals). An *overvalued* currency is one whose exchange rate is too high, resulting in a chronic trade deficit. The deficit can be covered by printing more money, which waters down the currency's value and brings down the exchange rate (assuming it is allowed to float freely). Because they see adjustments as harmless, liberals are not bothered by exchange rate changes such as the fall of the dollar relative to the euro. They view these changes as mechanisms for allowing the world economy to work out inefficiencies and maximize overall growth.

A unilateral move to reduce the value of one's own currency by changing a fixed or official exchange rate is called a **devaluation**. Generally, devaluation is a quick fix for financial problems in the short term, but it can create new problems. It causes losses to foreigners who hold one's currency (which suddenly loses value). Such losses reduce the trust people place in the currency. As a result, demand for the currency drops, even at the new lower rate. Investors become wary of future devaluations, and indeed such devaluations often follow one after another in unstable economies. In the first three weeks of 2009, Russia devalued its ruble six times, after the price of its main export, oil, plummeted. A currency may be devalued by being allowed to float freely after a period of fixed exchange rates, often bringing a single sharp drop in values. In general, any sharp or

POLICY PERSPECTIVES

President of China, Hu Jintao

PROBLEM *How do you balance international political pressures with domestic economic concerns?*

BACKGROUND   Imagine that you are the president of China. The Chinese economy has grown rapidly in the past decade. Growth rates rose to near 11 percent as of 2007, exceeding nearly all countries in the developing world. After a brief slowdown during the world financial crisis, near–double-digit growth returned to China in 2009. Chinese exports fell during the crisis, but have surged back, leading to massive trade surpluses in 2010.

Your position in the international economy is unique, because China's currency, the yuan, has been pegged to the U.S. dollar for nearly a decade (and to a basket of currencies, with just small adjustments, starting in mid-2005). Thus, even though the demand for the yuan may rise and fall, China's exchange rate does not change much.

Many feel your pegged currency is one explanation for your country's tremendous economic growth and trade surplus. The demand for the yuan is high (to pay for your exports), but because its value cannot rise relative to the dollar, the peg keeps the yuan low. The result is that Chinese exports are much cheaper on the world market, making your goods very attractive.

DOMESTIC CONSIDERATIONS   Economic growth is important for your country. Given its large population, increases in jobs are important to keep unemployment low. Higher wages help ensure low birthrates (through the demographic transition; see pp. 410–412). Exports are a key part of this picture, contributing heavily to economic growth and generating hard currency for your economy and creating jobs.

Recently, however, two dangers have appeared on the horizon. The first is economic. In 2010, your country experienced labor unrest from workers unhappy with their low pay rates. Responses to these protests could include higher wages, raising the costs of goods produced and potentially lowering exports. Both Europe and the United States have complained bitterly about your pegged exchange rate and your trade surplus. The United States has blamed the yuan-dollar peg for costing America 1.5 million jobs, further exacerbating political tensions. Although you have allowed your currency to rise a bit since 2006, this has not mollified American critics.

SCENARIO   Now imagine that the advanced-economy countries approach you with possible membership into the G8. Their condition is that you allow the yuan to float freely on international currency markets. Such a move would be very popular in international political circles and would lessen the chances that your own economy will "overheat" and become inflationary. In the long run, such a move will ensure your further integration into the international economy. In addition, a closer link to G8 states would provide significant prestige to your government.

Of course, there are also dangers in this course of action. If the yuan rises rapidly in value, your exports will be less competitive internationally, risking a stall in a key engine of your economy. You also become more vulnerable to international currency shocks, such as the 1997 Asian economic crisis, which you avoided in large part due to your pegged exchange rate.

CHOOSE YOUR POLICY   Do you remove the yuan-dollar peg? If yes, how do you make sure your economy stays on a moderate growth rate and your exports stay competitive? If no, how do you deal with the political pressure arising from your fixed exchange rate? Can you also run the risk that your economy will grow too fast, risking inflation and domestic discontent?

artificial change in exchange rates tends to disrupt smooth international trade and interfere with the creation of wealth.

Relatively stable exchange rates for international currency can be seen as a collective good, in that all members of the international economy benefit from a stable framework for making investments and sales, yet an individual country can benefit from devaluing its own currency. (Whether such benefits are actually economic, or merely political benefits tied to perceptions of national interest, does not matter here, as long as state leaders perceive that defection from existing exchange rates can benefit their countries.) According to the theory of collective goods, international exchange rate stability should be more readily achieved in two circumstances—under hegemony (the dominance principle) and under an arrangement among a small group of key states (where the reciprocity principle operates effectively). Hegemonic stability, in this theory, includes providing backing for world currency stability, using the hegemon's own economic clout and its influence over other great powers. Lacking a hegemon, collective goods are thought to be easiest to ensure if controlled by a small group. In the small-group setting, defectors stand out and mutual cooperation is more readily enforced.

Central Banks

Governments control the printing of money. In some states, the politicians or generals who control the government directly control the amounts of money printed. It is not surprising that inflation tends to be high in those states, because political problems can often be solved by printing more money. But in most industrialized countries, politicians know they cannot trust themselves with day-to-day decisions about printing money. To enforce self-discipline and enhance public trust in the value of money, these decisions are turned over to a **central bank**.[6]

The economists and technical experts who run the central bank seek to maintain the value of the state's currency by limiting the amount of money printed and not allowing high inflation. Politicians appoint the people who run the bank, but generally for long terms that do not coincide with those of the politicians. Thus, central bank managers try to run the bank in the national interest, a step removed from partisan politics. If a state leader orders a military intervention, the generals obey, but if the leader orders an intervention in currency markets, the central bank does not have to comply. In practice, the autonomy of central banks varies. For instance, the head of Thailand's central bank was fired by the prime minister in a dispute over interest rates in 2001.

In the United States, the central bank is the *Federal Reserve, or the Fed.* The "reserve" is the government's stockpile of hard currency. The Fed can affect the economy by releasing or hoarding its money. Internationally, it does this by intervening in currency markets (as described earlier). Multilateral interventions are usually coordinated by the heads of central banks and treasury (finance) ministries in the leading countries. The long-term, relatively nonpartisan perspective of central bankers makes it easier for states to achieve the collective good of a stable world monetary system.

Domestically, the Fed exercises its power mainly by setting the **discount rate**—the interest rate the government charges when it loans money to private banks. (Central banks have only private banks, not individuals and corporations, as their customers.) In effect, this rate controls how fast money is injected into the economy. If the Fed sets too

---

[6] Blinder, Alan S. *The Quiet Revolution: Central Banking Goes Modern.* Yale, 2004.

low a discount rate, too much money will enter into circulation and inflation will result. If the rate is set too high, too little money will circulate and consumers and businesses will find it hard to borrow as much or as cheaply from private banks; economic growth will be depressed.

Central bank decisions about the discount rate have important international consequences. If interest rates are higher in one state than in another, foreign capital tends to be attracted to the state with the higher rate. And if economic growth is high in a foreign country, more goods can be exported to it. So states care about other states' monetary policies. The resulting international conflicts can be resolved only politically (such as at G20 meetings), not technically, because each central bank, although removed from domestic politics, still looks out for its own state's interests.

Although central banks control sizable reserves of currency, they are constrained by the limited share of world money they own. Most wealth is controlled by private banks and corporations. As economic actors, states do not drive the direction of the world economy; in many ways they follow it, at least over the long run. Yet, as we have seen in the recent global economic crises, states still play a key role in the global economy. In the short run, states can adopt massive financial stimulus packages, can rescue private banks and corporations that teeter on bankruptcy, and can prosecute individuals who act illegally to cause economic hardship.

The World Bank and the IMF

Because of the importance of international cooperation for a stable world monetary system and because of the need to overcome collective goods problems, international regimes and institutions have developed around norms of behavior in monetary relations. Just as the UN institutionally supports regimes based on norms of behavior in international security affairs, the same is true in the world monetary regime.

As in security affairs, the main international economic institutions were created near the end of World War II. The **Bretton Woods system** was adopted at a conference of the winning states in 1944 (at Bretton Woods, New Hampshire). It established the *International Bank for Reconstruction and Development (IBRD)*, more commonly called the **World Bank**, as a source of loans to reconstruct the Western European economies after the war and to help states through future financial difficulties. (Later, the main borrowers were developing countries and, in the 1990s, Eastern European ones.) Closely linked with the World Bank is the **International Monetary Fund (IMF)**. The IMF coordinates international currency exchange, the balance of international payments, and national accounts (discussed shortly). The World Bank and the IMF continue to be the pillars of the international financial system. (The roles of the World Bank and the IMF in international development are taken up in Chapter 13.)[7]

Bretton Woods set a regime of stable monetary exchange, based on the U.S. dollar and backed by gold, that lasted from 1944 to 1971.[8] During this period, the dollar had a fixed value equal to 1/35 of an ounce of gold, and the U.S. government guaranteed to buy dollars for gold at this rate (from a stockpile in Fort Knox, Kentucky). Other states' currencies were exchanged at fixed rates relative to the dollar. These fixed exchange rates were set by

---

[7] Fischer, Stanley. *IMF Essays from a Time of Crisis: The International Financial System, Stabilization, and Development.* MIT, 2004. Copelovitch, Mark S. *The International Monetary Fund in the Global Economy.* Cambridge, 2010.

[8] Eichengreen, Barry. *Globalizing Capital: A History of the International Monetary System.* Princeton, 1996. Andrews, David M., C. Randall Henning, and Louis W. Pauly, eds. *Governing the World's Money.* Cornell, 2002.

the IMF based on the long-term equilibrium level that could be sustained for each currency (rather than short-term political considerations). The international currency markets operated within a narrow range around the fixed rate. If a country's currency fell more than 1 percent from the fixed rate, the country had to use its hard-currency reserves to buy its own currency back and thus shore up the price. If the price rose more than 1 percent, it had to sell its currency to drive the price down.

The gold standard was abandoned in 1971—an event sometimes called the "collapse of Bretton Woods." The term is not quite appropriate: the institutions survived, and even the monetary regime underwent more of an adjustment than a collapse. The U.S. economy no longer held the overwhelming dominance it had in 1944—mostly because of European and Japanese recovery from World War II, but also because of U.S. overspending on the Vietnam War and the outflow of U.S. dollars to buy oil. As a result, the dollar became seriously overvalued. By 1971, the dollar was no longer worth 1/35 of an ounce of gold, and the United States had to abandon its fixed exchange rate. President Nixon unilaterally dumped the dollar-gold system, and allowed the dollar to float freely. Soon it had fallen to a fraction of its former value relative to gold.

The abandonment of the gold standard was good for the United States and bad for Japan and Europe, where leaders expressed shock at the unilateral U.S. actions. The interdependence of the world capitalist economy, which had produced record economic growth for all the Western countries after World War II, had also created the conditions for new international conflicts.

To replace gold as a world standard, the IMF created a new world currency, the **Special Drawing Right (SDR)**. The SDR has been called "paper gold" because it is created in limited amounts by the IMF, is held as a hard-currency reserve by states' central banks, and can be exchanged for various international currencies. The SDR is today the closest thing to a world currency that exists, but it cannot buy goods—only currencies. And it is owned only by states (central banks), not by individuals or companies. The value of the U.S. dollar was pegged to the SDR rather than to gold, at a fixed exchange rate (but one that the IMF periodically adjusted to reflect the dollar's strength or weakness). SDRs are linked in value to a basket of several key international currencies. When one currency rises a bit and another falls, the SDR does not change value much; but if all currencies rise (worldwide inflation), the SDR rises with them.

Since the early 1970s, the major national currencies have been governed by the managed float system. Transition from the dollar-gold regime to the managed float regime was difficult. States had to bargain politically over the targets for currency exchange rates in the meetings now known as G6 summits. The G6 was later expanded to the G8 with the addition of Canada (in 1976) and Russia (in 1997). In 2009, it was announced that the G20, including far more developed and developing countries, would begin to replace the G8 in undertaking major financial deliberations.

The technical mechanisms of the IMF are based on each member state's depositing financial reserves with the IMF. Upon joining the IMF, a state is assigned a *quota* for such deposits, partly of hard currency and partly of the state's own currency (this quota is not related to the concept of trade quotas, which are import restrictions). The quota is based on the size and strength of a state's economy. A state can then borrow against its quota (even exceeding it somewhat) to stabilize its economy in difficult times and repay the IMF in subsequent years. In 2009, world leaders pledged an additional 1 trillion dollars to be paid to the IMF so it could help developing countries cope with the global financial crisis.

Unlike the WTO or UN General Assembly, the IMF and the World Bank use a *weighted voting system*—each state has a vote equal to its quota. Thus the advanced economies control the IMF, although nearly all the world's states are members. The United States has the single largest vote (17 percent), and its capital city is headquarters for both the IMF and the World Bank. In 2008, the IMF adjusted the voting formula, increasing modestly the quota and voting power of China (from about 3 to 3.7 percent of the total) and other developing countries.

Since 1944, the IMF and the World Bank have tried to accomplish three major missions. First they sought to provide stability and access to capital for states ravaged by World War II, especially Japan and the states of Western Europe. This mission was a great success, leading to growth and prosperity in those states. Second, especially in the 1970s and 1980s but still continuing today, the World Bank and the IMF have tried to promote economic development in poor countries. That mission has been far less successful—as seen in the lingering poverty in much of the global South (see Chapter 12). The third mission, in the 1990s, was the integration of Eastern Europe and Russia into the world capitalist economy. This effort posted a mixed record but has had general success overall.

State Financial Positions

As currency rates change and state economies grow, the overall positions of states relative to each other shift.

National Accounts

The IMF maintains a system of *national accounts* statistics to keep track of the overall monetary position of each state. A state's **balance of payments** is like the financial statement of a company: it summarizes all the flows of money in and out of the country. The system itself is technical and not political in nature. Essentially, three types of international transactions go into the balance of payments: the current account, flows of capital, and changes in reserves.

The *current account* is basically the balance of trade discussed in Chapter 8. Money flows out of a state to pay for imports and flows into the state to pay for exports. The goods imported or exported include both merchandise and services. For instance, money spent by a British tourist in Florida is equivalent to money spent by a British consumer buying Florida oranges in a London market; in both cases money flows into the U.S. current account. The current account includes two other items. *Government transactions* are military and foreign aid grants, as well as salaries and pensions paid to government employees abroad. *Remittances* are funds sent home by companies or individuals outside a country (see Chapter 13). For example, a Honda subsidiary in America may send profits back to Honda in Japan. Or a British citizen working in New York may send money to her parents in London.

NURTURING DEVELOPMENT

The World Bank works to stabilize and develop economies in poor and middle-income countries. Here, the Swiss president waters a plant in Kenya in 2006 after the World Bank negotiated a deal with Kenya's Green Belt Movement to purchase emissions reductions in Kenya that will help combat global warming. Looking on is the late leader of the movement, who won the 2004 Nobel Peace Prize for her environmental work.

Watch the **Video** "U.S.-China Trade Tensions" on **mypoliscilab.com**

The second category in the accounts, *capital flows*, are foreign investments in, and by, a country. Capital flows are measured in *net* terms—the total investments and loans foreigners make *in* a country minus the investments and loans that country's companies, citizens, and government invest in *other* countries. Most of such investment is private, although some is by (or in) government agencies and state-owned industries. Capital flows are divided into *foreign direct investment* (or *direct foreign investment*)—such as owning a factory, company, or real estate in a foreign country—and indirect *portfolio investment*, such as buying stocks and bonds or making loans to a foreign company. These various kinds of capital flows have somewhat different political consequences (see "International Debt" and "Foreign Direct Investment" later in this chapter), but are basically equivalent in the overall national accounts picture.

The third category, *changes in foreign exchange reserves*, makes the national accounts balance. Any difference between the inflows and outflows of money (in the current account and capital flows combined) is made up by an equal but opposite change in reserves. These changes in reserves consist of the state's purchases and sales of SDRs, gold, and hard currencies other than its own, and changes in its deposits with the IMF. If a state has more money flowing out than in, it gets that money from its reserves. If it has more money flowing in than out, it puts the money in its reserves. Thus, national accounts always balance in the end. At least, they almost balance; there is a residual category—errors and omissions—because even the most efficient and honest government (many governments are neither) cannot keep track of every bit of money crossing its borders.

International Debt

In one sense, an economy is constantly in motion, as money moves through the processes of production, trade, and consumption. But economies also contain *standing wealth*. The hard-currency reserves owned by governments are one form of standing wealth, but not the most important. Most standing wealth is in the form of homes and cars, farms and factories, ports and railroads. In particular, *capital* goods (such as factories) are products that can be used as inputs for further production. Nothing lasts forever, but standing wealth lasts for enough years to be treated differently from goods that are quickly consumed. The main difference is that capital can be used to create more wealth: factories produce goods, railroads support commerce, and so forth. Standing wealth creates new wealth, so the economy tends to grow over time. As it grows, more standing wealth is created. In a capitalist economy, money makes more money.

Interest rates reflect this inherent growth dynamic. *Real* interest rates are the rates for borrowing money above and beyond the rate of inflation (for instance, if money is loaned at an annual interest rate of 8 percent but inflation is 3 percent, the real interest rate is 5 percent). Businesses and households borrow money because they think they can use it to create new wealth faster than the rate of interest on the loan.

If a state's economy is healthy, it can borrow money from foreign governments, banks, or companies and create enough new wealth to repay the debts a few years later. But states, like businesses, sometimes operate at a loss; then their debts mount up. In a vicious circle, more and more of the income they generate goes to pay interest, and more money must be borrowed to keep the state in operation. If its fortunes reverse, a state or business can create wealth again and over time pay back the principal on its

---

[9] Kindleberger, Charles P. *International Capital Movements*. Cambridge, 1987.

debts to climb out of the hole. If not, it will have to begin selling off part of its standing wealth (buildings, airplanes, factories, and the like). The *net worth* of the state or business (all its assets minus all its liabilities) will decrease.

Failure to repay debts makes it hard to borrow in the future, a huge impediment to economic growth. In the 1970s and 1980s, debts accumulated in some developing countries to the point of virtual national bankruptcy. The debts became unpayable, and the lenders (banks and governments) had to write them off the books or settle them at a fraction of their official value. In 2001, when Argentina collapsed under more than $100 billion of debt accumulated over the prior decade (see pp. 325–326), creditors had to accept less than one-third of their money in a 2005 restructuring deal. In 2010 to 2012, financial markets repeatedly slumped in reaction to fears of a Greek default on large debts, which some feared would cause a chain reaction in other shaky European economies—Spain, Portugal, Ireland, and perhaps Italy—that could ultimately threaten the entire euro zone.

Why do states go into debt? One major reason is a trade deficit. In the balance of payments, a trade deficit must somehow be made up. It is common to borrow money to pay for a trade deficit. A second reason is the income and consumption pattern among households and businesses. If people and firms spend more than they take in, they must borrow to pay their bills. The credit card they use may be from a local bank, but that bank may be getting the money it lends to them from foreign lenders.

A third reason for national debt is government spending relative to taxation. Under the principles of **Keynesian economics** (named for economist John Maynard Keynes), governments sometimes spend more on programs than they take in from tax revenue— *deficit spending*—to stimulate economic growth. This has been the strategy adopted by many G8 countries in the current financial crisis, especially the United States. If this strategy works, increased economic growth eventually generates higher tax revenues to make up the deficit. If it does not, a state finds itself with a poor economy in even deeper debt.

Government decisions about spending and taxation are called **fiscal policy**; decisions about printing and circulating money are called **monetary policy**.[10] These are the two main tools available for government to manage an economy. There is no free lunch: high taxation

DRAGGED DOWN BY DEBT

Failure to make payments on international debt, called a default, is a very serious action because it can cut off a country's access to future investment and loans. Nonetheless, several states have defaulted on debts rather than inflict painful budget cuts that would hurt the population. In 2011, Greece contemplated a possible default on its huge debts, which could harm the euro zone that it belongs to. This trader reacts as Germany's stock market falls on fears of a Greek default.

---

[10] Kirshner, Jonathan, ed. *Monetary Orders: Ambiguous Economics, Ubiquitous Politics.* Cornell, 2003.

chokes off economic growth, printing excess money causes inflation, and borrowing to cover a deficit places a mortgage on the state's standing wealth. Thus, for all the complexities of governmental economic policies and international economic transactions, a state's wealth and power ultimately depend more than anything on the underlying health of its economy—the education and training of its labor force, the amount and modernity of its capital goods, the morale of its population, and the skill of its managers. In the long run, international debt reflects these underlying realities.

Shifts in financial fortune among the great powers often accompany changing power relations. Consider how the past decade has changed the financial positions of the United States, of Russia and Eastern Europe, and of Asia. (The position of Europe, including the new European currency, is discussed in Chapter 10.)

The Position of the United States

The United States is an extraordinarily wealthy and powerful state. Its most *unique* strengths may be in the area of international security—as the world's only superpower—but its economic strengths are also striking. It is not only the world's largest economy but also the most technologically advanced one in such growth sectors as computers, telecommunications, aviation and aerospace, and biotechnology. The U.S. position in scientific research and higher education is unparalleled in the world.

The U.S. position in the international economy, however, has shifted over the decades. U.S. hegemony peaked after World War II, then gradually eroded as competitors gained relative ground (especially in Western Europe and Asia). In the early 1950s, the U.S. economy (GDP) was about twice the size of the next six advanced industrial states *combined.* By the 1980s, its relative share of world GDP had dropped almost by half. In 1950, the United States held half of the world's financial reserves; by 1980, it held less than 10 percent. This long-term decline after the extraordinary post–1945 U.S. hegemony was a natural and probably unavoidable one. The shifting U.S. financial position since the 1980s is illustrated in Figure 9.1. In the early 1980s, the trade deficit (exports minus imports) grew from near zero to $200 billion in just a few years. The trade deficit shrank back, but then grew to more than $700 billion a year by 2007. After shrinking again during the 2008–2009 recession, the trade deficit began to grow again in 2010. The budget deficit meanwhile jumped to $300 billion per year in the early 1980s, then closed in the 1990s and briefly became a large surplus, only to hit a deficit of $1 trillion by 2008 as a result of war spending, tax cuts, and a Keynesian effort to stimulate economic growth during the economic recession. These trends have caused alarm regarding U.S. international economic leadership.[11]

The United States ended the 1990s with all-time low unemployment, low inflation, robust growth, stock market gains, and a budget surplus. Despite these successes, the U.S. expansion eventually ran out of steam, the bubble of Internet investment burst, and the United States was again in recession by 2001—this time joined by all the world's major economies, and hammered painfully home by the economic disruptions that followed the September 2001 terrorist attacks. Growth resumed during 2002–2006, but as growth slowed in 2007, the U.S. economic position grew increasingly tenuous. By the end of 2008, the American economy was in full recession, unemployment was at its

---

[11] Thorbecke, Willem. *The Effects of U.S. Budget Deficits on Financial Markets since 1980.* Edward Elgar, 2009. Dam, Kenneth W. *The Rules of the Global Game: A New Look at U.S. International Economic Policy Making.* Chicago, 2001.

FIGURE 9.1 U.S. Financial Position, 1970–2009

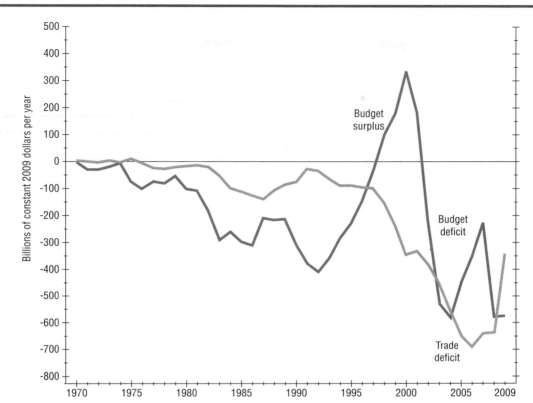

For decades the United States has imported more than it has exported (the current account balance or trade deficit), and its government has spent more than its income (the budget deficit). The budget deficit results in a large national debt.

highest rate in 25 years, consumer spending had plummeted, and several of the largest U.S. banks either merged with one another or were bailed out by the government. By 2010, the American economy had begun to grow again, yet unemployment remained relatively high.

In addition, the accumulated debt from 20 years of deficit spending remains. The U.S. government's **national debt** grew from about $1 trillion at the beginning of the 1980s to $3 trillion by the end of that decade, to $15 trillion in 2012. The interest payments are equivalent to what would otherwise be a healthy rate of economic growth. Not long ago, the United States was the world's leading lender state; now it is the world's leading debtor state.

These U.S. financial trends have profound implications for the entire world political economy. They first undermined (in the 1980s), then reconstructed (in the 1990s), and then undermined again (since 2000) the leading U.S. role in stabilizing international trade and monetary relations, in ensuring the provision of collective goods, and in providing capital for the economic development of other world regions. In a more decentralized, more privatized world economy with an uncertain U.S. role, collective goods problems would be harder to solve and free trade harder to achieve.

The Position of Russia and Eastern Europe

The United States provided limited capital (investments, loans, and grants) to help get the Russian and Eastern European region on its feet again after the Cold War. The United States has not repeated in Russia and Eastern Europe the aid program that stimulated new growth in Western Europe and Japan after World War II.

Instead, states in this region faced daunting challenges as they converted from centrally planned to capitalist economies and joined the world capitalist economy. These challenges included integrating into the world trading system (membership in the WTO, bilateral trade agreements, and so forth) and attracting foreign investment. Among the most difficult tasks were the attempts of states in this region to join the international monetary system. These matter greatly because having a stable and convertible currency is a key element in attracting foreign business and expanding international trade.

Most of the states of the former Soviet bloc became members of the IMF and were assigned quotas. But the IMF and the World Bank would not make loans available freely to these states until their governments took strong action to curb inflation, balance government budgets, and ensure economic stability. Such stability would have been easier to achieve with the foreign loans, however, creating a chicken-and-egg problem.

All the economies of the region experienced a deep depression (shrinking GDP) in the years following the end of the Cold War. The economies of the former Soviet Union shrank by half over seven years before climbing again (see Table 9.2). In general, the Eastern European countries have turned around their economies more effectively than have the former Soviet republics. Among the latter, Russia was better off than some others; it had inherited much of the Soviet Union's economic infrastructure and natural resources, especially oil, and was large enough to gain the attention of the West. But internal power struggles created political instability in Russia, discouraging foreign investment. Inflation reached 1,500 percent in 1992 but was brought down to less than 10 percent by 2006. Growth returned—more than 6 percent a year in 2000–2005—and a new flat tax on income boosted tax collections. By 2009, Russia had signed bilateral agreements, which precede WTO membership, with all WTO members except Georgia, which fought a war with Russia in 2008 and could single-handedly block Russia's joining.

TABLE 9.2 Economic Collapse in Russia and Eastern Europe

Country	Cumulative (10-Year) Change in GDP, 1990–1999
Russia/CIS	−50%
Former Yugoslavia	−35%
Estonia, Latvia, and Lithuania	−29%
Bulgaria	−29%
Romania	−28%
Albania	−12%
Czech Republic	−11%
Slovakia	−1%
Hungary	−1%
Poland	+21%

Source: Authors' estimates based on United Nations, *World Economic and Social Survey 1999*. United Nations, 1999, p. 263.

Organized crime emerged as a major problem in the 1990s. "Plutocrats" seized formerly state-owned companies and drained their wealth into private bank accounts. The chaos of transition also provided fertile ground for corruption among government officials. In 2004, Russia's largest oil company (Yukos) was shut down by then-President Vladimir Putin because of nonpayment of a $10 billion tax bill, only to have its assets purchased by a state-owned business. (Yukos's owner was an opponent of Putin.) The state has consolidated its control of major companies and the media again, using its powers to put the "plutocrats" under its control or push them aside.

Since a financial crisis in 1998, Russia has registered strong economic growth and reduced runaway inflation to less than 10 percent a year. Recently, high oil prices helped Russia (an oil exporter) to pay off debts and build large foreign reserves. Incomes are rising and poverty shrinking. However, structural obstacles remain, including corruption, weak rule of law, and political uncertainty as the government centralizes power and reasserts state control over business and the press. Russia was aggressive in attempting to stabilize its economy during the global recession and those efforts appeared to pay off as economic growth began to return by late 2009. The return of Vladimir Putin to the presidency in 2012 could provide greater economic stability (perhaps at the cost of freedoms), and Russia's joining the World Trade Organization should boost trade and foreign investment. Full integration into the world capitalist economy will require currency stability and convertibility, stronger rule of law, and reduced corruption.

The Position of Asia

Following decades of robust growth since the devastation of World War II, Japan by the 1980s seemed to be emerging as a possible rival to the United States as the world's leading industrial power. Japanese auto manufacturers gained ground on U.S. rivals when smaller cars became popular after the oil-price shocks of the 1970s. In electronics and other fields, Japanese products began to dominate world markets, and Japanese capital became a major economic force in nearby developing economies (such as China and Thailand) and even in the United States, where Japanese creditors financed much of the growing U.S. national debt.

These successes, however, masked serious problems. The economic growth of the 1980s drove prices of stocks and real estate to unrealistic levels based on speculation rather than inherent value. When these collapsed at the end of the 1980s, many banks were left with bad loans backed by deflated stocks and real estate. These losses were covered up, and the underlying problems—lax banking regulation, political cronyism, and outright corruption—persisted through the 1990s.

Despite the example of Japan's financial system, these mistakes were repeated almost exactly in the 1990s by other countries of East and Southeast Asia. Real estate and stocks became overvalued as rapid economic growth led to speculation and ever-rising expectations. Banks made massive bad loans based on the overvalued assets and got away with it because of political corruption and cronyism. In 1997, these economies suffered a serious financial crisis, which jumped across international borders and sent shock waves around the globe that reverberated for two years. The *1997 Asian financial crisis* began when currency speculators began selling off the currencies of Southeast Asian countries. Thailand, the Philippines, Malaysia, and Indonesia were forced to let their currencies be devalued. The currency problems of Asian countries led to stock market crashes in several of them. Other so-called *emerging markets* around the world—notably Brazil—suffered as investors generalized the problems in Asia.

The Philippines addressed the problem in the manner that international agencies and foreign investors preferred. After losing $1 billion in unsuccessfully defending its

BODY CHECK

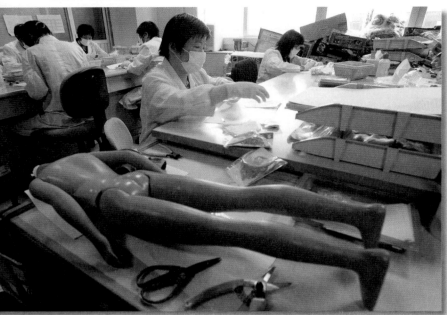

East Asia's economies have grown robustly in the decade since the 1997 financial crisis, but many of the causes of instability remain. Poor quality control in China's fast-growing export sector has sent tainted foods, drugs, and toys to Western markets. Authorities opened this toy-testing lab in response, 2007.

currency's value, the Philippines let its currency float and then asked the IMF for a $1 billion stabilization loan, which the IMF approved in a week. In return for the IMF loan, the Philippines' government agreed to keep interest rates high and budget deficits low (to reduce inflation), to pass a tax reform law, and to tighten control of banks that had made bad real estate loans. These kinds of tough measures create political problems, especially when banks are politically connected or when governments are corrupt. The Philippines, by addressing such problems, won international approval.

Other Asian countries did not act decisively and suffered greater economic setbacks. The currency speculators attacked Indonesia, which had to let its currency fall, raise interest rates, and let its stock market drop. Within months, Indonesia too sought tens of billions of dollars in IMF loans, with the usual conditions attached. But Indonesia resisted implementing the promised reforms, and its economy continued to slide (as did its political stability) in 1998. Riots and student protests eventually forced Indonesia's President Suharto to resign after 30 years of dictatorship. Overall, in Thailand, Malaysia, and Indonesia, stock markets lost about half their value and currencies about a quarter of their value.

When South Korea caught this "Asian flu" in 1997, its stock markets collapsed and its banks were saddled with $50 billion in bad loans based on cronyism. The IMF stepped in with a $60 billion international bailout—the largest ever—and Koreans elected a new reformist president. Thus in South Korea, as in Thailand and Indonesia, the financial crisis brought about reform as well as pain.

China escaped harm from the 1997 crisis, for several reasons: its economic growth had been less speculative (although rapid), its currency was not freely convertible, it held massive reserves of hard currency, and its government had shown the discipline necessary to bring inflation under control. The government reduced inflation from 20 percent to less than 4 percent in 1995–1997, and the engineer of this tight-money policy, Zhu Rongji, became the Chinese prime minister in 1998. (Successful inflation fighters also became presidents of Brazil and Argentina in the 1990s.)

In theory, the instant free flow of capital around the world—a result of global communications technologies—should stabilize economies. Investors can shift money quickly, and thus incrementally, as conditions indicate shifting strength and weakness of different currencies and economies. Instead of waiting for governments to devalue or revalue currencies when problems are far along, markets can gradually adjust values day by day. In practice, however, the global liquidity of capital has also shown a destabilizing tendency, as small events can be amplified and reverberate in distant locations. Thus the problems of Thailand became an Asian crisis and then an emerging-markets crisis, as liquid capital fled for cover at the speed of light. These events foreshadowed the financial crisis in 2008 when events in one country and sector again quickly spread worldwide.

Governments face a dilemma in that politically desirable policies—from stimulating growth and keeping taxes low to supporting banks and businesses owned by friends and relatives—tend to undermine currency stability. If allowed to continue, such policies may lead to an economic collapse and the loss of foreign investment, but tough policies to maintain currency stability may cause a government to lose power.

In all the regions just discussed—North America, Asia, Russia and Eastern Europe— the role of private businesses is expanding relative to that of the state. Throughout the remainder of the world, private business plays a role in the economy that exceeds that of the state. The remainder of this chapter considers the international political issues related to the operation of private businesses across state borders.

Multinational Business

Although states are the main rule makers for currency exchange and other international economic transactions, those transactions are carried out mainly by private firms and individuals, not governments. Most important among these private actors are MNCs.

Watch the **Video** **"Banking Interests and Regulatory Reform"** on **mypoliscilab.com**

Multinational Corporations

Multinational corporations (MNCs) are companies based in one state with affiliated branches or subsidiaries operating in other states. There is no exact definition, but the clearest case of an MNC is a large corporation that operates on a worldwide basis in many countries simultaneously, with fixed facilities and employees in each. There is also no exact count of the total number of MNCs, but most estimates are in the tens of thousands worldwide.

Most important are *industrial corporations*, which make goods in factories in various countries and sell them to businesses and consumers in various countries. The automobile, oil, and electronics industries have the largest MNCs. Almost all of the largest MNCs are based in G8 states.[12]

Financial corporations (the most important being banks) also operate multinationally— although often with more restrictions than industrial MNCs. Among the largest commercial banks worldwide, the United States does not hold a leading position—reflecting the traditional U.S. antitrust policy that limits banks' geographic expansion. The growing international integration of financial markets was spectacularly illustrated in 1995, when a single 28-year-old trader in Singapore lost $1 billion speculating on Japanese stock and bond markets and bankrupted his employer, a 200-year-old British investment bank.

Some MNCs sell *services*.[13] The McDonald's fast-food chain and American Telephone and Telegraph (AT&T) are good examples. So are the international airlines, which sell tickets in dozens of states (and currencies) for travel all over the world. More down-to-earth service businesses such as retail grocery stores can also become MNCs. The United States predominates in service MNCs as it does in industrial ones.

---

[12] United Nations. *World Investment Report 1994: Transnational Corporations, Employment and the Workplace.* United Nations, 1994.

[13] Mattoo, Aaditya, Robert M. Stern, and Gianni Zanini. *A Handbook of International Trade in Services.* Oxford, 2007.

DOING BUSINESS WORLDWIDE

Multinational corporations (MNCs) play important roles in international relations and are powerful actors with considerable resources in negotiating with governments. Here, Airbus, a division of a European MNC, shows off its new super-jumbo jet at the Singapore Airshow, 2008.

The role of MNCs in international political relations is complex and in some dispute.[14] Some scholars see MNCs as virtually being agents of their home national governments. This view resonates with mercantilism, in which economic activity ultimately serves political authorities; thus MNCs have clear national identities and act as members of their national society under state authority. A variant of this theme (from a more revolutionary world view) considers national governments as being agents of their MNCs; state interventions (economic and military) serve private, monied interests.

Others see MNCs as citizens of the world beholden to no government. The head of Dow Chemical once said he dreamed of buying an island beyond any state's territory and putting Dow's world headquarters there. In such a view, MNCs act globally in the interests of their (international) stockholders and owe loyalty to no state. In any case, MNCs are motivated by the need to maximize profits. Only in the case of state-owned MNCs—an important exception but a small minority of the total companies worldwide—do MNC actions reflect state interests. Even then, managers of state-owned MNCs have won greater autonomy to pursue profit in recent years (as part of the economic reforms instituted in many countries), and in many cases state-owned enterprises are being sold off (privatized).

As independent actors in the international arena, MNCs are increasingly powerful. Dozens of industrial MNCs have annual sales of tens of billions of dollars each (hundreds of billions of dollars for the top corporations such as ExxonMobil, Wal-Mart, and GM). Only about 35 states have more economic activity per year (GDP) than did the largest MNC in 2010, Wal-Mart. However, the largest *government* (the United States) has government revenues of $2 trillion—about seven times that of Wal-Mart. Thus the power of MNCs does not rival that of the largest states but exceeds that of many poorer states; this affects MNC operations in the global South (see pp. 476–478).

Giant MNCs contribute to global interdependence. They are so deeply entwined in so many states that they have a profound interest in the stable operation of the international system—in security affairs as well as in trade and monetary relations.[15] MNCs prosper in a stable international atmosphere that permits freedom of trade, of movement, and of capital flows (investments)—all governed by market forces with minimal government interference. Thus MNCs are, overall, a strong force for liberalism in the

[14] Doremus, Paul N., William W. Keller, Louis W. Pauly, and Simon Reich. *The Myth of the Global Corporation.* Princeton, 1998. Gilpin, Robert. *U.S. Power and the Multinational Corporation.* Basic Books, 1975.
[15] Brooks, Stephen G. *Producing Security: Multinational Corporations, Globalization, and the Changing Calculus of Conflict.* Princeton, 2005.

world economy, despite the fact that particular MNCs in particular industries push for certain mercantilist policies to protect their own interests.

Most MNCs have a world management system based on *subsidiaries* in each state in which they operate. The operations within a given state are subject to the legal authority of that state's government. But the foreign subsidiaries are owned (in whole or in substantial part) by the parent MNC in the home country. Thus, the parent MNC hires and fires the top managers of its foreign subsidiaries. The business infrastructure is a key aspect of *transnational relations*—linkages among people and groups across national borders.

In addition to the direct connections among members of a single MNC, the operations of MNCs support a global business infrastructure connecting a transnational community of businesspeople. A U.S. manager arriving in Seoul, South Korea, for instance, does not find a bewildering scene of unfamiliar languages, locations, and customs. Rather, he or she moves through a familiar sequence of airport lounges, telephone calls and faxes, international hotels, business conference rooms, and CNN broadcasts—most likely hearing English spoken in all.

Foreign Direct Investment

MNCs do not just operate in foreign countries, they also own capital there—buildings, factories, cars, and so forth. For instance, U.S. and German MNCs own some of the capital located in Japan, and Japanese MNCs own capital located in the United States and Germany. *Investment* means exchanging money for ownership of capital (for the purpose of producing a stream of income that will, over time, more than compensate for the money invested). Investments in foreign countries are among the most important, and politically sensitive, activities of MNCs. Figure 9.2 illustrates the growth of foreign direct investment. Although there is a strong trend toward more foreign direct investment, these flows rise and fall with the global economy.

Unlike portfolio investment (on paper), **foreign direct investment** involves tangible goods such as factories and office buildings (including ownership of a sizable fraction of a company's total stock, as opposed to a portfolio with little bits of many companies). Paper can be traded on a global market relatively freely, but direct investments cannot be freely moved from one state to another when conditions change. Direct investment is long term, and it is more visible than portfolio investment. Investments in the manufacturing sector usually entail the greatest investment in fixed facilities and in training workers and managers. Investments in the service sector tend to be less expensive and easier to walk away from if conditions change.[16]

Mercantilists tend to view foreign investments in their own country suspiciously. In developing countries, foreign direct investment often evokes concerns about a loss of sovereignty, because governments may be less powerful (and possibly less wealthy) than the MNCs that invest in their country. These fears also reflect the historical fact that most foreign investment in the global South once came from colonizers. Furthermore, although such investments create jobs, they also bring dislocations of traditional ways of life and cultures.

But because many poor and transitional states also desperately need capital from any source to stimulate economic growth, foreign direct investment is generally

[16] Jensen, Nathan M. *Nation-States and the Multinational Corporation: A Political Economy of Foreign Direct Investment.* Princeton, 2008.

FIGURE 9.2 Foreign Direct Investment, World Total, 1970–2009

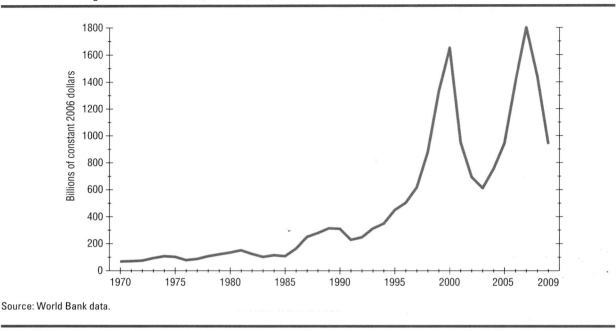

Source: World Bank data.

welcomed and encouraged despite the fears of economic nationalists (North-South investment is discussed further on pp. 476–478).[17] Most foreign direct investment (like most portfolio investment) is not in the global South, however, but in industrialized countries.

Economic nationalists in industrialized countries also worry about losing power and sovereignty due to foreign investment. In Canada, for instance, mercantilists are alarmed that U.S. firms own more than half of Canada's manufacturing industry and more than two-thirds of Canada's oil and gas industry. Canada is much smaller than the United States, yet it depends heavily on U.S. trade. In this asymmetrical situation, some Canadians worry that they are being turned into an annex of the United States—economically, culturally, and ultimately politically—losing their own national culture and control of their economy.

Meanwhile, U.S. economic nationalists have similar concerns over foreign direct investment in the United States. Partly this reflects alarm over the accumulation of U.S. debts. Mercantilists see a loss of power when foreign investors buy up companies and real estate in a debtor country. Such concerns seem stronger when a foreign MNC buys an existing company or building than when it builds a new factory or other facility. For example, in 2005, an outcry in the United States forced a Chinese oil company to withdraw its bid to buy the U.S. company Unocal, which ended up selling itself for a lower price to a U.S. company. (Chinese business and government leaders resented what they saw as a U.S. double standard.) But when Honda builds a new car factory in Ohio, adding jobs and facilities to the U.S. economy, Americans perceive no such loss.

---

[17] Cohen, Stephen D. *Multinational Corporations and Foreign Direct Investment: Avoiding Simplicity, Embracing Complexity.* Oxford, 2007.

Liberalism does not condone such arguments. Liberal economists emphasize that global efficiency and the increased generation of wealth result from the ability of MNCs to invest freely across international borders. Investment decisions should be made solely on economic grounds, not nationalistic ones. In the view of liberal economists, foreign investments in the United States help, rather than hurt, the U.S. economy. Many of the benefits of a profitable Japanese factory in the United States accrue to U.S. workers at the plant and U.S. consumers of its products, even if some profits go back to Japan (and even those profits may be reinvested in the United States). Because U.S. MNCs have more than $1 trillion of foreign direct investment outside the United States, the picture is by no means one-sided.

Host and Home Government Relations

A state in which a foreign MNC operates is called the **host country;** the state where the MNC has its headquarters is called its **home country**. MNC operations create a variety of problems and opportunities for both the host and home countries' governments. Conflicts between the host government and the MNC may spill over to become an interstate conflict between the host government and home government. For example, if a host government takes an MNC's property without compensation or arrests its executives, the home government may step in to help the MNC.[18]

Because host governments can regulate activities on their own territories, an MNC cannot operate in a state against the wishes of its government. Conversely, because MNCs have many states to choose from, a host government cannot generally force an MNC to do business in the country against the MNC's wishes. At least in theory, MNCs operate in host countries only when it is in the interests of both the MNC and the host government. Common interests result from the creation of wealth in the host country by the MNC. Both the MNC and the host government benefit—the MNC from profits, the government directly by taxation and indirectly through economic growth (generating future taxes and political support).

However, conflicts also arise in the relationship. One obvious conflict concerns the distribution of new wealth between the MNC and the host government. This distribution depends on the rate at which MNC activities or profits are taxed, as well as on the ground rules for MNC operations. Before an MNC invests or opens a subsidiary in a host country, it sits down with the government to negotiate these issues. Threats of violent leverage are largely irrelevant. Rather, the government's main leverage is to promise a favorable climate for doing business and making money; the MNC's main leverage is to threaten to take its capital elsewhere.

Governments can offer a variety of incentives to MNCs to invest. Special terms of taxation and of regulation are common. In cases of resource extraction, negotiations may revolve around the rates the government will charge to lease land and mineral rights to the MNC. National and local governments may offer to provide business infrastructure—such as roads, airports, or phone lines—at the government's expense. (An MNC could also offer to build such infrastructure if allowed to operate on favorable terms in the country.) Over time, certain locations may develop a strong business infrastructure and gain a comparative advantage in luring MNCs to locate there.

In addition to these relatively straightforward questions of distribution, MNC relations with host governments contain several other sources of potential conflict. One is

---

[18] Rodman, Kenneth A. *Sanctity versus Sovereignty: U.S. Policy toward the Nationalization of Natural Resource Investments in the Third World.* Columbia, 1988.

IT'S A JOB

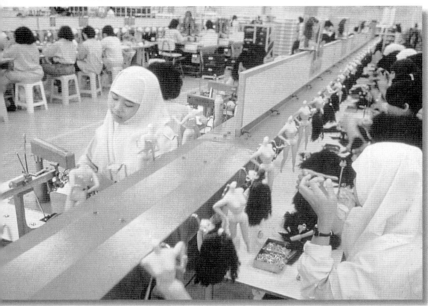

Foreign direct investment is often sought by host governments because it stimulates employment and economic growth, though at wages that home countries would not tolerate. Here, Muslim women in Indonesia assemble Barbies at a Mattel factory. Note that along with investment, a host country imports certain cultural trappings of the MNC's activity—such as Mattel's rendition of femininity in its doll. (This is a literal case of what postmodern feminists call the social construction of gender roles.)

the potential for governments to break their agreements with MNCs and change the terms of taxes, regulations, or other conditions. The extreme case is nationalization, in which a host government takes ownership of MNC facilities and assets in the host country (with or without compensation). In recent years, Russia, Venezuela, Bolivia, and Ecuador have all taken significant state ownership in what had been foreign assets in those countries' oil and gas sectors. Once an MNC has invested in fixed facilities, it loses much of its leverage over the government because it cannot move to another country without incurring huge expenses. However, governments hesitate to break their word with MNCs because then other MNCs may not invest in the future. In fact, for this reason foreign direct investment in Bolivia dropped by 90 percent from 1999 to 2005.[19] Nationalization of foreign assets is rare now.

Another source of conflict is the trade policies of the host government. Government restrictions on trade seldom help foreign MNCs; more often they help the host country's own industries—which often directly compete with foreign MNCs. Ironically, although they favor global free trade, MNCs may funnel direct investment to states that restrict imports, because MNCs can avoid the import restrictions by producing goods in the host country (rather than exporting from the home country). Trade restrictions are thus another form of leverage that states have in luring foreign direct investment.

Trade regulations often seek to create as many jobs and as much taxable income as possible within the host country. If Toyota assembles cars at a factory in the United States (perhaps to avoid U.S. import restrictions), the U.S. government tends to pressure Toyota to use more U.S. parts in building the cars (such "domestic content" rules were part of NAFTA). MNCs generally want the freedom to assemble goods anywhere from parts made anywhere; governments, by contrast, want to maximize the amount of wealth created on their own territories. With parts and supplies now routinely converging from many countries to go into a product completed in one country, it is very difficult to say exactly where the product was made. The question is a complex one that entails long negotiations between MNCs and host governments.

Monetary policy also leads to conflicts between MNCs and host governments. When a state's currency is devalued, imports suddenly become more expensive. A foreign MNC selling an imported product (or a product assembled from imported parts) in the host country can be

---

[19] Romero, Simon, and Juan Forero. Bolivia's Energy Takeover: Populism Rules in the Andes. *The New York Times*, May 3, 2006: A8.

devastated by such a change. For example, if the dollar falls relative to the yen, Toyota USA may have to charge more U.S. dollars for its cars in order to pay for the parts it brings in from Japan. Therefore, an MNC making a long-term investment in a host country wants the country's currency to be reasonably stable.

Finally, MNCs may conflict with host governments on issues of international security as well as domestic political stability. When an MNC invests in a country, it assumes that its facilities there will operate profitably over a number of years. If a war or revolution takes away the MNC's facility, the company loses not just income but capital—the standing wealth embodied in that facility. In 2001, ExxonMobil suspended operations at gas fields in Aceh province of Indonesia for three months until the Indonesian government—which earns $1 billion a year from the operation—brought in military forces to suppress armed separatists who had been attacking ExxonMobil. In 2003, Chevron Texaco, Shell, and TotalFinaElf had to shut down oil production in Nigeria for weeks owing to ethnic violence.

In negotiating over these various sources of conflict, MNCs use a variety of means to influence host governments. These generally follow the same patterns as those used by domestic corporations. MNCs hire lobbyists, use advertisements to influence public opinion, and offer incentives to host-country politicians (such as locating facilities in their districts). Such activities are politically sensitive because host-country citizens and politicians may resent foreigners' trying to influence them.

Corruption is another means of influence over host governments that cannot be overlooked. Nobody knows the full extent to which MNCs use payoffs, kickbacks, gifts, and similar methods to win the approval of individual government officials for policies favorable to the MNC. Certainly this occurs frequently with host governments in the global South (where government officials may be more desperate for income), but corruption also occurs regularly in rich industrialized countries.

MNCs have a range of conflicts with their home governments (where their headquarters are located), just as they do with their host states.[20] Some MNC conflicts with home governments resemble the conflicts with host governments. Taxation is an important one. Trade policies are another. A recurrent complaint of MNCs against home governments is that policies adopted to punish political adversaries—economic sanctions and less extreme restrictions—end up harming the home-country MNCs more than the intended target. Usually, a competing MNC from another country is able to step into the gap when a government restricts its own MNCs. Unless they are prohibited from doing so, MNCs tend to go on doing business wherever it is profitable, with little regard for the political preferences of their governments.

THE CHILDREN BEHIND THE CHOCOLATE

International business prospers in stable political environments in host countries, but the relationship of a host country with an investing MNC can be complex. Foreign investors are wary of putting money into business environments marked by inflation, crime, corruption, and especially armed violence that could hit their facilities and employees. Ivory Coast, the world's largest supplier of cocoa, not only suffered from civil war in recent years but depends on child labor to grow the cocoa that corporations ultimately market as chocolate products around the world. This 14-year-old works on a cocoa plantation, 2001.

---

[20] Pauly, Louis W. *Who Elected the Bankers? Surveillance and Control in the World Economy.* Cornell, 1997.

Sometimes governments do prevail, because MNCs often need the support of their home governments. In the 1990s, the U.S.-based Conoco oil company agreed to a billion-dollar oil development project in Iran, just when the U.S. government was trying to isolate Iran as a rogue state. Under pressure from the U.S. government, Conoco quickly decided to back out of the deal. This move saved Conoco a fight with its home government, but cost Conoco a lucrative contract that went instead to a European company.

The location of an MNC's headquarters determines its home nationality. The shareholders and top executives of an MNC are mostly from its home country. But as the world economy becomes more integrated, this is becoming less true. Just as MNCs are increasingly doing business all over the world and assembling products from parts made in many countries, so are shareholders and managers becoming more international in composition.[21]

All business activity takes place in an environment shaped by politics. The international business environment most conducive to the creation of wealth by MNCs is one of stable international security. It is difficult and risky to make money in a situation of international conflict, especially one that threatens to degenerate into violence and war. War destroys wealth, reduces the supply of labor, and distorts markets in many ways. Certainly some businesses profit from international instability and the threat of war—such as arms merchants and smugglers—but these are the exceptions.

Beyond these international security concerns, MNCs favor political stability in the broader rules of the game governing international business. In monetary policy, international business benefits from the stability of rates that the managed float system tries to achieve. In trade policy, business benefits from the stability of tariff levels in the slowly shifting WTO framework. In norms of international law, business benefits from the traditions holding governments responsible for their predecessors' debts and requiring compensation for nationalized foreign assets.

Occasionally, MNCs can get their home governments to provide security when host governments fail to do so. IR scholars continue to study the relationships between the international economic activities of MNCs and the international security activities of their home governments.[22]

Corporate alliances involving MNCs often have international implications. When business alliances in an industry that has international markets occur within a single state, the alliances may in effect promote economic nationalism. Increasingly, however, corporate alliances are forming across national borders. Such alliances tend to promote liberalism rather than economic nationalism.

These international business alliances undermine both economic nationalism and the concept of a world splitting into rival trading blocs based in Europe, North America, and East Asia. In fact, international business alliances create interdependence among their home states. National interests become more intertwined and interstate conflicts tend to be reduced. By operating in multiple countries at once, all MNCs have these effects to some degree. But because they are based in one home country, MNCs are foreigners in

[21] Bernhard, William T., and David Leblang. *Democratic Processes and Financial Markets: Pricing Politics.* Cambridge, 2006. Braithwaite, John, and Peter Drahos. *Global Business Regulation.* Cambridge, 2000.

[22] Krasner, Stephen D. *Defending the National Interest: Raw Materials Investments and U.S. Foreign Policy.* Princeton, 1978. Gibbs, David N. *The Political Economy of Third World Intervention: Mines, Money, and U.S. Policy in the Congo Crisis.* Chicago, 1991. Lipson, Charles. *Standing Guard: Protecting Foreign Capital in the Nineteenth and Twentieth Centuries.* California, 1985.

other countries. International alliances of MNCs, however, are at home in several countries at once.

We do not yet live in a world without national borders—by a long shot—but the international activities of MNCs are moving us in that direction. Chapter 10 explores some of the ways in which people, companies, and ideas are becoming globally integrated across states.

✓•⌐**Study**
and **Review**
the **Post-Test &**
Chapter Exam
at **mypoliscilab.com**

CHAPTER REVIEW

SUMMARY

- Each state uses its own currency (except 17 states share the euro). These currencies have no inherent value but depend on the belief that they can be traded for future goods and services.

- Gold and silver were once used as world currencies that had value in different countries. Today's system is more abstract: national currencies are valued against each other through exchange rates.

- The most important currencies—against which most other states' currencies are compared—are the U.S. dollar, the euro, and the Japanese yen.

- Inflation, most often resulting from the printing of currency faster than the creation of new goods and services, causes the value of a currency to fall relative to other currencies. Inflation rates vary widely but are generally much higher in the global South and former Soviet bloc than in the industrialized West.

- States maintain reserves of hard currency and gold. These reserves back a national currency and cover short-term imbalances in international financial flows.

- Fixed exchange rates can be used to set the relative value of currencies, but more often states use floating exchange rates driven by supply and demand on world currency markets.

- Governments cooperate to manage the fluctuations of (floating) exchange rates but are limited in this effort by the fact that most money traded on world markets is privately owned.

- Over the long term, the relative values of national currencies are determined by the underlying health of the national economies and by the monetary policies of governments (how much money they print).

- Governments often prefer a low (weak) value for their own currency, as this promotes exports, discourages imports, and hence improves the state's balance of trade. However, a sudden unilateral devaluation of the currency is a risky strategy because it undermines confidence in the currency.

- To ensure discipline in printing money—and to avoid inflation—industrialized states turn monetary policy over to semiautonomous central banks, such as the U.S. Federal Reserve. By adjusting interest rates on government money loaned to private banks, a central bank can control the supply of money in the national economy.

- The World Bank and the International Monetary Fund (IMF) work with states' central banks to maintain stable international monetary relations. From 1945 to 1971, this was done by pegging state currencies to the U.S. dollar and the dollar in turn to gold. Since then the system has used Special Drawing Rights (SDRs)—a kind of world currency controlled by the IMF—in place of gold.

- The IMF operates a system of national accounts to keep track of the flow of money into and out of states. The balance of trade (exports minus imports) must be balanced by capital flows (investments and loans) and changes in reserves.

- International debt results from a protracted imbalance in capital flows—a state borrowing more than it lends—to cover a chronic trade deficit or government budget deficit.

- The U.S. financial position declined naturally from its extraordinary predominance immediately after World War II. The fall of the dollar-gold standard in 1971 reflects this decline.

- The positions of Russia and the other states of the former Soviet bloc declined drastically as they made the difficult transition from communism to capitalism. Though the uncontrolled inflation of the early 1990s has subsided, the economies of the former Soviet republics are still not fully integrated into the world economy.

- Multinational corporations (MNCs) do business in more than one state simultaneously. The largest are based in the leading industrialized states, and most are privately owned. MNCs are increasingly powerful in international economic affairs.

- MNCs contribute to international interdependence in various ways. States depend on MNCs to create new wealth, and MNCs depend on states to maintain international stability conducive to doing business globally.

- MNCs try to negotiate favorable terms and look for states with stable currencies and political environments in which to make direct investments. Governments seek such foreign investments on their territories so as to benefit from the future stream of income.

- MNCs try to influence the international political policies of both their headquarters state and the other states in which they operate. Generally MNCs promote policies favorable to business—low taxes, light regulation, stable currencies, and free trade. They also support stable international security relations, because war generally disrupts business.

- Increasingly, MNCs headquartered in different states are forming international alliances with each other. These inter-MNC alliances, even more than other MNC operations across national borders, are creating international interdependence and promoting liberal international cooperation.

KEY TERMS

gold standard 322	devaluation 328	Keynesian economics 335
exchange rate 322	central bank 330	fiscal policy 335
convertible currency 323	discount rate 330	monetary policy 335
hyperinflation 323	Bretton Woods system 331	national debt 337
hard currency 323	World Bank 331	multinational corporations (MNCs) 341
reserves 324	International Monetary Fund (IMF) 331	foreign direct investment 343
fixed exchange rates 324	Special Drawing Right (SDR) 332	host country 345
floating exchange rates 324	balance of payments 333	home country 345
managed float 325		

CRITICAL THINKING QUESTIONS

1. Find a recent newspaper article about a change in currency exchange rates (usually located in the business section). Analyze the various influences that may have been at work in the change of currency values—monetary policies, the underlying state of national economies, the actions of central banks (separately or in coordination), and factors such as political uncertainty that affect investors' confidence in a currency.

2. The IMF's Special Drawing Rights (SDRs) are a world currency used only by governments for international currency management and national accounts. Do you think SDRs could become a currency used by businesses and individuals, and how could this happen (or why couldn't it)? What would be the effects on world business and on the ability of sovereign states to manage their own economies?

3. Many scholars and politicians alike think private international investment is the best hope for the economies of Russia and Eastern Europe. Given the current economic and political disarray in that region, what kinds of investors from the industrialized West might be willing to invest there? What actions could the governments of Western states take to encourage such investment? What pitfalls would the governments and investors have to watch out for?

4. If you were representing an MNC such as Toyota in negotiations over building an automobile factory in a foreign country, what kinds of concessions would you ask the host government for? What would you offer as incentives? In your report to Toyota's top management regarding the deal, what points would you emphasize as most important? If instead you were representing the host state in the negotiations and reporting to top state leaders, what would be your negotiating goals and the focus of your report?

5. Suppose that the head of Dow Chemical had his way and established Dow's world headquarters on an island outside all state territories. How do you think such a location would change Dow's strategies or business operations? What problems might it create for Dow?

Foreign Direct Investment: Engine of Growth or Tool of Exploitation?

Overview

Foreign direct investment (FDI) is a central part of the international economy. Well over a trillion dollars a year flows across borders as investments. Although much of that investment (almost $1.3 trillion in 2007) is investment between developed countries (such as Japan and the United States), an increasing amount (over $500 billion in 2007) flows from developed countries in the global North to developing countries in the global South.

Historically, most FDI flowed between countries in the global North. In fact, until the 1960s, the United States accounted for a large majority of FDI. Yet, with the growth of the global economy and the rise of globalization, FDI has become a global phenomenon. Throughout the 1970s and 1980s, FDI into developing countries remained low, averaging less than $20 billion as the 1990s approached. By the end of the 1990s, however, over $200 billion in investments entered into developing economies from abroad.

These flows to the global South are not without controversy. While some find these FDI flows necessary to spur economic growth, others argue that the money is not worth the political and social costs. Some states have attempted to lure FDI, especially from large Western MNCs, by undertaking domestic economic reforms. Other states do little to encourage FDI, fearful of potential negative environmental, social, and political impacts. Is FDI a positive resource for the developing world?

ARGUMENT 1

FDI Brings Positive Benefits to Developing Countries

FDI brings capital investment that is key to economic growth. What developing countries need more than anything to spur growth is capital. It is difficult for developing economies to generate this capital from within, so foreign investment is an excellent source of it to increase the potential for economic growth.

FDI brings more employment to developing economies. FDI often comes in the form of factories that bring increased employment for developing countries. While some argue that these jobs do not pay well, by local standards they often pay better than jobs generated locally.

FDI contributes to global interdependence. As firms and MNCs spread their manufacturing across the globe, this increases economic interdependence between states and thus fosters better relationships. As investors put more money into other states' economies, they may care more about those states' policies in other areas such as human rights or the environment. This could lead to pressure on FDI recipients to improve standards in areas such as labor practices or pollution.

FDI Brings Problems to Developing Countries

FDI's impact on developing economies is limited. Often, a very small number of individuals benefit from FDI, leaving the rest of the population unaffected by this external investment. Thus, even when FDI does add to economic growth, this growth is distributed very unevenly, leading to a large rich-poor gap in recipient states.

Policies to lure FDI hurt recipient states. To lure large amounts of foreign investment, states will often adopt policies to please investors such as large MNCs. These policies can include tax breaks (thus removing a source of state income), lax environmental standards (leading to problems such as pollution), or weak labor standards (leading to abusive labor practices such as child labor).

Jobs created by FDI are of poor quality. Regardless of their pay, jobs created by FDI are of poor quality. Almost all lack any significant benefits, and unionization is nearly always prohibited. The jobs can be very temporary as well—if a lower-cost labor supply is found, MNCs will pick up and move to other locations at a moment's notice. These are not the types of jobs that bring long-term stability to developing economies.

Questions

- On balance, do you believe that FDI is good or bad for developing countries? Given the expansion of MNCs and investment in this time of globalization, can a developing country forgo FDI if it hopes to achieve economic growth?

- Assuming that some harm comes to recipients of FDI, how can the harm be mitigated? Would it be easier to change the policies of the states that accept FDI or the behavior of the investors and businesses that invest in developing states?

- What leverage do leaders in developing countries have against MNCs that want to invest in their states? What are the dangers in making demands about the nature of FDI that enters the state?

For Further Reading

Jensen, Nathan. *Nation-States and the Multinational Corporation: A Political Economy of Foreign Direct Investment.* Princeton, 2008.

Cohen, Stephen D. *Multinational Corporations and Foreign Direct Investment: Avoiding Simplicity, Embracing Complexity.* Oxford, 2007.

Moran, Theodore. *Harnessing Foreign Direct Investment for Development: Policies for Developed and Developing Countries.* Center for Global Development, 2006.

Paus, Eva. *Global Capitalism Unbound: Winners and Losers from Offshore Outsourcing.* Palgrave, 2007.

CHAPTER 10 International Integration

European Parliament, 2011.

Globalization and Integration

Common to most discussions of globalization is a sense that there are forces in the world bringing us all closer together. Some of these forces are the result of state decisions—as we discussed in Chapter 8, states have attempted to integrate their economies through free trade agreements. Still other forces are factors such as technological changes that influence how states, nonstate actors, and even individual citizens function on a day-to-day basis.

This chapter discusses the sources of this "coming together." First, we will discuss state decisions to cooperate in order to create international organizations that are **supranational**—they subsume a number of states and their functions within a larger whole. The UN, as we have seen, has some supranational aspects, though they are limited by the UN Charter, which is based on state sovereignty. On a regional level, the European Union (EU) is a somewhat more supranational entity than the UN; other regional organizations have tried to follow Europe's path as well, but with only limited success. These IOs all contain a struggle between the contradictory forces of *nationalism* and *supranationalism*—between state sovereignty and the higher authority of supranational structures.

The other source of "coming together" we examine is technological change, specifically, the revolution in information technologies such as the Internet. These technologies may be even more far-reaching in that they operate globally and regionally across state boundaries without formal political structures. Nearly all of us have been affected by information technology that has brought us closer together within a state, across a region, or around the world.

Whether the sources of integration are from states or nonstate actors, the process of integration always involves transnational actors or issues. *Transnational actors* (for example, MNCs and NGOs) bridge national borders, creating new avenues of interdependence among states.[1] *Transnational issues* (for example, global warming or the spread of information technology) are processes that force states to work together because they cannot solve or manage the issue alone. This chapter explores how transnational actors and issues can lead to integration either through the actions of states or through technological change.

Integration Theory

The theory of international integration attempts to explain why states choose supranationalism, which challenges once again the foundations of realism (state sovereignty and territorial integrity). **International integration** refers to the process by which supranational institutions replace national ones—the gradual shifting upward of sovereignty from state to regional or global structures. The ultimate expression of integration would be the merger of several (or many) states into a single state—or ultimately into a single world government. Such a shift in sovereignty to the supranational level would probably entail some version of federalism, in which states or other political units recognize the sovereignty of a central government while retaining certain powers

---

[1] Rissen-Kappen, Thomas, ed. *Bringing Transnational Relations Back In: Non-state Actors, Domestic Structures, and International Relations*. Cambridge, 1995.

CROSSING THE BORDER

Integration processes in Europe and elsewhere are making state borders more permeable to people, goods, and ideas—increasing interdependence. The European Union is deepening economic integration while expanding eastward. Here, in 2006, the Tour de France crosses into Germany, passing only a road sign where in centuries past, great armies faced off across massive fortifications.

for themselves. This is the form of government adopted (after some debate) in the U.S. Constitution.

In practice, the process of integration has never gone beyond a partial and uneasy sharing of power between state and supranational levels. States have been unwilling to give up their exclusive claim to sovereignty and have limited the power and authority of supranational institutions. The UN certainly falls far short of a federal model (see Chapter 7). It represents only a step in the direction of international integration. Other modest examples of the integration process have been encountered in previous chapters—for example, NAFTA and the WTO. But these arrangements hardly challenge states' territorial integrity and usually challenge political sovereignty on only a handful of issues (such as trade).

The most successful example of the process of integration by far—though even that success is only partial—is the European Union. The regional coordination now occurring in Western Europe is a new historical phenomenon achieved only since World War II.[2]

● ┐ **Watch**
the **Video**
"Preventing Stagflation
in the Global Economy"
on **mypoliscilab.com**

Until 50 years ago, the European continent was the embodiment of national sovereignty, state rivalry, and war. For 500 years, until 1945, the states of Europe were locked in chronic intermittent warfare; in the 20th century alone two world wars left the continent in ruins. The European states have historical and present-day religious, ethnic, and cultural differences. The 27 members of the EU in 2011 spoke 23 different official languages. If ever there were a candidate for the failure of integration, Europe would appear to be it. Even more surprising, European integration began with the cooperation of Europe's two bitterest enemies over the previous 100 years, enemies in three major wars since 1870—France and Germany (references to "Germany" refer to West Germany from 1944 to 1990, and unified Germany since).

That Western European states began forming supranational institutions and creating an economic community to promote free trade and coordinate economic policies caught the attention of IR scholars, who used the term *integration* to describe what they observed. Seemingly, integration challenged the realist assumption that states were strictly autonomous and would never yield power or sovereignty.

---

[2] Eichengreen, Barry. *The European Economy since 1945: Coordinated Capitalism and Beyond.* Princeton, 2006. Moravcsik, Andrew. *The Choice for Europe: Social Purpose and State Power from Messina to Maastricht.* Cornell, 1998. Dinan, Desmond. *Europe Recast: A History of the European Union.* Rienner, 2004.

These scholars proposed that European moves toward integration could be explained by *functionalism*—growth of specialized technical organizations that cross national borders.[3] According to functionalists, technological and economic development lead to more and more supranational structures as states seek practical means to fulfill necessary *functions* such as delivering mail from one country to another or coordinating the use of rivers that cross borders. As these connections became denser and the flows faster, functionalism predicted that states would be drawn together into stronger international economic structures.

The European experience, however, went beyond the creation of specialized agencies to include the development of more general, more political supranational bodies, such as the European Parliament. **Neofunctionalism** is a modification of functional theory by IR scholars to explain these developments. Neofunctionalists argue that economic integration (functionalism) generates a *political* dynamic that drives integration further. Closer economic ties require more political coordination in order to operate effectively and eventually lead to political integration as well—a process called *spillover*.

Some scholars focused on the less tangible *sense of community* ("we" feeling) that began to develop among Europeans, running contrary to nationalist feelings that still existed as well. The low expectation of violence among the states of Western Europe created a **security community** in which such feelings could grow.[4] This is a prime example of the identity principle discussed in Chapter 1.

Elsewhere in the world, economies were becoming more interdependent at both the regional and global levels. In Asia, the Association of South East Asian Nations (ASEAN), founded in 1967, chalked up some successes in promoting regional economic coordination over several decades. The Andean Common Market, begun in 1969, promoted a limited degree of regional integration in the member states of Venezuela, Colombia, Ecuador, Peru, and Bolivia. Other South American countries (Argentina, Brazil, Paraguay, and Uruguay) founded Mercosur in 1991 to increase economic trade and integration. Most recently, the countries of Africa in 2002 formed the African Union, an ambitious plan to coordinate economic and foreign policies, elect an African parliament, and create a stronger infrastructure than the predecessor, Organization of African Unity (OAU). Of course, none of these organizations have experienced the success of the EU, but their aims are often similar.[5]

The new wave of integration in Europe and elsewhere encountered limits and setbacks. Integration reduces states' ability to shield themselves and their citizens from the world's many problems and conflicts. For example, in the early 1990s Venezuela found that its open border with Colombia brought in large transshipments of cocaine bound for the United States. Moreover, as states increasingly fear transnational terrorism, the prospects of open borders can give state leaders pause.

---

[3] Mitrany, David. *The Functional Theory of Politics*. London School of Economics/M. Robertson, 1975. Haas, Ernst B. *Beyond the Nation-State: Functionalism and International Organization*. Stanford, 1964. Ginsberg, Roy H. *Demystifying the European Union: The Enduring Logic of Regional Integration*. Rowman & Littlefield, 2007.

[4] Adler, Emanuel, and Michael Barnett, eds. *Security Communities*. Cambridge, 1998. Deutsch, Karl W., et al. *Political Community and the North Atlantic Area: International Organization in the Light of Historical Experience*. Princeton, 1957.

[5] Mattli, Walter. *The Logic of Regional Integration: Europe and Beyond*. Cambridge, 1999. Gleditsch, Kristian S. *All International Politics Is Local: The Diffusion of Conflict, Integration, and Democracy*. Michigan, 2002. Acharya, Amitav, and Alastair I. Johnston. *Crafting Cooperation: Regional International Institutions in Comparative Perspective*. Cambridge, 2007.

Integration can mean greater centralization at a time when individuals, local groups, and national populations demand more say over their own affairs. The centralization of political authority, information, and culture as a result of integration can threaten both individual and group freedom. Ethnic groups want to safeguard their own cultures, languages, and institutions against the bland homogeneity that a global or regional melting pot would create. As a result, many states and citizens, in Europe and elsewhere, responded to the new wave of integration with resurgent nationalism over the past decade.

Indeed, these forces have set in motion a wave of *disintegration* of states running counter to (though simultaneous with) the integrating tendencies in today's world. The wave of disintegration in some ways began with the decolonization of former European empires in Africa, Asia, and the Middle East after World War II. After the Cold War, disintegration centered on Russia and Eastern Europe—especially in the former Soviet Union and former Yugoslavia. States in other regions—Somalia, Democratic Congo, and Iraq—appear in danger of breaking into pieces, in practice if not formally. A challenge to integration theorists in the future will be to account for these new trends running counter to integration.

Throughout the successful and unsuccessful efforts at integration runs a common thread—the tension between nationalism and supranational loyalties (regionalism or globalism). In the less successful integration attempts, nationalism stands virtually unchallenged, and even in the most successful cases, nationalism remains a potent force locked in continual struggle with supranationalism. This struggle is a central theme even in the most successful case of integration—the European Union.

The European Union

◉━⌐ **Watch**
the **Video**
"The New European Union"
on **mypoliscilab.com**

Like the UN, the **European Union (EU)** was created after World War II and has developed since. But whereas the UN structure has changed little since its Charter was adopted, the EU has gone through several waves of expansion in its scope, membership, and mission over the past 50 years.[6] The EU today has nearly 500 million citizens and surpasses the U.S. economy in GDP.

✳━⌐ **Explore**
the **Simulation**
"Integration: You Are a Citizen of Europe"
on **mypoliscilab.com**

The Vision of a United Europe

Europe in 1945 was decimated by war. Most of the next decade was spent recovering with help from the United States through the Marshall Plan. But already, two French leaders, Jean Monnet and Robert Schuman, were developing a plan to implement the idea of functionalism in Europe—that future wars could be prevented by creating economic linkages that would eventually bind states together politically.

In 1950, Schuman as French foreign minister proposed a first modest step—the merger of the French and German steel (iron) and coal industries into a single framework that could most efficiently use the two states' coal resources and steel mills. Coal and steel were key to European recovery and growth. The Schuman plan gave birth in 1952 to the

---

[6] Sidjanski, Dusan. *The Federal Future of Europe: From the European Community to the European Union.* Michigan, 2000. Caporaso, James A. *The European Union: Dilemmas of Regional Integration.* Westview, 2000. Nelsen, Brent F., and Alexander Stubb. *European Union: Readings on the Theory and Practice of European Integration.* Rienner, 2003.

European Coal and Steel Community (ECSC), in which France and Germany were joined by Italy (the third large industrial country of continental Europe) and by three smaller countries—Belgium, the Netherlands, and Luxembourg (together called the *Benelux countries*). These six states worked through the ECSC to reduce trade barriers in coal and steel and to coordinate their coal and steel policies. The ECSC also established a High Authority that to some extent could bypass governments and deal directly with companies, labor unions, and individuals. Britain did not join, however.

If coal and steel sound like fairly boring topics, that was exactly the idea of functionalists. The issues involved were matters for engineers and technical experts, and did not threaten politicians. Since 1952, technical experts have served as the leaders of the integration process in other aspects of European life and outside Europe. (Of course, coal and steel were not chosen by accident, since both were essential to make war.) As mentioned in Chapter 7, technical IOs such as the Universal Postal Union came before political ones such as the UN.

International scientific communities deserve special mention in this regard. If German and French steel experts had more in common than German and French politicians, this is even truer of scientists. Today the European scientific community is one of the most internationally integrated areas of society. For example, the EU operates the European Space Agency and the European Molecular Biology Laboratory.

Although technical cooperation succeeded in 1952, political and military cooperation proved much more difficult. In line with the vision of a united Europe, the six ECSC states signed a second treaty in 1952 to create a European Defense Community to work toward integrating Europe's military forces under one budget and command. But the French parliament failed to ratify the treaty, and Britain refused to join such a force. The ECSC states also discussed formation of a European Political Community in 1953, but could not agree on its terms. Thus, in economic cooperation the supranational institutions succeeded, but in political and military affairs, state sovereignty prevailed.

The Treaty of Rome

In the **Treaty of Rome** in 1957, the same six states (France, Germany, Italy, Belgium, the Netherlands, Luxembourg) created two new organizations. One extended the coal-and-steel idea into a new realm, atomic energy. **Euratom**, the European Atomic Energy Community, was formed to coordinate nuclear power development by pooling research, investment, and management. It continues to operate today with an expanded membership. The second organization was the *European Economic Community (EEC)*, later renamed the *European Community (EC)*.

As discussed briefly in Chapter 8, there are important differences between *free trade areas*, *customs unions*, and *common markets*. Creating a **free trade area** meant lifting tariffs and restrictions on the movement of goods across (EEC) borders, as was done shortly after 1957. Today the *European Free Trade Association (EFTA)* is an extended free trade area associated with the European Union; its members are Norway, Iceland, Liechtenstein, and Switzerland.

In a **customs union**, participating states adopt a unified set of tariffs with regard to goods coming in from outside the free trade area. Without unified tariffs, each type of good could be imported into the state with the lowest tariff and then reexported (tariff free) to the other states in the free trade area; this would be inefficient. The Treaty of Rome committed the six states to creating a customs union by 1969. A customs union creates free and open trade within its member states, bringing great economic benefits.

PLANTING POLITICAL SEEDS

Under the free trade area first created by the 1957 Treaty of Rome, goods can move freely across European borders to reach consumers in any member country. In agriculture, creating an integrated free market in Europe has not been easy; the EC adopted a Common Agricultural Policy in the 1960s to address the problem. These Danish farmers took to the streets in 2011 to protest EU agricultural policies that put them at a disadvantage.

Thus, the customs union remains the heart of the EU and the one aspect widely copied elsewhere in the world.

A **common market** means that in addition to the customs union, member states allow labor and capital (as well as goods) to flow freely across borders. For instance, a Belgian financier can invest in Germany on the same terms as a German investor. Although the Treaty of Rome adopted the goal of a common market, even today it has been only partially achieved.

One key aspect of a common market was achieved, at least in theory, in the 1960s when the EU (then the EC) adopted a **Common Agricultural Policy (CAP)**. In practice, the CAP has led to recurrent conflicts among member states and tensions between nationalism and regionalism. Recall that agriculture has been one of the most difficult sectors of the world economy in which to achieve free trade (see p. 305). To promote national self-sufficiency in food, many governments give subsidies to farmers. The CAP was based on the principle that a subsidy extended to farmers in any member state should be extended to farmers in all EU countries. That way, no member government was forced to alienate politically powerful farmers by removing subsidies, yet the overall policy would be equalized throughout the community in line with the common market principle. As a result, subsidies to farmers today absorb about 40 percent of the total EU budget, with France as the main beneficiary, and are the single greatest source of trade friction between Europe and the United States (see pp. 293–294).

The next step in the plan for European integration, after a free trade area, customs union, and common market, was an *economic and monetary union (EMU)* in which the overall economic policies of the member states would be coordinated for greatest efficiency and stability. In this step, a single currency would replace the separate national currencies now in use (see "Monetary Union," later in this chapter). A possible future step could be the supranational coordination of economic policies such as budgets and taxes.

To reduce state leaders' fears of losing sovereignty, the Treaty of Rome provides that changes in its provisions must be approved by all member states. For example, France vetoed Britain's application for membership in the EEC in 1963 and 1967. However, in 1973 Britain did finally join, along with Ireland and Denmark. This action expanded the organization's membership to nine, including the largest and richest countries in the region.

In 1981, Greece was admitted, and in 1986 Portugal and Spain joined. Inclusion of these poorer countries with less industry and lower standards of living created difficulties in effectively integrating Europe's economies (difficulties that persist today). Richer European states give substantial aid to the poorer ones in hopes of strengthening the weak links. Yet, in 2011, the debt problems of these countries created the need for expensive new bailout funds and threatened the stability of the wider European economy.

Structure of the European Union

The structure of the EU reflects its roots in technical and economic cooperation. The coal and steel experts have been joined by experts on trade, agriculture, and finance at the heart of the community. The EU headquarters and staff have the reputation of colorless bureaucrats—sometimes called *Eurocrats*—who care more about technical problem solving than about politics. These supranational bureaucrats are balanced in the EU structure by provisions that uphold the power of states and state leaders.

Although the rule of Eurocrats follows the functionalist plan, it has created problems as the EU has progressed. Politicians in member states have qualms about losing power to the Eurocrats. Citizens in those states have become more uncomfortable in recent years with the growing power of faceless Eurocrats over their lives. Citizens can throw their own political leaders out of office in national elections, but the Eurocrats seem less accountable.

The EU's structure is illustrated in Figure 10.1. The Eurocrats consist of a staff of 25,000, organized under the **European Commission** at EU headquarters in Brussels, Belgium. The Commission has 27 individual members—one from each member state—who are chosen for four-year renewable terms. Their role is to identify problems and propose solutions to the Council of the European Union. They select one of their members as the commission president. These individuals are supposed to represent the interests of Europe as a whole (supranational interests), not their own states, but this goal has been only imperfectly met.

The European Commission lacks formal autonomous power except for day-to-day EU operations. Formally, the Commission reports to, and implements policies of, the **Council of the European Union** (formerly named the Council of Ministers). The Council is a meeting of the relevant ministers (foreign, economic, agriculture, finance, etc.) of each member state—politicians who control the bureaucrats (or who try to). For instance, in 2009 the 27 energy ministers met to approve EU efforts to restart natural gas supplies from Russia that had been shut off in a price dispute with Ukraine. This formal structure reflects states' resistance to yielding sovereignty. It also means that the individuals making up the Council of the European Union vary from one meeting to the next, and that technical issues receive priority over political ones. The arrangement thus gives some advantage back to the Commission staff. Recall the similar tension between politicians and career bureaucrats in national foreign policy making (see "Bureaucracies" on pp. 136–137).

The Council of the European Union in theory has functioned using weighted voting based on each state's population, but in practice it operated by consensus on major policy

FIGURE 10.1 Structure of the European Union (EU)

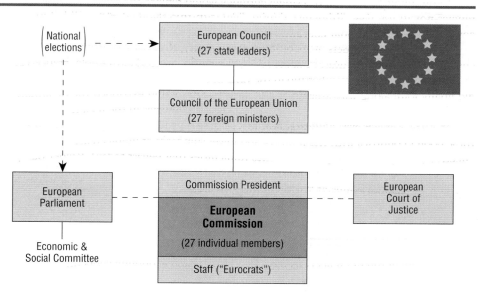

issues (all members must agree). After adoption of the Lisbon Treaty (see p. 369), nearly all issues are now decided by qualified majority voting. The Treaty's definition of a qualified majority is that at least 55 percent of EU members, representing 65 percent of EU citizens, must vote in favor to secure passage. The Council has a rotating presidency (with limited power). The Council of the European Union must approve the policies of the European Commission and give it general directions.[7]

In the 1970s, state leaders (prime ministers or presidents) created a special place for themselves in the EC, to oversee the direction of the community; this structure again shows state leaders' resistance to being governed by any supranational body. This *European Council* of the 27 state leaders meets with the European Commission president twice a year. They are the ones with the power to get things done in their respective national governments (which still control most of the money and power in Europe).

There is a **European Parliament**, which falls somewhat short of a true legislature passing laws for all of Europe.[8] At present it operates partly as a watchdog over the Commission, but with some power to legislate. It must approve the Commission's budget but cannot control it item by item. The parliament shares power with the Council under a "co-decision procedure" in such areas as migration, employment, health, and consumer protection. The 2009 Lisbon Treaty significantly expanded the areas in which the co-decision procedure applies. It also serves as a debating forum and a symbol of European unity. In 1999, an independent commission created by the parliament found waste and fraud in the Commission, leading all 20 commissioners to resign. Since 1979, voters throughout Europe have directly elected their representatives according to population—750 members representing nearly 500 million citizens. Political parties are organized across national lines.

The *Economic and Social Committee* discusses continent-wide issues that affect particular industries or constituencies. This committee is purely advisory; it lobbies the European Commission on matters it deems important. It is designed as a forum in which companies, labor unions, and interest groups can bargain transnationally.

The **European Court of Justice** in Luxembourg adjudicates disputes on matters covered by the Treaty of Rome—which covers many issues. Unlike the World Court (see pp. 256–258), the European Court has actively established its jurisdiction and does not serve merely as a mechanism of international mediation. The European Court can overrule national laws that conflict with EU law—giving it unique powers among international courts. In addition, it hears cases brought by individuals, not just governments. In hundreds of cases, the Court has ruled on matters ranging from discrimination in the workplace to the pensions of Commission staff members.

The Single European Act

European integration has proceeded in a step-by-step process that produces tangible successes, reduces politicians' fears of losing sovereignty, and creates pressures to continue the process. Often major steps forward are followed by periods of stagnation or even reversals in integration. The first major revision of the Treaty of Rome—the 1985 **Single European Act**—began a new phase of accelerated integration. The EU set a target date of the end of

---

[7] Kirchner, Emil Joseph. *Decision Making in the European Community: The Council Presidency and European Integration*. Manchester, 1992. Pollack, Mark A. *The Engines of Integration: Delegation, Agency, and Agenda Setting in the European Union*. Oxford, 2003.

[8] Judge, David, and David Earnshaw. *The European Parliament*. Palgrave, 2003. Kreppel, Amie. *The European Parliament and the Supranational Party System: A Study in Institutional Development*. Cambridge, 2002.

1992 for the creation of a true common market in Europe.[9] This comprehensive set of changes was nicknamed *Europe 1992* and centered on about 300 directives from the European Commission, aimed at eliminating nontariff barriers to free trade in goods, services, labor, and capital within the EC. The issues tended to be complex and technical. For instance, professionals licensed in one state should be free to practice in another, but Spain's licensing requirements for, say, physical therapists may have differed from those of Britain. The Commission bureaucrats worked to smooth out such inconsistencies and create a uniform set of standards. Each national government had to pass laws to implement these measures.

For example, a dispute raged for decades over the definition of chocolate. Belgium—famous for its chocolates—requires the exclusive use of cocoa butter for a product to be called chocolate; Britain and other countries use a cheaper process that partially substitutes other vegetable oils. With deepening integration and seamless trade, Belgium worried that it would lose its competitive advantage in the $30 billion worldwide chocolate market (half of which came from Europe). Britain and six other EU countries that joined the EU since 1973 won an exemption from the all-cocoa butter rule that applies to the other eight EU members. Under the pressure of integration, however, the EU is moving to unify standards such as food regulations. The chocolate wars illustrate that the seemingly simple concept of economic integration sets in motion forces of change that reach into every corner of society and affect the daily lives of millions of people.

The Single European Act also gave a new push to the creation of a European Central Bank (in Frankfurt, Germany), and a single currency and monetary system—long-standing goals that have since been accomplished. As long as the economies of the EU members were tied to separate states (with separate central banks), efforts to maintain fixed exchange rates were difficult. For example, British politicians in 1992 were reluctant to deepen a recession in order to save German politicians from inflation (the source of the controversial British devaluation discussed in Chapter 9).

The 1992 process moved economic integration into more political and controversial areas, eroding sovereignty more visibly than before. It also deepened a trend toward the EU's dealing directly with provinces rather than the states they belong to—thus beginning to "hollow out" the state from below (stronger provincial governments) as well as from above (stronger Europe-wide government). However, Europe 1992 continued to put aside for the future the difficult problems of political and military integration.

The Maastricht Treaty

The **Maastricht Treaty**, signed in the Dutch city of Maastricht in 1992, renamed the EC as the EU and committed it to further progress in three main areas. The first was monetary union (discussed shortly), in which the existing national currencies were abolished and replaced by a single European currency. A second set of changes, regarding justice and home affairs, created a European police agency and responded to the new reality that borders were opening to immigrants, criminals, sex traffickers, and contraband. It also expanded the idea of citizenship, so that, for example, a French citizen living in Germany can vote in local elections there. A third goal of Maastricht—political and military integration—was even more controversial. The treaty commits European states to work toward a common foreign policy with a goal of eventually establishing a joint military force.

---

[9] Moravcsik, Andrew. Negotiating the Single European Act: National Interests and Conventional Statecraft in the European Community. *International Organization* 45 (1), 1991: 19–56.

Some citizens of Europe began to react strongly against the loss of national identity and sovereignty implicit in the Maastricht Treaty.[10] As an amendment to the Treaty of Rome, Maastricht had to be ratified by all (then 12) members. The ratification process stirred up strong public feelings against closer European union in several countries. Suddenly, citizens and leaders in several countries seemed to realize that the faceless Eurocrats in Brussels were stripping away their national sovereignty! In the end, the EU implemented the Maastricht Treaty, although more slowly and with fewer participating countries than originally hoped. Economic and technical integration, including the new monetary union among 12 members, maintained momentum.

Europe's economic integration has begun to reshape political economy at a global level. The EU now sets the rules for access to one of the world's largest markets, for a vast production and technology network, and for the world's strongest currency. Europe's new power is illustrated in its environmental initiatives. The U.S. chemical industry operated under U.S. regulations that exempt 80 percent of chemicals. But the EU adopted stricter chemical regulations, requiring tests of health effects of all chemicals used in products and mandating efforts to substitute for toxic chemicals in everyday products. As a result, several major U.S. cosmetics companies reformulated their products to comply with new EU cosmetics regulations calling for removal of unhealthy substances. And Japanese car manufacturers adapted production processes to meet the EU's requirement that new cars consist of 85 percent recyclable components by 2006 (and 95 percent by 2015).[11]

Political and military integration have been much more problematic.[12] The struggle between nationalism and supranationalism seems precariously balanced between the two; the transition to supranationalism has not yet been accomplished in the realms of sovereignty and foreign and military policy. Even after 50 years of preparation, spillover from economic to political issues is elusive.

Monetary Union

A European currency, the **euro**, has replaced national currencies in 17 EU member states, as mandated in the Maastricht process. After several years as an abstract unit like the IMF's SDR (see p. 332), used by national governments and for international exchange, the euro came into full circulation in 2002 and the national currencies ceased to exist. The European Central Bank took over the functions of states' central banks.[13]

Monetary union is difficult for both economic and political reasons. In participating states, fundamental economic and financial conditions must be equalized. One state cannot stimulate its economy with low interest rates (for example, because of a recession) while another cools inflation with high interest rates (because of high economic growth). For example, in 2010 the unemployment rate was over 11 percent in Slovakia but only 5 percent in the Netherlands. In an integrated economy that is also politically centralized, the central government can reallocate resources, as the United States might do if Texas were booming and Massachusetts were in recession. But the EU does not have centralized powers of taxation or control of national budgets. This split of fiscal and monetary policy is unusual.

[10] Cowles, Maria Green, James Caporaso, and Thomas Risse, eds. *Transforming Europe: Europeanization and Domestic Change.* Cornell, 2001. Gstohl, Sieglende. *Reluctant Europeans: Norway, Sweden, and Switzerland and the Process of Integration.* Rienner, 2002.

[11] Schapiro, Mark. New Power for "Old Europe." *The Nation*, December 27, 2004.

[12] Duke, Simon. *The Elusive Quest for European Security: From EDC to CFSP.* St. Martin's, 2000. Salmon, Trevor C., and Alistair J. K. Shepherd. *Toward a European Army: A Military Power in the Making?* Rienner, 2003.

[13] Chang, Michele, Neill Nugent, and William E. Patterson, eds. *The Monetary Integration in the European Union.* Palgrave, 2009. De Grauwe, Paul. *The Economics of Monetary Union.* 5th ed. Oxford, 2004.

One solution is to work toward equalizing Europe's economies. For example, to reduce the disparity between rich and poor EU states, the Maastricht Treaty increased the EU budget by $25 billion annually to provide economic assistance to the poorer members. But the richer EU members pay the cost for this aid—in effect carrying the poor countries as free riders on the collective good of EU integration. Partly for this reason, $25 billion annually was far too small to truly equalize the rich and poor countries.

The main solution adopted at Maastricht was to restrict membership in the monetary union, at least in the first round, to only those countries with enough financial stability not to jeopardize the union. To join the unified currency, a state had to achieve a budget deficit of less than 3 percent of GDP, a national debt of less than 60 percent of GDP, an inflation rate no more than 1.5 percentage points above the average of the three lowest-inflation EU members, and stable interest rates and national currency values.

This meant hard choices by governments in France, Spain, Italy, and other countries to cut budgets and benefits and to take other politically unpopular moves. French workers responded with massive strikes on several occasions. Governments fell to opposition parties in several countries,

COOKED EURO?

The Maastricht Treaty called for a monetary union with a common currency. In 2002, the euro currency came into effect smoothly in 12 (now 17) countries and emerged as a world currency that rivals the U.S. dollar. This Italian chef celebrated the new currency in 2002 by making a pizza decorated with a euro symbol (€). But troubles threatened the euro in 2011.

but the new leaders generally kept to the same course. As a result of their newfound fiscal discipline, all 12 EU members that wanted to participate in the euro qualified. Slovenia joined in 2007, Cyprus and Malta in 2008, Slovakia in 2009, and Estonia in 2011. Lithuania and Latvia are preparing to adopt the euro next. Britain, Denmark, and Sweden opted to retain their national currencies.

Money is more political than steel tariffs or chocolate ingredients. A monetary union infringes on a core prerogative of states—the right to print currency. Because citizens use money every day, a European currency along these lines could deepen citizens' sense of identification with Europe—a victory for supranationalism over nationalism. When the euro went into circulation in 2002, people for the first time could "put Europe in their pocket." However, precisely for this reason, some state leaders and citizens resisted the idea of giving up the symbolic value of their national currencies. These problems were reflected in the task of designing euro banknotes and coins. How could any country's leaders or monuments become Europe-wide symbols? The solution was to put generic architectural elements (not identifiable by country) on the front of the banknotes and a map of Europe on the back. Coins come in various member-state designs (all valid throughout the euro zone).

Conflicts have arisen within the euro zone. In 2004, the European Commission challenged the EU member states for voting to let France and Germany break the euro rules by running high budget deficits. And Latvia's government lost power within six months of the country's joining the EU, under pressure of unpopular budget cuts needed to meet the euro rules within four years.

In 2010, new challenges to the euro arose. Greece, which had previously admitted to falsifying economic data in order to be admitted to the euro zone, began to suffer from a significant debt crisis. After Greece had for years borrowed more than it could repay, the global financial crisis brought new strains to the Greek economy that threatened all European countries. Because Greece used the euro, the country's financial difficulties influenced global investors' impressions of all euro states.

The Greek economic crisis brought more attention to EU economic woes after the global recession. In 2010, only two states in the EU (Finland and Luxembourg) actually met the EU targets for debt levels. Greece, Spain, Portugal, Ireland, and Italy all undertook large-scale economic reform due to their economic difficulties. Germany and France sparred over who would help bail out the euro states in trouble. After Germany's economic minister stated that Germany "would not offer Greece a cent," cooler heads prevailed and the EU countries banded together to support one another's economies. Soon Ireland also needed, and received, a massive bailout. By late 2011, responding to festering debt problems in Greece and beyond, the EU eventually came up with an expanded bailout fund worth more than a trillion dollars. But the EU's cumbersome decision process, and the resentments of Greeks citizens, put the plan in doubt. The EU debt crisis illustrates both the good and the bad of monetary integration: the euro is only as strong as its weakest member, yet if the euro states cooperate, they can assist one another through difficult times.

Despite these recent problems in the euro zone, the creation of a European currency is arguably the largest financial overhaul ever attempted in history, and in its first eight years it has been successful.

SEEKING THE COLLECTIVE GOOD

Bailing Out Greece
COLLECTIVE GOOD: European Financial Health

BACKGROUND: The 17 states that make up the euro zone have given up their national currencies in favor of a common one. As a result, each is affected by the financial policies of the others. For instance, deficit spending on politically popular programs would normally affect just that country's currency, but if the country is in the euro zone, then that effect is spread across all the other euro countries. To avoid the temptation to free-ride, the European Union set up rules for fiscal responsibility (including low deficits) before a country can adopt the euro. As later became clear, several countries, including Greece, fudged those requirements when they first joined the euro.

The health of the euro currency is thus a collective good depending on the fiscal discipline of its members.

Free riding threatens all euro zone members since an economic crisis in one country can easily spread to others through the common currency.

CHALLENGE: In 2010, Greek fiscal policies combined with the aftermath of the global recession to put Greece into a debt crisis, nearing bankruptcy. This instability threatened to spread to the other high-deficit euro members (Spain, Portugal, Ireland). The value of the euro began to drop and world financial markets fell as anxiety increased.

RECIPROCITY

IDENTITY

Expanding the European Union

The EU's success has attracted neighboring states that want to join. The EU has expanded from 15 members to 27 since 2004, with potentially far-reaching changes in how the EU operates.[14]

Spain and Portugal, admitted in 1986 as the 11th and 12th members, filled out the western side of Europe. In 1995, Austria, Sweden, and Finland joined the EU. They are located on the immediate fringe of the present EU area, and as relatively rich countries, they did not disrupt the EU economy. Norway applied to join and was accepted, but its citizens voted down the idea in a referendum in 1994, leaving the EU with 15 members after 1995—all but two of the main states of Western Europe. (Switzerland's plans to join were, like Norway's, halted by a popular referendum in the early 1990s.)

The EU's current expansion is guided by the 2000 Treaty of Nice, which came into effect in 2003 after Irish voters reversed an earlier vote and approved it (the last country to ratify it). Ten new members joined in 2004: Poland, the Czech Republic, Slovakia, Hungary, Slovenia, Estonia, Latvia, Lithuania, Malta, and Cyprus. The European Commission expanded to 25 members, without the five largest having two seats, and with new voting rules that move away from a requirement for consensus. In 2007, Romania and Bulgaria brought the EU's membership to 27. (But unlike with previous members, Britain and Ireland imposed work restrictions on the citizens of the new 2007 members.)

---

[14] Jacoby, Wade. *The Enlargement of the European Union and NATO: Ordering from the Menu in Central Europe.* Cambridge, 2004.

SOLUTION: In response, the European Union and IMF put together a $141 billion rescue package for Greece. To take effect, the package needed approval from all 16 at that time euro zone members. In Germany, where fiscal discipline is a tradition, angry voters did not want to bail out the irresponsible Greeks, and the governing party's slim majority in Parliament was threatened. The German government thus faced both domestic costs and a direct price tag of $28 billion for Germany's share of the bailout.

Identity played a role in the German government's decision to approve the deal. The European Union's identity as a continent in common meant that Germany saw the collective good of euro stability as its own good. However, reciprocity also played a role, since the German government supported the bailout only after the problem threatened to spread and destabilize the euro, directly harming Germany if it did not approve the deal. Just the thought of fellow

Greeks protest austerity measures taken as part of a bailout plan, 2010.

Europeans in need did not alone make Germany want to help.

Turkey continues to seek membership. Although it rebuffed Turkey in 2002, the EU later agreed to begin formal entry negotiations with Turkey in 2005—the start of a years-long process. The EU has not reached a consensus on admitting Turkey as a full member. Proponents note that Turkey has made major economic and political changes, including abolishing the death penalty and improving human rights, to try to win EU membership. Granting full membership would reward these changes, keeping an implicit promise to reciprocate Turkey's actions. Turkey's GDP, growing rapidly in recent years, would add about 5 percent to the EU's economy. And Turkish workers could help alleviate a labor shortage in Western Europe. Supporters also argue that Turkey as an EU member would serve as a bridge between Europe and the important but unstable Middle East region and as an example of secular democracy to other Middle Eastern countries.

Opponents note that Turkey would be the only Muslim country in the EU, yet would become the second most populous EU member after Germany. With 2 million Turks already living in Germany, opponents argue that EU membership would open the floodgates for immigration from a large, poor country, overwhelming the smaller and richer EU members. In France, opposition to Turkey's admission, and to immigration generally, created a backlash that helped derail the proposed EU constitution in 2005. In economic terms, Turkey would be the poorest member, even including the new Eastern European members (see Figure 10.2). Costs to subsidize Turkish farmers and expand social programs could reach tens of billions of euros.

FIGURE 10.2 Income Levels of Old and New EU Members, 2005

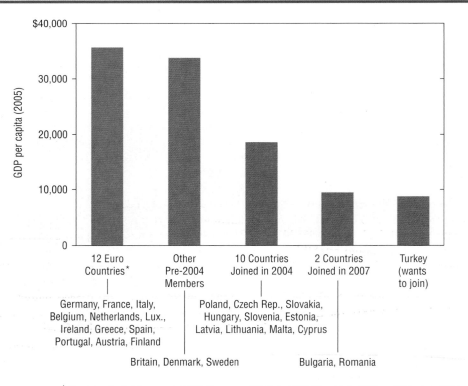

* Slovenia adopted the euro in 2007, Cyprus and Malta in 2008, Slovakia in 2009, and Estonia in 2011.

Source: World Bank data.

Turkey also carries a large debt-to-income ratio, twice as high as any current member. Finally, opponents want Turkey to remove its military forces from EU member Cyprus, where a Greek-Turkish partition has endured for decades.

As the new members joined the EU in 2004 and 2007, the ability of the EU to reach decisions by consensus became more complicated, a point underscored by Slovakia's single-handed veto of a massive euro bailout briefly in 2011. The working time required to make decisions in the Council of the European Union expanded, with potential conflicts and alliances on a particular issue among 27 rather than 15 members. Recall that collective goods are generally harder to provide in larger groups, where free riding is less obvious, than in smaller ones.

Furthermore, by Western European standards, the new members are relatively poor. Existing EU members are wary of being dragged down by these economies, most of which are still embroiled in the painful transition from socialism to capitalism and sometimes lack stable currencies. The tensions between nationalism and supranationalism might intensify, with more states pulling in more directions at once.

Perhaps as a result of these pressures, the EU in the last decade has shown signs of dividing into "inner" and "outer" layers—with states such as France and Germany joining a currency union and deepening their integration, and those such as Britain and perhaps the new members operating at the edges of the EU with more autonomy. Still, in some areas, there have been strides toward integration. Since 1995, the EU has established and expanded the *Schengen area*, a zone in which border controls have been abolished. Goods and people move freely within the zone without stopping at borders. The Schengen countries include the major EU states (except Britain, by its choice). Norway, Iceland, and Switzerland also belong although they are not EU members.

IMPERFECT UNION

The European Union added 12 members, mostly from Eastern Europe, in 2004 and 2007. Efforts to update European governance with the new Lisbon Treaty finally succeeded in 2009. But much complexity remains to be worked out, as shown in the muddled response to the Greek financial crisis in 2011. Here, protesters demonstrate at the European Central Bank in Frankfurt, Germany, 2011.

The Lisbon Treaty

To grapple with the implications of an expanding EU, the 25 leaders signed an EU constitution in late 2004, and the European Parliament gave it a strong vote of support in 2005. To take effect, it had to be ratified by all 25 states, including several requiring referenda. The constitution would establish a stronger president of the EU, as well as a foreign minister, and would replace the requirement for consensus in EU decision making with majority voting in more cases. It also guaranteed fundamental rights to all EU citizens. But voters in France and the Netherlands rejected the constitution and the process halted.

At the end of 2007, the EU moved forward with another new proposed constitution, the **Lisbon Treaty**. The treaty was similar to the previous constitution, but faced a popular referendum only in Ireland. (Lisbon did not require more state-level votes since it only amended previous EU treaties rather than replacing them as the constitution proposed to do.) The treaty came into force in 2009.

The treaty created numerous changes in both the structure and the day-to-day operations of the EU. Some of those changes promote more supranational decision making. For example, a charter of human rights was made legally binding on all member states. A new position called the High Commissioner on Foreign Affairs and Security Policy was created to better coordinate foreign policy among member states. (This position immediately became controversial when a relatively unknown British lord was chosen to fill the position.)

On the other hand, some changes allow state members and individual citizens to place more checks on EU power. Now, national parliaments can have more say in who is admitted to the EU (likely bad news for Turkey). National parliaments will now also receive draft legislation to evaluate and respond to before it is enacted in Brussels. The Treaty also attempts to increase transparency by requiring European Council meetings to be held in public. And in an attempt to engage EU citizens directly, the Commission must now take up any proposal or petition that receives 1 million signatures.

Beyond the EU itself, Europe is a patchwork of overlapping structures with varying memberships (see Figure 10.3). Despite the Single European Act, there are still many Europes. Within the EU are the "inner six" and the new arrivals, each with its own concerns. Around the edges are the EFTA states participating in the European Economic Area. NATO membership overlaps partly with the EU. Russia and even the United States are European actors in some respects but not others. One truly universal intergovernmental organization exists in Europe—the *Organization for Security and Cooperation in Europe (OSCE)*. Operating by consensus, with a large and universal membership of 56 states, the OSCE has little power except to act as a forum for discussions of security issues. In the late 1990s, the OSCE shifted into new tasks such as running elections, helping political parties in Bosnia and Kosovo, and providing various forms of monitoring and assistance in half a dozen Eastern European countries.

Thus, international integration is not a matter of a single group or organization but more a mosaic of structures tying states together. These various structures of the European political system, centered on the EU, are IGOs composed of states as members. But a less-tangible aspect of integration is the sense of identity that develops over time as economic (and other functional) ties bring people closer together across borders. Supranational identity, culture, and communication are also aspects of international integration. The remainder of this chapter considers how information technologies are bypassing states and bringing about this kind of integration globally.

The Power of Information

Global telecommunications are profoundly changing how information and culture function in international relations.[15] These technological advances, at the center of globalization, are bringing the identity principle to the fore as communities interact across distances and borders. Newly empowered individuals and groups are creating new transnational networks worldwide, bypassing states.

Connecting the World

New international political possibilities arise from technological developments. The media over which information travels—telephones, television, films, magazines, and so forth—shape the way ideas take form and spread from one place to another. The media with the strongest political impact are television, radio, phones, and the Internet.

---

[15] Hanson, Elizabeth C. *The Information Revolution in World Politics*. Rowman & Littlefield, 2008. Allison, Juliann E., ed. *Technology, Development, and Democracy: International Conflict and Cooperation in the Information Age*. SUNY, 2002. Pool, Ithiel de Sola. *Technologies without Boundaries: On Telecommunications in a Global Age*. Edited by Eli M. Noam. Harvard, 1990.

FIGURE 10.3 Overlapping Memberships of European States

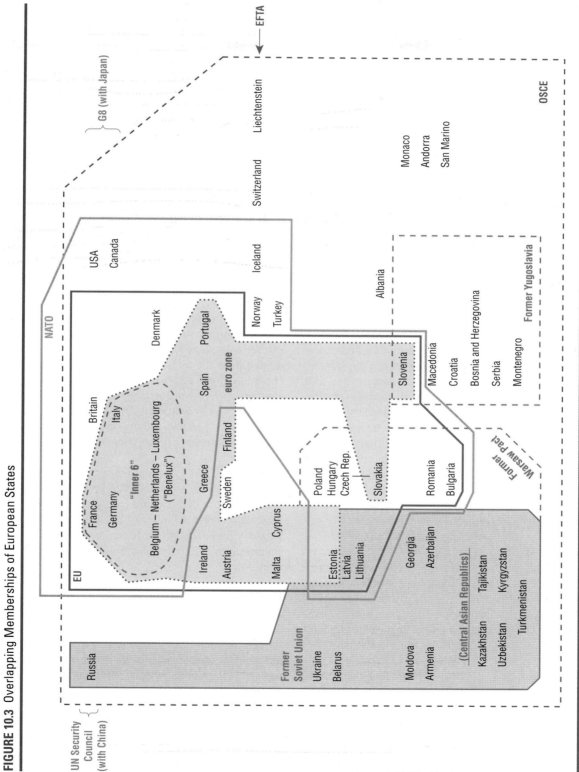

POLICY PERSPECTIVES

Chancellor of Germany, Angela Merkel

PROBLEM *How do you balance competing forces in the EU while satisfying domestic public opinion?*

BACKGROUND For decades, Turkey has desired full membership in the European Union. For many reasons, Turkey's application has been stalled. It would be the poorest member of the EU; it would be the only non-Christian EU member; it has not settled past conflicts with current members Cyprus and Greece; and it has never admitted its role in the genocide of Armenians during World War I.

Yet, many observers argue that Turkey is too important to leave out of the EU: it serves as a vital link between Europe and the Middle East; it is a NATO member; and it has successfully undertaken many of the reforms asked of it by EU states, in human rights, minority rights, and democracy. Your own country maintains extensive economic ties with Turkey as well—Germany is Turkey's top source of imports and biggest market for exports. An economically healthy Turkey in the EU would be good for German businesses.

Past German leaders have differed on their views on Turkey's application, ranging from outright opposition to strong support. You have attempted to provide a compromise solution: the idea of a "privileged partnership," which would provide some economic benefits to Turkey, but not full membership. Turkish leaders strongly oppose this option, and other European leaders have not supported your compromise to date.

While Turkey's application to the EU has supporters and detractors across Europe, no country opposes Turkish membership more than France. Its president, Nicolas Sarkozy, in 2007 campaigned on the platform of opposing Turkish membership in the EU. Recently, when France held the EU presidency, it demanded delays of Turkey's accession talks.

DOMESTIC CONSIDERATIONS Turkish membership in the EU is not popular domestically. Native Germans are concerned that immigrants could freely come to Germany and take jobs. They also fear that a wave of cheap exports from Turkey will undermine German workers. Already, more than 2.1 million Turks live in Germany, making them the largest ethnic minority in your country. There have been ethnic tensions between the Turkish immigrants and native Germans, leading for calls for tight restrictions on Turkish immigration. Yet, many of the Turks in Germany are voting and tax-paying citizens who have urged you to support Turkey's membership.

SCENARIO Imagine that France proposes to permanently kill Turkey's membership application to the EU. France asks for your support in ensuring that Turkey will never become a member of the EU. Upon hearing of France's proposal, ethnic Turks begin large protests in several cities in Germany to urge your support of Turkey's application.

CHOOSE YOUR POLICY Do you support France's attempt to keep Turkey out of the EU? Do you continue to push for your idea of a "privileged partnership" even though the idea has received little support at home or abroad? How do you balance demands from important EU partners with your own policy preferences and a difficult domestic situation?

TV and Radio   There are nearly 2 billion TV sets and 3 billion radio receivers in the world. The power of these media lies in their ability to reproduce a single source of information in many copies in many locations. Radio, and increasingly TV, reaches the poorest rural areas of the global South. Peasants who cannot read can understand radio. Shortwave radio—typically stations such as Voice of America (VOA) and the British Broadcasting Corporation (BBC)—is very popular in remote locations. TV is especially powerful. The combination of pictures and sounds affects viewers emotionally and intellectually. Independent TV news channels have attracted large audiences in India, Pakistan, and Nepal.

Ordinary over-the-air TV and radio signals are radio waves carried on specific frequencies. Frequencies are a limited resource in high demand, which governments regulate and allocate to users. Because radio waves do not respect national borders, the allocation of frequencies is a subject of interstate bargaining. International regimes have grown up around the regulation of international communications technologies.[16]

Satellite transmissions bypass the normal over-the-air radio spectrum and transmit signals over a huge area to dish-shaped antennas. This capability, bypassing states' control, fortifies transnational or supranational identity politics by allowing, for example, all Arabs in the world to see Arab satellite TV coverage of the Palestinian issue. The Qatar-based all-news satellite TV network al Jazeera, begun in 1996, has become a force in Middle Eastern politics. It reaches an influential audience across the region and world. In a 2006 poll in six Arab countries, citizens listed al Jazeera as their main source of international news by a large margin over any other satellite TV network.[17] Although it is criticized by Western governments for airing al Qaeda videos and anti-American propaganda generally, al Jazeera also occasionally broadcasts interviews with top U.S. officials.

Images and sounds are being recorded, reproduced, and viewed in new ways through video and cell phone cameras. These tools empower ordinary citizens to create their own visual records, such as videos of political demonstrations in one country that end up on TV in another country. In the 2011 Arab Spring revolutions, especially in Syria, cell phone videos played a critical role in winning the support of citizens, and the world, by showing how governments were brutally murdering unarmed protesters in the streets.

Telephone and Internet   Even more empowering of ordinary citizens are telephones and the Internet. Unlike TV and radio, these are two-way media through which users interact among themselves without any centralized information source. Telephones, perhaps more than any other technology, make individuals international actors. The minutes of international phone traffic worldwide quadrupled from 1991 to 2004. By 2009, a quarter of the world's population had computer access in the home. Both of these are clear indicators of globalization.

Growth of phones and Internet use worldwide has been explosive in the past decade (see Figure 10.4), with cell phones leading this explosion of connectivity. Over 4 billion people had cell phones in 2009, and nearly 2 billion used the Internet—in each case representing a doubling in the number of users in less than 5 years.

In Africa, cheap cell phones with cheap prepaid calling cards have let millions of relatively poor individuals bypass the very few land lines previously needed to communicate. In about a decade, sub-Saharan Africa has seen subscribers increase from near zero to nearly 300 million. Almost 90 percent of telephone users in Africa use cell phones rather than land lines (versus 60 percent in the United States).

---

[16] Franda, Marcus. *Governing the Internet: The Emergence of an International Regime*. Rienner, 2001. Braman, Sandra, ed. *The Emergent Global Information Policy Regime*. Palgrave, 2004.
[17] Sadat Chair, University of Maryland. Arab Attitudes toward Political and Social Issues, Foreign Policy and the Media. Available online at http://www.bsos.umd.edu/SADAT/PUB/Arab-attitudes-2005.htm.

FIGURE 10.4 World Phone and Internet Use, 1995–2010

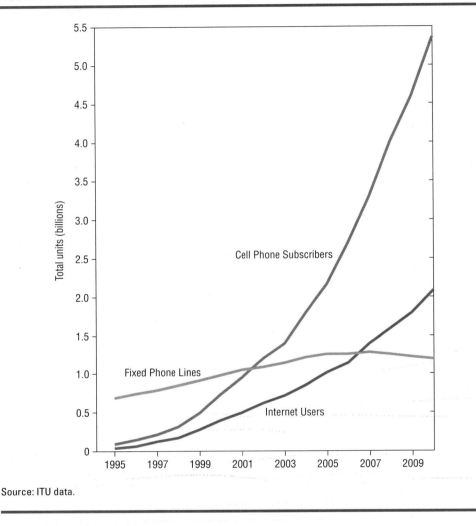

Source: ITU data.

The Digital Divide   Taken on its own, the addition of phone and Internet capability in poor countries is impressive. But in comparison with rich regions, the gap keeps growing (see Figure 10.5). A person living in the global North is four times as likely as a person in the global South to have a land line or cell phone, and eight times as likely to use the Internet. This gap, along with the gap in access to information technologies *within* countries, is known as the **digital divide**.[18]

As the Internet wires parts of the world into a tight network centered on the United States, Europe, and East Asia—where more than 90 percent of Web users live—other regions are largely left out. Poor countries and poor people cannot afford computers, which cost the equivalent of years' worth of wages for a typical person in a poor country. Users of the World Wide Web in 2010 made up 75 percent of the population in the United States,

[18] Norris, Pippa. *Digital Divide: Civic Engagement, Information Poverty, and the Internet Worldwide.* Cambridge, 2001. James, Jeffrey. *Bridging the Global Digital Divide.* Edward Elgar, 2003.

FIGURE 10.5 The North-South Digital Divide, 1994–2010

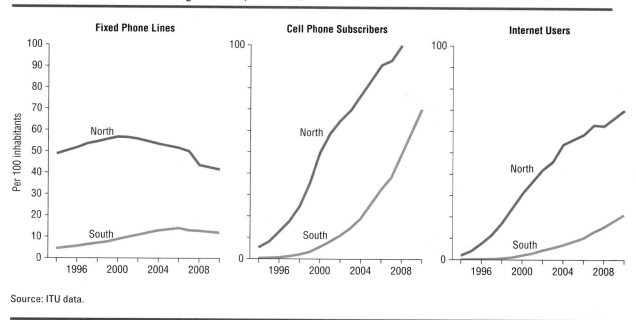

Source: ITU data.

40 percent in Russia, 15 percent in South Asia, and 10 percent in Africa. The explosive growth of Internet use is occurring mainly among the richest strata of the world's people.

World regions have their own digital divides. In Africa, three-quarters of the land lines in 2007 were in just five countries. Within the EU, the older members have nearly three times the Internet use per capita of the new Eastern European members, and eight times that of Russia and the other former Soviet republics.[19]

Some activists hope that the Internet can transform poor villages in the global South, partly by letting them produce traditional goods locally and market them globally. In one successful experiment in India in recent years, a businessman placed computer screens with pointing and clicking devices and high-speed Internet access in walls and kiosks in very poor slums. In each location, neighborhood kids quickly gathered, taught themselves to browse the Internet, and even invented their own terminology to describe the unfamiliar cursor and icons on the screen. This small-scale "hole in the wall experiment" shows that simple methods can go far to break down the digital divide between the world's rich and poor.

A model project in Cambodia in 2001 helped revive a village silk-weaving industry by marketing locally made scarves on a village Web site. However, critics noted that the project was feasible only because a satellite company owned by the Thai prime minister donated $18,000 per year of link time. A U.S. aid organization provided the computers, training, Web site design, and credit card processing required to sell scarves from the village. The reality is that most poor villages cannot afford the Internet, cannot read the language of most Web sites, and cannot maintain computers and Web sites without extensive training.[20]

In 2007, the One Laptop Per Child project began mass-producing an inexpensive Web-capable wireless personal computer, projected to drop to $100 in price over time.[21]

[19] Data on information access are from the International Telecommunication Union (ITU) unless otherwise noted.
[20] Chandrasekaran, Rajiv. Cambodian Village Wired to Future. *The Washington Post*, May 13, 2001: A1.
[21] See www.laptop.org/. Suroecki, James. Philanthropy's New Prototype. *Technology Review*, Nov./Dec. 2006.

WORTH A THOUSAND WORDS

Global communication, a very new capability on the time scale of the international system, is changing the rules of IR and empowering non-state transnational actors. Telecommunications could change the path of development in poor countries, possibly bypassing traditional infrastructure such as phone lines and leapfrogging to a wireless networked economy. And digital capabilities are illuminating political hotspots—cell phone videos fueled Arab protests in 2011, and these cameras, distributed to 700 children in Darfur, Sudan, by the UN, documented life in that conflict zone.

The computers, designed by an MIT professor, can communicate with Internet access points, such as at school, and network with each other to extend Internet access along a chain, say from school to students' homes. The laptops can be hand-powered, with one minute of exertion charging the battery for ten minutes of use. Several countries have ordered millions for their children and about 2 million have been shipped. In 2009, Uruguay completed an order for a laptop for every school-age child in that country (over 350,000). The project, however, has experienced problems, including the cancellation of a large order from Brazil, threats to back out of orders by other countries, and the laying off of half the project's staff in 2008. Still, the project continues to ship thousands of laptops throughout the world and in 2010, Peru ordered more than 250,000 laptops.

Information as a Tool of Governments

With more information traveling around the world than ever before, information has become an important instrument of governments' power (domestic and interstate).[22] Above all, governments want *access to information.* In 1992, U.S. secretary of state James Baker made his first visit to the newly independent Asian republics of the former Soviet Union (the poorest and most remote CIS members). At each stop, one of the first questions Baker was asked by the state leaders was, "How do I get CNN?"[23] CNN, state leaders hoped, would tie them directly to the Western world and symbolize their independence from Russia.

With today's information technologies, it is easier for governments to gather, organize, and store huge amounts of information. In this respect, the information revolution empowers governments more than ever. In the past, a wanted criminal, drug lord, or terrorist could slip over the border and take refuge in a foreign country. The terrorists who attacked the United States in 2001 demonstrated how easy this was. Today, however, it is more likely that a routine traffic ticket in the foreign country could trigger an instant directive to arrest the person. On the other hand, information technologies give repressive governments more power to keep tabs on citizens, spy on dissidents, and manipulate public opinion. Those technologies are now being mobilized in force to strengthen counterterrorism.

Just as citizens and terrorists find it harder to hide from governments, so are state governments finding it harder to hide information from each other. The military importance of satellite reconnaissance has been mentioned (see pp. 201–203). A powerful state such as the United States can increase its power through information technologies. It can and does monitor phone calls, faxes, data transmissions, and radio conversations in foreign countries.

[22] Roberts, Alasdair. *Blacked Out: Government Secrecy in the Information Age.* Cambridge, 2006.
[23] *The New York Times,* February 2, 1992: A10.

In the Arab Spring movements in 2011, protesters were not the only ones to deploy Internet capabilities; governments did as well. Egypt successfully blocked a choke point and cut off international Web access. And Syria's government used its own hackers to track down the identities of protesters anonymously posting antigovernment videos and messages on the Web. The U.S. government in response trained democracy activists in technologies of the Internet and social media and created shadow Internet and cell phone networks inside foreign countries whose governments were trying to shut down communications.

As the cost of information technology decreases, it comes into reach of more states. Now small states can gain some of the same capabilities electronically. Even sophisticated information is more available and cheaper—high-resolution satellite photos are now available commercially and are cheap or free. These images can be used for both military purposes and natural resource management—for example, knowing which states (including one's own) have such resources as oil, minerals, forests, and farmland, and the rate at which they are being used.

Most governments create explicit channels of information dissemination to influence domestic and international audiences. Stations such as Radio Moscow broadcast radio programs in dozens of languages aimed at all the world's regions. The United States operates the Voice of America (VOA) shortwave radio network, which is picked up in many remote regions. The United States also beams specialized programming into Cuba (TV/Radio Marti) and China, among others.

Governments spread false as well as true information as a means of international influence. This is called *disinformation*. In the 1930s, the Nazis discovered that the "big lie," if repeated enough times, would be accepted as truth by most people. It is harder to fool international audiences these days, but domestic ones can still respond to propagandistic misinformation.

Most governments (but not the U.S. government) own and operate at least one main TV station, and many hold a monopoly on TV stations. Thus TV signals often rank with military equipment and currency as capabilities so important to a government that it must control them itself. Indeed, in a military coup d'état, usually one of the first and most important targets seized is the television broadcasting facility.

Information as a Tool against Governments

Information can be used against governments as well, by foreign governments, NGOs, or domestic political opponents.[24] Governments, especially repressive ones, fear the free flow of information, for good reason. New information technologies have become powerful tools of domestic opposition movements and their allies in foreign governments. Television coverage has fed popular discontent regarding the current U.S. war in Iraq, as it did for the Vietnam War and the Russian war in Chechnya.

More than 500 million Chinese use the Internet, though not uncensored. In 2009, the Chinese government began blocking all access to YouTube after videos surfaced of Chinese military forces repressing pro-Tibet demonstrations. In Iran, where millions of people have used the Internet to discuss taboo topics such as sex, fashion, and politics, the government was widely criticized for cracking down on protesters after a disputed election in 2009. That crackdown was broadcast on Internet sites such as Twitter and Facebook as opposition members posted video and pictures of beatings and even the shooting death of a female protester. These methods were later adopted by the Arab Spring protesters.

---

[24] Jones, Adam. Wired World: Communications Technology, Governance, and the Democratic Uprising. In Comor, Edward A., ed. *The Global Political Economy of Communication: Hegemony, Telecommunication, and the Information Economy.* Macmillan, 1994.

HOT OFF THE PRESS

Information, which easily crosses state borders, is a major factor in both international and domestic politics and may even be laying technological foundations for a global identity. Governments have many ways to try to control information. Here a staff member of Kenya's daily newspaper surveys the damage after police—responding to unfavorable coverage of the president—stormed its offices and burned tens of thousands of copies, 2006.

In the Philippines in 2001, huge protests that swept a president from office were organized through text messages on cell phones. In Ghana, very popular talk shows on private FM radio programs—allowed after 1995—gave voice to ordinary people who then threw out the ruling party in 2000. The global peace demonstrations preceding the 2003 Iraq War used information technologies to turn out millions of people in dozens of countries on short notice. One U.S. group (moveon.org) used a Web site to schedule protesters' phone calls to their congressional representatives every minute of one day, the kind of coordinated action that would have required a large staff and budget in the past (moveon.org had a staff of four at the time).[25]

To counteract such uses of information, governments throughout the world try to limit the flow of unfavorable information—especially information from foreign sources. For example, China, like several other developing countries, channels all access to the Internet through a few state-controlled service providers, and filters the hundreds of billions of text messages exchanged annually among 300 million Chinese cell phone subscribers. In 2010, the United Arab Emirates announced it would shut down BlackBerry's services, but later reached a compromise allowing users to continue using the devices.

A major controversy over Web freedom also emerged in 2010 when the U.S. company Google announced that it would no longer comply with Chinese law that censors Internet searches by blocking politically sensitive words from its Chinese search engine. Later, Google compromised with the Chinese government, angering some U.S. critics.[26] U.S. secretary of state Hillary Clinton has been active at promoting Internet freedom as a core human right on her visits to countries that limit Internet access.

Information technologies have security implications. Capabilities such as fiber-optic cables or satellite communications serve governments in conducting their foreign and military policies (see "Evolving Technologies" on pp. 201–204). Nonstate actors such as terrorist organizations have also harbored the power of cellular phones and the Internet to recruit operatives, raise money, and coordinate attacks—even to detonate improvised explosive devices remotely with a cell phone's ring triggering the bomb when called. Recall that new "smart weapons" technologies empower foot soldiers

---

[25] Fathi, Nazila, and Erik Eckholm. Taboo Surfing: Click Here for Iran . . . And Click Here for China. *The New York Times,* August 4, 2002. Schmetzer, Uli. Cellphones Spurred Filipinos' Coup. *The Chicago Tribune,* January 22, 2001. Friedman, Thomas L. Low-Tech Democracy. *The New York Times,* May 1, 2001: A27.
[26] Goldsmith, Jack, and Tim Wu. *Who Controls the Internet? Illusions of a Borderless World.* Oxford, 2008.

relative to large weapons systems (see p. 204). New communications technologies may be doing the same for ordinary citizens relative to governments and political parties.

The Internet in many ways empowers small fringe groups relative to states, and leaves states vulnerable in new ways. Hackers have taken over control of U.S. government computers and have unleashed costly viruses against businesses and people worldwide. These cyberattacks by small-scale actors may target foreign countries. During the U.S.-China spy plane standoff in 2001, nationalistic Chinese hackers claimed to have put pro-Chinese graffiti on 1,000 U.S. Web sites, and U.S. hackers returned the favor. An Ohio school district found that its site now played China's national anthem. The Chinese communist party criticized "Web terrorism" and the crisis eased.[27] But the U.S. government worries that real terrorists could use the Internet to cause massive disruptions in U.S. economic life.

All in all, the tide of technology seems to be running against governments. Information gets through, and no political power seems capable of holding it back for long. As more and more communication channels carry more information to more places, governments become just another player in a crowded field.

THE WHOLE WORLD IS WATCHING

States do not control the global flow of information, which has become a potent force in world politics. Despite efforts by authoritarian governments, the young participants in the Arab Spring used Internet capabilities and social networking sites to publicize abuses and organize resistance. Graffiti on this wall in Tunisia, early in that country's successful nonviolent revolution in 2011, says "Thanks to the people! Thanks to Facebook!"

Telecommunications and Global Culture

As the information revolution continues to unfold, it will further increase international interdependence, making actions in one state reverberate in other states more strongly than in the past. Information is thus slowly undermining realists' assumptions of state sovereignty and territorial integrity. At the same time, by empowering substate and transnational actors, information technology is undermining the centrality of states themselves in world affairs.

The information revolution greatly increases *transparency* in international relations. As a result, states do not need to arm against unknown potential threats because they see the real threats. Similarly, the ability to monitor performance of agreements makes collective goods problems easier to resolve because cheaters and free riders can be identified. Moreover, the ability of governments to bargain effectively with each other and to reach mutually beneficial outcomes is enhanced by the availability of instant communications channels. In these ways, the increased transparency allowed by new technologies strengthens the reciprocity principle as a solution to IR conflicts. The complex monitoring and accounting required in international agreements based on reciprocity—from trade deals to arms control—comes much easier in a transparent world.

---

[27] Hockstader, Lee. Pings and E-Arrows Fly in Mideast Cyber-War. *The Washington Post*, October 27, 2000: A1. Cha, Ariana Eunjung. Chinese Suspected of Hacking U.S. Sites. *The Washington Post*, April 13, 2001: A13.

WORLD CULTURE

The power of information, opening up a wave of globalization in international business, is also strengthening global communities that cross or even transcend national borders. Some events, such as the British royal wedding in 2011, may be rooted in one nation but become global news stories followed by millions around the world.

Telecommunications, with its ability to connect communities beyond geographic space, is also strengthening the identity principle in IR because people's identities have new sources and new avenues of expression that often transcend national borders. In the past, nationalism has tapped into the psychological dynamics of group identity in a powerful way that has legitimized the state as the ultimate embodiment of its people's aspirations and identity. Now the information revolution may aid the development of transnational or supranational identities. Journalists, scientists, and church members, among others, work in communities spanning national borders. So do members of transnational movements, such as those linking women from various countries, or environmentalists, or human rights activists. The links forged in such transnational communities may create a new functionalism that could encourage international integration on a global scale.

Sports also create transnational communities. Citizens of different states share their admiration of sports stars, who become international celebrities. The Olympics (run by the International Olympic Committee, an NGO) is a global event with a worldwide audience.[28] The U.S.-Chinese rapprochement of 1971 was so delicate that political cooperation was impossible until the way had first been paved by sports—the U.S. table tennis team that made the first official U.S. visit to China.

Finally, tourism also builds transnational communities.[29] International tourists cross borders 500 million times a year. Tourism ranks among the top export industries worldwide. People who travel to other countries often develop both a deeper understanding and a deeper appreciation for them. Added to these contacts are exchange students and those who attend college in a foreign country.

Like international integration and globalization generally, global culture has its downside. The emerging global culture is primarily the culture of white Europeans and their descendants in rich areas of the world (mixed slightly with cultural elements of Japan and local elites in the global South). This cultural dominance has been referred to as **cultural imperialism**.[30] For many people, especially in the global South, the information revolution carrying global culture into their midst is, despite its empowering potential, an invasive force in practice. Because cultures are being subsumed, half of the world's nearly 7,000 languages risk extinction this century, according to UNESCO.

Above all, the emerging global culture is dominated by the world's superpower, the United States; U.S. cultural influence is at least as strong as U.S. military influence. Culture may be just another economic product, to be produced in the place of greatest comparative advantage, but culture also is central to national identity and politics. The prospect of cultural imperialism thus opens another front in the conflict of liberalism and mercantilism. Even the architecture of cyberspace assumes the United States as the default in such domain names as

---

[28] Pound, Richard. *Inside the Olympics: A Behind-the-Scenes Look at the Politics, the Scandals, and the Glory of the Games.* John Wiley, 2004. Schaffer, Kay, and Sidonie Smith. *The Olympics at the Millennium: Power Politics and the Games.* Rutgers, 2000.

[29] Leheny, David. *The Rules of Play: National Identity and the Shaping of Japanese Leisure.* Cornell, 2003.

[30] Maxwell, Richard. *Culture Works: The Political Economy of Culture.* Minnesota, 2001. Barber, Benjamin R. *Jihad vs. McWorld.* Times Books, 1995. Tomlinson, John. *Globalization and Culture.* Chicago, 1999.

.gov (U.S. government) and .mil (U.S. military). At the UN-sponsored World Summit on the Information Society in 2005, Europe and developing countries tried unsuccessfully to break the monopoly held by a U.S. consortium over registering domain names, including country-code domains such as ".uk" (Britain) and ".cn" (China) that states want to control as a matter of national sovereignty. By 2009, however, the Internet's governing body, the Internet Corporation for Assigned Names and Numbers (ICANN), announced that Internet addresses can now contain non-Latin characters. This will allow addresses to contain Chinese, Cyrillic, Japanese, Arabic, or any number of non-Latin based characters to form a Web address.

These supranational cultural influences are still in their infancy. Over the coming years and decades, their shape will become clearer, and scholars will be able to determine more accurately how they influence world politics and state sovereignty. We need not wait as long to see the effects of a different kind of supranational influence, however. Environmental problems, which rarely recognize national borders, have forced states into ever-closer cooperation as political leaders find that the only effective responses are at a supranational level. These issues occupy Chapter 11.

✓•⁻ **Study**
and **Review**
the **Post-Test &**
Chapter Exam
at **mypoliscilab.com**

CHAPTER REVIEW

SUMMARY

- Supranational processes bring states together in larger structures and identities. These processes generally lead to an ongoing struggle between nationalism and supranationalism.

- International integration—the partial shifting of sovereignty from the state toward supranational institutions—is considered an outgrowth of international cooperation in functional (technical and economic) issue areas.

- Integration theorists thought that functional cooperation would spill over into political integration in foreign policy and military issue areas. Instead, forces of disintegration tore apart previously existing states such as the Soviet Union.

- The European Union (EU) is the most advanced case of integration. Its 27 member states have given considerable power to the EU in economic decision making. However, national power still outweighs supranational power even in the EU.

- Since the founding of the European Coal and Steel Community (ECSC) in 1952, the mission and membership of what is now the EU have expanded continually.

- The most important and most successful element in the EU is its customs union (and the associated free trade area). Goods can cross borders of member states freely, and the members adopt unified tariffs with regard to goods entering from outside the EU.

- Under the EU's Common Agricultural Policy (CAP), subsidies to farmers are made uniform within the community. Carrying out the CAP consumes 40 percent of the EU's budget. EU agricultural subsidies are a major source of trade conflict with the United States.

- The EU has a monetary union with a single European currency (the euro) in 17 of the 27 EU states. It is the biggest experiment with money in history and had great success in its first years but hit a crisis in 2010–2011 over members' debts. Such a union requires roughly comparable inflation rates and financial stability in participating states.

- In structure, the EU revolves around the permanent staff of Eurocrats under the European Commission. The Commission's president, individual members, and staff all serve Europe as a whole—a supranational role. However, the Council of the European Union representing member states (in national roles) has power over the Commission.

- The European Parliament has members directly elected by citizens in EU states, but it has few powers and cannot legislate the rules for the community. The European Court of Justice also has limited powers, but has extended its jurisdiction more successfully than any other international court, and can overrule national laws.

- The 1991 Maastricht Treaty on closer European integration (monetary union and political-military coordination) provoked a public backlash in several countries against the power of EU bureaucrats.

- Twelve new members, mostly Eastern European, joined the EU in 2004 and 2007. The EU's structures and procedures are being adapted as it moves from 15 to 27 members. The EU faces challenges in deciding how far to expand its membership, particularly regarding Turkey.

- A different type of international integration can be seen in the growing role of communication and information operating across national borders. Supranational relationships and identities are being fostered by new information technologies—especially mass media such as TV, radio, and the Internet—although the process is still in an early stage.

- Governments use the dissemination of information across borders as a means of influencing other states. Government access to information can also increase the stability of international relationships, since the security dilemma and other collective goods problems become less difficult in a transparent world.

- The greater and freer flow of information around the world can undermine the authority and power of governments as well. Authoritarian governments find it hard to limit the flow of information into and out of their states.

- Telecommunications are contributing to the development of global cultural integration. This process may hold the potential for the development of a single world culture. However, some politicians and citizens worry about cultural imperialism—that such a culture would be too strongly dominated by the United States.

- Transnational communities in areas such as sports, music, and tourism may foster supranational identities that could someday compete with the state for the loyalty of citizens.

KEY TERMS

supranational 355	customs union 359	European Court of
international	common market 360	Justice 362
integration 355	Common Agricultural	Single European
neofunctionalism 357	Policy (CAP) 360	Act 362
security	European	Maastricht Treaty 363
community 357	Commission 361	euro 364
European Union	Council of the	Lisbon Treaty 369
(EU) 358	European	digital divide 374
Treaty of Rome 359	Union 361	cultural
Euratom 359	European	imperialism 380
free trade area 359	Parliament 362	

CRITICAL THINKING QUESTIONS

1. Functional economic ties among European states have contributed to the emergence of a supranational political structure, the EU, which has considerable though not unlimited power. Do you think the same thing could happen in North America? Could the U.S.-Canadian-Mexican NAFTA develop into a future North American Union like the EU? What problems would it be likely to face, given the experience of the EU?

2. Suppose you happened to be chatting with the president of the European Commission, who is complaining about the public reaction in European states against the growing power of the Commission's Eurocrats. What advice would you give? What steps could the Commission take to calm such fears without reversing the process of integration? How would your suggestions address the resentments that many European citizens or governments feel against Brussels?

3. Suppose the government of Turkey hired you as a consultant to help it develop a presentation to the EU about why Turkey should be admitted as a member. What arguments would you propose using? What kinds of rebuttals might you expect from the present EU members? How would you recommend that Turkey respond?

4. Information technologies are strengthening transnational and supranational communications and identity. However, they are also providing states with new instruments of power and control. Which aspect do you find predominant now? Are these new capabilities helpful or harmful to state governments? Why? Do you expect your answer to change in the future, as technology continues to develop?

5. What are the good and bad effects, in your opinion, of the emergence of global communications and culture? Should we be cheering or lamenting the possibility of one world culture? Does the answer depend on where one lives in the world? Give concrete examples of the effects you discuss.

Has European Integration Gone as Far as Possible?

Overview

Since the creation of the European Coal and Steel Community, there appears to be a forward-moving process of integration in Europe. The European Union is now the major political force in Europe. It is economically large, with an aggregate GDP greater than that of the United States. It is a powerful force diplomatically, mediating international disputes and conflicts, even those involving other great powers. It possesses significant influence inside and outside of Europe.

Yet, the EU has lately had difficulty furthering the integration process. After the adoption of the euro, the EU changed its focus from deepening integration (taking over more policy areas from member states) to broadening membership by admitting former Eastern European states to membership. This expansion has extended the economic and political power of the EU, but it has also resulted in challenges. Attempts to change EU rules to further extend the power of the European Parliament, to create a position to help unify European foreign policy, to make the EU's human rights charter legally binding, and to alter voting systems within the EU Council to remove the requirement for unanimous voting have all met with stiff resistance. The global economic recession also put strains on the EU, with the Hungarian prime minister warning in 2009 of a "new iron curtain" between rich (Western European) and poor (Eastern European) states.

Some now wonder if European integration has run its course. Have the last steps toward deepening integration already taken place? Are there more issues on which states will surrender their sovereignty in favor of supranationalism or is the EU left only to add more members?

ARGUMENT 1

The EU Integration Process Is Finished Progressing

Troubles with the proposed Constitution and new Lisbon Treaty prove there are difficulties. The rejection of the proposed European Constitution in 2007 and the initial rejection of the Lisbon Treaty in 2008 show that major challenges lie ahead when it comes to implementing major EU policy changes. Even the attempt to guarantee individual rights in Europe created controversy.

The number of members makes it nearly impossible to get major change. Many of the major EU changes, including the Single European Act and Maastricht, began when the EU had 12 or 15 members. Now, with 27 members, finding agreement among all the states will be extremely difficult, especially on issues where unanimous consent is required.

Public opinion is skeptical of further integration. "Euroskeptics," as they are labeled, are increasingly common in Europe. While public support may not directly influence EU policy, the public may begin to vote for leaders and political parties that will put a halt to EU integration (and possibly expansion as well).

The EU Integration Process Will Continue to Advance

Obstacles have been overcome in the past. Few observers gave the EU much of a chance to get the euro off the ground, yet it has succeeded in doing so. Soon after the defeat of the Lisbon Treaty in Ireland, a new agreement was reached to allow a second vote. EU ministers have been persistent and creative in their attempts to deepen the integration process.

External factors will drive deepening. With the failure to date of the Doha Round of WTO negotiations and tensions with the United States over when and where NATO forces should be used, the EU has strong incentives to deepen cooperation among its members. It now knows it cannot rely only on the WTO to further trade liberalization nor on the United States for military leadership.

The EU is flexible enough to deal with large numbers of members. Many cooks in the kitchen does not necessarily mean bad broth. The EU has been and remains flexible as to how member states respond to the deepening of cooperation. The euro is a perfect example—not all members use the euro, some from economic necessity but some by choice (for example, Britain). Thus, further integration does not require unanimous adoption of all policies.

Questions

■ Will the EU branch out into new issue areas or focus only on expanding to new members for the foreseeable future? Is there a natural geographic limit to the boundaries of the EU?

■ Could the EU separate into two tiers: the wealthier Western European states and the poorer Eastern European states? Would the EU be as important politically and economically if only certain states cooperated on some issues? Could a euro-like solution work in other policy areas?

■ What other functions could the EU attempt to perform? What would the prospects for success be in deepening military cooperation or budgetary coordination? How would increasing military cooperation fit with many EU states' existing commitment to NATO?

For Further Reading

Scott, James Wesley. *EU Enlargement, Region Building and Shifting Borders of Inclusion and Exclusion.* Ashgate, 2006.

Schimmelfennig, Frank. *The Politics of European Union Enlargement: Theoretical Approaches.* Routledge, 2005.

Sjursen, Helene. *Questioning EU Enlargement.* Routledge, 2006.

DeBardeleben, Joan. *The Boundaries of EU Enlargement: Finding a Place for Neighbours.* Palgrave Macmillan, 2008.

CHAPTER **11** | Environment and Population

Windmill and nuclear power plant, Britain, mid-1980s.

Interdependence and the Environment

Global threats to the natural environment are a growing source of interdependence. States' actions regarding pollution, conservation, and natural resources routinely affect other states. Because environmental effects tend to be diffuse and long term and because such effects easily spread from one location to another, international environmental politics creates difficult collective goods problems (see pp. 4–7). A sustainable natural environment is a collective good, and states bargain over how to distribute the costs of providing that good. The technical, scientific, and ethical aspects of managing the environment are complex, but the basic nature of states' interests is not. The collective goods problem arises in each issue area concerning the environment, resources, and population.

For example, the world's major fisheries in international waters are not owned by any state; they are a collective good. The various fishing states must cooperate (partly by regulating nonstate actors such as MNCs) to avoid depleting the stocks of fish. If too many states fail to cooperate, the fish populations decline and everyone's catch drops. And indeed, in 1997–2007, catches worldwide declined by about 15 percent. Further declines are projected for the coming years. Fishers have moved on to new species of seafood after depleting earlier ones, but have already depleted a third of the species, with the rest projected to go by midcentury (see Figure 11.1). Because the world's states did not solve the collective goods problem of world fisheries, they are paying $20 billion a year in subsidies to bankrupt fishing industries in their respective countries.[1]

Read and Listen to **Chapter 11** at **mypoliscilab.com**

✓ Study and **Review** the **Pre-Test & Flashcards** at **mypoliscilab.com**

FIGURE 11.1 Global Loss of Seafood Species

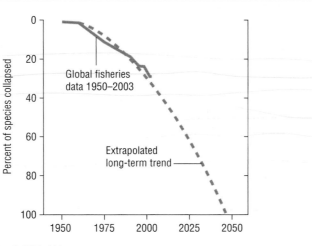

Source: *New York Times,* Nov. 3, 2006: A16.

---

[1] Food and Agriculture Organization. *State of World Aquaculture 2006.* FAO, 2006. Worm, Boris, et al. Impacts of Biodiversity Loss on Ocean Ecosystem Services. *Science* 314, November 3, 2006: 787–90. Black, Richard. "Only 50 Years Left" for Sea Fish. BBC News Web site, November 2, 2006.

👁️⊸⌐**Watch**
the **Video**
"Carteret's Climate
Refugees"
on **mypoliscilab.com**

This depletion occurred because each additional fishing boat—and the MNC that owns it as well as its state of origin—gains by catching an additional fish. The benefits of that fish go entirely to the one catching it, whereas the eventual costs of depleted stocks will be shared by all who fish there. But what is a state's fair quota of fish? No world government exists to decide such a question, so states must enter into multilateral negotiations, agreements, and regimes. Such efforts create new avenues for functionalism and international integration, but also new potentials for conflict and "prisoner's dilemmas."

In 1999, a UN-sponsored agreement among all the world's major fishing states set goals to reduce fleet overcapacity. (Four million fishing boats operate worldwide, of which 40,000 are ships larger than 100 tons.) Participating nations are capping the size of fishing fleets and then scaling them back gradually, while reducing subsidies. The pain of unemployment and economic adjustment should thus be shared. However, the agreement is voluntary, its implementation delayed, and its effect on collapsing fisheries probably too little, too late.

This type of collective goods dilemma has been called the **tragedy of the commons**.[2] Centuries ago, the commons were shared grazing land in Britain. As with fisheries, if too many people kept too many sheep, the commons would be overgrazed. Yet adding one more sheep was profitable to that sheep's owner. Britain solved the problem by **enclosure** of the commons—splitting it into privately owned pieces on each of which a single owner would have an incentive to manage resources responsibly. The world's states have taken a similar approach to coastal fisheries by extending territorial waters to put more fish under the control of single states (see p. 408). The *global commons* refers to the shared parts of the earth, such as the oceans and outer space.

As in other areas of IPE, the solution of environmental collective goods problems is based on achieving shared benefits that depend on overcoming conflicting interests.[3] *Regimes* are an important part of the solution (see pp. 90–92), providing rules based on the reciprocity principle to govern bargaining over who gets the benefits and bears the costs of environmental protection. Functional IOs specialize in technical and management aspects of the environment.[4]

Increasingly, these IOs overlap with broader communities of experts from various states that structure the way states manage environmental issues; these have been called *epistemic communities* (knowledge-based communities). For example, the transnational community of experts and policy makers concerned with pollution in the Mediterranean is an epistemic community.[5]

In global environmental politics, it is hard to manage collective goods problems because of the large number of actors. Collective goods are easier to provide in small

[2] Hardin, Garrett. The Tragedy of the Commons. *Science* 162, December 16, 1968: 1243–48.

[3] Tolba, Mostafa K., and Iwona Rummel-Bulska. *Global Environmental Diplomacy: Negotiating Environmental Agreements for the World, 1973–1992*. MIT, 2008. Speth, James Gustave, and Peter M. Haas. *Global Environmental Governance*. Island, 2006. Stevis, Dimitris, and Valerie J. Assetto, eds. *The International Political Economy of the Environment: Critical Perspectives*. Rienner, 2001. Schreurs, Miranda A., and Elizabeth Economy, eds. *The Internationalization of Environmental Protection*. Cambridge, 1997.

[4] Young, Oran R., Leslie A. King, and Heike Schroeder, eds. *Institutions and Environmental Change: Principal Findings, Applications, and Research Frontiers*. MIT, 2008. Young, Oran R., ed. *The Effectiveness of International Environmental Regimes: Casual Connections and Behavioral Mechanisms*. MIT, 1999. Peterson, M. J. *International Regimes for the Final Frontier*. SUNY, 2005.

[5] Haas, Peter M. *Saving the Mediterranean: The Politics of International Environmental Cooperation*. Columbia, 1990.

groups, in which individual actions have more impact on the total picture and cheating is more noticeable. The opposite is true with the environment. The actions of nearly 200 states (albeit some more than others) aggregate to cause indirect but serious consequences throughout the world.

Interest in the environment has grown steadily since the first Earth Day organized by environmental activists in 1970.[6] The first UN conference on the international environment took place in Stockholm, Sweden, in 1972. It adopted general principles—that one state's actions should not cause environmental damage to another, for instance—and raised awareness about international aspects of environmental damage. A second conference was held, with less publicity, in 1982 in Nairobi, Kenya (headquarters of the UN Environment Program). The larger and more ambitious 1992 Earth Summit in Rio de Janeiro, Brazil, brought together more than a hundred state leaders.

Sustainable Development

A major theme of these conferences is *sustainable* development. This refers to economic growth that does not deplete resources and destroy ecosystems so quickly that the basis of that economic growth is itself undermined. The concept applies to both the industrialized regions and the global South.[7]

The 1992 Earth Summit established the *Commission on Sustainable Development*, which monitors states' compliance with the promises they made at the Earth Summit and hears evidence from environmental NGOs such as Greenpeace. But it lacks powers of enforcement over national governments—again reflecting the preeminence of state sovereignty over supranational authority (see p. 355). The Commission has 53 member states. The Commission's ability to monitor and publicize state actions is supposed to discourage states from cheating on the Earth Summit plan and the follow-up 2002 Johannesburg Plan of Implementation. But progress has been slow.

China and other developing countries in Asia stand at the center of the debate over sustainable development. In the drive for rapid economic growth, these countries have created serious pollution and other environmental problems. Just to clear the air long enough to hold the 2008 Olympics, Beijing had to shut down industry and ban traffic. Because of China's size, any success in developing its economy along Western industrialized lines (for example, with mass ownership of automobiles) could create shocks to the global environment. In recent years, while China has been scouring the planet for raw materials, it has also become a leader in the development of "green" technology. For example, China now dominates the production of solar panels.

TOO MANY COOKS

Management of environmental issues is complicated by the large numbers of actors involved, which make collective goods problems hard to resolve (participants may be more tempted to free-ride). Here, 192 countries participate in global warming negotiations in Copenhagen, 2009.

[6] Desombre, Elizabeth R. *The Global Environment and World Politics: International Relations for the 21st Century.* Continuum, 2007. Bernstein, Steven F. *The Compromise of Liberal Environmentalism.* Columbia, 2001. Sprout, Harold, and Margaret Sprout. *The Ecological Perspective on Human Affairs, with Special Reference to International Politics.* Princeton, 1965.

[7] Brown, Lester R., et al. *State of the World* (annual). Norton/Worldwatch Institute.

NOT SUSTAINABLE

Pollution from industrialization caused great environmental damage in the Soviet Union, contributing to the stagnation and collapse of the Soviet economy—an unsustainable path. Many environmental problems remain in post-Soviet states, such as this heavily polluting nickel plant in Siberia. Today's poor countries will have to industrialize along cleaner lines to realize sustainable development.

Managing the Environment

Most global environmental problems are those that involve collective goods for all states and people in the world.[8]

The Atmosphere

Preserving the health of the earth's atmosphere is a benefit that affects people throughout the world without regard for their own state's contribution to the problem or its solution. Two problems of the atmosphere have become major international issues—global warming and depletion of the ozone layer.

Global Warming   Global climate change, or **global warming**, is a long-term rise in the average world temperature. Growing and compelling evidence shows that global warming is a real problem, that it is caused by the emission of carbon dioxide and other gases, and that it will get much worse in the future. The issue of global warm-

Watch
the **Video**
"Establishing Carbon Markets"
on **mypoliscilab.com**

Watch
the **Video**
"Deforestation in the Brazilian Amazon"
on **mypoliscilab.com**

ing rose high on the political agenda in 2005–2008 because of massive melt-offs of Arctic ice, high oil prices, and devastating hurricanes. In 2007, former U.S. Vice President Al Gore and the UN Intergovernmental Panel on Climate Change won the Nobel Peace Prize, and in 2009 President Obama vowed to redirect U.S. policy and work more closely with other countries to tackle global warming. Unfortunately, the international community has had little success solving the problem.

Over the next few decades, according to most estimates, global temperatures may rise by between 3 and 10 degrees Fahrenheit if nothing is done. The high end of this temperature range corresponds with the difference between today's climate and that of the last ice age; it is a major climate change. Possibly within a few decades, the polar ice caps will begin to melt and cause the sea level to rise by as much as a few feet. A study by British and American researchers in 2009 found that one Arctic ice shelf had vanished and that glaciers were melting at a faster rate than previously believed. Such a rise could flood many coastal cities and devastate low-lying areas such as the heavily populated coastal areas of Bangladesh and China. Urgent calls for action to avert global warming come from island states in the Pacific that will likely disappear this century. Indeed, reflecting an all too

---

[8] Pirages, Dennis Clark, and Theresa Manley DeGeest. *Ecological Security: An Evolutionary Perspective on Globalization.* Rowman & Littlefield, 2003.

realistic lack of faith in international action, the low-lying state of the Maldives created a fund to buy land in another country to move its 300,000 residents as its territory disappears.

Global climate change could also alter weather patterns in many regions, causing droughts, floods, freezes, and widespread disruption of natural ecosystems. It is also possible that climate changes could *benefit* some regions and make agriculture more productive. Melting of polar ice is opening new shipping routes north of Canada and Russia that could potentially cut weeks off the transit time from northern Europe or America to Asia (see Figure 11.2), a huge savings for global business. Furthermore, the Arctic seas are thought to hold large deposits of oil and gas, which would become commercially accessible if the ice melts (and, ironically, contribute to even more global warming). Still, overall, sudden environmental changes are usually much more destructive than helpful.

The **UN Environment Program (UNEP)**, whose main function is to monitor environmental conditions, works with the World Meteorological Organization to measure changes in global climate from year to year. Since 1989 the UN-sponsored *Intergovernmental Panel on Climate Change* (IPCC) has served as a negotiating forum for this issue. In 2007, the IPCC issued a report from scientists around the world, approved by more than 100 countries, calling global warming "unequivocal" and expressing "very high confidence" that humans are the main cause.[9]

It is costly to reduce the emissions of gases—mainly carbon dioxide—that cause global warming. These gases result from the broad spectrum of activities that drive an industrial economy. They are a by-product of burning *fossil fuels*—oil, coal, and natural gas—to run cars, tractors, furnaces, factories, and so forth. These activities create **greenhouse gases**— so named because when concentrated in the atmosphere, these gases act like the glass in a greenhouse: they let energy in as short-wavelength solar radiation but reflect it back when it tries to exit again as longer-wavelength heat waves. The greenhouse gases are *carbon dioxide* (responsible for two-thirds of the effect), *methane gas, chlorofluorocarbons* (CFCs), and *nitrous oxide*.

FIGURE 11.2 Potential Arctic Shipping Routes

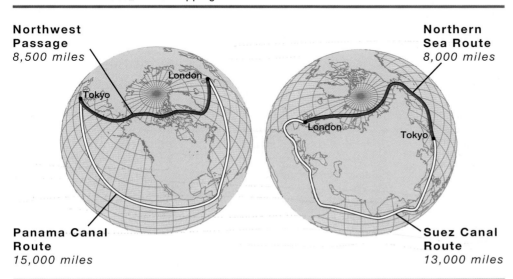

Northwest Passage
8,500 miles

Northern Sea Route
8,000 miles

Panama Canal Route
15,000 miles

Suez Canal Route
13,000 miles

[9] Intergovernmental Panel on Climate Change. *Climate Change 2007: The Physical Science Basis*. Cambridge, 2007. United Nations Environment Program. *Global Environment Outlook 3*. Oxford, 2002.

MELTING AWAY

International treaties have been much more successful at addressing ozone depletion than global warming, mostly because the costs of the latter are much higher. A 1997 conference in Kyoto, Japan, set goals for industrialized countries to reduce their output of carbon dioxide and related gases modestly over the next decade, but the goals are not being met. If global warming melts polar ice caps in the coming decades, sea levels could rise and devastate many cities. Polar bears are also endangered by the melting Arctic ice.

Thus reducing the greenhouse effect means curbing economic growth or shifting it onto entirely new technological paths, both of which are extremely expensive.[10] The political costs of such actions—which would likely increase unemployment, reduce corporate profits, and lower personal incomes—could be severe. If Arctic sea ice melts, polar bears may go extinct, but they do not have a seat at the table in international climate negotiations. Neither do today's children, who cannot vote but will live with the long-term consequences of their elders' actions.

For individual states, the costs of reducing greenhouse emissions are almost unrelated to the benefits of a solution. If one state reduces its industrial production or makes expensive investments in new technologies, this will have little effect on the long-term outcome unless other states do likewise. And if most states took such steps, a free rider that did not go along would save money and still benefit from the solution.

Global warming thus presents states with a triple dilemma. First, there is the dilemma of short-term (and predictable) costs to gain long-term (and less predictable) benefits. Second, specific constituencies such as oil companies and industrial workers pay the costs, whereas the benefits are distributed more generally across domestic society and internationally. Third, there is the collective goods dilemma among states: benefits are shared globally but costs must be extracted from each state individually.

This third dilemma is complicated by the North-South divide. How can the industrialization of today's poor countries (China and India in particular) take place without pushing greenhouse emissions to unacceptable levels? Greenhouse gases are produced by each state roughly in proportion to its industrial activity. Eighty percent of greenhouse gases now come from the industrialized countries—25 percent from the United States alone. U.S. carbon dioxide emissions amount to 20 tons per person annually, about twice the European rate and eight times China's (although China's aggregate emissions now exceed those of the United States). Yet the most severe impacts of global warming are likely to be felt in the global South. In densely populated countries such as Bangladesh, hundreds of millions of people stand to lose their homes and farmland under a rising sea. Offsetting these North-South divisions, however, is the emerging realization that global climate change could cause environmental catastrophes across both North and South.

All of these elements make for a difficult multilateral bargaining situation, one not yet resolved. The *Framework Convention on Climate Change* adopted at the 1992 Earth Summit set a nonbinding goal to limit greenhouse emissions to 1990 levels by the year 2000. That goal was not met. The treaty did not commit the signatory states to meet target levels of greenhouse emissions by a particular date, owing to U.S. objections to such a commitment. Western Europe and Japan have been more willing to regulate greenhouse emissions than has the United States (which burns more fossil fuel per person).

---

[10] Luterbacher, Urs, and Detlef F. Sprinz. *International Relations and Global Climate Change*. MIT, 2001. Fisher, Dana R. *National Governance and the Global Climate Change Regime*. Rowman & Littlefield, 2004.

FIGURE 11.3 Projected U.S. and Chinese Carbon Dioxide Emissions, 1990–2030

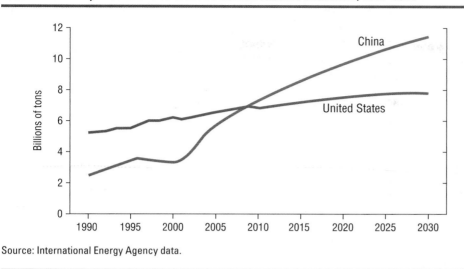

Source: International Energy Agency data.

The 1997 **Kyoto Protocol** adopted a complex formula for reducing greenhouse emissions to 1990 levels in the global North over about a decade.[11] Countries in the global South received preferential treatment because their levels (per capita) were much lower. Yet China, despite its low emissions per person, has total production of carbon dioxide higher than that of the United States, and China's fast-growing, coal-burning economy is a major factor in global warming (see Figure 11.3). China's emissions declined modestly in the late 1990s as China began switching away from its predominant fuel, coal. But China's rapid growth quickly pushed its total up again. India is another large source of carbon dioxide. The U.S. Congress refused to ratify the treaty when President Clinton submitted it, and President George W. Bush then declared the treaty "dead."

Moving forward without U.S. support, 160 countries in 2001 agreed to implement Kyoto. The agreement calls for 40 industrialized countries to reduce emissions to 5 percent below 1990 levels, by 2012, with binding penalties for failure. The EU pledged $400 million per year to help the global South reduce its emissions. The needed ratifications to put the treaty into effect (from states totaling 55 percent of world emissions) came when Russia ratified it in 2004, and the treaty entered into effect in 2005. Mandatory carbon cuts under the Kyoto Protocol began in 2008 and expire in 2012.

The European Union began operation of markets to trade carbon emission credits among 12,000 industrial facilities across Europe. And internationally, the treaty created trading in carbon credits, using free market principles to make reduction in carbon emissions more efficient. For example, a venture in Brazil earned carbon credits by burning methane gas from a garbage dump (to generate electricity) instead of venting it as a strong greenhouse gas. European investors bought the credits and could then sell them to, say, a polluting factory in Eastern Europe where reducing carbon might be especially expensive.[12]

---

[11] Von Stein, Jana. The International Law and Politics of Climate Change: Ratification of the United Nations Framework Convention and the Kyoto Protocol. *Journal of Conflict Resolution* 52 (2), 2008: 243–68. Victor, David G. *The Collapse of the Kyoto Protocol and the Struggle to Slow Global Warming.* Princeton, 2001. Grubb, Michael, and Duncan Brack, eds. *The Kyoto Protocol: A Guide and Assessment.* Royal Institute of International Affairs, 1999.
[12] Stowell, Deborah. *Climate Trading: Development of Greenhouse Gas Markets.* Palgrave, 2005.

In 2006, 180 states began negotiating on the question of what happens after 2012 when Kyoto expires. In 2009 the United States rejoined the climate change talks. The 2009 Copenhagen summit hoped to create an agreement similar to Kyoto to create binding emissions limits. Yet, Copenhagen ended in what some observers label a failure. The United States, China, India, Brazil, and South Africa agreed to reduce emissions, but they avoided making any binding commitments that would punish them should they fail to meet targets. This nonbinding agreement calls for states to limit the rise in global temperatures to no more than 2 degrees beyond preindustrial levels. Still, the agreement was a positive step and could pave the way for future cooperation on emissions.

Meanwhile, about half the states of the United States (notably California), and a number of cities, began taking steps to limit greenhouse emissions. Yet, none of these moves are enough, or soon enough, to decisively reverse the direction of climate change. The dilemma of global warming remains fundamentally unsolved, and with weak enforcement mechanisms, even the states that signed the Kyoto Protocol may not meet their targets by 2012. Indeed, even European states, which have the largest markets for carbon as an attempt to lower emissions, have yet to see any declines in carbon dioxide. Moreover, some EU leaders have questioned the operation of the cap-and-trade carbon market system, pushing for other alternatives to cut emissions.[13]

Ozone Depletion   A second major atmospheric problem negotiated by the world's governments is the depletion of the world's **ozone layer**.[14] Ozone high in the atmosphere screens

---

[13] Kanter, James. As Cap and Trade Falls Short, Europe Weighs New Tacks to Cut Carbon. *The New York Times*, May 25, 2010: B4.
[14] Litfin, Karen. *Ozone Discourses: Science and Politics in Global Environmental Cooperation*. Columbia, 1993.

SEEKING THE COLLECTIVE GOOD

Global Warming
COLLECTIVE GOOD: A New Climate Treaty

BACKGROUND: The prevention of global warming is a collective good that affects the entire world but results from the actions of the world's states individually. Those affected most actually will be those least responsible for causing it. Weather disasters such as the 2010 catastrophic floods in Pakistan would become more common if the world does not address the problem effectively.

The costs of required actions are high, however, and states have not been willing to pay them. Governments and businesses alike focus on short-term outcomes. Thus the international community has not yet been able to address the very serious problem of global warming. Major players such as the United States did not ratify the Kyoto Protocol, and the world's output of greenhouse gases has not slowed.

CHALLENGE: In late 2009, the world's states gathered in Copenhagen, Denmark, to negotiate a new treaty on global warming, to pick up where Kyoto had left off. Countries of the global North and global South differed on their approaches. Agreement proved elusive.

SOLUTION: One day, President Obama popped in on a meeting of the presidents of China, India, Brazil, and South Africa (that is, the global South).

DOMINANCE

out harmful ultraviolet rays from the sun. Certain chemicals expelled by industrial economies float to the top of the atmosphere and interact with ozone in a way that breaks it down. The chief culprits are CFCs, until recently widely used in refrigeration and in aerosol sprays. (Unfortunately, ozone produced by burning fossil fuels does not replace the high-level ozone but only pollutes the lower atmosphere.) As the ozone layer thins, more ultraviolet radiation reaches the earth's surface. Over Antarctica, a seasonal hole in the ozone grew larger year by year. If ozone levels kept rising, the increased radiation could eventually kill off vegetation, reduce agricultural yields, and disrupt ecosystems.

Clearly, this was another collective goods problem in that one state could benefit by allowing the use of CFCs in its economy, provided that most other states prohibited their use. But the costs of replacing CFCs were much lower than the costs of addressing global warming: CFCs could be replaced with other chemicals at relatively modest costs. Furthermore, the consequences of ozone depletion were both better understood and more immediate than those of global warming.

Perhaps because of these cost issues, states had much more success in negotiating agreements and developing regimes to manage ozone depletion than global warming. In the 1987 **Montreal Protocol**, 22 states agreed to reduce CFCs by 50 percent by 1998. In 1990, the timetable was accelerated and the signatories expanded: 81 states agreed to eliminate all CFCs by 2000. In 1992, as evidence of ozone depletion mounted, the schedule was again accelerated, with major industrial states phasing out CFCs by 1995. The signatories agreed in principle to establish a fund to help developing countries pay for alternative refrigeration technologies not based on CFCs. Without such an effort, the states of the global South would be tempted to free-ride and could ultimately undermine the effort. These countries were also given until 2010 to phase out production. The Montreal Protocol was revised and strengthened again in 1997 and 1999. Rich countries stopped making CFCs in 1996 and have contributed about $3 billion to the fund. This money,

The five then agreed on a deal that kept some momentum going although it fell far short of the hoped-for treaty in Copenhagen. The dominance principle came into play as a few big players from North and South worked out an agreement and presented it to the rest of the world. The position of the United States at the top of the dominance hierarchy is also reflected in the U.S. president's ability to barge in and get a deal.

Collective goods problems are easier to solve in smaller groups than in larger ones. Face-to-face interactions limit free riding and reinforce norms. In this case, five leaders made more progress than did the 192 participating states working as sovereign equals. Brazil's top climate negotiator commented, "Certain groups like G-77 are not happy when a few people make decisions." He continued, "It's not an inclusive exercise. Perhaps it can't be."*

Demonstrators in Copenhagen, 2009.

* Broder, John M. Many Goals Remain Unmet in 5 Nations' Climate Deal. *The New York Times*, December 19, 2009: A1.

supporting thousands of projects in more than a hundred countries, has helped the global South reduce emissions over the past decade. The ozone hole is projected to slowly shrink back over the coming 50 years if current arrangements continue.

The Montreal Protocol on CFCs is the most important success yet achieved in international negotiations to preserve the global environment. Indeed, UN secretary-general Kofi Annan called it "perhaps the single most successful international agreement to date." It showed that states can agree to take action on urgent environmental threats, can agree on targets and measures to counter such threats, and can allocate the costs of such measures in a mutually acceptable way and actually pay up when the bill comes. But the international cooperation on the ozone problem has not been widely repeated on other environmental issues.

Environmental negotiations resemble trade talks in that they rely on the reciprocity principle as the prime mover of agreement. If each country contributes, and all the others contribute, a goal such as restoring the ozone layer can be accomplished. As with trade, the agreements and regimes are complicated and require monitoring of compliance to prevent free riding. The biggest difference from trade talks is that when trade talks succeed in solving a collective goods problem, the participants get a short-term, tangible benefit of billions of dollars added to the world economy. When environmental collective goods problems are solved, the participants get a short-term, tangible bill to pay, and then long-term benefits. The size of that bill seems to be the major difference between very difficult, expensive global warming solutions and reasonably affordable ozone solutions. Reciprocity, evidently, solves collective goods problems better with low costs or tangible benefits (ozone; trade) than high costs and distant benefits (climate change).

Biodiversity

Biodiversity refers to the tremendous diversity of plant and animal species making up the earth's (global, regional, and local) ecosystems.[15] Because of humans' destruction of ecosystems, large numbers of species are already *extinct*. Extinction results from overhunting, overfishing, and introducing non-native species that crowd out previous inhabitants. But the most important cause is *loss of habitat*—the destruction of rain forests, pollution of lakes and streams, and loss of agricultural lands to urban sprawl. Because ecosystems are based on complex interrelationships among species, the extinction of a few species can cause deeper changes in the environment. For example, the loss of native microorganisms can lead to chronic pollution of rivers or to the transformation of arable land into deserts.

Because ecosystems are so complex, it is usually impossible to predict the consequences of a species' extinction or of the loss of a habitat or ecosystem. Generally the activities that lead to habitat loss are economically profitable, so real costs are associated with limiting such activities. Species preservation is thus a collective good resembling global warming; the costs are immediate and substantial but the benefits are long term and ill defined.

It has been difficult to reach international agreement on sharing the costs of preserving biodiversity. A UN convention on trade in endangered species has reduced but not eliminated such trade. At the 1992 Earth Summit, a treaty on biodiversity committed signatories to preserving habitats and got rich states to pay poor ones for the rights to use commercially profitable biological products extracted from rare species in protected habitats (such as medicines from rain forest trees). However, because of fears that the treaty

---

[15] Swanson, Timothy M., ed. *The Economics and Ecology of Biodiversity Decline: The Forces Driving Global Change*. Cambridge, 1998. Mulongoy, K. J., and S. Chape. *Protected Areas and Biodiversity Report: An Overview of Key Issues*. UNEP, 2004.

could limit U.S. patent rights in biotechnology, the United States never ratified it. As of 2010, the treaty had 193 member states. The United States does, however, participate in other biological treaties, such as a 1971 wetlands convention and the 1973 Convention on International Trade in Endangered Species (CITES).

International regimes to protect whales and dolphins have had limited success. The **International Whaling Commission** (an IGO) sets quotas for hunting certain whale species, but participation is voluntary and governments are not bound by decisions they object to.

The *Inter-American Tropical Tuna Commission* (another IGO) regulates methods used to fish for tuna, aiming to minimize dolphin losses. The United States, which consumes half the world's tuna catch, has gone further and unilaterally requires—in the Marine Mammal Protection Act—that dolphin-safe methods be used for tuna sold in U.S. territory. Other countries have challenged the act through international trade organizations as an unfair restriction on tuna exports to the United States. Such conflicts portend future battles between environmentalists and free trade advocates.[16] Free traders argue that states must not use domestic legislation to seek global environmental goals. Environmentalists do not want to give up national laws that they worked for decades to enact, over the opposition of industrial corporations.

For example, the U.S. Clean Air Act successfully reduced air pollution in U.S. cities, but the regulations had to be revised in 1997, on order of the WTO, to allow gasoline refined in Venezuela and Brazil to compete in U.S. markets. Environmentalists adopted the sea turtle as a symbol of their opposition to the WTO after the WTO overturned U.S. regulations that required shrimp to be caught in nets from which sea turtles (an endangered species) can escape. Recent conflicts have arisen over U.S. laws restricting imports of foods with pesticide residues, and over European laws on imports of genetically engineered agricultural and pharmaceutical products, which the United States wants to export worldwide.

Thus, unilateral approaches to biodiversity issues are problematic because they disrupt free trade; multilateral approaches are problematic because of the collective goods problem. It is not surprising that the international response has been fairly ineffective to date.

Forests and Oceans

Two types of habitat—tropical rain forests and oceans—are especially important to biodiversity *and* the atmosphere. Both are also reservoirs of commercially profitable resources such as fish and wood. They differ in that forests are located almost entirely within state territory, whereas oceans are largely beyond any state territory, in the global commons.

TAKE IT TO THE BANK

Some environmentalists criticize the World Bank and other international institutions promoting economic development in poor countries for interfering destructively in local ecosystems such as rain forests. The green revolution increased yields but shifted patterns of agriculture in complex ways, such as by increasing pesticide and fertilizer runoff. Now genetically engineered crops promise further increases in agricultural productivity—more food on the table—but with environmental consequences that are not fully understood. This gene bank in the Philippines stores rice varieties from around the world.

[16] Chambers, W. Bradnee, ed. *Inter-Linkages: The Kyoto Protocol and the International Trade and Investment Regimes.* Brookings, 2001. DeSombre, Elizabeth R. *Domestic Sources of International Environmental Policy.* MIT, 2000. Copeland, Brian R., and M. Scott Taylor. *Trade and the Environment: Theory and Evidence.* Princeton, 2003.

POLICY PERSPECTIVES

Prime Minister of Ireland, Enda Kenny

PROBLEM *How do you balance environmental and economic concerns?*

BACKGROUND Imagine that you are the president of Ireland. Genetically modified organisms (GMOs) are highly controversial in Europe, and this certainly includes your country. In 1997, for example, Ireland reluctantly approved a permit for the global MNC Monsanto to grow sugar beets near Dublin. After several legal attempts to halt the planting of the crop failed, activists destroyed the crop in the ground before it could be harvested.

Your country has quietly supported several Irish biotechnology firms in the past with joint ventures in research. These have produced a variety of advances that give Ireland a significant advantage in this field over other European states. Several MNCs stand to benefit from this research, providing you with investment and tax income.

DOMESTIC CONSIDERATIONS Unfortunately, this "positive but precautionary" approach is unpopular with the public. Some worry that Ireland's reputation as "the Green Island" will suffer, possibly posing a threat to tourism—a major source of income for your country. Others join the chorus of European opposition to GMOs based on concerns over the possible environmental effects of these products. A recent Eurobarometer poll found that 54 percent of European consumers consider GMO foods "dangerous."

In the spring of 2004, the European Union (EU) approved an end to the moratorium on GMO product sales (with your country voting in the majority), partially under a threat from the United States to enforce a WTO ruling that found the GMO ban illegal. The United States is your largest single trade partner, but other EU states combined are your most significant export market.

SCENARIO Imagine that the balance of power in the EU shifts against GMOs with the admission of new Central European states. Now, the EU will not approve the sale of GMO products within Europe. Thus, although it would still be legal to grow GMO crops, it would not be legal to export them to EU countries.

GMO crops could provide economic benefits to your country. Given your comparative technological advantage in this area, your economy stands to profit from expanding GMO use through increased agricultural output and increased business activity from MNCs. The United States has no regulations concerning the importation of GMO products and would be open to exports of these crops.

GMOs carry possible dangers as well. Some environmentalists warn that GMOs could have negative effects on ecology, wildlife, and human health. Many of your EU partners will shun your GMO products, robbing you of a large export market for these goods. Domestically, expanding the production of GMOs will be controversial.

CHOOSE YOUR POLICY Do you continue to quietly encourage the advance of GMO crops? Do you follow the new EU members in opposing GMOs, out of respect for the long-term environmental concerns raised by these products? Do you work with MNCs to use your comparative advantage for economic gain? How do you balance economic prosperity with a concern for the environment?

Rain Forests   As many as half the world's total species live in *rain forests*, which replenish oxygen and reduce carbon dioxide in the atmosphere—slowing down global warming. Rain forests thus benefit all the world's states; they are collective goods.

International bargaining on the preservation of rain forests has made considerable progress, probably because most rain forests belong to a few states. These few states have the power to speed up or slow down the destruction of forests—and international bargaining amounts to agreements to shift costs from those few states onto the broader group of states benefiting from the rain forests.

Although some rich states (including the United States) have large forests, most of the largest rain forests are in poor states such as Brazil, Indonesia, Malaysia, and Madagascar. Such states can benefit economically from exploiting the forests—freely cutting lumber, clearing land for agriculture, and mining.[17] Until recently (and still to an extent), leaders of rich states have been most interested in encouraging maximum economic growth in poor states so that foreign debts could be paid—with little regard for environmental damage.

Now that rich states have an interest in protecting rain forests, they are using development assistance as leverage to induce poorer states to protect their forests rather than exploit them. Under international agreements reached in the early 1990s, rich countries contribute hundreds of millions of dollars in foreign aid for this purpose. In some poor countries burdened by large foreign debts, environmentalists and bankers from rich countries have worked out "debt-for-nature swaps" in which a debt is canceled in exchange for the state's agreement to preserve forests. In 2006, for example, the U.S. government and NGOs helped Guatemala cancel more than $20 million in debts in exchange for expanded conservation programs. In 2005, Brazil announced that deforestation had fallen 50 percent since 2003, while in 2008 it announced that it planned to end deforestation by 2015. Environmentalists find the figure and the plan overly optimistic.

Oceans   The *oceans*, covering 70 percent of the earth's surface, are (like the rain forest) a key to regulating climate and preserving biodiversity. Oceans, like forests, are attractive targets for short-term economic uses that cause long-term environmental damage. Such uses include overfishing, dumping toxic and nuclear waste (and other garbage), and long-distance oil shipments with their recurrent spills. Unlike rain forests, oceans belong to no state but are a global commons.[18] This makes the collective goods problem more difficult because no authority exists to enforce regulations. Preserving the oceans depends on the cooperation of more than a hundred states and thousands of nonstate actors. Free riders have great opportunities to profit. For example, *drift nets* are huge fishing nets, miles long, that scoop up everything in their path. They are very profitable but destructive of a sustainable ocean environment. Most states have now banned their use (under pressure from the environmental movement). However, no state has the authority to go onto the **high seas** (nonterritorial waters) and stop illegal use of these nets.

One solution that states have pursued involves "enclosing" more of the ocean. Territorial waters have expanded to hundreds of miles off the coast (and around islands), so that state sovereignty encloses substantial resources such as fisheries and offshore oil and

[17] Dauvergne, Peter. *Loggers and Degradation in the Asia-Pacific: Corporations and Environmental Management.* Cambridge, 2001. Guimãraes, Roberto P. *The Ecopolitics of Development in the Third World: Politics and Environment in Brazil.* Rienner, 1991.
[18] Borgese, Elisabeth Mann. *The Oceanic Circle: Governing the Seas as a Global Resource.* UN University Press, 1999.

mineral deposits. This solution has been pursued in the context of larger multilateral negotiations on ocean management.[19]

The **UN Convention on the Law of the Sea (UNCLOS)**, negotiated from 1973 to 1982, governs the uses of the oceans. After more than a decade's delay and renegotiation of some of the deep-sea mining aspects, the United States signed UNCLOS in 1994, but has yet to ratify the treaty. The UNCLOS treaty established rules on territorial waters—12 miles for shipping and a 200-mile exclusive economic zone (EEZ) for economic activities, such as fishing and mining. The 200-mile limit placed a substantial share of the economically profitable ocean resources in the control of about a dozen states (see Figure 11.4).

Varying interpretations leave economic rights in dispute in a number of locations. In the East China Sea, China sent five warships in 2005 to back up its claim to an undersea gas field partly claimed by Japan, where China began drilling and Japan granted drilling rights to a Japanese company. China's claim under a Continental Shelf treaty conflicts with Japan's claim of an EEZ.

UNCLOS also developed the general principle that the oceans are a common heritage of humankind. A mechanism was created, through an International Sea-Bed Authority, for sharing some of the wealth that rich states might gain from extracting minerals on the ocean floor (beyond 200 miles).

Antarctica   Like the oceans, *Antarctica* belongs to no state.[20] The continent's strategic and commercial value is limited, however, and not many states care about it. Thus, states have been successful in reaching agreements on Antarctica because the costs were low and the players few. The *Antarctic Treaty of 1959*—one of the first multilateral treaties concerning the environment—forbids military activity as well as the presence of nuclear weapons or the dumping of nuclear waste. It sets aside territorial claims on the continent for future resolution and establishes a regime under which various states conduct scientific research in Antarctica. The treaty was signed by all states with interests in the area, including both superpowers. By 1991, Greenpeace had persuaded the treaty signatories to turn the continent into a "world park." Antarctica is largely a success story in international environmental politics.

Pollution

Pollution generally creates a collective goods problem, but one that is not often global in scale. Pollution is more often a regional or bilateral issue. With some exceptions—such as dumping at sea—the effects of pollution are limited to the state where it occurs and its close neighbors; U.S. industrial smokestack emissions cause acid rain in Canada but do not directly affect distant states. China's terrible air pollution kills nearly half a million Chinese a year, but few foreigners. Even when pollution crosses state borders, it often has its strongest effects closest to the source. This localized effect makes for a somewhat less intractable collective goods problem, because a polluting state can seldom free-ride, and few actors are involved.

In several regions—notably Western and Eastern Europe and the Middle East—states are closely packed in the same air, river, or sea basins. In such situations, pollution controls must often be negotiated multilaterally. In Europe during the Cold War, the international

---

[19] Webster, D. G. *Adaptive Governance: The Dynamics of Atlantic Fisheries Management*. MIT, 2008.
[20] Stokke, Olav Schram, and Davor Vidas, eds. *Governing the Antarctic: The Effectiveness and Legitimacy of the Antarctic Treaty System*. Cambridge, 1997.

FIGURE 11.4 State-Controlled Waters

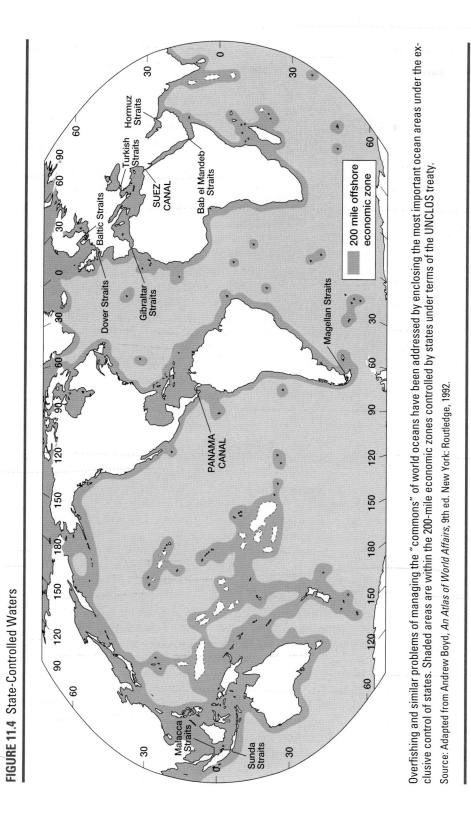

Overfishing and similar problems of managing the "commons" of world oceans have been addressed by enclosing the most important ocean areas under the exclusive control of states. Shaded areas are within the 200-mile economic zones controlled by states under terms of the UNCLOS treaty.

Source: Adapted from Andrew Boyd, *An Atlas of World Affairs*, 9th ed. New York: Routledge, 1992.

POISONED WATERS

Pollution easily crosses national borders. For example, here industrial waste and sewage in the New River crosses from Mexico into California, 2003.

pollution problem was exacerbated by the inability of Western European states to impose any limits on Eastern ones, whose pollution was notorious.

Several regional agreements seek to limit **acid rain**, caused by air pollution. European states—whose forests have been heavily damaged—have agreed to limit air pollution and acid rain for their mutual benefit. In 1988, 24 European states signed a treaty to limit nitrogen oxide emissions to 1988 levels by 1995. After long negotiations, the United States and Canada signed bilateral agreements to limit such pollution as well. These regional agreements have worked fairly well.

Water pollution often crosses borders as well, especially because industrial pollution, human sewage, and agricultural fertilizers and pesticides all tend to run into rivers and seas. For instance, in 2005, a huge chemical spill in northeast China polluted a river that flows into Russia. Long-standing regional agencies that regulate shipping on heavily used European rivers now also deal with pollution. The Mediterranean basin is severely polluted and difficult to manage because so many states border it.[21] In 2010, the largest oil spill in U.S. history occurred in the Gulf of Mexico. The spill resulted from an explosion on an oil platform, which resulted in a broken oil pipe 5,000 feet below the surface of the ocean. The leakage took months to contain and highlighted the dangers associated with deep-water oil drilling. British Petroleum, the company that operated the well, agreed to set aside billions of dollars to pay damages to residents of several southern U.S. states affected by the spill.

Toxic and *nuclear wastes* are a special problem because of their long-term dangers. States occasionally try to ship such wastes out of the country. However, international agreements now ban the dumping of toxic and nuclear wastes at sea (an obvious collective goods problem). But such wastes have been sent to developing countries for disposal, for a fee. For instance, toxic ash from Pennsylvania became material for bricks in Guinea, and Italian nuclear waste was shipped to Nigeria.

Norms have developed in recent years against exporting toxic wastes—a practice seen as exploitive of the receiving country. In 1989, 100 states signed a treaty under UN auspices to regulate shipments of toxic and nuclear wastes and prevent their secret movements under corrupt deals. Forty more countries, in Africa, did not sign the treaty but called for a complete halt to toxic waste shipments to Africa. Nonetheless, in 2006 a multinational company tried to dispose of toxic waste from a tanker ship in the Netherlands but took it back, on finding the cost to run into hundreds of thousands of dollars. Six weeks later, the ship unloaded the toxic sludge in Abidjan, Ivory Coast, where a

---

[21] Haas, Peter M. *Saving the Mediterranean* (see footnote 5 in this chapter).

local company dumped it at locations around the city. Thousands of residents got sick and eight people died.[22] In 2007 the company agreed to pay $200 million to settle claims.

In 1986, a meltdown at the Soviet nuclear power plant at **Chernobyl**, in Ukraine, created airborne radioactivity that spread over much of Europe, from Italy to Sweden. The accident exemplified the new reality—that economic and technical decisions made in one state can have grave environmental consequences for other countries. Soviet leaders made matters worse by failing to notify neighbors promptly of the accident.

On the various issues of water and air pollution, both unilateral state actions and international agreements have often been feasible and effective. In recent decades, river water quality has improved in most industrialized regions. Market economies have begun to deal with pollution as just another cost of production that should be charged to the polluter instead of to society at large. Some governments have begun to allocate "pollution rights" that companies can buy and sell on a free market.

In the former Soviet bloc, decades of centrally planned industrialization created more severe environmental problems.[23] With staggering environmental damage and human health effects, the economically strapped former Soviet republics had to bargain over limiting pollution and repairing the damage. For example, the severely polluted Aral Sea, formerly contained within one state, the Soviet Union, is now shared by two, Kazakhstan and Uzbekistan. Once the world's fourth-largest inland sea, it shrank in half, its huge fisheries destroyed, after a Soviet-era mega-irrigation project to grow cotton in the desert diverted the Aral Sea's inlet rivers and polluted them with pesticides. Former fishing towns found themselves many miles from the shoreline. After local and international political leaders failed to implement plans to address the problem, local populations suffered from widespread health effects of the disaster.

Natural Resources

The natural environment is not only a delicate ecosystem requiring protection, but also a repository of natural resources. Because the extraction of resources brings states wealth, these resources regularly fuel international conflicts.[24] Because they are mostly located within individual states, however, they do not present a collective goods problem. Rather, states bargain over these vital resources.

Three aspects of natural resources shape their role in international conflict. First, they are required for the operation of an industrial economy (sometimes even an agrarian one). Second, their sources—mineral deposits, rivers, and so forth—are associated with particular territories over which states may fight for control. Third, natural resources tend to be unevenly distributed, with plentiful supplies in some states and an absence in others. These aspects mean that trade in natural resources is extremely profitable; much additional wealth is created by such trade. They also mean that trade in resources is fairly politicized—creating market imperfections such as monopoly, oligopoly, and price manipulation, sometimes by cartels (see pp. 304–307).

Explore the Simulation "Transnational Issues: You Are an Environmental Consultant" on mypoliscilab.com

---

[22] Polgreen, Lydia, and Marlise Simons. Global Sludge Ends in Tragedy for Ivory Coast. *The New York Times*, October 2, 2006: A1.

[23] Feshbach, Murray. *Ecological Disaster: Cleaning Up the Hidden Legacy of the Soviet Regime*. Brookings, 1995. Weinthal, Erika. *State Making and Environment Cooperation: Linking Domestic and International Politics in Central Asia*. MIT, 2002.

[24] Zacher, Mark W., ed. *The International Political Economy of Natural Resources*. Elgar, 1993. Lipschutz, Ronnie D. *When Nations Clash: Raw Materials, Ideology, and Foreign Policy*. Ballinger, 1989. Bannon, Ian, and Paul Collier, eds. *Natural Resources and Violent Conflict: Options and Actions*. World Bank, 2003.

World Energy

Of the various natural resources required by states, energy resources (fuels) are central. The commercial fuels that power the world's industrial economies are oil (about 40 percent of world energy consumption), coal (30 percent), natural gas (25 percent), and hydroelectric and nuclear power (5 percent). The fossil fuels (coal, oil, gas) thus account for 95 percent of world energy consumption. Some energy consumed as electricity comes from hydroelectric dams or nuclear power plants, but most of it comes from burning fossil fuels in electric-generating plants.

Imagine a pile of coal weighing 75 pounds. The energy released by burning that much coal is equivalent to the amount of energy North Americans use per person every day. Wealthier people, of course, consume more energy per person than do poorer people, but 75 pounds is the average. The North American's pile of coal would be 10 times larger than that of a person in China, 20 times that of an African.

Table 11.1 shows energy consumption per person in the nine world regions. The four industrialized regions of the North use much more energy per person than those of the South. Because Asia and Africa have little industry, North America uses 25 times as much as those two continents. Among industrialized countries there are differences in the *efficiency* of energy use—GDP produced per unit of energy consumed. The least efficient are the former Soviet Republics; North America is also rather inefficient; Europe and Japan are the most energy efficient.

International trade in energy thus plays a vital role in the world economy. As Table 11.1 shows, the regions of the industrialized West are all large net importers of energy. The other six world regions are net exporters of energy. Although all forms of energy are traded internationally, the most important by far is oil, the cheapest to transport over long distances. Russia receives vital hard-currency earnings from exporting oil. Venezuela and Mexico (in Latin America) and Nigeria and Angola (in Africa) are also major oil exporters. But by far the largest source of oil exports is the Middle East—especially the

TABLE 11.1 Per Capita Energy Consumption and Net Energy Trade, 2007

	Per Capita Consumption (million BTU)	Total Net Energy Exports[a] (quadrillion BTU)
North America	385	−24
Europe	145	−37
Japan/Pacific	175	−23
Russia/CIS	160	+23
China	55	−6
Middle East	125	+42
Latin America	50	+5
South Asia	20	−1
Africa	16	+20
World as a whole	72	

[a]Net exports refers to production minus consumption. Net exports worldwide do not equal net imports for technical reasons.

Source: Calculated from data in U.S. Department of Energy. Energy Information Administration. See http://www.eia.doe.gov/iea/.

countries around the Persian Gulf (Saudi Arabia, Kuwait, Iraq, Iran, and the small sheik-doms of United Arab Emirates, Qatar, Bahrain, and Oman). Saudi Arabia is the largest oil exporter and holds the largest oil reserves (see Table 8.1 on p. 303). The politics of world energy revolve around Middle Eastern oil shipped to Western Europe, Japan/Pacific, and North America.

The importance of oil in the industrialized economies helps explain the political importance of the Middle East in world politics.[25] Not only is energy a crucial economic sector (on which all industrial activity depends), but it is also one of the most politically sensitive because of the dependence of the West on energy imported from the Middle East and the rest of the global South.

To secure a supply of oil in the Middle East, Britain and other European countries colonized the area early in the 20th century, carving up territory into protectorates in which European power kept local monarchs on their thrones. The United States did not claim colonies or protectorates, but U.S. MNCs were heavily involved in the development of oil resources in the area from the 1920s through the 1960s—often wielding vast power.[26] These U.S. and European oil companies kept the price paid to local states low and their own profits high, yet local rulers depended on the expertise and capital investment of these companies.

After World War II the British gave up colonial claims in the Middle East, but the Western oil companies kept producing cheap oil there for Western consumption. Then in 1973, during an Arab-Israeli war, the oil-producing Arab states of the region decided to punish the United States for supporting Israel. They cut off their oil exports to the United States and curtailed their overall exports. This supply disruption sent world oil prices sky-rocketing. OPEC realized its potential power and the high price the world was willing to pay for oil. This 1973 *oil shock* had a profound effect on the world economy and on world politics. Huge amounts of hard currency accumulated in the treasuries of the Middle East oil-exporting countries, which in turn invested them around the world (these were called *petrodollars*). High inflation plagued the United States and Europe for years afterward. The economic instability and sense of U.S. helplessness—coming on top of the Vietnam War—seemed to mark a decline in American power and perhaps the rise of the global South.

In 1979, the revolution in Iran led to a second oil shock. But higher oil prices led to the expansion of oil production in new locations outside of OPEC—in the North Sea (Britain and Norway), Alaska, Angola, Russia, and elsewhere. By the mid-1980s, the Middle East was rapidly losing its market share of world trade in oil. At the same time, industrialized economies learned to be more *energy efficient*. With supply up and demand down, oil prices dropped in the late 1980s to historic lows of less than $20/barrel.

In the late 1990s, the Caspian Sea region beckoned as a new and largely untapped oil source (see Figure 11.5). However, the oil must travel overland by pipeline to reach world markets (the Caspian is an inland sea). But the main pipeline from oil-producing Azerbaijan to the Black Sea (where tanker ships could load) traveled through war-torn Chechnya in southern Russia. Russia then built a bypass route around Chechnya that carries a large and growing amount of Caspian oil for export through the Black Sea. Western powers sought other pipeline routes that did not cross Russia, while Turkey sought to control a larger market share and reduce environmental damage to the Bosporus waterway (through which Russian tankers must travel). After long negotiations, in

---

[25] Kapstein, Ethan B. *The Insecure Alliance: Energy Crises and Western Politics Since 1944.* Oxford, 1990. Parra, Francisco R. *Oil Politics: A Modern History of Petroleum.* Tauris, 2004. Yergin, Daniel. *The Prize: The Epic Quest for Oil, Money, and Power.* Simon & Schuster, 1991.
[26] Vitalis, Robert. *America's Kingdom: Mythmaking on the Saudi Oil Frontier.* Verso, 2009.

FIGURE 11.5 Dividing the Caspian Sea

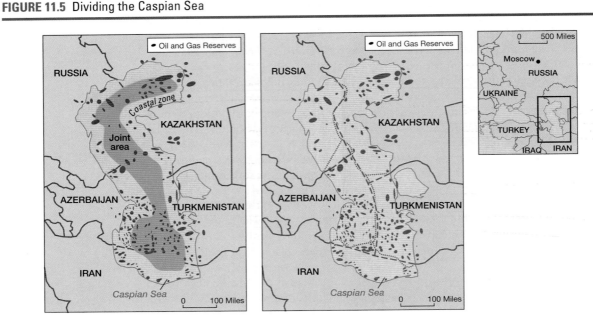

The Caspian Sea is the world's largest inland body of water. It could be defined under international law as either a lake or a sea.[a] A *lake* has a joint area in the middle (in green on the left panel) that can be exploited only if the countries agree on terms. There are also coastal zones under each country's sole control. In a *sea* less than 400 miles across, the bordering countries' 200-mile Exclusive Economic Zones (EEZs) split up the whole sea (right panel). If the whole area is split as in the map on the right, the sectors can be defined by median lines (dashed line) or by a division into five sectors of equal area (dotted line), giving Iran a larger sector.

In 2008, with major oil development underway in all five countries' coastal areas, the talks to draw final borders remained stalled. Russia had agreed with its neighbors, Azerbaijan and Kazakhstan, to use the median line on the seabed floor, though Russia proposes a different division for fishing purposes. Azerbaijan and Turkmenistan dispute ownership of an oil field along the dividing line between their sectors. Iran still wants one-fifth of the lake, and even sent a warship in 2001 to chase an oil exploration ship from Azerbaijan away from disputed waters. This conflict will be resolved not through dominance, but through reciprocity. Nobody benefits from a war and all five countries benefit from developing their oil resources. Solutions are enormously complicated—in this case factoring in additional elements like shipping, fishing, smuggling, and pipeline routes—and reaching agreement can take a very long time.

[a]Sciolino, Elaine. "It's a Sea! It's a Lake! No. It's a Pool of Oil!" *The New York Times,* June 21, 1998.

2002–2004, states and oil companies built a large-capacity pipeline, costing billions of dollars, through Azerbaijan and Georgia to Turkey's Mediterranean coast.

Violent conflicts make pipeline routes particularly complex. All three countries on the new pipeline route were at war in the past decade. A dozen other existing and proposed oil pipelines for Caspian Sea oil are no easier. Across the Caspian Sea, Turkmenistan wants to export natural gas to Pakistan, and from there to Asia, but a pipeline would have to cross war-torn Afghanistan. Meanwhile in 2003, a new $4 billion pipeline began carrying oil from Chad through Cameroon for export, promising to help both countries alleviate poverty, but as rebels based in Sudan attacked in Chad, oil money was diverted to military purposes. Although borders and geopolitics may be less and less important in communications and business, they still matter greatly in such international economic transactions as oil pipelines.

Oil prices stayed relatively high after 2000, ultimately shooting up to $140 a barrel in 2008 and pushing U.S. gas prices to more than $4 a gallon. These high oil prices had two major benefits. First, burning oil contributes to global warming, and high prices made it profitable to burn less oil and be more energy efficient. For instance, in 2008 sales of gas-guzzling SUVs dropped sharply while hybrids sold briskly. Second, high oil prices increase the export earnings of oil-producing countries. Countries such as Venezuela and Mexico count on oil revenues in their economic development plans and to repay foreign debts. These countries eased their debt problems as a result of higher prices, which also played a crucial part in Russia's economic recovery. Oil exporters can have too much of a good thing, however. The easy money concentrated in a few hands allowed dictators to rule and extremism to flourish in states such as Iran, Saudi Arabia, and Venezuela. More importantly, high oil prices helped drive the world economy into a severe recession, curtailing demand and forcing prices back down to $40 a barrel in a matter of months. The exporting countries and their recently rich governments suddenly found themselves cash poor. And the alternative energy sources like solar power, which had looked promising when oil was expensive, lost support when oil prices dropped, suggesting the start of a new cycle of dependence on oil imports in Western countries.

Minerals

To build the infrastructure and other manufactured goods that create wealth in a national economy, states need other raw materials in addition to energy. These include metals, other minerals, and related materials extracted through mining. The political economy of minerals—iron, copper, platinum, and so forth—differs from that of world energy. The value of international trade in oil is many times that of any mineral. Moreover, mineral supply is not so concentrated in one region of the world. Industrialized countries have also reduced their vulnerability by stockpiling strategic minerals.

Most important to industrialized economies are the minerals that go into making industrial equipment. Traditionally most important is iron, used to make steel. The leading producers of steel are the former Soviet Union, Japan, the United States, China, and Germany, followed by Brazil, Italy, South Korea, France, and Britain. Thus, major industrialized countries produce their own steel (Germany and Japan are the leading exporters worldwide). To preserve self-sufficiency in steel production, the United States and others have used trade policies to protect domestic steel industries (such as the U.S. steel tariffs; see p. 293). Some industrialized countries, notably Japan, depend heavily on importing iron ore for their steel industry. Iron ore is not concentrated in one location but is exported from developing and industrialized countries around the world.

For other important industrial minerals such as copper, nickel, and zinc, the pattern of supply and trade is much more diffuse than for oil, and the industrialized countries are largely self-sufficient. Even when poor states are the main suppliers, as with tin and bauxite, they have not gained the power of OPEC. There is a producer cartel in some cases (copper), a producer-consumer cartel in some (tin), and separate producer and consumer cartels in others (bauxite). China currently holds a near monopoly on the world's supply of "rare earth" minerals vital (in small amounts) to the production of electronics. China has cut exports at times to boost these minerals' price.

Certain agricultural products have spawned producer cartels such as the Union of Banana Exporting Countries (UBEC) and the African Groundnut Council. Like minerals, some export crops come mainly from just a few countries. These include sugar (Cuba), cocoa (Ivory Coast, Ghana, Nigeria), tea (India, Sri Lanka, China), and coffee (Brazil, Colombia). Despite the concentrations, producer cartels have not been very successful in boosting prices of these products, which are less essential than energy.

Water Disputes

In addition to energy and minerals, states need water. This need increases as a society industrializes, as it intensifies agriculture, and as its population grows. World water use is 35 times that of just a few centuries ago, and grew twice as fast as population in the 20th century. Yet water supplies are relatively unchanging and are becoming depleted in many places. One-fifth of the world's population lacks safe drinking water, and 80 countries suffer water shortages. Water supplies—rivers and water tables—often cross international boundaries; thus access to water is increasingly a source of international conflict. Sometimes—as when several states share access to a single water table—these conflicts are collective goods problems.

Water problems are especially important in the Middle East. For instance, the Euphrates River runs from Turkey through Syria to Iraq before reaching the Persian Gulf. Iraq objects to Syrian diversion of water from the river, and both Iraq and Syria object to Turkey's diversion.

The Jordan River originates in Syria and Lebanon and runs through Israel to Jordan. In the 1950s, Israel began building a canal to take water from the Jordan River to "make the desert bloom." Jordan and its Arab neighbors complained to the UN Security Council, but it failed in efforts to mediate the dispute, and each state went ahead with its own water plans (Israel and Jordan agreeing, however, to stay within UN-proposed allocations). In 1964, Syria and Lebanon tried to build dams and divert water before it reached Israel, rendering Israel's new water system worthless. Israeli air and artillery attacks on the construction site forced Syria to abandon its diversion project, and Israel's 1967 capture of the Golan Heights precluded Syria from renewing such efforts.[27] Thus, the dominance principle comes into play in resolving conflicts over natural resources.

Water also contains other resources such as fish and offshore oil deposits. The UNCLOS treaty enclosed more of these resources within states' territory—but this enclosure creates new problems. Norms regarding territorial waters are not firmly entrenched; some states disagree on who owns what. Also, control of small islands now implies rights to surrounding oceans with their fish, offshore oil, and minerals. A potentially serious international dispute has been brewing in the Spratly Islands, where some tiny islands are claimed by China, Vietnam, and other nearby countries (see p. 182). With the islands come nearby oil drilling rights and fisheries.

WATER, WATER EVERYWHERE

As population growth and economic development increase the demand for water, more international conflicts arise over water rights. Many important rivers pass through multiple states, and many states share access to seas and lakes. The Aral Sea, once part of the Soviet Union but now shared between Kazakhstan and Uzbekistan, was among the world's largest lakes until it was decimated by the diversion of its water sources to irrigate cotton. This scene shows the former seabed, now 70 miles from shore, in 1997.

---

[27] Conca, Ken. *Governing Water: Contentious Transnational Politics and Global Institution Building.* MIT, 2005. Selby, Jan. *Water, Power, and Politics in the Middle East.* Tauris, 2003.

A common theme runs through the conflicts over fuels, minerals, agricultural products, and territorial waters. They are produced in fixed locations but traded to distant places. Control of these locations gives a state both greater self-sufficiency (valued by mercantilists) and market commodities generating wealth (valued by liberals).

Of course, these resources can also be directly related to international security. IR scholars have expanded their studies of environmental politics to systematically study the relationship of military and security affairs to the environment.[28] One side of this relationship is the role of the environment as a source of international conflict. We have seen how environmental degradation can lead to collective goods problems among large numbers of states, and how competition for territory and resources can create conflicts among smaller groups of states.

Activities in the international security realm also affect the environment. Military activities—especially warfare—are important contributors to environmental degradation, above and beyond the degradation caused by economic activities such as mining and manufacturing. During the 1991 Gulf War, for example, Iraqi forces spilled large amounts of Kuwaiti oil into the Persian Gulf and then, before retreating from Kuwait, blew up hundreds of Kuwaiti oil wells, leaving them burning uncontrollably and covering Iraq and Iran with thick black smoke.

Population

Global population reached a record high today, as it does every day. World population, 7 billion in 2012, is growing by 80 million each year. Forecasting future population is easy in some respects. Barring a nuclear war or an environmental catastrophe, today's children will grow up and have children of their own. For the coming 20 to 30 years, world population growth will be driven, rather mechanistically, by the large number of children in today's populations in the global South. The projected world population in 2030 will be 8–9 billion people, and there is little anyone can do to change that projection.

Of the increase in population in that period, 96 percent will be in the global South. Currently, half the world's population growth occurs in just six countries: India, China, Pakistan, Nigeria, Bangladesh, and Indonesia. Among the world's poorest countries, population is expected to triple in the next 50 years, whereas many rich countries will see population shrinkage in that period.[29]

Forecasting beyond 25 years is difficult. When today's children grow up, the number of children they bear will be affected by their incomes (because of the "demographic transition," discussed shortly). To the extent that developing countries accumulate wealth—a subject taken up in Chapter 13—their populations will grow more slowly. A second factor affecting the rate of population growth will be government policies regarding women's rights and birth control.

Because of these two uncertainties, projections beyond a few decades have a range of uncertainty (see Figure 11.6). By 2050, world population could be 9 billion, with a final leveling out around 10 billion in the next 100 years. New data in 2002 showed that higher women's status and literacy are reducing population growth more than expected in large,

---

[28] Kahl, Colin H. *States, Scarcity, and Civil Strife in the Developing World*. Princeton, 2006. Dalby, Simon. *Environmental Security*. Minnesota, 2002. Homer-Dixon, Thomas F. *Environment, Scarcity, and Violence*. Princeton, 1999.

[29] UNFPA data. See United Nations. *State of World Population Report 2004*. UN, 2004.

FIGURE 11.6 World Population Trends and Projections

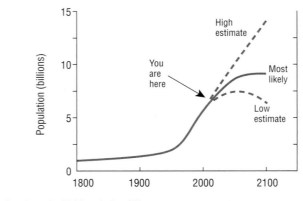

Source: Based on data from the UN Population Office.

poor countries.[30] The actions of states and IOs *now* will determine the earth's population in 200 years.

Two hundred years ago, the British writer Thomas Malthus warned that population tends to increase faster than food supply and predicted that population growth would limit itself through famine and disease. Today, experts and officials who warn against world overpopulation are sometimes called *Malthusian*. Critics of this view point out that technology has kept pace with population in the past, allowing more food and other resources to be extracted from the environment even as population keeps growing.

The Demographic Transition

Population growth results from the difference between rates of birth (per 1,000 people) and rates of death. In agrarian (preindustrial) societies, both birthrates and death rates are high. Population growth is thus slow—even negative at times when death rates exceed birthrates (during a famine or plague, for instance).

The process of economic development—of industrialization and the accumulation of wealth on a per capita basis—brings about a change in birthrates and death rates that follows a fairly universal pattern called the **demographic transition** (see Figure 11.7). First, death rates fall as food supplies increase and access to health care expands. Later, birthrates fall as people become educated, more secure, and more urbanized, and as the status of women in society rises. At the end of the transition, as at the beginning, birthrates and death rates are fairly close to each other, and population growth is limited. But during the transition, when death rates have fallen more than birthrates, population grows rapidly.

One reason poor people tend to have many children is that under harsh poverty, a child's survival is not assured. Disease, malnutrition, or violence may claim the lives of many children, leaving parents with no one to look after them in their old age. Having many children helps ensure that some survive.

As a state makes the demographic transition, the structure of its population changes dramatically. At the beginning and middle of the process, most of the population is young.

---

[30] Crossette, Barbara. Population Estimates Fall as Women Assert Control. *The New York Times*, March 10, 2002.

FIGURE 11.7 The Demographic Transition

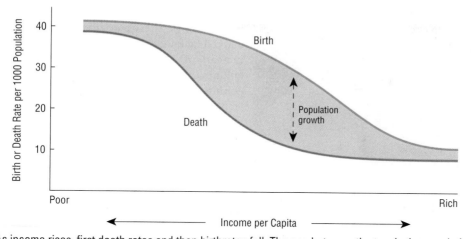

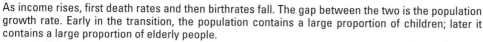

As income rises, first death rates and then birthrates fall. The gap between the two is the population growth rate. Early in the transition, the population contains a large proportion of children; later it contains a large proportion of elderly people.

Families have many children, and adults do not have a long life expectancy. Because children are not very productive economically, the large number of children in poor countries tends to slow down the accumulation of wealth. But by the end of the demographic transition, because adults live longer and families have fewer children, the average age of the population is much older. Eventually a substantial section of the population is elderly—a different nonproductive population that the economy must support.

The industrialized countries have completed the demographic transition and now have slow population growth. Russia, Europe, and Japan have shrinking populations. Most developing countries are in the middle of the transition and have rapid population growth.

The dilemma of the demographic transition is this: rapid population growth and a child-heavy population are powerful forces lowering per capita income. Yet the best way to slow population growth is to raise per capita income. Population growth thus contributes to a vicious cycle in many poor states. Where population rises at the same rate as overall wealth, the average person is no better off over time. Even when the economy grows faster than population, so that the *average* income rises, the total *number* of poor people may increase.

The demographic transition tends to widen international disparities of wealth. States that manage to raise incomes a bit enter an upward spiral—as population growth slows, income levels per capita rise more, which further slows population growth, and so forth. Meanwhile, states that do not raise incomes have unabated population growth; per capita incomes stay low, which fuels more population growth—a downward spiral.

Globally, this disparity contributes to the gap in wealth between the North and South (see Chapter 12). Within the South, disparities are also sharpened as a few countries manage to slow population growth and raise incomes while others fail to do so. Even within a single country, the demographic transition sharpens disparities. Cities, richer classes, richer ethnic groups, and richer provinces tend to have low birthrates compared to the countryside and the poorer classes, ethnic groups, and provinces. In countries such as France, Israel, and the United States, wealthier ethnic groups have much slower population growth than poorer ethnic groups.

RUB AND TUB

Because of the demographic transition, controlling population growth helps economic development and vice versa. Various countries use a wide range of population policies to this end, none stricter than China's one-child policy for urban couples. These Dutch babies enter a society well through the demographic transition, with plentiful resources for relatively few babies. Here, they cool down after a baby massage class, 2009.

In recent decades, the global South seems to be splitting into two groups of states. The first group, including China and India, entered the phase of the demographic transition marked by falling birthrates in the 1970s. But in nearly 70 other poor states, death rates kept falling faster than birthrates, leading to accelerating population growth. These population trends contributed to disparities within the global South that emerged in the 1990s, notably between Africa and Asia.

Population Policies

The policies that governments adopt—not just economic and demographic conditions—influence the birthrate. Among the most important policies are those regarding birth control (contraception). State policies vary widely.

At one extreme, China uses its strong government control to try to enforce a limit of one child per couple. Penalties for having a second child include being charged for services that were free for the first child. China has started to encourage wealthy and more educated families to have two children, and now, in some Chinese cities such as Shanghai, couples are allowed two-child families. Beyond two children, the penalties escalate. Contraceptives and abortions are free. China's policy has lowered growth rates considerably in the cities but less so in the countryside, where most people still live. Still, in a single decade (the 1970s), China's fertility rate fell from 6 children per woman to about 2.5, a dramatic change. (By 2011 it was 1.5.)

But the Chinese policy has drawbacks. It limits individual freedom in favor of government control. Forced or coerced abortions have been reported. In traditional Chinese society (as in some other countries), sons are valued more than daughters. Couples who have a daughter may keep trying until they have a son. In some cases, Chinese peasants have reportedly killed newborn daughters so that they could try for a son. Simply bribing or paying fines became more common routes around the one-child policy in the 1990s. Most often, parents in China (and some places in India) are using information technology—ultrasound scans—to determine their fetus's gender and abort it if female. China's 2000 census showed the percentage of female births at 0.85 per boy, rather than the normal 0.95, a difference that amounts to a million "missing" girls per year. In the countryside, the sex differential is twice as high as in the cities, reaching 140 men per 100 women in some areas where the one-child policy is strictly enforced. In recent years, hundreds of thousands of young women there have been kidnapped and sold as brides.[31]

---

[31] Dugger, Celia W. Modern Asia's Anomaly: The Girls Who Don't Get Born. *The New York Times*, May 6, 2001: Week in Review. Rosenthal, Elisabeth. Harsh Chinese Reality Feeds a Black Market in Women. *The New York Times*, June 25, 2001: A1. Hudson, Valerie M., and Andrea M. Den Boer. *Bare Branches: The Security Implications of Asia's Surplus Male Population.* MIT, 2004.

India's policies are less extreme but have been slower to have an effect. The birthrate fell from nearly 6 per woman to about 4.7 in the 1970s and 2.7 in 2011. India's government, strongly committed to birth control, has tried to make information and means widely available, but as a democracy it does not have China's extreme government control over society. Countries with somewhat higher incomes than India or China can succeed more easily. Mexico's strong but noncoercive family-planning program, adopted in 1974, cut birthrates in half over 15 years, to 2.7 per woman (and to 2.3 as of 2011).[32]

At the other extreme from China are governments that encourage or force childbearing and outlaw or limit access to contraception. Such a policy is called **pronatalist** (pro-birth). Traditionally, many governments have adopted such policies because population was seen as an element of national power. More babies today meant more soldiers later.

Today, only a few governments have strongly pronatalist policies, but many do not make birth control or sex education available to poor women. In some such states, population is not considered a problem (and may even be seen as an asset); in other states, the government simply cannot afford effective measures to lower birthrates. According to the United Nations Population Fund (UNFPA), 200 million women do not have access to effective contraception.

Birthrates are heavily influenced by the status of women in society. In cultures that traditionally see women as valuable only in producing babies, great pressures exist against women who stop doing so. Many women do not use birth control because their husbands will not allow them to. These husbands may think that having many children is proof of their manliness. However, as women's status improves and they can work in various occupations, own property, and vote, women gain the power as well as the education and money necessary to limit the size of their families. According to the UNFPA, improving the status of women is one of the most important means of controlling world population growth. Government policies about women's status vary from one state to another. International programs and agencies, such as the UN Commission on the Status of Women, are working to address this issue on a global scale.

Disease

Population growth is determined by the death rate as well as the birthrate. People die from many different causes at different ages. In poor countries, people tend to die younger, often from infectious diseases; in richer countries, people live longer and die more often from cancer and heart disease. The proportion of babies who die within their first year is the **infant mortality rate**. This rate is an excellent indicator of overall health because it reflects a population's access to nutrition, water, shelter, and health care. Infant mortality is 5 percent worldwide: 1 percent or less in rich countries but more than 10 percent in the poorest countries and even higher in local pockets of extreme poverty (especially in Africa and in recent war zones).

Although death rates vary greatly from one state or region to another, the overall trends are stable from decade to decade. Wars, droughts, epidemics, and disasters have an effect locally but hardly matter globally. In the poorest countries, which are just beginning the demographic transition, the death rate declined from nearly 30 deaths per thousand population in 1950 to less than 15 since 1990. In the industrialized countries, the death

[32] Anderson, John Ward. Six Billion and Counting—But Slower. *The Washington Post*, October 12, 1999: A1.

rate bottomed out around 10 per thousand by 1960, and now stands around 7 in the West. These stable trends in mortality mean that the death rate is not a means by which governments or international agencies can affect population growth—worsening poverty may cause famine and a rising death rate, but this is not a realistic way to control population growth. It would mean moving backward through the demographic transition, which would wreck any chance of lowering birthrates. Nor do wars kill enough people to reduce population growth. In short, most of the world is already at or near the end of the transition in *death* rates; the key question is how long birthrates take to complete the transition.[33]

Three mortality factors, however—HIV/AIDS, other infectious diseases, and smoking—deserve special attention because they exact very high costs even if they do not much affect global population trends. In these cases, actions taken in the short term have long-term and often international consequences, and once again there are short-term costs and long-term benefits.

HIV/AIDS   In the worldwide AIDS epidemic, one state's success or failure in limiting the spread of HIV (human immunodeficiency virus) affects infections in other states as well. There is a delay of five to ten years after infection by the virus before symptoms appear, and during this period an infected individual can infect others (through sex or blood). AIDS spreads internationally—through business, tourism, migration, and military operations—reflecting the interdependence of states.

By 2009, the HIV/AIDS epidemic had already killed more than 30 million people, and an estimated 33 million more were infected—though most of them did not know it. Two-thirds of them live in Africa and half of the rest in South Asia (see Table 11.2). The epidemic has also left 15 million orphans worldwide. Each year, about 2.7 million people

TABLE 11.2 Population and AIDS by World Region, 2010

Region[a]	Population (millions)	Population Growth Rate 1991–2008	HIV Infections (millions)
World	6,800	1.3%	33
Global North	1,400	0.3	4
Global South of which:	5,400	1.6	29
China	1,380	1.0	1
Middle East	450	2.1	0.2
Latin America	580	1.6	2
South Asia	2,150	1.9	4
Africa (sub-Saharan)	830	2.5	22

[a]Regions do not exactly match those used elsewhere in this book.

Source: Calculated from *World Development Indicators*. World Bank, 2010. *UNAIDS Reports on the Global AIDS Epidemic*. UNAIDS, 2009. In 2007, UNAIDS corrected earlier estimates, resulting in a significant drop in infection rates.

---

[33] Soubbotina, Tatyana P., and Katherine Sheram. *Beyond Economic Growth: Meeting the Challenges of Global Development*. World Bank, 2000.

are newly infected with HIV, and 2 million die from AIDS, including more than a quarter of a million children.

In Africa, already the world's poorest region, AIDS has emerged as one of several powerful forces driving the region backward into deeper poverty. About 5 percent of adults are infected with HIV, more than half of them women. In the most affected African countries in southern Africa, one in six adults has HIV (one in four for Botswana, the worst case). Infection is also rampant in African armies, with direct implications for international security. In Angola, it was the *end* of a long civil war that opened borders and increased traffic with neighboring states that had high HIV infection rates. As Angola's infection rate began to climb, military officers took the initiative to set up education programs and comprehensive HIV testing within the army. In contrast to other African states with high military infection rates, Angola's aggressive program kept the rate as low as in the general population, below 10 percent.

In North America and other industrialized regions, new drug therapies (which keep the virus in check for years) dramatically lowered the death rate from AIDS starting in the late 1990s. But these treatments were too expensive to help much in Africa and other poor regions. India and Brazil began to export cheap generic versions of these drugs, violating patent rights of Western drug companies. The U.S. government threatened to punish South Africa and other countries if they allowed import of these drugs without compensating U.S. corporations holding patents. It filed a complaint against Brazil with the WTO. In response, AIDS activists demonstrated loudly and mobilized public opinion to get the policies changed.

The United States withdrew its complaint against Brazil in 2001. Meanwhile, drug companies began offering lower prices to poor countries, but delivery of the drugs to millions of poor people remained painfully slow. In 2004, the international community finally initiated the large-scale delivery of antiviral drugs to AIDS patients in poor countries. Now, tremendous progress has been made in delivering these drugs. In the past four years, the number of people receiving treatment has increased fivefold, to over 3 million (over 2 million alone in sub-Saharan Africa).[34]

LIFE SAVER

AIDS has killed 30 million people and is spreading rapidly in Southeast Asia and Africa. The worldwide effort to slow AIDS, coordinated by the World Health Organization (WHO), illustrates how global-level problems such as AIDS are making IOs such as WHO more important. Currently, international efforts focus on trying to get antiviral medicines to more of the world's 40 million infected people, such as this woman in Swaziland, who began recovering after starting twice-a-day pills provided free each month, 2004. Millions of people who cannot afford the drugs and do not have access to a free program are dying of AIDS.

---

[34] UNAIDS. *2008 Report on the Global Aids Epidemic*. UNAIDS/WHO, 2008.

The global fight against AIDS has finally begun to receive the funding necessary to make progress against the disease, although it has taken some time. In 2001, during a special UN session on AIDS, Kofi Annan proposed a $7 billion to $10 billion per year global budget to combat AIDS (a fivefold increase in funding). The G8 states responded with pledges of a bit more than $1 billion—"laudable" but "not enough," in Annan's view.[35] In 2003, President Bush pledged $15 billion over five years to help slow AIDS in Africa. That program has since been expanded dramatically. Since 2003, the United States has provided nearly $20 billion to combat AIDS. Between 2009 and 2014, the U.S. government has pledged $48 billion to combat AIDS, tuberculosis (TB), and malaria. In 2006, five countries—France, Britain, Norway, Brazil, and Chile—agreed to raise $300 million a year to buy medications for children with AIDS, TB, and malaria. Most of it will come from taxing airline tickets (typically $5 coach and $50 first class). While observers have applauded these increased efforts, much more work remains, including care for the estimated 12 million children orphaned by AIDS in sub-Saharan Africa.

In some ways, AIDS has deepened the global North-South division. The 2001 UN session also revealed sharp differences between Western, secular states and a number of Islamic states that objected to any reference to gay people. This point was underscored when the president of Iran, in a 2007 speech at Columbia University, claimed there were no gay people in Iran. Catholic authorities worldwide have objected to programs that encourage condom use. As these examples show, some of the most effective prevention measures (public education, outreach to at-risk groups, condom distribution, free needles to drug users) are culturally and politically sensitive issues.

States must cooperate with each other if they are to bring the epidemic under control. These international efforts are coordinated primarily by WHO and funded mainly by the industrialized countries. But the entire WHO budget is equivalent to that of a midsize hospital in the global North. WHO depends on national governments to provide information and carry out policies, and governments have been slow to respond. Some governments falsify statistics to underreport the number of cases (lest tourists be driven away), and many governments are reluctant to condone or sponsor sex education and distribution of condoms because of religious or cultural taboos.

In recent years, HIV has spread rapidly in South Asia, China, and Russia/Eastern Europe, where prostitution and drug use are growing. Thailand was especially vulnerable because of its huge prostitution industry, acceptance of male promiscuity, and large tourism industry. It was one of the first developing countries to develop an effective anti-AIDS program, which focuses on public education, and it dramatically lowered the infection rate in the 1990s.[36]

In China, the government has been slow to act, and a stigma still prevents effective identification or treatment of the rapidly growing HIV-positive population. Unscrupulous cash-for-blood businesses, especially in one rural region, caused massive HIV infection. In rural China, medical practice relies heavily on shots—often with poorly sterilized needles—when other forms of treatment would be as effective. As a result, 60 percent of

[35] Annan, Kofi A. We Can Beat AIDS. *The New York Times*, June 25, 2001: A21.

[36] Shenon, Philip. Brash and Unabashed, Mr. Condom Takes on Sex Death in Thailand. *The New York Times*, December 20, 1992. Altman, Lawrence K. AIDS Surge Is Forecast for China, India, and Eastern Europe. *The New York Times*, November 4, 1997.

China's population has had hepatitis B, compared with 1 percent in the United States and Japan—a danger sign for the future growth of HIV in China.[37] China had an estimated 1 million infected people in 2011.

The international response to the AIDS epidemic is crucial in determining its ultimate course. AIDS illustrates the transnational linkages that make international borders less meaningful than in the past. Effective international cooperation could save millions of lives and significantly enhance the prospects for economic development in the poorest countries in the coming decades. But once again, a collective goods problem exists regarding the allocation of costs and benefits from such efforts. A dollar spent by WHO has the same effect regardless of which country contributed it.

Other Infectious Diseases   AIDS is the most severe epidemic of infectious disease in the world, but not the only concern. TB, malaria, hepatitis, dengue fever, and cholera have all reemerged or spread in recent decades, often mutating into drug-resistant forms that are increasingly difficult to treat. TB now kills 1.5 million people per year (in addition to AIDS patients who also contract TB). Malaria sickens hundreds of millions of people and kills more than a million per year, nearly all in Africa. New campaigns have distributed millions of mosquito nets in Africa to reduce malaria—a proven, cost-effective measure. A new vaccine being tested in 2011 could cut malaria cases in half. Meanwhile, new and poorly understood diseases have emerged, among them HIV, Ebola virus, hantavirus, and hepatitis C. Pneumonia, influenza, diarrhea-causing diseases, and measles all continue to be major problems but are not growing or spreading to the same extent. Vaccination programs have reduced the incidence of both polio and measles in recent years. A measles vaccination campaign now reaches 85 percent of infants worldwide, reducing deaths by 80 percent since 2000.

Iodine deficiency has historically received little attention although it affects as many as 2 billion people worldwide. Even moderate deficiencies in fetuses can lower intelligence by 10 to 15 I.Q. points, and serious deficiencies can stunt growth and cause

PANDEMIC PREVENTION

In 2009, H1N1 influenza (swine flu) spread rapidly across much of the world, testing the small and poorly funded international institutions devoted to global health, such as the World Health Organization. In Mexico City in 2009, where the epidemic gained speed and shut down normal life for weeks, this baptism went on but with flu precautions taken.

---

[37] Rosenthal, Elisabeth. Doctors' Dirty Needles Spreading Disease in China. *The New York Times*, August 20, 2001: A1.

mental retardation and goiter (enlarged thyroid gland). For about 5 cents per person yearly, iodine can be added to salt and completely prevent the deficiency, but many countries in the global South and former Soviet bloc still do not do so. An international campaign has increased the use of iodized salt from 25 percent of households worldwide in 1990 to 66 percent in 2006.[38]

Epidemics among animals have major effects as well. Currently, scientists fear that bird flu could mutate and spread person to person, sparking a global pandemic that could potentially kill millions.[39] In 2009–2010, swine flu spread quickly across the globe, rekindling fears of a global health epidemic and leading various countries to restrict travel to Mexico (where the flu originated). This strain of swine flu (H1N1) was found in many countries, many of which adopted quarantine policies for patients.

Smoking Worldwide, more than a billion people smoke, five-sixths of them in developing countries, and 5 million people a year die from tobacco-related disease. States that fail to curb the spread of nicotine addiction face high future costs in health care—costs that are just beginning to come due in many poor countries. The costs are largely limited to the state itself; its own citizens and economy pay the price. Nonetheless, the tobacco trade makes smoking an international issue. Tobacco companies' recent marketing campaigns targeting women in the global South could produce a huge increase in smokers in that group, according to the World Health Organization. The gender differences in smoking in developing countries are striking: around 4 percent of women smoke in most developing countries whereas the corresponding number for males runs as high as 60 percent (in China). By contrast, in the United States, about 24 percent of men smoke compared to 18 percent of women.[40]

In 2001, tobacco companies with some U.S. support sought to weaken a new proposed treaty, the Framework Convention on Tobacco Control, but in 2003 the United States dropped its objections and WHO member states adopted the treaty, which entered into force in 2005. Member states pledge to ban tobacco advertising and are encouraged to raise taxes on tobacco 5 percent a year above the inflation rate. The United States, alone among the world's major powers, still had not ratified the treaty in 2011.

Population issues are sometimes portrayed as simply too many people using up too little food and natural resources. However, the idea that overpopulation is the cause of hunger in today's world is not really accurate. Poverty and politics more than population are the causes of malnutrition and hunger today (see "World Hunger" on pp. 431–432). There is enough food, water, petroleum, land, and so forth—but these are unequally distributed.

This unequal distribution is directly related to the gap between the global North and the global South. Strains on the environment and on natural resources are global in scope, yet in the North they arise from industrialization (growing GDP per capita), whereas in the South they are more affected by growing populations. These differences in environmental impacts are by no means the only such North-South difference. The next two chapters turn to that global North-South divide.

✓•⊏Study
and **Review**
the **Post-Test &
Chapter Exam**
at **mypoliscilab.com**

---

[38] McNeil, Donald G., Jr. In Raising the World's I.Q., the Secret's in the Salt. *The New York Times*, December 16, 2006: A1.

[39] U.S. Central Intelligence Agency. *The Global Infectious Disease Threat and Its Implications for the United States* [National Intelligence Estimate 99–17D]. CIA, 2000.

[40] Marsh, Bill. A Growing Cloud Over the Planet. *The New York Times*, February 24, 2008: 4.

CHAPTER REVIEW

SUMMARY

- Environmental problems are an example of international interdependence and often create collective goods problems for the states involved. The large numbers of actors involved in global environmental problems make them more difficult to solve.

- To resolve such collective goods problems, states have used international regimes and IOs, and have in some cases extended state sovereignty (notably over territorial waters) to make management a national rather than an international matter.

- International efforts to solve environmental problems aim to bring about sustainable economic development.

- Global warming results from burning fossil fuels—the basis of industrial economies today. The industrialized states are much more responsible for the problem than are developing countries, but countries such as China and India also contribute to the problem. Solutions are difficult to reach because costs are substantial and dangers are somewhat distant and uncertain.

- Damage to the earth's ozone layer results from the use of specific chemicals, which are now being phased out under international agreements. Unlike global warming, the costs of solutions are much lower and the problem is better understood.

- Many species are threatened with extinction due to loss of habitats such as rain forests. An international treaty on biodiversity and an agreement on forests aim to reduce the destruction of local ecosystems, with costs spread among states.

- The UN Convention on the Law of the Sea (UNCLOS) establishes an ocean regime that puts most commercial fisheries and offshore oil under control of states as territorial waters.

- Pollution—including acid rain, water and air pollution, and toxic and nuclear waste—tends to be more localized than global and has been addressed mainly through unilateral, bilateral, and regional measures rather than global ones.

- Most Western states import energy resources, mostly oil, whereas the other world regions export them. Oil prices rose dramatically in the 1970s but declined in the 1980s as the world economy adjusted by increasing supply and reducing demand. Prices spiked again around 1991 and 2007–2008 before collapsing in 2008. Such fluctuations undermine world economic stability.

- The most important source of oil traded worldwide is the Persian Gulf area of the Middle East. Consequently, this area has long been a focal point of international political conflict.

- World population—now at 7 billion—may eventually level out around 10 billion. Virtually all of the increase will come in the global South.

- Future world population growth will be largely driven by the demographic transition. Death rates have fallen throughout the world, but birthrates will fall proportionally only as per capita incomes go up. The faster the economies of poor states develop, the sooner their populations will level out.

- Government policies can reduce birthrates somewhat at a given level of per capita income. Effective policies are those that improve access to birth control and raise the status of women in society. Actual policies vary, from China's very strict rules on childbearing to pronatalist governments that encourage maximum birthrates and outlaw birth control.

- The global HIV/AIDS epidemic creates huge costs for many poor states. Currently 33 million people are infected with HIV, and 30 million more have died. Most are in Africa, but new infections are growing rapidly in Asia and Russia.

KEY TERMS

tragedy of the
   commons   388
enclosure   388
global warming   390
UN Environment Program
   (UNEP)   391
greenhouse gases   391
Kyoto Protocol   393
ozone layer   394

Montreal Protocol   395
biodiversity   396
International Whaling
   Commission   397
high seas   399
UN Convention on
   the Law of the Sea
   (UNCLOS)   400
acid rain   402

Chernobyl   403
demographic
   transition   410
pronatalist   413
infant mortality
   rate   413

CRITICAL THINKING QUESTIONS

1. Given the collective goods problem in managing environmental issues—heightened by the participation of large numbers of actors—what new international organizations or agreements could be created in the coming years to help solve this problem? Are there ways to reduce the number of actors participating in the management of global problems such as global warming? What problems might your proposals run into?

2. Few effective international agreements have been reached to solve the problem of global warming. Given the several difficulties associated with managing this problem, what creative international solutions can you think of? What would be the strengths and weaknesses of your solutions in the short term and in the long term?

3. Does the record of the international community on environmental management reflect the views of mercantilists, liberals, or both? In what ways?

4. Some politicians call for the Western industrialized countries, including the United States, to be more self-sufficient in energy resources in order to reduce dependence on oil imports from the Middle East. In light of the overall world energy picture and the economics of international trade, what are the pros and cons of such a proposal?

5. Dozens of poor states appear to be stuck midway through the demographic transition: death rates have fallen, birthrates remain high, and per capita incomes are not increasing. How do you think these states, with or without foreign assistance, can best get unstuck and complete the demographic transition?

Stopping Global Warming: Who Should Pay?

Overview

The Kyoto Protocol has been the strongest attempt to date to control the pollutants that lead to global warming. Although the Protocol has been in effect for only a few years, it has already generated tremendous controversy. As discussed in this chapter, Kyoto uses a market mechanism to allocate caps on the amount of emissions that can come from various countries. Yet, only developed countries are required to meet the targets under Kyoto. Developing countries do not have binding caps on their emissions.

Some countries, such as the United States, object to the nonbinding targets for developing countries. In particular, the United States objects to China's classification as a developing state that does not need to abide by the limits of the treaty. It claims that China will be allowed to pollute while the United States pays a high economic cost to reduce global warming. These costs could run into the hundreds of billions of dollars over the long run.

Now, as the world attempts to design a new global warming treaty to replace the Kyoto Protocol when it expires, the question of who pays is again at the forefront of discussions. Should developing countries, such as China, be asked to contribute to stopping global warming? Who should be required to contribute to the provision of this public good?

ARGUMENT 1

Developing Countries Should Pay Their Share to Stop Warming

Developing countries contribute to warming, so they should pay. Developing countries contribute large amounts of carbon dioxide to the global atmosphere. They should not be allowed to free-ride on the efforts of the wealthy states who want to slow down global warming.

Technologies will keep costs low in the long run. While the cost to slow down global warming will be high initially, over time technology will help states keep costs low while lessening emissions. Thus, one should not be overly concerned that the costs of policy change in developing states will be overwhelming.

Developing countries could benefit economically from Kyoto-type agreements. If the Kyoto agreement is extended or future agreements have similar market-based mechanisms as Kyoto, developing countries could benefit economically. If these countries can bring emissions down enough to sell their extra cap space, they could actually recoup some of the costs of implementing the agreement.

Only Developed Countries Should Pay to Stop Warming

The costs to developing countries will undermine development. The costs of slowing global warming will be large. Placing even some of these costs on developing countries will lead to economic hardship, which will further undermine development, which could then increase emissions since these states would have no money to invest in better technologies or to develop cleaner industries.

Developed countries were allowed to pollute to develop. For many years, developed countries paid little attention to the environment as they built industries, achieved economic growth, and became successful. Now, with India and China threatening to become economically successful, Western states want to place limitations on how other states can develop and how they can treat the environment. Non-Western states should be allowed the same development path as Western states.

It is really the developed countries' pollution. Although developing countries do their fair share of polluting, many of these emissions come from industries that have been shipped from developed states. Western states did not want these polluting industries in their backyards, so they sent them abroad, and now demand that the host countries pay the bill for the cleanup.

Questions

- Should developing countries be bound by the Kyoto Protocol (or its successor) and forced to pay the cost of reducing emissions? Is such a requirement fair? Would this requirement make the success of the Kyoto Protocol more or less likely?

- Do you believe that environmental issues like global warming will be more or less difficult to solve during the current global economic crisis? Why or why not?

- Do you think that technological solutions will be developed to help solve the problem of global warming? Or will fundamental changes in how individuals consume energy be a better path to reduce the problem of global warming?

For Further Reading

Nordhaus, William D. *A Question of Balance: Weighing the Options on Global Warming Policies.* Yale, 2008.

Zedillo, Ernesto. *Global Warming: Looking Beyond Kyoto.* Brookings, 2008.

Sachs, Jeffrey D. *Common Wealth: Economics for a Crowded Planet.* Penguin, 2008.

Houser, Trevor, Rob Bradley, Britt Childs, Jacob Werksman, and Robert Heilmayr. *Leveling the Carbon Playing Field: International Competition and US Climate Policy Design.* Peterson Institute, 2008.

CHAPTER 12

The North-South Gap

Children displaced by flood in India, 2007.

The State of the South

This and the following chapter concern the world's poor regions—the global South—where most people live. States in these regions are called by various names, used interchangeably: third world countries, **less-developed countries (LDCs)**, *underdeveloped countries* (UDCs), or **developing countries**. This chapter discusses the gap in wealth between the industrialized regions (the North) and the rest of the world (the South). It develops the theories of imperialism introduced in Chapter 3 (pp. 103–104), which try to explain this gap in terms of historical colonization of the South by the North. Chapter 13 discusses international aspects of economic development in the South.

IR scholars do not agree on the causes or implications of poverty in the global South, nor on solutions (if any) to the problem. Thus, they also disagree about the nature of relations between rich and poor states (North-South relations).[1] Everyone agrees, however, that much of the global South is poor, and some of it extremely poor.[2]

In all, about a billion people live in abject poverty, without access to basic nutrition or health care. They are concentrated in Africa, where income levels have lagged for decades. Two decades ago the concentration was as strong in South Asia, but economic growth there has greatly reduced extreme poverty. Still, the average income per person in South Asia—home to 2 billion people—is only $2,700 per year, and in Africa only $2,000 (even after adjusting for the lower costs of living in these regions compared to richer ones). Although billions of people are rising out of poverty, because of population growth the number of very poor people nonetheless remains about the same.[3]

The bottom line is that every six seconds, somewhere in the world, a child dies as a result of malnutrition. That is 600 every hour, 14,000 every day, 5 million every year. The world produces enough food to nourish these children and enough income to afford to nourish them, but their own families or states do not have enough income. They die, ultimately, from poverty. Meanwhile, in that same six seconds the world spends more than $200,000 on military forces, a thousandth of which could save the child's life. Likewise, people lack water, shelter, health care, and other necessities because they cannot afford them. The widespread, grinding poverty of people who cannot afford necessities is less visible than the dramatic examples of starvation triggered by war or drought, but affects many more people.

The UN in 2000 adopted the **Millennium Development Goals**, which set targets for basic needs measures to be achieved by 2015 and measured against 1990 data. The first of the eight goals is to cut in half the proportion of the world's population living in "extreme poverty," defined as income of less than $1 per day (in 1990 dollars, or about $1.25 today). For the global South as a whole, that proportion fell from 31 percent to 20 percent between 1997 and 2007. China's rate has already dropped by half (33 to 14 percent), but Africa's is hardly changed, at around 50 percent.[4]

The five regions of the global South differ not only on poverty reduction, but also on income level and growth. As Figure 12.1 shows, the regions experiencing the fastest growth—China and South Asia—are neither the highest- nor the lowest-income

Read and **Listen** to **Chapter 12** at **mypoliscilab.com**

✔ **Study** and **Review** the **Pre-Test & Flashcards** at **mypoliscilab.com**

---

[1] Seligson, Mitchell A., and John T. Passe-Smith, eds. *Development and Underdevelopment: The Political Economy of Inequality*. 3rd ed. Rienner, 2003.

[2] UN Development Program. *Human Development Report*. Oxford, annual. World Bank. *World Development Report*. Oxford, annual.

[3] World Bank. *World Development Indicators 2006*. World Bank, 2006.

[4] United Nations. *The Millennium Development Goals Report 2008*. UN, 2008.

FIGURE 12.1 Income Level and Growth Rate by World Region

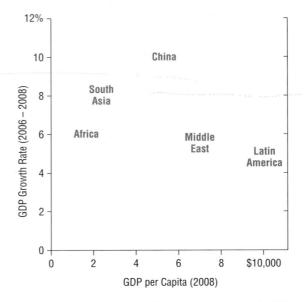

Note: For the global North overall, GDP per capita is $35,000.

Watch
the **Video**
**"Global Migration
and Employment"**
on **mypoliscilab.com**

regions. The Middle East is about as developed as China in terms of GDP per capita, but is growing at only half the rate. Chapter 13 will explore the reasons for these differences in economic growth, but here we note simply that the world's regions vary on both income and growth, with the two dimensions not correlated.

Experts disagree about how much poverty and inequality have decreased, with some arguing that poverty has been halved through rapid economic growth and that the global distribution of income is shifting from having rich and poor extremes to having a bell curve distribution with a large population at middle incomes—an emerging global middle class. The World Bank describes progress as slower.[5] Between 1990 and 2008, incomes per person (adjusted for inflation, in today's dollars) in the global South as a whole rose from about $3,000 to about $5,500. In the global North they rose from about $20,000 to about $31,000. Does this indicate a slow closing of the gap because the ratio fell from about 6.6 to 5.6 as the result of a higher rate of growth in the South? Or does it indicate a widening of the gap between a person in the North and one in the South because in absolute terms, it increased from $17,000 to over $25,000? Each has some truth.

Basic Human Needs

Some countries in the global South have made rapid progress in raising incomes, but others are caught in a cycle of poverty. Until incomes rise, the population will not move through the demographic transition (see pp. 410–412); population growth will remain high and incomes low.[6]

[5] Sala-i-Martin Xavier. *The World Distribution of Income (Estimated from Individual Country Distributions)*. NBER *Working Paper* No. 8933. National Bureau of Economic Research, 2002. Bhalla, Surjit S. *Imagine There's No Country: Poverty Inequality and Growth in the Era of Globalization*. Institute for International Economics, 2002.
[6] World Bank. *World Development Report 2004*. Oxford, 2004.

In order to put economic growth on a firm foundation, societies must meet the **basic human needs** of most of the population.[7] People need food, shelter, and other necessities of daily life in order to feel secure. Furthermore, as long as people in the global South blame imperialism for a lack of basic needs, extreme poverty fuels revolution, terrorism, and anti-Western sentiments.

Children are central to meeting a population's basic needs. In particular, education allows a new generation to meet other basic needs and move through the demographic transition.[8] Literacy—which UNESCO defines as the ability to read and write a simple sentence—is the key component of education. A person who can read and write can obtain a wealth of information about farming, health care, birth control, and so forth. Some poor countries have raised literacy rates substantially; others lag behind.

Great variation also exists in schooling. Primary-school attendance in 2008 was more than 90 percent in most world regions, though only 76 percent for Africa. Secondary education—middle and high school—is another matter. In the North, about 90 percent of secondary-age children are enrolled, but in most of the global South, fewer than two-thirds are. College is available to only a small fraction of the population.

In 2008 in the global South, according to UNICEF, one in four children suffered from malnutrition, one in seven lacked access to health care, and one in five had no safe drinking water. The AIDS epidemic is undoing progress made over decades in reducing child mortality and increasing education.[9]

Figure 12.2 shows the variation across regions in two key indicators of children's well-being at different stages—immunizations and secondary-school enrollments. In both cases, achievement of these basic needs for children roughly correlates with the regions' respective income levels.

Effective health care in poor countries is not expensive—less than $5 per person per year for primary care. For instance, UNICEF has promoted four inexpensive methods that together are credited with saving the lives of millions of children each year. One method is growth monitoring. Experts estimate that regular weighing and advice can prevent half of all cases of malnutrition. A second method is oral rehydration therapy (ORT), which stops diarrhea in children before they die from dehydration. A facility that produced 300 packets per day of the simple sugar-salt remedy, at a cost of 1.5 cents each, was built in Guatemala for just $550. Child deaths from diarrhea were cut in half in one year. The third method is

EXTREME POVERTY

Nearly a billion people in the global South—most of them in Africa and South Asia—live in abject poverty. The majority lack such basic needs as safe water, housing, food, and the ability to read. Natural disasters, droughts, wars, or other events that displace subsistence farmers from their land can quickly put large numbers at risk for their lives. These victims of drought and war in Somalia are among millions at risk there in 2011.

---

[7] Gough, Ian, and J. Allister McGregor, eds. *Wellbeing in Developing Countries: From Theory to Research.* Cambridge, 2007. Goldstein, Joshua S. Basic Human Needs: The Plateau Curve. *World Development* 13, 1985: 595–609. Moon, Bruce E. *The Political Economy of Basic Human Needs.* Cornell, 1991.

[8] Brown, Philip, and Hugh Lauder. Education, Globalization, and Economic Development. *Journal of Education Policy* 11 (1), 1996: 1–25.

[9] UNICEF. *The State of the World's Children 2009: Maternal and Newborn Health.* UNICEF, 2009.

FIGURE 12.2 Basic Needs Indicators by Region (2009)

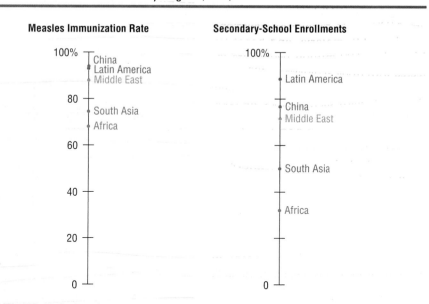

Data Source: World Bank. Regions do not exactly match those used elsewhere in this book.

immunization against six common deadly diseases: measles, polio, tuberculosis (TB), tetanus, whooping cough, and diphtheria. In recent decades, the number of children immunized in poor countries has risen from 5 percent to more than 50 percent. By 2008, the number of children immunized at least once against measles had climbed to 81 percent. The fourth method is the promotion of breast-feeding rather than the use of infant formula. Many poor mothers consider baby formula more modern and better for a baby—a view promoted at times by unethical MNCs eager to market formula to large developing countries.

Since 1990, despite the daunting problems of war and the HIV/AIDS epidemic, public health in the global South registered some important gains.[10] Infant tetanus deaths were halved, and access to safe water was extended to a billion more people. Polio was nearly eliminated, but resistance to vaccination in parts of Nigeria let the disease begin to spread again, with four countries having indigenous virus populations as of 2006.[11] In eight African countries in 2006, following successful trials in several other countries, authorities combined the distribution of insecticide-treated mosquito nets for malaria with measles and polio vaccines, deworming pills, vitamin A supplements, and educational materials—a combined approach proven to work. UNICEF reported in 2008 that deaths of children under five worldwide hit a record low, under 9 million, with the rate having dropped by more than half in the last 50 years. Just since 1999 measles deaths had decreased by 60 percent.[12]

Still, globally, the disparities in access to health care are striking.[13] The 75 percent of the world's people living in the global South have about 30 percent of the world's doctors and nurses. In medical research, less than 5 percent of world expenditures are directed at

[10] Esman, Milton J., and Ronald J. Herring, eds. *Carrots, Sticks and Ethnic Conflict: Rethinking Development Assistance.* Michigan, 2001. Thomas, Caroline, and Paikiasothy Saravanamuttu, eds. *Conflict and Consensus in South/North Security.* Cambridge, 1989.
[11] World Health Organization. Polio Endemic Countries Hit All-Time Low of Four [news release]. February 1, 2006.
[12] UNICEF, *Progress for Children,* December 2007: 18, 56. McNeil, Donald G., Jr. *The New York Times,* September 13, 2007: A9.
[13] World Health Organization. *World Health Statistics 2010.* WHO, 2010.

problems in developing countries, according to the WHO. The biggest killers are AIDS, acute respiratory infections, diarrhea, TB, malaria, and hepatitis. More than 600 million people are infected with tropical diseases—400 to 500 million with malaria alone. Yet, because the people with such diseases are poor, there is often not a large enough market for drug companies (MNCs) in the industrialized world to invest in medicines for them. And when poor countries need medicines developed for rich markets, the drugs may be prohibitively expensive—as with the AIDS drugs discussed in Chapter 11 (see pp. 414–417).

Safe water is another essential element of meeting basic human needs. In many rural locations, people must walk miles every day to fetch water. Note that access to water does not mean running water in every house, but a clean well or faucet for a village. In 2008, one in seven people worldwide, the great majority of them in rural areas, lacked access to safe drinking water. Even among those with access to safe drinking water, many lack sanitation facilities (such as sewers and sanitary latrines). Forty percent of the world's population does not have access to sanitation, and as a result suffers from recurrent epidemics and widespread diarrhea, which kill millions of children each year. Again, the situation is worse for rural areas, where up to 60 percent lack access to sanitation. The importance of sanitation was underscored in 2008 in Zimbabwe, when an economic collapse led to a shutdown of the water treatment system, quickly sparking a cholera epidemic that killed hundreds. Access to safe drinking water and sanitation has nonetheless improved since 1990, from 78 to 90 percent globally for drinking water and 49 to 68 percent for sanitation. But because of population growth, these improvements leave roughly the same absolute number of people lacking—about a billion for water and more than 2 billion for sanitation.[14]

Shelter is another key basic need. Of the world's 6.8 billion people, about one in six lives in substandard housing or is homeless altogether. For indicator after indicator, we find about a billion people left behind with nothing. The different indicators do not overlap perfectly, but basically the bottom billion of humanity, most living in rural areas, are in desperate poverty. The most important factors keeping these people in desperate poverty appear to be civil war, corruption, the "resource curse" (see p. 443), and landlocked locations without ready access to trade.[15]

In theory, providing for basic needs should give poor people hope of progress and should ensure political stability. However, that is not always the result. In Sri Lanka, a

DO THE MATH

Children are a main focus of efforts to provide basic human needs in the global South. Education is critical to both economic development and the demographic transition. Girls worldwide receive less education than boys, and in Afghanistan under the Taliban, they were banned from schools altogether. This math class in Kandahar, Afghanistan, in 2002 followed the Taliban's fall.

---

[14] World Health Organization and UNICEF. *Meeting the MDG Drinking Water and Sanitation Target.* UNICEF, 2004. World Health Organization. *World Health Statistics 2010.* WHO, 2010.

[15] Collier, Paul. *The Bottom Billion: Why the Poorest Countries Are Failing and What Can Be Done About It.* Oxford, 2007.

progressive-minded government implemented one of the world's most successful basic needs strategies, addressing nutrition, health care, and literacy. The policy showed that even a very poor country could meet basic needs at low levels of per capita income. Then an ethnic civil war broke out. The war became more and more brutal—with death squads and indiscriminate reprisals on civilians—until it consumed the progress Sri Lanka had made.

War in the global South—both international and civil war—is a leading obstacle to the provision of basic needs. War causes much greater damage to society than merely the direct deaths and injuries it inflicts. In war zones, economic infrastructure such as transportation is disrupted, as are government services such as health care and education. Wars drastically reduce the confidence in economic and political stability on which investment and trade depend.

Figure 12.3 maps the rates of access to safe water and food. The worldwide pattern somewhat resembles the map of wars in progress on p. 154. If indeed there is a relationship

FIGURE 12.3 Rates of Access to Water and Food, 2005

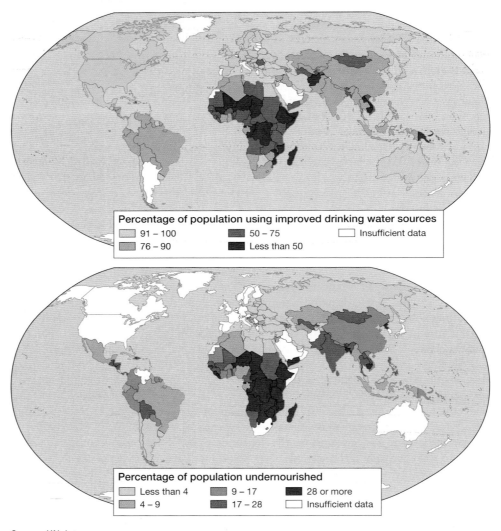

Source: UN data.

between recent or present warfare and a lack of basic needs (in turn correlated with income level), what really causes what? Does being at war keep a society poor and prevent it from meeting its population's basic needs? Or does being poor, with unmet basic needs, make a society more war-prone? Probably both are true. War is often part of a vicious circle for states unable to rise out of poverty.

The fragility of life in poor countries was demonstrated all too starkly in 2010 when a major earthquake devastated Haiti, already the poorest country in the Western hemisphere, with annual GDP of $1,300 per person. Because of poor construction, many buildings collapsed, and because of poor health and sanitation facilities, survivors faced desperate conditions. More than 100,000 people died and millions were left homeless. Haitians could only hope that international aid would help them rebuild from scratch in the coming years.

World Hunger

Of all the basic needs of people in the global South, the most central is *food*. **Malnutrition** (or malnourishment) refers to the lack of needed foods including protein and vitamins. The term *hunger* refers broadly to malnutrition or outright undernourishment—a lack of calories. Hunger does not usually kill people through outright starvation, but it weakens them and leaves them susceptible to infectious diseases that would not ordinarily be fatal.[16]

Some 830 million people—about one in eight worldwide—are chronically undernourished (see Table 12.1). Their potential contribution to economic accumulation is wasted because they cannot do even light work. And they are a potential source of political instability—including international instability—as long as they stay hungry. Record food prices in 2011 made the problem worse. At the World Food Summit in 1996, world leaders adopted a goal to cut hunger in half by 2015. But 13 years later, there were

TABLE 12.1 Who's Hungry?
Chronically Undernourished People by Region, c. 2008

Region	Number (millions)	Percentage of Population	15 Years Earlier
South Asia	330	20%	22%
Southeast Asia	75	14%	24%
China	130	10%	18%
Africa	220	23%	26%
Latin America	45	8%	12%
Middle East	30	7%	6%
Developing World	830	15%	20%

Notes: Data are from 2006–2008 and 1990–1992. Chronic undernourishment means failing to consume enough food on average over a year to maintain body weight and support light activity.

Source: Based on Food and Agriculture Organization. *The State of Food Insecurity in the World 2011.* FAO, 2011, pp. 44–47.

---

[16] Leathers, Howard D., and Phillips Foster. *The World Food Problem: Tackling the Causes of Undernutrition in the Third World.* 3rd ed. Rienner, 2004. Dréze, Jean, Amartya Sen, and Athar Hussain, eds. *The Political Economy of Hunger: Selected Essays.* Oxford, 1995.

more hungry people, not fewer. As a proportion of a growing population, however, the rate of hunger dropped from 14 to 13 percent from 1995 to 2006.[17] In 2006, UNICEF reported that China had made great progress in reducing child malnutrition, but progress in South Asia had been very slow and Africa was not moving forward. A quarter of the world's children under age 5—and nearly half those in India—were underweight. Of the world's 150 million underweight children, half lived in India, Pakistan, and Bangladesh.[18]

Traditionally, rural communities have grown their own food—**subsistence farming**. Colonialism disrupted this pattern, and the disruption has continued in postcolonial times. States in the global South shifted from subsistence to commercial agriculture. Small plots were merged into big plantations, often under the control of wealthy landlords. By concentrating capital and orienting the economy toward a niche in world trade, this process is consistent with liberal economics. But it displaces subsistence farmers from the land. Wars displace farmers even more quickly, with similar results.

Commercial agriculture relies on machinery, commercial fuels, and artificial fertilizers and pesticides, which must be bought with cash and often must be imported. To pay for these supplies, big farms grow **cash crops**—agricultural goods produced for export to world markets.[19] Such crops typically provide little nutrition to local peasants; examples include coffee, tea, and sugar cane. When a plantation is built or expanded, subsistence farmers end up working on the plantation at very low wages or migrating to cities in search of jobs. Often they end up hungry. Ironically, the higher food prices in 2007–2008 have provided increased income for farmers in rural areas, yet at the cost of many being unable to afford food.

Natural disasters can exacerbate food shortages. The threat of major food shortages threatened Pakistan after devastating floods in the summer of 2010. According to the UN's Food and Agriculture Organization, well over 700,000 hectares of crops were lost in the Pakistan flood, leaving food in short supply for people and farm animals. States, IGOs, and NGOs rushed food to Pakistan after the floods, hoping to avert a major humanitarian catastrophe.

International food aid itself can sometimes contribute to these problems.[20] Agricultural assistance may favor mechanized commercial agriculture. And if an international agency floods an area with food, prices on local markets drop, which may force even more local farmers out of business and increase dependence on handouts from the government or international community. Also, people in a drought or famine often have to travel to feeding centers to receive the food, halting their work on their own land.

Rural and Urban Populations

The displacement of peasants from subsistence farming contributes to a massive population shift that typically accompanies the demographic transition. More and more people move to the cities from the countryside—**urbanization**. This is hard to measure exactly; there is no standard definition of when a town is considered a city. But

---

[17] Food and Agriculture Organization. *The State of Food Insecurity in the World 2009*. FAO, 2009.
[18] UNICEF. Progress for Children: A Report Card on Nutrition. Number 4, May 2006. UNICEF, 2006.
[19] Barkin, David, Rosemary L. Batt, and Billie R. DeWatt. *Food Crops vs. Feed Crops: Global Substitution of Grains in Production*. Rienner, 1990.
[20] Webb, Patrick. *Food as Aid: Trends, Needs, and Challenges in the 21st Century*. World Food Program, 2004.

industrialized states report that about 70 to 90 percent of their populations live in cities. By contrast, China is only 40 percent urbanized—a level typical of Asia and Africa. Most Middle Eastern states are a bit more urban (45 to 55 percent), and South American ones are 70 to 85 percent urban.

Urbanization is not caused by higher population growth in cities than in the countryside. In fact, the opposite is true. In cities, the people are generally better educated, with higher incomes. They are further along in the demographic transition and have lower birthrates than people in the countryside. Rather, the growth of urban population is caused by people moving to the cities from the countryside. They do so because of the higher income levels in the cities—economic opportunity—and the hope of more chances for an exciting life. They also move because population growth in the countryside stretches available food, water, arable land, and other resources.

In many cities, the influx of people cannot be accommodated with jobs, housing, and services. In slums, basic human needs often go unmet. Many states have considered policies to break up large land holdings and redistribute land to poor peasants for use in subsistence farming—**land reform**.[21] The main opponents of land reform are large landowners, who often wield great political power because of their wealth and international connections to markets, MNCs, and other sources of hard currency.

LANDLESS

Subsistence farmers displaced from their land risk chronic hunger and sometimes starvation. This woman in Darfur, Sudan, in 2009 goes to a water distribution point to get water brought in by donkey from a source an hour and a half away.

Women in Development

Economic development in poor countries is closely tied to the status of women in those societies.[22] This is a relatively recent revelation; most attention for decades had focused on men as supposedly the main generators of capital. Governments and international reports concentrated on work performed by male wage earners. Women's work, by contrast, often is not paid for in money and does not show up in financial statistics. But women in much of the world work harder than men and contribute more to the economic well-being of their families and communities. Women are key to efforts to improve the lot of children and reduce birthrates. In nutrition, education, health care, and shelter, women are central to providing the basic needs of people in poor countries.

Yet women hold inferior social status to men in the countries of the South (even more so than in the North). For instance, when food is in short supply, men and boys often eat first, with women and girls getting what is left.

[21] Dorner, Peter. *Latin American Land Reform in Theory and Practice*. Wisconsin, 1992. Deininger, Klaus W. *Land Policies for Growth and Poverty Reduction*. Oxford, 2003.

[22] Boserup, Ester, Nazneed Kanji, Su Fei Tan, and Camilla Toulmin. *Woman's Role in Economic Development*. Earthscan, 2007. Jaquette, Jane S., and Gale Summerfield. *Women and Gender Equality in Development Theory and Practice: Institutions, Resources, and Mobilization*. Duke, 2006. Afshar, Haleh, and Deborah Eade. *Development, Women, and War: Feminist Perspectives*. Oxfam, 2004. Aguilar, Delia D., and Anne E. Lacsamana. *Women and Globalization*. Humanity, 2004. Beneria, Lourdes. *Gender, Development, and Globalization: Economics as if All People Mattered*. Routledge, 2003.

WOMEN'S POWER

The status of women in countries of the global South affects their prospects for economic development. Women are central to rural economies, to population strategies, and to the provision of basic human needs, including education. Here, a women's cooperative in Mauritania makes small loans to its members, 2006.

Discrimination against girls is widespread in education and literacy. Worldwide, nearly twice as many women as men are illiterate. Across the global South, only in Latin America do women's literacy rates approach those of men. In Pakistan, three-quarters of boys but little more than half the girls receive primary education. Throughout Asia, Africa, and the Middle East (but not in Latin America), more boys receive education, especially at the secondary level, though the gap has closed considerably in recent years. At the university level, only 30 percent of students in China and the Middle East are women, a bit more than 20 percent in South Asia and Africa (but 45 percent in Latin America). The Taliban regime in Afghanistan (1996–2001) took extreme measures against women's education, banning all girls from school and all women from paid work.

States and international agencies have begun to pay attention to ending discrimination in schooling, ensuring women's access to health care and birth control, educating mothers about prenatal and child health, and generally raising women's status in society (allowing them a greater voice in decisions). These issues occupied the 1995 UN women's conference in Beijing, China, attended by tens of thousands of state and NGO representatives.

For example, international agencies help women organize small businesses, farms, and other income-producing activities. UNICEF has helped women get bank loans on favorable terms to start up small businesses in Egypt and Pakistan as well as cooperative farms in Indonesia. Women have organized cooperatives throughout the global South, often in rural areas, to produce income through weaving and other textile and clothing production, retail stores, agriculture, and so forth.[23] In the slums of Addis Ababa, Ethiopia, women heads of household with no land for subsistence farming had been forced into begging and prostitution. Women taking part in the Integrated Holistic Approach Urban Development Project organized income-producing businesses in areas such as food processing, cloth weaving, and garment production. These profitable businesses earned income for the women and helped subsidize health and sanitation services in the slums.

Migration and Refugees

The processes just outlined—basic needs deprivation, displacement from land, and urbanization—culminate in one of the biggest political issues affecting North-South relations: **migration** from poorer to richer states.[24] Millions of people from the global South have crossed international borders, often illegally, to reach the North.

Someone who moves to a new country in search of better economic opportunities, a better professional environment, or better access to his or her family, culture, or religion

[23] Lopez, T. *Women and Rural Development: New Employment Sources and Cooperatives in Less Favored Areas.* FAO, 2007. Rahman, Aminur. *Women and Microcredit in Rural Bangladesh: An Anthropological Study of Grameen Bank Lending.* Westview, 2001.

[24] Stalker, Peter. *Workers without Frontiers: The Impact of Globalization on International Migration.* Rienner, 2000. Meyers, Eytan. *International Immigration Policy: An Empirical and Theoretical Analysis.* Palgrave, 2004.

is engaging in migration (emigration from the old state and immigration to the new state). Such migration is considered voluntary. The home state is not under any obligation to let such people leave, and, more important, no state is obligated to receive migrants. As with any trade issue, migration creates complex patterns of winners and losers. Immigrants often provide cheap labor, benefiting the host economy overall, but also compete for jobs with (poor) citizens of the host country.

Most industrialized states try to limit immigration from the global South. Despite border guards and fences, many people migrate anyway, illegally. In the United States, such immigrants come from all over the world, but mostly from nearby Mexico, Central America, and the Caribbean. In Western Europe, they come largely from North Africa, Turkey, and (increasingly) Eastern Europe.[25] Some Western European leaders worry that the loosening of border controls under the process of integration (see pp. 355–358) will make it harder to keep out illegal immigrants. Indeed, fear of immigration is one reason why Swiss voters rejected membership in the EU. In 2004–2006, tens of thousands of migrants and refugees from sub-Saharan Africa came to Morocco and climbed over razor-wire fences to enter two tiny Spanish enclaves there. Once on Spanish soil, they could not be sent home if they kept authorities from determining their nationality. The increase in migrants trying to reach the enclaves in Morocco followed Spanish efforts to stem the flow of migrants crossing in boats from North Africa to Spain itself near the Gibraltar straits. In turn, when Spain cracked down on the crossings at the Moroccan enclaves, Africans set out in boats and rafts to reach the Spanish-owned Canary Islands in the Atlantic off Morocco.

International law and custom distinguish migrants from **refugees**, people fleeing to find refuge from war, natural disaster, or political persecution.[26] (Fleeing from chronic discrimination may or may not be grounds for refugee status.) International norms obligate countries to accept refugees who arrive at their borders. Refugees from wars or natural disasters are generally housed in refugee camps temporarily until they can return home (though their stay can drag on for years). Refugees from political persecution may be granted asylum to stay in the new state. Acceptance of refugees—and the question of which states must bear the costs—is a collective goods problem.

ON THE MOVE

Refugees are both a result of international conflict and a source of conflict. In addition to those fleeing war and repression and those seeking economic opportunity, hundreds of thousands of people each year cross borders as sex and labor slaves. These refugees crossing from war-torn Libya into Tunisia in 2011 show their Bangladesh passports.

---

[25] Aleinikoff, Alexander, and Douglas Klusmeyer, eds. *From Migrants to Citizens: Membership in a Changing World*. Carnegie Endowment for International Peace, 2000. Massey, Douglas S., and J. Edward Taylor. *International Migration: Prospects and Policies in a Global Market*. Oxford, 2004.

[26] UN High Commissioner for Refugees. *The State of the World's Refugees*. Oxford, annual. Haddad, Emma. *The Refugee in International Society: Between Sovereigns*. Cambridge, 2008. Zolberg, Aristide R., and Peter Benda. *Global Migrants, Global Refugees: Problems and Solutions*. Berghan, 2001. Loescher, Gil. *The UNHCR and World Politics: A Perilous Path*. Oxford, 2001.

TABLE 12.2 Refugee Populations, 2010

Region	Millions	Main Concentrations
Middle East and Asia	12	Afghanistan, Iraq, Pakistan, Thailand, Iran
Palestinians under UNRWA	4	Palestine, Jordan, Lebanon, Syria
Africa	10	Somalia, Uganda, Sudan, D.R. Congo
Latin America	4	Colombia
Europe	3	Germany
World Total	33	

Note: Includes refugees, asylum seekers, returned refugees, and internally displaced people.

Source: UN High Commissioner for Refugees (UNHCR).

This problem came into sharp focus in 2011 when tens of thousands of refugees from Tunisia and Libya poured into Italy, from which they could pass freely into other nearby European countries. France stopped accepting them, and EU leaders reviewed their free-movement rules.

The number of international refugees in the world was about 10 million in 2011. About 15 million more people were displaced within their own countries. Three-fourths of these internally displaced persons (IDPs) resided in Colombia, Congo, Somalia, Sudan, Iraq, and Afghanistan. An additional 4 million Palestinian refugees fall under the responsibility of the UN Relief and Works Agency (UNRWA). The majority of refugees and IDPs have been displaced by wars (see Table 12.2).

The political impact of refugees has been demonstrated repeatedly. The most politicized refugee problem for decades has been that of Palestinians displaced in the 1948 and 1967 Arab-Israeli wars (and their children and grandchildren). They live in "camps" that have become long-term neighborhoods, mainly in Jordan, Lebanon, and the Palestinian territories of Gaza and the West Bank. Economic development is impeded in these camps because the host states and Palestinians insist that the arrangement is only temporary. The poverty of the refugees in turn fuels radical political movements among the inhabitants. The question of Palestinian refugees' right to return to what is now Israel has challenged every attempt at a comprehensive peace settlement for years.

It is not always easy to distinguish a refugee fleeing war or political persecution from a migrant seeking economic opportunity. Illegal immigrants may claim to be refugees in order to be allowed to stay, when really they are seeking better economic opportunities. In recent decades this issue has become a major one throughout the North.

In Germany, France, Austria, and elsewhere, resentment of foreign immigrants has fueled upsurges of right-wing nationalism in domestic politics. Germany, with lax regulations for asylum seekers (they could live for years at state expense while applications for refugee status were processed), became a favored destination for immigrants.

Remittances   A crucial aspect of migration and immigration is **remittances**—money sent home by migrants to relatives in their country of origin. They are an important source of income for many poor countries with large numbers of immigrant workers.[27]

---

[27] Terry, Donald F., and Steven R. Wilson. *Beyond Small Change: Making Migrant Remittances Count.* Inter-American Development Bank, 2005.

POLICY PERSPECTIVES

President of Botswana, Seretse Khama Ian Khama

PROBLEM   *How do you confront a regional humanitarian crisis without sacrificing the well-being of your own population?*

BACKGROUND   Imagine that you are the president of Botswana. Your neighbor to the east, Zimbabwe, has undergone years of political, economic, and social turmoil. Most recently, a contested presidential election set off waves of violence and protest there. These violent clashes sent waves of refugees fleeing from their homes. Besides the political violence, a food shortage crisis affects up to half of the 12 million inhabitants of Zimbabwe. Economically, Zimbabwe is in collapse as well, with an inflation rate above 200 million percent. Finally, Zimbabwe has experienced several outbreaks of cholera, which have killed thousands who lack basic health care in the midst of the crisis. These terrible political, social, and economic conditions have led many to flee Zimbabwe looking for temporary (or in some cases permanent) relief from the conditions in that country.

DOMESTIC CONSIDERATIONS   Your own political and economic situation, however, is quite different. Over the past decade, your country has gone from being one of the poorest in Africa to one with a per capita GDP of $15,000 per person. The economic situation of your country is solid and the political situation is relatively stable. This new wealth has let you put in place a comprehensive program to address the very high rate of HIV/AIDS infection (one in three adults) in your country, and to begin reducing the high unemployment rate (40 percent by some estimates).

While your political and economic situation is certainly better than Zimbabwe's, it is not clear that you would be able to provide assistance or refuge for the tens of thousands of Zimbabweans fleeing to your country. In particular, your health care system, already strained by the AIDS epidemic, would be quickly overtaxed by refugees streaming in from Zimbabwe infected with cholera. And while your own public has some tolerance for a limited number of refugees, they would oppose accommodating all Zimbabweans who want assistance.

SCENARIO   Now imagine that the political situation in Zimbabwe worsens. Another cholera outbreak occurs, which spurs tens of thousands of additional refugees to pour into Botswana. Your health minister implores you to shut down the border because of the cholera threat. But you are under some pressure from the international community to accept the refugees. The UN High Commissioner for Refugees has promised to help pay the costs for hosting those fleeing from Zimbabwe no matter how long it takes to restore political stability to Zimbabwe (which could be years).

CHOOSE YOUR POLICY   What do you do with the refugees? Do you forcefully stop them from leaving Zimbabwe? This could add to the political and economic instability of Zimbabwe. Do you allow the refugees to stay in Botswana? This could lead to resentment on the part of your own population if the refugees take jobs, drain food supplies, or burden your health care system. How do you balance humanitarian needs with a concern for your own people's physical and economic well-being?

Remittances are important for states in many regions of the world. In the Philippines, remittances account for well over 10 percent of GDP, and for Lebanon nearly 25 percent of GDP. For some smaller economies, such as Tajikistan, remittances can comprise nearly half of the GDP.

Remittances are becoming an increasingly important part of the global economy (see Figure 12.4).[28] Unlike FDI, remittances are not transferred between companies or wealthy individuals, but usually between families. Thus, remittances cannot be withdrawn from a recipient economy. They also are not handed out by governments and thus, not subject to corruption or governmental waste. Also, unlike foreign aid, remittances are not subject to conditions from donors. They are given freely from family to family. These characteristics of remittances (as well as their growing size) make them important, yet also difficult to study.

Remittances help states in the global South. They give poorer households more disposable income. They have helped some poorer states, such as the Philippines and Bangladesh, improve their investment ratings and sell bonds, luring more foreign direct investment. However, remittance levels are very vulnerable to economic downturns in wealthy countries. Remittances also continue the cycle of dependency of poor states on wealthy ones. Should wealthy states close their borders or expel migrant populations, this would create hardships for individual families as well as the economies of developing countries.

Trafficking   In addition to migration and refugees, a growing number of people—estimated at about 700,000 annually—are trafficked across international borders against their will. They include both sex slaves and labor slaves, with each category including females and males, adults and children. Perhaps 20,000 of these people are trafficked to

---

[28] Singer, David A. Migrant Remittances and Exchange Rate Regimes in the Developing World. *American Political Science Review* 104 (2): 307-323.

SEEKING THE COLLECTIVE GOOD

The Refugee Regime
COLLECTIVE GOOD: The Well-Being of Refugees

BACKGROUND: Wars and disasters regularly displace millions of people from their homes, as they seek safety and survival by fleeing. Not infrequently, they show up at an international border seeking to cross and find refuge on the other side. A state that lets them in incurs costs in doing so. The world as a whole is served by helping refugees (which heads off political and economic instability, as well as public health risks, that a desperate population out of control could pose). The care of refugees is thus a collective good for the world's states.

CHALLENGE: In 2011 the world had about 10 million refugees (and another 15 million displaced but still within their countries). Eighty percent were in the global South. With most wars happening in poor regions of the world, the neighboring countries that are expected to absorb refugee populations often lack the resources to provide for them. There is thus a temptation to free-ride and turn refugees away at the border.

SOLUTION: The identity principle can play a role, as when refugees are a persecuted minority who cross the border into a country where their ethnic group is a majority. The host country then identifies with them and is more

RECIPROCITY

FIGURE 12.4 Global Flows of Remittances, 1970–2008

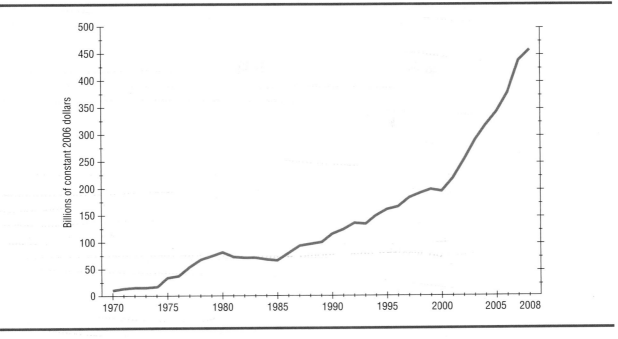

the United States annually. In 2010, the U.S. State Department listed 13 countries making insufficient efforts to stop human trafficking, including friends such as Kuwait, Malaysia, and Saudi Arabia.[29]

---

[29] U.S. Department of State. *Trafficking in Persons Report 2009*. Dept. of State, 2009.

willing to provide for them. The main approach, however, is reciprocity—neither expecting countries to take in refugees just from the goodness of their hearts, but also not threatening them or forcing them to do so.

The world's refugee regime is a reciprocity-based set of rules that the world's states have agreed to. All states are supposed to follow the same rules, which require them to take in war refugees. In order to help the host countries, the international community has an international organization, the UN High Commissioner for Refugees (UNHCR), to help take care of refugee populations. UNHCR funding is itself a collective goods problem, and the agency often runs short of desperately needed supplies when the good is not provided.

Refugees from Kyrgyzstan are separated when Tajikistan closes the border, 2010.

In general, South-North migration of all types creates problems for the industrialized states that, it seems, can be solved only by addressing the problems of the South itself.

Theories of Accumulation

● Explore
the Simulation
"International
Development: You Are
the Minister of Trade
and Finance"
on mypoliscilab.com

How do we explain the enormous gap between income levels in the world's industrialized regions and those in the global South? What are the implications of that gap for international politics? There are several very different approaches to these questions; we will concentrate on two contrasting theories of wealth accumulation, based on more liberal and more revolutionary perspectives.

Economic Accumulation

A view of the problem from the perspective of capitalism is based on liberal economics—stressing overall efficiency in maximizing *economic growth*. This view sees the global South as merely lagging behind the industrialized North. More wealth creation in the North is a good thing, as is wealth creation in the South—the two are not in conflict.

A different view of things, from the perspective of socialism, is concerned with the distribution of wealth as much as the absolute creation of wealth. It sees the North-South divide as more of a zero-sum game in which the creation of wealth in the North most often comes at the expense of the South. It also gives politics (the state) more of a role in redistributing wealth and managing the economy than does capitalism. Socialism thus parallels mercantilism in some ways. But socialists see economic classes rather than states as the main actors in the political bargaining over the distribution of the world's wealth. And mercantilism promotes the idea of concentrating wealth (as a power element), whereas socialism promotes the broader distribution of wealth.

For socialists, international exchange is shaped by capitalists' exploitation of cheap labor and cheap resources—using states to help create the political conditions for this exploitation. (Some socialists focus on workers in poor countries, some on workers in richer industrialized countries, and some on both.) Thus, whereas mercantilists see political interests (of the state) as driving economic policies, socialists see economic interests (of capitalists and of workers) as driving political policies. In Latin America in recent years, several states have elected leftist presidents committed to changing course away from free market capitalism and toward a socialist philosophy with more state-owned industries. These countries are Venezuela, Bolivia, Ecuador, and Nicaragua.

Capitalist and socialist approaches are rather incompatible in their language and assumptions about the problem of poverty and its international implications. This chapter somewhat favors socialist approaches, focusing on the past history of imperialism as a central cause of the North-South divide, and on revolutionary strategies and massive redistribution of wealth as solutions to it. Chapter 13, in turn, leans toward capitalist approaches.

In reality, no state is purely capitalist. Almost all have some form of mixed economy that includes both private and state ownership.[30] In most capitalist countries the government balances the inhuman side of capitalism by redistributing some wealth downward. A "welfare state" provides education, certain health benefits, welfare for the poor, and so

---

[30] Freeman, John R. *Democracy and Markets: The Politics of Mixed Economies*. Cornell, 1989.

forth. In the 2008–2009 financial crisis, some of the largest capitalist economies, including the United States and Great Britain, found themselves spending money to buy portions of private companies, such as insurance companies, automakers, and banks, to keep these businesses from going into bankruptcy.

Economic development is based on *capital accumulation*—the creation of standing wealth (capital) such as buildings, roads, and factories. In order for human populations and their capital to grow, they must produce an **economic surplus** by using capital to produce more capital. This is done by investing money in productive capital rather than using it for consumption. The more surplus an economy produces, the more resources are available for investment above the minimum level of consumption needed to sustain human life.

The Industrial Revolution of several centuries ago greatly accelerated the process of world accumulation, drawing on large amounts of energy from fossil fuels. But industrialization has occurred very unevenly across the world regions. The North has accumulated vast capital. Though the South produces spurts of wealth and has pockets of accumulation, in most areas it remains a preindustrial economy—the reason why the North consumes nearly ten times as much commercial energy per person as the South does (see Table 11.1 on p. 404).

LOW-TECH

Production in the global South uses relatively little capital and much labor (at low wages), reflecting an early stage of industrialization. To develop economically, poor countries must generate self-sustaining capital accumulation. Agriculture, energy, and textiles are classic export products from the global South, relatively low-capital and labor-intensive. In Morocco, textiles such as these for sale in 2010 are a major source of export revenue.

Information technology now is making a fuel-burning infrastructure relatively less important in the advanced economies. The countries of the global South may need to pass through a phase of heavy industrialization, as countries in the North did, or perhaps they can develop economically along different paths, using new technology from the start. The problem is that, just as industrial infrastructure is located mostly in the North, so is the world's information infrastructure (see pp. 376–377). While a generation of students in industrialized countries go online, poorer countries still struggle to extend literacy to rural populations.

The World-System

The global system of regional class divisions has been seen by some IR scholars as a **world-system** or a *capitalist world economy*.[31] This view is Marxist in orientation (focusing on economic classes; see Chapter 3) and relies on a global level of analysis. In the world-system, class divisions are regionalized. Regions in the global South mostly extract

[31] Wallerstein, Immanuel. *The Modern World-System*. 3 vols. Academic, 1974, 1980, 1989. Frank, André Gunder. *World Accumulation, 1492–1789*. Monthly Review Press, 1978. Chew, Sing C., and Robert A. Denemark, eds. *The Underdevelopment of Development: Essays in Honor of André Gunder Frank*. Sage, 1996.

raw materials (including agriculture)—work that uses much labor and little capital, and pays low wages. Industrialized regions mostly manufacture goods—work that uses more capital, requires more skilled labor, and pays workers higher wages. The manufacturing regions are called the *core* (or *center*) of the world-system; the extraction regions are called the *periphery*.

The most important class struggle today, in this view, is that between the core and the periphery of the world-system.[32] The core uses its power (derived from its wealth) to concentrate surplus from the periphery, as it has done for about 500 years. Conflicts among great powers, including the two world wars and the Cold War, basically result from competition among core states over the right to exploit the periphery.

The core and periphery are not sharply delineated. Within the periphery, there are also centers and peripheries (for instance, the city of Rio de Janeiro compared to the Amazon rain forest) as there are within the core (such as New York City compared to the Mississippi Delta). The whole global structure is one of overlapping hierarchies. The concentration of capital and the scale of wages each form a continuum rather than a sharp division into two categories.[33]

In world-system theory, the *semiperiphery* is an area in which some manufacturing occurs and some capital concentrates, but not to the extent of the most advanced areas in the core. Eastern Europe and Russia are commonly considered semiperipheral, as are some of the newly industrializing countries (see pp. 461–462) such as Taiwan and Singapore. The semiperiphery acts as a kind of political buffer between the core and periphery because poor states can aspire to join the semiperiphery instead of aspiring to rebel against domination by the core.

Over time, membership in the core, the semiperiphery, and the periphery changes somewhat, but the overall global system of class relations remains. Areas that once were beyond the reach of Europeans, such as the interior of Latin America, become incorporated as periphery. Areas of the periphery can become semiperiphery and even join the core, as North America did. And core states can slip into the semiperiphery if they fall behind in accumulation, as Spain did in the late 16th to early 17th centuries. Because world-system theory provides only general concepts but not firm definitions of what constitutes the core, semiperiphery, and periphery, it is hard to say exactly which states belong to each category.[34]

The actual patterns of world trade support world-system theory to some extent. The industrialized West fits the profile of the core, exporting more than it imports in machinery, chemicals, and similar heavy manufactured goods. In the 1990s, all the other regions imported more than they exported in such goods. But in the 2000s, China (and other Asian countries) also became a net exporter of heavy manufactured goods. Asia also still has a niche in exporting light manufacturing including textile production. Such a pattern fits the semiperiphery category. The industrialized West imports these light manufactures. The shift of export-oriented manufacturing from the industrialized countries to Asia reflects globalization.

The industrialized West's net imports of energy are an enormously important type of trade and another indication of globalization. Asia now also imports energy. The Middle East specializes in exporting oil, and Russia, Latin America, and Africa all export energy on balance as well. This is an extraction role typical of the periphery. Latin America has net

---

[32] Boswell, Terry, ed. *Revolution in the World-System.* Greenwood, 1989.

[33] Boswell, Terry, and Christopher Chase-Dunn. *The Spiral of Capitalism and Socialism: Toward Global Democracy.* Rienner, 2000.

[34] Thompson, William R., ed. *Contending Approaches to World System Analysis.* Sage, 1983. Hopkins, Terence K., and Immanuel Wallerstein. *The Age of Transition: Trajectory of the World-System, 1945–2025.* Zed, 1996.

exports in food, agricultural products, and minerals—also typical of the periphery. These regions' patterns of specialization must be kept in perspective, however. All regions both import and export all these types of goods, and the net exports listed in the table amount to only a small part of the world's total trade.

Semiperiphery regions, which export manufactured products, are just those—China and South Asia—that have been growing very rapidly in recent years (see Figure 12.1 on p. 426). The three regions that engage with the globalizing world economy primarily as raw-material exporters (Africa, the Middle East, and Latin America) are growing more slowly.

Having exportable natural resources would seem a big plus for an economy, but in fact the problems of basing economic growth on resource exports have been called the **resource curse**.[35] Even in a middle-income country, Chile, the quadrupling of the price of its main export commodity, copper, in 2003–2006 was a mixed blessing. Protesters demanded that the billions of dollars be spent on social services for the poor, but the president (although a socialist) warned against spending what could be a temporary windfall. Meanwhile the high export earnings strengthened Chile's currency, making it harder for other industries to export their products.[36] Then in late 2008, the global recession caused a crash in copper prices, drastically cutting Chile's income.

Imperialism

Watch the **Video** "Zimbabwe's Economic Crisis" on mypoliscilab.com

Both the disparities in wealth between the global North and South and the regions' export specializations have long histories. In Chapter 3 we discussed Marxist theories of imperialism, which give a particular kind of explanation for how the North-South gap evolved. Here we review how **imperialism** affected the South over the centuries and how its aftereffects are still felt around the world. Imperialism, especially in the 16th to mid-20th centuries, structured world order starkly around the dominance principle, with masters and slaves, conquerors and conquered peoples with their land, labor, and treasures. At the same time, imperialism depends on the identity principle to unite the global North around a common racial identity that defines nonwhite people as an out-group. (Although identity issues today are more complex, racism still affects North-South relations.)

World Civilizations

The present-day international system is the product of a particular civilization—Western civilization, centered in Europe. The international system as we know it developed among the European states of 300 to 500 years ago, was exported to the rest of the world, and has in the last century subsumed virtually all of the world's territory into sovereign states. Other civilizations existed in other world regions for centuries before Europeans ever arrived. These cultural traditions continue to exert an influence on IR, especially when the styles and expectations of these cultures come into play in international interactions (see Figure 12.5).[37]

---

[35] Humphreys, Macartan, Jeffrey D. Sachs, and Joseph E. Stiglitz. *Escaping the Resource Curse*. Columbia, 2007. Lujala, Palvi, Nils Peter Gleditsch, and Elisabeth Gilmore. A Diamond Curse? Civil War and Lootable Resources. *Journal of Conflict Resolution* 49 (4), 2005: 538–62.

[36] Rohter, Larry. Chile Copper Windfall Forces Hard Choices on Spending. *The New York Times*, January 7, 2007: 4.

[37] Barraclough, Geoffrey, ed. *The Times Atlas of World History*. Hammond, 1978. Mozaffari, Mehdi, ed. *Globalization and Civilizations*. Routledge, 2002. Abu-Lughod, Janet. *Before European Hegemony: The World System, a.d. 1250–1350*. Oxford, 1989. Hodgson, Marshall G. S. *The Venture of Islam: Conscience and History in a World Civilization*. Chicago, 1974. Bozeman, Adda. *Politics and Culture in International History*. Princeton, 1960.

FIGURE 12.5 World Civilizations

	Before A.D. 1000	A.D. 1000–1250	1250–1500	1500–1750	1750–2000
Japan	Korean and Chinese influences	samurai; shoguns →	→	Tokugawa isolation →	Meiji restoration; WWII; prosperity
China	Dynasties; Great Wall begun; Taoism; Buddhism; paper, gunpowder	Sung dynasty	Mongol dynasty	Ming dynasty; Manchu dynasty	European dominance; People's Republic
S. Asia	Emergence of Hinduism, Buddhism; Ancient India; Arab conquest	Turkish period		Taj Mahal built; European colonialism	European colonialism →; independence
Africa	Kingdom of Ghana	Yoruba, Mali, Benin (kingdoms)	Congo; Zimbabwe; slave trade	Buganda; Ashanti; slave trade →	→ European colonialism; independence
Middle East	Mesopotamia, Egypt, Persia; Jews, Christians; Greeks/Romans; Islam	Crusades; Arab empire →	→	Ottoman Empire →	Arab nationalism; European colonialism; Islamic rev.
W. Europe	Ancient Greece; Roman Empire; Vikings; Feudalism	"Dark Ages"	Venice	Renaissance; Protestantism; Empires →	French Revolution; German/Italian unifica-tions; WWI/II; loss of empires
Russia & E. Europe	Khazars		Genghis Khan	Ivan the Terrible; czars →	Lenin USSR; WWII; CIS
N. America	(Preagricultural)			Columbus; European colonization	American Revolution; U.S. Civil War; westward expansion; WWII; Cold War
Latin America	Mayans	Aztec & Inca Empires →	→	Portuguese & Spanish conquest; colonialism →	European & U.S. interventions; independence; wars, debts, dictators, revolutions

North America's indigenous cultures were largely exterminated or pushed aside by European settlers. Today's North American population is overwhelmingly descended from immigrants. In most of the world (especially in Africa and Asia), however, European empires incorporated rather than pushed aside indigenous populations. Today's populations are descended primarily from indigenous inhabitants, not immigrants. These populations are therefore more strongly rooted in their own cultural traditions and history than are most Americans.

European civilization evolved from roots in the Eastern Mediterranean—Egypt, Mesopotamia (Iraq), and especially Greece. Of special importance for IR is the classical period of Greek city-states around 400 B.C., which exemplified some of the fundamental principles of interstate power politics (reflected in Thucydides's classic account of the Peloponnesian Wars between Athens and Sparta). By that time, states were carrying out sophisticated trade relations and warfare with each other in a broad swath of the world from the Mediterranean through India to East Asia. Much of this area came under Greek influence with the conquests of Alexander the Great (around 300 B.C.), then under the Roman Empire (around A.D. 1), and then under the Arab caliphate (around A.D. 600).

China remained an independent civilization during all this time. In the "warring states" period, at about the same time as the Greek city-states, sophisticated states (organized as territorial political units) first used warfare as an instrument of power politics. This is described in the classic work *The Art of War*, by Sun Tzu.[38] By about A.D. 800, when Europe was in its "dark ages" and Arab civilization in its golden age, China under the T'ang dynasty was a highly advanced civilization quite independent of Western influence. Japan, strongly influenced by Chinese civilization, flowered on its own in the centuries leading up to the Shoguns (around A.D. 1200). Japan isolated itself from Western influence under the Tokugawa shogunate for several centuries, ending after 1850 when the Meiji restoration began Japanese industrialization and international trade. Latin America also had flourishing civilizations—the Mayans around A.D. 100 to 900 and the Aztecs and Incas around 1200—independent of Western influence until they were conquered by Spain around 1500. In Africa, the great kingdoms flowered after about A.D. 1000 (as early as A.D. 600 in Ghana) and were highly developed when the European slave traders arrived on the scene around 1500.

The Arab caliphate of about A.D. 600 to 1200 plays a special role in the international relations of the Middle East. Almost the whole of the region was once united in this empire, which arose and spread with the religion of Islam. European invasions—the Crusades—were driven out. In the 16th to 19th centuries, the Eastern Mediterranean came under the Turkish-based Ottoman Empire, which gave relative autonomy to local cultures if they paid tribute. This history of empires continued to influence the region in the 20th century. For example, *Pan-Arabism* (or Arab nationalism), especially strong in the 1950s and 1960s, saw the region as potentially one nation again, with a single religion, language, and identity. Iraq's Saddam Hussein during the Gulf War likened himself to the ruler who drove away the Crusaders a thousand years ago. The strength of Islamic fundamentalism throughout the region today, as well as the emotions attached to the Arab-Israeli conflict, reflect the continuing importance of the Arab caliphate.

Europe itself began its rise to world dominance around 1500, after the Renaissance (when the Greek and Roman classics were rediscovered). The Italian city-states of the period also rediscovered the rules of interstate power politics, as described by an advisor to

---

[38] Sun Tzu. *The Art of War*. Translated by Samuel B. Griffith. Oxford, 1963.

Renaissance princes named Niccolò Machiavelli. Feudal units began to merge into large territorial nation-states under single authoritarian rulers (monarchs). The military revolution of the period created the first modern armies.[39] European monarchs put cannons on sailing ships and began to "discover" the world. The development of the international system, of imperialism, of trade and war, were all greatly accelerated by the Industrial Revolution after about 1750. Ultimately the European conquest of the world brought about a single world civilization, albeit with regional variants and subcultures.[40]

History of Imperialism, 1500–2000

European imperialism got its start in the 15th century with the development of oceangoing sailing ships in which a small crew could transport a sizable cargo over a long distance. Portugal pioneered the first voyages of exploration beyond Europe. Spain, France, and Britain soon followed. With superior military technology, Europeans gained control of coastal cities and of resupply outposts along major trade routes. Gradually this control extended farther inland, first in Latin America, then in North America, and later throughout Asia and Africa (see Figure 12.6).

In the 16th century, Spain and Portugal had extensive empires in Central America and Brazil, respectively. Britain and France had colonies in North America and the Caribbean. The imperialists bought slaves in Africa and shipped them to Mexico and Brazil, where they worked in tropical agriculture and in mining silver and gold. The wealth produced was exported to Europe, where monarchs used it to buy armies and build states.

These empires decimated indigenous populations and cultures, causing immense suffering. Over time, the economies of colonies developed with the creation of basic transportation and communication infrastructure, factories, and so forth. But these economies were often molded to the needs of the colonizers, not the local populations.

Decolonization began with the British colonists in the United States, who declared independence in 1776. Most of Latin America gained independence a few decades later. The new states in North America and Latin America were, of course, still run by the descendants of Europeans, to the disadvantage of Native Americans and African slaves.

New colonies were still being acquired by Europe through the end of the 19th century, culminating in a scramble for colonies in Africa in the 1890s (resulting in arbitrary territorial divisions as competing European armies rushed inland from all sides). India became Britain's largest and most important colony in the 19th century. Latecomers such as Germany and Italy were frustrated to find few attractive territories remaining in the world when they tried to build overseas empires in the late 19th century. Ultimately, only a few non-European areas of the world retained their independence: Japan, most of China, Iran, Turkey, and a few other areas. Japan began building its own empire, as did the United States, at the end of the 19th century. China became weaker and its coastal regions fell under the domination, if not the formal control, of European powers. Europe colonized most of the world's territory at one time or another (see Figure 12.7).

---

[39] Howard, Michael. *War in European History*. Oxford, 1976. Parker, Geoffrey. *The Military Revolution: Military Innovation and the Rise of the West, 1500–1800*. 2nd ed. Cambridge, 1996. Black, Jeremy, ed. *The Origins of War in Early Modern Europe*. Donald, 1987.

[40] Cipolla, Carlo M. *Guns, Sails and Empires*. Pantheon, 1965. Anderson, Perry. *Lineages of the Absolutist State*. NLB, 1974. Braudel, Fernand. *Civilization and Capitalism, 15th–18th Century*. 3 vols. Harper & Row, 1984.

FIGURE 12.6 History of Imperialism, 1500–2000

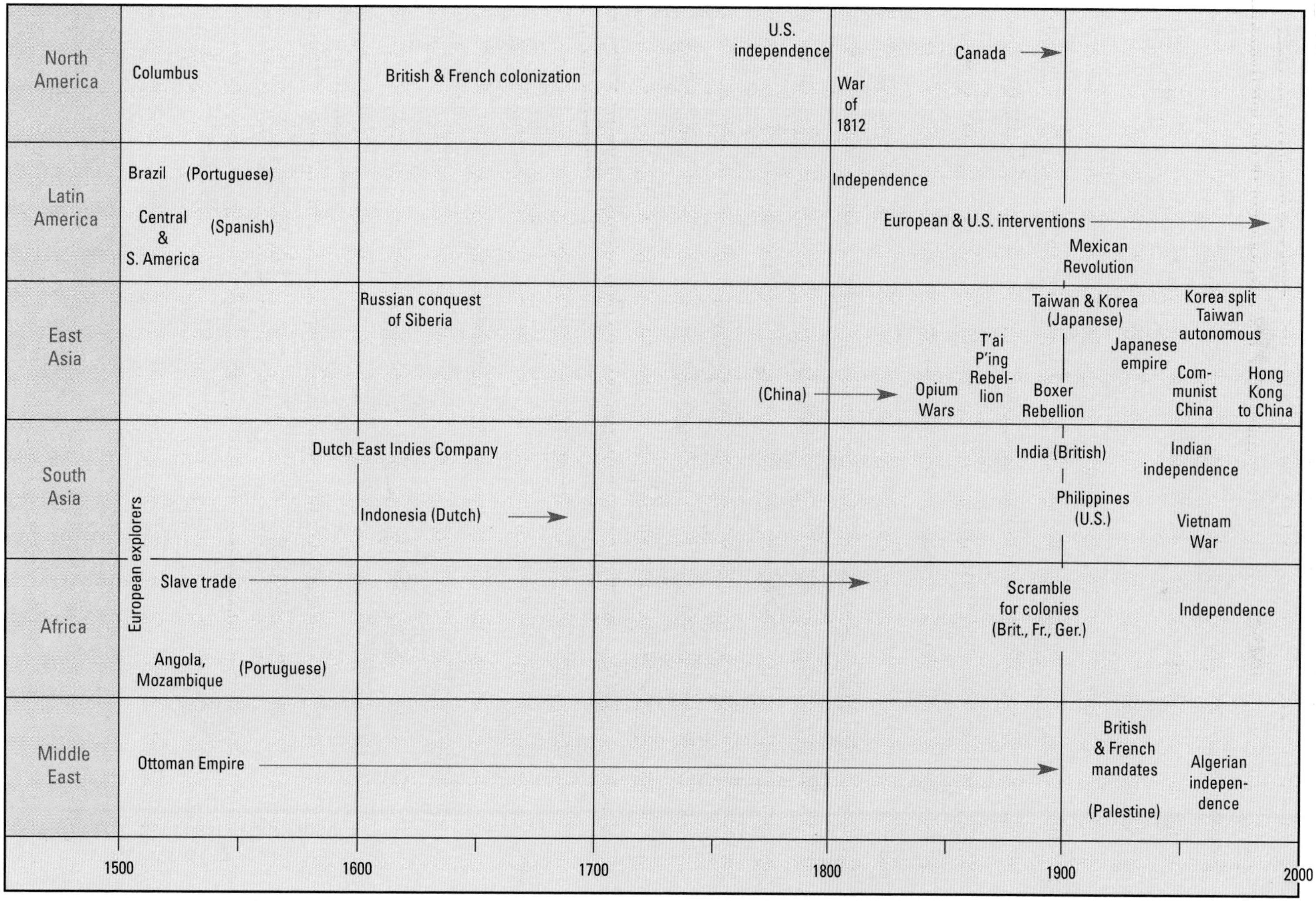

	1500	1600	1700	1800	1900	2000
North America	Columbus	British & French colonization		U.S. independence / War of 1812	Canada →	
Latin America	Brazil (Portuguese) / Central & S. America (Spanish)			Independence	European & U.S. interventions / Mexican Revolution →	
East Asia		Russian conquest of Siberia		(China)	Opium Wars / T'ai P'ing Rebellion / Boxer Rebellion / Taiwan & Korea (Japanese) / Japanese empire / Korea split / Taiwan autonomous / Communist China / Hong Kong to China	
South Asia		Dutch East Indies Company / Indonesia (Dutch) →			India (British) / Philippines (U.S.) / Indian independence / Vietnam War	
Africa	Slave trade / Angola, Mozambique (Portuguese)				Scramble for colonies (Brit., Fr., Ger.) / Independence	
Middle East	Ottoman Empire				British & French mandates (Palestine) / Algerian independence	

European explorers

FIGURE 12.7 Conquest of the World

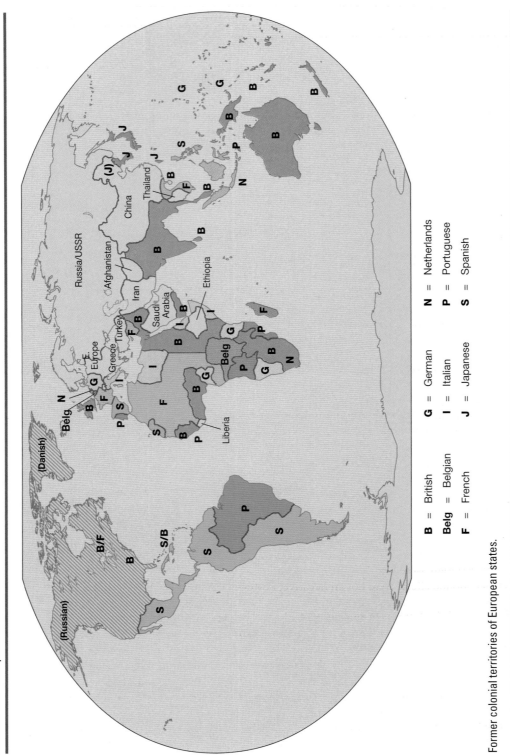

B = British

Belg = Belgian

F = French

G = German

I = Italian

J = Japanese

N = Netherlands

P = Portuguese

S = Spanish

Former colonial territories of European states.

In the 20th century, the world regions formerly dominated by Europe gained independence, with their own sovereign states participating in the international system. Independence came earlier in the Americas (around 1800). In Latin America, most of the 19th century was absorbed with wars, border changes, the rise and fall of dictatorships and republics, a chronic foreign debt problem, revolutions, and recurrent military incursions by European powers and the United States to recover debts.

In the wave of decolonization after World War II, it was not local colonists (as in the Americas) but indigenous populations in Asia and Africa who won independence. Decolonization continued through the mid-1970s until almost no European colonies remained. Most of the newly independent states have faced tremendous challenges and difficulties in the postcolonial era because of their colonial histories.

Effects of Colonialism

For most states in the global South, the history of having been colonized by Europeans is central to their national identity, foreign policy, and place in the world. For these states—and especially for those within them who favor socialist perspectives—international relations revolves around their asymmetrical power relationships with industrialized states. (Capitalist perspectives tend to pay less attention to history and to focus on present-day problems in the South such as unbalanced economies, unskilled workforces, and corrupt governments.)

Being colonized has a devastating effect on a people and culture. Foreigners overrun a territory with force and take it over. They install their own government, staffed by their own nationals. The inhabitants are forced to speak the language of the colonizers, to adopt their cultural practices, and to be educated at schools run under their guidance. The inhabitants are told that they are racially inferior to the foreigners.

White Europeans in third world colonies in Africa and Asia were greatly outnumbered by native inhabitants but maintained power by a combination of force and (more important) psychological conditioning. After generations under colonialism, most native inhabitants either saw white domination as normal or believed that nothing could be done about it. The whites often lived in a bubble world separated from the lives of the local inhabitants.

Colonialism also had negative *economic* implications. The most easily accessible minerals were dug up and shipped away. The best farmland was planted in export crops rather than subsistence crops, and was sometimes overworked and eroded. The infrastructure that was built served the purposes of imperialism rather than the local population—for instance, railroads going straight from mining areas to ports. The education and skills needed to run the economy were largely limited to whites.

The economic effects were not all negative, however. Colonialism often fostered local economic accumulation (although controlled by whites). Cities grew. Mines were dug and farms established. It was in the colonial administration's interest to foster local cycles of capital accumulation. Much of the infrastructure that exists today in many third world countries was created by colonizers. In some cases (though not all), colonization combined disparate communities into a cohesive political unit with a common religion, language, and culture, thus creating more opportunities for economic accumulation. In some cases, the local political cultures replaced by colonialism were themselves oppressive to the majority of the people.

Wherever there were colonizers, there were anticolonial movements. Independence movements throughout Africa and Asia gained momentum during and after World War II,

FIGURE 12.8 Areas of White Minority Rule in Africa, 1952–1994

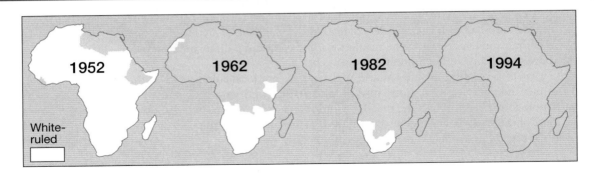

Formal colonialism was swept away over 40 years. However, postcolonial dependency lingers on in many former colonies.
Source: Adapted from Andrew Boyd, *An Atlas of World Affairs.* 9th ed. NY: Routledge, 1992, p. 91.

when the European powers were weakened. Through the 1960s, a wave of successful independence movements swept from one country to the next, as people stopped accepting imperialism as normal or inevitable. Within a few decades, nearly all of Africa overthrew white rule (see Figure 12.8).

Although many third world countries gained independence around the same time, the methods by which they did so varied. In India, the most important colony of the largest empire (Britain), Gandhi led a movement based on nonviolent resistance to British rule (see p. 110). However, nonviolence broke down in the subsequent Hindu-Muslim civil war, which split India into two states—India mostly with Hindus, and Pakistan (including what is now Bangladesh) mostly with Muslims.

Some colonies—for example, Algeria and Vietnam—won independence through warfare to oust their European masters; others won it peacefully by negotiating a transfer of power with weary Europeans. In Algeria, France abandoned its colonial claims in 1962 only after fighting a bitter guerrilla war. Some colonial liberation movements fought guerrilla wars based on communist ideology. The Viet Minh, for instance, defeated the French occupiers in 1954 and established communist rule in all of Vietnam by 1975. The Soviet Union supported many such movements, and the United States opposed them. But in most cases the appeal of liberation movements was the general theme of anticolonialism rather than communist ideology.

Across the various methods and ideologies of liberation movements in the global South, one common feature was reliance on nationalism for strong popular support. Nationalism was only one idea that these movements took from Europe and used to undermine European control; others included democracy, freedom, progress, and Marxism. Leaders of liberation movements often had gone to European universities. Under European control many states also developed infrastructures, educational and religious institutions, health care, and military forces based on the European model. Europe's conquest of the global South thus contributed tools to undo their conquest.[41]

---

[41] Barraclough, Geoffrey. *An Introduction to Contemporary History.* Chap. 6. Penguin, 1964.

Postcolonial Dependency

If imperialism concentrated the accumulation of wealth in the core and drained economic surplus from the periphery, one might expect that accumulation in the global South would take off once colonialism was overthrown. Generally, however, this was not the case. A few states, such as Singapore, have accumulated capital successfully since becoming independent. But others, including many African states, seem to be going backward, with little new capital accumulating to replace the old colonial infrastructure. Most former colonies are making only slow progress in accumulation. Political independence has not been a cure-all for poor countries.

One reason for these problems is that under colonialism, the training and experience needed to manage the economy were often limited to white Europeans, leaving a huge gap in technical and administrative skills after independence.

Another problem faced by newly independent states was that as colonies, their economies had been narrowly developed to serve the needs of the European home country. Many of these economies rested on the export of one or two products. For Zambia, it was copper ore; for El Salvador, coffee; for Botswana, diamonds. Such a narrow export economy would seem well suited to use the state's comparative advantage to specialize in one niche of the world economy. But it leaves the state vulnerable to price fluctuations on world markets (see the "resource curse" on p. 443). The liberal free trade regime based around the WTO corrected only partially for the North's superior bargaining position in North-South trade. And the WTO has allowed agriculture (exported by the periphery) to remain protected in core states, while promoting liberalization of trade in manufactured goods exported by the core (see p. 297).

It is not easy to restructure an economy away from the export of a few commodities. Nor do state leaders generally want to do so, because the leaders benefit from the imports that can be bought with hard currency (including weapons). In any case, coffee plantations and copper mines take time and capital to create, and they represent capital accumulation—they cannot just be abandoned. In addition, local inhabitants' skills and training are likely to be concentrated in the existing industries. Furthermore, infrastructure such as railroads most likely was set up to serve the export economy. For instance, in Angola and Namibia the major railroads, built in colonial times, lead from mining or plantation districts to ports (see Figure 12.9).

The newly independent states inherited borders that were drawn in European capitals by foreign officers looking at maps. As a result, especially in Africa, the internal rivalries of ethnic groups and regions made it very difficult for the new states to implement coherent economic plans. In a number of cases, ethnic conflicts within former colonies led to civil wars, which halted or reversed capital accumulation.

Finally, governments of many postcolonial states did not function very effectively, creating another obstacle to accumulation. In some cases, corruption became much worse after independence (see "Corruption" on pp. 475–476). In other cases, governments tried to impose central control and planning on their national economy, based on nationalism, mercantilism, or socialism.

In sum, liberation from colonial control did not change underlying economic realities. The main trading partners of newly independent countries were usually their former colonial masters. The main products were usually those developed under colonialism. The administrative units and territorial borders were those created by Europeans. The state continued to occupy the same peripheral position in the world-system after independence as it had before. And in some cases it continued to rely on its former colonizer for security.

For these reasons, the period after independence is sometimes called **neocolonialism**—the continuation of colonial exploitation without formal political control (see pp. 61–63).

FIGURE 12.9 Borders, Railroads, and Resources in Angola and Namibia

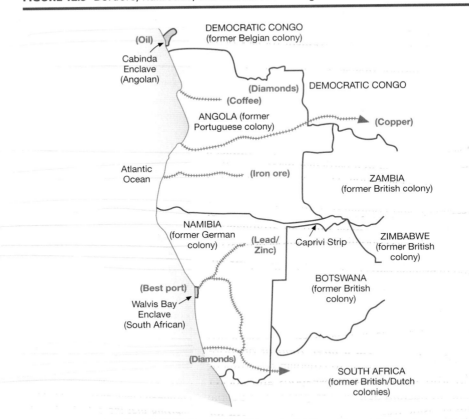

Despite the independence of Angola and Namibia, colonial times shaped the borders and infrastructure in the region.

This concept also covers the relationship of the global South with the United States, which (with a few exceptions) was not a formal colonizer. And it covers the North-South international relations of Latin American states, independent for almost two centuries.

Dependency Marxist IR scholars have developed **dependency theory** to explain the lack of accumulation in the third world.[42] These scholars define dependency as a situation in which accumulation of capital cannot sustain itself internally. A dependent country must borrow capital to produce goods; its debt payments then reduce the accumulation of surplus. (Dependency is a form of international interdependence—rich regions need to loan out their money just as poor ones need to borrow it—but it is an interdependence with an extreme power imbalance.)

---

[42] Cardoso, Fernando Henrique, and Enzo Faletto. *Dependency and Development in Latin America.* Translated by Marjory Mattingly Urquidi. California, 1979. Evans, Peter. *Dependent Development: The Alliance of Multinational, State, and Local Capital in Brazil.* Princeton, 1979. Foweraker, Joe, and Todd Landman. Economic Development and Democracy Revisited: Why Dependency Theory Is Not Yet Dead. *Democratization* 11 (1), 2004: 1–20.

Dependency theorists focus not on the overall structure of the world-system (center and periphery) but on how a peripheral state's own internal class relationships play out. The development (or lack of development) of a third world state depends on its local conditions and history, though it is affected by the same global conditions as other countries located in the periphery.

One historically important configuration of dependency is the **enclave economy**, in which foreign capital is invested in a third world country to extract a particular raw material in a particular place—usually a mine, oil well, or plantation. Here the cycle of capital accumulation is primed by foreign capital, is fueled by local resources, and completes itself with the sale of products on foreign markets. Such an arrangement leaves the country's economy largely untouched except to give employment to a few local workers in the enclave and to provide taxes to the state (or line the pockets of some state officials). Over time, it leaves the state's natural resources depleted.

Angola's Cabinda province, located up the coast from the rest of Angola, is a classic enclave economy. Chevron pumps oil from a large field of offshore wells, with the money going to Angolan government officials, who spend some on weapons and pocket large sums in flagrant acts of corruption. The people of Cabinda, aside from a tiny number who work for Chevron, live in poverty with crumbling infrastructure, few government services, few jobs, and recurrent banditry by unpaid soldiers. Inside the Chevron compound, however, U.S. workers drive on paved roads, eat American food, and enjoy an 18-hole golf course. They spend 28 days there, working 12-hour days, then fly back to the United States for 28 days of rest. Traveling the 12 miles to the airport by helicopter, the Americans rarely leave the fenced compound, which Chevron reportedly surrounded with land mines.

MY DOLL, MY SELF

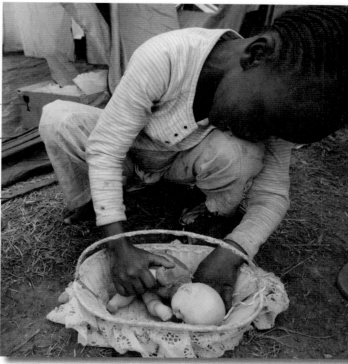

European colonialism worldwide promoted values and norms implying that the colonizer's culture was superior to the indigenous culture. Lingering effects remain in postcolonial societies. This girl displaced by violence in Kenya, a former British colony, plays with a light-skinned doll, 2008.

A different historical pattern is that of nationally controlled production, in which a local capitalist class controls a cycle of accumulation based on producing export products. The cycle still depends on foreign markets, but the profits accrue to the local capitalists, building up a powerful class of rich owners within the country. This class—the local bourgeoisie—tends to behave in a manner consistent with the interests of rich industrialized countries (on whose markets the class depends). They are not unpatriotic, but their interests tend to converge with those of foreign capitalists. For instance, they want to keep local wages as low as possible, to produce cheap goods for consumers in the rich countries. The local capitalists, in alliance with political authorities, enforce a system of domination that ultimately serves the foreign capitalists. This is another form of dependency.

After World War II, a third form of dependency became more common—penetration of national economies by MNCs. Here the capital is provided externally (as with enclaves), but production is for local markets. For instance, a GM factory in Brazil produces cars mostly for sale within Brazil. To create local markets for such manufactured goods, income must be concentrated enough to create a middle class that can afford such goods. This sharpens disparities of income within the country (most people remain poor). The cycle of accumulation depends on local labor and local markets, but because MNCs provide the foreign capital, they take out much of the surplus as profit.

According to dependency theory, the particular constellation of forces within a country determines which coalitions form among the state, the military, big landowners, local capitalists, foreign capitalists (MNCs), foreign governments, and middle classes such as professionals and skilled industrial workers. On the other side, peasants, workers, and sometimes students and the church form alliances to work for more equal distribution of income, human and political rights, and local control of the economy. These class alliances and the resulting social relationships are not determined by any general rule but by concrete conditions and historical developments in each country. Like other Marxist theories, dependency theory pays special attention to class struggle as a source of social change.

Some people think that under conditions of dependency, economic development is almost impossible. Others think that development is possible under dependency, despite certain difficulties. We will return to these possibilities in Chapter 13.

Revolutionary Movements

Poverty and lack of access to basic human needs are prime causes of revolutions, especially when poor people see others living much better.[43] Most revolutionary movements espouse egalitarian ideals—a more equal distribution of wealth and power.

During the Cold War years, the classic revolutionary movement was a communist insurgency based in the countryside. Usually "U.S. imperialism" or another such foreign presence was viewed as a friend of the state and an enemy of the revolution. Sometimes the U.S. government gave direct military aid to governments facing such revolutionary movements. In a number of countries, U.S. military advisors and even combat troops were sent to help put down the revolutions and keep communists from taking power. For its part, the Soviet Union often armed and helped train the revolutionaries. Thus, the domestic politics of poor countries became intertwined with great power politics in the context of the North-South gap. In reality, many of these governments and revolutions had little to do with global communism, capitalism, or imperialism. They were local power struggles—sometimes between the haves and the have-nots, sometimes between rival ethnic groups—into which great powers were drawn.[44]

By the early 1990s, these communist revolutions seemed to have played themselves out—winning in some places, losing in others, and coming to a stalemate in a few countries. The end of the Cold War removed superpower support from both sides, and the collapse of the Soviet Union and the adoption of capitalist-oriented economic reforms in China undercut the ideological appeal of communist revolutions. Several Marxist revolutionary movements linger, however, including in Colombia, Peru, and

---

[43] Skocpol, Theda. *Social Revolutions in the Modern World*. Cambridge, 1994. Skocpol, Theda. *States and Social Revolutions: A Comparative Analysis of France, Russia, and China*. Cambridge, 1979. Gurr, Ted Robert. *Why Men Rebel*. Princeton, 1970. McAdam, Doug, Sidney Tarrow, and Charles Tilly. *Dynamics of Contention*. Cambridge, 2001. Goodwin, Jeff. *No Other Way Out: States and Revolutionary Movements, 1945–1991*. Cambridge, 2008.
[44] McClintock, Cynthia. *Revolutionary Movements in Latin America*. U.S. Institute of Peace, 1998. Dominguez, Jorge. *To Make a World Safe for Revolution: Cuba's Foreign Policy*. Harvard, 1989.

India.[45] In Nepal, Maoist rebels fought for a decade until a 2006 peace agreement, then won elections and became the country's governing party.

In foreign policy, revolutionary governments often start out planning radically different relationships with neighbors and great powers. The pattern of international alliances often shifts after revolutions, as when a Cold War client of one superpower shifted to the other after a change of government. But the new government usually discovers that, once it holds power, it has the same interest as other states in promoting national sovereignty and territorial integrity. The rules of the international system now work for the revolutionaries instead of against them, once they control a state. Their state also has the same geographical location as before, the same historical conflicts with its neighbors, and the same ethnic ties. So it is not unusual over time to find similar foreign policies emanating from a revolutionary government as from its predecessor. Thus, although revolutions create short-term shifts in foreign policy, over the longer term the rules of international relations have tended to triumph over revolutionary challenges.

RARE SUCCESS

South Africa's former president, Nelson Mandela (here shown at a march of the African National Congress in Boipatong, 1992), had unusual success in making the difficult transition from revolutionary to state leader, and then leaving office peacefully. He had the advantage of coming to power nonviolently (relatively speaking), enjoying tremendous world respect, and leading a country that is relatively prosperous (though with huge inequalities) in a very poor continent.

Overall, North-South relations show how difficult it has become to separate political economy from international security. The original political relations contained in European imperialism led to economic conditions in the South—such as high population growth, urbanization, and concentrations of wealth—that in turn led to political movements for independence, and later to revolutions. The various aspects of the North-South gap considered in this chapter—including hunger, refugees, and the structure of commodity exports—all contain both economic and political-military aspects.

Marxists emphasize that the economic realities of accumulation, or the lack of accumulation, lie beneath all the political struggles related to global North-South relations. But Marxists' strategies—from armed revolutions to self-reliance to state ownership—have not been successful at changing those realities. Chapter 13 therefore turns in depth to the question of how economies in the South can develop the accumulation process and what role the North can play in that process.

✓•⌈**Study** and **Review** the **Post-Test & Chapter Exam** at **mypoliscilab.com**

[45] Stavig, Ward. *The World of Túpac Amaru: Conflict, Community, and Identity in Colonial Peru.* Nebraska, 1999. Gorriti, Ellenbogen Gustavo. *The Shining Path: A History of the Millenarian War in Peru.* North Carolina, 1999.

CHAPTER REVIEW

SUMMARY

- Most of the world's people live in poverty in the global South. About a billion live in extreme poverty, without access to adequate food, water, and other necessities.

- Wealth accumulation (including the demographic transition discussed in Chapter 11) depends on the meeting of basic human needs such as access to food, water, education, shelter, and health care. Third world states have had mixed success in meeting their populations' basic needs.

- Hunger and malnutrition are rampant in the global South. The most important cause is the displacement of subsistence farmers from their land because of war, population pressures, and the conversion of agricultural land into plantations growing export crops to earn hard currency.

- Urbanization is increasing throughout the global South as more people move from the countryside to cities. Huge slums have grown in the cities as poor people arrive and cannot find jobs.

- Women's central role in the process of accumulation has begun to be recognized. International agencies based in the North have started taking women's contributions into account in analyzing economic development in the South.

- Poverty in the South has led huge numbers of migrants to seek a better life in the North; this has created international political frictions. War and repression in the South have generated millions of refugees seeking safe haven. Under international law and norms, states are generally supposed to accept refugees but do not have to accept migrants.

- War has been a major impediment to meeting basic needs, and to wealth accumulation generally, in poor countries. Almost all the wars of the past 50 years have been fought in the global South.

- Moving from poverty to well-being requires the accumulation of capital. Capitalism and socialism take different views on this process. Capitalism emphasizes overall growth with considerable concentration of wealth, whereas socialism emphasizes a fair distribution of wealth.

- Most states have a mixed economy with some degree of private ownership of capital and some degree of state ownership. However, state ownership has not been very successful in accumulating wealth. Consequently, many states have been selling off state-owned enterprises (privatization), especially in Russia and Eastern Europe.

- Since Lenin's time, many Marxists have attributed poverty in the South to the concentration of wealth in the North. In this theory, capitalists in the North exploit the South economically and use the wealth thus generated to buy off workers in the North. Revolutions thus occur in the South and are ultimately directed against the North.

- IR scholars in the world-system school argue that the North is a core region specializing in producing manufactured goods and the South is a periphery specializing in extracting raw materials through agriculture and mining. Between these are semiperiphery states with light manufacturing.

- Various world civilizations were conquered by Europeans over several centuries and forcefully absorbed into a single global international system initially centered in Europe. Today's North-South gap traces its roots to the past colonization of the southern world regions by Europe. This colonization occurred at different times in different parts of the world, as did decolonization.

- Because of the negative impact of colonialism on local populations, anticolonial movements arose throughout the global South at various times and using various methods.

These culminated in a wave of successful independence movements after World War II in Asia and Africa. (Latin American states gained independence much earlier.)

- Following independence, third world states were left with legacies of colonialism, including their basic economic infrastructures, that made wealth accumulation difficult in certain ways. These problems still remain in many countries.

- When revolutionaries succeed in taking power, they usually change their state's foreign policy. Over time, however, old national interests and strategies tend to reappear. After several decades in power, revolutionaries usually become conservative and in particular come to support the norms and rules of the international system (which are favorable to them as state leaders).

KEY TERMS

less-developed countries (LDCs)   425
developing countries   425
Millennium Development Goals   425
basic human needs   427
malnutrition   431

subsistence farming   432
cash crop   432
urbanization   432
land reform   433
migration   434
refugees   435
remittances   436

economic surplus   441
world-system   441
resource curse   443
imperialism   443
neocolonialism   451
dependency theory   452
enclave economy   453

CRITICAL THINKING QUESTIONS

1. In what ways does the North American Free Trade Agreement (NAFTA), discussed in Chapter 8, reflect the overall state of North-South relations as described in this chapter? How would capitalism and socialism as general approaches to the theory of wealth accumulation differ in their views of the agreement?

2. The zones of the world economy as described by world-system theorists treat the North as a core and the South as largely a periphery. Can you think of exceptions to this formula? How seriously do such exceptions challenge the overall concept as applied to North-South relations generally? Be specific about why the exceptions do not fit the theory.

3. In North and South America, independence from colonialism was won by descendants of the colonists themselves. In Asia and Africa, it was won mainly by local populations with a long history of their own. How do you think this aspect has affected the postcolonial history of one or more specific countries from each group?

4. Suppose you lived in an extremely poor slum in the global South and had no money or job—but retained all the knowledge you now have. What strategies would you adopt for your own survival and well-being? What strategies would you reject as infeasible? Would you adopt or reject the idea of revolution? Why?

5. Currently incomes in the global North are five times as high, per person, as in the global South. If you could magically redistribute the world's income so that everyone had equal income ($10,000 per person per year), would you? What effects would such a change make in the North and South?

Immigration Reform: Should Illegal Immigrants in the United States Have a Path to Citizenship?

Overview

The movement of people across borders is one of the important issues that blends domestic politics and international relations. Although much of the debate is couched in terms of immigrants' (and migrants') impact on the economy of the host state, a variety of international factors shape the incentives of individuals to migrate, including global economic conditions, political conditions in neighboring states, and the status of military conflicts within and between states.

Nearly every country in the world engages in debates over immigration. In part, these issues are nettlesome because they combine important elements of economics (will immigrants drive down wages or take jobs?) with elements of national identity (who are we as a country and who will we be in the future?). Immigration policy must balance empathy for those abroad with a responsibility for those already here. Whether the debate is over war refugees in Africa, economic immigrants in Europe, or victims of natural disasters in Latin America, immigration policy is always a matter of intense debate.

The debate over immigration in the United States is no exception. The question of immigration policy has become one of extremely divided opinions in the United States—opinions that cross traditional ideological and political party lines. Particularly controversial is the idea of granting a way for immigrants currently in the United States illegally to earn a way to become citizens, giving them rights to vote, to education, and to social programs. Should the U.S. government provide a way for these illegal immigrants to become American citizens?

ARGUMENT 1

The U.S. Government Should Provide a Path to Citizenship for Illegal Immigrants

Legalizing illegal immigrants will lead to increases in tax revenue for governments. Because illegal immigrants often do not pay income taxes, they are a large untapped source of tax revenue. Many of these immigrants use social services, such as education, so allowing them to earn citizenship will allow them to "pay" for these services through taxes.

Remittances will help development in the immigrants' home countries. Workers who earn money inside the United States often send significant portions back to their home countries. This money helps to stabilize home countries economically, providing opportunities for family members and improving their quality of life.

Illegal immigrants are essential to the U.S. workforce. Absent immigration, the population of the United States is declining. Without the presence of these working immigrants (legal and illegal), some industries (agriculture and construction in particular) would experience labor shortages, driving up prices for all Americans.

The U.S. Government Should Not Provide a Path to Citizenship for Illegal Immigrants

Granting citizenship awards illegal behavior. There is already a legal path to citizenship that has been taken by millions of Americans. It would be unfair to reward with citizenship those who illegally entered the country after so many Americans had to undergo a long, arduous process to earn their rights.

Illegal immigrants compete for jobs in difficult economic times. During economic downturns, layoffs increase and jobs are harder to come by. Illegal immigrants compete for these scarce jobs. This competition is especially damaging to Americans of lower socioeconomic status, who are already threatened in other ways by the economic downturn.

Increases in immigration resulting from the policy would create security risks. If a path to citizenship encourages surges in future immigration, it will be difficult to keep U.S. borders secure, leading to security risks. In this age of global terrorism, any factor increasing the large numbers of individuals passing across state borders can threaten a state's security.

Questions

- Do you think the U.S. government should provide a way for illegal immigrants to earn their citizenship? Are there other arguments you find convincing in this debate?

- Think about the NAFTA and EU member states. Why do you think the EU has been more willing to open borders to one another? Do you believe the EU will move to close borders in the future? Will NAFTA become more open in the future?

- How much do you feel that the arguments in this debate are influenced by international factors such as the state of the world economy? Do these factors affect the similar debates concerning the rights of immigrants in other countries?

For Further Reading

Givens, Terri E., Gary P. Freeman, and David L. Leal, eds. *Immigration Policy and Security: U.S., European, and Commonwealth Perspectives.* Routledge, 2008.

Cornelius, Wayne A., Philip L. Martin, and James F. Hollified. *Controlling Immigration: A Global Perspective.* 2nd ed. rev. Stanford, 2004.

Ngai, Mae M. *Impossible Subjects: Illegal Aliens and the Making of Modern America.* Princeton, 2005.

Guskin, Jane, and David L. Wilson. *The Politics of Immigration: Questions and Answers.* Monthly Review, 2007.

CHAPTER 13

International Development

Shanghai bullet train, 2007.

Experiences

Chapter 12 discussed the situation in the global South and how it came to be; this chapter takes up the question of what to do about it. **Economic development** refers to the combined processes of capital accumulation, rising per capita incomes (with consequent falling birthrates), increasing skills in the population, adoption of new technological styles, and other related social and economic changes.[1] The most central aspect is the accumulation of capital (with its ongoing wealth-generating potential). The concept of development has a subjective side that cannot be measured statistically—the judgment of whether a certain pattern of wealth creation and distribution is good for a state and its people. But one simple measure of economic development is the per capita GDP—the amount of economic activity per person. This measure was the horizontal axis in Figure 12.1 (p. 426), and change in this measure was on the vertical axis.

By this measure, we can trace the successes and failures of the South as a whole and, more important, its regions and countries. The latter is more important because it contains the seeds of possible lessons and strategies that could build on the South's successes in the future. Most of the global South made progress on economic development in the 1970s, but per capita GDP *decreased* in the 1980s in Latin America, Africa, and the Middle East, with only China growing robustly. In the 1990s, real economic growth returned across much of the South—about 5–6 percent annual growth for the South as a whole, and even higher for China, compared to 2–3 percent in the global North. China stood out among the regions of the South as making rapid progress toward economic development.

In the new century, growth has accelerated in the South and now outpaces the North (see Figure 13.1). This growth has been uneven, however. South Asia joined China in rapid growth of 8–9 percent annually. Because China and South Asia together contain the majority of the population in the global South, this development is very important. This new growth shows that it is possible to rise out of poverty to relative prosperity. South Korea did so, followed by China, and India appears to be starting on the same curve (see Figure 13.2). Even in Africa, according to the World Bank, economies grew by more than 5 percent annually from 2005 to 2007 (led by, but not limited to, oil- and mineral-exporting nations). And although the 2008–2009 global economic crisis threatened the developing world, most states in the global South have emerged more quickly than their wealthy counterparts in the global North.

The Newly Industrializing Countries

Before China took off, a handful of poor states—called the **newly industrializing countries (NICs)**—achieved self-sustaining capital accumulation, with impressive economic growth.[2] These semiperiphery states, which export light manufactured

Read and Listen to **Chapter 13** at **mypoliscilab.com**

Study and **Review** the **Pre-Test & Flashcards** at **mypoliscilab.com**

---

[1] Stiglitz, Joseph, and Gerald Meier. *Frontiers in Development.* Oxford, 2000. Stone, Diane. *Banking on Knowledge: The Genesis of the Global Development Network.* Routledge, 2001. Bates, Robert H. *Prosperity and Violence: The Political Economy of Development.* Norton, 2001. Helpman, Elhanan. *The Mystery of Economic Growth.* Belknap, 2004.

[2] Amsden, Alice. *The Rise of the "Rest": Challenges to the West from Late-Industrializing Economies.* Oxford, 2001. Haggard, Stephan. *Developing Nations and the Politics of Global Integration.* Brookings, 1995.

FIGURE 13.1 Real GDP Growth of Selected Countries, 2010

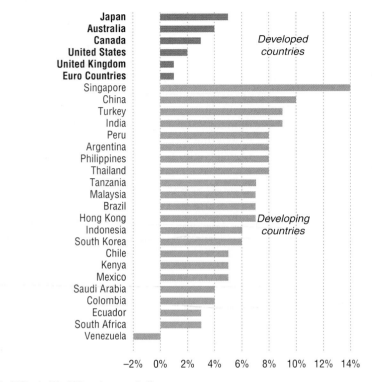

Source: World Bank, *World Development Indicators.*

Watch
the **Video**
**"India's New
Middle Class"**
on **mypoliscilab.com**

Watch
the **Video**
"China's New Rich"
on **mypoliscilab.com**

Explore
the **Simulation**
**"The North-
South Gap:
You Are a
Coffee Farmer"**
on **mypoliscilab.com**

goods, posted strong economic growth in the 1980s and early 1990s (see "The World-System" on pp. 441–443). They suffered a setback in the 1997 Asian financial crisis because growth had been too fast, with overly idealistic loans, speculative investments, and corrupt deals (see pp. 339–341). But the NICs quickly resumed growth and have developed much further and faster than most of the global South.

The most successful NICs are the **"four tigers" or "four dragons"** of East Asia: South Korea, Taiwan, Hong Kong, and Singapore. Each succeeded in developing particular sectors and industries that were competitive on world markets.[3] These sectors and industries can create enough capital accumulation within the country to raise income levels not just among the small elite but across the population more broadly. Scholars do not know whether the NICs are just the lucky few that have moved from the periphery to the semi-periphery of the world-system (see p. 440) or whether their success can eventually be replicated throughout the world.

South Korea, with iron and coal resources, developed competitive steel and automobile industries that export globally, creating a trade surplus (see pp. 286–287). Taiwan

---

[3] Minami, Ryoshin, Kwan S. Kim, and Malcolm Falkus, eds. *Growth, Distribution, and Political Change: Asia and the Wider World.* St. Martin's, 1999. Berger, Mark T. *The Battle for Asia: From Decolonization to Globalization.* RoutledgeCurzon, 2004.

FIGURE 13.2 Per Capita GDP of South Korea, China, India, and Ghana, 1960–2009

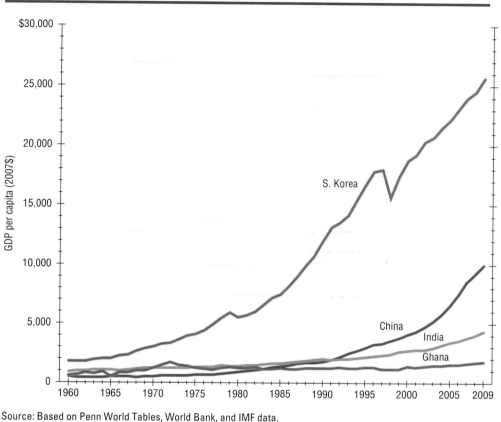

Source: Based on Penn World Tables, World Bank, and IMF data.

also used a strong state industrial policy, specializing in the electronics and computer industries and in other light manufacturing. Hong Kong—controlled by China since 1997—also has world-competitive electronics and other light industries, but its greatest strengths are in banking and trade. Singapore is a trading city located at the tip of the Malaysian peninsula—convenient to the South China Sea, the Indian Ocean, and Australia.

For different reasons, each of these states holds a somewhat unusual political status in the international system. South Korea and Taiwan were hot spots of international conflict that came under the U.S. security umbrella during the Cold War. Both were militarized, authoritarian states intolerant of dissent that later became democratic. U.S. spending in East Asia during the Cold War benefited South Korea and Taiwan. In these cases military conflict did not impede development.

Hong Kong and Singapore have a different political profile. They are both former British colonies. They are more city-states than nation-states, and their cities are trading ports and financial centers. Although not as repressive or as militarized as South Korea and Taiwan during the Cold War era, Hong Kong and Singapore were not democracies either. Hong Kong was ruled by a British governor (and since 1997 by the government in Beijing), and Singapore by a dominant individual.

A TIGER

Singapore is one of the "four tigers" (with Hong Kong, Taiwan, and South Korea). Even after the setback of a 1997 financial crisis, their growth has made them prosperous by the standards of the global South. Other countries are trying to emulate the success of these NICs. But no single, simple lesson applicable to other states emerges from the NICs.

Beyond the four tigers, other Southeast Asian countries have tried, since the 1980s, to follow in their footsteps. These countries include Thailand, Malaysia, and Indonesia. Because their experiences vary, they are discussed later with other Asian economies (see pp. 469–472).

The Chinese Experience

If there was ever doubt that the successes of the NICs could be replicated elsewhere and on a larger scale, China ended those doubts. China has 1.3 billion people, and this size alone makes China's efforts to generate self-sustaining accumulation worthy of study. But China has also had the world's fastest-growing economies over the past two decades.

Between the communist victory of 1949 and the Cultural Revolution of the late 1960s, in the era of Chairman Mao Zedong, Chinese economic policy emphasized national self-sufficiency and communist ideology. The state controlled all economic activity through central planning and state ownership. An "iron rice bowl" policy guaranteed basic food needs to all Chinese citizens (at least in theory).

After Mao died in 1976, China under Deng Xiaoping instituted economic reforms and transformed its southern coastal provinces into *free economic zones* open to foreign investment and run on capitalist principles. Peasants worked their own fields, instead of collective farms, and got rich (by Chinese standards) if they did well. Entrepreneurs started companies, hired workers, and generated profits. Foreign investment flooded into southern China, taking advantage of its location, cheap labor, and relative political stability. Other areas of China gradually opened up to capitalist principles as well. The state required more industries to turn a profit and gave more initiative to managers to run their own companies and spend the profits as they saw fit. Economic growth has been rapid since these policies were instituted. Standards of living have risen substantially.

However, China has also re-created some of the features of capitalism that Mao's revolutionaries had overturned. New class disparities emerged, with rich entrepreneurs driving fancy imported cars while poor workers found themselves unemployed. Unprofitable state-owned industries laid off 10 million workers in the 1990s, with more coming each year. In the countryside, areas bypassed by development still contain 200 million desperately poor Chinese peasants. Social problems such as prostitution returned, as did economic problems such as inflation (since largely tamed). Most frustrating for ordinary Chinese is the widespread official corruption accompanying the get-rich atmosphere.

Popular resentment over such problems as inflation and corruption led industrial workers and even government officials to join students in antigovernment protests at Beijing's

Tiananmen Square in 1989. Authorities used the military to violently suppress the protests, killing hundreds of people and signaling the government's determination to maintain tight political control while economic reform proceeded. Party leaders have repeatedly reaffirmed this policy of combining economic reform with political orthodoxy, and felt vindicated by subsequent economic performance. China then weathered the 1997 Asian financial crisis despite its widespread problems with bad bank loans, money-losing state industries, and corruption.

MNCs' foreign investments primed rapid growth in Chinese exports—to $250 billion in 2000 and over $1.1 trillion in 2009 (down from 2008 due to the global economic crisis). In the coming years, China is poised to join the United States, Japan, and Germany as a major automobile exporter. China's WTO membership since 2001 is accelerating these trends.

By 2006, with a new generation of Chinese leaders in charge—led by President Hu Jintao—China had continued rapid economic growth (over 10 percent annually) year after year, with the help of large government infrastructure expenditures. Hu's top priority is to address the growing inequality between the country's newly rich strata and the hundreds of millions left in poverty in the countryside or laid off from jobs in state-owned industries in the cities (along with migrants from the countryside who cannot find work in the cities). In rural villages, hundreds of "mass incidents of unrest" took place each day in 2004, ranging from protests to full-scale riots put down by lethal force, as peasants reacted to land seizures, taxes, pollution, and corruption by local officials. The government suppressed news of these protests in mass media and over the Internet.

China's membership in the WTO raises new questions about how the ongoing Chinese opening of its economy to the world can coexist with continued political authoritarianism under communist rule. China's hundreds of millions of new Internet users and cell phone subscribers will be able to communicate with overseas partners, monitor shipments, and follow economic trends globally. They will also be able to bypass government-controlled sources of political information. Some observers expect economic integration in an information era to inexorably open up China's political system and lead to democratization, whereas other experts think that as long as Chinese leaders deliver economic growth, the population will have little appetite for political change.

China's economic success has given it both more prestige in the international system and a more global perspective on international relations far from China's borders. In 2004–2006, President Hu and other Chinese leaders made high-profile visits to resource-rich areas of the global South, notably Africa and Latin America, making large-scale deals for minerals and energy to fuel China's growth, while boosting China's foreign aid to these areas. In 2007, China announced $3 billion in preferential loans to Africa, which, China emphasized, "carry no political conditions" (unlike Western loans, which often demand such policies as respect for human rights or fighting corruption).[4] Several months earlier, China had hosted a meeting for 48 African leaders. China is also a key

CAR CULTURE

China's rapid economic growth has raised incomes dramatically, especially for a growing middle class. These successes followed China's opening to the world economy and adoption of market-oriented reforms. However, as exports slow down in a global recession, China must develop its domestic market and consumer spending rather than relying so heavily on exports to fuel growth. Here, 700,000 Chinese consumers do their part as they mob the Shanghai auto show in 2011, hoping to get in on China's growing infatuation with that ultimate big-ticket consumer item, the automobile.

---

[4] Rotberg, Robert I., ed. *China Into Africa: Trade, Aid and Influence.* Brookings, 2008. Brautigam, Deborah. *The Dragon's Gift: The Real Story of China in Africa.* Oxford, 2009.

member of the Group of 20 (G20) organization. In 2009, the large Western economies announced that the G20 would replace the G8 as the key international body to deal with questions of economic coordination, opening up a potentially new avenue of influence for China. China also has close economic ties with other Asian countries (see Figure 13.3). China's rising international standing is also reflected in the selection of Beijing to host the 2008 Olympics, which were enormously successful.

FIGURE 13.3 China's View of Its Neighborhood

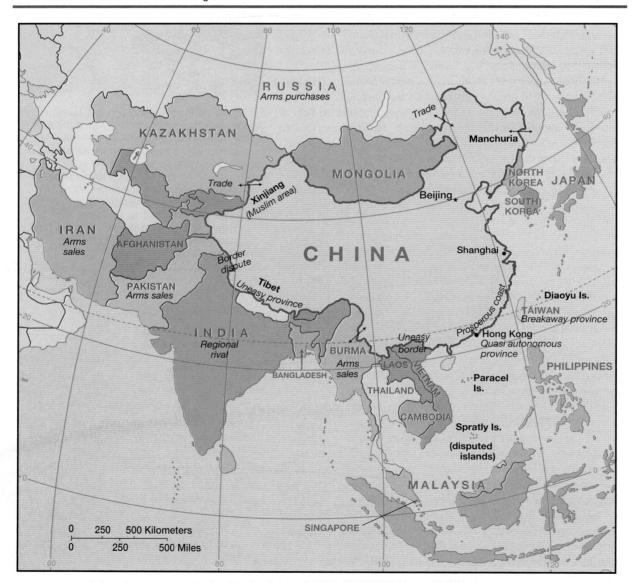

China's continuing growth is the leading example of success of economic development in the global South. China's future path will affect all of Asia.

For years it appeared that China's huge population would supply limitless cheap labor to foreign investors making goods in China. In recent years, however, China's growth has begun to squeeze the available labor force and push wages up somewhat. MNCs have begun to move some light manufacturing to other Asian countries with even cheaper labor, such as Vietnam.

China's economic miracle did hit a bump in the 2008–2009 economic crisis. China's investments in the United States, made with the trade surpluses China had accumulated over the years, lost a substantial fraction of their value in the financial meltdown. Chinese leaders announced a major stimulus package aimed at spurring domestic consumption in China, but this faced problems in the short term, including the cultural problem of getting people with a history of poverty to spend instead of saving, and the economic problem of reorienting an export-driven economy to produce for domestic markets. Yet, despite these dangers and risks, China's economy has forged ahead out of the economic crisis. For example, by mid-2010, Chinese exports to the United States had returned to pre-recession levels.

It is unclear what lessons China's economic success over the past decade holds for the rest of the global South. The shift away from central planning and toward private ownership was clearly a key factor in its success, yet the state continued to play a central role in overseeing the economy (even more than in the NICs). These topics are being debated vigorously as China navigates its new era of rising prosperity and rising expectations, finds its way in the newly turbulent world economy, and as other poor states look to China's experience for lessons.

India Takes Off

India, like China, deserves special attention because of its size and recent robust growth. From 1996 to 2008, India's average annual growth rate exceeded 7 percent. India's decade of success still does not compare to China's nearly three decades, and India's GDP per person is still not much more than half of China's. But India's success has started it toward what could be, in the coming years, a repetition of China's rise out of poverty.

India's economy was for decades based loosely on socialism and state control of large industries but on private capitalism in agriculture and consumer goods. The state subsidizes basic goods and gives special treatment to farmers. Unlike China, India has a democratic government, but a fractious one, with various autonomy movements and ethnic conflicts. India's government has suffered from corruption, although this has improved in recent years.

AT YOUR SERVICE

India has grown rapidly in recent years, using its large, well-educated, English-speaking population to generate export revenues in the service sector—software companies, call centers serving American customers, and professional services in such areas as accounting, architecture, engineering, and medicine. This radiologist in Bangalore, India's technology capital, reads body scans from a U.S. hospital sent via the Internet and discusses the results by phone with the patient's doctor in Connecticut, 2004.

Indian state-owned industries, like those elsewhere, were largely unprofitable. To take an extreme example, 12 years after a fertilizer plant was built, it employed 3,000 workers but had not produced any fertilizer. India's socialist philosophy and widespread poverty also limited the growth of a middle class to support capital accumulation and state revenue: less than 1 percent of the population paid any income tax. Furthermore, bureaucracy in India discouraged foreign investment. In the 1990s, China received many times the foreign investment that India did. The 1991 collapse of the Soviet Union—India's major trading partner—threw India into a severe economic crisis that nearly caused it to default on its international debts. India sought help from the IMF and the World Bank and committed itself to far-reaching economic reforms such as reducing bureaucracy and selling money-losing state-owned industries (see "IMF Conditionality," pp. 480–481). Although reforms were imperfectly carried out, India saw robust economic growth return in the late 1990s. Recent economic growth comes despite continuing corruption and bureaucracy in India's government; Indians joke that the economy grows at night while the government is asleep.

In the era of globalization, India's niche in the globalized world economy is in the service and information sectors. Although the service sector accounts for less than 30 percent of India's labor force (most of which is still in agriculture), it contributes 60 percent of GDP. Whereas South Korea specialized in exporting heavy manufactured goods and China in light manufactured goods, India specializes in exporting information products such as software and telephone call center services. Each country uses its labor force to add value to products that are exported worldwide, especially to the large American market. In India's case the labor force is well educated and speaks English. India also uses its location to advantage by working during the nighttime hours in North America. Software companies can hand off projects daily for the India shift to work on overnight, and American hospitals can send medical notes for overnight transcription. MNCs widely use India's labor force to answer phone calls from around the world, such as technical support calls for the company's products.

India's future success or failure will bear strongly on several competing theories about economic development. In particular, China has had success under a harsh, centralized political system whereas India has a free-wheeling democracy. If India cannot sustain growth, then maybe authoritarian government helps development, and democracy should wait until a later stage (an argument we discuss shortly). If India continues to succeed, however, then clearly authoritarian government is not a precondition.

Figure 13.4 compares China's and India's progress on two key indicators—infant mortality (a good overall measure of public health) and the fertility rate (see pp. 409–413). In both cases, China was able to make dramatic improvements very quickly because of its authoritarian government, whose control (in theory) extended to every village and every bedroom. In the 1950s, China ordered mass campaigns in which citizens exterminated pests and set up sanitation facilities. As a result, in the 1960s China's rates of epidemic diseases such as cholera and plague dropped, and so did the infant mortality rate. In the 1970s, with its heavy-handed one-child policy, China forced down the fertility rate. Women who objected could be forcibly sterilized. Thus, China relied on the dominance principle to force individuals to take actions that were in society's interest. Its successes in improving public health and lowering fertility provided a foundation for China's subsequent economic success, although obviously at a cost to individual freedom.

India, by contrast, has relied more on the identity principle, getting people to change their preferences and *want* to have fewer children and help improve public health. Without a dictatorship to force compliance, India's progress has been slower. However, over time India is moving toward the same results as China, albeit decades later, and doing so without giving up its own national identity as a democracy.

FIGURE 13.4 Comparing Chinese and Indian Development

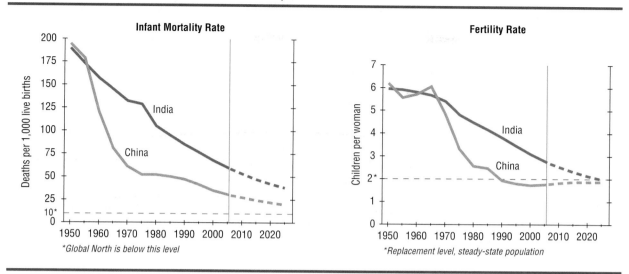

Other Experiments

Other sizable developing countries have pursued various development strategies, with mixed successes and failures. The best results have come from Asia. Figure 13.5 shows the income levels and growth rates of the 16 largest countries by population in the global South. The graph parallels that for world regions in Figure 12.1 (p. 427). Clearly the large countries of the South vary widely in income level. The five highest-income countries (Turkey, Iran, Thailand, Mexico, and Brazil) come from three of the four regions and are growing at 3–6 percent. The fastest-growing countries (India, Vietnam, Ethiopia, and Democratic Congo) at 7–9 percent are at the lower end of the income scale. Clearly China is developing faster than the other 15 large countries of the global South, although all posted solid growth, 5–9 percent for most. (These growth rates declined in 2008 and 2009 as the global economic crisis spread to the developing world, but have since began to climb again.) Clearly, too, regional location makes a difference. The fact that the five regions of the global South can be mapped onto single contiguous zones on this figure shows that whole regions are moving together in distinct patterns.

In Asia, three of the first to try to follow the NICs were Indonesia, Malaysia, and Thailand. Indonesia set a goal in 1969 to become an NIC by 1994. It fell short of that goal, but made some progress in attracting foreign investment. With 250 million people and a GDP per capita near India's, Indonesia's major assets are cheap labor (a minimum wage of less than 50 cents per hour) and exportable natural resources, including oil. But Indonesia has had to import oil since 2004 because of decreasing production. The position of the Philippines resembles that of Indonesia. After navigating the 1997 crisis smoothly, the Philippines got onto a growth curve, currently about 5 percent a year, that is positive but not fast enough to address the widespread poverty in the country.

Malaysia also set out to follow closely in the footsteps of the tigers. Although it exports oil and gas, Malaysia focused its export industry heavily on electronics. It was hit hard by the information sector dot-com crash of 2001–2002, but came back to grow at 5–7 percent per year in 2004–2008. With income per person of $15,000, Malaysia has successfully risen to a middle-income level.

FIGURE 13.5 Largest Countries' Income Levels and Growth Rates, 2010

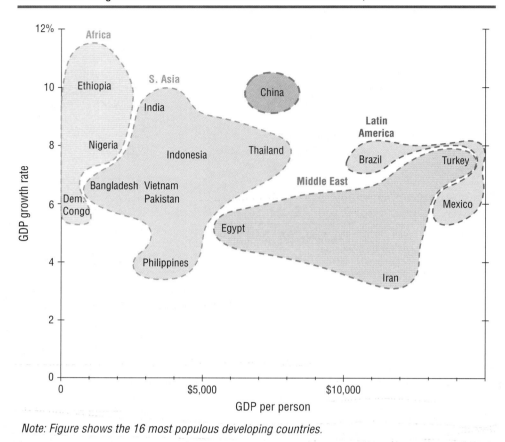

Note: Figure shows the 16 most populous developing countries.

Source: World Bank, *World Development Indicators.*

Thailand was often suggested as a potential "fifth tiger." It received enormous foreign investment in the 1980s (mostly from Japan) and created a sizable middle class. But its growth masked serious problems that put Thailand at the center of the 1997 financial crisis. Thailand recovered and posted strong growth, despite continuing problems with bad loans. But a coup in 2006 and political instability over the past three years has made Thailand somewhat less attractive for foreign investment.

Since 2001 several Southeast Asian countries have also had to address problems of terrorism within their borders, and Indonesia faced simmering ethnic unrest in several islands (although the active secessionist war in Aceh province has ended). These factors held back the economic development of the would-be NICs of Southeast Asia.

Vietnam has found success similar to India's. Vietnam is a communist state following a reform model modeled on China's. Like China, Vietnam has few worries about terrorism and was largely unaffected by the 2008 economic crisis. Vietnam's growth since 1997 has averaged about 7 percent per year. This period of fast growth follows liberalization of the economy, which had been held back by decades of devastating war and centralized communist rule. Vietnam, which particularly exports textiles, joined the WTO in 2007. As with China, Vietnam did a good job at meeting basic human needs at very low average income levels and has reduced extreme poverty despite remaining a poor country.

The large Asian states of Bangladesh and Pakistan are more deeply mired in poverty and have dimmer prospects for capital accumulation in the coming years. They face problems with state bureaucracies, corruption, and political instability. Nonetheless at the end of 2008, Bangladesh successfully emerged from emergency rule with fair elections that saw a huge turnout and brought new hopes for development and the curtailing of corruption. Pakistan, by contrast, continued to struggle with instability in areas bordering Afghanistan. Massive flooding in the summer of 2010 brought further unrest as Islamist groups stepped in to provide relief to flood victims, capitalizing on anger over the government's slow response.

In Latin America, the major countries start from higher income levels but lower growth rates than in China and South Asia. Brazil and Mexico are the largest. Brazil built up a sizable internal market by concentrating income in a growing middle and upper class. However, its cities are still ringed with huge slums filled with desperately poor people. Brazil received $71 billion in IMF loans in 1998 and 2002. The election of a leftist president, Lula da Silva, raised fears that spending on social programs would undermine Brazil's financial position, but instead he reined in spending, brought down inflation, and stabilized Brazil's financial position in 2003, at the short-term cost of economic recession—proving that in Brazil, as in China, socialists can make good capitalists. Brazil hopes its selection to host the 2016 Olympic games will increase its economic and political prestige.

Mexico undertook similar economic reforms in the 1980s. Like Brazil, Mexico had pockets of deep poverty and a sizable foreign debt but, unlike Brazil, had oil to export. Mexico had also enjoyed relative political stability, though corruption was a problem. A reformist president from outside the long-standing ruling party was elected in 2000, and a similarly minded president succeeded him after a contested election in 2006.[5] In the 15 years since NAFTA, despite periodic political and economic upheavals, Mexico has seen neither a breakthrough nor a disaster. However, the country faces a growing problem of drug-related violence that could undercut political and economic stability.

In Africa, Nigeria is the largest country and, with oil to export, should be one of the less impoverished. But at $2,000 per person, its income is quite low, and corruption takes a steady toll on the economy. Nigeria seems to suffer from the "resource curse" (see p. 443). Oil provides 95 percent of export earnings and pays two-thirds of the government's budget. After years of military dictatorship, elections were held in 1999, and Nigeria has enjoyed more political stability in the new century, notwithstanding new ethnic violence in 2001 and armed rebels in the oil-rich Niger delta region. Nigeria reached an agreement with the IMF in 2000 but broke it in 2002 after failing to meet targets. Nigeria's condition remains fragile.

Elsewhere in Africa, matters hardly look better. The next-largest countries, Ethiopia and Democratic Congo, are growing fast but starting from great poverty, with GDPs at or less than $1,000 per person. Democratic Congo was poised to recover from decades of war, but the emergence of violence recently has threatened economic and political progress there. South Africa has a relatively high income ($11,000 per person) but tremendous inequality and high rates of HIV/AIDS.

In the Middle East, Israel has developed economically in an unusual manner. It received sustained infusions of outside capital from several sources—German reparations, U.S. foreign aid, and contributions from Zionists in foreign countries. This outside assistance was particular to the history of German genocide against Jews during World War II and the efforts of Jews worldwide to help build a Jewish state afterward. Few if any developing countries could hope to receive such outside assistance (relative to Israel's small

---

[5] MacLeod, Dag. *Downsizing the State: Privatization and the Limits of Neoliberal Reform in Mexico.* Penn State, 2004.

GLOBALIZE THIS

Globalization is creating winners and losers while sharpening income disparities. Debt, currency crises, IMF conditionality, and the privatization of state-owned enterprises are among the sources of upheaval and poverty in many third world countries. This striking worker in South Africa asks his government to halt cheap Chinese imports, 2005.

size). In common with other NICs, however, Israel had a strong state involvement in key industries and carved out a few niches for itself in world markets (notably in cut diamonds, computer software, and military technology).

The small countries with large oil exports—such as Saudi Arabia, Kuwait, Bahrain, and the United Arab Emirates—have done well economically. But they are in a special class; their experience is not one that others without oil can follow. Iran began to grow robustly and to attract foreign investment after the Iran-Iraq War ended in 1988. Most of the economy is state-controlled, however. In addition, Islamic radicalism creates frictions with Western powers and makes investors wary.

Turkey was somewhat successful in developing its economy without oil revenues. Like South Korea and Taiwan, Turkey was an authoritarian state for many years but has allowed political liberalization since the 1990s. It has developed under a U.S. security umbrella (NATO) and has received considerable U.S. foreign aid. Like Mexico, Turkey is trying to join its richer neighbors—the EU (see pp. 367–369). Turkey suffered recession in 2000–2001 and received a $30 billion IMF bailout. Since 2003, Turkey's economy has grown solidly and its debt position has improved, although Turkey's exports suffered during the recent financial crisis.

Egypt is mired in poverty despite substantial U.S. aid since the late 1970s. The state owns much of the industry, operates the economy centrally, imposes high import tariffs, and provides patronage jobs and subsidized prices in order to maintain political power. Reforms in the 1990s brought economic growth, but remaining problems include high unemployment, a trade deficit, and widespread corruption. After the overthrow of its authoritarian ruler in 2011, Egypt looked forward to restarting its economy, which was seriously disrupted by the instability of the Arab Spring.

Lessons

 **Watch the Video** "Kenya's Developmental Challenge" on mypoliscilab.com

The largest developing countries are following somewhat different strategies with somewhat different results. But several common themes recur. These themes concern trade, the concentration of capital, and corruption.[6]

Import Substitution and Export-Led Growth

Throughout the global South, states are trying to use international trade as the basis of accumulation. For the reasons discussed in Chapter 8, a policy of self-reliance or autarky is at best an extremely slow way to build up wealth. But through the creation of a trade surplus, a state can accumulate hard currency and build industry and infrastructure.

---

[6] Easterly, William R. *The Elusive Quest for Growth: Economists' Adventures and Misadventures in the Tropics.* MIT, 2001.

One way to try to create a trade surplus, used frequently a few decades ago, is through **import substitution**—the development of local industries to produce items that a country had been importing. These industries may receive state subsidies or tariff protection. This might seem to be a good policy for reducing dependency—especially on the former colonial master—while shrinking a trade deficit or building a trade surplus. But it is against the principle of comparative advantage and has not proven effective in most cases. Some scholars think that import substitution is a useful policy only at a very early phase of economic development, after which it becomes counterproductive. Others think it is never useful.

More and more states have shifted to a strategy of **export-led growth**, a strategy used by the NICs. This strategy seeks to develop industries that can compete in specific niches in the world economy. These industries may receive special treatment such as subsidies and protected access to local markets. Exports from these industries generate hard currency and create a favorable trade balance. The state can then spend part of its money on imports of commodities produced more cheaply elsewhere. Such a strategy has risks, especially when a state specializes in the export of a few raw materials (see "Postcolonial Dependency" on pp. 451–454). It leaves poor countries vulnerable to sudden price fluctuations for their exports.

Thus, states have looked to exporting manufactured goods, rather than raw materials, as the key to export-led growth. However, in seeking a niche for manufactured goods, a developing country must compete against industrialized countries with better technology, more educated workforces, and much more capital. It is not enough to subsidize and protect an industry until it grows in size; someday it has to be able to stand its own ground in a competitive world or it will not bring in a trade surplus.

Concentrating Capital for Manufacturing

Manufacturing emerges as a key factor in both export-led growth and self-sustaining industrialization (home production for home markets). To invest in manufacturing, these countries must *concentrate* what surplus their economies produce. Money spent building factories cannot be spent subsidizing food prices or building better schools. Thus the concentration of capital for manufacturing can sharpen disparities in income. Furthermore, because manufacturing industries in poor countries are not immediately competitive on world markets, one common strategy is to first build up the industry with sales to the home market (protected by tariffs and subsidies). But home markets for manufactured goods do not come from poor peasants in the countryside or the unemployed youth in city slums. Rather, wealth must be concentrated in a *middle class* that has the income to buy manufactured goods. These disparities may result in crowds rioting in the streets or guerrillas taking over the countryside.

Capital for manufacturing can come instead from foreign investment or foreign loans, but this reduces the amount of surplus available to the state in the long term. Another way to minimize capital needs is to start out in low-capital industries. These industries can begin generating capital, which can then be used to move into somewhat more technologically demanding and capital-intensive kinds of manufacturing. A favorite starter industry is *textiles*. The industry is fairly labor-intensive, giving an advantage to countries with cheap labor, and does not require huge investments of capital to get started. In 2005, textile tariffs were removed worldwide, so textile exporters in developing countries gained access to Western markets but faced intensified competition from China.

A related approach to capitalization in very poor countries, growing in popularity in recent years, is **microcredit** (or *microlending*). Based on a successful model in Bangladesh (the Grameen Bank, which won the 2006 Nobel Peace Prize, and now operates more than 2,100 branch offices), microcredit uses small loans to poor people, especially women, to support economic self-sufficiency. The borrowers are organized into small groups and

CAPITAL INVESTMENT

Foreign investment, international debt, and domestic inequality all can help concentrate the necessary capital for manufacturing. In recent years, microcredit—very small loans made directly to very poor people—provides a way to use capital more diffusely. These women in Bangladesh bought a cell phone with a loan and rented time on it to villagers in 1997. The Grameen Bank in Bangladesh and its founder won the 2006 Nobel Peace Prize for developing microcredit.

take responsibility for each other's success, including repaying the loans. Repayment rates have been high, and the idea has spread rapidly in several regions. In one popular application, village women used small loans to start businesses renting cell phone time. Rural farmers used the phone time to find out market conditions before making a long trek to sell their products. Thus, bringing the information revolution to isolated villages raised incomes for the farmers and the women alike, and the bank got its loans repaid. Microcredit is now being applied on a macro scale. Tens of millions of families have received loans from thousands of institutions worldwide. Microcredit is the opposite of a trickle-down approach—it injects capital at the bottom of the economic hierarchy. A loan to buy a goat or cell phone may do more good, dollar for dollar, than a loan to build a dam.[7]

Capitalists tend to favor the concentration of capital as a way to spur investment rather than consumption (and to realize economies of scale and specialization). In line with liberalism, capitalists favor development paths that tie developing countries closely to the world economy and international trade. They argue that although such development strategies defer equity, they maximize efficiency. Once a state has a self-sustaining cycle of accumulation under way, it can better redress poverty in the broad population. To do so too early would choke off economic growth, in this view. The same concept applies broadly to the world's development as a whole. From a capitalist perspective, capital accumulation is concentrated in the North. This unequal concentration creates faster economic growth, which ultimately will bring more wealth to the South as well. There is no practical way, in this view, to shift wealth from the North to the South without undermining the free market economics responsible for global economic growth.

Socialists, by contrast, argue that meaningful economic development should improve the position of the whole population and of the poor—sooner rather than later. Thus, socialists tend to advocate a more equitable distribution of wealth; they dispute the idea that greater equity will impede efficiency or slow down economic growth. Rather, by raising incomes among the poorer people, a strategy based on equity will speed up the demographic transition and lead more quickly to sustained accumulation. On a global level, socialists do not see the North-South disparities as justified by global growth benefits. They favor political actions to shift income from North to South in order to foster economic growth in the South. Such redistribution, in this view, would create faster, not slower, global economic growth—as well as more balanced and stable growth.

The capitalist theory that unequal income distributions are related to higher economic growth is only weakly supported by empirical evidence. Many states with fairly equitable income distributions have high growth rates (including South Korea, Taiwan, Singapore, and Hong Kong); many with unequal distributions have grown slowly if at all (Zambia, Argentina, and Ghana). But there are also cases of relatively equitable countries that grow slowly and inequitable ones that grow

[7] Yunus, Muhammad. *Creating a World Without Poverty: Social Business and the Future of Capitalism.* Public Affairs, 2009. Smith, Philip, and Eric Thurman. *A Billion Bootstraps: Microcredit, Barefoot Banking, and the Business Solution for Ending Poverty.* McGraw-Hill, 2007.

rapidly. The World Bank reviewed evidence on the effect of income inequality on economic growth and concluded that inequality holds back growth by wasting human potential. The Bank recommends extending access to health care, education, and jobs—as well as to political power—to the poorest people in societies of the global South in order to spur faster economic growth.[8]

Corruption

Corruption is an important negative factor in economic development in many states. Corruption centers on the government as the central actor in economic development, especially in its international aspects.[9] Through foreign policy, the government mediates the national economy's relationship to the world economy. It regulates the conditions under which MNCs operate in the country. It enforces worker discipline—calling out the army if necessary to break strikes or suppress revolutions. It sets tax rates and wields other macroeconomic levers of control over the economy. And in most developing countries, it owns a sizable stake in major industries—a monopoly in some cases.

State officials decide whether to let an MNC into the country, which MNC to give drilling rights to, and what terms to insist on (leasing fees, percentages of sales, etc.). These are complex deals struck after long negotiations. Corruption adds another player, the corrupt official, to share the benefits. For instance, a foreign oil company can pay off an official to award a favorable contract, and both can profit. In 2003, U.S. prosecutors indicted a Mobil Oil executive for paying $78 million to two senior officials in Kazakhstan—with a kickback of $2 million for the Mobil executive—to secure Mobil's billion-dollar stake in a huge oil field there. He pleaded guilty to tax evasion, received a prison sentence, and had to pay taxes on the $2 million.

Corruption is by no means limited to the global South. But for several reasons, corruption has a deeper effect in poor countries. First, because there is simply less surplus to keep economic growth going, accumulation is fragile. Another difference is that in developing countries dependent on exporting a few products, the revenue arrives in a very concentrated form—large payments in hard currency—presenting a greater opportunity for corruption than in a more diversified economy. This is a major element in the "resource curse" (see p. 443). Furthermore, in developing countries incomes are often so low that corrupt officials are more tempted to accept payments.

Corruption in the global South presents a collective goods problem for states and MNCs in the global North: individually, MNCs

(see p. 443)

CLEAN IT UP!

Corruption is a major impediment to economic development in both rich and poor countries but is more devastating to economies in the global South and to transitional former communist economies. In India, widespread corruption has held back economic development and equality for years. These demonstrators in 2011 are part of a major new movement to turn back corruption in Indian society and government.

---

[8] World Bank. *World Development Report 2006: Equity and Development.* World Bank, 2006.

[9] Uslaner, Eric M. *Corruption, Inequality, and the Rule of Law: The Bulging Pocket Makes the Easy Life.* Cambridge, 2008. Johnston, Michael. *Syndromes of Corruption: Wealth, Power, and Democracy.* Cambridge, 2006. Manion, Melanie F. *Corruption By Design: Building Clean Government in Mainland China and Hong Kong.* Harvard, 2004.

and their home states can profit by clinching a deal with a private payoff, but collectively, the MNCs and states of the North lose money by having to make these payoffs. Therefore, there is an incentive to clamp down on corruption only if other industrialized states do likewise. The United States in recent decades has barred U.S. companies from making corrupt deals abroad, but other countries of the North had not done so until recently. Germany and Canada even allowed their companies to deduct foreign bribes on their taxes.

Transparency helps solve collective goods problems (see pp. 4–5). A Berlin-based NGO called Transparency International pushed successfully for action to stem corruption in international business deals. The group publishes annual surveys showing the countries that business executives consider most corrupt. The top five on the list in 2008 were Somalia, Burma, Iraq, Haiti, and Afghanistan. In 1997, the world's 29 leading industrialized states agreed to forbid their companies from bribing foreign officials. And the Extractive Industries Transparency Initiative, a coalition of states, NGOs, and MNCs launched by Britain in 2002, fights corruption in the especially vulnerable oil, gas, and mineral sectors worldwide by getting companies to release information on payments they make to developing countries.

In Chad in 1999, a consortium led by ExxonMobil and backed by World Bank loans struck a deal to build a $4 billion oil pipeline, with oil revenues going through a Citibank account in London to avoid corruption. Chad promised to use 72 percent of the money to reduce poverty. But in 2005, as the oil money flowed in, Chad's government—under attack by rebels based in Sudan—pulled out of the deal to use the money for its military, and the World Bank suspended its loans.

North-South Capital Flows

● Watch
the **Video**
"Fair Trade Coffee"
on mypoliscilab.com

Capital from the global North moves to the South and potentially spurs growth there in several forms—foreign investment, debt, and foreign aid. The rest of this chapter discusses these capital flows from North to South.

Foreign Investment

Poor countries have little money available to invest in new factories, farms, mines, or oil wells. Foreign investment—investment in such capital goods by foreigners (most often MNCs)—is one way to get accumulation started (see "Foreign Direct Investment" on pp. 343–345). Foreign investment has been crucial to the success of China and other Asian developing countries. Overall, private capital flows to the global South were nearly $600 billion in 2008—six times the amount given in official development assistance.[10]

Foreigners who invest in a country then own the facilities; the investor by virtue of its ownership can control decisions about how many people to employ, whether to expand or shut down, what products to make, and how to market them. Also, the foreign investor can usually take the profits from the operation out of the country (repatriation of profits). However, the host government can share in the wealth by charging fees and taxes, or by leasing land or drilling rights (see "Host and Home Government Relations" on pp. 345–349).

Because of past colonial experiences, many governments in the global South have feared the loss of control that comes with foreign investments by MNCs. Sometimes the presence of MNCs was associated with the painful process of concentrating capital and

---

[10] World Bank data.

the sharpening of class disparities in the host state. Although such fears remain, they are counterbalanced by the ability of foreign investors to infuse capital and generate more surplus. By the 1980s and 1990s, as models based on autarky or state ownership were discredited and the NICs gained success, many poor states rushed to embrace foreign investment. China has been the most successful of these by far.

One way in which states have sought to soften the loss of control is through *joint ventures,* companies owned partly by a foreign MNC and partly by a local firm or the host government itself. Sometimes foreign ownership in joint ventures is limited to some percentage (often 49 percent), to ensure that ultimate control rests with the host country. The percentage of ownership is usually proportional to the amount of capital invested; if a host government wants more control, it must put up more of the money. Joint ventures work well for MNCs because they help ensure the host government's cooperation in reducing bureaucratic hassles and ensuring success (by giving the host government a direct stake in the outcome).

MNCs invest in a country because of some advantage of doing business there. In some cases, it is the presence of natural resources. Sometimes it is cheap labor. Sometimes geographical location is a factor. Some states have better *absorptive capacity* than others—the ability to put investments to productive use—because of more highly developed infrastructure and a higher level of skills among workers or managers. As these are most often middle-income states, the funneling of investments to states with high absorptive capacity tends to sharpen disparities *within* the global South. MNCs also look for a favorable *regulatory environment* in which a host state will facilitate, rather than impede, the MNC's business.

MNC decisions about foreign investment also depend on prospects for *financial stability,* especially for low inflation and stable currency exchange rates. If a currency is not convertible, an MNC will not be able to take profits back to its home state or reinvest them elsewhere. Of equal importance in attracting investment is *political stability* (see p. 348). Banks and MNCs conduct *political risk analyses* to assess the risks of political disturbances in states in which they might invest.

Beyond these financial considerations, a foreign investor producing for local markets wants to know that the host country's economic growth will sustain demand for the goods being produced. Similarly, whether producing for local consumption or export, the MNC wants the local *labor supply*—whether semiskilled labor or just cheap—to be stable. Foreign investors often look to international financial institutions, such as the World Bank and the IMF, and to private analyses, to judge a state's economic stability before investing in it.

FOREIGN INVESTORS

Foreign investment is an important source of capital for economic development in the global South. The relationship of foreign investors and host countries transcends economics and draws in culture, politics, and identity. These Japanese executives visit their Honda factory in India, where Honda has invested $400 million, in 2008.

Technology transfer refers to a poor state's acquisition of technology (knowledge, skills, methods, designs, and specialized equipment) from foreign sources, usually in conjunction with foreign direct investment or similar business operations. A developing country may allow an MNC to produce certain goods in the country under favorable conditions, provided the MNC shares knowledge of the technology and design behind the product. The state may try to get its own citizens into the management and professional workforce of factories or facilities created by foreign investment. Not only can physical capital accumulate in the country, but so can the related technological base for further development. But MNCs may be reluctant to share proprietary technology.

Most poor states seek to build up an educated elite with knowledge and skills to run the national economy. One way to do so is to send students to industrialized states for higher education. This entails some risks, however. Students may enjoy life in the North and fail to return home. The problem of losing skilled workers to richer countries, called the **brain drain**, has impeded economic development in states such as India, Pakistan, and the Philippines (where more nurses emigrated than graduated nursing school in 2000–2004).

North-South Debt

Borrowing money is an alternative to foreign investment as a way of obtaining funds to prime a cycle of economic accumulation. If accumulation succeeds, it produces enough surplus to repay the loan and still make a profit. Borrowing has several advantages. It keeps control in the hands of the state (or other local borrower) and does not impose painful sacrifices on local citizens, at least in the short term.

Debt has disadvantages too. The borrower must service the debt—making regular payments of interest and repaying the principal according to the terms of the loan. *Debt service* is a constant drain on whatever surplus is generated by investment of the money. With foreign direct investment, a money-losing venture is the problem of the foreign MNC; with debt, it is the problem of the borrowing state, which must find the money elsewhere. Often, a debtor must borrow new funds to service old loans, slipping further into debt. Debt service has created a net financial outflow from South to North in recent years, as the South has paid billions more in interest to banks and governments in the North than it has received in foreign investment or development aid.

Failure to make scheduled payments, called a **default**, is considered a drastic action because it destroys lenders' confidence and results in cutoff of future loans.[11] Rather than defaulting, borrowers usually attempt **debt renegotiation**—reworking the terms on which a loan will be repaid. By renegotiating their debts with lenders, borrowers seek a mutually acceptable payment scheme to keep at least some money flowing to the lender. If interest rates have fallen since a loan was first taken out, the borrower can refinance. Borrowers and lenders can also negotiate to restructure a debt by changing the length of the loan (usually to a longer payback period) or the other terms. Occasionally state-to-state loans are written off altogether—forgiven—for political reasons, as happened with U.S. loans to Egypt after the Gulf War.

North-South debt encompasses several types of lending relationships, all of which are influenced by international politics. The *borrower* may be a private firm or bank in a developing country, or it may be the government itself. Loans to the government are somewhat more common because lenders consider the government less likely to default than a private borrower. The *lender* may be a private bank or company, or a state (both are important).

---

[11] Tomz, Michael. *Reputation and International Cooperation: Sovereign Debt Across Three Centuries.* Princeton, 2007.

Usually banks are more insistent on receiving timely payments and firmer in renegotiating debts than are states. Some state-to-state loans are made on artificially favorable *concessionary* terms, in effect subsidizing economic development in the borrowing state.

Debt renegotiation has become a perennial occupation of the global South. Such renegotiations are complex international bargaining situations, like international trade or arms control negotiations. If a borrowing government accepts terms that are too burdensome, it may lose popularity at home. But if the borrowing state does not give enough to gain the agreement of the lenders, it might have to default.

For lenders, debt renegotiations involve a collective goods problem: all of them have to agree on the conditions of the renegotiation but each really cares only about getting its own money back. To solve this problem, state creditors meet together periodically as the **Paris Club**, and private creditors as the **London Club**, to work out their terms.

Through such renegotiations and the corresponding write-offs of debts by banks, developing countries have largely avoided defaulting on their debts. However, in 2001, Argentina in effect defaulted. By then, financial institutions had adjusted psychologically to the reality that Argentina could not pay its debt. Indeed, Argentina recovered—its economy growing 9 percent a year since 2001—and in 2005 offered its creditors a take-it-or-leave-it deal for repayment of less than 30 cents on the dollar. Most took it. Still, default is a risky course because of the need for foreign investment and foreign trade to accumulate wealth. Lenders too have generally proven willing to absorb losses rather than push a borrower over the edge and risk financial instability. But in 2008, Ecuador defaulted on its $10 billion in foreign debt, which the leftist president called "immoral and illegitimate."

In 2010–2012, these debt problems jumped to the global North as the euro zone grappled with the heavy indebtedness of some of its poorer members—especially Greece, as well as Portugal, Spain, and Ireland. In a 2011 bailout agreement, bankers holding Greek debt had to accept 50 cents on the dollar; even so, Greek voters expressed anger toward budget cuts required to meet conditions for the bailout.

Despite stabilization, developing countries have not yet solved the debt problem. As shown in Table 13.1, the South owes $3 trillion in foreign debt, and pays more than $1 trillion a year to service it. The debt service (in hard currency) absorbs almost a third of the entire hard-currency export earnings in Latin America—the region most affected. For the entire global South, it is 20 percent of exports.

TABLE 13.1 Debt in the Global South, 2010

Region	Foreign Debt		Annual Debt Service	
	Billion $	% of GDP[a]	Billion $	% of Exports
Latin America	1,000	23%	300	30%
Asia	1,400	17	550	18
Africa	200	21	60	16
Middle East	800	32	200	18
Total "South"	3,400	23	1,100	20

[a]GDP not calculated at purchasing-power parity.

Notes: Regions do not exactly match those used elsewhere in this book. Africa here includes North Africa. Asia includes China.

Source: IMF. *Statistical Appendix to World Economic Outlook,* April 2011.

In recent years, activists and NGOs have called for extensive debt forgiveness for the poorest countries, most of which are in Africa. Critics say such cancellations just put more money in the hands of corrupt, inept governments. But G7 members in 2005 agreed to eliminate all debts owed by 37 very poor countries to the World Bank and IMF—cutting almost in half the poorest countries' estimated $200 billion in debt. The first $40 billion, owed by 18 countries, began to be written off in 2006. Between 2005 and 2009, over $100 billion in debt had been forgiven.

IMF Conditionality

The International Monetary Fund (IMF) and the World Bank have a large supply of capital from their member states (see "The World Bank and the IMF" on pp. 331–333). This capital plays an important role in funding early stages of accumulation in developing countries and in helping them get through short periods of great difficulty. And, as a political entity rather than a bank, the IMF can make funds available on favorable terms.

The IMF scrutinizes developing countries' economic plans and policies, withholding loans until it is satisfied that the right policies are in place. Then it makes loans to help states through the transitional process of implementing the IMF-approved policies. The IMF also sends important signals to private lenders and investors. Its approval of a state's economic plans is a "seal of approval" that bankers and MNCs use to assess the wisdom of investing in that state. Thus, the IMF wields great power to influence the economic policies of developing countries.

An agreement to loan IMF funds on the condition that certain government policies are adopted is called an **IMF conditionality** agreement; implementation of these conditions is referred to as a *structural adjustment program*.[12] Dozens of developing countries have entered into such agreements with the IMF in the past two decades. The terms insisted on by the IMF are usually painful for the citizens (and hence for national politicians). The IMF demands that inflation be brought under control, which requires reducing state spending and closing budget deficits. These measures often spur unemployment and require that subsidies of food and basic goods be reduced or eliminated. Short-term consumption is curtailed in favor of longer-term investment. Surplus must be concentrated to service debt and invest in new capital accumulation. The IMF wants to ensure that money lent to a country is not spent for politically popular but economically unprofitable purposes (such as subsidizing food). It also wants to ensure that inflation does not eat away all progress and that the economy is stable enough to attract investment. In addition, it demands steps to curtail corruption.

Because of the pain inflicted by a conditionality agreement—and to some extent by any debt renegotiation agreement—such agreements are often politically unpopular in the global South.[13] On quite a few occasions, a conditionality agreement has brought rioters into the streets demanding the restoration of subsidies for food, gasoline, and other essential goods. Sometimes governments have backed out of the agreement or have broken their promises under such pressure. Occasionally, governments have been toppled.

---

[12] Peet, Richard. *Unholy Trinity: The IMF, World Bank and WTO.* Zed, 2003. Fischer, Stanley. *IMF Essays in a Time of Crisis: The International Financial System, Stabilization, and Development.* MIT, 2004. Vines, David, and Christopher L. Gilber. *The IMF and Its Critics: Reform of Global Finance Architecture.* Cambridge, 2004.
[13] Haggard, Stephan, and Robert R. Kaufman, eds. *The Politics of Economic Adjustment: International Constraints, Distributive Conflicts, and the State.* Princeton, 1992. Vreeland, James R. *The IMF and Economic Development.* Cambridge, 2003.

In Egypt, where the same word is used for bread and for life, cheap bread is vital to political stability, at least in the government's view. An annual subsidy of $3.5 billion provides a supply of bread at one-third its real cost for Egypt's large and poor population. These costs distort the free market, encouraging Egyptians to eat (and waste) more bread than they otherwise would, driving up the need for imported wheat, and offering widespread opportunities for corruption by diverting subsidized flour or bread to black markets. But when the government tried to raise the price of bread in 1977, street riots forced a reversal. Instead, the government has subtly changed the size and composition of loaves, and in 1996 began secretly mixing cheaper corn flour into state-milled wheat flour.[14]

Of course, these IMF conditions have also proved unpopular in developed countries that needed assistance during the 2008–2009 recession. After receiving a $6 billion rescue package from the IMF, Iceland was forced to make fundamental reforms to its banking sector. Greece, which received over $133 billion from the IMF, agreed to eliminate several paid holidays while cutting all wages of all public workers by 3 percent. This led to massive street protests and numerous strikes by workers.

MIRACLE OF LOAVES

IMF conditionality agreements often call for reducing subsidies for food, transportation, and other basic needs. In Egypt, bread prices are heavily subsidized, forcing the government to use hard currency to import wheat. But public resistance to bread price increases is so strong that the government has not brought itself to cut the subsidy. Here, bread is delivered in Cairo during opposition protests in 2011.

The South in International Economic Regimes

Because of the need for capital and the wealth created by international trade, most states of the global South see their future economic development as resting on a close interconnection with the world economy, not on national autarky or regional economic communities. Thus poor states must play by the rules embedded in international economic regimes (see Chapters 8 and 9).

The WTO trading regime sometimes works against poor states, however, relative to industrialized ones. A free trade regime makes it harder for poor states to protect infant industries in order to build self-sufficient capital accumulation. It forces competition with more technologically advanced states. A poor state can be competitive only in low-wage, low-capital niches—especially those using natural resources that are scarce in the North, such as tropical agriculture, extractive (mining and drilling) industries, and textiles.

Yet just those economic sectors in which poor states have comparative advantages on world markets—agriculture and textiles in particular—were largely excluded from free trade rules for decades (see pp. 294–298). Instead, world trade deals concentrated on free trade in manufactured goods, in which states in the North have comparative advantages. As a result, some developing countries had to open their home markets to foreign products, against which home industries were not competitive, yet see their own export products shut out of foreign markets. Current WTO negotiations are attempting to remedy this inequity, but so far without success.

[14] Slackman, Michael. Bread, the (Subsidized) Stuff of Life in Egypt. *International Herald Tribune*, January 16, 2008.

Another criticism leveled at the WTO centers on the trade dispute system, in which states may bring complaints of unfair trading practices. Such legal disputes can cost millions of dollars to litigate, requiring expensive lawyers and a large staff at WTO headquarters in Geneva. Few states in the global South can afford this legal process, and therefore few use it to help their own industries knock down unfair barriers to trade. Recall that even if a state wins a WTO dispute, it gains only the right to place tariffs on the offending country's goods in an equal amount. For small states, this retaliation can inflict as much damage on their own economies as on the economies of the offending states.

To compensate for these inequities and to help poor states use trade to boost their economic growth, the WTO has a Generalized System of Preferences (see p. 295). These and other measures—such as the Lomé conventions in which EU states relaxed tariffs on goods from the global South—are exceptions to the overall rules of trade, intended to ensure that participation in world trade advances rather than impedes development.[15] Nonetheless, critics claim that poor states are the losers in the overall world trade regime.

Countries in the South have responded in several ways to these problems with world economic regimes. In the 1970s, OPEC shifted the terms of trade for oil—bringing huge amounts of capital into the oil-exporting countries. Some states hoped such successes could be repeated for other commodities, resulting in broad gains for the global South, but this did not occur (see pp. 302–304 and pp. 407–409).

Also in the 1970s, many poor and middle-income states tried to form a broad political coalition to push for restructuring the world economy so as to make North-South economic transactions more favorable to the South. A summit meeting of the nonaligned movement (see pp. 70–71) in 1973 first called for a *New International Economic Order (NIEO)*.[16] Central to the NIEO was a shift in the terms of trade to favor primary commodities relative to manufactured goods. The NIEO proposal also called for the promotion of industrialization in the global South and for increased development assistance from the North. The NIEO never became much more than a rallying cry for the global South, partly because of the South's lack of power and partly because disparities within the South created divergent interests among states there.

Countries in the South continue to pursue proposals to restructure world trade to benefit the South. These efforts now take place mainly through the *UN Conference on Trade and Development (UNCTAD)*, which meets periodically but lacks power to implement major changes in North-South economic relations.[17] Attempts to promote South-South trade (reducing dependence on the North) have proven largely impractical. China sometimes uses the South-South solidarity argument in wooing new friends in Africa. And efforts continue to boost cooperation and solidarity in the global South through a variety of groups such as the nonaligned movement and the UN.[18] Nonetheless, such efforts have done little to change the South's reliance on the North.

[15] Flint, Adrian. *Trade, Poverty, and the Environment: The EU, Cotonou and the African-Caribbean-Pacific Bloc.* Palgrave, 2008.

[16] Hudson, Michael. *Global Fracture: The New International Economic Order.* Pluto, 2005. Murphy, Craig N. *The Emergence of the NIEO Ideology.* Westview, 1984.

[17] Lavelle, Kathryn C. Participating in Governance of Trade: The GATT, UNCTAD, and the WTO. *International Journal of Political Economy* 33 (4), 2003: 28–42.

[18] Page, Sheila. *Regionalism among Developing Countries.* Palgrave, 2000. Folke, Steen, Niels Fold, and Thyge Enevoldsen. *South-South Trade and Development: Manufacturers in the New International Division of Labour.* St. Martin's, 1993. Erisman, H. Michael. *Pursuing Postdependency Politics: South-South Relations in the Caribbean.* Rienner, 1992.

POLICY PERSPECTIVES

Prime Minister of Turkey, Recep Tayyip Erdogan

PROBLEM *How do you balance the demands of domestic actors and international financial institutions?*

BACKGROUND Imagine that you are the prime minister of Turkey. Your economy suffered from the recent global recession but has emerged from that crisis in strong shape. GDP growth was more than 7 percent in 2010. Exports comprise a significant portion of your economy and are diverse: agricultural products, automotive and electronic parts, as well as textiles, are some of your most popular exports.

Your country has undergone extensive privatization over the past decade, as you sold ownership in key industries to private investors. Indeed, most major manufacturing industries in your country are now privately owned, a significant change from 20 years ago. Much of this privatization was encouraged by the International Monetary Fund (IMF) after a significant economic crisis in 2001.

One area of your economy that has not liberalized as fast as the industrial sector is the financial and banking sector. The financial and banking industries are still protected by extensive regulation that limits foreign ownership. These regulations have discouraged foreign direct investment (FDI) from wealthy EU states, the United States, and Japan.

DOMESTIC CONSIDERATIONS You are an incredibly popular prime minister, having recently won an unprecedented third term in office. Much of your popularity, however, is based on the economic success you have engineered. Voters have continued to support your privatization and economic liberalization efforts, mostly because the Turkish economy has remained strong.

Business elites, however, continue to support strong regulation efforts in the finance and banking sector in order to insulate Turkey from international economic crises. These regulations also protect their own advantageous financial positions within the Turkish economy. International investors, however, would like more freedom to invest in these sectors of your economy.

SCENARIO Now imagine that one of the key sources of capital for your economy, the EU, continues to struggle with debt crisis issues in Greece, Spain, Portugal, and Italy. As a result of these EU struggles, FDI to your country declines precipitously. Moreover, exports fall due to declining economic fortunes in your key trading partners in Europe. The economy that bolstered your popularity and international standing is now becoming a major problem for your administration.

One potential solution to your economic problems would be to loosen the regulatory controls in the finance and banking sector. Western observers and the IMF have suggested that such a policy change will provide a much needed injection of capital into your economy, which could lift the Turkish economy out of its current downturn.

CHOOSE YOUR POLICY Do you loosen your investment rules in order to encourage more FDI? Do you risk the domestic political backlash of this move, which would cause key economic supporters to oppose you? Do you expose Turkey to the potential to be subject to additional economic crises? Or do you wait and hope the EU recovery will happen soon and revive your own economic fortunes? Do you keep Turkey isolated from additional capital flows that could help increase economic growth?

Foreign Assistance

Watch
the **Video**
"Disaster
Relief in Haiti"
on **mypoliscilab.com**

Foreign assistance (or *overseas development assistance*) is money or other aid made available to help states speed up economic development or simply meet basic humanitarian needs.[19] It covers a variety of programs—from individual volunteers lending a hand to massive government packages.

Different kinds of development assistance have different purposes, which often overlap. Some are humanitarian, some are political, and others are intended to create future economic advantages for the giver. The state or organization that gives assistance is called a *donor*; the state or organization receiving the aid is the *recipient*. Foreign assistance creates, or extends, a relationship between donor and recipient that is simultaneously political and cultural as well as economic.[20] Foreign assistance can be a form of power in which the donor seeks to influence the recipient, or it can be a form of interdependence in which the donor and recipient create a mutually beneficial exchange. The remainder of this chapter examines the patterns and types of foreign assistance, the politics involved, and the potential impact of foreign assistance.

Patterns of Foreign Assistance

Large amounts of foreign assistance come from governments in the North. Of the roughly $100 billion in governmental foreign assistance provided in 2008, more than 90 percent came from members of the **Development Assistance Committee (DAC)**, consisting of states from Western Europe, North America, and Japan/Pacific. Several oil-exporting Arab countries provide some foreign development assistance, and in 2003, transition economies became a net "exporter" of financial aid. Three-quarters of the DAC countries' government assistance goes directly to governments in the global South as state-to-state **bilateral aid**; the rest goes through the UN or other agencies as **multilateral aid**.

The DAC countries have set themselves a goal to contribute 0.7 percent of their GNPs in foreign aid. But overall, they give less than half this amount. Only Norway, Sweden, Denmark, the Netherlands, and Luxembourg meet the target. In fact, Oxfam International reported that industrialized countries' aid dropped from 0.48 percent of income in 1960–1965 to 0.34 percent in 1980–1985 and then to 0.24 percent in 2003.[21]

The United States gives the lowest percentage of GNP—about two-tenths of 1 percent—of any of the 30 states of the industrialized West that make up the OECD. In total economic aid given ($22 billion), the United States has recently regained the lead over Japan (which cut foreign aid to $12 billion). Germany, Britain, and France each give about $10 billion. U.S. and other decreases brought the world total in foreign assistance down substantially in the 1990s (see Figure 13.6). After the 2001 terrorist attacks, Britain proposed a $50 billion increase in foreign aid, nearly doubling current levels, and the United States raised its aid budget sharply. In 2002, rock star Bono took U.S. treasury secretary Paul O'Neill on a two-week tour through Africa to

---

[19] Crawford, Gordon. *Foreign Aid and Political Reform: A Comparative Analysis of Democracy Assistance and Political Conditionality.* Palgrave, 2001. O'Hanlon, Michael, and Carol Graham. *A Half Penny on the Federal Dollar: The Future of Development Aid.* Brookings, 1997. Lumsdaine, David H. *Moral Vision in International Politics: The Foreign Aid Regime, 1949–1989.* Princeton, 1993.

[20] Ensign, Margee M. *Doing Good or Doing Well? Japan's Foreign Aid Program.* Columbia, 1992.

[21] Oxfam International. *Paying the Price: Why Rich Countries Must Invest Now in a War on Poverty.* Oxfam, 2005, p. 6.

argue for increased U.S. foreign assistance. O'Neill lost his job later that year, but the U.S. foreign aid budget rose by more than 15 percent a year in 2003–2005 (although it has since dropped back somewhat).

Another major source of foreign assistance is *UN programs*. The place of these programs in the UN structure is described in Chapter 7 (see pp. 236–241). The overall flow of assistance through the UN is coordinated by the **UN Development Program (UNDP)**, which manages 5,000 projects at once around the world (focusing especially on technical development assistance). Other UN programs focus on concentrating capital, transferring technology, and developing workforce skills for manufacturing. UNIDO works on industrialization, UNITAR on training and research. But most UN programs—such as UNICEF, UNFPA, UNESCO, and WHO—focus on meeting basic needs.

UN programs have three advantages in promoting economic development. One is that governments and citizens tend to perceive the UN as a friend of the global South, not an alien force, a threat to sovereignty, or a reminder of colonialism. Second, UN workers may be more likely to make appropriate decisions because of their backgrounds. UN workers who come from the global South or have worked in other poor countries in a region may be more sensitive to local conditions and to the pitfalls of development assistance than are aid workers from rich countries. Third, the UN can organize its assistance on a global scale, giving priority to projects and avoiding duplication and the reinvention of the wheel in each state.

A major disadvantage faced by UN development programs is that they are funded largely through voluntary contributions by rich states. Each program has to solicit contributions to carry on its activities, so the contributions can be abruptly cut off if the program displeases a donor government. Also, governments that pledge aid may not follow through. For instance, the UN complained in early 2005 that only 5 percent of the $500 million pledged for southern Sudan by the international community five months earlier had actually been paid. A second major disadvantage of UN programs is their reputation for operating in an

FIGURE 13.6 Foreign Assistance as a Percent of Donor's Income, 2009 and 1960–2009

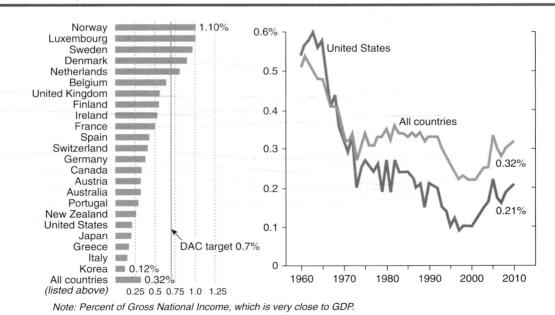

Note: Percent of Gross National Income, which is very close to GDP.

Source: *The New York Times;* www.oecd.org/dac/stats.

HELPING OUT

Governments provide more than $50 billion annually in foreign assistance, and private donors more than $10 billion in additional aid. In the West, the United States gives among the least amount of foreign aid as a percentage of GDP, despite recent increases. Here, a U.S. Peace Corps volunteer works in Panama, 2001.

inefficient, bureaucratic manner, without the cohesion and the resources that governments and MNCs in the North take for granted.

Types of Foreign Assistance

Bilateral aid takes a variety of forms. *Grants* are funds given free to a recipient state, usually for some stated purpose. *Technical cooperation* refers to grants given in the form of expert assistance in some project rather than just money or goods. *Credits* are grants that can be used to buy certain products from the donor state. For instance, the United States regularly gives credits that can be used to purchase U.S. grain. If people in a recipient country become accustomed to products from the donor state, they are likely to buy those same products in the future.

Loans are funds given to help in economic development, which must be repaid in the future out of the surplus generated by the development process (they too are often tied to the purchase of products from the donor state). Unlike commercial loans, government-to-government development loans are often made on concessionary terms, with long repayment times and low interest rates. Although still an obligation for the recipient country, such loans are relatively easy to service.

Loan guarantees, which are used only occasionally, are promises by the donor state to back up commercial loans to the recipient. If the recipient state services such debts and ultimately repays them, there is no cost to the donor. But if the recipient cannot make the payments, the donor has to step in and cover the debts. A loan guarantee allows the recipient state to borrow money at lower interest from commercial banks (because the risk to the bank is much lower).

Military aid is not normally included in development assistance, but in a broad sense belongs there. It is money that flows from North to South, from government to government, and it does bring a certain amount of value into the economies of the global South. If a country is going to have a certain size army with certain weapons, getting them free from a donor state frees up money that can be used elsewhere in the economy. However, of all the forms of development assistance, military aid is certainly one of the least efficient and most prone to impede rather than help economic development. It is also geared almost exclusively to political alliances rather than actual development needs.

The main agency dispensing U.S. foreign economic assistance (but not military aid) is the State Department's *Agency for International Development (USAID)*, which works mainly through the U.S. embassy in each recipient country. Major recipients of U.S. foreign aid include Israel, Egypt, and Turkey—all important strategic allies in the volatile Middle East.

The U.S. **Peace Corps** provides U.S. volunteers for technical development assistance in developing countries. They work at the request and under the direction of the host state but are paid an allowance by the U.S. government. Started by President Kennedy in 1961, the Peace Corps now sends nearly 8,000 volunteers to 76 countries, where they participate in projects affecting about a million people.

In foreign aid, the donor must have the permission of the recipient government to operate in the country. This goes back to the principle of national sovereignty and the history of colonialism. National governments have the right to control the distribution of aid and the presence of foreign workers on their soil. Only occasionally is this principle violated, as when the United States and its allies provided assistance to Iraqi Kurds against the wishes of the Iraqi government following the Gulf War. International norms may be starting to change in this regard, with short-term humanitarian assistance starting to be seen as a human right that should not be subject to government veto.

Private Aid   Private donations provide a smaller amount, although sometimes a significant one. For instance, the Bill and Melinda Gates Foundation contributes more than $1 billion annually to world health campaigns. Private aid is an important source of aid for the global South. By 2008, according to the OECD, private aid flows from DAC countries neared $130 billion. This figure was equal to official development assistance given by state governments.

There are many sources of private aid. Individuals in wealthy states may give as individuals (like Bill Gates or George Soros). Individuals may give to charities that send money or food abroad such as the Red Cross, Doctors without Borders, or their local church. One of the major private charitable groups is **Oxfam America** (one of seven groups worldwide descended from the Oxford Committee for Famine Relief, founded in 1942 in Britain).

Oxfam has developed a unique model of foreign assistance. Originally devoted to short-term aid to famine victims, and still active in that effort, Oxfam America realized that over the longer term, people need not just handouts of food but the means to feed themselves—land, water, seeds, tools, and technical training.

The distinctive aspect of the Oxfam model is that it relies on local communities to determine the needs of their own people and to carry out development projects. Oxfam does not operate projects itself but provides funding to local organizations. Nor does Oxfam call itself a donor and these organizations recipients. Rather, it calls both sides "project partners"—working together to accomplish a task. In this model, a little outside money can go a long way toward building sustained local economic development. Furthermore, projects help participants empower themselves by organizing to meet their own needs.

For example, Oxfam America helped the Ethiopian women's cooperative mentioned on pp. 433–434. Oxfam did not design or organize the project; women in Addis Ababa did. But when their garment-making workshop became profitable and was ready to expand and employ twice as many women, Oxfam gave the group a $15,000 grant to build a new building.

The relationship between North and South—groups such as Oxfam and their project partners—is likened to a good marriage in which decisions are made jointly and dependency does not develop. In this model, economic development is not charity; it is in the interests of people in the rich countries as well as the poor. A cooperative relationship between North and South is essential for a peaceful and prosperous world. Even in a narrow economic sense, development in the global South creates new markets and new products that will enrich the industrialized countries as well. In economics, the creation of wealth is a positive-sum game.

The Oxfam approach seeks to reconceptualize development assistance to focus on long-term development through a bottom-up basic needs strategy and the political

PARTNER IN DEVELOPMENT

The Oxfam model of foreign assistance emphasizes support for local groups that can stimulate self-sustaining economic development at a local level. A mutually beneficial North-South partnership is the global goal of such projects. These women show off a mill they purchased with microcredit from an Oxfam-affiliated group in Gambia, 2001.

empowerment of poor people. The group's philosophy of a "rights-based approach to development" has drawn praise from human rights NGOs. Because of disappointment with the political uses of foreign aid in the past, Oxfam has tried to minimize the role in its projects of governments in both the North and South. For instance, Oxfam does not accept government funds, nor does it make grants to governments.

The general goals of the Oxfam model of foreign aid are consistent with a broader movement in the global South toward grassroots *empowerment*. Efforts such as those of Oxfam partners are organized by poor people to gain some power over their situation and meet their basic needs—not by seizing control of the state in a revolution but by means that are more direct, more local, and less violent. The key to success is getting organized, finding information, gaining self-confidence, and obtaining needed resources to implement action plans.

For example, in India, local women's groups using only the power of persuasion and logic have persuaded some landowners to give them land for cooperative income-generating projects such as vegetable farming and raising silkworms. Elsewhere in India, women working as gatherers of wood and other forest products got organized to win the legal minimum wage for 250,000 female forest workers—three times what they had been paid before. In this case, government action was necessary, but the pressure for such action came from local organizing. The women took their case to the public and the press, staging protest marches and getting an art exhibit relating to their cause displayed in the provincial capital.

Such examples do not mean that national and foreign governments are unimportant. On the contrary, government policies affect millions of people more quickly and more widely than do grassroots efforts. Indeed, grassroots organizing often has as an ultimate goal the restructuring of national political and social life so that policies reflect the needs of poor people. But the successes of grassroots empowerment show that poor communities can be more than victims of poverty waiting to be saved, or passive bystanders in North-South relations. Nor do poor people need to place their hopes for change in violent revolutions aimed at toppling national governments—revolutions that lead to greater suffering more often than to stable economic development.

The Oxfam model to date has been tested on only a small scale. Although the model may be effective in the local communities it reaches, it would have to be adopted widely and replicated on a much larger scale in order to influence the overall prospects for development. In the case of assistance to survivors of the 2004 tsunami, Oxfam's $12 million in contributions compares with about 50 times that amount pledged by the U.S. government. It is unclear whether the principles that the model embodies, from a reliance on local community organizers to an avoidance of government involvement, would work on a massive scale. A model that bypasses governments also bypasses the majority of money spent for foreign aid globally.

One advantage of private aid giving, like that of Oxfam, is the flexibility with which it can be given. Private aid organizations may also be more efficient (due to their smaller size) and better able to create partnerships with local recipients. Unfortunately, private aid organizations' lack of size and official government status can also be a disadvantage. They can be barred from entering a country (Zimbabwe recently expelled all private NGOs providing assistance), and they may have difficulty providing large-scale relief in times of crisis. They also may promote development policies that are at odds with government policy, putting them in conflict with other donor governments.

The Politics of Foreign Assistance

Many governments and private organizations provide ongoing development assistance in the form of projects in local communities in the South that are administered by agencies from the North to help meet basic needs. Such charitable programs are a useful means by which people in the North funnel resources to people in the South, but may create unanticipated problems. For example, the programs do not address the causes of poverty, the position of poor countries in the world economy, or local political conditions such as military rule or corruption. In addition, although photos of a hungry child may stare at the reader from a magazine page while the accompanying text notes that a few cents a day can "save" the child may raise awareness in the North of the extent of poverty in the South, at worst they tend to be exploitive and to reinforce racist and paternalistic stereotypes of the helplessness of people in the global South.

Moreover, although the motivation for foreign aid is to help those who are less fortunate, donor states have discovered that foreign aid is also an important tool of leverage over recipient states. Many donor states thus try to use some types of foreign aid to create economic and political changes in recipient countries.

Like almost all donor states, the United States uses the promise of foreign aid, or the threat of cutting it off, as leverage in political bargaining with recipients. For example, when Pakistan proceeded in the late 1980s with a nuclear weapons program despite U.S. warnings, a sizable flow of U.S. aid was terminated. Then when Pakistan supported U.S. military action in next-door Afghanistan in 2001, U.S. aid was restored.

In 2004, the United States launched the Millennium Challenge Corporation (MCC), which increases U.S. aid but only to governments with certain policies, such as rule of law, control of corruption, investment in education, and sound fiscal management. After potential recipients apply for aid, a board composed of government and private officials reviews the applications. The applicants are then reviewed for their suitability for aid based on a set of criteria established by the MCC. In this way, the United States hopes to reduce the aid lost to corruption and waste.

Of course, foreign assistance is also a complicated domestic political process. For example, in recent years, aid advocates in the United States have fought a U.S. law requiring that food sent to hungry people in Africa be grown in the United States and shipped in U.S. vessels. Instead of this simple handout system, they proposed using U.S. funds to buy food locally in Africa, which would save a lot of money, get aid to the hungry people months faster, and help African farmers. But the proposal was opposed by the so-called Iron Triangle of food aid—U.S. agribusiness that profits from selling the food to the government, U.S. shipping companies that profit from shipping it, and U.S. charities (including CARE and Catholic Relief Services) that fund a healthy fraction of their budgets by selling in Africa some of the grain they ship from the United States. The charities, by becoming international grain merchants and flooding local markets with cheap food (both sold and given away), compete with local farmers and drive down local prices, harming long-term recovery. Yet because of the Iron Triangle's lobbying power, Congress killed off the proposal to allow purchase of local food in Africa.

The one type of foreign assistance that is the *least* politically motivated is disaster relief. It is the kind of foreign assistance given when poor people are afflicted by famine, drought, earthquakes, flooding, or other such natural disasters. (War is also a disaster and can compound naturally occurring disasters.) When disaster strikes a poor state, many people are left with no means of subsistence and often without their homes. **Disaster relief** is the provision of short-term relief to such people in the form of food, water, shelter, clothing, and other essentials.

Disaster relief is very important because disasters can wipe out years of progress in economic development in a single blow. Generally, the international community tries to respond with enough assistance to get people back on their feet. The costs of such assistance are relatively modest, the benefits visible and dramatic. Having a system of disaster relief in place provides the global South with a kind of insurance against sudden losses that could otherwise destabilize economic accumulation.

Disasters generally occur quickly and without much warning. Rapid response is difficult to coordinate. International disaster relief has become more organized and better coordinated in the past decade but is still a complex process that varies somewhat from one situation to the next. Contributions of governments, private charitable organizations, and other groups and agencies are coordinated through the *UN Office of the Disaster Relief Coordinator (UNDRO)* in Geneva. In 2006, the UN set up a $500 million fund to enable it to respond quickly to disasters without waiting to raise funds first each time disaster strikes. Typically, international contributions make up no more than about one-third of the total relief effort, the remainder coming from local communities and national governments in the affected states.

SEEKING THE COLLECTIVE GOOD

Trick or Treat for UNICEF
COLLECTIVE GOOD: Money to Help Poor Children around the World

BACKGROUND: The world's children—2 billion people under age 18—have special humanitarian needs. The future depends on them, yet they are among the most vulnerable members of their societies, and are most prone to preventable deaths from disease. The great majority of the world's children live in the global South, including large numbers in abject poverty in the poorest countries.

The international community has addressed children's needs through agencies for humanitarian, public health, and economic development assistance—notably through the UN Children's Fund, UNICEF. This benefit is enjoyed by humanity regardless of how much anyone contributes to it. If too many free-ride, however, UNICEF will lack resources and so will needy children.

CHALLENGE: In 2000, the UN adopted the Millennium Development Goals (MDGs) for reducing poverty in the global South. Most of the MDGs affect

children, and UNICEF is a core participant. Ten years later, and two-thirds of the way to the target date of 2015, world leaders met to review progress. Some important progress had been made, but "unmet commitments [and] inadequate resources" had led the process to fall short of goals in key areas.* In the global South, 26 percent of children were underweight, down from 31 percent in the 1990s but still too high to meet the 15 percent target for 2015. In primary-school enrollment, the global South rose from 82 to 89 percent but was not on track to reach the goal of near 100 percent in 2015.

SOLUTION: The dominance principle does not help the world's children, who occupy the low ranks on the world's hierarchies. Nor does UNICEF have the quality of mutual, reciprocal obligation

IDENTITY

Disaster relief is something of a collective good because the states of the North do not benefit individually by contributing, yet they benefit in the long run from greater stability in the South. Despite the potential collective action problem with a large number of actors, disaster relief is generally a positive example of international cooperation to get a job done—and an example of the use of the identity principle to solve a collective goods problem. Food donated by the World Council of Churches may be carried to the scene in U.S. military aircraft and then distributed by the *International Committee of the Red Cross (ICRC)*. Embarrassing failures in the past—of underresponse or overresponse, of duplication of efforts or agencies working at cross-purposes—became rarer in the 1990s, and in the new century, groups coordinate their actions more effectively.[22]

The devastating earthquake in Haiti in 2010 showed the progress and the limitations of international relief efforts. Overnight, millions lost family members, homes, possessions, safe drinking water, and ways of life. With no functioning government or medical care system, initial relief efforts were chaotic and international aid poorly coordinated. Many victims died as planes stacked up over the small airport, unable to deliver supplies. In days, however, U.S. military forces took over the airport, and massive international assistance flowed in. Governments and NGOs pledged billions of dollars to help Haiti get back to its feet under UN guidance.

Both IOs and NGOs quickly mobilized to carry out what has been termed the "largest relief effort in human history." The efforts by these organizations were coordinated through

---

[22] Maynard, Kimberly A. *Healing Communities in Conflict: International Assistance in Complex Emergencies.* Columbia, 1999.

and monitoring of commitments found in a reciprocity-based organization such as the WTO. Rather, UNICEF relies on voluntary contributions, two-thirds of them from governments and the rest from foundations, NGOs, and individuals. The identity principle works well in this situation because all the world's people were once children and can identify with children.

To play up this identity aspect, UNICEF began a campaign in 1950 called "Trick or Treat for UNICEF." As American schoolchildren collect treats on Halloween each year, they also collect contributions for UNICEF in an orange cardboard box. Currently, the campaign raises almost $5 million a year. More importantly, it has reinforced an identity link of Americans with UNICEF over the decades, helping produce almost $20 million more from U.S. foundations and grants as well as $130 million from the U.S. Congress. The top four donors to UNICEF after the United States are Norway, the Netherlands, Britain, and Sweden—all countries where humanitarian aid is a strong element of national identity.

Actress Selena Gomez launches the UNICEF Trick-or-Treat drive, 2009.

*United Nations. *The Millennium Development Goals Report 2010.* New York: UN, 2010.

a variety of relief agencies, including the International Committee of the Red Cross, the International Organization for Migration, the UNHCR, and Oxfam. Initially, it appeared as though the United States would coordinate its own relief efforts apart from the UN, but after reconsideration, the United States ceded the lead role in relief to the UN. This somewhat spontaneous coordination of states, IOs, and NGOs seems contrary to the anarchical international system.

The relationship between disasters and economic development is complex, and appropriate responses vary according to location, type and size of disaster, and phase of recovery.[23] Different resources are needed in the emergency phase (for example, food and medical supplies) than in the reconstruction phase (for example, earthquake-resistant housing designs). Responses that are too small in scale or too short-term may fail to meet critical needs, but those that are too large or prolonged can overwhelm the local economy and create dependency (reducing incentives for self-help).

International norms regarding states' legal obligations to assist others in times of natural disaster and to accept such assistance if needed are changing. Some have even suggested extending the idea of the responsibility to protect to the area of disaster relief.[24] This idea became particularly relevant in the wake of Cyclone Nargis, which struck Burma in 2008. An estimated 130,000 people died in that natural disaster, yet the repressive government of Burma delayed or denied efforts of the international community to provide assistance to those affected by the cyclone. While aid did eventually flow into Burma, weeks were wasted while the government denied the needed assistance for coping with the cyclone.

The Impact of Foreign Assistance

There is a danger in providing foreign assistance—especially in large-scale governmental aid programs—that people from the North may provide assistance inappropriate for a developing country's local conditions and culture. This danger is illustrated by an experience in Kenya in the 1970s. Nomadic herders in the area of Lake Turkana near the Sahara desert—the Turkana tribe—were poor and vulnerable to periodic droughts. Western aid donors and the Kenyan government decided that the herders' traditional way of life was not environmentally sustainable and should be replaced by commercial fishing of the abundant tilapia fish in Lake Turkana. Norway, with its long experience in fishing, was asked to teach fishing and boat-building methods to the Turkana. To create a commercially viable local economy, Norwegian consultants recommended marketing frozen fish fillets to Kenya and the world. Thus in 1981 Norway finished building a $2 million, state-of-the-art fish freezing plant on the shores of Lake Turkana and a $20 million road connecting the plant to Kenya's transportation system.

There were only three problems. First, with temperatures of 100 degrees outside (a contrast with Norway!), the cost of operating the freezers exceeded the income from the fillets. So after a few days, the freezers were turned off and the facility became a very expensive dried-fish warehouse. Second, Turkana culture viewed fishing as the lowest-status profession, suitable only for those incompetent at herding. Third, every few decades, Lake Turkana shrinks as drought reduces the inflow of water. Such a drought in 1984–1985 eliminated the gulf where the fishing operations were based. The Norwegians might have foreseen these problems by doing more homework instead of just transplanting what worked in Norway. When the drought hit, the 20,000 herders who had been brought to the lake to learn fishing were left in an overcrowded, overgrazed environment in which every tree was cut for firewood

[23] Pelling, Mark. *Natural Disaster and Development in a Globalizing World*. Routledge, 2003.
[24] Cooper, Richard H., and Juliette V. Kohler. *Responsibility to Protect: The Global Moral Compact for the 21st Century*. Palgrave, 2009. Bellamy, Alex J. *Responsibility to Protect*. Polity, 2009.

and most cattle died. Instead of becoming self-sufficient, the Turkana people became totally dependent on outside aid.[25]

In the past decade, many scholars have undertaken research to understand whether foreign aid is effective at creating economic growth and alleviating poverty in the global South. Heated debates now occur among academics and policy makers as to whether aid is effective and, therefore, whether more or less should be given. On one side, scholars suggest increasing foreign assistance in order to deal with the crushing inequalities between the global North and the global South. Because the global South cannot reliably sustain capital accumulation, assistance from the North is necessary to jump-start economic growth.[26]

Countering this position, however, is research suggesting that aid does not always help poor countries develop. In particular, unless recipient countries possess institutions that practice good government, aid will largely be wasted or fall into the hands of corrupt leaders.[27] This research has been the inspiration for the United States' MCC policies as well as more IMF conditionality.

MOUTHWASH FOR MAURITANIA

Sometimes foreign assistance contributes goods to third world economies with little understanding of local needs or long-term strategies. Here, free supplies including cartons of mouthwash are delivered by the U.S. ambassador and the captain of a U.S. Navy ship participating in Project Handclasp, 1989.

Other critics of aid suggest that it should be reduced in general. They contend that the flow of aid has allowed leaders in poor states to avoid difficult policy changes that would pave the way for long-term economic growth. They argue that in some African countries, the massive infusion of foreign assistance after decolonization led to increased poverty and dependence on charity, rather than increased wealth and independence.[28]

Confronting the North-South Gap   The giving and receiving of foreign assistance is political, even if the motivations for giving it are not. Perhaps most important is that people in the North become aware of the tremendous gap between North and South and try to address the problem. Poverty can seem so overwhelming that citizens in rich countries can easily turn their backs and just try to live their own lives.

But in today's interdependent world, this really is not possible. North-South relations have become a part of everyday life. The integrated global economy brings to the North products and people from the South. The information revolution puts images of poverty on TV sets in comfortable living rooms. Security relations and political economy alike have shifted in the post–Cold War era to give new prominence to the global South.

✔ Study and **Review** the **Post-Test & Chapter Exam** at **mypoliscilab.com**

---

[25] Harden, Blaine. *Africa: Dispatches from a Fragile Continent.* Norton, 1990.

[26] Sachs, Jeffrey D. *The End of Poverty: Economic Possibilities for Our Time.* Penguin, 2006.

[27] Burnside, Craig and David Dollar. Aid, Policies, and Growth. *American Economic Review* 90 (4), 2000: 847-68.

[28] Easterly, William. The White Man's Burden: *Why the West's Efforts to Aid the Rest Have Done So Much Ill and So Little Good.* Penguin, 2007.

CHAPTER REVIEW

SUMMARY

- Economic development in the global South has been uneven. In recent years many poor countries, led by China, have grown robustly. And while the 2008–2009 recession hurt the global South, growth has begun to return.

- Evidence does not support a strong association of economic growth either with internal equality of wealth distribution or with internal inequality.

- The newly industrializing countries (NICs) in Asia—South Korea, Taiwan, Hong Kong, and Singapore—show that it is possible to rise out of poverty into sustained economic accumulation.

- China has registered strong economic growth in the past 25 years of market-oriented economic reforms. Though still poor, China is the world's leading success story in economic development.

- Export-led growth has largely replaced import substitution as a development strategy. This reflects the experiences of the NICs and China as well as the theory of comparative advantage.

- The theory that democratization would accompany and strengthen economic development has not been supported by the actual experiences of poor countries. But the opposite theory—that authoritarian government is necessary to maintain control while concentrating capital for industrialization—has also not been supported.

- Government corruption is a major obstacle to development throughout the global South.

- Given the shortage of local capital in most poor states, foreign investment by MNCs can be a means of stimulating economic growth. MNCs look for favorable local conditions, including political and economic stability, in deciding where to invest.

- Debt, resulting largely from overborrowing in the 1970s and early 1980s, is a major problem in the global South. Through renegotiations and other debt management efforts, the North and South have improved the debt situation in recent years. However, the South remains $2 trillion in debt to the North.

- The IMF makes loans to states in the South conditional on economic and governmental reforms. These conditionality agreements often necessitate politically unpopular measures such as cutting food subsidies.

- The WTO trading regime works against the global South by allowing richer nations to protect sectors in which the global South has advantages—notably agriculture and textiles. The Generalized System of Preferences (GSP) tries to compensate by lowering barriers to exports from the global South.

- Foreign assistance, most of it from governments in the North, plays an important part in the economic development plans of the poorer states of the South.

- Only a few states in the North meet the goal of contributing 0.7 percent of their GNPs as foreign assistance to the South.

- Most foreign aid consists of bilateral grants and loans from governments in the North to specific governments in the South. Such aid is often used for political leverage and promotes the export of products from the donor state.

- Donors in the global North use various relief models to distribute aid to the developing world, each with advantages and drawbacks.

KEY TERMS

economic
  development   461
newly industrializing
  countries
  (NICs)   461
"four tigers"/"four
  dragons"   462
import
  substitution   473
export-led growth   473
microcredit   473

technology
  transfer   478
brain drain   478
default   478
debt renegotiation   478
Paris Club   479
London
  Club   479
IMF conditionality   480
foreign
  assistance   484

Development Assistance
  Committee
  (DAC)   484
bilateral aid   484
multilateral aid   484
UN Development
  Program
  (UNDP)   485
Peace Corps   487
Oxfam America   487
disaster relief   490

CRITICAL THINKING QUESTIONS

1. How might the strong economic growth of the Asian NICs and of China affect proposals for an Asian free trade area similar to NAFTA and the EU? What would be the interests and worries of Japan, of China and the NICs, and of the poor states of the region in such an arrangement?

2. Past successes in economic development have depended heavily on developing a manufacturing base, which requires access to scarce capital. Do you think the information revolution and the increasing role of services in the world economy are changing this pattern? What does India's experience say about the feasibility of finding a niche in these growing sectors of the world economy and perhaps bypassing manufacturing?

3. How does the global South's debt problem compare with the U.S. debt, discussed in Chapter 9, in magnitude and effect? Do the two debt problems arise from similar causes? Which problem do you consider more serious, and why?

4. Some scholars criticize the IMF for imposing harsh terms in its conditionality agreements with poor states. Others applaud the IMF for demanding serious reforms before providing financial resources. If you were a leader negotiating with the IMF, what kinds of terms would you be willing to agree to and what terms would you resist? Why?

5. If the states in North America, Western Europe, and Japan/Pacific all met the target of providing 0.7 percent of GNP in foreign assistance, what might the effects be? How much additional aid would be made available? To whom would it likely go? What effects might it have on the recipient states and on economic development overall?

Foreign Aid: A Solution to Development or a Source of Problems?

Overview

Billions of dollars per year in foreign aid flow from developed countries to developing countries. Yet, as discussed in this chapter, the amount of foreign aid from the Development Assistance Committee (DAC) has fluctuated greatly over time. When measured as a percentage of DAC countries' GDP, the amount of foreign aid has steadily fallen in the past four decades. Yet, when measured by absolute dollars, the amount has risen. Is the current giving by DAC countries enough?

Non-DAC foreign assistance has increased in absolute dollars. Multilateral agencies (such as investment banks and the UN) give nearly $12 billion to the global South. Private donors from DAC countries now provide over $300 billion in aid flows as well, more than three times the official assistance provided by DAC countries.

Recently, a controversy has emerged regarding the question of how much aid to give. Some prominent economists and political figures have called for large increases in foreign aid given by DAC countries, larger than the increases seen after the 9/11 attacks. There are some who doubt the wisdom of this course of action, however. While these skeptics do not necessarily call for decreasing foreign assistance, they argue that increasing the level of foreign aid would not help to achieve the ultimate goal of much of the aid, economic development. Should DAC countries significantly increase their foreign aid budgets? Would this increase in aid be a help or a hindrance to development?

DAC Countries Should Significantly Increase Foreign Aid

Foreign aid can help solve important problems. From health care crises, infrastructure maintenance, and literacy programs to food assistance, foreign aid can be essential to help poorer states kick-start the development process. Higher levels of assistance would increase the quality of life for millions of people living in poverty abroad.

Increasing foreign aid will increase goodwill. As the United States and the EU compete for influence with China in places like Africa and Latin America, increasing foreign assistance will create tighter economic, political, and social bonds between DAC countries and recipient states, potentially preventing China from gaining allies in the developing world.

More foreign assistance will increase Western security. By providing money and other resources to stabilize poor countries, DAC countries decrease the chances that disaffected individuals in those countries will blame the West for their problems. This resentment often leads to anti-Western behavior—in the extreme case, support for terrorism.

DAC Countries Should Not Significantly Increase Foreign Aid

Large amounts of foreign aid are wasted or stolen. Some economists estimate that in some cases, half of aid packages are stolen by corrupt leaders or state officials, while other times, the aid is simply wasted. Increasing foreign assistance will not help developing countries. It is just throwing good money after bad.

Large foreign aid flows will create dependencies. Developing countries may get used to receiving large amounts of aid and neglect to develop internal programs to provide education, health care, or infrastructure maintenance. This dependency is dangerous for developing countries since it leaves them vulnerable to the policies of aid donors.

Foreign aid can violate recipients' sovereignty. Most assistance programs come with strings (conditions) attached. Thus, as a condition for receiving aid, developing states must promise to make certain changes or perform particular tasks. This is a particularly egregious violation of sovereignty since it is done under the guise of helping the recipient states.

Questions

- Should DAC countries significantly increase their foreign aid budgets? Will this aid be a hindrance or a help to development?
- Can DAC countries afford to significantly increase foreign aid? What stops DAC countries from giving more foreign aid?
- Private NGOs (churches, the Gates Foundation, etc.) also now provide extensive amounts of aid to help developing countries. How should states and NGOs cooperate to maximize their efforts to provide foreign aid? Do you think private NGOs will be better at some tasks, while states will be better at others?

For Further Reading

Easterly, William. *The White Man's Burden: Why the West's Efforts to Aid the Rest Have Done So Much Ill and So Little Good.* Penguin, 2007.

Sachs, Jeffrey. *The End of Poverty: Economic Possibilities for Our Time.* Penguin, 2006.

Whitfield, Lindsay. *The Politics of Aid: African Strategies for Dealing with Donors.* Oxford, 2009.

Moyo, Dambisa. *Dead Aid: Why Aid Is Not Working and How There Is a Better Way for Africa.* Farrar, Straus and Giroux, 2009.

CHAPTER 14

Postscript

Australian peacekeeper with digital camera in East Timor, 2007.

Ultimately the conflicts and dramas of international relations are the problems of human society—struggles for power and wealth, efforts to cooperate despite differences, social dilemmas and collective goods problems, the balance between freedom and order, and trade-offs of equity versus efficiency and of long-term versus short-term outcomes. These themes are inescapable in human society, from the smallest groups to the world community. The subject of international relations is in this sense an extension of everyday life and a reflection of the choices of individual human beings. IR belongs to all of us—North and South, women and men, citizens and leaders—who live together on this planet.

This book has shown that in IR, more than other social settings, collective goods problems pose formidable challenges to successful cooperation among the large number of independent (state and nonstate) actors. With no central government to enforce order, actors in IR have developed three kinds of solutions to collective goods problems—our three core principles. Countries turn to the dominance principle most often in international security affairs, especially military force (Chapter 6). The identity principle matters most in the remarkable process of integration (Chapter 10). Most important, however, is the reciprocity principle, which underlies international treaties, law, and organizations from the UN to the WTO. Characteristic solutions based on the reciprocity principle are complicated, take forever to agree upon, and require extensive monitoring of compliance thereafter. But woven together, these reciprocity-based agreements offer the basis for an international system that has moved over centuries from extreme war-proneness to ever stronger peace and prosperity—notwithstanding the world's many serious remaining problems.

One major theme of this book is the nature of the international system as a well-developed set of rules based on state sovereignty, territoriality, and "anarchy"—a lack of central government. Yet the international system is becoming more complex, more nuanced, and more interconnected with other aspects of planetary society. State sovereignty is now challenged by the principle of self-determination. International norms have begun to limit the right of government to rule a population by force against its will and to violate human rights. Territorial integrity is also problematic, because national borders do not stop information, environmental changes, or missiles. Information allows actors—state, substate, and supranational—to know what is going on everywhere in the world and to coordinate actions globally.

Technological development is just one aspect of the profound, yet incremental, changes taking place in international relations. New actors are gaining power, long-standing principles are becoming less effective, and new challenges are arising for states, groups, and individuals alike. Technology is profoundly changing the utility and role of military force. Technology plays key roles on both sides in counterinsurgency wars such as in Afghanistan and the other 11 active wars in the world.

Nonmilitary forms of leverage, particularly economic rewards, have become much more important power capabilities. The post–Cold War era is a peaceful one, yet the peace is fragile. Will this era, like past postwar eras, lapse slowly into the next prewar era, or will it lead to a robust and lasting "permanent peace" such as Kant imagined?

In IPE, we see simultaneous trends toward integration and disintegration among states. People continue to speak their own language, to fly their own flag, and to use their own currency with its pictures and emblems. Nationalism continues to be an important force. At the same time, however, although people identify with their state, they also now hold competing identities based on ethnic ties, gender, and (in the case of Europe) region. In international trade, liberal economics prevails because it works so well. States have learned that to survive, they must help the creation of wealth by MNCs and other actors.

Environmental damage may become the single greatest obstacle to sustained economic growth in both the North and South. Because of high costs, the large number of actors, and collective goods problems, international bargaining over the environment is difficult.

Meanwhile, North-South relations are moving to the center of world politics. Demographic and economic trends are sharpening the global North-South gap, with the North continuing to accumulate wealth while much of the South lags. Ultimately, the North will bear a high cost for failing to address the economic development of the South. Perhaps, by using computerization and biotechnology innovations, poor states can develop their economies more efficiently and sustainably than did Europe or North America.

The future is unknowable now, but as it unfolds you can compare it—at mileposts along the way—to the worlds that you desire and expect. For example, you could ask questions such as the following (asking yourself, for each one, why you answer the way you do for your desired future and expected future):

1. Will state sovereignty be eroded by supranational authority?
2. Will norms of human rights and democracy become global?
3. Will the UN evolve into a quasi-government for the world?
4. Will the UN be restructured?
5. Will World Court judgments become enforceable?
6. Will the number of states increase?
7. Will China become democratic?
8. What effects will information technologies have on IR?
9. Will weapons of mass destruction proliferate?
10. Will military leverage become obsolete?
11. Will disarmament occur?
12. Will women participate more fully in IR? With what effect?
13. Will there be a single world currency?
14. Will there be a global free trade regime?
15. Will nationalism fade out or continue strong?
16. Will many people develop a global identity?
17. Will world culture become more homogeneous or more pluralistic?
18. Will the EU or other regional IOs achieve political union?
19. Will global environmental destruction be severe? How soon?
20. Will new technologies avert environmental constraints?
21. Will global problems create stronger or weaker world order?
22. Will population growth level out? If so, when and at what level?
23. Will the poorest countries accumulate wealth? How soon?
24. What role will the North play in the South's development?

The choices you make and actions you take will ultimately affect the world you live in. You cannot opt out of involvement in international relations. You are involved, and year by year the information revolution and other aspects of interdependence are drawing you more closely into contact with the rest of the world. You can act in many ways to bring the world you expect more into line with the world you desire. You can empower yourself by finding the actions and choices that define your place in international relations.

Now that you have completed the studies covered in this book, don't stop here. Keep learning about the world beyond your country's borders. Keep thinking about the world that might exist. Be a part of the changes that will carry this world through the coming decades. It's your world: study it, care for it, make it your own.

Glossary

acid rain   Rain caused by air pollution that damages trees and often crosses borders. Limiting acid rain (via limiting nitrogen oxide emissions) has been the subject of several regional agreements. (p. 402)

airspace   The space above a state that is considered its territory, in contrast to outer space, which is considered international territory. (p. 184)

alliance cohesion   The ease with which the members hold together an alliance; it tends to be high when national interests converge and when cooperation among allies becomes institutionalized. (p. 64)

Amnesty International   An influential nongovernmental organization that operates globally to monitor and try to rectify glaring abuses of political (not economic or social) human rights. (p. 268)

anarchy   In IR theory, a term that implies not complete chaos but the lack of a central government that can enforce rules. (p. 50)

Antiballistic Missile (ABM) Treaty (1972)   A treaty that prohibited either the United States or the Soviet Union from using a ballistic missile defense as a shield, which would have undermined mutually assured destruction and the basis of deterrence. (p. 221) See also *mutually assured destruction (MAD)* and *Strategic Defense Initiative (SDI)*.

arms race   A reciprocal process in which two or more states build up military capabilities in response to each other. (p. 74)

autarky   A policy of self-reliance, avoiding or minimizing trade and trying to produce everything one needs (or the most vital things) by oneself. (p. 291)

balance of payments   A summary of all the flows of money into and out of a country. It includes three types of international transactions: the current account (including the merchandise trade balance), flows of capital, and changes in reserves. (p. 333)

balance of power   The general concept of one or more states' power being used to balance that of another state or group of states. The term can refer to (1) any ratio of power capabilities between states or alliances, (2) a relatively equal ratio, or (3) the process by which counterbalancing coalitions have repeatedly formed to prevent one state from conquering an entire region. (p. 52)

balance of trade   The value of a state's exports relative to its imports. (p. 286)

ballistic missile   The major strategic delivery vehicle for nuclear weapons; it carries a warhead along a trajectory (typically rising at least 50 miles high) and lets it drop on the target. (p. 211) See also *intercontinental ballistic missiles (ICBMs)*.

basic human needs   The fundamental needs of people for adequate food, shelter, health care, sanitation, and education. Meeting such needs may be thought of as both a moral imperative and a form of investment in "human capital" essential for economic growth. (p. 427)

bilateral aid   Government assistance that goes directly to third world governments as state-to-state aid. (p. 484)

biodiversity   The tremendous diversity of plant and animal species making up the earth's (global, regional, and local) ecosystems. (p. 396)

Biological Weapons Convention (1972)   An agreement that prohibits the development, production, and possession of biological weapons, but makes no provision for inspections. (p. 215)

brain drain   Poor countries' loss of skilled workers to rich countries. (p. 478)

Bretton Woods system   A post–World War II arrangement for managing the world economy, established at a meeting in Bretton Woods, New Hampshire, in 1944. Its main institutional components are the World Bank and the International Monetary Fund (IMF). (p. 331)

burden sharing   The distribution of the costs of an alliance among members; the term also refers to the conflicts that may arise over such distribution. (p. 64)

cartel   An association of producers or consumers (or both) of a certain product, formed for the purpose of manipulating its price on the world market. (p. 301)

cash crop   An agricultural good produced as a commodity for export to world markets. (p. 432)

central bank   An institution common in industrialized countries whose major tasks are to maintain the value of the state's currency and to control inflation. (p. 330)

centrally planned economy   An economy in which political authorities set prices and decide on quotas for production and consumption of each commodity according to a long-term plan. (p. 311)

chain of command   A hierarchy of officials (often civilian as well as military) through which states control military forces. (p. 224)

Chemical Weapons Convention (1992)   An agreement that bans the production and possession of chemical weapons and includes strict verification provisions and the threat of sanctions against violators and nonparticipants in the treaty. (p. 215)

Chernobyl   A city in Ukraine that was the site of a 1986 meltdown at a Soviet nuclear power plant. (p. 403)

civil-military relations   The relations between a state's civilian leaders and the military leadership. In most countries, the military takes orders from civilian leaders. In extreme cases, poor civil-military relations can lead to military coups. (p. 225)

civil war   A war between factions within a state trying to create, or prevent, a new government for the entire state or some territorial part of it. (p. 155)

Cold War   The hostile relations—punctuated by occasional periods of improvement, or détente—between the two superpowers, the United States and the Soviet Union, from 1945 to 1990. (p. 31)

collective goods problem   A tangible or intangible good, created by the members of a group, that is available to all group members

regardless of their individual contributions; participants can gain by lowering their own contribution to the collective good, yet if too many participants do so, the good cannot be provided. (p. 5)

collective security   The formation of a broad alliance of most major actors in an international system for the purpose of jointly opposing aggression by any actor; sometimes seen as presupposing the existence of a universal organization (such as the United Nations) to which both the aggressor and its opponents belong. (p. 90) See also *League of Nations*.

Common Agricultural Policy (CAP)   A European Union policy based on the principle that a subsidy extended to farmers in any member country should be extended to farmers in all member countries. (p. 360)

common market   A zone in which labor and capital (as well as goods) flow freely across borders. (p. 360)

comparative advantage   The principle that says states should specialize in trading goods that they produce with the greatest relative efficiency and at the lowest relative cost (relative, that is, to other goods produced by the same state). (p. 288)

compellence   The threat of force to make another actor take some action (rather than, as in deterrence, refrain from taking an action). (p. 73)

Comprehensive Test Ban Treaty (CTBT) (1996)   A treaty that bans all nuclear weapons testing, thereby broadening the ban on atmospheric testing negotiated in 1963. (p. 221)

conditionality   See *IMF conditionality*.

conflict   A difference in preferred outcomes in a bargaining situation. (p. 157)

conflict and cooperation   The types of actions that states take toward each other through time. (p. 11)

conflict resolution   The development and implementation of peaceful strategies for settling conflicts. (p. 131)

constructivism   A movement in IR theory that examines how changing international norms and actors' identities help shape the content of state interests. (p. 121)

containment A policy adopted in the late 1940s by which the United States sought to halt the global expansion of Soviet influence on several levels—military, political, ideological, and economic. (p. 31)

convertible currency The guarantee that the holder of a particular currency can exchange it for another currency. Some states' currencies are nonconvertible. (p. 323) See also *hard currency*.

cost-benefit analysis A calculation of the costs incurred by a possible action and the benefits it is likely to bring. (p. 74)

Council of the European Union A European Union institution in which the relevant ministers (foreign, economic, agriculture, finance, etc.) of each member state meet to enact legislation and reconcile national interests. Formerly known as the Council of Ministers. When the meeting takes place among the state leaders, it is called the "European Council." (p. 361) See also *European Commission*.

counterinsurgency An effort to combat guerrilla armies, often including programs to "win the hearts and minds" of rural populations so that they stop sheltering guerrillas. (p. 196)

coup d'état French for "blow against the state"; a term that refers to the seizure of political power by domestic military forces—that is, a change of political power outside the state's constitutional order. (p. 226)

crimes against humanity A category of legal offenses created at the Nuremberg trials after World War II to encompass genocide and other acts committed by the political and military leaders of the Third Reich (Nazi Germany). (p. 270) See also *dehumanization* and *genocide*.

cruise missile A small winged missile that can navigate across thousands of miles of previously mapped terrain to reach a particular target; it can carry either a nuclear or a conventional warhead. (p. 212)

Cuban Missile Crisis (1962) A superpower crisis, sparked by the Soviet Union's installation of medium-range nuclear missiles in Cuba, that marks the moment when the United States and the Soviet Union came closest to nuclear war. (p. 32)

cultural imperialism A term critical of U.S. dominance of the emerging global culture. (p. 380)

customs union A common external tariff adopted by members of a free trade area; that is, participating states adopt a unified set of tariffs with regard to goods coming in from outside. (p. 359) See also *free trade area*.

cycle theories An effort to explain tendencies toward war in the international system as cyclical; for example, by linking wars with long waves in the world economy (Kondratieff cycles). (p. 159)

debt renegotiation A reworking of the terms on which a loan will be repaid; frequently negotiated by third world debtor governments in order to avoid default. (p. 478)

default Failure to make scheduled debt payments. (p. 478)

dehumanization Stigmatization of enemies as subhuman or nonhuman, leading frequently to widespread massacres or worse. (p. 164) See also *crimes against humanity* and *genocide*.

democratic peace The proposition, strongly supported by empirical evidence, that democracies almost never fight wars against each other (although they do fight against authoritarian states). (p. 95)

demographic transition The pattern of falling death rates, followed by falling birthrates, that generally accompanies industrialization and economic development. (p. 410)

dependency theory A Marxist-oriented theory that explains the lack of capital accumulation in the third world as a result of the interplay between domestic class relations and the forces of foreign capital. (p. 452) See also *enclave economy*.

deterrence The threat to punish another actor if it takes a certain negative action (especially attacking one's own state or one's allies). (p. 73) See also *mutually assured destruction (MAD)*.

devaluation A unilateral move to reduce the value of a currency by changing a fixed or official exchange rate. (p. 328) See also *exchange rate*.

developing countries States in the global South, the poorest regions of the world—also called third world countries, less-developed countries, and undeveloped countries. (p. 425)

Development Assistance Committee (DAC)   A committee whose members—consisting of states from Western Europe, North America, and Japan/Pacific—provide 95 percent of official development assistance to countries of the global South. (p. 484) See also *foreign assistance*.

difference feminism   A strand of feminism that believes gender differences are not just socially constructed and that views women as inherently less warlike than men (on average). (p. 137)

digital divide   The gap in access to information technologies between rich and poor people, and between the global North and South. (p. 374)

diplomatic immunity   A privilege under which diplomats' activities fall outside the jurisdiction of the host country's national courts. (p. 262)

diplomatic recognition   The process by which the status of embassies and that of an ambassador as an official state representative are explicitly defined. (p. 261)

direct foreign investment   See *foreign direct investment*.

disaster relief   Provision of short-term relief in the form of food, water, shelter, clothing, and other essentials to people facing natural disasters. (p. 490)

discount rate   The interest rate charged by governments when they lend money to private banks. The discount rate is set by countries' central banks. (p. 330)

diversionary foreign policy   Foreign policies adopted to distract the public from domestic political problems. (p. 144)

Doha Round   A series of negotiations under the World Trade Organization that began in Doha, Qatar, in 2001. It followed the *Uruguay Round* and has focused on agricultural subsidies, intellectual property, and other issues. (p. 296)

dominance   A principle for solving collective goods problems by imposing solutions hierarchically. (p. 5)

dumping   The sale of products in foreign markets at prices below the minimum level necessary to make a profit (or below cost). (p. 293)

economic classes   A categorization of individuals based on economic status. (p. 128)

economic development   The combined processes of capital accumulation, rising per capita incomes (with consequent falling birthrates), the increasing of skills in the population, the adoption of new technological styles, and other related social and economic changes. (p. 461)

economic liberalism   In the context of IPE, an approach that generally shares the assumption of anarchy (the lack of a world government) but does not see this condition as precluding extensive cooperation to realize common gains from economic exchanges. It emphasizes absolute over relative gains and, in practice, a commitment to free trade, free capital flows, and an "open" world economy. (p. 284) See also *mercantilism* and *neoliberal*.

economic surplus   A surplus created by investing money in productive capital rather than using it for consumption. (p. 441)

electronic warfare   Use of the electromagnetic spectrum (radio waves, radar, infrared, etc.) in war, such as employing electromagnetic signals for one's own benefit while denying their use to an enemy. (p. 203)

enclave economy   A historically important form of dependency in which foreign capital is invested in a third world country to extract a particular raw material in a particular place—usually a mine, oil well, or plantation. (p. 453) See also *dependency theory*.

enclosure   The splitting of a common area or good into privately owned pieces, giving individual owners an incentive to manage resources responsibly. (p. 388)

"ethnic cleansing"   Euphemism for forced displacement of an ethnic group or groups from a territory, accompanied by massacres and other human rights violations; it has occurred after the breakup of multinational states, notably in the former Yugoslavia. (p. 180)

ethnic groups   Large groups of people who share ancestral, language, cultural, or religious ties and a common identity. (p. 162)

ethnocentrism   The tendency to see one's own group (in-group) in favorable terms and an out-group in unfavorable terms. (p. 164)

Euratom   An organization created by the Treaty of Rome in 1957 to coordinate nuclear power development by pooling research, investment, and management. (p. 359)

euro   Also called the ECU (European currency unit); a single European currency used by 16 members of the European Union (EU). (p. 364)

European Commission   A European Union body whose members, while appointed by states, are supposed to represent EU interests. Supported by a multinational civil service in Brussels, the commission's role is to identify problems and propose solutions to the Council of Ministers. (p. 361) See also *Council of the European Union*.

European Court of Justice   A judicial arm of the European Union, based in Luxembourg. The court has actively established its jurisdiction and its right to overrule national law when it conflicts with EU law. (p. 362)

European Parliament   A quasi-legislative body of the European Union that operates as a watchdog over the European Commission and has limited legislative power. (p. 362)

European Union (EU)   The official term for the European Community (formerly the European Economic Community) and associated treaty organizations. The EU has 25 member states and is negotiating with other states that have applied for membership. (p. 358) See also *Maastricht Treaty*.

exchange rate   The rate at which one state's currency can be exchanged for the currency of another state. Since 1973, the international monetary system has depended mainly on floating rather than fixed exchange rates. (p. 322) See also *convertible currency; fixed exchange rates;* and *managed float*.

export-led growth   An economic development strategy that seeks to develop industries capable of competing in specific niches in the world economy. (p. 473)

fiscal policy   A government's decisions about spending and taxation, and one of the two major tools of macroeconomic policy making (the other being monetary policy). (p. 335)

fissionable material   The elements uranium-235 and plutonium, whose atoms split apart and release energy via a chain reaction when an atomic bomb explodes. (p. 209)

fixed exchange rates   The official rates of exchange for currencies set by governments; not a dominant mechanism in the international monetary system since 1973. (p. 324) See also *floating exchange rates*.

floating exchange rates   The rates determined by global currency markets in which private investors and governments alike buy and sell currencies. (p. 324) See also *fixed exchange rates*.

foreign assistance   Money or other aid made available to third world states to help them speed up economic development or meet humanitarian needs. Most foreign assistance is provided by governments and is called official development assistance (ODA). (p. 484) See also *Development Assistance Committee (DAC)*.

foreign direct investment   The acquisition by residents of one country of control over a new or existing business in another country. Also called *direct foreign investment*. (p. 343)

foreign policy process   The process by which foreign policies are arrived at and implemented. (p. 103)

"four tigers"/"four dragons"   The most successful newly industrialized areas of East Asia: South Korea, Taiwan, Hong Kong, and Singapore. (p. 462)

free trade   The flow of goods and services across national boundaries unimpeded by tariffs or other restrictions; in principle (if not always in practice), free trade was a key aspect of Britain's policy after 1846 and of U.S. policy after 1945. (p. 286)

free trade area   A zone in which there are no tariffs or other restrictions on the movement of goods and services across borders. (p. 359) See also *customs union*.

game theory   A branch of mathematics concerned with predicting bargaining outcomes. Games such as prisoner's dilemma and Chicken have been used to analyze various sorts of international interactions. (p. 75)

gender gap   Refers to polls showing women lower than men on average in their support for military actions, as well as for various other issues and candidates. (p. 141)

General Agreement on Tariffs and Trade (GATT) A world organization established in 1947 to work for freer trade on a multilateral basis; the GATT was more of a negotiating framework than an administrative institution. It became the World Trade Organization (WTO) in 1995. (p. 295)

General Assembly See *UN General Assembly*.

Generalized System of Preferences (GSP) A mechanism by which some industrialized states began in the 1970s to give tariff concessions to third world states on certain imports; an exception to the most-favored nation (MFN) principle. (p. 295) See also *most-favored nation (MFN)*.

genocide An intentional and systematic attempt to destroy a national, ethnic, racial, or religious group, in whole or part. It was confirmed as a crime under international law by the UN Genocide Convention (1948). (p. 166) See also *crimes against humanity* and *dehumanization*.

geopolitics The use of geography as an element of power, and the ideas about it held by political leaders and scholars. (p. 49)

globalization The increasing integration of the world in terms of communications, culture, and economics; may also refer to changing subjective experiences of space and time accompanying this process. (p. 19)

global warming A slow, long-term rise in the average world temperature caused by the emission of greenhouse gases produced by burning fossil fuels—oil, coal, and natural gas. (p. 390) See also *greenhouse gases*.

gold standard A system in international monetary relations, prominent for a century before the 1970s, in which the value of national currencies was pegged to the value of gold or other precious metals. (p. 322)

government bargaining model A model that sees foreign policy decisions as flowing from a bargaining process among various government agencies that have somewhat divergent interests in the outcome ("where you stand depends on where you sit"). Also called the "bureaucratic politics model." (p. 106)

great powers Generally, the half-dozen or so most powerful states; the great power club was exclusively European until the 20th century. (p. 54) See also *middle powers*.

greenhouse gases Carbon dioxide and other gases that, when concentrated in the atmosphere, act like the glass in a greenhouse, holding energy in and leading to global warming. (p. 391)

Gross Domestic Product (GDP) The size of a state's total annual economic activity. (p. 14)

groupthink The tendency of groups to validate wrong decisions by becoming overconfident and underestimating risks. (p. 111)

guerrilla war Warfare without front lines and with irregular forces operating in the midst of, and often hidden or protected by, civilian populations. (p. 155)

hard currency Money that can be readily converted to leading world currencies. (p. 323) See also *convertible currency*.

hegemonic stability theory The argument that regimes are most effective when power in the international system is most concentrated. (p. 58) See also *hegemony*.

hegemonic war War for control of the entire world order—the rules of the international system as a whole. Also known as world war, global war, general war, or systemic war. (p. 153)

hegemony The holding by one state of a preponderance of power in the international system, so that it can single-handedly dominate the rules and arrangements by which international political and economic relations are conducted. (p. 58) See also *hegemonic stability theory*.

high seas The portion of the oceans considered common territory, not under any kind of exclusive state jurisdiction. (p. 399) See also *territorial waters*.

home country The state where a multinational corporation (MNC) has its headquarters. (p. 345) See also *host country*.

host country A state in which a foreign multinational corporation (MNC) operates. (p. 345) See also *home country*.

human rights The rights of all people to be free from abuses such as torture or imprisonment for their political beliefs (political and civil rights), and to enjoy certain minimum economic and social protections (economic and social rights). (p. 264)

hyperinflation An extremely rapid, uncontrolled rise in prices, such as occurred in Germany in the 1920s and some third world countries more recently. (p. 323)

idealism An approach that emphasizes international law, morality, and international organization, rather than power alone, as key influences on international relations. (p. 43) See also *realism*.

identity A principle for solving collective goods problems by changing participants' preferences based on their shared sense of belonging to a community. (p. 6)

IMF conditionality An agreement to loan IMF funds on the condition that certain government policies are adopted. Dozens of third world states have entered into such agreements with the IMF in the past two decades. (p. 480) See also *International Monetary Fund (IMF)*.

immigration law National laws that establish the conditions under which foreigners may travel and visit within a state's territory, work within the state, and sometimes become citizens of the state (naturalization). (p. 261)

imperialism The acquisition of colonies by conquest or otherwise. Lenin's theory of imperialism argued that European capitalists were investing in colonies where they could earn big profits, and then using part of those profits to buy off portions of the working class at home. (p. 443)

import substitution A strategy of developing local industries, often conducted behind protectionist barriers, to produce items that a country had been importing. (p. 473)

industrialization The use of fossil-fuel energy to drive machinery and the accumulation of such machinery along with the products created by it. (p. 309)

industrial policy The strategies by which a government works actively with industries to promote their growth and tailor trade policy to their needs. (p. 304)

infant mortality rate The proportion of babies who die within their first year of life. (p. 413)

infantry Foot soldiers who use assault rifles and other light weapons (mines, machine guns, etc.). (p. 194)

information screens The subconscious or unconscious filters through which people put the information coming in about the world around them. (p. 129) See also *misperceptions, selective perceptions*.

intellectual property rights The legal protection of the original works of inventors, authors, creators, and performers under patent, copyright, and trademark law. Such rights became a contentious area of trade negotiations in the 1990s. (p. 305)

intercontinental ballistic missiles (ICBMs) The longest-range ballistic missiles, able to travel 5,000 miles. (p. 211) See also *ballistic missile*.

interdependence A political and economic situation in which two states are simultaneously dependent on each other for their well-being. The degree of interdependence is sometimes designated in terms of "sensitivity" or "vulnerability." (p. 187)

interest groups Coalitions of people who share a common interest in the outcome of some political issue and who organize themselves to try to influence the outcome. (p. 96)

intergovernmental organization (IGO) An organization (such as the United Nations and its agencies) whose members are state governments. (p. 15)

International Committee of the Red Cross (ICRC) A nongovernmental organization (NGO) that provides practical support, such as medical care, food, and letters from home, to civilians caught in wars and to prisoners of war (POWs). Exchanges of POWs are usually negotiated through the ICRC. (p. 274)

International Court of Justice See *World Court*.

International Criminal Court (ICC) A permanent tribunal for war crimes and crimes against humanity. (p. 272)

international integration The process by which supranational institutions come to replace national ones; the gradual shifting upward of some sovereignty from the state to regional or global structures. (p. 355)

International Monetary Fund (IMF) An intergovernmental organization (IGO) that coordinates international currency exchange, the balance of international payments, and national accounts. Along with the World Bank, it is a pillar of the international financial system. (p. 331) See also *IMF conditionality.*

international norms The expectations held by participants about normal relations among states. (p. 233)

international organizations (IOs) Intergovernmental organizations (IGOs) such as the UN and nongovernmental organizations (NGOs) such as the International Committee of the Red Cross (ICRC). (p. 234)

international political economy (IPE) The study of the politics of trade, monetary, and other economic relations among nations, and their connection to other transnational forces. (p. 12)

international regime A set of rules, norms, and procedures around which the expectations of actors converge in a certain international issue area (such as oceans or monetary policy). (p. 89)

international relations (IR) The relationships among the world's state governments and the connection of those relationships with other actors (such as the United Nations, multinational corporations, and individuals), with other social relationships (including economics, culture, and domestic politics), and with geographic and historical influences. (p. 3)

international security A subfield of international relations (IR) that focuses on questions of war and peace. (p. 12)

international system The set of relationships among the world's states, structured by certain rules and patterns of interaction. (p. 14)

International Whaling Commission An intergovernmental organization (IGO) that sets quotas for hunting certain whale species; states' participation is voluntary. (p. 397)

irredentism A form of nationalism whose goal is to regain territory lost to another state; it can lead directly to violent interstate conflicts. (p. 178)

Islam A broad and diverse world religion whose divergent populations include Sunni Muslims, Shi'ite Muslims, and many smaller branches and sects from Nigeria to Indonesia, centered in the Middle East and South Asia. (p. 169)

Islamist Political ideology based on instituting Islamic principles and laws in government. A broad range of groups using diverse methods come under this category. (p. 169)

issue areas Distinct spheres of international activity (such as global trade negotiations) within which policy makers of various states face conflicts and sometimes achieve cooperation. (p. 11)

just wars A category in international law and political theory that defines when wars can be justly started (*jus ad bellum*) and how they can be justly fought (*jus in bello*). (p. 263) See also *war crimes.*

Keynesian economics The principles articulated by British economist John Maynard Keynes, used successfully in the Great Depression of the 1930s, including the view that governments should sometimes use deficit spending to stimulate economic growth. (p. 335)

Kyoto Protocol (1997) The main international treaty on global warming, which entered into effect in 2005 and mandates cuts in carbon emissions in 2008–2012. Almost all the world's major countries, except the United States, are participants. (p. 393)

land mines Concealed explosive devices, often left behind by irregular armies, that kill or maim civilians after wars end. Such mines number more than 100 million, primarily in Angola, Bosnia, Afghanistan, and Cambodia. A movement to ban land mines is underway; nearly 100 states have agreed to do so. (p. 196)

land reform Policies that aim to break up large land holdings and redistribute land to poor peasants for use in subsistence farming. (p. 433)

League of Nations An organization established after World War I and a forerunner of today's United Nations; it achieved certain humanitarian and other successes but was weakened by the absence of U.S. membership and by its own lack of effectiveness in ensuring collective security. (p. 27) See also *collective security.*

less-developed countries (LDCs) The world's poorest regions—the global South—where most people live; also called underdeveloped countries or developing countries. (p. 425)

liberal feminism A strand of feminism that emphasizes gender equality and views the "essential" differences in men's and women's abilities or perspectives as trivial or nonexistent. (p. 138)

limited war Military actions that seek objectives short of the surrender and occupation of the enemy. (p. 155)

Lisbon Treaty A European Union agreement that replaces a failed attempt at an EU Constitution with a similar set of reforms strengthening central EU authority and modifying voting procedures among the EU's expanded membership. (p. 369)

London Club See *Paris Club.*

Maastricht Treaty A treaty signed in the Dutch city of Maastricht and ratified in 1992; it commits the European Union to monetary union (a single currency and European Central Bank) and to a common foreign policy. (p. 363) See also *European Union (EU).*

malnutrition A lack of needed foods including protein and vitamins; about 10 million children die each year from malnutrition-related causes. (p. 431)

managed float A system of occasional multinational government interventions in currency markets to manage otherwise free-floating currency rates. (p. 325)

Marxism A branch of socialism that emphasizes exploitation and class struggle and includes both communism and other approaches. (p. 128)

mediation The use of a third party (or parties) in conflict resolution. (p. 131)

mercantilism An economic theory and a political ideology opposed to free trade; it shares with realism the belief that each state must protect its own interests without seeking mutual gains through international organizations. (p. 283) See also *economic liberalism.*

microcredit The use of very small loans to small groups of individuals, often women, to stimulate economic development. (p. 473)

middle powers States that rank somewhat below the great powers in terms of their influence on world affairs (for example, Brazil and India). (p. 55) See also *great powers.*

migration Movement between states, usually emigration from the old state and immigration to the new state. (p. 434)

militarism The glorification of war, military force, and violence. (p. 133)

military governments States in which military forces control the government; they are most common in third world countries, where the military may be the only large modern institution. (p. 226)

military-industrial complex A huge interlocking network of governmental agencies, industrial corporations, and research institutes, all working together to promote and benefit from military spending. (p. 97)

Millennium Development Goals UN targets for basic needs measures such as reducing poverty and hunger, adopted in 2000 with a target date of 2015. (p. 425)

misperceptions, selective perceptions The selective or mistaken processing of the available information about a decision; one of several ways—along with affective and cognitive bias—in which individual decision making diverges from the rational model. (p. 129) See also *information screens.*

Missile Technology Control Regime A set of agreements through which industrialized states try to limit the flow of missile-relevant technology to third world states. (p. 214)

mixed economies Economies such as those in the industrialized West that contain both some government control and some private ownership. (p. 312)

monetary policy A government's decisions about printing and circulating money, and one of the two major tools of macroeconomic policy making (the other being fiscal policy). (p. 335)

Montreal Protocol (1987) An agreement on protection of the ozone layer in which states pledged to reduce and then eliminate use of chlorofluorocarbons (CFCs). It is the most successful environmental treaty to date. (p. 395)

most-favored nation (MFN) A principle by which one state, by granting another state MFN status, promises to give it the same treatment given to the first state's most-favored trading partner. (p. 295) See also *Generalized System of Preferences (GSP)*.

multilateral aid Government foreign aid from several states that goes through a third party, such as the UN or another agency. (p. 484)

multinational corporation (MNC) A company based in one state with affiliated branches or subsidiaries operating in other states. (p. 341) See also *home country* and *host country*.

multipolar system An international system with typically five or six centers of power that are not grouped into alliances. (p. 56)

Munich Agreement A symbol of the failed policy of appeasement, this agreement, signed in 1938, allowed Nazi Germany to occupy a part of Czechoslovakia. Rather than appease German aspirations, it was followed by further German expansions, which triggered World War II. (p. 27)

Muslims See *Islam*.

mutually assured destruction (MAD) The possession of second-strike nuclear capabilities, which ensures that neither of two adversaries could prevent the other from destroying it in an all-out war. (p. 220) See also *deterrence*.

national debt The amount a government owes in debt as a result of deficit spending. (p. 337)

national interest The interests of a state overall (as opposed to particular parties or factions within the state). (p. 74)

nationalism Identification with and devotion to the interests of one's nation. It usually involves a large group of people who share a national identity and often a language, culture, or ancestry. (p. 160)

nation-states States whose populations share a sense of national identity, usually including a language and culture. (p. 14)

neocolonialism The continuation, in a former colony, of colonial exploitation without formal political control. (p. 451)

neofunctionalism A theory that holds that economic integration (functionalism) generates a "spillover" effect, resulting in increased political integration. (p. 357)

neoliberal Shorthand for "neoliberal institutionalism," an approach that stresses the importance of international institutions in reducing the inherent conflict that realists assume in an international system; the reasoning is based on the core liberal idea that seeking long-term mutual gains is often more rational than maximizing individual short-term gains. (p. 86) See also *economic liberalism*.

neorealism A version of realist theory that emphasizes the influence on state behavior of the system's structure, especially the international distribution of power. (p. 56) See also *realism*.

newly industrializing countries (NICs) Third world states that have achieved self-sustaining capital accumulation, with impressive economic growth. The most successful are the "four tigers" or "four dragons" of East Asia: South Korea, Taiwan, Hong Kong, and Singapore. (p. 461)

nonaligned movement A movement of third world states, led by India and Yugoslavia, that attempted to stand apart from the U.S.-Soviet rivalry during the Cold War. (p. 70)

nongovernmental organization (NGO) A transnational group or entity (such as the Catholic Church, Greenpeace, or the International Olympic Committee) that interacts with states, multinational corporations (MNCs), other NGOs, and intergovernmental organizations (IGOs). (p. 15)

Non-Proliferation Treaty (NPT) (1968) A treaty that created a framework for controlling the spread of nuclear materials and expertise, including the International Atomic Energy Agency (IAEA), a UN agency based in Vienna that is charged with inspecting the nuclear power industry in NPT member states to prevent secret military diversions of nuclear materials. (p. 217)

nonstate actors   Actors other than state governments that operate either below the level of the state (that is, within states) or across state borders. (p. 15)

nontariff barriers   Forms of restricting imports other than tariffs, such as quotas (ceilings on how many goods of a certain kind can be imported). (p. 293)

norms   The shared expectations about what behavior is considered proper. (p. 50)

North American Free Trade Agreement (NAFTA)   A free trade zone encompassing the United States, Canada, and Mexico since 1994. (p. 300)

North Atlantic Treaty Organization (NATO)   A U.S.-led military alliance, formed in 1949 with mainly West European members, to oppose and deter Soviet power in Europe. It is currently expanding into the former Soviet bloc. (p. 65) See also *Warsaw Pact.*

North-South gap   The disparity in resources (income, wealth, and power) between the industrialized, relatively rich countries of the West (and the former East) and the poorer countries of Africa, the Middle East, and much of Asia and Latin America. (p. 21)

optimizing   Picking the very best option; contrasts with satisficing, or finding a satisfactory but less than best solution to a problem. The model of "bounded rationality" postulates that decision makers generally "satisfice" rather than optimize. (p. 110)

organizational process model   A decision-making model in which policy makers or lower-level officials rely largely on standardized responses or standard operating procedures. (p. 106)

Organization of Petroleum Exporting Countries (OPEC)   The most prominent cartel in the international economy; its members control about half the world's total oil exports, enough to significantly affect the world price of oil. (p. 303)

Oxfam America   A private charitable group that works with local third world communities to determine the needs of their own people and to carry out development projects. Oxfam does not operate the projects but provides funding to local organizations to carry them out. (p. 487)

ozone layer   The part of the atmosphere that screens out harmful ultraviolet rays from the sun. Certain chemicals used in industrial economies break the ozone layer down. (p. 394)

Paris Club   A group of first world governments that have loaned money to third world governments; it meets periodically to work out terms of debt renegotiations. Private creditors meet as the London Club. (p. 479)

peacebuilding   The use of military peacekeepers, civilian administrators, police trainers, and similar efforts to sustain peace agreements and build stable, democratic governments in societies recovering from civil wars. Since 2005, a UN Peacebuilding Commission has coordinated and supported these activities. (p. 248)

Peace Corps   An organization started by President John Kennedy in 1961 that provides U.S. volunteers for technical development assistance in third world states. (p. 487)

peace movements   Movements against specific wars or against war and militarism in general, usually involving large numbers of people and forms of direct action such as street protests. (p. 135)

positive peace   A peace that resolves the underlying reasons for war; not just a cease-fire but a transformation of relationships, including elimination or reduction of economic exploitation and political oppression. (p. 133)

postmodern feminism   An effort to combine feminist and postmodernist perspectives with the aim of uncovering the hidden influences of gender in IR and showing how arbitrary the construction of gender roles is. (p. 138)

postmodernism   An approach that denies the existence of a single fixed reality, and pays special attention to texts and to discourses—that is, to how people talk and write about a subject. (p. 102)

power   The ability or potential to influence others' behavior, as measured by the possession of certain tangible and intangible characteristics. (p. 45)

power projection   The ability to use military force in areas far from a country's region or sphere of influence. (p. 198)

power transition theory   A theory that the largest wars result from challenges to the top position in the status hierarchy, when a rising power is surpassing (or threatening to surpass) the most powerful state. (p. xxx)

prisoner's dilemma (PD)   A situation modeled by game theory in which rational actors pursuing their individual interests all achieve worse outcomes than they could have by working together. (p. 75)

prisoners of war (POWs)   Soldiers who have surrendered (and who thereby receive special status under the laws of war). (p. 273)

proliferation   The spread of weapons of mass destruction (nuclear, chemical, or biological weapons) into the hands of more actors. (p. 216)

pronatalist   A government policy that encourages or forces childbearing, and outlaws or limits access to contraception. (p. 413)

prospect theory   A decision-making theory that holds that options are assessed by comparison to a reference point, which is often the status quo but might be some past or expected situation. The model also holds that decision makers fear losses more than they value gains. (p. 110)

protectionism   The protection of domestic industries against international competition, by trade tariffs and other means. (p. 291)

proxy wars   Wars in the third world—often civil wars—in which the United States and the Soviet Union jockeyed for position by supplying and advising opposing factions. (p. 32)

public opinion   In IR, the range of views on foreign policy issues held by the citizens of a state. (p. 141)

"rally 'round the flag" syndrome   The public's increased support for government leaders during wartime, at least in the short term. (p. 144)

rational actors   Actors conceived of as single entities that can "think" about their actions coherently, make choices, identify their interests, and rank the interests in terms of priority. (p. 74)

rational model   A model in which decision makers calculate the costs and benefits of each possible course of action, then choose the one with the highest benefits and lowest costs. (p. 105)

realism   A broad intellectual tradition that explains international relations mainly in terms of power. (p. 43) See also *idealism* and *neorealism*.

reciprocity   A response in kind to another's actions; a strategy of reciprocity uses positive forms of leverage to promise rewards and negative forms of leverage to threaten punishment. (p. 5)

refugees   People fleeing their countries to find refuge from war, natural disaster, or political persecution. International law distinguishes them from migrants. (p. 435)

remittances   Money sent home by migrant workers to individuals (usually relatives) in their country of origin. (p. 436)

reserves   Hard-currency stockpiles kept by states. (p. 324)

resource curse   The difficulties faced by resource-rich developing countries, including dependence on exporting one or a few commodities whose prices fluctuate, as well as potentials for corruption and inequality. (p. 443)

responsibility to protect (R2P)   Principle adopted by world leaders in 2005 holding governments responsible for protecting civilians from genocide and crimes against humanity perpetrated within a sovereign state. (p. 269)

satisficing   The act of finding a satisfactory or "good enough" solution to a problem. (p. 110)

Secretariat   See *UN Secretariat*.

secular (state)   A state created apart from religious establishments and in which there is a high degree of separation between religious and political organizations. (p. 168)

security community   A situation in which low expectations of interstate violence permit a high degree of political cooperation—as, for example, among NATO members. (p. 357)

Security Council   See *UN Security Council*.

security dilemma A situation in which actions states take to ensure their own security (such as deploying more military forces) are perceived as threats to the security of other states. (p. 52)

service sector The part of an economy that concerns services (as opposed to the production of tangible goods); the key focus in international trade negotiations is on banking, insurance, and related financial services. (p. 307)

Single European Act (1985) An act that set a target date of the end of 1992 for the creation of a true common market (free cross-border movement of goods, capital, people, and services) in the European Community (EC). (p. 362)

Sino-Soviet split A rift in the 1960s between the communist powers of the Soviet Union and China, fueled by China's opposition to Soviet moves toward peaceful coexistence with the United States. (p. 31)

sovereignty A state's right, at least in principle, to do whatever it wants within its own territory; traditionally, sovereignty is the most important international norm. (p. 50)

Special Drawing Right (SDR) A world currency created by the International Monetary Fund (IMF) to replace gold as a world standard. Valued by a "basket" of national currencies, the SDR has been called "paper gold." (p. 332)

state An inhabited territorial entity controlled by a government that exercises sovereignty on its territory. (p. 12)

state-owned industries Industries such as oil-production companies and airlines that are owned wholly or partly by the state because they are thought to be vital to the national economy. (p. 312)

state-sponsored terrorism The use of terrorist groups by states, usually under control of a state's intelligence agency, to achieve political aims. (p. 207)

stealth technology The use of special radar-absorbent materials and unusual shapes in the design of aircraft, missiles, and ships to scatter enemy radar. (p. 203)

Strategic Defense Initiative (SDI) A U.S. effort, also known as "Star Wars," to develop defenses that could shoot down incoming ballistic missiles, spurred by President Ronald Reagan in 1983. Critics call it an expensive failure that will likely be ineffective. (p. 220) See also *Antiballistic Missile (ABM) Treaty*.

subsistence farming Rural communities growing food mainly for their own consumption rather than for sale in local or world markets. (p. 432)

subtext Meanings that are implicit or hidden in a text rather than explicitly addressed. (p. 128) See also *postmodernism*.

summit meeting A meeting between heads of state, often referring to leaders of great powers, as in the Cold War superpower summits between the United States and the Soviet Union or today's meetings of the Group of Eight on economic coordination. (p. 31)

supranational Larger institutions and groupings such as the European Union to which state authority or national identity is subordinated. (p. 355)

tariff A duty or tax levied on certain types of imports (usually as a percentage of their value) as they enter a country. (p. 293)

technology transfer Third world states' acquisition of technology (knowledge, skills, methods, designs, specialized equipment, etc.) from foreign sources, usually in conjunction with direct foreign investment or similar business operations. (p. 478)

territorial waters The waters near states' shores generally treated as part of national territory. The UN Convention on the Law of the Sea provides for a 12-mile territorial sea (exclusive national jurisdiction over shipping and navigation) and a 200-mile exclusive economic zone (EEZ) covering exclusive fishing and mineral rights (but allowing for free navigation by all). (p. 183) See also *high seas* and *UN Convention on the Law of the Sea (UNCLOS)*.

third world countries See *less-developed countries (LDCs)*.

total war Warfare by one state waged to conquer and occupy another; modern total war

513

originated in the Napoleonic Wars, which relied on conscription on a mass scale. (p. 153)

tragedy of the commons   A collective goods dilemma that is created when common environmental assets (such as the world's fisheries) are depleted or degraded through the failure of states to cooperate effectively. One solution is to "enclose" the commons (split them into individually owned pieces); international regimes can also be a (partial) solution. (p. 388)

transitional economies   Countries in Russia and Eastern Europe that are trying to convert from communism to capitalism, with various degrees of success. (p. 312)

Treaty of Rome (1957)   The founding document of the European Economic Community (EEC) or Common Market, now subsumed by the European Union. (p. 359)

truth commissions   Governmental bodies established in several countries after internal wars to hear honest testimony and bring to light what really happened during these wars, and in exchange to offer most of the participants asylum from punishment. (p. 156)

United Nations (UN)   An organization of nearly all world states, created after World War II to promote collective security. (p. 236)

UN Charter   The founding document of the United Nations; it is based on the principles that states are equal, have sovereignty over their own affairs, enjoy independence and territorial integrity, and must fulfill international obligations. The Charter also lays out the structure and methods of the UN. (p. 237)

UN Conference on Trade and Development (UNCTAD)   A structure established in 1964 to promote third world development through various trade proposals. (p. 252)

UN Convention on the Law of the Sea (UNCLOS)   A world treaty (1982) governing use of the oceans. The UNCLOS treaty established rules on territorial waters and a 200-mile exclusive economic zone (EEZ). (p. 400) See also *territorial waters*.

UN Development Program (UNDP)   A program that coordinates the flow of multilateral development assistance and manages 5,000 projects at once around the world (focusing especially on technical development assistance). (p. 485)

UN Environment Program (UNEP)   A program that monitors environmental conditions and, among other activities, works with the World Meteorological Organization to measure changes in global climate. (p. 391)

UN General Assembly   A body composed of representatives of all states that allocates UN funds, passes nonbinding resolutions, and coordinates third world development programs and various autonomous agencies through the Economic and Social Council (ECOSOC). (p. 237)

UN Secretariat   The UN's executive branch, led by the secretary-general. (p. 239)

UN Security Council   A body of five great powers (which can veto resolutions) and ten rotating member states that makes decisions about international peace and security including the dispatch of UN peacekeeping forces. (p. 239)

Universal Declaration of Human Rights (UDHR) (1948)   The core UN document on human rights; although it lacks the force of international law, it sets forth international norms regarding behavior by governments toward their own citizens and foreigners alike. (p. 266)

urbanization   A shift of population from the countryside to the cities that typically accompanies economic development and is augmented by displacement of peasants from subsistence farming. (p. 432)

Uruguay Round   A series of negotiations under the General Agreement on Tariffs and Trade (GATT) that began in Uruguay in 1986 and concluded in 1994 with agreement to create the World Trade Organization. The Uruguay Round followed earlier GATT negotiations such as the Kennedy Round and the Tokyo Round. (p. 296) See also *World Trade Organization (WTO)*.

U.S.-Japanese Security Treaty   A bilateral alliance between the United States and Japan, created in 1951 against the potential Soviet threat to Japan. The United States maintains troops in Japan and is committed to defend Japan if attacked, and Japan pays the United

States to offset about half the cost of maintaining the troops. (p. 67)

war crimes   Violations of the law governing the conduct of warfare, such as by mistreating prisoners of war or unnecessarily targeting civilians. (p. 270) See also *just wars*.

Warsaw Pact   A Soviet-led Eastern European military alliance, founded in 1955 and disbanded in 1991. It opposed the NATO alliance. (p. 65) See also *North Atlantic Treaty Organization (NATO)*.

weapons of mass destruction   Nuclear, chemical, and biological weapons, all distinguished from conventional weapons by their enormous potential lethality and their relative lack of discrimination in whom they kill. (p. 209)

World Bank   Formally the International Bank for Reconstruction and Development (IBRD), an organization that was established in 1944 as a source of loans to help reconstruct the European economies. Later, the main borrowers were third world countries and, in the 1990s, Eastern European ones. (p. 331)

World Court (International Court of Justice)   The judicial arm of the UN; located in The Hague, it hears only cases between states. (p. 256)

world government   A centralized world governing body with strong enforcement powers. (p. 134)

World Health Organization (WHO)   An organization based in Geneva that provides technical assistance to improve health conditions in the third world and conducts major immunization campaigns. (p. 253)

world-system   A view of the world in terms of regional class divisions, with industrialized countries as the core, poorest countries as the periphery, and other areas (for example, some of the newly industrializing countries) as the semiperiphery. (p. 441)

World Trade Organization (WTO)   An organization begun in 1995 that expanded the GATT's traditional focus on manufactured goods and created monitoring and enforcement mechanisms. (p. 294) See also *General Agreement on Tariffs and Trade (GATT)* and *Uruguay Round*.

zero-sum games   Situations in which one actor's gain is by definition equal to the other's loss, as opposed to a non-zero-sum game, in which it is possible for both actors to gain (or lose). (p. 75)

Photo Credits

Name Index

Note: Entry format is page number followed by footnote; 144n52 refers to page 144, footnote 52.

Subject Index

Note: **Boldface** entries and page numbers indicate key terms. Entries for tables and figures are followed by "*table*" and "*fig.*," respectively.

as tool of governments, 376–377

UN coordination of, 237

Information screens, 129–130

Information technologies. *See also* Global telecommunications

electronic information in warfare, 203–204

nationalism and, 378–379

North-South gap and, 441

security and, 378–379

supranationalism and, 379–381

territorial state system and, 50

trade restrictions on, 292

transparency and, 91

In-group bias, 166, 167

Integrated Holistic Approach Urban Development Project, 434

Integration theory, 355–358

Intellectual property rights, 305–306

Intelligence, governmental, 130, 200–201, 225

Intelsat, 235

Inter-American Court of Human Rights, 268

Inter-American Tropical Tuna Commission, 397

Intercontinental ballistic missiles (ICBMs), 211

Interdependence, 87, 387–389

Interest groups, 138

foreign policy and, 138–139

legislative influence of, 145–146

trade policies and, 304–307

Interest rates, 330–331, 334

Intergovernmental organizations (IGOs), 15. *See also* specific IGOs

global, 235

as IOs, 234

as nonstate actors, 16 *(table)*

regional, 235, 300, 302

supranationalism and, 355

in world (1815-2005), 235 *(fig.)*

Intergovernmental Panel on Climate Change (IPCC), 390, 391

Internally displaced persons (IDPs). *See* Refugees

International Air Transport Association, 235

International Atomic Energy Agency (IAEA), 217–218, 253

International Bank for Reconstruction and Development (IBRD). *See* World Bank

International Bill of Human Rights, 267

International Civil Aviation Organization (ICAO), 253

International civil service, of diplomats and bureaucrats (UN), 250

International Committee of the Red Cross (ICRC), 234, 274, 491

International Convention on the Elimination of All Forms of Racial Discrimination (CERD), 267–268

International Convention on the Protection of the Rights of All Migrant Workers and Members of Their Families (CMW), 268

International Court of Justice. *See* World Court (International Court of Justice)

International Covenant on Civil and Political Rights (CCPR), 267

International Covenant on Economic, Social, and Cultural Rights (CESCR), 267

International Criminal Court (ICC), 35, 99, 270–273, **272,** 275

International economic regimes, South in, 481–482

International Energy Agency (IEA), 304

International institutions, regimes in, 92

International integration, 355–381. *See also* European Union (EU)

globalization and, 355

global telecommunications and, 370, 373–381

governments and information, 376–379

integration theory, 355–358

International Labor Organization (ILO), 253, 313

International law, 254–261. *See also* World Court

(International Court of Justice)

diplomacy and, 261–263

on disaster relief, 492

earliest development of, 276

enforcement of, 255–256

human rights and, 264–270

just-war doctrine, 263–264

national courts, 259–261

on sanctions, 256

on seiges, 274

sources of, 254–255

state sovereignty and, 261–264

war crimes and, 270–274

International level of analysis, 18, 18 *(table)*

International Maritime Organization (IMO), 253

International Monetary Fund (IMF), 331. *See also* specific countries

Asian financial crisis, 340

conditionality of, 480–481, 493

debt relief and, 480

formation of, 311

former Soviet bloc members of, 338

missions of, 333

national accounts, 333–334

as supranational institution, 20

weighted voting system of, 327, 332–333

World Bank and, 331–333

world economy and, 254

International norms, 233–236

constraint of state actions and, 101

disaster relief and, 492

world order and morality, 90, 101, 233–234, 492

in World War I, 28 *(fig.)*

International Olympic Committee, 235. *See also* Olympic Games

International order. *See* World order

International Organization for Migration, 492

International organizations (IOs), 16

International organizations (IOs), 234. *See also* specific organizations

disaster relief efforts, 490–492

Maps

World States and Territories

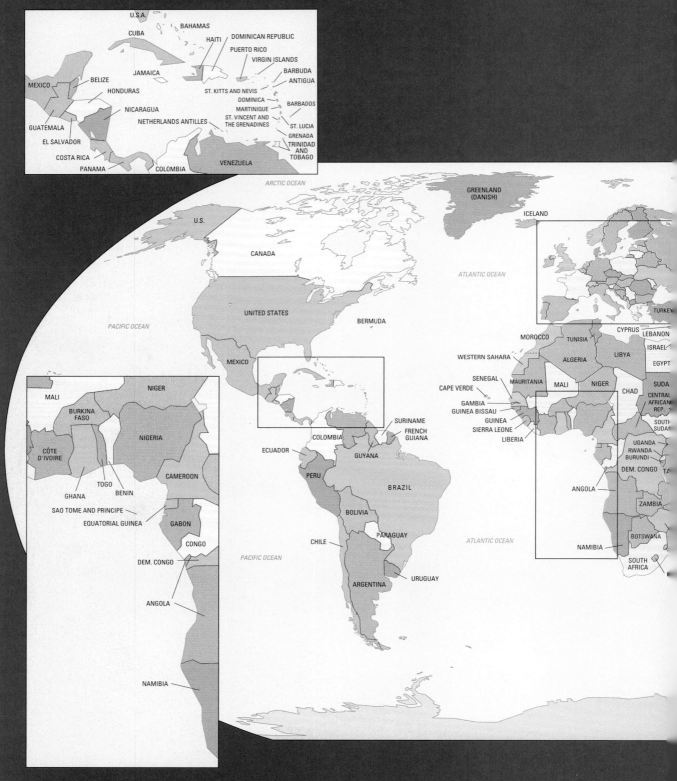

U.S.A.
BAHAMAS
CUBA
HAITI
DOMINICAN REPUBLIC
PUERTO RICO
VIRGIN ISLANDS
JAMAICA
BARBUDA
ANTIGUA
MEXICO
BELIZE
HONDURAS
ST. KITTS AND NEVIS
DOMINICA
BARBADOS
NICARAGUA
MARTINIQUE
GUATEMALA
NETHERLANDS ANTILLES
ST. VINCENT AND
THE GRENADINES
ST. LUCIA
EL SALVADOR
GRENADA
COSTA RICA
TRINIDAD
AND
TOBAGO
PANAMA
COLOMBIA
VENEZUELA

ARCTIC OCEAN
GREENLAND
(DANISH)
ICELAND
U.S.
CANADA
ATLANTIC OCEAN
PACIFIC OCEAN
UNITED STATES
BERMUDA
TURKEY
MOROCCO
TUNISIA
CYPRUS
LEBANON
ISRAEL
WESTERN SAHARA
ALGERIA
LIBYA
EGYPT
MEXICO
SENEGAL
MAURITANIA
SUDA
CAPE VERDE
MALI
NIGER
CHAD
CENTRAL
AFRICAN
REP.
GAMBIA
GUINEA BISSAU
GUINEA
SURINAME
SOUTH
SUDA
COLOMBIA
FRENCH
GUIANA
SIERRA LEONE
LIBERIA
UGANDA
RWANDA
BURUNDI
ECUADOR
GUYANA
DEM. CONGO
PERU
TA
BRAZIL
ANGOLA
BOLIVIA
ZAMBIA
MALI
NIGER
PARAGUAY
BURKINA
FASO
NIGERIA
CÔTE
D'IVOIRE
CHILE
ATLANTIC OCEAN
BOTSWANA
CAMEROON
TOGO
BENIN
NAMIBIA
GHANA
SOUTH
AFRICA
SAO TOME AND PRINCIPE
ARGENTINA
URUGUAY
EQUATORIAL GUINEA
GABON
CONGO
PACIFIC OCEAN
DEM. CONGO
ANGOLA
NAMIBIA

562

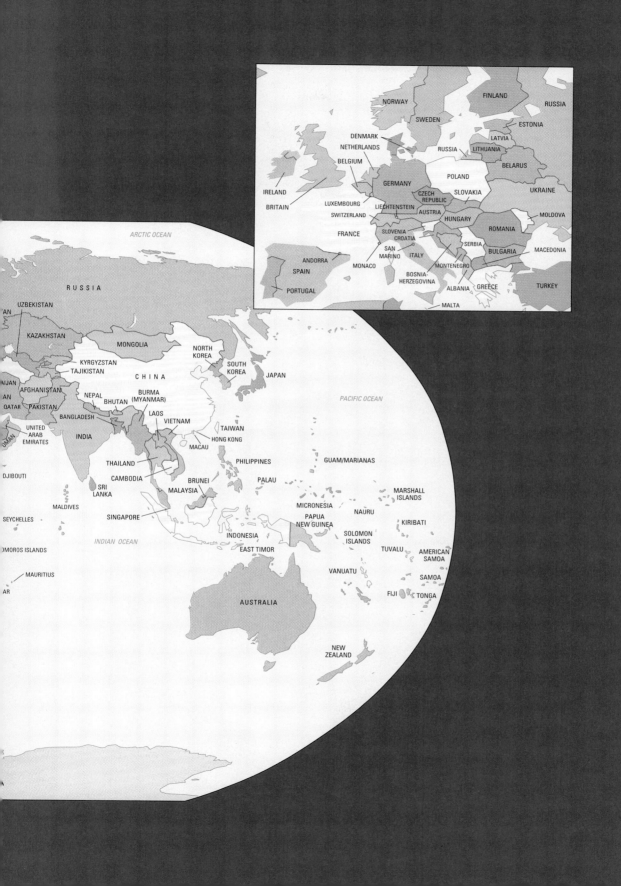

ARCTIC OCEAN

NORWAY
FINLAND
RUSSIA
SWEDEN
ESTONIA
DENMARK
LATVIA
NETHERLANDS
RUSSIA
LITHUANIA
BELGIUM
BELARUS
POLAND
GERMANY
IRELAND
CZECH
REPUBLIC
SLOVAKIA
UKRAINE
BRITAIN
LUXEMBOURG
LIECHTENSTEIN
AUSTRIA
MOLDOVA
SWITZERLAND
HUNGARY
ROMANIA
FRANCE
SLOVENIA
CROATIA
SERBIA
BULGARIA
MACEDONIA
ANDORRA
SAN
MARINO
ITALY
MONTENEGRO
SPAIN
MONACO
BOSNIA-
HERZEGOVINA
ALBANIA
GREECE
TURKEY
PORTUGAL
MALTA

RUSSIA

UZBEKISTAN
KAZAKHSTAN
MONGOLIA
NORTH
KOREA
AN
KYRGYZSTAN
SOUTH
KOREA
TAJIKISTAN
CHINA
JAPAN
AIJAN
AFGHANISTAN
PACIFIC OCEAN
AN
NEPAL
BURMA
(MYANMAR)
QATAR
PAKISTAN
BHUTAN
LAOS
BANGLADESH
VIETNAM
UNITED
ARAB
EMIRATES
INDIA
TAIWAN
HONG KONG
MACAU
OMAN
THAILAND
PHILIPPINES
GUAM/MARIANAS
DJIBOUTI
CAMBODIA
PALAU
SRI
LANKA
BRUNEI
MALAYSIA
MICRONESIA
MARSHALL
ISLANDS
MALDIVES
NAURU
SEYCHELLES
SINGAPORE
PAPUA
NEW GUINEA
KIRIBATI
INDONESIA
SOLOMON
ISLANDS
OMOROS ISLANDS
INDIAN OCEAN
EAST TIMOR
TUVALU
AMERICAN
SAMOA
MAURITIUS
VANUATU
SAMOA
AR
FIJI
TONGA
AUSTRALIA

NEW
ZEALAND

North America

Central America and the Caribbean

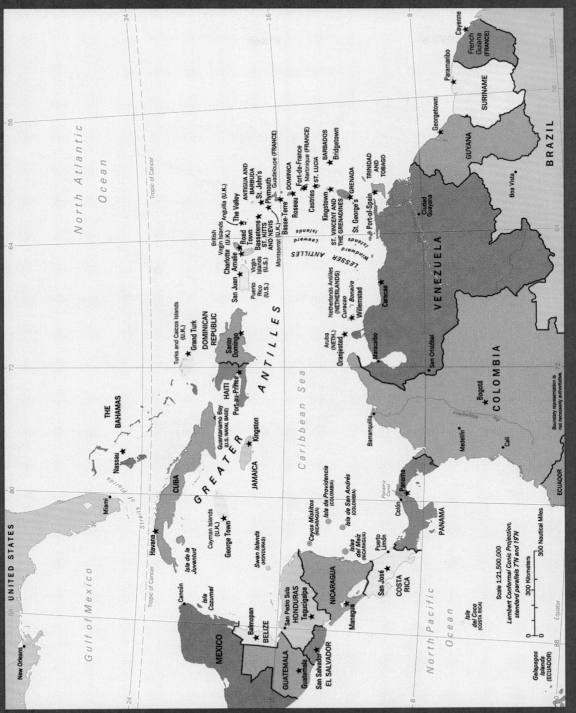

South America

Africa

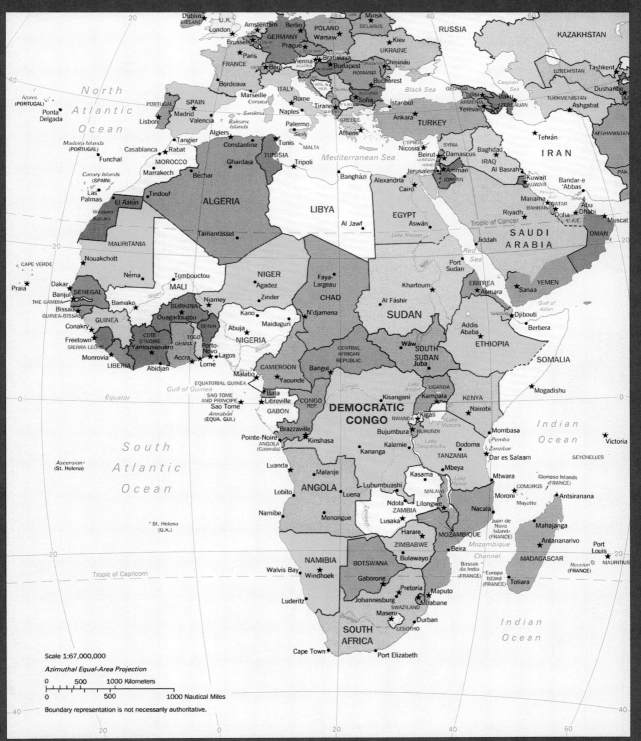

Northern Africa and the Middle East

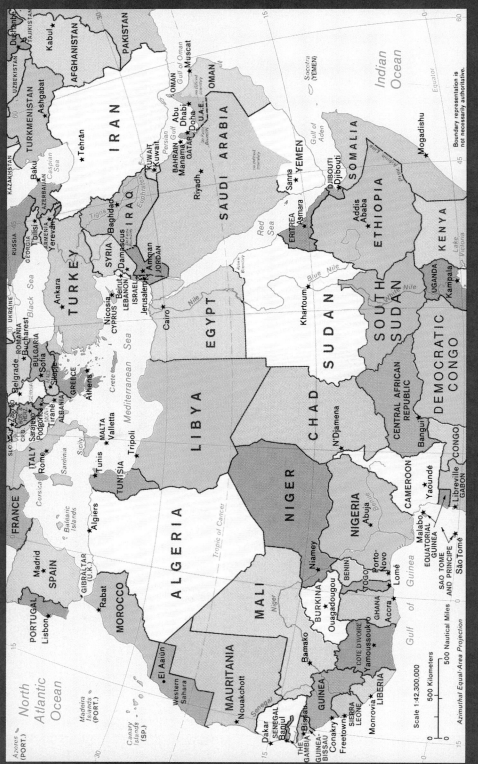

Europe

Asia

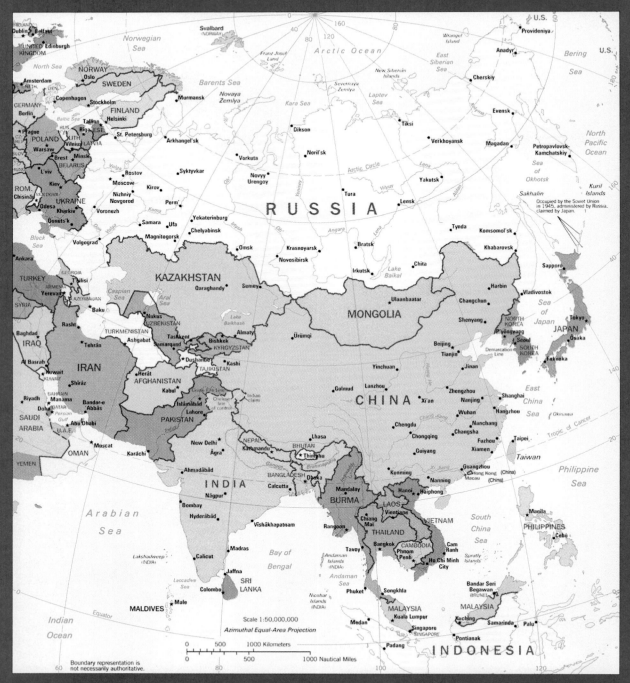